Around the Square

The Story of Ennis Hurling

For Rita McCormack
Best regards
Ollie Byrne

Against the Wind
We Were Running Against the Wind
We were young and strong, we were
Running against the Wind

Against the Wind
I'm still running against the Wind
I'm older now but still running against the Wind

Well I'm Older now and still running
Against the Wind

Bob Seger

Dedication

51 years ago hurling in Ennis reached a low ebb.
A group of young men went out and did something
about this sad state of affairs.
They rejuvenated hurling; they injected new life into it.
This book is dedicated to that group of men.

Around the Square

The Story of Ennis Hurling

Ollie Byrnes

First published in 2003 by
Ollie Byrnes
Ennis, Co. Clare
Ireland

ISBN
0 9546172 0 7 (hardback)
0 9546172 1 5 (paperback)

Typeset in 11pt. Optima

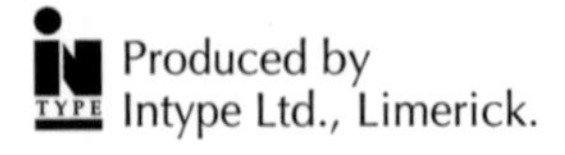
Produced by
Intype Ltd., Limerick.

Contents

Acknowledgements

The following publications were consulted during research for this book:-

2000 Years of Hurling in Ireland by Art Ó Maolfabhail – Dundalgan Press Ltd., (1973).

A Lifetime in Hurling – The Tommy Doyle Story by Raymond Smith – Hutchinsons, (1955).

An Ennis Miscellany – Edited by Joseph Power (1990).

Babs – The Michael Keating Story – Michael Keating with Donal Keenan.

Eamon De Valera and The Banner County - by Kevin J. Browne – Glendale (1982).

Farna's Hurling Story (St. Finbarr's Farranferris) – by Tim Horgan.

Fermoy GAA History by Michael Barry, (1995).

For the Record – Clare GAA 1887 – 2002 by Des Crowe, (2002).

From Silence to Speech – By Sr. Nicholas Griffey – Dominican Publications.

History of England, Part III by George Carter, Relfe Brothers Ltd. (1909).

History of Hurling by Carbery (Paddy Mehigan), published by The Kerryman, (1946).

Hurling Giants – Brendan Fulham – Wolfhound Press (1994).

Irish Film – 100 Years – by Arthur Flynn – Kestrel Books.

Irish Voices – an Informal History 1916/'66 – by Peter Somerville-Large.

Munster GAA History.

No Hurling at the Dairy Door – Billy Rackard, Blackwater Press.

Over 50 Years of Clare Hurling Teams, The Pa Howard Collection, Edited by Jimmy Smyth (2002).

Shell Book of the McCarthy Cup – Owen McCann – Oisín Publications.

The Banner – edited by Thomas Dillon (1963).

The Football Immortals – Raymond Smith – Bruce Spicer Ltd. (1968).

The Guinness Book of Hurling by David Guiney and Padraig Puirseal, publised by Arthur Guinness and Co. Ltd., (1964).

The Kilkenny GAA Bible – by Gerry O'Neill.

'The Nash' 1897 – 1997 Scéal Scoile – Edited by Risteard Ua Croinín & Garry Stack (1997).

Films/Documentaries, etc.

A Sense of Belonging – The Market Reunion – 2002 – Brooks Studios.
Guns in the Heather – Walt Disney – based on the novel by Lockhard Amerman.
St. Michael's Villas – Celebrating 50 years of Community Spirit. (We had it All.) – St. Michael's Committee – Paschal Brooks.
Telefís Scoile Documentary – Ennis, presented by Patrick Gallagher, RTE – 1968.
Clare Searchlights (1925 – 1936). Notes from the Banner County – a special feature to the Limerick Leader – by Patrick J. Crimmins (1861 – 1937).

Club Histories and other Assorted Publications

A Proud Past – Newmarket.
Toonagh Year Book - 1983.
Clare Football Annual – 1973. Dalton Printing Co. Limerick.
Clare GAA Annuals – Editor Pádraig Mac Mathúna.
Clare Journal.
Cumann Dal gCais – 1934. Printed to honour Cusack's County and the Founding of the G.A.A.
Cumann na mBunscoil an Chláir – 1964 – 2000. Edited by Brendan Vaughan.
Éire Óg 1952 – '67 by Johnny McCarthy/Michael Brennan. Clare Champion Ltd.
Éire Óg GAA Bulletins.
Ennis Rovers Reunion – 1990/St. John's H.C. Grand Reunion 1986.
Feakle by Kieran Sheedy.
Gaelic Sport Magazines.
Gaelic World Magazines.
Images and Memories – Clooney, Quin, Maghera, Dangan. Pr. 1994 Clare Champion.
Kilnamona and its People.
Na Bráithre Críostaí Inis – 1827 – 1977.
Barefield National School Centenary 1895-1995.
Ruan Celebration Brochure - 1986.
Cusack Park Souvenir Brochure - June 1980.
Ruan Souvenir Programme - June 1971.
The Tulla Ceili Band 1946-1997 – by Chris Keane.
Our Games Annuals – 1963, 1966, 1967, 1972, 1973.

Technical School Student Magazine. Produced by Nuala O'Driscoll and Mary Margaret Scanlan.
The Banner Magazine. Published by The Kerryman. Editor Gerry Colleran.
The Claret and Gold – Tulla.
The Clash of the Ash in Ruan.
The GAA in Clarecastle – by Joseph Power.
The GAA in Whitegate & Mountshannon – by Patrick Madden.
Treasured Memories – O'Callaghan's Mills GAA Story.
West Coast Radio.

Additional Articles

15 Years Agrowing – by Johnny McCarthy/Michael Brennan.
1962 Harty Final – A Game to Remember – Bobby Burke.
40 Years of the Red Shadows – John Mungovan.
A Dazzling Decade by Seán Guinnane.
A Record Year – by Dalcassian (Joe Madigan).
A Remarkable Era 1957/'73 – by Val Arthur.
A Rover in the 1960s – Michael Brennan.
A Town I Know So Well – Brian Dinan.
Beagles, Soccer, Hurling & the Rovers – by Paschal O'Brien.
Changing Face of Ennis Hurling – by T. d E.
Colleges Scene 1962 – by Peadar O'Brien.
Éire Óg players stick to their guns – by Jupiter.
Éire Óg & St. Joseph's Rivalry – Johnny McCarthy.
Ennis CBS Nursery – Michael Carmody (Éire Óg).
History of Doora/Barefield – Michael McNamara.
Hunger Strike 1917 – by Col. Austin Brennan.
Paddy Duggan Remembers.
P. J. O'Dea – The Man with the Multi-Coloured Record – by Seán Ó Riain.
Politics in Ennis 1914 – 1920 – by Gráinne Ryan.
Remembering Brian Borus by Gerry Quinn.
Rovers & Friendship – Michael Butler.
Roving with the Rovers – Kyran Kennedy.
St. Joseph's – A Proud History – by Michael Carmody (St. Joseph's).
The late Matt Nugent - by Michael Carmody (St. Joseph's).
The First Clare Cup Final - by Val Arthur.
Paddy Reidy - A simple man with a fertile brain - by Frank Custy.
Down Memory Lane (Reflections of Ruan Hurling Club) by Michael Henchy.

The Christian Brothers in Ennis – by Bro. S. Whelan.
The Old Townies – Brian Dinan.
Three Days with Bannermen in Hammersmith and Kilburn – by Aidan Tuttle.
Tim Smythe – by Bobby Burke.
T. V. Honan in Tune with his Times – by Seán Spellissy.
Willie McAllister and the CBS Dean Ryan – Seán Ó Liodáin.
Some Famous Ennis Hurling Families by Johnny McCarthy and Michael Brennan.

Newspapers

Irish Examiner	Irish Star	Irish Press
Irish Independent	Celtic Times	Saturday Record
Clare Journal	Clare Courier	Irish Times
Limerick Leader	Clare Champion	Clare Advertiser
Clare County Express	Clare News	Clare People
Gaelic Weekly	Gaelic Sport	Tipperary Nationalist

Other Sources

Seamus Hayes	Sean King	Gerry McInerney
Tom O'Riordan	Seamus O'Reilly	Gerry Slevin
Gerry Quinn		

Song Lyrics

'La maison ou j'ai grandie' by Marnay/Calentano/Beretta/DelPrate. As recorded by Françoise Hardy in 1966 – A cover version, Tar and Cement was made famous here by Joe Dolan in the Summer of 1967.

Lyrics to *'Against the Wind'* by Bob Seger. Seger led a wonderful group called "The Silver Bullet Band", out of Detroit, Michigan in the 1970s.

The Stone Outside Dan Murphy's Door was composed by Feakle native Johnny Patterson. Ruby Murray and Kate Purcell have interpreted his songs.

The Foggy Dew was written by Fr. O'Neill.

Dicey Riley is a traditional Dublin street song as recorded by Sweeney's Men, and Frank Harte.

Sleeve Notes from the LP "The Book of Invasions" by Horslips recorded in 1976.

Poetry by Christy Murphy.

Photographs Courtesy of:

The Pat Brennan Collection
Paddy Flynn
Seán Heaslip
Johnny Murphy
Frank O'Malley
Seamus O'Reilly Collection
Catherine Glynn
Paschal Brooks (R.I.P.) Collection
Esther Gilligan
Colm Keating
Val McGann
Ollie O'Regan
Michael Mulcaire
Photo-World, High Street

Additional photographs, programmes, books, memorabilia and general help:

Kevin Arthur, Michael Arthur, Larry Blake, Teresa Blake, John Boyd, Kate Browne, George Bradley, Cyril Brennan, Willie Byrnes (R.I.P.), Michael Butler, Nuala Collins, Seán Cooley, Tony Considine, Jim Costello, Teresa Cronin, Seán Connolly, Paddy Crowe, P.J. Curtis, Seán Custy, Pat Daly, Michael Doherty, Kevin Damery, Bro. Liam de Róiste, George Dilger, Yvonne Flynn, Finbarr and Marion Gardé, Liam Harvey, Ann Glynn, Mary Hanly, Kieran Hennessy (R.I.P.), Michael Henchy, Bríd Hynes, Mattsie Hogan, Karen Gregory, Maura Keane (R.I.P.), Peter Keane, John D. Kelly, Gerry Kelly, Noelle Kenny, Suzanne King, Michael Leahy, John Lynch, Pat Lynch, Ger Morrissey, Kathleen Metcalfe, Michael McCarthy, Joe and Maureen McDonagh, Gerry McInerney, John Nevin (R.I.P.), Paddy Molony (R.I.P.), Marie Molony, Peter Maher, Tony Maher, Seán Mounsey, John Mungovan, Flan McMahon (R.I.P.), Padraig Mac Mathúna, Catherine McNicholas, Charlie Nono, Michael G. O'Brien, Peadar O'Brien, Dermot O'Loughlin, Eddie O'Loughlin, George O'Halloran, Gerry Quinn, John Russell, Gretta Ryan, Barry Smythe, Michael J. Spellissy, Seán Spellissy, Siobhán Spellissy, Paschal Sheridan, Tom Tuohy, Brian Twomey, Paddy White, Gerry Woods. Thanks to Francis O'Gorman, Maureen Comber and Peter Beirne at the Manse.

I would like to acknowledge the following photographers whose work has enhanced this publication. Liam McGrath (R.I.P.) Denis Wylde (R.I.P.), John Kelly, Eamon Ward – all Clare Champion. Seamus O'Reilly (County Express), Michael Mulcaire, Paschal Brooks Snr. (R.I.P.), George Dilger, Michael Keane, Owen J. Moroney, Shepherds Bush, Clare Advertiser, John D. Kelly.

A special thank you to Pat Brennan, Kate Browne, Caroline Collins, Peter Cronin, Brian Dinan, Geraldine Dinan, Seán Heaslip, Maura Leyden, Jimmy Mahony (R.I.P.), Christy Murphy, Johnny McCarthy, Paddy McDonnell, Frankie O'Gorman, Seamus O'Reilly, Joe Shannon, Jimmy Smyth.

Finally my thanks to all who gave their time to be interviewed for this book.

Front Cover:
Action shot involving Paschal O'Brien in the Munster Championship v. Cork in 1966. *Courtesy of Clare Champion.*

O'Connell Square. *Courtesy of John Nevin.*

Paddy Flynn carried shoulder high following Ennis CBS victory in the 1962 Harty Cup. *Courtesy of Brooks Studios.*

Éire Óg Senior team of 1959 pictured on County Final day. Back row, left to right: Ralphie Burns (former great), Aidan Lynch, Colm Madigan, Stephen Loftus, Paddy Kerin, Paddy Loftus, Michael Blake, Pat Tynan, Paschal Brooks, 'Aoner' Sheridan (former great). **Front row, left to right:** Jimmy Cronin, Brendan Doyle, Michael Dilger, Bobby Burke, Michael Guerin, Johnny McCarthy, Paddy Duggan. **Mascot:** Jimmy Brennan.
Courtesy of Clare Champion.

Back Cover:
Tull Considine captain of 1928 winning championship team.
Courtesy of Flan Hynes.

Éire Óg Feile na nGael champions, 1999. *Courtesy of Gerry Kelly.*

Spine:
Features Declan Coote (top) and Seán Heaslip in action for Éire Óg.
Courtesy of Clare Champion.

Cover Design by Intype Ltd.

Foreword

Johnny McCarthy

At last the history of Gaelic Games in Ennis has been written. A century-long void has finally been filled. For years, many of us have spoken of the need for such a history, but it has taken a man of exceptional skill, determination, patience and sheer persistence, to tackle, and bring to fruition, this mammoth task.

Ollie Byrnes has already distinguished himself in this field. His history of Clare Hurling from earliest times to the present day – *"Against the Wind"* – is a tour-de-force and already acknowledged as the definitive work on the subject. *"Blue is the Colour"* – his book on the history of hurling in St. Flannan's is equally accomplished. Described by the great Jimmy Smyth as a "weaver of dreams, and lighter of the lamp of memory on many grand and glorious incidents and games", Ollie Byrnes again brings his many skills to bear on this, his latest work – painstaking research, attention to detail, easy, relaxed style, remarkable photographs, memorable quotes from great players and characters of the town, little snippets that give us a flavour of the daily life of Ennis people down the generations, and a love of his subject that illuminates every page. We have been given a window into the past, and a timely reminder of the many great warriors who, in hard times, quarried a proud, unyielding spirit that made Ennis hurling and football respected everywhere.

This is a book for every Ennis person to savour. It is particularly important that our present generation of players read it. Tradition is a powerful and motivating factor in our games. In a rapidly expanding town, it is vital that we keep in touch with our roots. We surely won't know where we're going if we don't know where we've come from!

Tá muintir na hInse faoi chomaoin ag Ollie Byrnes.

About the Author

Ollie Byrnes is a native of Ennis. He was educated at Ennis CBS primary school and Rice College. A love of hurling was instilled by his parents and teachers. Along with Tony Garland, Ollie was very involved with West Coast Radio and headed the group at the I.R.T.C. hearings on March 9th, 1989. He is the author of 'Against the Wind' (Memories of Clare Hurling) published by Mercier Press, edited by Michael Garry, 1996, and 'Blue is the Colour' (Hurling at St. Flannan's), published in 2001. He also devotes much of his time to his other passion Music. *Courtesy of Michael Mulcaire.*

Introduction

The idea of documenting hurling first occurred to me in 1988, when several well known hurlers were interviewed on the then independent station, West Coast Radio.

I acquired a general love of History and English during my time at Ennis CBS and I would like to acknowledge my history teachers, Bro. Power, Bro. Bridges, Cyril Brennan, Seán O'Brien and Mannix Berry. Many of my best memories of schooldays concern hurling. The section "Days of the Old Schoolyard" was a pleasure to write. It brought back great memories and also the realisation of the contribution made by the Christian Brothers to Ennis.

Other influences include a History of Éire Óg 1952 – 1967, written by John McCarthy and Michael Brennan. This book fired my imagination and helped give me a general understanding and love of Ennis hurling.

Much of the material in this book came from my research for the County book – "Against the Wind" (Mercier, 1996). In January 1997, I began work on the Ennis project and, with the exception of the 18 months spent on "Blue is the Colour" – a history of hurling at St. Flannan's, I have worked consistently on it.

In November 1997, I contacted Brian Dinan, Jimmy Smyth, Paddy McDonnell and Christy Murphy asking them to submit articles. All agreed and I received their contributions immediately. This really helped kick start the book.

The section "Caruso's Ennis" goes back to my time on West Coast Radio. And, though the station was unsuccessful, it gave me the greatest education of my life in the ways of the world. It is important to include this interview, taken from 12 hours of tape, as the social and political history of the town complements the hurling. It was a pleasure to talk to Jimmy Mahony.

My thanks to all who gave me photographs. Pat Brennan of the Clare Champion allowed me access to their archive. Yvonne Flynn lent me her father Paddy's wonderful collection. Esther Gilligan as always came up trumps, contributing many outstanding photographs. A special thanks to Seamus O'Reilly of Clare County Express for access to his archive.

To my mother, Bridie, for her understanding over the years. To Pat Brennan who went from pillar to post to get the finance to pay for this publication. To Caroline Collins for her unselfish help with typing, ideas, proof reading and general layout. To Johnny McCarthy for his solid advice. A word of appreciation to Maura Leyden (typist) and to Kevin FitzGerald and Audrey Barry of Intype for their professionalism. To Gerard Kennedy and his colleagues at Leader for their support.

While the 23 profiles at the back feature many great Ennismen, it should not be interpreted that these are the best and the greatest. These men simply epitomise the very best from every era in living memory.

While Éire Óg has enjoyed recent success at Gaelic Football, it should never be forgotten by the football fraternity that the club was founded as a hurling club and nothing else.

I sincerely hope I've done justice to Ennis and to the fine old families that came from the town. I hope also that this publication records for posterity the story of hurling in Ennis, and that it serves to stimulate interest in the local community and serve as a reference point for future historians. I hope that it illustrates the richness of Ennis and will hopefully inspire passion and interest in Gaelic games and in the town, a town which in many ways has lost its soul.

Ollie Byrnes, September 2003.

"Where are the meadows, tar and cement,
where are the lilacs, tar and cement,
Laughter of children, tar and cement,
Nothing but acres of tar and cement."

PART ONE

Iomáint

Iomáint, a lovely Irish word for hurling, translates as the art of driving, hurling, pressing, or urging forward. Hurling goes back into the mists of time. The book of Leinster tells us that the game enjoyed an outstanding place in the lives of the people. It had close associations with weddings, betrothals, match-making and coming of age.

It was at a hurling match that Gráinne, the daughter of King Cormac Mac Airt, placed Diarmuid Ó Duibhne under a 'geassa' (a sacred magic obligation) to elope with her. This love story forms the basis of the book Toruigeacht Diarmuda agus Ghráinne.

The Tuatha De Danann – the peoples of the Goddess Danann, occupied this country, living in peace and harmony until the coming of the Clanna Míle. The Tuatha were a mystical race, handsome and learned, elegantly dressed, expert in every art and science and supreme masters of wizardry. The rival forces met at Moytura. As a prelude to battle "Three Times Nine" hurlers from the Clanna Míle stepped forward and met an equal number from the Tuatha De Danann.

Hurling is mentioned in the Cattle Raid of Cooley and the Book of Invasions (Leabhar Gabhála Éireann), a 12th century chronicle of the myriad pre-Christian colonisations of Ireland. The mythical characters abound. Hurling survived the Vikings, the Normans and the Tudor colonisation.

The Anglo Saxons and gentry took to the game. They patronised it. They placed wagers on teams. Clare and Galway met at a place called Turloughmore in October 1759. "The teams marched from Gort preceded by a 'band of musick', a French horn, a running footman and a fellow in a harlequin dress. The procession closed with many carriages and horsemen. None of the hurlers were in the least hurt, the greatest harmony having subsisted. The Clare hurlers were elegantly entertained the following night and a hundred guineas was proposed to be hurled for at a re-match"! So wrote the 18th century newspaper Pue's Occurrences. English travel writers for the most part praised the game. Arthur Young and S. C. Hall left many positive accounts of hurling.

The travel writer Edward Wakefield wrote in 1812: - "In Tipperary,

Limerick and Queen's County, the Irish language is very common. The men are strong limbed, and seem to be more active than those of Cork. Hurling is a prevailing amusement. Children, as soon as they are able to follow each other, run about in bands of a dozen or more, with balls and hurls, eagerly contending for victory." S. C. Hall and his young wife toured the South-land 30 years later. Hall left this account. "The great game in Kerry, and indeed throughout the South, is the game of 'Hurley', a game rather rare, although not unknown in England. It is a fine manly exercise with sufficient danger to produce excitement, and is indeed, par excellence, the game of the peasantry of Ireland. To be an expert hurler, a man must possess athletic powers of no ordinary character; he must have a quick eye, a ready hand, and a strong arm; and he must be a good runner, a skilful wrestler, and withal patient as well as resolute". Dr. Samuel Johnson (1709-1784) was less charitable. In his lexicography he gives the following definition: - *"Hurling is a game played by wild Irishmen with sticks".*

The Clare Journal of September 22nd, 1842 certainly concurs with the above remarks. From the Letters Page we glean *"a hurling match played at Newmarket-on-Fergus 15 years since, the brother was opposed to the brother, and the father against the son, it was awful to look at, to see the savage fury of the combatants, yelling and shouting, and but for the timely interference of some of the neighbouring clergymen, several lives would be lost, as it was there was one or two killed, besides numbers dreadfully mangled! On what day did this take place? On a Sunday. Again about eight years back, another great hurling match took place at Loughville, within a mile of this town, a fight took place. It terminated in the death of a man, who left a wife and six or seven children to bewail his loss, as usual, it occurred on a Sunday...I am afraid, Mr. Editor, that I have trespassed much on your valuable time, but I hope that I may be the cause of parents in preventing their children and friends from following such practices especially on the Sabbath. I am, Sir, with respect, (y)our obedient servant" – Signed B.B. Ennis – September 20th 1842.* A number of things are interesting during the period 1830 to 1880. The idea that hurling seems to have been a cyclical thing, unpopular for a number of years, then revived. The fact that the police and clergy were so down on it would indicate a certain subversive enjoyment of a forbidden sport by young people. The injuries seem to have been savage, and if B.B. is to be believed, the matches seem to have been an excuse for faction fights, and the onlookers thought of it as all part of the sport. We can only speculate where the field at Loughville is!

The famine of 1845 – 1847 destroyed everything including language, customs and native pastimes. To quote Carbery: *"Then out of the Barony*

Éire Óg - Senior hurling team 1983, one of the best ever to represent Ennis. Back row left to right: *Pete Barry, Sean Lynch, Michael Glynn, Paschal McMahon, Joe Barry, Tony Nugent, Francis Heaslip, Noel Ryan.* **Front row:** *Pat Lynch, Gerry Barry, Colm McMahon, Martin Nugent, Seamus Durack, Pat Kelly, Declan Coote, Sean Heaslip.* **Mascot:** *Brian Lynch.*

of the Burren in Northern Clare, swept by the Atlantic, came a man of independent Fenian mind, rich in Gaelic language and tradition. His name was Cusack – Michael Cusack, a teacher by profession. He wielded a terse and trenchant pen. He decided to bring "the hurling back to Ireland". Well appointed in sturdy athletic body and vigorous mind, he put his thoughts on papers to which he had access, 'The Celtic Times' and 'United Ireland'." Cusack's love of hurling can be seen from his many letters published by the Clare Journal, circa 1903: *"To me personally, it matters little what team wins. I am content that Ireland's game of hurling is as safe as it was when the Milesians took it over from the glorious Tuatha De Danann race."*

What's in a Name

Clubs have come and gone in Ennis hurling circles over the past 116 years. Unlike other parishes Ennis has had a tradition of changing names. The strange thing about it is that the name Ennis has seldom been used.

One of the earliest clubs was ***Thomas Davis***, called after a founding father of the 'Repeal of the Union' Movement. Davis, along with William Smith O'Brien and Gavan Duffy, felt that Repeal would be carried, and Ireland would have a parliament of her own. Charles Stewart Parnell continued the struggle. One of his greatest supporters was the Nationalist MP, ***Alexander Martin Sullivan***. The very first hurling club in Ennis (AM Sullivan's) was named after the Bantry man.

Faughs was considered a virile club who often put the fear of God into opposing teams. The name ***Faughs*** is derived from the Gaelic phrase 'Faugh A' Balleagh' meaning 'clear the way'.

The ***Ennis Hurling Club*** (essentially the Dalcassians) won the Championship in 1911. Named after the Dal gCais, whose forebears are believed to have come to this region from Spain and Portugal, the Dalcassian territory spread well beyond the boundaries of Clare, which was in the heart of the ancient territory of Thomond.

The ***Thomond Club*** represented the town at the turn of the 20th Century, contesting the County Final of 1903. The ***Commercial Club*** was founded about 1942. However, by 1943 they were asked to join forces with the Dals. This they did and the town senior team fielded under the name of *Commercial Dalcassians* for a number of years. The Dalcassian name has made sporadic comebacks. From 1971 – 1974 a new minor club was fielded by the town under the Dalcassian name. The *Banner Club* lent assistance to Éire Óg in 1978 and 1980 under the name ***Éire Óg Dals***.

Rovers was formed in 1926 in Old Mill Street. Hugely respected, they won Intermediate honours the following year. The Old Mill Street hurlers remained a strong force in Intermediate throughout the thirties, dominating the Street Leagues. They sported the most beautiful Irish name – *Cumann Iomána Fanaithe na hInse*. It's very probable that Rovers

Éire Óg seniors pictured prior to the 1965 County Final against Newmarket-on-Fergus. *The 1965 Final is considered by purists of the game to be amongst the greatest finals ever played in terms of polished hurling and sportsmanship.* ***Back row, left to right:*** *Des Loftus, Garry Stack, Noel Pyne, Des Neylon, Brian Fitzgerald, Gerry Roche, Massey Dilger, Vincent Loftus, Jim McMahon, Martin Bradley, Paschal O'Brien, Pat Brennan.* ***Front row:*** *John Nevin, Michael Hanrahan, Johnny McCarthy, John Dunne (captain), Aidan Lynch, Dick Pyne, Paddy Carney, Tom Murray, Johnny Guerin.*

Courtesy of Pat Brennan.

preceded the great Cork City club, Glen Rovers, as the boys of Blackpool only really hit their stride when Christy Ring joined them from Cloyne. Likewise the name ***Éire Óg*** is widely used. Cork, Kilkenny, Tipperary and Carlow also field clubs called Éire Óg. The Éire Óg Ennis club was founded in 1952. This historic name is yet another link with Thomas Davis and the Young Ireland Movement. ***The Faughs*** club was reformed in Steele's Terrace in 1943. They quickly became a force in Gaelic Football, winning four senior football titles between 1946 and 1955. The hurling side of the club captured the Intermediate title in 1945. They played Senior Hurling Championship in 1950 and 1951.

Cumann Naomh Eoin ***(St. John's)*** was founded by a group of enthusiastic youths from the Francis Street area. St. John's met with great success. They too were a credit to the town. Many felt they should have gone senior. ***Turnpike*** fielded useful intermediate teams in the fifties. Under this name they contested the finals of 1951 and 1956. *The Market* represented the town in Junior (A) during the mid-1940s. The first new wave of building began in 1935 with the erection of Connolly Villas and Considine's Terrace houses. The 46 Connolly Villas' houses were completed in 1935 with the official ceremony performed by Seán T. O'Kelly. 18 years later a neighbouring scheme was completed in what became known as St. Michael's Villas. With these and other estates such

'St. John's set very high standard'. Juvenile champions 1960 and Dr. Stuart Shield champions pictured on a trip to Dublin sponsored by John Player Cigarettes. Back row, left to right: *Paddy McInerney (mentor), James Ball, Conor Smythe, Ml. Flaherty, Noelie Kelly, Paddy Brigdale, Haulie Molloy, Bernard Carroll, Pat Coffey, Tommy Blake, Des McCullough (mentor).* ***Front row:*** *Ben Sheehan, Peter Brigdale, Frankie Moloney (O'Connell St.), Paschal O'Brien, Ml. Hanrahan (captain), Brian Higgins, Michael Piggott, Seamie Murphy, Eric Hanrahan, Frankie Moloney (St. Flannan's Terrace). (Clare juvenile final St. John's 6-3 Ennis Rovers 3-2).* *Courtesy of Peter Brigdale.*

as Hermitage and Marian Avenue, the town began to spread out. A new hurling competition, the Inter Parish League, was inaugurated during the late 1960s. Ennis fielded two teams – ***St. Michael's*** and ***Hermitage***. St. Michael's made overtures to form a separate independent club. This didn't happen. Nonetheless, St. Michael's and the 'Tage provided evidence that a lot of hurling talent existed in these areas.

The Banner club was formed in 1977 during a hurling fever. The Clare County Senior team won 2 national hurling league titles, capturing the imagination of the country with their attractive brand of play. The *Banner Club* adapted the name of the Banner County. The origin of the Banner (County) goes back to the war of the Spanish Succession (1701 - c. 1709). There were three principal theatres in the war - in the Netherlands and South Germany, Northern Italy and Spain. One of the bloodiest battles in this conflict was at Ramillies in 1706 and in the battle which ensued, the French, under General Villeroi were defeated.

It was after the French had retreated that their allies, the Irish Brigade, engaged the enemy. They routed a Scottish regiment and also defeated an

English regiment, capturing the *Regimental Banners* of both, which were then left with the Irish Benedictine Nuns at Ypres by Murrough O'Brien, Lieutenant Colonel of the Clare Regiment. Clare's Dragoons were the most famous regiment in the Irish Brigade. It was a cavalry regiment. The men and officers were mostly Claremen. They were initiated at Carrigaholt and transported from there to France. The original incident at the Battle of Ramillies is mentioned by Thomas Davis in his rousing poem 'Clare's Dragoons' and it is from this period that the term *The Banner County* originates.

Regardless of what name was in vogue, Ennis club teams have always given of their best, in a sporting and vigorous manner.

GENERAL HARDWARE, SEEDS AND ALL HOUSEHOLD GOODS

Wallpaper and Wedding Presents A Speciality

J. SPELLISSY

56, 58 & 68 Parnell Street - Ennis

Jack Spellissy ran a hardware store in these premises in the 1940s and '50s, he also "sold hurleys at the right price".

Notes on Clubs

In some instances, an abbreviated form of the club name is used. The Newmarket-on-Fergus Club is referred to as simply 'The Blues'. The Ennis Dalcassian Club is referred throughout as 'The Dals'. 'The Mills' refers at all times to O'Callaghan's Mills. The Clarecastle hurlers are known affectionately as 'The Magpies'; the same term applies to the Doonbeg footballers.

For those who don't follow hurling as some of us do, the following is a list of grades. At adult level, the grades are: -

Senior
Intermediate
Junior A
Junior B.
U-21 refers to hurling at under 21 level.
Minor is played at under 18 level.
Juvenile refers to under 16 and under 15 respectively.

If a club wins a Junior B title that club then has the right to play Junior A the following season. A winning Junior A team is upgraded to Intermediate and naturally a winning Intermediate team is promoted to Senior status.

It Started with the Sullivan's

1887 – 1911

"A busy little narrow streeted foreign looking town".
William Makepeace Thackerey (1811-1863) - English Novelist.

"The Lithe Ennis Lads ran on to the pitch sporting their new rich blue jersey's, with a gold hoop and black nicks, with a white stripe down the side".
Clare Journal, 1904

Records for the period 1887-1911 show that there were three senior hurling clubs in Ennis. These were A.M. Sullivan's; Thomas Davis and the Faughs. The Faughs were considered to be the most prominent of the three with newspaper reports of the time describing them as the strongest and most virile.

The first County Convention of the Clare G.A.A. took place in the Town Hall, Ennis on February 14th, 1887. The Convention was attended by representatives of twenty one clubs. The first Clare County Board was elected on that date consisting of a Chairman, Secretary and five other members.

The A.M. Sullivan's Club was called after the Bantry born Nationalist politician, Alexander Martin Sullivan. A.M. Sullivan and his brothers Donal and T.D. belonged to Parnells Irish Party. A.M. Sullivan died a few years before the Parnell split. This was the first Ennis club to affiliate under the auspices of the G.A.A. The name A.M. Sullivan's was proposed by Thomas O'Neill who said that "he was certain that the members would be proud to honour the memory of a man whose genius and other virtues exalted the Irish character, and whose name was written in the most enduring pages of history." All those present heartily concurred and the motion was passed unanimously. The first captain of the club was Paddy Carmody.

A. M. Sullivan's first game in 1887 was against Robert Emmet's from Tulla, with the East Clare men winning easily. Shortly afterwards the Tulla men were invited for a return match in Martin Daly's field, Lifford. A large crowd turned out to see a much improved Ennis side, but again they failed to match Tulla in over 80 minutes. The final score was 1-4 to nil. This match was the first played in Ennis since the founding of the association. At the end of the game both teams formed in processional order and marched through the streets of Ennis to the Town Hall, where a meal was prepared for the teams. The A.M. Sullivan's continued their preparations for the championship with a game against Wolfe Tones of Kilmaley, at Mrs. Roughan's field in Clonroad, on March 20th, 1887. On an exceptionally fine day the Ennis men had their first victory, 2-4 to nil. Prominent for A.M. Sullivan's were Peter Burke, Thomas Fahy, Moloney, Finn, Paddy Carmody, Lyons and Logan. The Clare Journal humorously reported "The mentors made a more judicious selection, though some of the Ennis men were more ornamental than useful". After the game the visitors were entertained at the rooms of the A.M. Sullivans Club at the Town Hall. The band of the St. Patrick's Temperance Society headed by Honest James McMahon entertained. Despite this victory A.M. Sullivan's lost to Barefield by 2-1 to nil in the championship. Twenty two clubs entered the first championship. The teams were divided into districts to cut down on travel.

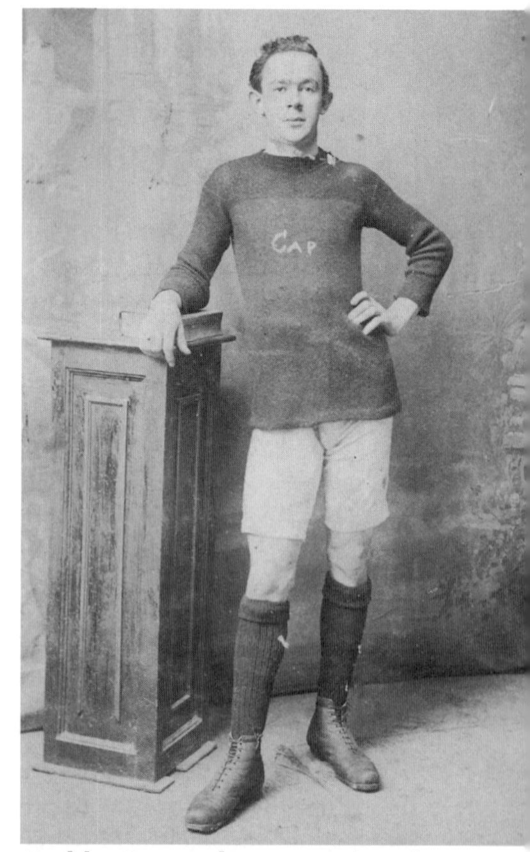

***Paddy Carmody** - captain of Alexander Martin Sullivans Hurling Club. The A.M. Sullivan Branch was the first hurling club affiliated under the auspices of the G.A.A. in Ennis.*

About this time, P.J. Linnane, President of A. M. Sullivan's, organised an Ennis Hurling Tournament including a long puck competition which included many notable players of the day to test their strength and skill in rising and striking the ball. The winner was Thomas Shea of the Feakle Club who drove the ball a distance of 99 yards, with Bonfield, McGuane, Kenny and Moloney also doing well. Though A.M. Sullivan's made little headway in the Championship, they won the Lahinch Tournament, beating Kilfenora in the final. They also won the Junior Cup beating Lisheen in the decider at Hogan's field, Doora. Both competitions were won in late 1887. Witnessed by a large crowd, the Ennismen won by a good margin on a score of 3-3 to 1-1. The Saturday Record reported - "The gallant little boys of the St. Patrick's Temperance Society headed by the soldierly form of Honest James McMahon delighted the hurlers as well as the general public with music as Irish as the G.A.A. itself. The A.M. Sullivan's added another victory to the many other such records already to their credit".

The earliest mention of the Thomas Davis Club appears to be in the Saturday Record, regarding a game with Lord Edward's (Barefield). "The Thomas Davis players including Martin and Mike Ryan, Conlon, Quinlivan and the Dillons, mustered in Jail Street all wearing blue and white striped costumes and caps to match, headed by the St. Patrick's Fife and Drum Band marched through the town. Having met their rival club Lord Edward's, who sported green and white, they joined the processional order and proceeded to the field. In a game lasting 80 minutes, Lord Edward's triumphed by 2-4 to nil."

Michael Cusack attended the game between Thomas Davis and Lord Edwards and thankfully he left us a very atmospheric account of proceedings, published in the Celtic Times in 1887. "Precisely at two o'clock the stirring strains of National music were heard, and away at Ballycoree cars laden with enthusiastic Gaelic men were seen approaching, followed by the members of the Thomas Davis Hurling Club, walking two abreast in picturesque blue and white, a procession of enormous dimensions from Ennis followed and on its arrival at the Two-Mile-Gate they were received with a volley of cheers by the Kilraghtis men, while the fair sex waved their handkerchiefs in welcome of the visitors. Through a difficulty in procuring a suitable ball, play did not commence until ten minutes before three o'clock, and both teams having entered the arena crossed camáns, the ball was thrown in by referee, Mr. Pat McInerney, of Ennis." The Barefield men won easily.

Notwithstanding the result for the Thomas Davis, a splendid time was had by all as Cusack continues - "Immediately afterwards, all marched to the rooms of the Barefield Club, where the visitors were sumptuously entertained, and after spending a very pleasant evening, they left for home amid the enthusiastic cheering of the people of Kilraghtis."

Ennis Faughs from Old Mill Street entered an independent team in various tournaments as early as 1887. One of the earliest recorded was at Fushagh in the townland of Kilcross near Ennis. Seven teams competed - Corofin, Lord Edwards, Kilmaley, Dysart, Kilnamona, A.M. Sullivan's and Faughs. The winners were Kilnamona who received a prize of a fat sheep. Like the Fushagh tournament, Ruan too organised a tournament in 1888. The winning prize in this case was a pony. Ennis Faughs overcame Corofin and Barefield (second string) to win a place in the semi-final against the hosts. The Saturday Record reported on November 25th "Old Mill Street was astir at about 1 o'clock . 6 'buses' and 7 short cars headed by the St. Patrick's Temperance Fife and Drum Band dashed through the streets en route for the scene of the contest. As soon as the Ennis men entered Ruan they were greeted with 3 cheers from the thousands assembled there. As was customary Faughs drew first blood with a point from the throw in. By half time Faughs led Ruan by 1-3 to 0-2 with Frawley the Faughs goalkeeper in fine form. Faughs were well on top at the end - with darkness falling."

Contemporary reports describe every match in the series as a 'grueller' but none more equalled the final between Faughs and Kilnamona. After normal time the sides were level, so 30 minutes extra time was played to decide ownership of the pony. Faughs won after what was described "as fierce and terrible rushes by both sides". Faughs included Martin Moloney, Jack Casey, Stephen Kenny, Harry Moloney and Matt Ryan in their line up. They suffered their first defeat in these tournaments (which were taken as seriously as the official championships) when they went under to Robert Emmets by 3-6 to 1-1. In the 1889 Doora tournament, Tulla confirmed their superiority over Faughs winning easily by 4-9 to 2-1, in Carrahan, on June 22, 1889.

Amalgamation of A.M. Sullivans and Thomas Davis

Towards the close of the 19th century, emigration was a sad fact of life in Ireland. The dwindling numbers of young men who left Ireland to seek their fortunes abroad meant that the game of hurling suffered with fewer men available to play. In Ennis the shortage of players led to the amalgamation of two clubs – A.M. Sullivan's and Thomas Davis. This effectively ended the name A.M. Sullivan's. Speaking to the Saturday Record newspaper at the time, the President of A.M. Sullivan's said "We used to have two teams but now we can hardly get a handful to play - because the railway stations are full during the summer with Gaels leaving Ireland" Perhaps also, hurling at that time didn't have the glamour and excitement that it has today. Interestingly, a comment made by a colleague of P.J. Linnane's, a Mr. Madigan gives us an insight into the views of the time when he criticised the young men of Ennis who considered that "hurling was not dignified for them".

G.A.A. Split

The G.A.A. almost met an early demise in 1891 due to the split in the association which evolved out of the Charles Stewart Parnell/Katherine O'Shea affair. It seems that no area of Irish life remained unaffected by the ripples from this famous episode, the affair became enmeshed in a web of British political opportunism, hypocrisy and outrage. The affair split the Irish party and ultimately the whole of Ireland. Parnell, the champion of Home Rule, saw his power and achievements dwindle away before his early death in 1891, aged only 45. In 1891 the Gaelic Athletic Association broke into two bitterly opposed sections. Many County Boards were dissolved, in Clare no official County Championships took place from 1891-1895. In 1896 the County Board was re-established, with Pat O'Neill as secretary, and Clare took part again in the championships. It's interesting to note that the other Munster counties continued to participate during the Parnell split.

Prominence of Gaelic Football

During the 1890's, Ennis had a famous football club, the Ennis Dalcassians. In 1897, the Dalcassians won their first senior championship and between the years 1897 and 1911, numerous senior football titles came to the club. At this time, great rivalry existed between the Dals and Kilrush Shamrocks. Stalwarts of the Ennis side included Joe Nono, Paul Hayes, Michael Hayes, Tom Clohessy, Jim Clohessy, Patrick Considine, Paddy Kenny, Pako Malone, Michael Smyth, Fred McMahon, John Griffey. Practically all of these men wore the Clare colours at senior level. Much of the success of football in Ennis was due to the mentors James Coughlan and James Hayes. The latter also gave five sons to the game.

Despite the incredible success at football, success at hurling continued to elude Ennis hurling teams. In 1903 Thomonds of Ennis reached the County Final after a series of good wins. Pitted against Kilnamona and with players of the calibre of 'Napper' Cullinan, Marrinan, Malone and O'Neill, great things were expected of them, but carelessness and over-confidence proved their undoing. Thomonds could only muster 12 players on County Final day and had to borrow five hurlers from the huge attendance to complete their 17-man line-up.

The Journal Correspondent tells us that "Great crowds assembled at Fushagh on 5th January, 1904 numbering amongst them some hoary heads who delighted to speak of the hurling of yesterday, and who reasonably expected to witness a closely contested match, but a more one-sided affair, and a poorer exhibition of hurling for a final, neither they nor I have ever beheld. It does not speak very well for a team when they have to borrow the weapons of war from their opponents, and to pick youths from the side-line to complete their numbers."

Kilnamona had little difficulty in destroying the feeble challenge of Thomonds on a score of 4-14 to nil. However, hurling affairs can't have been that bad in the capital town as the Dalcassians and Kilmaley, Kilnamona and Ruan served up excellent fare in a double header in June, 1904 at the Dals field off the Old Mill Street. "Both matches were of good character and friendship displayed on all sides. They were models of what hurling matches should be. The Kilmaley and Ennismen were first to line up. The lithe Ennis lads ran out on the pitch sporting their new rich blue jerseys, with a gold hoop and black nicks. And after a highly entertaining match Ennis succumbed to the Kilmaley men by 3-4 to 1-5." (Journal).

The Ennis team was: - Mack (Goalie), John Cullinan (Capt.), Pako Malone, Forde, Willie 'Dodger' Considine, Marrinan, Steve Kenny, Fitzgerald, Moran, Tom Clohessy, McCormack, Michael 'Beezer' Spellissy, Steve Millar, Moloney, Dave O'Donnell, Slattery, O'Neill.

In the 1906 Championship Ennis Dals travelled to the unlikely venue of Lahinch to play Cloonanaha (Inagh) on a splendid day, but a strong breeze blew off the swelling bay, interfering with play. 'Dodger' Considine was in form notching 1-2, with the Ennismen winning 2-4 to 2-1.

Following this, Ennis and Kilnamona clashed in the semi-final of the Redmond Cup, at the Showgrounds. A share of 'unnecessary heat' was introduced into the game, with a number of players being cautioned and one sent off. Kilnamona staged a great rally to force a draw on a scoreline of 4-9 to 4-9.

Erratic Reporting of Sporting Fixtures

During the early years of the 20th century, reports of games in the Clare Journal were very erratic and confusing. The paper refers to the town senior team as the Ennis Hurling Club, but in other reports the correspondent calls them The Dalcassians. This newspaper highlighted international news to a greater extent. Copious accounts of the Boer War (1899-1902), General Buller's advance, etc. was published. Naturally the Home Rule issue received huge coverage including the positive speeches of Colonel Arthur Lynch, MP for West Clare, on the subject. The obituary of the American Frontier Sheriff, Pat Garrett, (1850-1908) also received headlines. Garrett, who had many years earlier shot Billy the Kid, was assassinated on a mountain pass near El Paso.

Dublin Hurlers Visit Showgrounds

On June 28, 1908 the Dublin Hurling Team visited Clare. The metropolitan side selected from the Kickhams, Faughs and Thomas Davis clubs was invited to the Banner County to play Clare in a tournament game in aid of the Quin presbytery. The Dublin team brought a big following with them. Many taking advantage of the glorious weather, travelled down by special excursion trains. The teams were played on to the pitch at the Showgrounds by the St. Patrick's Temperance Society Band, and despite good displays from 'Dodger' Considine, Paddy Kenny, Dunny O'Callaghan (Mills), Clare lost by 2-14 to 1-10. Again in that year in the County Championship, Ennis lost to Kilmaley by 3-7 to 1-4.

To conclude on this short section it's interesting to note that neither Ennis, Clarecastle nor Newmarket-on-Fergus between them won a Senior Hurling Championship during the years 1887-1910. Up to 1908 Clarecastle only played Gaelic football. It was only then that Clarecastle started to hurl. Likewise Newmarket were very strong in Gaelic Football. The rural parishes seemed better able to undertake hurling. They had ash trees. They were better off. They could make their own hurleys. Wealth always determines what you can do.

Ennis Dals Make Their Name

1911 – 1923

After a number of fruitless years, the Ennis Hurling Club reached the county senior final in 1911. In that game, the Ennis team was pitted against the seasoned hurlers of O'Callaghan's Mills who included in their ranks Paddy Kelleher, Sonny McInerney, and several other county hurlers in Tom 'Dagger' Cooney, Ned Grace and 'Fowler' McInerney.

Staged at the Showgrounds, the teams were played on to the pitch by the St. Patrick's Temperance band. From once the ball left the hands of the referee, Thomas Kinnane of Clarecastle, the game was well contested with early 'Mills' raids contained by 'Dodger' Considine, Jim Marrinan, Grealish and Mack. The Journal reported "now and again, Pako Malone was called on to save, which he did in splendid style, winning the admiration of all. After an even first half, the teams retired with Ennis leading by one point, and though the 'Mills got through for a second half goal, they were forced to play a defensive game to curb the spirited onslaughts of the Ennis forwards". In the end, the Ennis Hurling Club ran out winners by 3-1 to 1-2. The team was captained by Willie 'Dodger' Considine and included his brother, Brendan, a youth of fourteen.

The 1911 win is also interesting because it was the final year of the seventeen a side competition before the whip forward position became redundant and hurling standardised to fifteen a side. It was the beginning of a great era in town hurling and once again the street league was the catalyst.

In the Clare Journal of February 2nd 1912, Slieve Callan in his column, called for the adoption of Parish Rule, (The rule that states that one can only play for the parish one was born in or one is living in), 'I say that in order to keep hurling alive, Gaels must stand up for the adoption of Parish Rule.' He also condemned the amount of rancour amongst certain clubs and called on the Clare selectors to pick the best talent in the county. As County Champions the Ennis Club had four votes on the County Selection Committee of seven members.

Ennis Dals - Newmarket Rivalry

June 11th, 1911 saw the beginning of a long and sporting rivalry between Ennis and Newmarket. The balance of power was beginning to shift from clubs such as O'Callaghan's Mills, Kilnamona and Tulla. The Newmarket club was reorganised in 1908 when they adapted as their colours the royal blue of Munster with a saffron band.

In 1911 the Blues contested the Willie Redmond Cup Final (Senior League). They won their first senior championship in 1912 beating Ennis along the way in a 'needle' game. The referee Mr. Wallace cautioned both teams before the throw in.

Newmarket met Ennis Dals in the 1913 Championship at St. Flannan's College grounds. The Ennis club now run in conjunction with the very successful football club came out easy winners by 8-1 to 3-1. The Blues had their best players in Rob Doherty, Michael Killeen and Jim Clancy. The Clare Journal wrote - "Paddy Kenny must be congratulated on his own and his team's display. It is a proud distinction to lower the prestige of such a team as Newmarket, who have such a record."

In April, 1914, Ennis consolidated their dominance over Newmarket when they beat the Blues by 6-2 to 1-1 in a tournament game in aid of the Ennis Temperance Society. A handsome set of medals were presented to the Ennismen. A novel feature of the programme was a tug of war contest for the championship of Clare. Kilmaley emerged the winners beating off the challenge of Clarecastle, Doora and Ennis.

In 1914 and 1915 Ennis Dals won senior championships back to back at the expense of Newmarket. The 1915 decider wasn't played until October 1916.It appears that both clubs favoured playing the final at the Market's Field (Limerick), but the County Board ordered the game to be played at a Clare venue, the finalists then agreed on Killaloe. A special train was laid on at a cost of ½ a crown. Both sides played to form with the Dals holding out for a 3-4 to 2-4 win, with Martin Moloney and Sham Spellissy best for Ennis.

Again the 1916 final was much delayed. The Blues and Dals reached the final for the third season in succession. The clubs agreed to toss for the choice of venue. However, when Newmarket won the toss Ennis Dals reneged on their promise to go to Newmarket should they lose the toss. After a heated County Board meeting, Tull Considine told the Board he had done everything in his power to persuade his team to play in Newmarket but to no avail. The Kilkishen and Barefield venues were then put forward. 'Sham' Spellissy told the delegates that Ennis Dals had been blackguarded in Kilkishen in the past. The County Board refuted this allegation and protested against Sham Spellissy's observation. Finally, Considine, Spellissy and Halpin (Newmarket) retired for a private meeting. The County Board Chairman Fr. Michael Crowe, then added if Ennis won't go to Barefield they will have to play in Newmarket or risk being expelled from the 1916 Championship. The Dals had no option then but to travel to Newmarket.

The Ennis Dals arrived at Flanagan's field in Newmarket in two parties, one led by 'Dodger' Considine and the other led by Martin 'Handsome' Moloney. The Dals, who played with a stiff wind in the first half, drew first blood with a point by Tull Considine, but the Blues got on top to lead at the interval by 5-1 to 1-2. The Dals tried to make a match of it in the third quarter but were totally out-classed by their opponents, losing by 8-2 to 2-2.

SELECTED PEN-PICTURES OF ENNIS DALS – 1914/1915 WINNING CHAMPIONSHIP TEAMS

Willie 'Dodger' Considine: Made his Clare debut about 1902. "One of the old guard, a safe and strong player." - Clare Journal. 'Dodger' won senior championships with Ennis in 1911, 1914 and 1915. As well as winning a Munster and All-Ireland in 1914 he won a Croke Cup with the Banner County in 1908. He represented Clare almost constantly until April, 1916 when The Banner County lost to Dublin in the Croke Cup Final of 1915.

Martin 'Handsome' Moloney: "An ideal type, generous, broad-minded and amiable to a degree. Universally popular, a friend to all. Well and nobly did he play his part in the Munster Final win over Cork." Clare Champion, 1935. "Very reliable with a great turn of speed, Moloney was a beautiful hurler and a lovely striker of the ball". (Brendan Considine).

Martin Moloney made his inter-county debut in 1909 and represented the Banner county until 1918. He won three senior championships 1911, 1914, 1915.

Brendan Considine: "Made his Championship debut versus Limerick in 1914 and did so well to justify his inclusion in the premier team for the rest of the championship. He is fast and useful". –Clare Journal.

A brother of 'Dodger', Brendan was the youngest member of the 1914 team. He later won All-Ireland honours with Dublin in 1917 and a Munster Senior championship medal with Cork in 1920. He later represented Waterford before returning to the Banner county 1928-1930.

James 'Sham' Spellissy: Born 1896, one of the youngest members of the 1914 team. Made his senior debut v Kerry in the opening round at Listowel. A regular member of the Clare team from 1914 to 1920, 'Sham' Spellissy won three senior medals in 1914, 1915 and 1924 before transferring to Dublin to work. He also won a senior football medal with the Dals in 1914 and a Munster Senior Championship with the Clare Footballers in 1917. Sham's brothers Jack and Michael 'Beezer' also played hurling. Jack won All-Ireland Junior in 1914 and played senior in the Croke Cup 1915/16. 'Beezer' emigrated to the States in 1911. His family live in Lowell, Massachusetts. 'Sham' later excelled at hockey with Railway Union and 3 Rock Rovers.

Dan Minogue: Captain of the Clare Junior team. "One of the most reliable backs in Clare. Very cool in the most trying circumstances, he is reliable and in the wing where he plays never fails to beat off an attack." Clare Journal, 1915.

Paddy Gordon: "A clever player, his left handers are always well directed, and when it comes to fighting for the leather, Paddy is always in the thick of it, and invariably comes out on top." (Clare Journal) Paddy Gordon made his debut with the Dalcassians in 1911.

Jack Spellissy: "Possibly the most stylish hurler on the Clare Junior team. Like his brother, Sham, he plays an intelligent game, always cool and effective, and the outstanding feature is that every stroke is turned to advantage." Clare Journal

Edward (Ted) Lucid: "A strong, determined player, with great dash, he is very useful, and when he strikes in the forward line the custodian has his work well cut out for him. A member of the Ennis team for the past three or four seasons." Clare Journal. Ted Lucid later married Annie Spellissy, a sister of Jack and James.

Michael J. Baker: "M.J. is a very consistent player, having spent some time in Dublin, where he was very popular, he joined the Ennis team on his return, with which he has been playing for a number of years. All-Ireland Junior Medallist in 1914." Clare Journal

1914 All-Ireland Senior Hurling Champions

With the success of Clare teams in recent years, maybe it's now time to look back on one of Clare's finest moments in hurling – the winning of the 1914 All-Ireland title. The men of 1914 had a fine balance of youth and experience. The team, trained by Jim O'Hehir, was one of the best prepared ever to represent the Banner County. The Clare Journal of April 20th, 1914 applauded all concerned with Clare hurling. "A step in the right direction has been taken by the Committee of the Quin Club, who offered a set of medals for competitions amongst the teams of the sub-division of the County Board to hold a series of inter-divisional matches in Quin, with a view to bringing out the best blood in Clare, so that the selection committee may have an opportunity of seeing all the probably inter-county players, thus assisting them to choose the best team to do battle for the county later on." Mid-Clare, represented by Ennis, Quin, Barefield, Crusheen, Kilnamona and Ruan, lost to South-Clare by 5-4 to 3-4. The Ennis players on view were Willie and Brendan Considine, Paddy Kenny, Paddy Gordon, Sham Spellissy, Pako Malone and Michael McElligott. A couple of weeks later, Mid-Clare played East Clare. At least 10 members of the Dals Club were tried in this match, including Dan Minogue, Johnny Coote, Steve Millar and James Marrinan. The 1914 Dals team was outstanding in that 13 of them played senior or junior hurling for Clare in the 1914 championships. Those that definitely represented the juniors included Michael J. Baker, Freddy Garrihy, Paddy Gordon, Johnny Coote, Ted Lucid, Dan Minogue, James Marrinan and Jack Spellissy. Michael J. Spellissy, a son of (James) Sham, recalled to me – "I always remember my father saying that the senior and junior teams of that year were of equal ability." Before facing Clare in the All Ireland Final, Laois had impressive wins over Wexford, Dublin and Kilkenny. Their style of hurling had changed from the old bustling methods to a more 'scientific style' modelled on the clean striking of Kilkenny. The gates of Jones Road, now Croke Park, opened promptly at 1 p.m. and admission to all parts of the grounds was by ticket only. It seems that there were villains and touts around in those days too as the GAA warned patrons not to purchase tickets from any persons not wearing the official badges of green, white and gold. A special tram service ran from Nelson's Pillar to Ballybough. The members of the Faughs, Fianna, St. Laurence O'Toole and Purveyor Clubs acted as stewards for the big game.

On their way to the championship, Clare accounted for Kerry, Limerick, Cork and finally Laois. The team was backboned by Ennis Dalcassians, O'Callaghan's Mills, Quin and Newmarket. The Dals had five representatives in the Considines, Martin 'Handsome' Moloney, James 'Sham' Spellissy and Paddy Kenny. Kenny, a regular Clare hurler since 1907

Paddy Kenny.

and captain of the 1912 team, played in Clare's victory over Limerick but took no further part in the Championship that year.

Willie 'Dodger' Considine was one of the most senior members of the panel, having made his debut in 1902. His brother Brendan, the youngest member of the team "took his bow" at inter-county hurling in the second round of the championship of 1914. Likewise, Sham Spellissy made his debut in the 1914 series. The fifth member from the Dals club was Martin Moloney introduced to senior fare in 1909. Likewise, the Blues had a big representation on the team in John Fox, Robert Doherty, James Clancy and Jim Guerin. The latter was outstanding in the final, scoring three goals. The captain of the Newmarket club, Rob Doherty made his first inter-county appearance in 1912, while John Fox and Jim Clancy were first introduced in 1914. Clancy was first seen in the Clare colours on April 5th, playing against Kilkenny in Athlone. O'Callaghan's Mills was one of the strongest clubs in Clare at this time. The 'Mills' produced Ned Grace, Thomas McGrath, Patrick 'Fowler' McInerney and John Shaloo. Edward Grace "a safe and sure player" was highly experienced. He was a member of the Croke Cup winning team and had been on the scene since 1906. Tom McGrath "a fast and resourceful player" made his county debut in 1907. Like Grace, John Shaloo was a member of the county team since the Croke Cup success of 1908. Shaloo played with distinction in all of Clare's victories in 1914. While Pat 'Fowler' McInerney, the goalkeeper made his debut versus Galway on February 13th, 1914 in Gort. He too would play in all of Clare's 1914 championship games.

This brings us to the Quin hurling club, who supplied Amby Power, his brother Joe, and Michael Flanagan. By this time, the Powers had given great service to Clare. Joe was a county man since 1903, with Amby making his debut at the tender age of sixteen. Their colleague Michael Flanagan made his senior debut in 1912. Some of the other panel members included the Whitegate club captain, Patrick McDermott "a play anywhere type", McDermott starred in the 1913 Thomond Shield. Patrick Moloney, the Feakle club captain made his first appearance in the Clare jersey against Tipperary in Ennis in 1912. "A strenuous player", Moloney played in the provincial final win over Cork. An injury curtailed his chances of starting the 1914 All-Ireland final. However, he replaced the injured John Fox during the course of the game. John 'Langer' Rodgers was Tulla's sole representative. A regular on the county team since 1911, Rodgers came on in the first half against Laois for the injured Sham Spellissy, who suffered a severe knee-cap injury. Like Paddy Kenny, F. Brady played in Clare's win over Limerick but didn't feature again.

Despite the score-line of five goals and a point to a goal, it must be

Ennis Dalcassians, winners of Clare senior championships 1914, 1915. Back row, left to right: *Paddy Kenny, Martin Moloney, G. Kelly, Tull Considine, Willie 'Dodger' Considine, M. Hanrahan, Patrick Moloney.* ***Middle row:*** *James (Sham) Spellissy, Paddy Connell, Freddie Garrihy, Jim Marrinan, Jack Spellissy, Edward Lucid.* ***Front row:*** *Michael J. Baker, Dan Minogue (captain), Paddy Gordon. Courtesy of Ml. J. Spellissy.*

said that Laois put up a good show, but their forwards failed to break down a stone-wall Clare defence, marshalled by 'Dodger' Considine.

After the game, Mr. M.J. Crowe presented the Great Southern Challenge Cup to the Clare captain, Amby Power. Mr. William Redmond MP for East Clare was then asked by the Clare team to visit the Laois dressing room. This Willie Redmond did and spoke on behalf of the Clare team. He said that "the Claremen desire to compliment you on a fair and manly challenge. It is their opinion that you could not have been more fair and honourable opponents".

The Scorers for Clare were:

Jim Guerin	-	3-0	Martin Moloney	-	1-0
Jim Clancy	-	1-0	Brendan Considine	-	0-1

Other sources credit Patrick Moloney with one of the goals and Guerin with 2 goals.

Colours – Clare-White Jersey with Green Sash. Laois – Amber Jersey with Black Bars

Referee – Mr. J. Lawlor, Kilkenny.

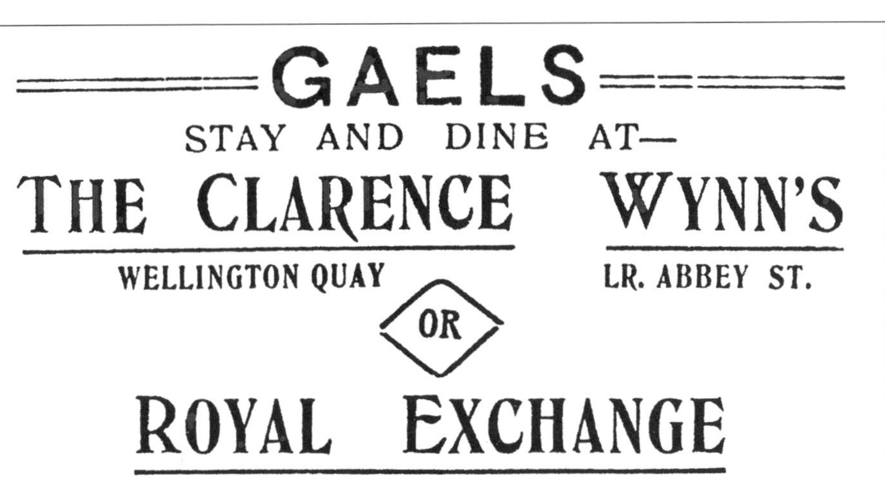

An advertisement placed in the 1914 All-Ireland Hurling Final programme.

Successful Town League

A successful Town League was run off in 1917, comprising four teams captained by the Spellissys, James Wylde and Tull Considine. Despite this activity, hurling in the town seemed to dip with the East Clare Clubs of Scariff, O'Callaghan's Mills, and Clonlara taking the laurels.

Tull Considine and Sham Spellissy were selected on the Clare Team for the Croke Park Tournament in 1920 and with wins over Limerick and Tipperary, Clare qualified to meet Dublin at headquarters, where they lost by 5-5 to 3-6. Others to star for Clare in the Croke Park Tournament were Dan Flannery, Dan Tracey and Pat McSweeney. With the political situation as it was during the years 1917-1923 and with Ennis under martial law, sporting pastimes were thrown into chaos. The County Board was suspended during 1921-22 with no championships taking place. The inactivity of these years led to the deterioration of standards. The Mills and Ennis contested the 1920 County Final (played 1922) with Ennis winning by 2-4 to 1-1 at Clooney. However, the Mills objected and the County Board ordered a replay. The Ennis Dals Team failed to show up for the replay as several of their players were involved in a Junior Football Final in Kilkee. The Board then declared the 1920 County Final null and void. By 1924, with life getting back to some form of normality, the Dalcassian Club was re-organised with Bill and Eddie Fahy and Jack Duffy, amongst the prime movers.

Random Thoughts of Ennis Long Ago

Martin Cronin

As an Ennisman I would like to give some impressions of Ennis long ago, which I'm sure will be appreciated by all Ennis-born natives.

My longest memory concerns the burial in Ennis Pro-Cathedral of Most Rev. Dr. McRedmond in 1904 and I had to march from the Boys' National school with a lot of others my own age to attend the Requiem Mass and burial. As my family grew up we were up to every devilment and as a consequence we got into many scrapes.

Many games were played in the Market and our favourite was Abinababina but we had hurling matches, peggina tops and rounders and on Shrove Tuesday nights we battered everyone's door with tin cans tied with a rope. It was the custom to bang each bachelor's door but we had to vent our feelings by banging every door irrespective of whether they were married or not.

Darcy's Forge was a favourite meeting place for all the gang but Jack Darcy and his helper, Jim Quinn were never molested. In fact we all took a hand in blowing the bellows and doing some of the sledging for them. At that time a large turf fire for wheel bands to redden was a treat we all appreciated very much.

Films and Opera

The Irish Animated Picture Company brought the pictures to the Town Hall occasionally, but the people of Ennis had treats in store when Easter Grime Opera Company, George Mallon's Dramatic Company and William Dobell's Dramatic Company used to visit the town.

Very few people are now aware that Ennis produced a great sculptor during the 19th Century. His name was Matt Cabey and it was he cut the stone and O'Connell's figure at the top of the monument in O'Connell Square. Matt Cabey also did some lovely work at the National Bank, opposite the Post Office, bunches of grapes cut out in stone can be seen around the main door and windows.

On May 20th, 1910, a great meeting was held in Ennis by the Nationalist or Home Rule Party and John Redmond, MP, was the principal speaker. Every Sunday morning the lovely band of the Clare

A once prominent Ennis business and G.A.A. sporting family name, of Belgian origin.

Artillery or Militia paraded from the Barracks at Kilrush Road to 10 o'clock Mass in the Cathedral. It was a wonderful sight to see over 1,000 men in spiked helmets and in peace-time uniforms march down the New Line which was the name we used for the Kilrush Road. I knew all the marches off by heart and in later years had the pleasure of playing some of them in the Temperance Band, of which I became a member in 1910. At that time a fife and drum band was formed in the Labour Hall in Lower Market Street and 'Bacchus' McCarthy was a bandmaster, and every Saturday night he gave a solo selection in the Market; the people living in the vicinity of Darcy's Forge would gladly give hours listening to the rendering of the Dear Irish Boy. He certainly was a great Bandmaster.

On February 25, 1909, I became an altar boy at the Pro-Cathedral and was very thankful to Mickey Hastings who was then Clerk of the Parish. The men's Confraternity Meeting was held every Monday night and our section was St. Patrick's which was also the section for Market Street residents, and the section leader or Prefect was Jim Moloney. While a member of the Temperance Band, all the members put in two hours practice every night and the music played by the band under the baton of Bob Lennon was second to none. Every Sunday the Temperance Band attended various outings including hurling matches, house shows, etc. and some of the band were not so temperate by the time we arrived back in Ennis that night.

Hurling Matches

The hurling balls we used were purchased from Matt Higgins for 1d and 2d and at that time he could supply an All-Ireland hurling ball for 6d. Matt was a tanner by trade.

The hurling matches that took place from time to time in Clonroad Fairgreen were hectic affairs and we who lived in the Market were bombarded with challenges from Corkally Lane, the Turnpike, Old Mill Street and the Boreen. We used to hurl with 'spocks' and the only people who were blessed with real hurleys were the Considines and Fahys of the Turnpike. The Market almost always came out on top and instead of hurling for one hour, the matches often took three hours, as the team who scored the first 12 goals were declared winners. While a schoolboy at Ennis National School, I remember many a knock and the Master, who was Mr. John P. Mackey, was a strict disciplinarian. Once you entered the school precincts in the morning you could consider yourself a prisoner until school was over in the evening. 'Craney' Duggan was head teacher and he was very handy with the cane and all the hard chaws had a very rough time under him. Seán Gordon, who replaced Craney, was a toff and trained some of the boys to sing Irish songs and he took us to various Feiseanna all over the county to compete. We did not let him down.

Our principal shop was Guiton's and one could get as much sweets from Mrs. Guiton for 1d. A special biscuit called a Napper-Nathy could be purchased for ½d and 12 soldiers buttons cost 1d (old penny).

Dances were held in Enright's yard off Mill Street two or three times weekly. The dances were run by Tommy Redmond who was a famous piccolo player and was known far and wide as Redmond's hop. It was a pleasure to take part in a set of lancers, quadrilles or Caledonians or to watch the dancers who knew how to dance. We paid the princely sum of 4d for admission.

The Circus

Several visited the town from time to time in my young days and the charge of 2d for admission applied to the day shows and if one had 2½d one could buy a bar of Brown Rock from Mr. Murphy for ½d (old half-penny), which one could keep munching throughout the performance.

Hanneford's Circus was really good, and the others included Buff Bill's, Lloyd's, Poole's, Bosco's and Duffy's were always welcome, but to find the entrance fee a boy would have to start saving for over a week.

Sixpence (6d) admitted a person to the night shows. It was really lovely to watch the circus procession wind its way through the town at 1 p.m. on the day the circus was billed to perform.

In January 1910, I left the Boys' National School and was accepted as a pupil by the Christian Brothers. Brother Xavier Doyle was headmaster and at that time he impressed upon all the pupils how necessary it was to bring 1d school money every Monday morning, as the Brothers were not state aided then.

Bro. T. B. Cronin was a great organiser of Gaelic games and he started a league with four teams from the school. The four captains were Brendan Considine, Paddy Colgan, Tim O'Leary and (Dr.) Tommy Daly, the celebrated hurling goalie. The first league final took place on November 11th, 1911 and was won by Paddy Colgan's team. The teams were then reshuffled and Brendan Considine's team won the second final played at the Fairgreen on February 10th, 1912. I was lucky to have been selected on both winning teams and the little medals which we were presented with could not have cost more than 1 shilling each.

Frank Gordon who afterwards emigrated to the USA was my teacher in my second year at the CBS. He was a first class musician and played the piano at all school concerts and functions. He was the first person who introduced "It's a long way to Tipperary" and another old favourite "Casey Jones". He was killed in France during the First World War, fighting with the American Forces.

On July 15, 1912, I joined the Sappers and it was at the Ordnance Survey Office in Ennis that I came into contact with another of the Gordon family. He was Patrick Gordon and was father of both Seán and Frank. The survey of Ireland was completed in 1913 and in consequence all the staff at the Ennis office was transferred to various offices in England, Dublin and Belfast, and my destination was Dublin. During my time in Dublin I saw all the various regiments being mobilised for the war. The happiest day of my life was October 18, 1914, when I was at Croke Park to see Clare win the All-Ireland Hurling Final by 5-1 to 1-0 for Laois.

I returned to Ennis early in 1916 and took a commercial course at St. Flannan's College at the time that Rev. Fr. O'Connell was President. Up to the outbreak of the 1916 Rebellion the people were all staunch Redmondites but quite a change took place when the leaders were executed and soon the majority of the people of Clare were supporters of the Sinn Féin movement. As all Clare people are aware, the most important election since Daniel O'Connell was elected MP in 1828 took place with Eamon de Valera representing Sinn Féin and Patrick Lynch, KC, who represented the Redmondites. The East Clare election took place on July 10, 1917, owing to the death of William Redmond, who was killed in France earlier that year. The election was bitterly fought and the Market was de Valera's stronghold – we even called the street de Valera Street.

The volunteers were organised by the Brennan brothers and each night 500 or 600 young men marched through the town of Ennis behind Thomas Ashe and Bill Mackey of Clonmel. Prior to the election all Sinn Féin supporters congregated in the Market after the route march each night and all the Sinn Féin songs were sung with gusto until the early hours of the morning, and if a Redmondite happened to be seen he would have been in for a very lively time.

Clare Election

On the morning of the election I had the pleasure of wishing Mr. de Valera good luck. He stayed in the Old Ground Hotel and was up and about at 3 a.m. During the election campaign many fierce tussles took place and on one occasion I had the satisfaction of beating up one of Mr. Lynch's supporters because he had in turn beaten up one of my brothers. I always consider that we had a great following on Dev's side and I could never forget the heroism, which was rampant at that time. It must be remembered that a lot of Redmondite followers came to Ennis to help Mr. Lynch, especially those who arrived from Limerick. Amongst the Sinn Féin followers I must mention 'Gessler' Keane for pride of place and Freddie Garrahy, William 'Dodger' Considine and Peter O'Loughlin. These four supporters were outstanding and helped in no small way to secure Dev's return. There were lots of others who did their fair share but they are too numerous to mention. When the result of the poll was announced, I cycled from the Courthouse at a speed Bernie Donnelly would envy with the great news – de Valera 5,010, Lynch 2,035.

After the election the Volunteers got down to business and on each occasion that we went drilling we were followed by the Peelers. One evening we had a route march to Claureen and we decided to give the RIC some running so we went in to Martin Halloran's wood and we were still followed. Our leader gave orders to some of the Volunteers to get back on the main road and cut the tyres and tubes of the Peelers' bicycles while the main body of Volunteers kept the RIC well in touch.

All the leaders were arrested later and each received a sentence of six months. Jimmy Griffey was the first to be arrested. Frank Shinnors was next and then Jimmy Madigan, Tom Browne, Bill McNamara, John Joe Egan, 'Gessler' Keane and Art O'Donnell, but still we carried on.

Two tinkers were fighting outside Daffy's Pub in the Market but a crowd of the boys rescued the tinkers from the police. After a short time about fifty police patrolled the street but we all escaped, including the tinkers.

A crowd of Market boys met at Ned Sheehan's corner one night and a patrol of Peelers came along from Carmody Street. One of the crowd,

Eamon de Valera addressing supporters at the Court House during the Clare election of 1917. De Valera won the East Clare seat following the death of Willie Redmond. Courtesy of Clare Co. Library.

who was none other than Jacko Flanagan, shouted "to hell with the Saxon foes'. The RIC gentlemen charged us. They were fully armed and we had no choice but to run for it. We were followed out the New Line and out across by Cahercalla up the Rocky Road until we finally made our escape, but we had to wait quite a while until we were sure the Peelers were gone, before we returned home.

There's no doubt but Ennis is a very prosperous town and although I've been domiciled away from the old town for a good number of years I still retain happy memories of the good old times I had as a boy. Every day of my life my thoughts go back to the grand old stock I left behind.

In conclusion I wish to state my happiness would be completed if Clare win the All-Ireland Hurling title this year, 1966, and that the County Board reinstate Jim Cullinan of Newmarket, whom I consider to be the best hurler in Ireland.

Martin Cronin was a native of Garraunakilla, Upper Market Street. This article is compiled from essays he wrote for the Clare Champion and the Clare County Express. It is reproduced with the permission of his nephew Peter Cronin.

Caruso's Ennis

Oh, had they died by Pearse's side
Or fought with Cathal Brugha
Their names we would keep
Where the Fenian's sleep
'Neath the shroud of the foggy dew

Jimmy Mahony was born in Ennis in 1900. His father was John Mahony, a tailor at Our Lady's Psychiatric Hospital, and his mother was Sarah nee (McNamara), whose family was originally from Newmarket-on-Fergus. Jimmy attended the CBS and later served an apprenticeship as a jeweller and watchmaker at Maurers. He married Margaret Corry from the Clonroad in Ennis in 1925. Two years later they emigrated to the United States. In 1988 Jimmy spoke to Ollie Byrnes and Michael Keane on West Coast Radio. He recalled his school days and the cultural, social and political history of Ennis during the turbulent years of 1910 – '27. Jimmy died in New York on January 5, 1995. The interviews, which were kept on tape, went as follows:-

Jimmy Mahony pictured in September, 1924.

Q. What are your recollections of life in the town about 1910?

J.M. The town was very quiet. The only excitement was looking forward to the passage of the Home Rule Bill. We had the Clare Militia in the Military Barracks. They had Sunday parades. They had a band attached which put on quite a show. Apart from that, the big interest was Gaelic Games. Gaelic football was very strong in Ennis. There were a lot of street leagues in hurling, which produced some of the successful senior and junior players of 1914. The County Champions, Ennis Dalcassians, had the pick and they selected some from Newmarket, Amby Power from Quin and Tom McGrath. They made a very good choice. They were clean cut lads. They practised every evening and they learned how to handle a stick from the old-timers in the Turnpike. Turnpike was the bedrock of athletics. You had great families, the Considines – Tull, Brendan and Willie (Dodger), the Spellissys at the top of Gaol Street – Jack, father of Seán in the bookshop, 'Sham' and 'Beezer'. Old Mill Street had a hurling team and their most prominent players were Steve Millar, Martin 'Handsome' Moloney and Paddy Kenny.

Q. Why all the nicknames?
J.M. You were hardly in Ennis 24 hours when someone gave you a nickname, and it was something that applied to you, they would dub you. It seemed to be a town of nicknames, but they were affectionate.

Q. Had you one yourself?
J.M. I escaped! Actually, they called me 'Caruso'. I loved to sing and there was a girl named Chrissy Slattery, who was a lovely pianist and she was into the classics. There wasn't a benefit in the county that we didn't attend. Concerts were very common.

Q. Do you remember much about the victory in 1914?
J.M. It was 'a nine day wonder'. People were jubilant obviously. The local pubs were packed with people celebrating. M. J. Baker, a member of the Clare Junior Team, had a pub in Lifford (now James O'Keeffe's).

Q. What are your memories of Ennis as a town?
J.M. I loved it. The people were very generous and shared whatever they had.

Q. What part of town did you come from?
J.M. The back of Considines in Mill Street. It's a parking lot now. It was then known as Barrett's Lane. The Boreen was all thatched and so was the Turnpike. You had great families – the Molloy's, McGraths, Collins, Freeman's, Coughlan's, Caulfields. Tom Coughlan was connected with the Texas Oil Company. I can remember Steele's Terrace being built in 1912.

Q. Before we started the tape recorder, you were relating a little anecdote about the Courthouse.
J.M. The belief was that the Courthouse was never meant for Ennis. The plans were sent to Ennis and the building went up accordingly, but the

plans were meant for some part of India. This is what we believed. I think Ennis is worthy of the Courthouse because the First Master of the Rolls, Sir Michael O'Loughlen, came from Templemaley. He was from a prominent family and became Master of the Rolls after Catholic Emancipation. I remember during my days at Ennis CBS, we had a Christian Brother who brought us to the Courthouse every Friday to hear the cases. You'd be surprised at the education one can pick up. I enjoyed my days at the Brothers. At that time we were not confirmed until about the age of 14. Then in 1910, Pope Pius X decreed that children reached the age of reason at the age of 7, and they could be prepared for the sacraments. I was nearly 10 and I hadn't made my First Holy Communion. I first received Communion on 8 December, 1910. After that the ceremony became a lot more cheerful and a lot of people took an interest in the little children. At 14, we began preparing for Confirmation.

Q. Do you remember the Brothers?
J.M. Yes. Brothers Lucey, Mahony, Murphy, Coughlan, Kerrigan and Doyle. Bro. Xavier Doyle was the Principal. I also remember Professor O'Connor.

Q. Were you taught through Irish?
J.M. No – it wasn't a must. Remember, this was before 1916. The idea of moving towards Irish wasn't on. National Schools never heard of it but in the CBS we had about a half an hour per week. Later in secondary school, we had Irish as a language.

Q. How did people feel when Home Rule was deferred?
J.M. The Home Rule Act was due to come into being in 1912. It had gone through the House of Lords twice. Edward Carson objected. They played around with it for two years and then the 1914-'18 war broke out. We were very disappointed but hopeful it would come. After the 1916 Rising and the execution of the leaders and the atrocious murder of James Connolly, people became more Republican. The public perception changed after 1916.

Q. Did many young men join the British Army during the Great War?
J.M. Yes. John Redmond and his brother William Redmond (MP for East Clare) encouraged many to go to France; they advocated that people should join the army and everything would be all right after the war. In other words, we were going to get Home Rule on a platter. Many more joined because of economic reasons. People needed food on the table as conditions were very bad. The 'Separation Women' drew money while their husbands and sons fought in France.

Q. What did Home Rule mean to the people of Ennis? What did they envisage Home Rule doing to enhance their lives?

J.M. We would have our own government presiding over a 32-county State, though we'd still be part of the British Empire, with dominion status, something like Canada used to be. This was a time of change. Ennis was very active and people tuned in very early to the political situation as it was changing or about to change. Shortly after the Rising of 1916, one could see great change in the attitude of people towards the new form of government – the rebel government, if you like, of Patrick H. Pearse. There was also a very strong leaning towards William Redmond, who was a brother of John Redmond, Chairman of the Nationalist Party, the party that was inherited from Charles Stewart Parnell. You had a lot of followers of Parnell who remained loyal to John Redmond. There was a grudge carried from 1914 because of the postponement of Home Rule until after the war, the people didn't like it. So, loyalty to the Redmond Party was waning. When fighting broke out in Dublin in 1916, there was excitement in the town.

John Redmond leader of the Irish Nationalist party and brother of Willie Redmond M.P. for East Clare (1891-1917).

Q. What was the atmosphere like when news filtered through?

J.M. For the first week there were rumours. Everybody ran to the Post office hoping for a bulletin. Then we had news that the revolution was crushed.

Q. Could it have spread around the Country? Was Liam Mellows active in Galway?

J.M. Mellows was active with the rebels in Dublin. I only know of one man who was active in Ennis. He was Tom Browne and he was also in Dublin at the time. There was great anxiety about whether or not he took part in Easter week, but he brought all the first hand news home to Ennis. The press was still leaning towards the Old Nationalist crowd; we had the Saturday Record. Then the Clare Champion was run by one Sarsfield

Maguire, who became a real republican and his headlines were bringing out all the news about the execution of the rebel leaders. He convinced a group here that there was a change in national policy.

Q. What was the initial reaction of the public?
J.M. Those in public life expressed their indignation at the Rising of 1916, that it was all a waste. They felt the rebels were just a bunch of stragglers who went in unequipped. The news was very slanted towards British propaganda, but after the executions, opinion began to change. Once in a while you would hear of a rally. They brought in a couple of people from Dublin and the next thing they were organising here. Oscar Hopstead was one who began to seek out the old people who were familiar with the Fenians. There was one in the Market named (Frank) Shinnors, Commander of the Ennis Volunteers. His father, Dick Shinnors, was a prominent Fenian. Shinnors was a saddler round from Guitons' Corner. There was another named Sullivan, who was also a saddler from Mill Street. Also there was (Patrick) Considine from Turnpike, father of the famous hurling family (Dodger, Tull, Brendan and Sylvie). These men expounded the new theory, plus you had Dan McFarlane, Paddy O'Loughlin; he had a public house in front of the Old Bow Lane, Corney Mungovan, T.V. Honan in the Square and one of the Clohessy's opposite the Courthouse. They nominated De Valera for the 1917 election. Other prominent businessmen like Peter Moylan and Pat Howard nominated Paddy Lynch from Latoon.

Q. Was there a lot of resentment towards the new party?
J.M. Yes. When people are poor and they have half a loaf of bread, you don't change unless you're given a loaf – so the people had to be brought into the republican orbit slowly.

Q. Did you play an active part yourself?
J.M. No, not really. Maybe indirectly a couple of times.

Q. Eamon De Valera and Paddy Lynch contested the election of 1917. How did this come about?
J.M. William Redmond, MP, represented East Clare. He held a commission in the British Army and was killed in action in France in 1917 so his seat became vacant. To choose a candidate, those who were familiar with Easter 1916 and the new movement decided on De Valera; he was nominated on the steps of the Courthouse. De Valera had a great record of being a good fighting man. He was the last to surrender in Boland's Mills.

***A group of Ennis men who worked for the election of Eamon de Valera in Clare, pictured in New York, 1928. Back row, left to right:** Denis Quinn, Drumbiggle, Garrett Barry, Parnell St., George O'Neill, Turnpike, 'Tado' Smyth, Carmody St., John O'Loughlin, Barrack St., Patrick Flemming, Turnpike, Freddie Garrihy, Market St., John O'Halloran, Market St., – Quinn, Drumbiggle. **Front row:** 'Heybo' Flynn, Market St., B. Doyle, Lifford, Joe Flynn, Market St., Ernie Fahy, Turnpike, Paddy Callinan, Market St., – –, Frank Keane, Kilrush Road. Courtesy of Clare Co. Library.*

Q. Had he any previous connections with Clare?

J.M. Absolutely none. When he first came, the people had a hard time pronouncing his name. Finally, they settled for Dev.

Q. Why was he so popular?

J.M. Sarsfield Maguire was the man. There is no individual more powerful to mould public opinion than the editor of a paper, and the paper was "The Champion" because "The Record" was on its way out. The Champion came out with blazing headlines about the new party and how it should be supported. Maguire was also involved in the nominating of De Valera. "The Freeman's Journal" too was in favour of the revolution. "The Irish Times" and "The Sketch" could be wrapped together and called British. Clare was impatient. We felt let down because the Home Rule Act was postponed until after the war. We felt there would be so many problems, we'd never be heard of. So now's the time to grab the opportunity and put up Dev for election. When Dev was elected the town was jubilant for the most part. But you had a good many people from Ennis who were members of the British armed forces. Naturally, their people at home were loyal to them. You could not convince these people that De Valera was their "bread and butter" while their wives and mothers drew "separation" money from those in the army. When Dev came to Ennis, he was accompanied by the Newmarket-on-Fergus Brass Band. He came with five or six cars and he was in the lead car. People lined the streets; they wanted to get a look at him whether they voted for him or not.

Q. As someone present, were you impressed by him?

J.M. Yes, very much so, but also by his retinue. The election was observed by every secret service man they could afford to send down from Dublin. At that time, there was plenty of room to house these people because you didn't have many members in the police force. It was only after that election that the town became deeply fortified with British troops. If Dev had been defeated, I don't think half the troops would have occupied the town. Dev became the leader of the new Party when the prisoners were released after the war between England and Germany ended. The political prisoners got amnesty and many of them were elected as absentees. Then, there was a general election and they swept the country. Practically all the nationalists were swept out of power. The first night, Dev stayed in the Old Clare Hotel, but The Old Ground was his election headquarters. His workers took over part of the hotel for communications and literature. Tommy Keane and I gave out literature.

Q. Was there open public support for the (Old) IRA at this time?

J.M. Not open, but a lot of sympathisers. There was no law in the country; we were under martial law. One had to be at home by eight o'clock. You had to post the names of everyone in your family and their ages inside your front door. If one more person was present, he was arrested. You couldn't leave the town to go as far as Limerick without a permit. You needed a police permit from the Barracks. Clare suffered very much; four miles was the limit outside the town. This was 1920-1921 before the truce. An assembly of any amount over six was illegal. It bore a great hardship on the people. Men who were going to fairs had to get a permit and tell their business.

Q. What are your memories of the truce?

J.M. It was very unsettled in Ennis; there was for and against. The Bishop of course was pro-truce; he said Ireland was tired and that they should accept the truce. This generation had done a lot for the independence of Ireland from 1916-1921, and people needed a rest to get back to stability. I was in the Town Hall when the news came through. There was great jubilation and all forces were confined to barracks. When Dev was elected, I was seventeen. My father was a Parnellite and you couldn't change him, which meant he was with Paddy Lynch and the Nationalist Party. My uncle was the opposite; he was with Dev. So, when the split came, the result in my uncle's branch of the family was that he went with the rejection and lost his life. He was executed in the Home Barracks by the Free State Army with my first cousin, Paddy Mahony and his friends Willie O'Shaughnessy and Christy Quinn. When the Free State was established one of the things that disappointed me most was that the people who stepped into the breach to operate locally were not active in the struggle for independence. In America, these people are called Carpetbaggers. The set themselves up as law and order.

Q. Did you know Tommy 'Gessler' Keane?

J.M. Yes, very well. 'Gessler' was an out-and-out Republican. He got his 'schooling' from Jacko Keane, Mickie D'Arcy, the Garrihys and the Fordes. 'Gessler' advocated and preached and one night, while making a speech outside Bredin's in Barrack Street, he was arrested. When a kid of sixteen is arrested and put in gaol, people become resentful. They begin to see the cruelty of the enforcing group. The military had to curb the Black and Tans on occasion. The Tans filled in the ranks of the dwindling R.I.C. and the Auxiliaries were ex-officers of the British army who served in France. The town would have been burned to the ground if they were let loose. We had a very good military commander in Major Kershaw. He was a very fair man and he kept 'the Tans' in check. One Sunday, there was general communion for the Confraternity. As we were going to Mass, we were called to halt by the soldiers, lined up and put into lorries like sheep. When they had enough, they took us to the Cornmarket. We had been fasting for Mass, but a Mrs. Coote from the Cornmarket – she was a hero – and she figured that we'd be there for some time, so she had bucket of tea for us. We were than taken to Darragh, because trees had been felled and the main road cut up to make it impossible for the British to pass. Our job was to remove the trees and fill in the holes so that the military could use the main road. I was working with Jimmo Cronin from the Market. Towards noon, we were getting used to it, though we'd received nothing to eat. Then some shots were fired by the IRA who resented the British forcing civilians to do their work. To avoid a nasty situation, they brought us back.

Q. Were there many reprisals by the British?

J.M. There would have been many more reprisals and burnings in the town, because an ambush within so many miles created a situation whereby Ennis had to suffer. I remember T.V. Honan in the Square. All their stock was taken out and burned at the Monument by the armed forces in front of the Honan's small children. I want to be impartial in my recollection. The Crown Solicitor at that time, under British rule, was William Healy and he lived in Springfield House over in Harmony Row. His family held great influence with Major Kershaw. I'm sure his influence saved Ennis from getting a worse beating than it did.

Q. Did the Tans have any local co-operation?
J.M. They didn't need co-operation. When they wanted something they took it. They were jumpy and guns were drawn going into shops. The R.I.C. were on the way down and they had no control over the Tans. The Tans created trouble, but the Army was disciplined and they had friends in town.

Q. Were the Tans many in number?
J.M. They had as many as the Barracks would hold.

Q. Can you recall them arriving in Ennis?
J.M. No. I don't believe anybody ever saw them coming. You woke up on the morning and they were there.

Q. What was normal life like?
J.M. Under these circumstances, normal life didn't exist. We had no social life, but we had good home life, which was a blessing.

Q. What contribution did the Catholic Church and the Church of Ireland make?
J.M. They urged people to remain peaceful and pray that the situation would ease.

Q. What did the people do, to while away the long nights during curfew?
J.M. We read by candlelight, played checkers, did homework if you were still at school. The average bedtime was eleven o'clock. We got resigned to curfew after a while.

Q. What was it like after the cease-fire?
J.M. People were glad to get some form of relief. The dance halls opened, we 'struck up the band' and people were beginning to enjoy themselves. After the Treaty was accepted, most of the occupying forces pulled out. Then came the split between accepting or rejecting the Treaty

within the Irish Government. Those who rejected the Treaty walked out of the House and became very militant. During that crisis (the beginning of the Civil War) there was a rush for all of the places that were vacant. Those who favoured acceptance of the Treaty took the Home Barracks, because the stronghold was there, and they were handed whatever arms and ammunition they required to maintain law and order and establish the Free State. The Irregulars occupied the Barracks. The Free State forces tried to negotiate peacefully to get the Irregulars out, but they refused to go. They took whatever equipment was left by the police and they burned the place. These men were then hunted because they were carrying arms against the establishment of the Free State. They formed groups and became the Irregulars.

Q. Were they numerous in Clare?
J.M. They were numerous enough to create trouble. You must realise that the men who were enforcing the law and the men objecting to this Treaty had fought side by side. The Free Staters opened up the Home Barracks for recruits for the new army of the Constitution. Some of them had fought in the British Army during the Great War and came home and joined up. They recruited them because they needed men who could use the 'ten round rapid'. There was one ex-soldier called Sanafarian O'Neill from Corrovorrin; he was a real soldier of fortune and helped to establish the army here. Then he went to America and joined the army there. He was a very colourful character.

Q. What was public opinion at the time?
J.M. The man on the street didn't want the Civil War. The leaders wanted it and they got recruits to do the work for them.

Q. How did the peace come around, especially in Ennis?
J.M. Very slow reconciliation. The town had a very good spiritual leader in Bishop Michael Fogarty who was a man of vision. He was very close to the leaders during the struggle for independence. He could not see them separated over ideology and he wanted to get the country back to stability. His opinion was very much respected by all the parties, irrespective of their political feeling. He was responsible for maintaining peace among factions. When the easing-off part came, a lot of men had to be reconciled with the Church. The Franciscans were very charitable and kind and they led many of the dissenters back to the Church. This was done very slowly; it takes a long time for the wounds of war to heal. Of course, Lloyd George held the ace with his threat of immediate war if Ireland didn't accept the Treaty.

Q. When the Civil War came to an end, was the return to normality a slow process?

J.M. We had a great deal of unemployment here, very little progress was being made. There was a Labour Party in Ennis and one in Kilrush. There was a contest here in Ennis and Paddy Hogan was elected. The county now had five seats. Originally Clare had only two seats, East Clare and West Clare. Willie Redmond was representative for East Clare and Colonel Arthur Lynch for West Clare. In the new scheme of things, proportional representation came in, which meant everybody would get a fair crack. Now P.R., in our estimation at that time, was all right in Dublin or any cosmopolitan area, but it split parties, and there was so much confusion, even in the counting of votes under P.R. it caused a lot of confusion. Who's your first preference? Who's your second, etc.? The electorate was accustomed to voting for one candidate. That's all there was to it. We had the Labour Party, The Farmers Party and the Free State Party in Common Language and the Irregulars which was De Valera. Things were settling more as far as government was concerned. But it took Ennis a long time to pick up and a lot of people sold out.

Q. In your day growing up, there was no radio, etc. You mentioned dances.

J.M. We had a dancehall in Enright's yard; there's a little bow-way going into the car park coming down from Kennedy's lane in the Market. There was a dancehall belonging to Enright. A man called Tommy Redmond came from Dublin and he set up a dancing studio there. He taught ballroom dancing and sets. The fee for this was 4d (four old pence) per night but girls were free. There was one stipulation – the girls couldn't refuse to dance! We were all sent there to learn how to dance, he introduced the Caledonian. The nicest dance of all was the Quadrille, a military dance. He taught poise and turned out Munster finalists in Martin Flanagan and Gretta Morrissey from Lysaght's Lane and Bridie Reidy from Orchard Lane; this was about 1915. Twice a year he'd run a Ball called the 'Cinderella Ball'. He brought great culture to Ennis. In the Quadrilles you had to bow to your partner, even is she was your sister!

Q. What about traditional music?

J.M. Traditional music was scarce. Fr. Maloney, a native of Cork, was a great traditionalist. He introduced Irish dancing and his musicians included Mr. and Mrs. Jimmy Ball, who played fiddle and accordion. We had two top choirs, one at the Cathedral and one at the Friary. There was great competition between them; they had the pick of the talent. We developed the two into a Choral and Dramatic Society. We had about

MAJOR WILLIE

Redmond Anniversary •

Ennis—Sunday, 13th June, 1926.

The ORATION will be delivered by Mr.

J. P. HAYDEN, ex M.P.

100 members and we did Gilbert & Sullivan's 'Trial by Jury' in 1923 and 'H.M.S. Pinafore', 'The Pirates of Penzance' and 'The Mikado' in 1926. The talent was there and everything was authentic. We would practice for about two months right after Autumn and present it around February or March. I didn't miss one of those Operettas. I got my knowledge of all this from Chrissy Slattery; she could play piano and I rehearsed with her. It was conducted by the Bindon St. residents. Mrs. Knox from Clare Road was a powerful pianist and John Bredin in the Market conducted. The O'Beirnes in O'Connell Street were gifted singers. I became very interested in the Classics from all of this. I also had a great phonograph collection. I used to write to London for them. I went into it very deeply and I still listen to them. I have the complete Operas, Tosca, La Boheme, Rigoletto, La Traviata, with all the great singers. A good record cost 3s/6d (17.5p) for a 78RPM. Then, the 10" came out. Chrissy Slattery, later Mrs. Bazzler of Steele's Terrace, and I learned our music at the Temperance Hall.

Q. Why was classical and operatic music so popular?

J.M. Mainly because of the influence of travelling companies, operatic music was popular. Lizzy Blake was another fine singer. She had a great voice. She was a jolly individual with razor sharp wit, bordering on the theatrical. Lizzy could always be relied upon to lend her powerful singing voice at local events. The market was a hamlet of colourful characters straight out of a storybook.

Q. Apart from opera, are you interested in other music?

J.M. Yes, mainly Irish traditional music.

Q. Where was the Temperance Hall?
J.M. In Chapel Lane. It was once the Cathedral and it had fallen into decay. Old Morgan McInerney roofed it and put in side seats. Those frequenting it observed total abstinence. A Brass & Reed Band was formed by the children of the original members.

Lizzy Blake "a jolly character with razor sharp wit".

Q. What about licensed premises?
J.M. The way I remember a bar in those days, when one started drinking, one was very careful about the bar one frequented, because one wouldn't go into a bar where one's father drank. You showed him that respect and you could be married. I had a brother older than I who took a drink, but never in the presence of my father.

Q. Were family values much better in those days?
J.M. Yes. You had no diversions, no media. Everything was discussed at meal times.

Q. Did you come from a big family?
J.M. I was one of nine.

Q. Did you have many trades in those days?
J.M. Yes, we had about twenty tailors, eight or ten shoemakers, about six to eight blacksmiths, Malone, Morgan, and Carroll was a big builder; he built what is Carroll's bridge by the Post Office, no small stuff here. In the trades, many of the apprentices lived in. The Cahir's lived here where we're speaking (West Coast Radio, Parnell Street). John Cahir ran a drapery shop here. He had four boys and five girls. Plus he employed four men and one woman. It was thriving. In the Cash Co. apprentices also lived in.

Q. Did you work as an apprentice?
J.M. After leaving the C.B.S. at about 16, I served my apprenticeship in the jewellery business at Maurers. I was there for nine years.

Q. Did you have class distinction in Ennis?
J.M. You had about six different classes. Ennis had many clubs; the

Country Club was frequented by the Protestant ruling class. The Farmer's Club over in Harmony Row had the professional classes; doctors, lawyers and big farmers socialised there. The Abbey Club opposite the Abbey gate had the major business men. The Odd-fellows Club in Arthur's Lane was frequented by the crowd that worked for those who drank at the Abbey Club. The O'Connell Club and the Forrester's Club in O'Connell Street were frequented by blue collar workers. And you had the Labourer's Club near the roundabout at Paddy White's. Jack Spellissy's grandfather, the old Bull Spellissy, was one of the big shots at the Odd-fellows Club, and many a story is told about him. The police were chasing Parnell one time during the evictions and Bull Spellissy, who looked like Parnell, jumped into a car and took off towards Inch with the police in pursuit. Meanwhile, Parnell made his getaway down the Clare Road.

Q. Was Charles Stewart Parnell a frequent visitor to Ennis?
J.M. Parnell was very much liked in Ennis. One of his greatest supporters was Michael Hanrahan from Mill Street. My father was also a great Parnellite. The Freeman's Journal often put out supplements of historical events and my father used to frame these – Robert Emmet, Grattan's Parliament, Daniel O'Connell – of course O'Connell was a story everyone had.

Q. Who was responsible for the O'Connell Monument?
J.M. Mickie Considine lived at Brewery Lane, at the back of T.V. Honans. He organised the money to pay for the monument, he was a painter by trade. There were a couple of others as well, but he was in charge from beginning to end. Mickie Considine was the secretary and president until he got that money. The monument was built on the site of the Old Courthouse.

Q. Was there a reason for that site?
J.M. O'Connell was nominated on the steps of the Old Courthouse. He defeated Vesey Fitzgerald.

Q. The lanes off Parnell Street and O'Connell Street – Lysaght's Lane, Cook's Lane - were these named after real people?
J.M. They were. We called Lysaght's Lane 'Scabby Lane'. Even the kids who came from there called it Scabby Lane. It would be nice if plaques with names on them were put up – Arthur's Row, Cook's Lane, etc.

Q. Did the Gaiety Cinema exist then?
J.M. We saw movies at the Old Town Hall – and concerts too. The

Movie House was upstairs under the management of Mary Kate Boland. The site that later became the Gaiety Cinema was a skating rink (now Dunnes Stores).

Q. You emigrated in 1928.
J.M. Emigration was widespread then. Everybody I went to school with emigrated. There was an exodus. They didn't leave because they wanted to. They left because they had to. It took me about two months to find work. The Wall Street Crash came in 1929. It was a rough time. The effect of the Crash was being felt long beforehand. Companies were beginning to feel it. General Electric, for example, was letting people off.

Q. What was your first job?
J.M. Operating an elevator. I tried my own profession (jeweller), but it's a closed shop in the States. I later went to High School by night and I became a lab technician. My wife and I were able to put our four children through College. We lived well during the Depression because my job was steady. The opportunities in America were great.

Q. How long were you away before you came back for the first time?
J.M. Twenty eight years. I came back in 1956.

Q. As a native of Ennis living in the States for 60 years, do you find that Ennis has changed?
J.M. Very much. The first observation is economic. There was a lot of poverty when I was young. It was very conspicuous. Now everybody seems to have a few pounds and there's no sign of poverty. The town has enlarged. When I left, Ennis had a population of 6,600. The houses are in very good shape compared to the rows of little thatched cottages that there were up in Old Mill Street and the Turnpike. They were homely and great families came out of these houses.

Q. Was Tony Mahony, the musician, a relation of yours?
J.M. A first cousin. His father lived up near the market; he was a shoemaker.

Q. After all that you saw in the War of Independence and the Civil War, does it sadden you to see the conflict in the North?
J.M. People can live together irrespective of their religious beliefs, provided that you educate them. Their so-called leaders are bigots. In any society all men are equal. I've lived beside Jews, Italians, Germans. We all go to our different places of worship. We all have the same needs. We need each other.

Q. We have an unemployment problem at the moment. Was that prevalent when you were growing up?
J.M. A lot of people in my time had nothing. Have the conditions improved? You will find a lot of young people from Ireland practically hiding over in America. At least, in my time, you could go over there freely, but in the old days you didn't have social welfare. Once grown, you had to go.

Q. Jimmy, we would like to thank you for sharing your memories with us over a considerable period of time. It's been a pleasure talking to you.
J.M. It's also my pleasure. From the first day that I went to America 60 years ago, I don't believe I ever fell asleep at night without thinking of Ennis. Ennis will always be home to me.

Flan McMahon and Tony Mahony (violin).

NOTES ON CARUSO'S ENNIS

Jimmy Mahony had great recall. His memories were positive and they bear out with the recollections of Elizabeth Crimmins, Christy O'Connell, Padraig O'Heithir, Martin Cronin, Kevin J. Browne, Michael J. Fitzgerald and Sr. Nicholas Griffey O.P. from this time.

Jimmy refers to great families in the Turnpike and Boreen. The following families lived in the Boreen, Steele's Terrace and Gort Road, circa 1935/1940.

Steele's Terrace

No. 1. Jim Mackey, 2, Tom Strand, 3. Connellans, 4. Frank Moloney, 5. Miss Lewis, 6. Miss Garvey, 7. Jack Kerin, 8. John Burley, 9. Jackie Duffy, 10. Pappy Garrihy, 11. Lynch's, 12. Miko Duggan, 13. Websters, 14. Miss O'Flaherty (Private School), 15. O'Grady's, 16. Moroney's, 17. O'Connell's, 18. Kearney's, 19. Egan's, 20. Miss K. Cahill, 21, Hoares, 22. Miss Duggan, 23. Miss O'Brien (Music Teacher), 24. M.J. McMahon (shop), 25. Nicholas McMahon, 26. Carroll's, 27. Lynch's, 28. Arthur O'Donnell, 29. Elizabeth and Eileen O'Donoghue, 30. J.Walsh.

Boreen

J. Hartnett, Mrs. Partridge, Miss McMahon, Miss Lucas, John O'Connell, Harry Fleming, Paddy Kelly/Johnny Coughlan (the Quarry), Mrs. Molly McMahon, Mrs. Mary Geoghegan, P. Molloy, Nurse Carroll, Christy O'Loughlin, Moll Molloy, John Flynn, Joe and Jim Coughlan, Miko Ensko (the Lane), Frank Duggan, Pat Coughlan, Hanrahan's, Kenneally's, Paddy Caulfield, Mrs. McGrath, Freeman's, Collins, Miss McGrath (Laundry), Jack Sullivan, Paddy Reidy, John Fahy, Paddy Carmody, Paddy Scales, Nonie Ensko, John-Joe Scales, Whites, John McMahon (Road Overseer), Mick Curtin, John McMahon (shop), Katy Bowles.

Gort Road Cottages

No. 1 McMahon's, 2. Clohessy's, 3. Andy and Barbara Carmody.

- The above list was compiled by John Leyden (RIP) of Lifford and Birmingham, published in the Clare County Express c. 1986.
- Major Kershaw – Jimmy also offered the name Major Kirkshaw as an alternative.

Bishop Michael Fogarty was a native of Kilcolman, Nenagh, Co. Tipperary. He succeeded Dr. McRedmond as Bishop of Killaloe in September, 1904. Dr. Fogarty served as Bishop of the Diocese until his death in 1955.

William Vesey Fitzgerald (1783-1843). A son of James Fitzgerald of Ennis and Catherine Vesey, he was born in Ennis and educated at Oxford. In 1829, he ran against Daniel O'Connell for the Clare seat and was well and truly beaten. The Clare Journal tells us that polling in the 1829 election lasted for five days, and O'Connell's majority grew more and more decisive. He was outvoted by O'Connell supporters by more than two votes to one. Fitzgerald was given a peerage in 1835 and was still in public office at the time of his death.

West Coast Radio was founded in 1984 by Tony Garland, Paddy O'Donoghue, Paul and Ollie Byrnes. A native of Brighton, England, Tony Garland was the catalyst. Initially WCR broadcast from the Upper Market Area. Later they acquired offices in Parnell Street. While there were no legal structures in place at that time for the granting of a radio licence, they thought it better to have an application on the Minister's table when such structures were established. In July 1987, A. Gerard Moylan & Company, Solicitors, Galway and Loughrea applied on behalf of Ollie Byrnes to Mr. Ray Burke, TD, Minister for Energy & Communications for such a licence. West Coast Radio received a positive response from the Minister's office regarding the future granting of this licence. By 1988, with investment from Ennis businessmen, Paul Flynn and Frank Flaherty, WCR could be heard as far away as Mallow, Co. Cork. Ollie Byrnes headed the group at the Independent Radio and Television Commission hearings at Jury's hotel, Limerick on March 9th, 1989, under the chairmanship of Brendan Vaughan. In spite of good media reviews and a detailed submission, West Coast Radio was unsuccessful in its bid for the local radio licence of Clare.

Enrico Caruso (1873-1921) made his debut at La Scala in 1900. He mastered scores of operatic roles and enjoyed unparalleled success.

'The Foggy Dew', possibly the finest of all the 1916 songs. The words are by Fr. P.O'Neill. Luke Kelly's version is definitive.

The Clare Champion was reborn in March 1903 from the ashes of the Clare Man. The Nationalist newspaper the Clareman was forced to close because of a libel action. Tom Galvin's first editorial read "The Champion will stand as the inveterate foe of landlordism, shoneenism, grabbers and castle hacks. The wants of the people will be espoused until their grievances are redressed. They shall agitate for an Irish Ireland and an Irish Parliament to govern and make laws for the Irish people." Tom Galvin died on 7th December 1903. On his death the management of the paper was taken over by his sister, Mrs. Josephine Maguire, with her husband Sarsfield Maguire as editor. Despite threats, the bold policy of the paper was continued. In 1918 a detachment of military entered the premises of the newspaper and removed sections of machinery. From April to September, 1918 no paper was published. Sarsfield Maguire refused to guarantee that his paper would not print 'subversive' and 'seditious' articles.

Jimmy Mahony refers to characters 'straight our of a story book'. 'The Bowler' Duggan and his wife Nanc, ran an eating house in Chapel Lane. Later Josie Cronin ran a shop in the same premises. Jackie Duggan (1923-2001) a son of William and Nanc became a costume designer with the BBC. Michael Tierney was another much loved character around town. A flamboyant colourful character, Michael distributed newspapers. He ran Magical Mystery Tours during his leisure hours.

The Ennis Temperance Band was founded in 1875.

William Redmond MP (1861-1917) William Hoey Kearney Redmond was the second son of William Archer Redmond MP for Wexford. A brother of John, Willie Redmond joined the Irish Parliamentary Party led by Charles Stewart Parnell in 1883. Before representing East Clare, Willie Redmond had earlier represented Fermanagh North Division during the years 1883-1891. Redmond practised what he preached. He was killed in action in France in 1917.

The Gaiety Cinema

This splendid cinema was located in O'Connell Street. In its heyday the Gaiety provided a window to the magical world of film and was one of the towns principal attractions during the years c.1940-1973. The cinema was renowned for its colourful staff members such as Mary Kate Boland, Josie Cronin and Anthony Noonan. Late of Hermitage Road, Anthony Noonan passed away in 1987.

Letter from America

I was 14 years old, when my parents, my brother, John and my sisters, Christina and Frances left Ennis for the United States. That was in November, 1920. We lived at 35 Lower Market Street. They were troubled times in Ennis then. I remember we had to take a car to Limerick Junction as there were no trains coming into Ennis, as roads and bridges were being blown up. Along with the British passport we had to have a Sinn Fein passport also and it was printed in Irish. There were plenty of Black and Tans around. We arrived in Brooklyn, N.Y. around December

__Clare H.C. of New York - 1925.__ Team includes: John Fitzgerald, 2nd from right, back row. Jack Malone, 5th from left, middle row. Billy 'Botch' Fahy, 2nd from left, front row. Freddie Garrihy, 2nd from left, middle row, his brother is pictured, front row, 2nd from right.
Also pictured are two McTigue's from Kilnamona, brothers of Mike McTigue the world light heavy weight boxing champion, one is in the back row, 5th from right, while the other is in the middle row, 3rd from right.
The photo was sent to the County Express in May, 1981 by Ml. J. Fitzgerald, New York and formerly of Ennis. Michael emigrated in 1920 at the age of 14.

10 and we were met by my brother, *Peter and by my sister Annie, as she was in the States about two years before us.

About my years in Ennis, I don't remember too much. I went to the CBS. My teacher was *Bro. Moloney. Paddy Collins was there also with me. I was a good friend of Peter McDonnell, R.I.P. and also his brothers, James, John and Edward. Also, John Burns, John Frawley and Joseph Moloney, all from the Market.

I remember going to the movies upstairs at the Town Hall, and some of the kids would open the windows and let the light in. We would all holler to close them. Another time I was in the Rink movies and there was a fire in the stables in the back of the Rink, so they brought some hoses out through the people in the audience.

I have been a pioneer since June, 1930. My wife who is American born and I attend Queen of Angels church here in Sunnyside. On June 6th, 1981, we will be married 50 years, thank God. I am the church trustee. I am also a Eucharistic minister at the 5 o'clock mass every Saturday. We have a wonderful pastor, Rev. James M. Cavanagh, his parents came from Co. Cavan. We have five priests altogether. I have worked in the cosmetic business for about 46 years with Elizabeth Arden Inc., of which I am now retired. When I lived in Brooklyn, I kept in touch with my good friends Simon Frawley and Paddy Armstrong, his father was a pawnbroker in Ennis. Other friends here are Danny Sullivan and his wife the former May Stack. I was the godfather to her brother Garrett in Ennis. Last but not least is my good friend in Ennis, Maureen Rice, who keeps me informed about the old town and she sends me the Clare Express which is wonderful.

Michael J. Fitzgerald
New York City.

Published in the Clare County Express in May, 1981.

*Bro. Moloney died around this time
*Peter Fitzgerald – served in France with the United States Army during the great war.

Dals, Newmarket and Feakle Dominate

1924 –1944

"Of all the years 1929 is undoubtedly the one that stands head and shoulders above all others"
Joe Madigan

The early 1920's saw little hurling played due to the political turmoil of the time. The Civil War and the War of Independence had raged, leaving the country ravaged and with little time for sports.

However, in 1924, the game of hurling was re-organised in Ennis. A report in the Clare Champion of June 14th, 1924 wrote of a local derby at the Fair Green between the Dals and the Faughs, with the Dals defeating the Faughs by a considerable margin. Whether this game was league, championship or challenge, we don't know. But what we do know is that the Dals were magnificent during the Summer of 1924 with the Clare Champion describing them as "the best team in the county". Prominent names in town hurling at this time included Fahy, the brothers Billy, Eddie, Mickie and Wally as well as Joe Madigan and the names of Coote and Molloy.

Johnny 'Joker' Coote.

The County final of 1924 saw the Dals meet a strong Newmarket side, who were favourites to win. But a determined and intelligent Dals team beat off the strong opposition by 7-2 to 3-2. Eddie Fahy, Freddie Garrihy and 'Joker' Coote excelled in defence and Mickey White and Jackie Duffy were reliable forwards.

National League Inaugurated

The National League, which has become an integral part of the G.A.A. calendar was inaugurated in 1926. This inter-county competition was to run from the autumn to spring of each year. Clare won Division II of the league in its first year, with Cork taking the premier competition. A number of Ennis players assisted the county team in its Division II honours and they included Tull Considine, Jackie Duffy, Eddie and Billy

Fahy, Paddy 'Boo' Doherty and Freddie Garrihy. Tom 'Hawker' Blake was sub to goal-keeper George O'Dea.

Club Hit by Emigration

Throughout the 1920's there was wide-spread emigration from Ireland. Like other hurling clubs, the Dals lost many of it's players. Among them were Freddie Garrihy, Billy Fahy and John Murphy who emigrated overseas and James Spellissy and Eddie Fahy who moved to Dublin. To fill the vacancies, a very young Larry Blake was called on to the Dals senior team in 1926. Other relative newcomers included Joe Doherty and Mike Ensko. The Clare Champion tells us that 'Dodger' Considine was recalled for a short spell. Is it possible that Larry Blake and Willie 'Dodger' Considine played on the same team? The Clare Champion of 1926 certainly supports this claim.

The Dals defeated Clarecastle by 6-2 to 2-4 in the Divisional final of the 1926 championship. However, they were knocked out by the Newmarket Blues in the later stages on a score of 4-6 to 2-3.

Dublin Visit Showgrounds

Playing in Division I of the league in 1927, Clare entertained Dublin who inflicted a 12 point defeat on the Bannermen at the Showgrounds. Indeed, the Dublin team included six Clare men in their line-out: - Tommy Daly, Pa 'Fowler;' McInerney, Eddie Fahy, Tom Burnell, Rob Doherty and Jack Gleeson.

Dublin went on to win the All-Ireland Senior Championship in 1927. With the relaxation of 'the non-resident rule', in senior championship hurling, Clare would field one of their best ever sides from 1928-1932.

Tull Considine.

Other Notable Events of 1927

In 1927, Old Mill Street captured the Town League and a handsome set of medals was presented to the Cloughleigh side at the Dals AGM by Tull Considine. In the same year, Clare lost the Munster hurling final to Cork by 5-3 to 3-4. The Dals representation on the team included Joe Madigan, Tull Considine and Mickey White.

Mickie White.

The Dals and Blues renew rivalry

Parish Rule (the rule that states that one can only play for the parish one was born in or are living in) was introduced in 1910 and continued until 1927. By 1927 the Newmarket Blues had won their third consecutive senior county championship when they easily defeated the Dals in the county final.

By all accounts, it was proposed at a County Board meeting that a number of amalgamations should come together to improve the general standard, and to possibly stop Newmarket dominating. Newmarket, who made the most of this rich period contesting ten county finals in a row from 1924-1933, didn't object and several combinations came into being for the 1928 series. These included:

1. **Ennis**/Clarecastle.
2. **Bodyke**/Scariff/Ogonnelloe
3. **O'Callaghan's Mills**/Kilkishen/Kilbane
4. **Feakle**/Killanena/Mountshannon
5. **Newmarket**

(Note, the Ennis/Clarecastle arrangement lasted just one season).

Many other clubs dropped down to intermediate and junior ranks. The Clare Champion Cup more commonly known as the Clare Cup was presented to the G.A.A. by Sarsfield Maguire of the Clare Champion in 1928 for a senior league competition.

Jackie Duffy.

1928 – 'DALS' win double

In the Clare Cup final and the County Final of 1928, the Ennis Dals clashed with Newmarket. The Ennis Brass and Reed band led the opposing teams onto the magnificent Showgrounds pitch before approximately 1,000 spectators. The Ennis combination opened in great style with goals from Jackie Duffy and Pa Corry before John Joe Doyle replied with a glorious point from the wing. The Dals easily won the championship on a score line of 4-1 to 0-3 and the Clare Cup by 3-3 to 1-4. A feature of the Cup final was that the entire Dals score line was grabbed by three Clarecastle men, Pa Corry (2-1), Christy 'Swaddie' McMahon (1-0) and Vincent Murphy (0-2). Others to shine in the double over Newmarket were Larry Blake, William Hackett and Tull Considine. The Clarecastle/Ennis partnership was quickly dissolved after the Cup final. Ennis had to find replacements for the Clarecastle contingent. A further problem arose when it was discovered that 'Joker' Coote was ineligible to play for

Larry Blake.

Tom Blake.

Ennis for the 1929 championship as he was working in Barefield and living in Clarecastle. 'Joker' declared for 'The Magpies' in 1929.

1928 Irish tour by United States Hurling Team

In August 1928, the Irish international team entertained the U.S.A. in the Tailteann games at Croke Park. The Irish selection who won by 5-9 to 4-3 included three Clare men, Tommy Daly (Dublin), J.J. Kinnane (Limerick) and Tull Considine. The American team which included hurlers from Cork, Kilkenny, Offaly, Laois, Tipperary and big Jim Burke from Tulla travelled to Ennis on September 22nd to play the Banner county at the Showgrounds.

The Exile party led by James O'Duffy, president of the G.A.A. in American and a native of Inch was officially welcomed at the railway station by Rev. Fr. Michael Hamilton, chairman of the Clare County Board. The Ennis Brass and Reed band played the Exiles to their hotel. A crowd of 9,000 turned out at the Showgrounds to see the States defeat the Banner county by 4-7 to 2-6. (This unique game was preceded by the quarter final of the Clare senior football championship with the Dals inflicting a 7 point defeat on Kilrush).

The Tailteann games took place in 1924, 1928 and 1932. Many of the greatest players of all time lined out in these internationals. The 1932 Irish side included Jim Hurley and Dinny Barry Murphy of Cork, Mattie Power (Kilkenny) and John Joe 'Goggles' Doyle of Clare. John Joe recalled those great occasions to me *"the Tailteann games were marvellous. They were real internationals. Because of widespread emigration, America had a fine team, we beat them in Croke Park"*.

1928 Munster Championship – Clare defeat Tipperary

Such was the richness and magnificence of the Ennis Dals and Newmarket Blues teams of the late 1920's that they provided the backbone of the Clare Senior Hurling team. In 1928, Clare defeated Tipperary by 5-5 to 2-5 in the early stages of the championship at Thurles Sports Field.

In the Munster final, Clare drew with Cork, but lost the replay when the celebrated Clare forward line was held by the Cork defence in spite of tremendous play by Brendan Considine at centre forward.

The team rebounded in 1929 to defeat Cork by 4-5 to 3-2 and Tipperary, 7-5 to 3-4 to win the prestigious Thomond Feis (a four county championship involving Tipperary, Clare, Limerick and Cork).

The Railway Cup

The Railway Cup inter-provincial competitions for hurling and football came into existence in 1926 following a proposal made at that years annual congress on April 3rd by the then Cork County secretary Padraig O'Caoimh. The two perpetual trophies were presented by the Great Southern Railway Company. Tull Considine, John Joe Doyle and later Larry Blake were practically automatic choices on the Munster teams of these years. Sean Harrington, a Tipperary native won a winners medal in 1935. The popular Dals hurler taught at Ennis C.B.S. for some years before transferring to Feakle.

Telifis Scoile in Ennis

In 1968 Patrick Gallagher presented two half hours programmes for R.T.E. on the history and development of Ennis. The programmes included footage of Frank 'Diver' McNamara and Frank Malone. 30 years later I spoke to Frank Malone about the making of this documentary and about his work as a farrier. *"it was the hardest work you could get. You were pulled around from morning till night. Patrick Gallagher was with me for an hour. I had a very difficult horse, I had to be very careful. R.T.E came at the wrong time. Had I known, I could have worked on a different horse and closed my eyes. Patrick Gallagher was delighted with the result. There's huge changes since that film was made. Many of the old characters are gone including 'Diver' McNamara. The town is nearly a city now, where are all the people coming from"?* I then changed the subject to hurling in Ennis in 1920's and 1930's. Vincent Sheridan chipped in – *"The Fahy's were good hurlers. Vincent, Bill and Eddie. Bill worked at Webster's in Abbey Street and Eddie joined the Gardaí. 'Pharoah' Mahony never wore boots. I remember him hurling on big Jim Burke. Dinny 'Lals' Rice was good. Ralphie Burns was very sticky. Larry Blake was out on his own. The Blues were dominant. They had a great team, Mickey Arthur, Tony Nealon, John Joe Doyle and Andy Callinan. Newmarket and Ennis were great rivals. I remember fantastic games at the Showgrounds. Tull and Brendan Considine, 'Joker' Coote and Paddy Kenny, you had Martin Moloney in Mill Street, a butcher by trade and a great hurler. I knew Steve and Johnny Millar and their sister Esther, the best swimmer in Ireland. Ennis was full of good hurlers going back to my father's time (Tom Sheridan) with the Faughs".*

1929 - A RECORD YEAR *by Joe Madigan (written 1967)*

The games of the Gael – hurling and football – have been firmly established in Ennis for many years. In that period very good teams have represented the capital in both codes, winning championships, assisting county selections and attaining inter-provincial and Ireland honours.

Of all these years 1929 is undoubtedly the one that stands head and shoulders above all others, as in that year the Ennis Dals club again completed the elusive double by winning the senior football and hurling championships, repeating the feat of the great 1914 teams which had so many star players. The quality of the players of that year and their performances in the senior championships, were very likely inferior to those of other years but their achievements in winning Clare senior football and hurling championships, together with the two other premier competitions – viz, the Clare Champion Cup in Hurling and the Cusack Cup in football – proved them worthy of an honoured place in G.A.A. annals in Ennis.

Joe Madigan - as I remember him from my days in CBS.

The previous year, 1928, Ennis Dalcassians amalgamated with Clarecastle. The amalgamation succeeded in winning the senior championship. The Clarecastle players in the final were Patrick McInerney, Vincent Murphy, Dick Cole, Patrick Corry, Bernie Power and 'Swaddie' McMahon – Albert Murphy being the sub goalie.

This partnership was dissolved after the final. The 1929 championship was run on a league system. The Dals were defeated by Tulla in their first match by 5-2 to 3-4 after a hectic encounter in Newmarket. This setback, instead of demoralising the team, caused them to set about training in earnest for their second round clash with their co-partners of the previous year. Great interest was manifest in this game as both sides had several out field players from the 1928 final. Then, as now, a clash with 'the magpies' brought out the very best in Ennis and after a dour and hectic hours hurling the Dals emerged winners by a handsome winning margin – flattering, as later encounters showed. The sole topic of conversation in G.A.A. circles was the meeting of Tulla and Clarecastle. Could the latter defeat Tulla and bring Ennis back into the reckoning. True to tradition, 'the magpies' rose to the occasion and their win left the three teams level on points. From the draw Ennis obtained the bye, so Clarecastle and Tulla met again on the knock-out system. The latter again failed to overcome erstwhile conquerors and so the stage was set for another 'magpies' clash. This fixture was at Newmarket and attracted a huge crowd who were treated to a rugged, dour and at times rough exhibition of hurling. Ennis played the second half with thirteen players and Clarecastle finished with fourteen. The 'magpies' showed much more spirit and determination in this match, but still the town side was again victorious – even though their opponents reduced the winning margin by half, viz. 11 points.

Senior Football Championship

In the meantime the footballers were continuing the good work of the hurlers and had victories over Kilrush and Cooraclare, but came a cropper to Miltown in their third match. Miltown also had wins over Kilrush and Kilkee. Thus, it came as a big surprise when Miltown was beaten by Cooraclare. The Dals trained hard for their final match against Kilkee and were rewarded by a good win over the West Clare Blues. Miltown and Ennis thus finished level at the top of the league with six points each – Cooraclare having lost two matches. Ennis and Miltown were left to contest the county final. This match was held up for a considerable time as Ennis had to fulfil its engagements in senior hurling and champion cup games.

The Blues

Newmarket won out in division two, so it was a Dals versus Blues final, which was fixed for the Showgrounds, Ennis, with Monsignor Michael Hamilton as referee. *However, for some reason unknown to writer of this article, Newmarket refused to play and Ennis received a walkover. While the outcome of an objection lodged by Newmarket to awarding the county final to Ennis was awaited, the matches in the Clare Champion Cup were being played and resulted in wins for Ennis Dals over the Gardai, Kilkishen and Tulla. Ennis and Clarecastle had then to meet for the third time that year to claim the right to enter the Clare Cup final against Newmarket.

Fixed for Miltown

It is hard to imagine such a thing happening now, but the match between two neighbouring parishes was played in Miltown Malbay, of all places. The seaside pitch almost proved fatal for Ennis. The team gave its worst performance of the year, failing to produce the form that had won all the other games for them. Even the stars of the team failed to shine and were it not for a late goal scored from fully seventy yards by left half back, Larry Blake, in the dying minutes, Ennis would have lost. It was the most subdued of the three meetings and yielded very little good hurling and it was 'the magpies' who provided this. The final score was Dals 3-2, Clarecastle 2-2.

**Clarecastle had appealed to the Munster Council over the previous Dals/Clarecastle result. Newmarket the finalists refused to play until this objection was heard.*

Ennis and Newmarket for another final a fortnight later at the showgrounds with Seamus Malone as referee. The eagerly awaited result of the Newmarket objection came to light. The County Board decided that if Ennis win, they retain the senior championship, but if defeated they play Newmarket for the county final. An appeal against this decision was lodged by Ennis with Munster council. This appeal was held up by the latter body but it was thought County Board would appeal to Central council – so the matter seemed to be still undecided.

Training Routine

Ennis had displayed very poor form in Cup semi-final and such an important match was due for decision just 14 days later. The captain, Tull Considine, and Reverend Michael Crowe, chairman of the club took charge of the training. As it was late in the year, training had to begin at 4 o'clock in the evening. The chairman and captain contacted all employers of the players in the town and I'm delighted to say all players were permitted to get off at 3.30p.m. Training in Fairgreen each evening and morning consisted of a bout of hurling, running and sprinting. The team then met in the Town Hall at 8p.m. for an hours physical drill followed by a sharp brisk walk from Town Hall to Barefield and back again. This routine was followed until the Tuesday when it was reduced to short sprints, evening and morning and nightly walk. Soon many doubts existed as to the merits of both teams that a record crowd flocked to the Showgrounds for the final which was to decide so many outstanding questions. A win for Ennis would prove them worthy of a further meeting with the Blues. A win for the latter would show them superior to the champions and give them a chance to wrest championship from the Dals.

The pace was a cracker from the start and no quarter was asked or given. The superior speed of the Ennis team was evident from the start and each player threw himself with reckless abandon into the fray. Play ranged fast and furious, but Ennis were gradually attaining the upper hand when the game came to an abrupt end after 24 minutes. Ennis then led by 2-1 to 1-0, with a goal disallowed. A Newmarket player was ordered off for striking an Ennis player with his hurley. The player in question refused to obey the referee who had then no option but to award the match to Ennis.

The spectators really enjoyed what they had seen but were disappointed a full hour of such hurling was not played. Most were of the opinion that Ennis would have won as they were out hurling and out running their slower and heavier opponents.

The Ennis team was:

Tom Blake

Paul Cronin	Paddy Kenny	Vinnie Considine
Jacksie Darcy	Gerry Cronin	Larry Blake
Tull Considine (capt)		Mickey White
Joe Madigan	Michael Malone	Tony 'Topper' Morrissey
Peter Cunningham	Paddy Doherty	Jackie Duffy

Having disposed of Newmarket, the senior footballers, including eight of the victorious hurling team, set out on a similar training routine for the county final with Miltown in Kilrush. As was the case with the senior hurlers, the footballers turned out a very fit fifteen, fully determined to bring back the senior title to Ennis after a lapse of 12 years. Ennis had good support when they took the field and even though Miltown were favourites, the Ennis team and followers were quietly confident. The strenuous course of training that Ennis had put in gave them the edge in fitness and speed and this allied to the town teams craft brought them victory.

Tony 'Topper' Morrissey. 'Topper' is listed amongst a select group of eight Ennis hurlers/footballers who swept the boards in 1929. Tony Morrissey is pictured here in later life.

Miltown played with the advantage of the wind in the first half and led by three points to nil at half time. It was in the second half that Ennis showed the result of their long hours of training. The Dals equalised by scoring a goal and with 10 minutes to go, scored the all important point. They easily withstood spasmodic Miltown pressure from then to the final whistle.

The winning senior football team was:-

Joe Davis

Paul Cronin	Tull Considine (capt)	James McInerney
Larry Blake	Paddy Callinan	Michael Malone
Anthony Moroney		Jacksie Darcy
Joe Madigan	Thomas O'Halloran	Tony 'Topper' Morrissey
Jackie Duffy	Con Levin	Jack Doherty

Great credit for this dual success must be given to Reverend Fr. Michael Crowe C.C., the chairman of the club, who was present at every training session to encourage and advise the players as only he could. He was later transferred as parish priest to Corofin where he died. Naturally there was great rejoicing in Ennis having brought off the double – a feat that was not accomplished since 1914 – so it appears as if 1929 will long remain a glorious and unique year in Ennis G.A.A. annals.

The eight players who won Senior Hurling Championship, Clare Champion Cup, Senior Football Championship and Cusack Cup were:

Paul Cronin, Tull Considine, Larry Blake, Michael Malone, Joe Madigan, Tony 'Topper' Morrissey, Jacksie Darcy, Jackie Duffy.

– Joe Madigan

1930 –

After the incredible success of 1929, the Dalcassian club began the 1930 season in style by inflicting a decisive defeat on Tulla by 7-1 to 2-3 in the championship. As in 1929, 'the magpies' again brought out the best in Ennis in the Clare cup semi-final of 1931 in a fast and highly charged encounter. "Tensions ran high in the second half when Clarecastle came within a point of Ennis. Tull Considine did well in his new position at full back while Joe Madigan, Sean Harrington and Larry Blake were in great form. In the end Clarecastle were unable to cope with the skill and speed of the Dals. The final score read Ennis 3-4, Clarecastle 0-6" (Clare Champion 1931).

In the 1931 Clare cup final Newmarket again edged out the Dals by 5-5 to 3-6. The Blues would hold a vice-like grip on the Clare Champion Cup until 1934.

In a cracking county championship final, played before an attendance of 5,000 patrons, John Joe Doyle proved to be the difference between the Blues and the Dals as the former continued to torment the Ennis men. Doyle gave probably the greatest performance of his career as the Blues had seven points to spare 3-4 to 1-3 at the end of a sporting contest. The Clare Champion reported "both teams left the field together after the game amid great jubilation and hand shaking all around. The atmosphere in which the county final was played proved that even great rivals can even be great friends".

1932 Cup Shock

In the Clare Cup semi-final of 1932, the Dals were shocked by Kilkishen on a score line of 3-6 to 4 goals in a sterling contest. The result caused great jubilation amongst the supporters of the Kilkishen team. However, 1932 was a great year for the Clare senior hurling team and three Ennis men formed part of that team – the great Tull Considine, Larry Blake, and Joe Madigan. In June of 1933, Ennis Dals lost to Clooney by 2-3 to 2-2 in the cup, while they lost interest in the championship after Newmarket inflicted a 5-3 to 3-4 defeat on them.

1934 - Dals Champions Again

The 1934 championship was run off in a divisional system and the Dals were pitted against Newmarket, Clonlara and Tulla. In their opening game, Ennis went under to the Blues by 4-1 to 2-3. Instead of demoralising the side, they retaliated by inflicting a 6-2 to 2-3 win over the holders Tulla, followed by 4-3 to 2-1 defeat of Clonlara. In the meantime, the Dals gained some measure of revenge when they defeated the Blues in the Kilkishen tournament. This win by Ennis over Newmarket seemed to inspire them as they defeated the Blues again by 2-6 to 2-4 in the divisional final of the championship. The successful Town League of 1934 was also a major factor as the series of games threw up many notable hurlers including Jack Carroll, 'Aoner' Sheridan, 'Click' Houlihan and James Kearney. A depleted Clonlara side who had earlier made great strides in the Clare cup lost to Ennis by 9 points in the semi-final of the championship.

Mick Hennessy re-organised the dormant Clooney hurling club in 1932. Between 1934-1944, Hennessy with tremendous energy, charisma, enthusiasm and leadership, created the golden age of Clooney hurling and camogie. Mick was the driving force which brought the Clooney club to 10 senior finals, 5 in the championship and 5 in the Clare Cup in a 10

1935/1936 Dals Senior team featuring many of the 1934 winning team. Front row, left to right: *Larry Blake, Tadgh Quirke, Aoner Sheridan, Ralphie Burns, Mickie White, George Morgan.* ***Centre:*** *Mick Linnane, Jacksie Darcy, Paddy Flynn, Seán Guinnane, John Joe Quinn, Paddy Hynes.* ***Standing:*** *Joe Madigan, Jimmy Kearney, Christy 'Click' Houlihan, Miko Malone, Tull Considine (capt.), Gerry Cronin, Peadar Dervan, Paddy Howard, Paddy Kenny.* ***Insets:*** *Jack Quirke, Seán Harrington.* ***Missing:*** *Jack Carroll.*

Courtesy of Seán Spellissy.

Old Mill Street dominated the Leagues during the years 1933-1935. Tull Considine is pictured with Cup. 'Pharaoh' Mahony is pictured second on left, seated. Mick Linnane, back row, first hurler on left. Christy 'Click' Houlihan can be seen in centre row, second hurler from right.

year spell. Initially in 1932, Clooney Utd., received assistance from Ruan, Tubber, Barefield and Crusheen. By 1934, with just the aid of Ruan, they won the Clare Champion Cup. This was the side that Ennis Dals faced in the County Championship final.

On County Final Day Clooney won the toss and elected to play with the stiff wind. Their early pressure was rewarded when Wally Healy found the net. The Dals, slow to settle down, found their feet with Blake, Darcy, Harrington and Hynes in magnificent form. "The Dals bombarded the Clooney goal mouth but rotten luck attended their efforts. Miko Malone then struck with a goal. Tull Considine at full back and James Kearney in goal were good. At the interval, Clooney led by 2-1 to 1-1. In the second half, Cusack, Duggan, Healy, Lynch and Hennessy continued to torment, but the Ennis backs were up to it". (Clare Champion reporter).

A goal by George Morgan brought Ennis back into it. Morgan was later replaced by Tony Considine. The winning goal came from Peadar Flanagan after 'Aoner' Sheridan and Joe Madigan linked up to put Flanagan through. As the final whistle sounded, the Dals led by 4-2 to 3-1.

1934 ENNIS DALS PEN PICTURES
From the Pages of the Clare Champion, unless otherwise stated.

Larry Blake: Regarded as one of the best players in the game, a young man in years, but a veteran in achievement, plays with a wonderful sense of position.

Ralphie Burns: A versatile hurler, he is regarded as one of Clare's bright hopes for the future. Position – corner and full-back or centre field. He later made his inter-county debut in 1935 and played senior championship in 1936 and 1937.

Jack 'Buster' Carroll: Very prominent in the early rounds of the 1934 championship. He later served as chairman of the Faughs hurling club 1945-1946.

Tony 'Tonnie' Considine: Came on during the course of the 1934 championship. A regular Dals player throughout the late 1930's and early 1940's. He won further honours in 1937 (Clare Cup) and 1941 senior championship.

Tull Considine: A brilliant sticksman, possessor of a deadly body swerve, when on the move he is fast and clever, a genius at converting the half chance into a score. Right or left, in the air or on the ground, it doesn't matter to Tull as he can split a defence wide open with a darting weaving run *(Irish Press).*

Gerry Cronin (Right Half Back): A fast and resourceful player. He possesses a keen sense of anticipation. He has helped the Dals to many victories. Holder of four senior hurling medals with the Dals in 1924, 1928, 1929 and 1934. Regular on the Clare team of the 1925/1930 era.

Jacksie Darcy (Left Full Back): Though young in years he is playing remarkably well this year. A strong left and right sided player, very reliable". A dual member of the Dals teams of 1929 that swept the boards in senior hurling and football.

Peadar Dervin: A striker with great power and accuracy. He should partner Jack Quirke as centre field. A native of Galway, he came to prominence with the Boreen hurlers. He later played senior championship with Clare in 1935 and 1938.

Christy 'Click' Houlihan: A highly regarded member of the Old Mill Street hurlers, Christy won intermediate with the Rovers in 1927 and won numerous awards in the Gilroy and Mackey cups in the Town Leagues.

Paddy Hynes: Highly rated by contemporaries, came to prominence in the leagues of 1934. "Made senior debut in 1934. He is fast and fearless. A young player with a great future."

Sean Harrington: A native of Templederry, Co. Tipperary. Made his debut with the Dals in 1930. Played senior hurling with Clare from 1933 – 1938. He joined the Feakle club about 1935 after transferring from Ennis C.B.S. In the words of team mate Flan Purcell, "Sean Harrington was brilliant, resourceful. He had speed, he had skill, he had everything."

Jimmy Kearney (Goalie): He can play anywhere, brainy and accurate. He is fast to clear his lines and is one of our hopes for the future. Jimmy is a product of the local leagues." In the words of Bernie Woods, "Jimmy Kearney was one of the best hurlers ever to play for Ennis.

Peadar Flanagan: A student at St. Flannan's and a native of Tipperary. He is a fast and forceful forward, he got vital scores during the championship. Highly rated by fellow players. To quote 'Aoner' Sheridan, "We talk about the hurlers of to-day but you'd want to see Peadar Flanagan hurl, he was great, a flaking hurler" Peadar Flanagan was called on to the Clare team of 1934/1935.

Joe Madigan: An accurate and effective forward. Adept at tackling and knows no fear. Gave a lifelong service to hurling in Ennis. Represented Clare in the great years 1927-1932. He won five county hurling plus one football, at least three Clare Cups and one Cusack Cup.

George Morgan: The stylist of the team. A dynamic player, possesses great ability. Though very young, he is regarded as one of the fastest men in the game today. A born hurler.

Mick Linnane: Member of the Rovers club. Won intermediate in 1927 and numerous awards with Old Mill Street. Played mostly at left corner back. Great ground striker. A brother-in-law of 'Click' Houlihan.

Miko 'Mixer' Malone: A very accurate forward, a straight shooter, he never misplaces a ball. Malone will fill the full forward position. One of the select group of eight that won senior hurling/football, Clare and Cusack cups in 1929. A feat unlikely to be achieved again.

Paddy Kenny: Highly rated and respected by opponents. Regularly plays in the full back line. A very seasoned player. Paddy Kenny won three senior championships and three Clare cups with the Dals. A nephew of Paddy Kenny of the 1911-1916 era.

Jack Quirke: A tower of strength and finished exponent of the game. A great opportunist, he plays a dashing kind of game. Jack Quirke played senior championship for Clare in 1935, 1936 and 1937.

Tadhg Quirke : A fast and slick striking player, possesses great powers of endurance. A brother of Jack's. He learned his hurling in St. Flannans and represented Clare at minor, junior and senior.

Michael 'Aoner' Sheridan: An outstanding ground hurler, remarkably fast and accurate. He represented Clare at all grades, minor, junior, intermediate and senior in 1934. A regular on the county teams of the 1935 – 1940 era.

Mickey White: "A sweet, swift striker of the ball, one of the most spectacular players in the game today", Clare Champion. A beautiful wing forward, he had neither the towering height of Cork's Jim Hurley or the bustling physique of Mick Mackey. White relied on his art". (Padraig O'Beachain).

Other members of the 1934 panel included Paddy Flynn, John Joe Quinn and Paddy Howard. According to 'Aoner' Sheridan all these men were very reliable and capable of coming on at any time and doing justice to the Dals.

Michael Cusack Commemoration 1934

1934 proved to be a memorable year in the story of Ennis G.A.A. Great effort was put into the Town Leagues. On September 22nd, 1934, Clare honoured the memory of one of her most famous sons, Michael Cusack. Work also commenced on the development of Howard's Field which was officially opened on Sunday 25th May, 1936 as Cusack Park by Mr. Bob O'Keefe, President of the G.A.A.

The Dals opened the 1935 championship with Crusheen and though they trailed by 4 points at the interval, the Ennis side took complete control after the restart thanks to terrific play from 'Click' Houlihan, Peadar Dervin and Sean Guinnane. The final score read 9-3 to 3-2. The Dals followed with a victory over Clooney, before losing to Feakle. However, Feakle then lost to Clooney and the Dals overcame the challenge of Bodyke, setting up a semi-final pairing of Ennis/Feakle and 'the Blues'/'Mills' in the other section. Played at Kilkishen, Feakle continued their recent dominance of the Dals with a five point victory margin. The sides had retired level at the interval, mainly due to the brilliance of Paddy Kenny at fullback. The Feakle men took control early in the second half with two flashing goals. "A terrific struggle now ensued with every Ennis man playing his part with a special word of praise for Paddy Kenny. Hurleys clashed as men went down on both sides. For Feakle, Flan Purcell, Tom Moloney, Brud McGrath and John Jones were outstanding". (Clare Champion) In the County Final, Feakle had 10 points to spare over Newmarket. Feakle also ended the Dals interest in the Clare Cup. On the domestic scene, Old Mill Street captured the honours in the Town Leagues.

1936/1937 Mixed Fortunes

In 1936, the Dals continued with a good run in the Clare Cup before losing to top-side Feakle in the semi-final. In the early stages of the championship Ennis and Clarecastle played a gruelling draw (2-5 to 2-5). After this display, Clarecastle 'the Magpies' were installed as serious contenders for senior honours. "Clarecastle fought every inch of the way with their more experience rivals. Merciless tackling and great pace was the order of the day. 'Swaddy' McMahon was the spearhead of the Clarecastle attack. Clarecastle shaded the issue in the replay. "Dals form not what it used to be. The team lacks balance in the absence of Paddy Kenny" wrote the local press.

Clare Cup Champions Again

A fine run in the 1937 Clare Cup saw the Ennismen record victories over Clarecastle, Newmarket and Feakle. The Dals/Newmarket clash revived great memories of the heyday of these clubs, with Ennis coming out on top by 5-3 to 4-5. The Cup Final clash with O'Callaghan's Mills was originally fixed for August 29th at Newmarket. At 'the Mills' request, the game was deferred due to the staging of the all Ireland semi-final at Cusack Park. The local match was later re-fixed but due to a disagreement over the Newmarket venue, 'the Mills' forfeited the match. Rev. Fr. Michael Hamilton, Chairman of the County Board, stated "the Cup Final and venue must stand as fixed, and no question of further postponement can be considered". The Clare Cup was then awarded to Ennis Dals.

The Magpies and Clooney ended the Dals interest in the senior championship. Again in 1938, the Dals had a good run in the Clare Cup beating Eire Og (an amalgamation of Ballyea, Ballynacally, Barefield, Crusheen and Kilnamona) and Clarecastle, to share the spoils with Feakle. Such was the strength in depth of Ennis hurling that the Dals could afford to field a second string in intermediate (B) and the Rovers were amongst the top- dogs in intermediate (A).

Feakle/Dals Cup Replay

Feakle and Ennis crossed swords again in the Clare Cup of 1938. Played in a downpour, Feakle built a seven point lead before a great goal by Denny 'Lals' Rice brought the Dals back into the reckoning. There was tremendous excitement on the part of the spectators. Hats and flags went flying in the air when the East Clare men added another goal to give them a fairly safe lead. Mickey White from a free knocked the rain from the net to intensify the excitement. But Feakle with the Loughnane's and Flan Purcell stood up to the Dals onslaughts. This was a splendid game with top class discipline observed by both teams. The same cannot be said for the spectator's as, during the progress of the game, there were two or three scenes in which fist fights took place. For Ennis, Blake, 'Paddence' O'Loughlin, Dervin,Sheridan and White were outstanding.

Feakle went on to win the Cup beating Tulla by 6-2 to3-2. This was the first time since the inauguration of the competition, that the Clare Cup went to an East Clare club.

Dals/Feakle again - *The Clare Champion* reported

"In the divisional final of the senior championship, Ennis had one point to spare over Clarecastle, (1-5 to 1-4) before again meeting Feakle in another gruelling encounter. The hectic struggles between Feakle and Ennis have been a feature of this year's senior championship, never has competition been so equal since the G.A.A. was founded. The sides provided a splendid exhibition of fine striking as Feakle succeeded in wearing down the stubborn challenge of the Dals by 4-2 to 3-1. The game featured great exchanges between M.P. Loughnane and Sean Guinnane. 'Paddence' O'Loughlin and Ralphie Burns were also very much to the fore for Ennis". Feakle went on to add the senior championship title to their Cup win."

1939/1940 Huge Effort

A huge push was made by the Dalcassian club in 1939/1940 to once again bring senior honours to the town. The local town league was again the catalyst. It was agreed by the organisers that all hurlers working in Ennis would be eligible to play with the team of their particular district in which they worked. This gave all hurling fans the opportunity to witness the displays of such prominent players as John Daly, Paddy Markham, Albert Murphy, Michael Murphy, Mick Shea and Tom Neylon in action.

In spite of a huge effort, the Dals again lost to Feakle in a replay by a narrow margin. The town side was also prominent in the Ennis Cathedral Tournament, a competition involving Clooney, Tulla, Feakle and the Dals.

1941 Senior Championship

Ennis opened their season with a 14 point win over Newmarket in the Cup. Their clash in the championship was a much closer affair but the Dals prevailed by 3-3 to 2-2. Following this win, Ennis had 8 points to spare over Broadford. In the semi final, 'Aoner' Sheridan was recalled for his first game of the season. Sheridan proved to be the hero of the hour scoring 2-3. Ruan who were unlucky to lose by four points were best served by Jimmy Forbes and Tommy Keating. In the other side of the draw, Clooney had wins over Cratloe, Clarecastle and Tulla but were held to a draw by Scariff. On their way to the final both Ennis and Clooney trained very hard and consistently and the high standard of play was fully reflected in the exhibition given. A crowd of 6,000 witnessed one of the cleanest and manliest county finals ever played. Though the Dals trailed by a goal at the interval, they put in a storming second half. Johnny Fleming, grabbing possession in the corner, bobbed and weaved his way through the Clooney defence to score a great goal, changing the complexion of the game. The Ennis Dals secured one of their greatest victories by 5-2 to 2-1.

Kieran Hennessy from Quin was then a ten year old staunch Clooney supporter. Kieran told me *"the first big hurling match I saw in Ennis was the All Ireland Semi-Final between Limerick and Galway in 1940 and being held up by Jack Conway to see Mick Mackey, who had thrown away his boots. The other big game I remember was the 1941 County final. This was the first year I really followed Clooney everywhere. They won the Clare cup in Tulla. We regarded Clooney as a certainty to win the final against Ennis Dals. We regarded the Dals as no hopers. That's how thick we were. The old timers told us about the Dalcassians. What a revelation that was. My memory of the game is not just of all the subs that came on, but of the Ennis goalie who was outstanding – a man called Arthur Power. Clooney were outplayed. They had no excuses. I think over confidence let them down. A couple of their players like John Gaffney and Jimmy Kelly were clerical students and were gone back to Maynooth. They couldn't play because of 'the clerical ruling'. I think that is why Mick Hennessy played in goal. We were very disappointed with the result. There is little doubt that Clooney were favourites going into the final. Clooney had a fine team in players of the calibre of Tom Halloran, Joe Kilmartin, Paddy and Joe McNamara and Paddy Joe Reynolds. P.J. Reynolds was a star with St. Flannans. He had a great spell on the Clare team from around 1933 – 1936. He worked in Alf Hogan's Turf Accountants. He was a lovely man".*

In the 1941 Championship the Dals defeated Tulla, Broadford, Newmarket, Ruan and the Cup Champions, Clooney. The County Final with Clooney produced hurling of the highest quality and is regarded as one of the greatest hurling finals ever played.

PEN PICTURES

These pin pictures are based around match reports from the 1941 championship.

Arthur Power: Reliable and effective goalkeeper. Made a crucial save in the game with Newmarket – diverting a ground shot over the bar at the expense of a point.

Michael 'Paddence' O'Loughlin: Outstanding Clare minor of 1937, 1938 and 1939. Has played sterling games at corner back for the Dals over the last 2 to 3 years. Without doubt the definite No. 2 on the Dals team.

John 'Brudsy' McCarthy: Has held down the No. 4 jersey for some time now. Represented both Rovers and Dalcassians, at adult level. Part of a formidable full-back line. 'Brudsy' gave a marvellous display in their win over Newmarket. Has represented the County at senior level.

Jim Quinlivan: Previously represented his native Tulla and has represented the County on many occasions. A product of St. Flannan's.

Ralphie Burns: A regular Clare inter-county hurler. Like McCarthy he too shone against Newmarket. He later played senior football for Kilfenora in 1941. Winner of two senior hurling and two senior football medals. "Ralphie was a man of great wit and smiling disposition. His hurling skills matched the best, Mackey, Considine or Ring would have been proud to have him on their team and indeed, Maureen Potter would gladly have Ralphie in her comedy act." Clare County Express, 1980.

Tom Neylon: The former inspiration of the Kilmaley Club, Tom has represented Clarecastle and Éire Óg in past championships. A big acquisition to the Dals.

Christy Glynn: Whether at corner or centre-back Christy is always one of the cornerstones of the defence. A link with the Cup team of 1937.

Ennis Dalcassians, 1941 Clare Senior Champions. Back row, left to right: *John Hynes, Tom Neylon, Michael 'Paddence' O'Loughlin, Christy Glynn, Johnny Fleming, Jim Quinlivan, Brudsy McCarthy, Seán Moloney, Tull Considine, Ralphie Burns.* ***Front row:*** *Tony Glynn, Arthur Power, Bruddy Mann, Miko Ball, Seán Guinnane, 'Tonnie' Considine, Joe Madigan, 'Aoner' Sheridan, Eddie 'Bucky' Flynn. Missing from photograph Mickey White, Larry Blake.*

Tony 'Tonnie' Considine: Outstanding athlete, a product of Ennis CBS. Has represented the Munster Colleges.

Larry Blake: Returned this year after a long absence. Like Quirke, he too has lost nothing of his craft and accuracy. Blake has 15 years of top class hurling behind him.

Michael Sheridan: Returned after a long layoff. Made an outstanding contribution against Ruan. 'Aoner' is a forward of fast movement and resource.

Johnny Fleming: A young promising forward. Could yet prove a match winner.

Miko Ball: Fast and clever forward. Always good for a score.

Maurice and Bruddy Mann: The brothers Mann are full of hurling ability allied with lots of enthusiasm.

Jack Quirke: A centre-field man of great presence and strength, he gets great distance into his deliveries. According to 'Aoner' Sheridan and 'Paddence' O'Loughlin the introduction of Jack Quirke as a sub won the County Final for the Dals.

Mickey White: A veteran, still clever and reliable. He scored the Dals third goal, which sunk Newmarket.

Edward Flynn: A regular for many years, a nippy forward.

Joe Madigan: Another veteran, going back to the days of '27. Could yet play his part.

Other members of the 1941 panel included: Tony Glynn, Sean Moloney, and W. Moroney, players noted for their penetrating and piercing runs through opposing defences.

Big Representation on County Team

The Dals had a big representation on the Clare team of 1941/1942, with Larry Blake, Sean Guinnane, Arthur Power, 'Brudsy' McCarthy, 'Aoner' Sheridan, Johnny Fleming and Eddie Flynn all honoured by the selectors in either league or championship. The Dals added the Spring Hurling league to their senior championship.

Huge Interest in Juveniles 1941 – 1942

The five traditional areas of the town battled it out in one of the most exciting juvenile competitions in 1941. After three series of games, Boreen and Old Mill Street remained unbeaten. The Old Mill Street team, the eventual winners had the pick of Cloughleigh and Carmody Street. The Boreen selection extended in Abbey Street and Bindon Street. Such was the interest shown in the juveniles that the Clare Champion published copious accounts of the exploits of these youngsters. "The final rounds should be classics. These contests are attracting an increasing attendance of spectators, and excitement was so tense on Monday evening last that many of their elders lost their tempers". However, I'm sure, few could crib with the refereeing of T.J. Meehan, the organiser of these leagues. A valuable set of medals was on display in Maurer's window and many longing eyes were most likely cast on the display as the young contestants passed to and fro from school. These magnificent medals were purchased from the sale of programmes at the recent Clare/Limerick Munster Championship clash. The programmes were sold by the enterprising juveniles. The stars in these leagues included Billy Power, J.J. Clohessy, John Joe Keane and P.J. Dilger.

Ennis Dalcassians Juvenile Champions, 1942. Back row, left to right: *T.J. Meehan (secretary), Simon O'Donnell, Tommy Moloney, Phil Murphy, Johnny Tuohy, P.J. Dilger, John Joe Keane, Josie Doherty, J.J. Clohessy, Fr. Ml. Hamilton (Chairman of County Board).* ***Front row:*** *Bonaventure Morgan, Seán Mounsey, 'Brack' Halloran, Philim Cronin, Billy Power, Gerry Cronin, Flan Smyth.*

Remembering the 23rd Battalion

While the Ennis Dals took their last title in 1941, a new force arrived in Clare hurling in the form of the Army team known as the 23rd Battalion. The army unit stationed in Dromoland fielded one of the strongest club teams in the mid forties. Reports of their great tussles with Clarecastle, Clooney and Tulla are documented in the pages of the Clare Champion during this period. Though affiliated to the County Board since 1941, it wasn't until 1943 that they, with the influx of new blood made a big impact on Clare club hurling and at least three of their members were called onto the Clare team – Jimmy Duggan, Paddy Ryan and Phil Byrnes. In 1943, the Army team lost the Clare Cup final but the following year they bounced back to win the Clare Champion Cup beating Newmarket, Cratloe, Ennis Commercial Dalcassians and Clooney along the way. Pouring over old dusty newspapers, rarely gives one the full picture of times gone by. Through a mutual friend, Brian McMahon, I was introduced to Kevin Damery, of Cobh, who played at wing back with the army team for five years. I spoke to Kevin over a couple of pints on the eve of the 1997 Munster final in Cork. He recalled with great accuracy the names of team mates and opponents. *"We won the Clare Champion Cup, the Dr. Daly Memorial cup and the Fr. Murphy Tournament. In goal we had Willie Mackey. Mick Walsh was usually full back. Ned Daunt was left full back and I played on the other wing with Phil Shanahan, at centre back. Our centre field usually consisted of Brian Moore and Paddy Ryan. Joe Harrington, a grand hurler from Dungarvan was our centre forward. He was class hurler and a product of Mount Sion C.B.S. Fr. Creed practically ran the team on his own. He may have been from the Kilkishen area as I believe he had a brother living there. We had fine players in Brian Moore, Mick Walsh, Jimmy Duggan and Gus Mayberry of Kerry. Mick Walsh later married a girl from Clooney and hurled for them. Jimmy Duggan played for Clare in the 1944 championship. Jim Devitt also played for us for a short spell. He later captained Tipperary. Ennis Dalcassians were very much out of it. They won very little while I was there. Clarecastle, Clooney, Newmarket, Feakle and Tulla were very strong. I often played on Tommy Considine of Clarecastle. Paddy Markham was a grand hurler and John Daly was a great goal keeper and a nice fellow. Others I recall include Sean Guinnane, Jimmy Forbes and Mick Hennessy. Ruan were good previous to 1948 though they fielded a great team afterwards. Towards the end of 1945, the army unit at Dromoland was demobilised."*

Ennis Commercial Dalcassians

In 1943 the Ennis Dals club was re-organised. The Commercials had arranged to form a new club but, as a result of a meeting with the Dalcassians, it was agreed to unite and call the new club the Ennis Commercial Dalcassians. While the Commercials assisted the Dals at senior level, it is unclear if they fielded an independent team in the junior grade. Ennis Commercial Dalcassians had a 16 point win over Ruan in the 1943 County Championship. In 1943 and 1944, the Commercial Dalcassians were knocked out of the Cup and championship by Clooney and the 23rd Battallion.

Decline of the Dalcassians

By 1944, the Dals continued to dominate the minor grade. Boasting players of the calibre of Sean Mahon, Sean Guinnane (New Road), Phelim Cronin and the free scoring John Joe Keane accounted for Tulla in the final. In the face of their superiority in juvenile hurling, little came out of it as with few work opportunities on offer, Ennis was hit by widespread emigration. Allied to this, a serious row split the Dalcassian club hastening the slow decline of a great hurling club.

On April 5th, 1969, it was decided at a meeting of Ennis UDC to call the new housing estate, Turnpike Road, after the Dalcassian Hurling Club. The proposal was made by Michael Considine and seconded by Tim Smythe and 'Aoner' Sheridan. The new 132-house scheme became known as Dalcassian Park, Dalcassian Drive and Dalcassian Avenue.

Golden Days of the Town Leagues

1933 - 1948

The earliest reference I found regarding the Ennis hurling leagues was a tie between Jail Street and Church Street, reported in the Clare Journal of November 26, 1911. Jail Street, strengthened by the Considine Brothers and Jack Spellissy, led at the interval by 3-1 to 1 goal, thanks to the splendid work of their whips, (played in the days of 17 a side, the Whips seem to have been additional inside forwards). Church Street fought back gallantly in the second half but failed to break through for the vital scores. Jail Street went on to win by a comfortable margin (6-2 to 2-0) despite the best efforts of Johnny 'Joker' Coote, Paddy Gordon, the Cash brothers, Hoare and Marrinan. It is unclear if the leagues continued regularly throughout these years but in 1917 a meeting was called in the Town Hall to re-vamp the leagues. The main organisers were Tull Considine, James Wylde and James Spellissy. Four captains were chosen to select players of their choice under the names of Pearses, McDonaghs, O'Rahillys and Dalys. The captains were Jack Spellissy (Pearses), James 'Sham' Spellissy (McDonaghs), Tull Considine (O'Rahillys) and James Wylde (Dalys). The influence of the 1916 leaders is evident in the names of the teams.

All four teams went into training at the Fairgreen before the competition was run off in ideal weather conditions. The outcome of this league is unclear but O'Rahillys defeated McDonaghs by 7-1 to 5-0. The prominent players included Steve Millar and 'Joker' Coote (Pearses), Pako 'Brophy' Malone, John O'Loughlin, Martin Kennedy (McDonaghs), Joe Madigan (O'Rahillys), Ed Lucid, Paddy Gordon, Wally Fahy (Dalys) plus their respective captains.

Without doubt the golden age of the leagues was the years 1933-1948 when at least six of the traditional areas fielded teams. The great thing about town leagues was the ability of the average hurler to rise above his station and occasionally roast a star or inter-county hurler in these local derbies. Old Mill Street (the eventual winners in 1933), underwent a careful course of training for their opening joust with the Turnpike.

The Rovers took to the field looking fit and spectacular in their newly acquired colours of saffron and blue, but the 'Pike' led at the interval 4-3

Turnpike beaten Town League finalists 1948. Back row, left to right: *Seán Brody, John Shannon, Jackie Moroney, Josie Doherty, Seán Tuttle, Frank Cosgrove, Joe O'Grady, Jackie Darcy.* ***Middle row:*** *Des Cullinan, Billy O'Halloran, Frank 'Soapy' Higgins, Christy Shannon, Paddy Kenny, John Torpey, Vince Cosgrove.* ***Front row:*** *Paddy Doherty, Josie Kennedy, Michael Broderick, Seán Dinan, Michael Doherty.* *Courtesy of Pat Brennan.*

to 2-1. With full-time approaching the Rovers had forged ahead 4-4 to 4-3, thanks to the brilliance of Bernie Woods in the Mill Street goal. *"Keane playing on the right wing pounced on a ball in fine style and sent it to Tull Considine. Considine the astute and seasoned veteran spotting the course of the ball connected to drive the ball home for the insurance goal"*, wrote the Clare Champion reporter. Meanwhile the Market overcame Clare Road by 6-6 to 5-5 with 'Aoner' Sheridan and Mickie White to the fore. The Boreen beat Turnpike 5-4 to 1-2 but lost to Old Mill Street 5-8 to 4-7 before an attendance of 800 people. Old Mill Street held a vice-like grip on the Gilroy Perpetual Challenge Cup over the next couple of years. Prominent for Old Mill Street in those years were Paddy Kenny, Christy 'Click' Houlihan, Michael 'Pharaoh' Mahony, Denny 'Lals' Rice, Mick 'Soot' Coote, John Joe 'Doll Dido' Gilligan and George Morgan. This was the era of the Old Mill Street harriers and other out-door activities such as fishing, shooting and swimming. The late Vincent Sheridan, a brother of the then inter-county hurler, Michael 'Aoner' spoke to me at length: "*The leagues attracted great crowds to the Fairgreen, the Showgrounds and Cusack Park. People came from far and near. The standard was very high as many inter-county hurlers took part – Ralphie*

Burns, Sean Guinnane, Jim Quinlivan, Mick Hennessy, Paddy Markham, Peadar Dervan from Galway and Sean Harrington, a Tipperary man. Mickie White was a beautiful hurler, he had great hands. Larry Blake was out on his own. I remember the final of '48, that was a hot game."

In April 1935 'Abbeymore' reported in the Champion: *"Mill street are in training, likewise Clare Road, the Market men have been patronising the Fairgreen. Boreen have been conspicuous by their inactivity. One would incline to the thought that the wearers of the green and white would be foremost in setting an example in activity. We have not heard how the 'Pike' have been faring"*. In the same issue 'Fergus' wrote, *"Apart from senior leagues, we propose to run minor and secondary leagues for those beyond the age of minor but who have never played senior."*

Mill Street Hurlers Victory Ceili

The Gilroy Cup was presented at the Ennis Labour Hall by the Garda Siochana, together with a splendid set of medals put up by the Ennis Dals Club. Fr. Michael Hamilton presided and delivered an eloquent speech. Mill Street lost their opening tie to the Market; stung by this defeat they took to training and in their final match they disposed of the Turnpike, to become the holders of the Gilroy Cup. The fifteen members of the Mill Street team helped the Senior, Intermediate and Junior Dalcassian sides in the Champion Cup and County Championship engagements.

Without doubt, the most famous league was that of 1948. Old Mill Street set the pace early on when they overcame the Boreen at Cusack Park with Sean Mounsey, George Summerly and P. J. O'Dea doing well. However, they failed to the Clare Road by 3-3 to 3-2 before a large crowd. For Clare Road, F. Milner and P. J. Morgan were the pick. After eight rounds of games, Turnpike were on top with 15 points following seven wins and one draw and with the Market in second place the stage was set for a showdown. Such was the interest generated that the Clare Champion published abundant accounts on the final.

Johnny McCarthy, though only a boy of 9 years has memories of the 1948 final. *"The extraordinary thing about 1948 is that Josie Doherty was flown from Dublin to assist the 'Pike."* Michael Doherty too has vivid memories of the 1948 town Final: *"Cusack Park was full at 6 pence a time. There was a lot of money placed on the outcome. I was only 15, most of the Market lads, including Gerry Moroney, were in their early twenties. They had 'the drop on us' in that. We (the Turnpike) had a great record coming into the final. A remarkable feature of the game was that my brother, Josie, was flown from Dublin to play. Brendan Spellissy was a great patron of Turnpike. He was responsible for flying Josie down that morning. The Market team and supporters couldn't believe it when they*

***Market Street (Town League Champions 1948). Back row, left to right:** Mickie White, Michael Mackey, Paddy 'Polo' Guilfoyle, Gerry Moroney, Flan Smyth, Bernie O'Shea, John Hanley, John Kearney, Paddy Kearney, Peter 'Slavery' Guilfoyle. **Middle row:** Paddy White, Dan Lynch, Martin Murphy, Hauley Dargan, Bob Kearney, John Joe McInerney. **Front row:** Josh Dilger, Seán Dargan, Martin Casey, John Joe Keane (captain), Leo Clohessy, Bernie Woods. **Mascots:** John White, Michael Mackey, Gerry Woods.*

saw him. It was like Neil Armstrong and 'Buz' Aldrin landing on the Moon in Apollo 11. Josie was a ten second man at centre-field but he was suffering from jet-lag so they moved him to full-forward."

Paddy White, a son of Mickie remembers the preparation put in by both sides. *"My father knew that Turnpike were the better team. He called a meeting of the Market players to discuss tactics. Turnpike had class hurlers; every night he'd have the expected Turnpike team written out and he'd shuffle the Market side to bring down the supposed deficit. A feature of the game was the brilliant goalkeeping of Sean Brody and Bernie Woods."*

Michael Doherty of the Turnpike continues: *"After the '48 final, hurling disintegrated. Bitterness crept in. The 'Pike' and the Market wouldn't agree. The Rovers had a junior team of their own, so the town was divided. Ennis Dals just barely produced a team during those years. I played with the Dals though I was only in minor ranks."* The celebrated Kilrush, Clare and Munster footballer, P. J. O'Dea played hurling for Old Mill Street. P. J. told me: *"Hurling is my number one game. I never enjoyed anything as much as the street leagues; they were terrific. Hurling wasn't new to me. We loved the game in West Clare where we had a useful junior team. I also played junior hurling in Cork with Churchtown. The Old Mill Street Rovers were the greatest group of players I ever played with. They were great characters. Sean Mounsey was the star of the Rovers, a lovely hurler, Tony McEnery, Johnny and Paschal Molloy also stood out."*

For the record, the 1948 teams that contested the final lined out as follows, as per the Clare Champion:

The Market: Bernie Woods, Bernie O'Shea, Gerry Moroney, John Joe McInerney, J. Dinan, Flan Smith, John Hanley, John Kearney, Dan Lynch (Kilmaley), John Joe Keane, Sean Dargan, Leo Clohessy, Martin Casey, Haulie Dargan and Paddy 'Polo' Guilfoyle. **Subs:** Paddy White, Martin Murphy, Paddy Kearney.

Turnpike: Sean Brody, Liam Torpey, Josie Grady, Paddy Kenny, Michael Doherty, Paddy Doherty, Vince Cosgrove, Josie Doherty, Frank Cosgrove, Jackie Moroney, Des Cullinan, Frank 'Soapy' Higgins, Sean Dinan, Christy Shannon and Josie Kennedy. **Subs:** D. Ryan, Sean Tuttle, Billy O'Halloran, Michael Broderick, John Shannon.

Though 1948 is generally regarded as the high point of the leagues, they continued to serve the town well, especially in the off-season, keeping lads fit. The 1954 league was of great advantage to Éire Óg with the Clare Road beating Boreen by 6-8 to 2-2 in the final.

It is impossible to record all the fine hurlers that took part in the leagues but others included Martin Campbell, Phelim Cronin, Danno Coote, Haulie Coote, Haulie Cullinan, Bonaventure Morgan, Johnny Tuohy, Peter Skerritt, Andy, Jamesy and Bernie Woods, Georgie and Flan Summerly, Paddy White and Kevin Doherty.

Other highly rated hurlers included Jackie Molloy and Josie McCarthy, both of whom played for Rovers. Josie was selected on the St. John's/Ennis representative side that beat the Tony O'Shaughnessy led St. Mary's, Cork, 4-7 to 4-5 in 1955. Josie was a big loss to hurling when he emigrated to England shortly afterwards.

The Town Leagues were an integral part of the early days of Éire Óg and again in the 1980 – 1984 era when Éire Óg and the Banner came together to organise highly successful leagues, with well over 100 hurlers taking part during the spring and early summer. These leagues bore fruit with Senior Championships coming to the town in 1980 and 1982 during a great spell in Ennis hurling.

Great Days of Town Leagues in Ennis

Kevin J. Browne

(Previously published in the Souvenir programme to mark the occasion of the re-opening of Cusack Park on 29th June, 1980. Re-produced with the permission of Catherine Browne.)

Ennis always produced great hurlers and I am convinced that the old town leagues of the late 1920s, 1930s and the 1940s played a major part in keeping the national pastime not only alive but very virile in the town. For this reason I would like to see a revival of the old spirit that could field teams in six of the towns old areas such as The Market, Old Mill Street, Turnpike, Clare Road, Boreen and Drumbiggle. With all said, areas now expanded population-wise, this should not be an exaggerated job and would not alone do great work in promoting a wider interest in the game but also in the making of better players. Of course I am writing about forty to fifty years ago and the events in the town of those years. There have been many good hurlers in Ennis since then but there would be a lot more if the leagues had been continued. There are many reasons why this happened, the 'Emergency', which took many to look for work in England, the radio and in more recent times television, not to mention the lack of playing fields. For instance in those times you not alone had the Fairgreen, Cusack Park but also the roads and yards of people of the town. To put it gently Ennis was still a hurling town and when things went right for the GAA there was always the Showgrounds.

Kevin J. Browne.

'Tull' Considine, The Great from Turnpike

But while I like to look to the future I can only in this article reminisce about the abundance of hurlers the town leagues produced. I well know that the leagues did not have to come to make for happy memories for many of them, but even though some of the players had made their names on Munster and All-Ireland teams, they still gave the leagues that class which brought the crowds to the Fairgreen and Cusack Park. Take Tull Considine for instance. He had made his name in GAA circles long before, as had his brother Willie 'Dodger', who was on the county winning All-Ireland team of 1914. Tull also played in the All-Ireland final against Kilkenny in 1932, but while that elusive medal did not come his way he won every other award in the game. A Turnpike man, he played for five years 1927 – 1931 with Munster and was also selected on one occasion on the Railway Cup Football panel in 1927. But Tull did not let fame get in his eyes and was more than willing to play with his native Turnpike. When he later came to reside in the Cusack Road, he turned out for Old Mill Street. This was the inspiration he gave then and which Ennis could well do with in these years.

Who can forget the blonde Larry Blake, another Turnpike man who never forgot where he was born even though All-Ireland fame came his way. Larry was a constant member of the Munster Railway Cup teams from 1931 – 1938 but he also played for Ennis in County Championships and the Turnpike. He was another man who fame did not take from his love of the game. Before I leave the Turnpike I must recall some other great sportsmen who came from the same area. I remember Eddie Fahy playing great hurling for Clare and his brother Wally playing for Ennis DALS. Wally, incidentally, was the owner of 'Manhattan Harmony' who was beaten in a very disputed final of the Irish Cup (Greyhounds) in 1950. Others from the Turnpike who honoured Clare and Ennis as well as the 'Pike' were Sean Guinnane, Tony 'Topper' Morrissey, Paddy Kenny, Denny O'Grady and 'Coppernob' Goulding. I know I am forgetting many but I am certain the 'Pike' district will still continue to produce the right stuff if the old town leagues come back.

Old Mill Street

Now for the district that gave us the (Old) Faughs and later the Rovers with their famous black and white jerseys. In this period the team was known as the Old Road and gave Ennis such hurling stalwarts as Jack Doherty, Mick Linnane, John 'Brodsy' McCarthy. The Old Road had many great hurlers and many of them had nicknames like Michael 'Pharaoh' Mahony, Christy 'Click' Houlihan, Denny 'Lalls' Rice and 'Font' Tobin. Others I recall include Mick Coote, John Joe Cullinan, Bernie and Andy Woods, Jack Moloney and Michael 'Paddence' O'Loughlin. The latter and 'Brodsy' McCarthy were selected on the successful DALS team of 1941.

Paddy White with the Gilroy Cup for Town League pictured with Gerry Moroney, one of the great Ennis stalwarts (c.1998). The Gilroy Cup was first presented in 1933 and won by Old Mill Street in its initial year. It was played for continuously until 1948 when it was won by The Market. Courtesy of Michael Keane.

Market Men

Now I must go to the Market and I suppose most of the credit for this team must go to three men, Joe 'Juler' Madigan, Michael 'Aoner' Sheridan and 'Ralphie' Burns. Of course Jacksie Darcy was also a sound full-back in later days; Jim Quinlivan, Buddy Costelloe, Gerry Moroney and Ownie Griffin came to the assistance of the district. I could never write memories of the Ennis Town Leagues without thinking of Michael 'Mixie' Malone who also gave great service to the DALS.

The Boreen

And now for the Boreen which district produced Jackie Duffy who not alone gave sterling service to Clare but also to the spirit of hurling in his Fairgreen area. He was just "going off" when the 1932 Clare team was picked. Mick Ensko, Jack 'Buster' Carroll, Paddy Flynn and the Fleming brothers Christy and Johnny and Sean Moloney. Others from this area who kept the game alive in what I like to remember as the Christian Brothers and Fairgreen side of the town include Sean Harrington and Peadar Dervin, both inter-county men.

Clare Road and Drumbiggle

When I recall the Clare Road, Jack and Tadgh Quirke come to mind. Both were real stylists while Paudge and Flan Hynes were another pair to give great service to this area. Before going to the Drumbiggle, whose town league efforts were short, I must remember Christopher 'Dabber' Pilkington of the Clare Road. Drumbiggle did not compete for very long and were given leave to pick a few from outside the area. Dermot McKee, a first class goalkeeper from Slaveen and Jack Maher, a raking forward are two I recall. The town area also produced a few excellent hurlers in Jimmy Kearney, Tom Kelly and Georgie Morgan. Georgie also had the distinction of winning an All-Ireland Minor Football medal with Clare in 1929.

The Changing Times

Times were certainly different when hurling and football were the be all and end all in Ennis. The town was closer together then and to have a son playing for his local area was a pride and joy. Today's town is spreading out and with the industrialisation there are more sporting ventures. The national pastimes have suffered as a result and the sooner we come back to the old pastimes the better. In other words there has been a slackening of hurling and football in the town and we could do with a few greats like 'Tull' Considine and Larry Blake. We could also do with a Mackey and Gilroy Cup and maybe a Long Puck contest now and then.

Recollections of Miko Ball

The name Miko Ball is synonymous with music and entertainment. Now enjoying his retirement at home in Ennis, Miko entertained the masses for over 60 years playing at functions and weddings. In an illustrious career Miko played with the Gaiety Dance Band, the Bud Clancy Orchestra, Clem Browne and the Savoy Dance Band, Mickie Hogan, the Castledangan Ceili Band, the Kilfenora, the Sweet Rhythm Band - all this before forming the Red Shadows.

Miko and Chrissie Ball at home in Ennis in 1978.

Growing up in Ennis Miko like all his contemporaries played hurling in the Street Leagues before picking up a senior championship medal with the Dalcassians in 1941. Later an intermediate medal would come his way in 1945 when he lined out with the Faughs.

Many local musicians of this era were influenced by the wonderful big bands led by Victor Sylvester and Joe Loss.

Popular Ennis man Michael Nihill speaking at a social occasion in the 1980s. Miko Ball (accordion) is on his right, Flan McMahon (sax) is on his left.

In 1985 Miko and Chrissie Ball[1] spoke to Denis Canty on West Coast Radio. The programme, broadcast at Christmas, was introduced by Chrissie singing a fine version of 'The Dying Rebel'. Miko then recounted his memories to Denis - "The first band I played with was Freddie Cronin and the Paramount Dance Band. I played the drums at that stage but I loved the accordion so I played that instrument from then on. My parents were musical. My father was violinist with the Miko Hoare Gaiety Dance Band and my mother the former Fanny Lawlor played the concertina and melodeon. I'm self taught myself. I took up the accordion one night in Miko Hoare's house, (21 Steele's Terrace) and played a tune straight away. I was born in Vinegar Lane. We had great neighbours. Paddy Flynn had a garage and by putting up a partition it was turned into a dance hall. It cost 2 old pence to get in. Mickie Reddan collected the money at the door and if you didn't have it you could pay the next week."

Freddie Cronin.

The Sweet Rhythm band was one of the most popular dance bands of their time. At one time or another the band possibly included Freddie Cronin (piano), his brother Louis (drums), Bill Colgan (sax), Jimmy Kelly (sax), Paschal Hanrahan (sax), Tony Mahony (violin), Michael and Flan McMahon and Miko Ball (accordion). Jimmy Kelly and Bill Colgan read

The Glen of Ennis Big Band. From left: *Jimmy Enright, Michael McMahon (accordion), Christy McAllister, Ozzy Connolly (drums), Paschal Hanrahan (sax), Flan McMahon, Jimmy Kelly (sax), 'Mixie' McGuane (vocals).*

Courtesy of Mattsie Hogan.

music and they used to buy the sheet music at Nono's, opposite the Old Ground. But sometimes they had to send to Dublin for it. The Sweet Rhythm played the world of dance dates and marquees. In the old days, dances would last from nine o'clock until three in the morning. This was hard, gruelling work for any band. Bands today don't play those kind of hours. Miko added "I hate to see young people drinking before going dancing. This is false courage for many people. I'm not sure when exactly we formed the Red Shadows. At one time or another several members of my family played with the Red Shadows - Michael, James (vocals), Marion, Chris, Patrick (R.I.P.) (Drums) and I. It was almost a family show. The other members included Flan McMahon[2] (sax), what a man, Michael Whyte and Hughie Benn. It was the first showband in town. We had to play everything, foxtrots, sambas, tangos, quicksteps and all the modern music. I love all music but I hate noise. You had to be able to dance otherwise you wouldn't be asked up. When I was a kid, Pearl Garvey from the Clare Road and Maudy Reidy from the back cottages taught me to dance. That's how I met my wife. I'm in favour of ballroom dancing, providing they also include some Irish dancing. I think both should go together. Over the years we had great fun. I'd do it all again. I loved making people happy."

[1] Formerly Chrissie Murphy.

[2] Flan McMahon, a multi instrumentalist passed away in March 2002. Flan was a brother of Michael, likewise a talented musician and record collector. Michael died about 1997.
Flan and Michael McMahon also played with the Kilfenora Céilí Band, the Coasters Combo, The Glen of Ennis. Some of the musicians in these groups included Christy McAllister, Patsy Quinn, Noel Carmody, Tony Mahony (drums), 'Mixie' McGuane, Seán T. Keane, Brendan Barnes, Liam Madigan and Patrick Mulqueen.

Interview with Simon O'Donnell Faughs and Éire Óg

Simon O'Donnell served with the Faughs and Eire Og clubs in the late 1940's and early 1950's. He is one of the founding fathers of Eire Og. On June 19th, 1997, he spoke to Ollie Byrnes at his home in the Kilrush Road.

Q. By the late 1940's, the Dals struggled to field teams at senior level. Was hurling in trouble at this time in Ennis?

S.O'D. Hurling went into a decline at senior level in 1946. The Dals were beaten in the Clare Cup by possibly the 23rd Battalion and though they drew with Scariff in the championship, the Dals failed to field a team for the replay.

Q. The Faughs played senior hurling championship during the late 1940's. Can you tell me the origin of the Faughs?

S.O'D. The Faughs Club was formed in Steele's Terrace about 1943. They formed because the players from that area felt they weren't being looked at by the Dals selectors. There was opposition to the formation of the Faughs. They lost in 1943 to Dysart. Mick Hennessy (Co. Secretary) then entered them in the junior football championship. I was part of the Faughs Football team that won the Intermediate championship in 1946, though I didn't play in the final. I was doing exams at the time. I remember most of the lads who were involved with the Faughs - Tony Strand, Sean Moloney, Reggie Connellan, Johnny Fleming, John Leyden, Roy Coote and Maurice and Bruddy Mann. Roy Coote, a son of 'Joker' was a brilliant goalkeeper. Roy was inter-county material and Mick Hennessy, tried to interest him more. Roy was very quiet. He later disappeared off the scene. The hurling team won the Intermediate in 1945. The hurlers were confined to the Lifford area of town and many of them were former pupils of Ennis CBS. The salt of the earth and the greatest people on earth lived in the Boreen.

Q. Faughs had success at Gaelic football but limited success at hurling. Why was this the case?

S.O'D. Faughs had the pick of the town for senior football. Football

Ennis Faughs 1945 Intermediate Hurling Champions. Back row, left to right: *Tim Smythe, Flan Hynes, 'Bruddy' Mann, Michael Considine, Reggie Connellan, Tony Glynn, Vinnie Strand, 'Brudsy' McCarthy, Seán Leyden, Jack 'Buster' Carroll.* ***Middle row:*** *Simon O'Donnell, Tommy Collins, Michael Mackey, Seán Moloney, Johnny Fleming, Maurice Mann, Tommy Moloney, Christy Fleming.* ***Front row:*** *Paddy Duggan, Ralphie Burns, 'Aoner' Sheridan, Miko Ball, Tony Strand.*

fever took over. The Faughs had fine players in Paddy Dowling, Sean Connolly, Gerry Moroney, Brian Quinn and later Matt Nugent and Bobby Burke. To me, Matt Nugent was a nicer footballer than a hurler. He'd have made a great soccer player. He could do anything with 'a dead ball'.

Q. Eire Og was formed as a hurling club in 1952. Was this a conscious decision to get away form the Dals and the Faughs?

S.O'D. The club was formed because it was felt among many active players that not enough was being done to further the game of hurling. Some meetings were held of an exploratory nature and the formation of a new independent club was always the key issue of discussion. These meetings were possibly held in Paddy Duggan's house in Steele's Terrace. I was invited by a number of them to be Chairman. I vividly remember a meeting at the Queen's Hotel. No it wasn't a conscious decision to get away form the Dalcassian name, though some of the younger lads were disillusioned with the older men who were running things. They probably disagreed with their methods.

Q. Who were the key people?

S.O'D. Two of the key people at that time were Paddy Duggan and Tony

Cusack. Officers were elected and it was decided that the name of the club would be Éire Og. The officers decided were - Chairman: Simon O'Donnell, vice Chairman Sean Guinnane, Hon. Secretary, Hugh O'Donnell, Treasurer, Tony Hickey. And the committee consisted of Michael 'Dot' Halloran, Richard 'Dick' Ensko, a brother of Mary Allen, Paddy Duggan, Sean Caulfield, Tony Cusack and Jackie Kelly.

Q. Did you play hurling?
S.O'D. Yes. We entered a team in the junior grade and the first match we played was against Kilnamona. I played in goal in that game. We beat Kilnamona. Later we lost to Corofin at Ruan. The team travelled up on the back of a lorry. There was a Munster Championship match on the same day and we couldn't get cars to hire.

Q. Were things much simpler then?
S.O'D. We had a lot of club activities. We trained in the Fairgreen. We went to the countryside looking for ash to make hurleys. We had flag days and church gate collections. It was also a time of religious fervour. We had a committee to erect the Marian Grotto, beside the Courthouse. Your father (Martin Byrnes) was involved in the building of the grotto.

Q. You mentioned the making of hurleys. Did the club make all your hurleys then?
S.O'D. The hurleys used in our first match were made by Paddy Honan and his brother in law, Con Tierney.

Q. After just one year in junior ranks, Eire Og applied for senior status. This was a great leap, was it seen as madness?
S.O'D. They went senior in 1953. I didn't see the move as madness because they were the finest bunch of young fellows I had ever come across. Also we had limitations as to who we could play in our first year. But once we became a senior club these limitations were lifted.
Ennis fielded other teams - The Rovers in junior and Turnpike in Intermediate. Some influential people within the GAA in the town came to my father who had something to do with the GAA in the past to ask us to stop the club. I helped get Eire Og off the ground in the administration side of things. I had gained a lot of experience with the Faughs as the right hand man to Tommy Collins.
My involvement with Eire Og ceased within a short time and it was mainly due to a disagreement over the handling of an objection against Castle Rovers in the Tournament final.

1944 - 1959

"Gruggie Dilger was as fast as lightning. His brother, Bernie, and Michael Blake were pure class. They were mighty hurlers".
Sean Custy

About 1943, a split occurred in the Dalcassian Club. Many hurlers were disenchanted with the situation within the Dals Club. They felt local players were being dropped to accommodate hurlers who had come in to work in the town.

After a meeting in Moloney's house in Steele's Terrace the Faughs hurling Club came into being. The new hurling club was for the most part confined to the Lifford area. After the Faughs hurlers lost to Dysart in 1944, Mick Hennessy entered the Club in the football championship.

Subsequent to this period, the Faughs became a strong force in Intermediate hurling ad senior football while with the loss of so many key players, the Dalcassian Club began to go into decline.

Despite the lack of success at senior grade, Ennis continued to field several teams at adult level including the Commercials and the Market. Playing in Junior 'A' ranks, the Market lost heavily to Ruan in the championship. In the second round, Market Street conceded in walk over to Tradaree. The Faughs with Fleming, Sheridan, Leahy, Houlihan and Mahon to the fore defeated Newmarket by 7-5 to 3-1 in the first round of the Intermediate League, *"Fast hard pulling characterised the first half, the issue was never in doubt in the second half"* - reported the Clare Champion. The Faughs won the Intermediate Championship of 1945, playing against Broadford.

The Clare Champion of the day reported: "A huge crowd cheered the Faughs to victory, perhaps the biggest for an Intermediate final. Playing in only their second season the bulk of the Faughs team hailed from the Courthouse end of town, led at the interval by 6-0 to 1-2, thanks mainly to the supremacy of Johnny Fleming at centre-field. Mid-way through the second half a great recovery from Boradford, saw the East Clare men reduce the leeway to four points. However, inspired by 'Brudsy' McCarthy, Seán Moloney, Roy Coote, Miko Ball and 'Bruddy' Mann, the Faughs finished strongly to win by 10-3 to 3-5. Wild jubilation ensued when the team arrived home from Tulla with bonfires blazing along the Boreen and Steele's Terrace".

The Intermediate success by Faughs was all the more meritorious as

Exciting Times - *Val McGann, Paddy Duggan, 'Kansas' Keane, Raymond Greene. Courtesy of Val McGann.*

they defeated the same opposition which qualified for the senior championship final. The Faughs later defeated Newmarket by 8-2 to 5-1 in the Clare Cup.

In March 1946, representatives of both the Dalcassion and Faughs met and discussed in detail the various points of dispute. Following this successful meeting, chaired by Jack Spellissy, it was agreed the Dalcassians could pick from the Faughs for senior competition. On July 14th the Dals and Scariff drew (2-6 to 2-6) in the championship, with the Ennismen equalising in the last minute. Though the East Claremen lost the services of the Whitegate players due to the introduction of 'parish rule', they still fielded a strong team with players of the calibre of J.J. Bugler, Des Carroll, Dan McInerney, Tom & Paddy Minogue and Joe Whelan. The highlight of the game was the superb goalkeeping of Rodgers (Scariff) and Morgan.

Following the drawn game with Scariff, Ennis Dals defeated Tulla in the Cusack Shield and they also played Clarecastle in the Cup. Due to injuries, the Dals appealed to the County Board for a postponement of the championship replay with Scariff. The appeal fell on deaf ears. Ennis failed to field a team for the replay. The Dals claimed they gave due notice to both the County Board and Scariff. The referee was also notified that Ennis couldn't travel. The game was awarded to Scariff but the Dalcassians felt that the Board's decision was unprecedented in so far as no other club in similar circumstances would have a similar decision given against them. The County Board's decision was final and Scariff went on to win the championship.

Meanwhile, the Faughs (the holders) reached the semi-final of the Intermediate Championship when they went under to Ruan by 5-3 to 4-1. Regardless of the addition of Dermot Solon (Whitegate), Jimmy Walker (Tralee) and Paddy Markham (Ballyea), the Dals were well beaten by Feakle in the 1947 Senior Championship.

Despite a lack of success at adult level, the Dals minor team captured their fourth county title in a row. At the A.G.M., Frank O'Gorman paid tribute to the minors and thanked the Faughs for their co-operation during the year. The Chairman also in his address paid glowing tributes to Tom Neylon - the popular and energetic Secretary and to Peter Fitzgerald and Christy Glynn.

In 1948 the minors added yet another County 'A' title, with the Market doing extremely well in the Junior 'A' division, but the seniors were trounced by Ruan. The Clare Champion of July 31st, 1948 reported - *"Ennis outclassed in hurling championship. Ruan led from the start and gave Ennis little chance to offer a serious challenge. The Ruan XV were well trained and they threw zest into the game for the full hour."* Though Ennis had some good individual players in Christy Glynn, Seán Mounsey, Paddy Markham, Seán Mahon, Ralph Burns, P.J. O'Dea, and Flan Smyth, they didn't combine well.

In 1949, Ennis hurling continued in the doldrums when Clarecastle whipped the Dals by 9-3 to 1-4 in the Clare Cup. Such was the disunity in town hurling that the club was forced to concede a walk over to Ruan in the 2nd round of the Cup. Michael Doherty, who was thrown into the thick of senior hurling at the tender age of 15, recalls - "After the Town League Final of '48, hurling disintegrated. There was no unity. The Rovers from Old Mill Street had a team of their own. The Dals just barely fielded a team. There was bitterness in the town." The famed Dalcassian Club probably received their worst ever beating in 1949 at the hands of Bodyke by 8-7 to 0-3.

A Clare Champion reporter writing in his column 'Clubs and their Affairs' had this to say about the state of Ennis hurling in 1949 - "How can we expect a hurling resurgence in Clare in the absence of a real worth-while contribution from the capital town. When small parishes can field first class teams, it is difficult to explain how the association has reached such a moribund state in Ennis. It is a pity, that Ennis which was one of Clare's hurling strongholds, appears unable to put a team on the field worthy of its great traditions. Bodyke, though not extended, will need to show improvement if they are to regain the Senior Championship. No reputations were made last Sunday."

To Revive Hurling in Ennis

At the Faughs A.G.M. of January 15th, 1950, it was agreed that the Faughs affiliate a Senior Hurling team and to link up all the hurling talent in the town so as to build a team worthy of representing Ennis. The speakers included Seán Guinnane, Murt O'Shea, Seán Kelly and Tony Strand. Murt O'Shea felt - "That as hurling is the premier game in Ennis they should do everything to bring it to the fore again." Tony Strand believed that all the hurlers in town were in favour of the Faughs Club taking over senior hurling and football and Seán Kelly felt - "it mattered little what name the club was called."

On March 5th, 1950 the Faughs took the field against Clarecastle in the Clare Cup, losing, 3-13 to 2-5. Though well beaten by 'the Magpies', many felt there was room for optimism with Mick Murphy, the former Clare and Tipperary player, to the fore, as were Tony Strand, Des Cullinan and Seán Moloney.

This was Tom Mannion's first game for Faughs since coming to Ennis from Mulcaire Rovers in Tipperary. In the second round of the Clare Cup, the Faughs drew with Cup specialists Newmarket, 4-5 to 5-2. Ger Keane impressed in goal as did Johnny Fleming at centre-forward.

Meanwhile a resurgent Clooney team featuring Kevin Doherty, Martin and Seán Byrnes shocked Newmarket in the senior championship with seven points to spare. Also in the championship Faughs and Ardnacrusha drew, 4-6 to 4-6. Ardnacrusha beat Faughs in the replay.

Brian MacMahon was the only Ennisman selected on the Clare team which ran Tipperary to 2-13 to 3-7, after a gruelling full-blooded, but sporting game. Brian MacMahon was part of the half-back line with 'Tolly' Guinnane and Donal O'Grady on a side trained by Larry Blake.

Dals Minors

The Ennis minor teams great run of victories came to an end in the 1950 minor championship when a Clarecastle Regional selection beat the Faughs, 5-6 to 3-3. The Faughs minors were honoured with a big selection on the county minor team with Michael Doherty, Michael McMahon, Seán Tuttle, Seán and Brendan Madigan and Gerry Cronin all selected.

An early Éire Óg committee. Standing, left to right: *Tony Conroy, Val McGann, Eugene Ryan, Seán Caulfield, Larry Blake.* ***Sitting:*** *Kevin O'Callaghan, Michael Blake, Tommy Brennan, Paddy Duggan.*

The Clare Cup of 1951 brought little joy to Faughs when they were whipped by St. Joseph's, 8-4 to 1-4, with only Michael Doherty, Gerry Moroney and Johnny Fleming shining. For this game Faughs could only muster twelve players for the first half. On a brighter note their goalkeeper Seán Keane was selected for the county junior team. Following this setback with St. Joseph's, Fr. Denis Kelly and Fr. Brady called for an enquiry into the state of Ennis hurling on May 9th at the Scout Hall.

Meanwhile, Rovers were causing a stir in junior 'B' ranks when beating Ennistymon, (3-1 to 2-1), before losing to Clonlara, (7-4 to 7-3) in what the Champion described as - *"One of the best games seen for some time with a high standard of hurling befitting two senior teams."* After an objection by the Rovers over illegal players, a replay was ordered. Clonlara again won by the narrowest of margins, 3-2 to 3-1. Rovers included George Summerly, Seán Mounsey, James Mulqueen, Tony McEnery and Paddy Loftus in their ranks at this time. Despite the apparent apathy amongst the Faughs seniors, their minors inflicted a crushing defeat on Clarecastle by 10-7 to 1-3 with *"an attractive brand of hurling. Michael Doherty was a tower of strength at centre-back feeding the wing players Cyril Brennan and Frank Costelloe who had a hand in every score."*

The Turnpike

In 1951 the Turnpike offered another glimmer of hope when they reached the Intermediate Final when losing to the up and coming Sixmilebridge team by one point. At their A.G.M. the Chairman thanked the people of the 'Pike for giving the club financial aid for the purpose of buying jerseys and togs. A vote of thanks was passed to the Rovers, Faughs and St. Joseph's. Michael Doherty recalled the 1951 Intermediate Championship - "The 'Pike could pick from different parts of Ennis. I played in some of the early rounds, we beat 'Our Lady's' and O'Callaghans Mills along the way. Some of the Market lads who played for us included Gerry Moroney, Eugene Ryan and Seán Tuttle." The team also included Kevin Doherty.

Michael Doherty feels the material was there to field a good senior team. –"The hurlers were there, Paddy Loftus, Josie (Mc)Carthy, Seán Mounsey and Johnny Tuohy were all good enough for the senior team.

Michael Considine and Mick Murphy were great players. Murphy's best position was wing back, a beautiful hurler, a stylist. I was suspended for playing rugby. I emigrated to London. The standard of London club hurling was very high, as you know they beat the Clare junior team in the 1949 All Ireland Final by 3-7 to 3-6. This was in effect Clare's second team. I went over in 1954, everybody was emigrating, it was a golden age in England. I played with St. Mary's, Pearses and later Michael Cusack's. Michael Cusack's had a fine side comprised mostly of Claremen, Paddy Duggan, Jimmy Walker, Tom Melody, Frank Corbett and Paddy Hewitt. Jimmy Walker, though from Tralee, had earlier played hurling and football for the Faughs".

A historic meeting was called in the home of Paddy Duggan in Steele's Terrace on the last week of February 1952. It was decided to form a new club and to enter a team in the junior B Championship. Jerseys for the new club - white with a green shamrock - were made available thanks to the generosity of the residents of Steele' Terrace. It only now remained to name the infant club Éire Óg. The name was so obviously appropriate that it was accepted unanimously.

Éire Óg played their first game under the new banner on May 4th, 1952, defeating Kilnamona in the junior B championship. They were beaten in the quarter final by Corofin in July in a game of good fast hurling. Best for Éire Óg were Michael Blake, Hugh O'Donnell, Christy

Michael Cusacks team London 1957/1958. The team featured mostly Claremen. Back row, left to right: *K. Corbett (Killaloe), Tim Hayes (Ogonnelloe), Batt Dillon (Clarecastle), Michael Doherty (Ennis), Michael McNamara (Ennis), Joe O'Grady (Ennis), Pakie Pender (Clondegad), Christy Tobin (Ennis), Tony Casey (Sixmilebridge).* ***Front row:*** *Paddy Rodgers (Scariff), Tom Melody (Scariff), Larry Blake (Ennis), Paddy Hewitt (Ennis), J. Collins (Bodyke), Paddy Duggan (Ennis), Jimmy Walker (Tralee).*

Courtesy of Owen & Moroney, Shepherds Bush.

Shannon, Con O'Donnell and the captain, Paddy Duggan. Éire Óg went on to contest the Corofin tournament, beating a physically stronger Tubber side by 4-5 to 4-1 with Seán (Mc)Mahon getting the winning scores. In the final they lost to Castle Rovers by 2-6 to 2-3.

While Éire Óg hadn't won anything major, they were going well. A group of them approached the Dals committee with a view to taking over senior hurling in town. Gerry Cronin, Joe Madigan and Larry Blake (Snr.) gave them all the help they required. They decided to stick with the name Éire Óg. They felt they were successful and weren't going to part with some of that success. Then in a bold move Éire Óg decided to go senior. The decision was endorsed at their A.G.M. held in January, 1953 with Tim Smythe elected trainer.

As yet this movement was in its infancy, being no more than a group of young hurlers, many of them attending school, gathering together on a Sunday to play a match for the pure joy of it.

In March 22, 1953, Éire Óg made their senior debut in the Clare Cup against Clooney. The team lined out as follows:

Tony Cusack

Tony Conroy	Gerry Moroney	Eugene Ryan
Val McGann	Michael Blake	Michael Doherty
Gerry Cronin		Tony Keaty
Seán Madigan	Larry Blake	Paddy Duggan
Bobby Burke	Seán (Mc)Mahon	Frankie Cassidy

A physically stronger Clooney led by 3-1 to 1-4 at the interval. Two quick second half goals failed to upset Clooney who were backboned by the Doherty brothers, Kevin, Brian and Michael. The final score was Clooney 7-2, Éire Óg 4-5.

Though hurling in Ennis at senior level was at a low ebb, the town by 1953/54 was fielding four minor teams. Ennis Dalcassians (A and B), Rovers and the newly formed St. John's. It's interesting to note that these minor teams were trouncing all and sundry in the under 18 grade. Some of the prominent players included - Michael Garry, Paddy Hewitt, Val McGann, Eddie George, Raymond Duggan, Noel Bane, George Dilger and John Loftus.

Though Éire Óg scored 6 goals against the Blues in their first Senior Championship encounter, they still came out at the wrong end in a high scoring game by 10-3 to 6-4. *"The Ennis half-forward line of Michael Dilger, Larry Blake and Paddy Duggan excelled with Duggan's many spectacular solo runs winning the applause of the crowd. Michael Dilger's magnificent 80 yard solo to the edge of the square before dispatching the ball to the roof of the net will certainly be talked about for a long time."* - wrote the Clare Champion reporter.

On March 7th, 1954, Éire Óg defeated Tulla in the semi-final of the Gaelic League Tournament. This was Éire Óg's first win in senior ranks and significantly the power house of the team on that day (and many days to come) was the half-back line of Bernie Dilger, Michael Blake and Gerry Cronin.

Éire Óg were pitted against rivals St. Joseph's in the first round of the championship. "Éire Óg came on to the field looking very spruce in their blood red jerseys and played in the first half against a strong tricky wind they trailed 2-6 to 0-3 at the break. On the resumption Paschal Sheridan set up Brooks for a goal to put the game out of reach. The final score of 3-7 to 0-3 didn't flatter the Barefield men." In their second divisional game Éire Óg put up a good showing, 5-4 to 3-3 against a strong Ruan side. To keep the morale of the players high a very successful town league was run off with the Clareroad defeating the Boreen by 6-8 to 2-2 in the final on November 1st, 1954. In early Spring 1955 a much improved Éire Óg side shocked the County champions, St. Joseph's, in a tournament game.

With the addition of Pat Kirby, Paddy Kerin, Dermot Leahy and Mick Morrissey, Éire Óg had become a strong force and it was only a matter of time before major honours came their way. Éire Óg opened the 1955 championship with a great win over Ruan, 7-6 to 2-2. The large crowd was greatly impressed by the text book hurling of Michael Blake and Michael Dilger. At half time the Ennismen, playing first time ground hurling were totally on top - 3-4 to a solitary point. Two further goals from Éire Óg from the hard pulling Tony Keaty put Éire Óg into an unassailable 18 point lead before Jimmy Smyth and Willie Kitson put a respectable look on the scoreboard. - "Ruan though not a shadow of their great sides of the last few years suffered greatly from the absence of the Leahy brothers, Miko Neylon, Joe McDonnell and other past masters." Éire Óg followed the victory with a good win over 'the Magpies', 7-7 to 4-4. They again accounted for Clarecastle in the Ennis Feis Tournament final by 6-9 to 5-2 at Cusack Park. A set of medals was presented to the Éire Óg Captain Paddy Duggan (who incidentally played in goal) by Rev. Bro. Ó Cinnéide amidst great rejoicing. Duggan was then carried from the pitch by Éire Óg's fanatical supporters.

Val McGann of Kilmaley, one of the founders of Éire Óg , pictured in Albert Park, playing for Young Irelands (Australia), shortly after emigrating in 1957.

Meanwhile in the Clare Cup, Éire Óg chalked up further victories over Whitegate, 6-9 to 4-4 and Sixmilebridge, 6-5 to 2-6. Éire Óg went on to win the 1955 Clare Cup (played in April 1956) by beating a fancied Feakle side by 4-6 to 2-3. The East Clare Club, trailing by 4 points at the interval could not break down the stonewall defence of Gerry Moroney, Paddy Kerin and Paddy Loftus and when Paschal Brooks and Gerry Cronin took over at centre-field, Éire Óg finished very strongly with goals from Larry Blake, Paddy Duggan and Seán Madigan. The Clare Champion Cup was presented to Paddy Duggan by Fr. Corry.

St. Joseph's Team

The Mental Hospital Club and Doora/Barefield amalgamated for senior competition under the banner of St. Joseph's in 1949. The main instigators behind St. Joseph's were Dr. Thomas Loughnane, John Moran, Paddy McInerney, Paddy Ryan, Rev. Edward Maxwell, Gerry Browne and John O'Connell. Prior to that Barefield fielded a successful junior team with players of the calibre of Alfie O'Connell and Jack O'Dea. It was decided to amalgamate the existing junior club in Barefield with Our Lady's Hospital. This new senior team was called St. Joseph's after a Holy Well situated between Our Lady's Hospital and Barefield.

By 1951 St. Joseph's began to make a serious challenge for senior honours, and that year they had a decisive three point win over Cup specialists, Newmarket in the Championship. Donal O'Grady at centre-back, Matt Nugent, Gerry Browne, Flan Hynes and Terry Millar were amongst the big names in their 2-8 to 2-5 win over the Blues. St. Joseph's would have to wait another two years for their first success when they captured the Clare Champion Cup at the expense of Newmarket in 1953.

Beginning of St. Joseph's/Éire Óg rivalry

Neighbours Éire Óg and St. Joseph's clashed in the third round of the championship (divisional final) of 1955, at Cusack Park. This eagerly awaited game was originally fixed for Newmarket, but at St. Joseph's behest it was brought to Ennis. With Matt Nugent and Johnny Purcell lording it in their respective positions, St. Joseph's were well on top, 6-2 to 3-1, when a row broke out amongst rival supporters 13 minutes into the second half. The disturbances spilled out into the pitch forcing referee Michael Quaine to abandon the game. Speaking to the Champion reporter shortly afterwards Quaine said, - "This was the first time I called off a game. I am sorry to say that it would take more force than we in our position could offer to clear or shift some of the spectators I happened to see in action. There were two whom I saw use hurleys freely on players and spectators alike. The troublemakers were not confined to St. Joseph's or Éire Óg. I valued my life more than to take the names of those two bullies. Its about time that the gates of all sports fields were locked to such troublemakers."

A County Board meeting was called to investigate the matter. By a margin of two votes (11-9) it was decided to replay the game. The St. Joseph's officials were incensed by the judgement and stormed out. The replay was fixed for Newmarket, Éire Óg travelled but St. Joseph's didn't show up at the venue. Though in hindsight, St. Joseph's were probably wrong to pull their team from the championship, it was hard not to sympathise with them as they were 10 points up with 17 minutes to play.

Paschal Sheridan made his senior debut with St. Joseph's in 1952. Paschal recalled the rivalry between Éire Óg and St. Joseph's. - "Everyone thought the match would be awarded to St. Joseph's, but a replay was ordered. We were anxious to go back and play but some of our players were against it. The decision to pull out, put us back as we had a fine team, probably the best we had then. In the 1954 semi-final we trailed Tulla by 14 points with 20 minutes to go and beat them by 3 points. Tulla were good, they had many new faces, a sprinkling of the old team in Jimmy 'Whacky' Murphy, Pakie Mac and Paddy Floyd, plus young fellows like Charlie Murphy. The spirit in our club died somewhat after the row with Éire Óg in 1955. The 'Mills' later beat us in the Cup. We should never have pulled out of the championship. There was tension amongst some of the rival players but there was never bitterness. We often met afterwards and that was it."

With St. Joseph's now out of contention, the semi-final meeting between Tulla and Éire Óg produced sparkling hurling. Tulla led at the interval by 4-2 to 2-4, but once Michael Dilger and Paschal Brooks took over at centre-field the writing was on the wall for Tulla, as Éire Óg pulled away to win, 4-7 – 4-2.

So an Ennis side was through to a Senior final for the first time in 14 years. The opposition was Newmarket-on-Fergus. The teams were led onto the pitch by the Ennistymon Pipe-Band and the Newmarket Brass-Band. The Ennis selectors dropped a bombshell with the omission of Michael 'Gruggy' Dilger from the starting line out. And though Éire Óg lead by 6 points at the interval, a Newmarket blitz yielding 2-3 early in the second half paid off for the Blues. The Newmarket win was fashioned by Jimmy Halpin, Jackie Green, Billy Halpin, Pádraig Crimmins, and Mick Grace at full back. The decisive moment was the move of Jimmy Carney to mid-field. With the exception of Paddy Duggan and Gerry Moroney this was a very young Éire Óg team. Many of their players were in the 19-23 age group. Though beaten by 3-9 to 3-3 in an entertaining and sporting struggle, Éire Óg had arrived.

Éire Óg quickly put the 1955 County Final behind them and early in 1956, they played the Ennis CBS Harty Cup team before a large crowd at Cusack park. Following this Éire Óg introduced Aidan Raleigh, the Limerick hurler, at centre-field. Subsequently they defeated Smith O'Brien's by 6-3 to 3-3. As a warm up for the Championship, Éire Óg beat Brian Boru's (London) by 8-8 to 6-5 in Kilkee for the Corca Baiscín Cup. The London/Irish Club was over on a short tour and had earlier defeated Newmarket by 6-4 to 3-10. Éire Óg's form slumped once more when they lost to the Blues by 7-3 to 4-1 in the Clare Cup. After the game with the Blues, Éire Óg defeated Ruan, 5-1- to 3-5. 'The Magpies' had 4

Éire Óg County Senior Champions 1956. Back row, left to right: *Bernie Dilger, Colm Madigan, Jack Daly, Michael Morrissey, Gerry Moroney, Paddy Loftus, Paddy Kerin, Jimmy Cronin, Paschal Brooks, Hugh Ensko.* ***Front row, left to right:*** *Pat Kirby, Tony Keaty, Ml. Blake, Paddy Duggan, Gerry Cronin, Larry Blake, Sean Madigan, Bobby Burke, Hugh O'Donnell, Ml. Dilger.*
Courtesy of Brooks Studios.

goals to spare over the Blues and then beat the 'Bridge, who had earlier withdrawn from all competitions because of the objection to Jimmy Carney. (Doonbeg footballer Jimmy Carney had earlier left the Newmarket club to join the 'Bridge). Clarecastle defeated Whitegate in the semi-final, 8-7 to 3-3 to contest the County Final with Éire Óg. For the final the Ennis selectors dropped another bombshell when they omitted Tony Keaty from the starting line out. By all accounts a large Tipperary crowd came to Cusack Park to see the popular Keaty in action. It is interesting to note that Éire Óg clocked up 16-18 in just three games coasting into the final.

1956 Munster Championship – Limerick do it again

To prove that the 1955 Munster final defeat was no freak, Limerick again inflicted a deep scar on Clare hurling when they overcame the Banner by 1-15 to 2-6 before 24,000 patrons. The Clare Champion reported that Clare can have no excuses now - *"It proved a bitter disappointment for Clare supporters, and they were there in their thousands, but the decision was clear cut and decisive. People did not go about seeking excuses for their team afterwards as they did leaving the Ennis Road grounds last year. They saw it happening before their very eyes again."* The team included Éire Óg men Michael Blake and Aidan Raleigh.

1956 County Final Éire Óg v Clarecastle

"Sprightly Éire Óg are champions this time. Stamina and speed bring a 9th Senior title to Ennis. Clarecastle trail throughout" reported the Clare Champion. Éire Óg led by 7 points entering the final quarter when they were subjected to a sizzling final onslaught by 'the Magpies'. But Michael Blake, the man of the match was everywhere, and the Ennis defence stood up to the Clarecastle threat. Amongst the heroes of the hour for Éire Óg were Colm Madigan, who scored 2 goals, Gerry Cronin and Larry Blake.

An Éire Óg backed Turnpike team contested the County Intermediate final of 1956. Under the rules Turnpike could field nine players from senior ranks. Some of the others included Seán Malone, Seán Dinan, Brian Cronin and Monty Keane. Parteen and Turnpike served up tremendous fare at Tulla with the South East Claremen winning by the narrowest of margins, 5-1 to 3-6.

Éire Óg showed little mercy in the opening round of the 1957 Senior Championship when playing with great team understanding, they annihilated O'Callaghan's Mills, 6-11 to 1-0. But shortly afterwards the Turnpike, again backed by Éire Óg, lost heavily to Bauroe, 6-8 to 3-4 in the Intermediate grade.

Round Two of the Senior Championships tossed up old rivals, St. Joseph's. Éire Óg had to pull out all the stops to force a late draw (3-2 to 2-5) with a Pat Kirby goal from a 21 yard free. For the replay the Ennis selectors called on the services of four St. John's players.

Johnny McCarthy recalls - "I played juvenile with the Dals in the early 50's. Though the Dals senior team was defunct, Frank Burns and Joe Madigan ran the juvenile club. When the Dals minor club collapsed we went to St. John's. The latter won Minor 'A', Junior 'A' and Intermediate and performed very well in the Clare Cup. When a senior club exists in a parish I think they can oppose the formation of another senior club. Looking back on it, it was detrimental, St. John's weren't allowed to play senior championship. Four of the St. John's team were selected for the replay with St. Joseph's in 1957, Jack Daly, Brendan Doyle, Joe Ensko and I. With the extra four players Éire Óg won the replay. Pat Kirby started at centre-field and the selectors put Hugh (Joe) Ensko into goal, a great move. Kirby was powerful. That led on to the gold Watch Tournament in 1958, three games with St. Joseph's. The attendances were bigger than county finals. The mentors at St. John's, Frank O'Gorman and Des McCullough were very upset about four of their players going to Éire Óg. They felt Éire Óg were poaching from St. John's for the work they had done which was a legitimate point. St. John's went into a decline because of this but also because Ennis Rovers were beginning to flex their muscles. Rovers were outstanding, Michael Brennan and P.J. Summerly were the chief movers."

Apart from the inclusion of the St. John's players the selectors recalled Hugh O'Donnell to the side. Hugh O'Donnell opened the scoring, giving the town team a tonic start. This game produced tremendous man-to-man hurling, the highlights being the tussles between Michael Blake and Matt Nugent, Flan Hynes and Seán Madigan, Paschal Sheridan and Gerry Cronin. The replay also produced a few fireworks with Tony Keaty and Mick Hayes being sent to the line. In the end Éire Óg prevailed by 3-7 to 3-3.

After the game Matt Nugent visited the Éire Óg dressing room to congratulate the winners and wished them well for the remainder of the season. Nugent said - "there is a belief that bitterness exists between the clubs, but to-day's game has proved the spirit that binds Éire Óg and St. Joseph's."

Éire Óg gave their best display of the 1957 championship when overcoming the 'Bridge by 2-9 to 1-5 in the semi-final with Jimmy Cronin curbing inter-county star Jimmy Carney. Michael Dilger as always stood out with recent newcomer Johnny McCarthy *"weaving, dodging and deadly accurate. Jack Daly was very effective at full-forward."* Reported the Clare Champion.

The superb training methods of Tim Smythe paid off in the final when Éire Óg were out of sight of Whitegate leading, 5-6 to 0-2 by half time. The expected Whitegate comback never materialised with Éire Óg winning easily by 5-9 to 2-3. Patrons were streaming out long before the final whistle. Rev. John Corry presented the Hamilton Cup for the first time ever to Éire Óg captain, Gerry Cronin.

Victory Social

At the Éire Óg Victory Dinner at the Queen's Hotel, Dr. Harry Bugler thanked the St. John's club for releasing players for duty with Éire Óg as they had lost the services of Colm Madigan, Mick Morrissey, Dermot Leahy, Paddy Duggan (to emigration) and Michael Blake.

Éire Óg introduced a number of newcomers for senior duty during the Winter League, including Jim Blake, George Dilger and Steve Loftus. Again Éire Óg were in winning form beating Whitegate, 4-4 to 2-3 and St. Joseph's, 2-8 - 2-2 in a tension filled tie.

The final between St. Joseph's and Éire Óg was held up for several minutes while rival supporters were involved in an altercation along the sideline. The decisive move of the game was the switch of Tony Keaty to full-forward in the second half. Shortly after these incidents several supporters were notified by the County Board that they would be debarred from the side line unless they apologised for their bad conduct at games. This game was awarded to St. Joseph's on a technicality.

There is little doubt that to be involved with Éire Óg in these years was a joyful experience. Larry Blake (jnr.) remembers - "We were close friends. Friends for life. We socialised together. They were exciting times because we were young. We played in varous tournaments. The seven-a-side tournaments against Castle Rovers and Corofin were great. We usually travelled - with Jim Woodhouse or 'Coco' Broderick. Later we had great games with St. Joseph's. Our supporters were tremendous, especially the women. Florrie Malone washed our jerseys. Mrs. Loftus was a wonderful supporter. It was Florrie Malone who lit the bonfires at Captain Mac's Cross after we beat Clarecastle in the 1956 County Final. They were great times".

"The Magpies thought they were going to win - Parly Boo
The Magpies thought they were going to win - Parly Boo
The Magpies thought they were going to win
But Éire Óg gave 'em a right suck in, Inky, Binky, Parly Boo."
Peter 'Slavery' Guilfoyle

Val McGann was another important player in all of this. Val recalled these exciting times to Me. 'Having played juvenile for Kilmaley, I then transferred to Ennis. I was involved in the formation of Éire Óg and I later played senior for them. Playing for the Market in the Town Competition was a real highlight, these games were fiercely competitive. After suffering a severe knee injury I took up cycling with the Coffey brothers, God rest them, they died far too young, I did this to strengthen my knee. Afterwards I emigrated to Australia and played hurling for the Young Ireland's Club in Victoria for six years. The state featured seven hurling clubs.

With the exception of one player from Antrim, the Young Irelands comprised all Munster men.

To be involved in hurling in Ennis during the early 1950's was an exciting time playing in the company of Michael and Larry Blake, Bobby Burke, Syl Cosgrove, Bernie Dilger, Paddy Duggan and many others".

The following are pen pictures of the Éire Óg players of 1955-1957, that contested three County Finals in addition to the Clare Champion Cup of 1955. These pen pictures are compiled by a member of this Éire Óg team.

Michael Blake: A product of Ennis CBS. Represented Clare at minor, junior and senior level. A vital member of the Clare senior team of 1956-

1960. He didn't play in the final stages of the 1957 Championship because of injury. His tussles with Matt Nugent at the height of the St. Joseph's - Éire Óg' rivalry were a joy to watch. Immensely strong Michael Blake won Senior Championship Medals in 1956, 1957 and Clare Cup Medals in 1955 and 1959.

Larry Blake: A brother of Michael. Holder of minor, senior and two Cup Medals. Represented the Michael Cusack's Club in London, 1957/58. Returned to Éire Óg in 1959. One of the fastest players in the county, delightful opportunist but always ready to combine. Played minor, junior and senior for the county.

Jimo Blake: Reliable corner-back, also figured in goal. (Cousin of Larry and Michael) Represented the Rovers. Seamus gave great service to Éire Óg over a 10 year spell. A link with the 1966 team.

Paschal Brooks: Played mostly at centre-field. Like many others he learned his hurling at the C.B.S. town leagues. Paschal was described to me by Jimmy Smyth as "a very formidable opponent." He fulfilled early promise and won two Championships, two Clare Cups, O'Doherty Tournament and numerous other awards.

Bobby Burke: Equally at home in defence or attack. Represented Éire Óg over a 12 year spell '53 - '64. Dual player with Faughs and part of the Clare Minor squad of '53 that contested the Minor Final v. Mayo. Played senior championship with Clare hurlers in 1958. Later served as Treasurer of the Board.

Jimmy Cronin: Took over from Michael Blake at centre-back in the final stages of the 1957 Championship. The loss of Michael Blake was expected to weaken Éire Óg - in fact his displays at centre-back - particularly in the Semi-Final v. Sixmilebridge when he out-played Jimmy Carney completely - was the cornerstone of Éire Óg's campaign in 1957. Jimmy Cronin represented Clare at all levels.

Gerry Cronin: Had great games at centre-field - overhead striking and reach were far greater than one would expect for one of his stature. A very accurate striker. Won two Senior Championships. A brother of Jimmy.

Tony Conroy: A very consistent and effective corner-back of the 1953/55 era. Played in 1955 Final v. Newmarket.

Éire Óg winners of O'Doherty Cup and Gold Watch Tournament, Nov. 2nd., 1958. Back row, left to right: *Paschal Brooks, Bobby Burke, Hugh Ensko, Paddy Kerin, Michael Blake, Paddy Loftus, Noel Gilligan, Des Loftus, Jimmy Cronin.* ***Front row:*** *Brendan Doyle, Johnny McCarthy, Michael Dilger, Tony Keaty, Pat Kirby, Bernie Dilger.* ***Mascots:*** *Seamus Mulqueen and Thomas Mulqueen. Courtesy of Esther Gilligan.*

Michael 'Doc' Doherty: One of the cutest forwards ever to play for Ennis. Also at home in defence. Great Gaelic and soccer player! Got a trial for some of the 1st Division Clubs in England. 'Doc' represented St. John's at juvenile level. He played senior for the county team and travelled with them to England for the Wembley Tournament.

Jack Daly: Came to prominence with C.B.S. Ennis Harty Cup team in 1956 and St. John's minor team. A determined forward, his combination and distribution were a threat to any defence. Jack went on to become a very successful Chairman of the County Board - streamlined the long-winded marathon sessions that had been a feature of County Board meetings before his tenure of office.

Bernie Dilger: A regular on Éire Óg Club team from 1953-'59. A 'real dynamo'. A recurring knee injury blighted a promising career at club and inter-county level. One of the few wing-backs in the country who could handle Jimmy Doyle. Bernie played for Clare 1957/58. Holder of two Senior and one Clare Cup.

Paddy Kerin: Part of a very strong full-back line. Made Senior debut in 1955. 2 Senior and 2 Clare Cup Medals.

Paddy Hewitt: Played in Clare Cup and Corca Baiscín Cup 1956. Prominent in quarter final win over Smith O'Brien's.

Michael Dilger: Fast, fit, intelligent and skilled, he was more than a match for the best in the country. A stylist with a great turn of speed and body swerve. 'Gruggy' represented Clare at Senior Championship level. A vital member of the Éire Óg side from 1953-'59.

Paddy Duggan: Full of tricks, impossible to mark or to shoulder! Powerful slap of a ball! His greatest service to the club was in coaching underage teams that dominated the underage championships for years. Paddy captained the Clare Cup winning team of '55 at corner forward!

Brendan Doyle: A fast determined product of CBS highly rated Harty team of 1956. Regarded as one of the tightest wing-backs of the era. Brendan won Minor, Junior, Intermediate and Senior Championship and Clare Cup Medals with either St. John's or Éire Óg. He continued to assist Éire Óg at junior level until 1964.

Hugh Ensko: The move that sent Hugh Ensko to goal and brought Pat Kirby to centre-field was inspired (1957 Campaign v. St. Joseph's). A versatile player and very effective in goal, Hugh represented the Munster Colleges in the inter-provincial series while a student at Ennis C.B.S.

Noel Gilligan: Versatile player. Could play in goal, centre-field or attack. Played excellent hurling v St. Joseph's in 'Watches'. Represented Clare in National League, 1958. A brother of Brendan who later played for Clare.

Tony Keaty: The best full-forward Éire Óg ever had - feared by goal-keepers - tough as teak - could give it and take it. Cool as ice in the heat of battle! Great tussles with Mick Hayes of St. Joseph's. A product of St. Flannan's.

Pat Kirby: A native of Tuamgraney. Great goalkeeper and centre-field player. Represented Clare at minor, Junior and senior level. Played for

New York for many years. Holder of three Clare Senior Championship Medals. Kirby's eye was so good he could snap a 21 on the goal-line - even from the likes of Nugent or Smyth! A world class handballer.

Colm Madigan: A powerful ground hurler. Captain and star of the 1956 CBS Harty team. Represented Clare Minors and the Munster Colleges inter-provincial team.

Seán Madigan: A fast, lively forward and wonderful opportunist. Won honours at all levels.

Dermot Leahy: An intelligent, strong and forceful centre-forward. Won Clare Cup in 1955 (played April '56). Represented Faughs at senior football.

Gerry Moroney: One of the recognised stalwarts of the game in Ennis. Great leadership qualities. Gerry represented Dals, Rovers, Turnpike and Éire Óg in hurling. Member of successful Faughs football sides of 1947 and 1948.

Michael Morrissey: Great strength and presence. Seldom failed to get a score. A great acquisition to Éire Óg in 1955/56. A produce of Adare C.B.S.

Johnny McCarthy: A fast striking forward with a flashing turn of speed. A product of Ennis Dals and St. John's Juvenile Clubs. Johnny represented Clare at Minor level in 1956 and 1957 and played Senior inter-county between 1958 and 1965. A link with the 1966 team.

Paddy Loftus: A powerful defender. Made his senior debut in 1955. Represented Clare at senior level as did his brothers Steve, Des and Vincent. A product of the Rovers Club.

Tom Murray: Joined the club in 1957 from Loughrea. A strong and determined forward.

Hugh O'Donnell: A utility player, figured prominently in defence and attack. Represented Clare at Minor Hurling and Football.

Aidan Raleigh: A lovely ballplayer and stylist. Had a very short career with Éire Óg. Represented Clare in Thomond Feis and Munster Championship in 1956.

Seán Spring: A determined defender with the courage of a lion. A member of the 1954/1955 squad.

Declan Ensko (brother of Hugh): Excellent colleges player. A member of the 1955 squad.

After a number of years at the top, apathy, overconfidence and carelessness crept into the Éire Óg camp and in April, 1958 they were dumped out of the Championship by the Blues at Newmarket. *"Sixteen year old Pat Cronin was one of Newmarket's heroes adding spice to the forward entertainment. A great goal by Conleth Conroy from a ground shot after Noel Gilligan had saved twice turned the game in favour of the Blues, 4-1 to 1-4. Others to shine for Newmarket were Michael Arthur and Pat Greene. Meanwhile back in Ennis the Éire Óg players were licking their wounds and seeking answers for this reversal. The main reason was they saw too little of the training ground"* - wrote the Clare Champion scribe. This defeat was followed by a bad beating at the hands of Whitegate (6-4 to 1-5) in the Clare Cup semi-final. It would take this sight of the St. Joseph's jerseys to bring out the best in this Éire Óg team.

O'Doherty Cup + Gold Watch Tournament

Paschal Sheridan of St. Joseph's has fond memories of this era. He spoke with great passion about the many tournaments and leagues which were taken as seriously as the championship. *"We had the O'Doherty Cup and Gold Watch Tournament, Dr. Daly Cup, McKaigney Cup (which was presented by the Queen's Hotel) and the Winter League. The hurling was tougher then. We played Éire Óg five times in 1958, the Dr. Daly Cup was never replayed. The Cup was later awarded to us. The Gold Watch Tournament was taken seriously. Dessie Loftus and I had many a tussle. Michael Blake, 'Gruggy' Dilger, Paddy Kerin, Paddy Loftus, and Bobby Burke were great hurlers. Brendan Doyle was a fine wing back, Gerry and Jimmy Cronin, Seán Madigan and Tony Keaty was a great character. The Dr. Daly final ended, 2-6 to 2-6. I remember there was a Fleadh Cheoil on in Tulla. St. Joseph's and Éire Óg were big crowd pullers."*

The O'Doherty Cup attracted the top 8 clubs in the county and it was run off in Championship format. Once again St. Joseph's and Éire Óg clashed in the final. "The crowd was intense but in a good-humoured mood as the starting time approached. It roused the spirits of old and young alike and will be talked about for many a day. Many sported their colours and each team had their cheer group." Wrote the Clare Champion. The sides finished level, 2-5 to 2-5. For the replay, the St. Joseph's players wore black armlets in respect of the memory of John

Highly charged action from a St. Josephs/Éire Óg clash of 1958, involving Tony Keaty, extreme left and Mick Hayes, St. Joseph's goalkeeper.

Moran of Barefield. He was a founder member of the Our Lady's Hospital Club. In his young days he played with Barefield and Ennis Rovers. The game again finished square. The final score was unusually low for hurling - Éire Óg 0-4, St. Joseph's 1-1.

2nd Replay of Gold Watch Tournament

The second replay of the Gold Watches saga ended prematurely with the town team leading, 2-6 to 1-7, after 53 minutes of play. The early whistle disappointed everyone including the Éire Óg crowd. The hurling was good with outstanding performances on both sides. The Champion reporter 'Fergus' described Pat Kirby at centre-field and Hugh Ensko in goal as outstanding. Obviously St. Joseph's appealed but their enquiry was defeated by 6 votes to 4. Rule 132 states the time for actual play at club level is 1 hour and an interval not exceeding 10 minutes may be allowed at half time. The game started at 3.10 and finished at 4.20. Afterwards, speaking to the Champion reporter 'Fergus', the referee Tommy Casey said - "When I blew the full time whistle I was under the impression that playing time was exhausted." Obviously the interval must have lasted at least 17 minutes.

End of St. Joseph's/Éire Óg - Rivalry

Paschal Sheridan recalls - "We were down 2-6 to 1-7 with a fair breeze behind us, the best was to come. Tommy Casey, the referee, blew the whistle seven minutes before full time. He made a human mistake, that's all. In the Clare Cup in 1960 we beat Éire Óg easily by 4-13 to 1-9. Then a lot of our team retired. It was hard to replace Matt Nugent, Johnny Purcell and Gerry Browne. St. Joseph's won two Minor 'A' Championships but very few came out of it for senior. Overall hurling was very good to me."

Ruan/Éire Óg

The parish of Ruan boasts one of the County's proudest hurling traditions. The game was documented in Ruan as early as 1786. The earliest documented game featuring Ruan in GAA times took place about 1890 when they lost by a single point to Ennis Faughs. Ruan continued as a force in the early decades of the twentieth century. They had great duels with Tulla, 'the Mills', Carrahan and Ennis Dals. And, though major honours eluded Ruan in the 1920s, they produced fine hurlers in Sean and Paul Hayes, Tom and Paddy Meaney, Paddy Casey and Martin O'Donoghue. From 1926 to 1940 Paddy Reidy was secretary of the club. Paddy knew every law and bye-law in the Treoraí Oifigiúil and was one of the most respected club secretaries in the association.

Paddy Reidy was succeeded as club secretary by Joe Hurley from 1940 – 1945. Joe filled me in on much of the background of the Ruan club. *"Ruan and Dysart amalgamated about 1925. Around this time juvenile hurling was played under the name of schoolboys. You could be any age as long as you attended national school. Paddy Reidy and Paddy O'Brien were prominent in the club in the 1930s and they helped bring the juvenile and junior championships to the parish in 1932. Afterwards, we amalgamated with Clooney for senior purposes in 1934. Ruan won the intermediate title in 1940 and then went senior in 1941. In the mid-40s Ruan had assistance from Tubber. Tubber supplied Paddy Carney, the Cunninghams and possibly Matt Nugent."*

I then asked Joe about the others he remembered and heard of. *"I remember Jimmy Lillis, Tim Custy, father of Sean and Frank. Ned 'Sailor' Grey from Cork played for Ruan from about 1932 to 1935. He was a*

Action from the Ruan/Éire Óg County Final 1959.

sergeant stationed in Maurice's Mills. He was possibly 'going off a bit' when he hurled for Ruan. I'm sure he played for Cork prior to that. Tommy Keating was a great goalkeeper. Keating played senior championship for Clare. He'd be better in today's game as fellows can't charge the goalkeeper now. He died a young man. Gerard Smyth, an older brother of Jimmy's, was good."

The guiding lights of Ruan were Miko Lyons, Fr. Leamy and Fr. Gunning. These men had a great love for the game. Fr. William Leamy was a useful hurler in his younger days with Silvermines and St. Flannan's as well as being honoured by the Tipperary minor selectors. Jimmy Smyth described Fr. Gunning and Fr. Leamy as two great priests. "*They were powerful men. Fr. Leamy was more of an intellectual type. We had great confidence in them. Ruan is a hurling parish. I was reared with hurling. There is no person in Ruan who hasn't some relation who was involved with hurling. The records go back to the seventeenth century. Hurling is a hard, tough, skilled game. I got my first hurley from Mick Hennessy. Before that we played with sticks. Ruan made a breakthrough in 1948. We had a very high standard with players of the calibre of Sean and Mick Leahy, Ger Kelly, Joe McDonnell, Christy Courtney, Paddy McNamara, Paddy Leahy and Joe Hassett. Joe 'Jazzer' Meaney and Joe McDonnell played for the Clare seniors and Christy Courtney was up to the standard. The strange thing about it, you always had encroachments onto the pitch.*

It happens with new teams coming through for the first time. Fellows get excited and they rush out onto the pitch. Later on they get more sophisticated. We had a second great spell in the late 50s. A new crop came through from Castle Rovers. They made a big contribution." It was this second crop that lay in wait for Éire Óg in 1959.

After the great rivalry between St. Joseph's and Éire Óg a new force was emerging in Ruan. Seán Custy, one of the Ruan stalwarts filled me in on their background. "There was a lull in Ruan after the great years of 1948-'52. All the fuss was about that team and very little was done with our juveniles for seven or eight years. Ruan continued to play an old team. The selectors were very slow to bring in younger players, even players like Frannie Lyons and Willie Kitson. In the Cup Final of 1956, Ruan still had the remnants of the 1948-1952 team. We then came with a couple of good minor teams. Ruan won the minor title with the minor goalkeeper from Ennis, Paddy Hewitt, playing in goal and you talk of hurling being civilised! Frank (Custy) was in goal up to the final. The amount of cheating was unbelievable at juvenile and minor level. Fellows playing under false names. They would have their 'mother's' maiden name written on their hurley incase they were asked. There were a lot of objections. They were different times. At senior level Ruan started to come again in 1958 when we reached the semi-final of the Clare Cup. We gave 'plenty of it' to St. Joseph's. Ruan had a very young team in 1959, seven or eight of us were under twenty. Kevin Smyth, Pat Henchy, Frank (Custy) and Tony Meaney came from the County Minor Teams of 1957 and 1958. Jimmy Smyth was a great trainer. We had Tommy and Jimmy Barrett from Lisdoonvarna. Éire Óg's star forward Michael 'Gruggy' Dilger got hit accidentally going down for a low ball. 'Gruggy' was as fast as lightning. He was as fast and lively as James O'Connor but not as tough. His brother Bernie at wing-back was pure class and Michael Blake in the centre, two mighty hurlers."

Seán's team mate Tony Meaney remembers - "Jimmy Smyth got the interest going in Ruan. Smyth was training for the Munster Railway Cup team, and he came to the village one evening and he asked a few of us to go to the pitch. We were just hanging around 'pitching and tossing'. A couple of weeks later we had eight or nine training and it took off from there, the interest grew. My brother Joe 'Jazzer' came out of retirement. Éire Óg were good in 1959. The game was different then. It was more man to man, more physical. Things didn't go well for Éire Óg in the final. We had five great years with this Ruan team. We trained about five nights a week. We had excellent athletes in Kevin Smyth and Pat Henchy. Tommy and Jimmy Barrett from Lisdoonvarna were a big addition. They fitted in well, and were dedicated."

In 1959, Éire Óg introduced new blood in Steve Loftus, Aidan Lynch, Brian Malone and Michael Guerin. They helped get the season off to a bright start with wins in the Clare Cup and gold Watch tournaments. In the latter Éire Óg beat Smith O'Brien's, 4-11 to 2-6 and Clarecastle, 3-7 to 2-8 in May. In the Senior Championship at Tulla the Ennis side overcame Feakle, 2-7 to 1-6 (despite a late goal from J.J. Naughton) with impressive performances from Paschal Brooks and Pat Tynan at centre-field and Michael Guerin and Michael Dilger in the attack. Following this Éire Óg had 9 points to spare over Whitegate with Pat Tynan outstanding on the '40' mark, (4-3 to 1-3). Meanwhile Ruan were making steady progress with big wins over Smith O'Brien's, Newmarket and Clarecastle. In their semi-final tussle, Éire Óg defeated Sixmilebridge by 2-8 to 2-2.

Without doubt the Ennismen entered the final as favourites with a mixture of youth and experience. Newcomers to the side included Ollie Ball just 19, Aidan Lynch (17), Steve Loftus (21) and Michael Guerin (20). Plus with Larry Blake and Paddy Duggan back from England and the versatile Noel Gilligan, Éire Óg looked the best bet.

A record crowd paid £720.00 at the turnstiles. *"After leading 1-4 to 0-3 at the interval, Ruan had their backs to the wall for much of the second half. Frank Custy stood head and shoulders over all by the magnificence of his performance. With uncanny anticipation and great courage he blocked one bullet-like shot after another. Custy proved a real lifesaver, worth his weight in gold to Ruan."* -wrote the Clare Champion reporter. Éire Óg forced three 21 yard frees but all efforts at goal were saved by the Ruan defence. The Éire Óg's full-forward Michael Guerin remembers, - "I doubled on a ball and kept running, it hit the toe of Custy's boot and came back out as I was running in. I thought Custy would be picking it out of the net. Frank Custy played great in goal." This seemed to sum up Éire's Óg's fortunes in the decider. The late Michael Gallagher of Clare F.M. Sports recalled, - "Ruan were exceptional from 1959-62. They were as good a club as ever I saw. The Éire Óg/Ruan Final of 1959 was one of the best. Michael Dilger was lethal at that time but Éire Óg met an exceptionally good Ruan team. Ruan were physically stronger and very committed, masterful in defence. They shackled the Éire Óg attack." In the final quarter, Ruan got on top at centre-field. Following a free by Tony Meaney, his brother 'Jazzer' drove the ball to the net to leave Ruan ahead, 2-6 to 0-4. Following the final whistle Jimmy Smyth was carried from the field by jubilant Ruan supporters.

In spite of the County Final reversal Éire Óg got back in winning mood to contest the Clare Champion Cup Final. Played in a blinding rainstorm Éire Óg fought back from an 8 point deficit to force a draw with Clarecastle, (3-3 to 2-6). Following good work by Michael Blake, Patsy

O'Loughlin started the comeback with a goal. Then after Éire Óg forced a 21 yard free the ball was stopped on the line by a packed 'Magpie' defence, with the in-rushing Johnny McCarthy flashing the re-bound to the net.

Paddy Duggan recalled the Cup replay. - "In 1959 we defeated our great rivals and neighbours, Clarecastle, in a replay at Newmarket-on-Fergus on November 1st to take the honours. It was not a great game really until the final quarter when Clarecastle staged a good rally to reduce the deficit. Up to that point we had dominated throughout the field and had chalked up a big lead. At one stage we led by 14 points. In the final quarter of the game, Clarecastle scored 3-1 but they never looked like beating us. Michael Blake switched from centre-forward to centre-back in the second half, and, together with Jimmy Cronin, Brendan Doyle and Bobby Burke, gave little scope to the Clarecastle forwards. Clarecastle had the man of the match in Paddy Mullins at midfield, but Colm Madigan and Johnny McCarthy did well here for us. Pat Tynan and Patsy O'Loughlin were two of our forwards to impress on the day. Michael Slattery, Christy 'Wax' Guinnane and Michael McNamara had some good moments for Clarecastle. After the game the Cup was presented by Seán Guinnane to Bobby Burke."

With victory in the Clare Cup in 1959, the decade which began on such a bleak note ended on a high. Since 1955 Éire Óg had contested four County Finals. Rovers and St. John's had won numerous championships and brought great honour to the capital town. Such was the talent in Ennis that many hurling followers feel Ennis should have fielded two senior clubs. The one common denominator in almost every interview I have done concerning hurling in Ennis during this era was the amount of local talent apparently ignored at senior level by the Dals and Éire Óg to accommodate incoming talent to Ennis to take up positions in professional areas. Was this snobbery on the part of the Dalcassian or Éire Óg selectors or was it just an economic thing? It's possible this happened everywhere; and we must remember the state of the economy, lads coming into town, any town, working in professional areas were often thought to be superior and automatically played before locals. Whether it was snobbery, or an inferiority complex on the part of the selectors we'll never know. But one thing we do know is that many of the incoming players made a fine contribution to Ennis hurling at some stage during the fifties and early sixties. Some of those who spring to mind include - Jimmy Conroy, Dermot Kelly, Pat Kirby, Dermot Leahy, Mick Morrissey, Tom Murray, and Jack Heaslip.

Cadhráns, Éire Óg and Kilkee

Paddy McDonnell
PRO, West Clare Hurling Board

A hurling involvement with its origin between "The Two Hills" in Moveen, carried along in Kilkee, with a long sojourn in Dublin, and the Éire Óg connection. An unlikely concept but nevertheless the route laid out for this humble scribe, along the pathway of a love affair with the greatest field game in the world, that is undiminished, indeed intensified, over a period of 47 years. It began in 1954 when I lived in Moveen and Clare had a great team, which won the Oireachtas Cup, beating Tipp and Wexford after a replay. The old Mullard Radio was the conduit for tremendous commentary by Micheál Ó Muircheartaigh, and the seed was sown.

Paddy McDonnell.

A present of a hurley from Mike "Bones" Hedderman, bought for 1/6d at Chrissie McNamara's, sister of Brother Seán, well known for his endeavours on behalf of Clare GAA supporters in Dublin, and I was up and running. No sliotar, but plenty of "cadhráns" or small hard lumps of turf in abundance on Moveen Hill, which were a useful substitute, later on an old tennis ball or sponge.

Coming to live in McSweeney Terrace, Kilkee towards the end of 1955, after Clare's great run in the Munster Championship, defeating Cork and Tipp, but losing to Limerick in the Munster Final. At that time Tom Haugh promoted hurling in Kilkee and organised a strand league, which aroused tremendous interest, and was encouraged by Vincent Murphy of Clarecastle, a member of the County Board and Munster Council, who had a summer job in the town. The legendary Jimmy Smyth was a frequent summer visitor to the town as well, which gave added profile.

Thus the hurling proper came to fruition. We were then travelling by hackney, driven by Johnsey Foran, to watch Clare playing, but the inter-county players were still rather remote to West Clare. In 1956, Brian Boru's hurling team from London came to Ireland, and a game was organised through Mike Woods, Danny Gleeson and Marty Marrinan, to play Éire Óg in the "Old Field" for the Corca Baiscinn Cup. The Clonbony Pipe Band led the two teams from the town to and around the field, before a big crowd, and we had a close up of some great players. Bernie and Michael "Gruggy" Dilger together with Pat Kirby later to become World Handball Champion, and Michael Blake were all to wear the saffron and blue of Clare. Pat Kirby played in goal and his puck outs were prodigious on a windy day, landing frequently in the square; he even drove a couple wide.

Jimmy Smyth refereed the game, which was won by Éire Óg on a score of 8-8 to 6-5, and Boru's were captained by Paddy Ryan who was a legendary figure in London hurling circles. There was an Éire Óg presence in Kilkee every summer for a number of years, as the Ennis Boy Scouts camped in the East End. Georgie and Massey Dilger were around our own age, and would join in with us hurling on the strand or up in the field. None of us had any great idea of hooking or blocking, and Georgie used to give us demonstrations on how to do it. Bernie and "Gruggy" were well known to us through their basketball exploits with Ennis CYMS, and they frequently competed in the old Olympia Hall. Michael Blake was a great basketball player, and another Éire Óg man, Ollie Ball was another tremendous exponent.

The road of life took me to Dublin where St. Brendan's was my team and, as I was never more than a trier, no major honours came my way. But my passion was undimmed, and my enjoyment limitless. After a sojourn in England and encouraged by Tom Malone, I became involved with Kilkee/Bealaha, who had been formed to compete in the West Clare Hurling League. Successful in County Junior 'C' Championship and League, we had our first County Junior 'B' success against Éire Óg in 1984. Bernie O'Brien starred for Éire Óg and 'Pudsy' Ryan scored 1-1.

I would like to thank John Russell, Eoin McMahon and Seamus Durack for the time and effort they put in to the promotion of hurling in Kilkee in the 1980s. Hurling remains in my soul and while this is 'big ball territory' the ancient game is firmly entrenched, and we no longer feel out in the cold when Clare does battle for highest honours.

Cumann Iomána Fánaithe na h-Inse
Ennis Rovers Hurling Club

Founded 1926

"Ennis was full of good hurlers,
the Rovers were nice characters and fine hurlers."
Johnny Moloney, Scariff

"John Kearney was the heart and soul of the Rovers.
His house was a great meeting place, a great house for visitors."
Paschal Molloy

Old Mill Street was always different. It was clannish in the best sense of the word. It was like a parish within a parish. It was renowned for its outdoor lifestyle of fishing, shooting, hurling, beagles, soccer, greyhounds. The characters there abounded. In short, it was a distinct part of Ennis.

A great togetherness and community spirit existed there, which Martin Cronin described as 'village atmosphere'. *"When one turned at 'Long's Corner' to go up Old Mill Street, one turned immediately to fame, culture and sport for which our town was renowned. At Long's Corner you arrived at the Stone outside Dan Murphy's door, immortalised by Johnny Patterson (a Feakle man) in song.*

'There's a sweet garden spot in my memory
It's the place I was born and reared
Tis' long years ago since I left it
And return there I will if I'm spared'

After going further on, you arrived at what I would regard as a sort of village, because the people had a lifestyle built around a different type of sport and activities, all of which were a fulfilment of their different lifestyles."

Gretta Gilligan married Miko Ryan in 1929. Gretta followed hurling and the Rovers in her young days. Her two brothers, John Joe 'Doll-dido' and Freddie 'Coggie' played for Rovers. Gretta told me in the summer of 1997: *"Almost all the Rovers team came from Old Mill Street. The exceptions were John Joe O'Grady (Clare Road), Tommy Fitzpatrick (Kilnamona or Dysart), and Mick Hynes. Miko (Ryan) and I came home*

Ennis Rovers County Intermediate Champions 1927. Back row, left to right: *Frankie O'Halloran, Mick Hynes, Tommy Fitzpatrick, Dan Meehan, Mick Linnane, Richard Barron, Frank O'Gorman.* **Middle row:** *Mick 'Soot' Coote, Christy Coleman, Johnno Guerin, Paddy Molloy, John Joe 'Dole dido' Gilligan, Christy 'Tar' Meehan, Phil Houlihan.* **Front row:** *Michael 'Pharoah' Mahony, Paddy Guerin (captain), John Joe O'Grady.* Courtesy of Pat Brennan.

from London in 1932; there was little work in Ennis then. It was all fishing and shooting. Miko came from the same street as me. He was a gardener. There was no work for the men. The women were the mainstay. The men only had casual work. There were no houses being built until Considine's Road in 1933. Miko followed hurling, boxing, and rugby. He was involved with the Rovers."

Fisherman Josie White also recalls the healthy outdoor lifestyle. *"Though I never hurled, I followed the Rovers; they had a field in Shanaway called the Ranch. Our pastimes were fishing and shooting; at nights watching geese and wild duck. I was a gillie for Mr. Staunton for 36 years. A gillie's job is to support the fisherman on the boat. I'd organise the boat. I had great dogs, very civilised; they'd talk to you. My Labrador was a genius. I got my love of fishing from my father. Fishing and shooting was a way of life then. It was a great life, we'd sell the salmon to the hotels and keep the trout."* I listened with great interest to Josie as he spoke of a lifestyle now almost gone; *"the game isn't there anymore,"* Josie said softly. Then his mind wandered back to the hurlers he knew – *"Christy 'Click' Houlihan, Michael 'Pharaoh' Mahony, the Kings, Johnny and 'Kelso' were deadly, John Hynes, George Morgan was a fine goalkeeper, 'Doll-dido' Gilligan was good too, but 'Pharaoh' (Mahony) was a genius."*

The Rovers hurling club was founded in 1926 by Tom Casey, John Joe Flanagan, Joe Kenny, John McCarthy, Frank O'Gorman and others who helped out in the administration of club affairs in the early days of its existence. The club took its inspiration from the (Old) Faughs hurlers, one of the most virile clubs in the town during the early days of the GAA.

Up to the early 1960's one had to be from the Old Mill Street / Hermitage / Buttermarket and Cornmarket areas to represent the Rovers. About 1961 things began to change. Summerhill was built and the club started to play hurlers from the O'Connell Street and Summerhill areas.

In their first season in existence the Rovers captured the Intermediate title for 1927. The Rovers opened their championship campaign versus Kilnamona at the Ennis Showgrounds. Played in a downpour, Ennis easily defeated their opponents by 6-5 to 0-2. Following this they defeated Crusheen, 3-5 to 3-2 in a divisional final. The Crusheen club objected to Rovers in a strongly worded letter lodged by Liam O'Halloran to the Clare Champion on August 6th 1927. John O'Loughlin replied informing Crusheen *"that Ennis are only concerned with winning the game on the field and as far as we are concerned we did exactly that."* The Crusheen objection was ruled out of order by the County Board. For their joust with Clarecastle, Rovers trained hard at the 'Ranch' in Shanaway under the guidance of Frank O'Gorman and Paddy Kenny.

Having accounted for Clooney, Barefield and Newmarket, Clarecastle was installed as favourites to beat Ennis Rovers in the final. From the moment the referee, George O'Dea, threw in the ball the match was a thriller. At the change of ends the sides were level at one goal each. On resumption of play, Rovers scored 1-2, but Clarecastle didn't lie down and 'the Magpies' came back strongly with a goal by Vincie Murphy. From then to the end exchanges were hard but fair with the Rovers holding out to win the Intermediate Championship by 3-3 to 2-1.

The Rovers continued as a strong force in Intermediate Championship and Clare Champion Cup (senior league) through the following years. In the local leagues of 1929, the Rovers lost by a point 4-3 to 4-2 to the Turnpike. Also in 1929 Rovers caused one of the biggest shocks in Clare hurling circles when they trounced the Dals (County Champions) by 8-0 to 1-3 in the Clare Cup with Mick Linnane, John Joe O'Grady, Christy Coleman outstanding. The Rovers went on to defeat Tulla in the same competition.

1930's Town Leagues

Folklore has it that the Rovers concentrated on the Town Leagues during the 1930s. These leagues were of a very competitive nature and oftentimes more interest was placed on these competitions than the County Championships. The Rovers, known as Old Mill Street, dominated the town leagues during the years 1933 – 1935, winning the Dr. Mackey Challenge Cup and the Gilroy Perpetual Trophy.

Backboned by 'Click' Houlihan, Mick Linnane, Paddy Guerin, 'Pharaoh' Mahony, Old Mill Street won the Mackey and Gilroy Cups for 1933. *"Tull Considine at full-back for Mill Street impressed time and time again as he stemmed the fierce onslaughts of the Market forwards. He was ably assisted by Browne, Wally O'Brien and Mick Linnane. Mill Street combined well – obviously they spent a lot of time at the training ground"* wrote the Champion.

For the 1934 Town League final, huge effort was put in to honour Michael Cusack – *"who won the hearts and enthralled the minds of successive generations of Gaels."*

The victorious fifteen Old Mill Street players assisted the Dalcassian Senior, Intermediate and Junior teams in the Champion Cup and County Championships. Ralphie Burns, Christy 'Click' Houlihan, Mick Linnane and George Morgan were honoured by the Dals senior selectors on a 24-man panel, which brought the Senior Championship back to the capital town.

In 1937/1938 Rovers proved strong opposition to all comers in Intermediate 'A' ranks, while the Dals' second string played in the Intermediate 'B' Division. Powered by the 'old Stagers of 27' in Michael 'Pharaoh' Mahony, Mick Linnane and Mick Coote, Rovers accounted for Kilkishen and Crusheen in the Championship. On the 15th May 1937 the Clare Champion reported, *"the Rovers have beaten all comers, but in Sixmilebridge they will meet different stuff in Bobby Flynn and company"*. The Bridge too fell to the Rovers. It was Tubber who proved the stumbling block with the 'Yank' Lee and Wally MacMahon in their ranks. After a lively first half, Tubber led by 3-0 to 0-2; then following an incident in the 33rd minute, the referee ordered a player to the line. Indignation was expressed at his decision and finally the game was called off. It was never replayed, but I believe the game was awarded to Tubber.

Rovers gained some consolation in 1938 when, with goals from Grady, Coffey and Moroney, they accounted for Tubber by 3-2 to 1-1. In the build up to their game with Scariff, the Rovers defeated Éire Óg by 4-1 to 1-0. Rovers bowed out in the latter stages, possibly in the final to Scariff.

Scariff publican Johnny Moloney had a lifelong love of hurling. Johnny and I spoke of hurling in the back room of his bar in Scariff one

Rovers Committee who organised the 1990 Re-Union. Back row: *Paschal Molloy, Paddy Loftus, Eddie Breen, Pat Brennan.* **Front row:** *Gerry Moloney, Ml. 'Darby' Cullinan, P.J. Summerly, John Bradley. Missing - Terry Hennigan, T.J. McNamara, Tony Maher.*

summer's evening. The great names of the game slipped from Johnny's lips. *"My earliest memories of county finals would be the 1927/30 era at the Showgrounds. I remember the combination of Ennis and Clarecastle beating Newmarket. I was so young and so thrilled to be in Ennis. It was an event, a day out. Newmarket and Ennis were dominant then. They had great teams. Ennis was full of good hurlers. Ralphie Burns, Mickie White, Pharaoh Mahony and Gerry Cronin. Gerry's sons too were nice hurlers. In later years I rated the Dilgers, Noel Pyne, Tom Ryan and Paschal O'Brien. The first breakthrough we made in my time in Scariff was beating the Rovers in the Intermediate Final of 1938. The Rovers were nice characters and fine hurlers."*

Following the 1938 Intermediate Championship little is known of the Rovers. Scant mention is found in the pages of the Clare Champion. It is not known if the club existed (outside of the Old Mill Street league teams) during the forties. In the late 1940s, the club was reformed in 'Pharaoh' Mahony's house and John 'Dugger' Kearney was elected Chairman.

The club was affiliated in Junior 'B' and Minor 'B' ranks. The first junior game played by the 'new' Rovers was against Kilnamona in May 1951, and later on in June Rovers beat Ennistymon by 3-1 to 2-1. In the semi-final Rovers lost by 7-4 to 7-3 to Clonlara; however, a replay was ordered on the grounds that Clonlara fielded three illegal players, but the south-east Claremen still won by 3-2 to 3-1. The minor team lost to Ballyea by 4-3 to 3-2.

In the 1953 Junior 'B' Championship the Rovers scored an 8-point victory over Kilmaley (3-9 to 2-4) but lost to Smith O'Brien's in the semi-final.

Some of the stars of the Rovers included Seán Mounsey, George and Flan Summerly, Tony McEnery, John Molloy and Paddy Loftus. Paddy recalled that it was extremely difficult for an *"outsider to gain access to the inner sanctum of this close-knit community."* Residing in close proximity to Old Mill Street, he was allowed to play for the club. Paddy Loftus was also the first Rover to be selected on the newly formed Éire Óg team. He was part of the panel that reached the County Final in 1955 and an integral part of the team that won senior titles back-to-back in 1956, 1957.

Coming of Minor Success

Rovers began to emerge in 1955 as a force in Minor Hurling. In that year they reached the Minor 'B' Semi-Final but lost in a local derby to St. John's by 4-2 to 4-0. St. John's progressed to Minor 'A' in 1956.

An outstanding exhibition of ground hurling saw Rovers capture the 1956 Minor 'B' Championship at the expense of Cratloe by 3-8 to 3-2. A feature of the game were the outstanding displays of Steve and Des Loftus, Niall McCullough and Paddy Vaughan. The latter would later star for his native Crusheen.

Social Club

As we all know, clubs don't just run themselves; finance has to be raised by over-worked committees. At their sixth Annual General Meeting held on 21st January 1956, a record attendance was present to hear John Loftus, Treasurer, state that the Rovers Club was well off financially – showing a credit balance of £55-10-6. The Rovers' Committee in the years 1955/56 included John Kearney (Chairman), Ralph Burns (Vice-Chairman), John Loftus (Treasurer), George Summerly (Secretary and Club Captain). The backroom also included Denis Rice, P. J. Summerly, Jackie Molloy and Peter Skerritt.

Brian Dinan, then a juvenile with the club, filled me in on their background and social scene. *"We played hurling in Terry O'Loughlin's field. It wasn't a recognised venue but with his goodwill we played there. The Rovers had a distinctive red jersey with a white collar and a big lace. John 'Dugger' Kearney's house was the focal point of the Rovers. Players met there. Hurleys were left there. 'Dugger's' wife, Ellen washed the jerseys. We travelled to games in Jim Woodhouse's big American 'Dodge', the type of car you'd see in the gangster movies. We felt very important travelling in the lap of luxury, eight juveniles and all our gear. The Summerlys were a great family; P. J., Haulie, Georgie, Anthony were all involved in hurling. P. J. was a great organiser and mentor. To raise funds for the club, Joe Hehir and P. J. came up with the idea of staging the play 'A Man of Ideas' by P. J. O'Dea (not our P. J. O'Dea in Kilrush). We paid royalties for the privilege of staging it. I played the part of Molly Brannigan. It was a comedy, a farce. The Rovers staged an annual dance at Paddy Cons to raise funds. GAA clubs then weren't allowed run modern dances but by putting down Ennis Rovers' Supporters Club or Social Club we got away with it. P. J. broke new ground by introducing this form of entertainment. He was a great club official and a master of those type of tactics."*

P. J. Summerly added: - *"I got involved with the Rovers in the mid-fifties. John Loftus was in charge then. Our catchment area was Parnell Street, the Buttermarket, Drumbiggle, Old Mill Street and Loughville. It was a fairly defined area. On the junior side we had Michael MacMahon, Joe Brooks, Jackie Molloy, Paddy Loftus, Josie McCarthy, Johnny Tuohy, Seán 'Bacchus' McCarthy, 'Bomber' Moloney, Peter Wilkie, Michael John Mulqueen and Pádraig MacMáthúna. Our minor stars at that time included Steve and Des Loftus, Mikie Hassett, Willie Molloy, Frank Cullinan and Brian McMahon. At juvenile we boasted Vincent Loftus, John Nevin, Eddie Browne, Des Neylon, Kyran Kennedy and Tony and Noel O'Loughlin. John 'Dugger' Kearney's house was the focal point. Paddy 'Wheesie' Carmody was secretary for years. There was money in the club. We had a Dramatic Society. We put on two plays and a pantomime; 'A Man of Ideas' was a sort of farce starring Brian Dinan and Michael 'Darby' Cullinan. We did a lot of extra-curricular activity. To raise money we also put on dances at Paddy Cons' (the New Hall)."*

John Kearney

The 'new' Rovers club came into being about 1951 and John Kearney from Hermitage is considered by many to have been the father-figure, inspiration and back-bone of the club.

Paschal Molloy was one of the Rovers prominent players in the early fifties. Paschal recalled the early days of the club and the part played by John Kearney. *"The new Rovers Club was formed about 1951. The main people behind the club were Jackie Molloy, Georgie Summerly and John Kearney. Eddie Breen was another good club man. I played at junior level; Seán Mounsey, Josie (Mc) Carthy, Johnny Tuohy were great hurlers but they never got their place on the Éire Óg senior team. Rovers had a*

Rovers H.C. present the Blake Cup for U/21 Championship 1964. Left to right: *Paddy Sheehan, Chris Ball, Brian Ensko, John 'Dugger' Kearney, Ben McAllister, Fr. John Carroll, Pat Brennan, Jimmy McEnery, Paschal Molloy.*

healthy rivalry with St. John's. No quarter was given. The early 1960's was the beginning of a great spell at Minor and later Under-21. We had great players. I was part of the committee with P. J. Summerly, Anthony Summerly, Pat and Michael Brennan and John Kearney. They were great clubmen and John and Ellen Kearney's home in Hermitage, near the Marian Grotto, was used for meetings. The meetings were social occasions. It was a great house for visitors. John Kearney was the heart and soul of the Rovers."

Michael Brennan added: *"In later years Gary Stack (Snr.) came in but 'Dugger' Kearney was the main man. It's hard now, 40 years on, to imagine how hurling meant so much to any area of the town but the corner 'round Dugger's house was a hive of activity and was the centre of all that was best in the Rovers at the time. The plotting and the planning of so many a team's downfall was set up at 'Dugger's' house. Nobody minded the long meetings as Ellen always had the kettle on the boil and 'tis many a row she broke up with a call for a tea break."*

Michael Butler remembers: *"After training most evenings many of the hurlers used to visit the home of our great friend, John Kearney and his wife Ellen. They were held in the highest esteem by everyone."*

Paschal O'Brien recalled: *"John 'Dugger' Kearney provided clubhouse, wit, and a burning desire to have his club achieve the pinnacle of success. Anyone who ever met him will remember how wonderful a personality he was."* And when it came to wit, personality and enthusiasm, Paschal would have recognised these traits, as he had them himself in abundance.

Medals Presented

It was not until the late fifties that the Rovers put their name on the record books again with victories in the juvenile and minor championships. These championship wins were but a prelude to a record-breaking run of success in the sixties – a record which will hardly be surpassed, if indeed even equalled.

On Friday 7th September, 1957, over 200 guests attended a social function when the 1956 medals were presented to the juvenile and minor team winners. The guests included Fr. W. O'Donoghue, CC, Fr. Carthage, OFM, Fr. Justin, OFM, Brother Gerard Murphy and Brother O'Grady from the CBS. Fr. O'Donoghue made the presentations while Pakie McCullough congratulated the teams on their success. Brother O'Grady and John Loftus also spoke.

In May 1957, Rovers juveniles, captained by Eddie Browne, won the postponed 1956 final. Michael 'Darby' Cullinan remembers it like this: *"We won the County (B) title as we thought but the County Board in its wisdom decided to stage a deluxe final with Kilkee. With players of the calibre of Eddie McNamara, Willie Molloy and Johnny Hassett we easily outclassed Kilkee. We played Juvenile (A) in 1957 without any success. We later beat a stylish St. John's in the Minor (A) decider. My brother Frank was at centre-back, Francie McMahon and Seán White in goal. Rovers had great identity."*

Town Leagues

A cup for the purposes of a Town League was presented in 1958 by Patrick McCullough of O'Connell Street. The Clare Road, Market Street, Boreen, Mill Street and Ard na Gréine (St. Michael's) all entered teams. Also around this time the Rovers club ran a 9-a-side league. In the decider Massey Dilger's IX defeated Tony Butler's IX by 6-5 to 3-1.

1960 Juvenile Final

Juvenile finals were usually played as a curtain raiser to the senior hurling finals, but in 1960 in the Rovers/St. John's juvenile final, some controversy was created when the game was switched to Tulla, much to the annoyance of the Rovers' mentors. The smaller pitch, they believed, would suit St. John's and sure enough Rovers were beaten by the in-form St. John's by 6-3 to 3-2. St. John's were best served by Michael Hanrahan, Ben Sheehan, Peter and Paddy 'Bom' Brigdale and a rampant Frankie Moloney at wing-forward, while Vincent Loftus, Noel Pyne, Des Neylon and Frank Rice battled for the Rovers.

Domination of Minor and Under-21 Championships

The early sixties was a great spell for hurling in Ennis – with the CBS and St. Flannan's dominant in the Harty and Dean Ryan competitions. A very young Rovers side qualified for the 1961 Minor 'A' Final after beating Broadford, 1-6 to 1-2 in the semi-final. The final was played two weeks before Christmas in Tulla against Newmarket, who had beaten St. John's in the other semi-final in a classic encounter. The Blues were firm favourites to take the championship but, coached by Bro. Jim Hennessy, the Rovers shocked Newmarket by 4-5 to 2-1 to take the Cup.

Afterwards at a function in the Queen's Hotel, Treasurer, P. J. Summerly, congratulated the players on bringing the minor title to Ennis. The Rockmount Stompers, who were making their first public appearance, supplied the dance music for the night.

1962 Rovers County Minor (A) Champions. Front row, left to right: *James Ball, Brian Higgins, Seán Coffey, John Nevin, Derry Dinan, Jimmy Lillis, Garry Stack, Dickie Pyne.* ***Back row:*** *Gerry Moloney (selector), Pat Brennan, Paddy Flynn, Des Neylon, Vincent Loftus, Jim McMahon, Ml. Hanrahan, Paddy McInerney. Missing from photo: Pat Coffey, Noel Pyne, Peter Brigdale, T.J. McNamara, Frank Brennan.* Courtesy of Brooks Studios.

Tony Maher captained the 1961 Rovers team and he remembers: - *"I started hurling at the school leagues in Ennis CBS. Then a friend of mine, Tommy Fitzpatrick, introduced me to the Rovers Club at 14. We had Under-15 and Minor at that stage in grades 'A' and 'B'. In my final year at minor I captained the Rovers winning Minor 'A' team beating Newmarket at Tulla. The Rovers went on to win five minor championships and two Under-21s. 1961 was a great year for me. I was a member of the Éire Óg senior team and the Clare minor team. I also enjoyed playing for Ennis CBS in the Dr. Rodgers and Dr. Harty Cup teams. I played in goal in the Harty Cup of 1960. We lost to Charleville CBS. With the introduction of Bro. (Jim) Hennessy we became a force. I missed out on both winning teams, Rodgers 1961 and Harty 1962. I played Harty Cup 1959/60 and 1960/61. I'd love to have won one or both. I came on to the Éire Óg senior team in 1961 and remained until 1963. I went to Dublin in 1964 and played for Young Ireland's and later on I represented Eoghan Rua. With Eoghan Rua the famous Fran Whelan was wing forward, I was centre and Joe Towell was the other half-forward, so I was in exalted company. I really enjoyed the hurling then. I was in Dublin until 1974. There was a lot of talent within Éire Óg in 1965/66, but with training I'd have been there or there about."*

Financing the Club – Ciste na Banban

Outside the usual door-to-door collection around Hermitage, Cornmarket, Buttermarket and Summerhill, Rovers ran the odd concert; P. J. Summerly produced an annual Pantomime. All these endeavours, however, paled when compared to *'keeping the book'*. In the early 1960's, Ciste na Banban from Cork ran a weekly pools exclusively for the GAA, and this was adopted as the main financial support of the Rovers, and in the latter half of the sixties by Éire Óg. The book consisted of all local participants in the pools, which reached a high at one time of over 600 names. Much organisation was needed to keep this system in operation. The book was divided with many collectors 'doing the rounds' every weekend, returning monies collected to the club on Tuesday nights at Dugger's house.

A regular advertisement run by Ciste na Banban read as follows: -

"Please help us to continue the good work we have undertaken.
Join our pools and participate in a weekly draw for £1,000.
Profits devoted entirely to GAA Schemes.

We can be contacted at 13A Parnell Place, Cork.
32 Bachelor's Walk, Dublin."

St. John's Cease as a Minor Club

Despite the amazing success at juvenile and minor level, St. John's ceased as a minor club in 1962 and at a Rovers AGM in that year, a motion was passed to amalgamate Rovers and St. John's players to form one club for minor teams.

Sweeping all before them, Rovers again reached the County Final. The 'Bridge were expected to test them but they collapsed, 9-9 to 1-0. The Clare Champion reported: *"It's a pity that Ennis Rovers are so good, at least for the sake of the Clare Minor Hurling Championship. This was demonstrated when they completely outhurled Sixmilebridge in the final. In fact the Ennis boys did as they pleased throughout the hour. It's impossible to find fault with them and they made it clear that nobody but themselves were rightly champions. Throughout the season they played textbook hurling and had easy wins over Corofin, Newmarket and O'Callaghan's Mills."*

Rovers lined out as follows: -

Seán Coffey

Jimmy Lillis   Frank Brennan   Paddy Flynn

Jim McMahon   John Nevin   Pat Brennan

Garry Stack   Brian Higgins

Michael Hanrahan (4-0)   Vincent Loftus (1-4)   Noel Pyne (0-3)

Dick Pyne   James Ball (2-1)   Pat Coffey (2-1)

Subs included Peter Brigdale, T. J. McNamara, Des Neylon – all used.

After victories in the Minor (A) Championship of 1961 and 1962, there was no doubt Rovers would win their third in a row in 1963. Fielding 10 of the Clare Minor team, Rovers hammered Feakle in the decider.

1963 Minor Championship

In the 1963 Minor Hurling Championship, Clare, featuring ten Rovers players, was most unlucky to lose to a star studded Cork team by one point. The Cork minor team at that time featured numerous players who later won All-Ireland senior hurling medals with Cork in 1966. They included Charlie, Gerald and Justin McCarthy, Seanie Barry, Tony Maher, Con Roche and Eddie O'Brien. This Cork Minor team also included Tom McAuliffe of St. Finbarr's, Farranferris at full forward. Donal Clifford also went on to play senior championship for Cork in the 1970s. It is important to emphasise the calibre of the Rovers players at this time, given the standard of the opposition.

The following is a synopsis of the Clare Champion report: -

CLARE PRESENT CORK WITH MINOR VICTORY

Cork 2-7 . . . Clare 3-3

"While the weather may not have suggested it, one was forced to think it was Christmas time, the time of present making, at the Gaelic Grounds, Limerick, on Sunday last when the Clare Minor hurlers made a present of their Munster Championship game with Cork. With two minutes left for play and playing with a strong breeze, Clare, leading by 3-3 to 1-6, looked destined for the second round, but then a typical rally from the Leesiders saw the Clare lead of three points go by the board. Indeed after being literally camped in the Cork half for most of the second period it would not at all have been against the run of play to see Clare enjoy a 6 goal lead going into the latter stages; instead it was another disastrous blow to Clare hurling.

Playing with the breeze in the first half, the Corkonians were fairly held by the Clare defence, many of whom let it be known from an early stage that they were not going to accept any nonsense or messing around with the ball. In a number of instances the game got out of hand and play was held up for a number of minutes shortly after the restart when a melee developed in the Clare goalmouth. The result of it all was that Clare's winning hopes got a severe setback when Vincent Loftus, who gave the impression that he was king of all he surveyed at fullback, got his marching orders with a Cork forward.

Up to this, Loftus had been the key figure in the Clare defence and was hardly ever beaten for possession and cleared with ease. From the start to the time of his forced retirement, Loftus was in powerful form and would have been a match winner on his own were it not for the misfortunate incident in the goalmouth. With Loftus, John Nevin hurled a fine hour at centre-back and was well up to his usual high standard. Michael Considine of Newmarket and Jim Hanrahan, a St. Flannan's College star, played effectively at wing back and corner back, respectively. Noel Pyne, Michael Hanrahan and Peter Brigdale were the stars of the attack. Brigdale was in fine form at corner-forward where his first time pulling and determination made him a forward to be respected.

A feature of the game was the policing of the much feared Seanie Barry by Rovers man Pat Brennan. Barry also had a spell at corner-forward on Michael Donnelly who also kept a tight rein on another of Cork's big guns, Charlie McCarthy. The speed and power packed hurling of Brennan and the first time pulling of Michael Donnelly made certain that no scoring effort from the Cork side would develop from their wing."

The Clare selectors came in for heavy criticism in that they left P. J. Ryan of Rovers, a seasoned midfielder with the Ennis CBS Harty Cup team, on the sideline for the entire hour. Many felt that Ryan should have been on the actual line-out; one found it difficult to understand why his services were not called upon even after 10 minutes.

The Clare Minor Team (10 from Rovers) was: -

	Liam Moloney *(Feakle)*	
Jim (Seamus) Hanrahan *(Feakle)*	Vincent Loftus	Michael Donnelly *(Clarecastle)*
Michael Considine *(Newmarket)*	John Nevin	Pat Brennan
Seán Coffey		Brian Higgins
Pat Coffey (1-0)	Michael Hanrahan (2-1)	Noel Pyne (0-2)
Haulie Molloy	Sean Flannery *(Kilrush)*	Peter Brigdale

Sub: Brendan O'Connor *(Tubber)*

Inauguration of Under-21 Championships

The Under-21 grade in hurling and football was inaugurated in 1964 at inter-county and club level. The initial tests at inter-county level were won by Tipperary (hurling) and Kerry (football). On the local scene Rovers became the first team to win the club title.

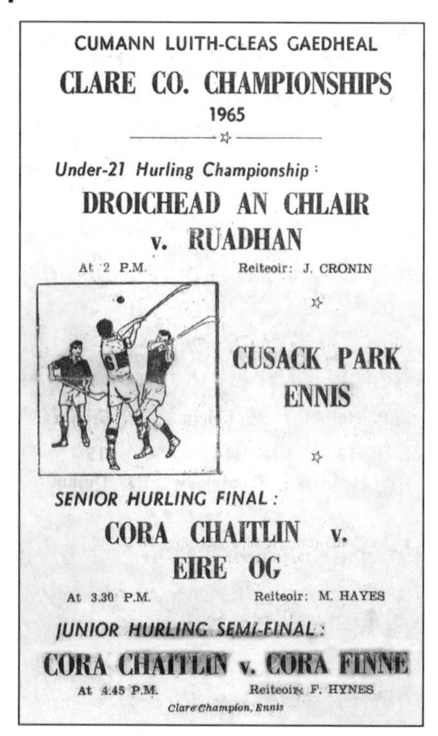

In preparation for the Minor and Under-21 Championships of 1964 Rovers travelled to Tipperary to take on the Tipperary U-21 Champions, Roscrea. The Tipperary side, featuring Tadhg O'Connor and Francis Loughnane had a narrow win over the Ennis side.

In September 1964, Rovers tasted their first defeat in Minor Championship in four years when they lost 5-7 to 4-6 to Clarecastle in the County Final at Newmarket. It was the Magpies' first Minor Championship title since 1950. Rovers bounced back and defeated Clarecastle by 8-7 to 4-7 in the Under-21 grade before accounting for the Blues, 5-4 to 1-7 in the final.

Rovers Retain the U/21 Title

In September 1965, Rovers' Under-21 team was the backbone of the Éire Óg team that contested the County Senior Final with the Blues. Played in September 1966, Newmarket held Rovers to a 4-7 to 4-7 draw in the final of the delayed 1965 Under-21 decider. In the replay, played the following week, Newmarket paid the penalty by failing to put Rovers away in the first quarter. During this spell Newmarket, with Jimmy McNamara in flying form, was well on top. Shortly after John Nevin was switched over onto McNamara and helped curb the elusive Newmarket man. The fullback line of Terry Hurson, Des Neylon and Seán O'Driscoll and goalkeeper, Paschal O'Brien, were in great form and much improved from the drawn game. Michael Hanrahan and Dickie Pyne were the pick of the attack.

Minor Champions Again

Rovers continued their stranglehold on under-age hurling when they regained the 1965 title. Forced to play with 14 players for most of the game Rovers, showing great character, pipped Newmarket in a great final by 3-9 to 3-7. Best for Rovers were Bonaventure McCullough at wingback, Vincent O'Shaughnessy, Donal Kenny and P. J. Kelly. Rovers retained the O'Byrne Cup in 1966 when they again edged out the Blues by one point in the final replay. The Champion wrote: *"They say General Custer's 'last stand' was quite a fight. But for sheer courage and determination, Rovers' heroic second half performance – during which they survived incessant Newmarket barrages, was defiance itself. The Rovers clambered to a fantastic victory in this throbbing, thrilling Minor Hurling Final at chilly Ruan, by 3-0 to 1-5."*

Out on a Winning Note

Though the Rovers affiliated a team to participate in the 1966 Under-21 grade, the Championship did not take place until 1967 by which time the Club was dormant. Éire Óg Under-21's, consisting mainly of all former Rovers, went on to win a third in a row for Ennis. Many reasons are put forward for the decline of this club, depending on whom you talk to; lack of officers, lack of funds or not let go senior. Paschal Molloy told me it was the end of his involvement with hurling. He never bothered again.

Ennis Rovers and St. John's made a great contribution to hurling in Ennis and the day that these clubs are re-awakened will be a great day for Ennis. Rovers won numerous championships but more importantly, the club was run without the trappings of distant officialdom. The players felt themselves a part of their club, in their own place, representing in a proud way their own town. It had historic connections with previous generations from the Old Mill Street area, namely the Old Rovers and (Old) Faughs – Cumann Inis Fág a' Bheallach. When hurling lost the Rovers, Ennis lost a fighting spirit that comes from playing for closely-knit communities.

UP THE TAGE *by Christy Murphy*
Well the Tage boys are out and we'll never look back,
We've just played a match and we're having the craic,
We've built up our thirst playing hard at the game
And don't give a damn about fortune or fame.

We'll play any game and always have fun,
Tage lads are as cute with a rod or a gun.
Whatever the sport, shur we'll all have a go
And after each game the black beer it will flow.

Hurling or soccer it's all odds to us,
Two seconds notice we're away on the bus.
The girls as well will all come along
They're as good as the lads at the deadly singsong.

Go up to the Tage and it's there that you'll find
All the auld townies so good and so kind,
We come from the Bullrings, the Backs, the Grotto
And the Tage boys will play come sunshine or snow.

Up the Diamond and the Island we sharpened our play,
We'd start in the morning and stay there all day,
Then come the weekend we were off to the Green,
That the Tage boys were good shur 'twas plain to be seen.

We've played 'gainst the Avenue, St. Michael's as well,
Of many's the great match tales we could tell,
But win, lose or draw at the end of the day
The Tage boys don't care just as long as we play.

Now if you're with the Tage boys do come and join in,
We'll sing 'til it's bright dawn make a hell of a din.
Later we'll ramble back up the Tage hill
But now my game boys drink up a good fill.

All you old boys and young boys sing while you can,
Lift up your glass like a good Ennis man,
Drink to the Tage boys and never give up
Til back to the old hill we bring the next cup.

Cumann Iomána Naomh Eoin St. John's – Founded 1953

On a Saturday afternoon in late October 1952, Causeway residents, Sean O'Gorman, Michael Brodie, Michael Nihill and Sean Cleary took the first steps in forming a new under-age hurling club in Ennis. To start this club they took up a door-to-door collection in their street, which amounted to 11 shillings and 6 pence.

In November 1995, Michael Nihill vividly recalled the humble beginnings of this club to me: *"After taking up the collection we were standing outside the Franciscan Church and discussing plans about forming a club of our own to enter the Clare Championships. Pako Malone (former Clare hurling goalkeeper and farrier) was standing at his door and he called across to us and said 'what are ye doing', we replied we're forming a hurling club so he said 'ye're outside the Franciscan Church why don't ye call it the St. Francis Club'. After a further debate we felt St. Francis H. C. wouldn't sound right so we decided, as there were two Michaels and two Johns, we'd toss for it. The John's side won, so we called it St. John's. We recruited Paddy McInerney and we put the wheels in motion to form a club. We got in touch with Paschal Brooks, John O'Donoghue, basically people who were GAA followers but had no involvement with the DALS. We got our first set of jerseys from Ennis CBS, blue with a gold hoop, and entered teams in the Minor 'B' and Juvenile Championships."*

Other main movers behind the scenes included Frank O'Gorman, Jack and Joe Daly, Rev. Fr. Carthage, Rev. Fr. Justin, Des McCullough and Frank Tierney. In their first year in competition St. John's reached the County Juvenile Final of 1953 (played on 17th January 1954) against local town rivals the DALS.

After trailing by 3-2 to 1-0 at the interval, St. John's attacked incessantly after the break but the DALS held out to win by the narrowest of margins 3-4 to 4 goals.

The St. John's team lined out as follows: - Brendan Considine, Pat Mangan, Jack Daly, Paschal Moloney, Michael Nihill, Brendan Doyle, Steve Loftus, Joe Noone, Seamus McMahon, Joe Ensko, Tony McInerney, Michael Greene, Richard Kennedy, Paddy Browne and Frank Kennedy.

St. John's Junior 'A' team 1956. Back row, left to right: *Noel Bane, Ml. (Haulie) Casey, Gerry Roche, Seán O'Gorman, Seamus McMahon, Noel Gilligan, Declan Ensko, Michael O'Shaughnessy, Joe Daly, Michael Greene.* ***Front row:*** *Raymond Duggan, Tony Blake, Tom Cosgrove, Brendan Doyle, Peadar McNamara, Richie Kennedy, Johnny McGann, John Tatton, Jim Ball, Danny Kelly, George Dilger. Courtesy of Esther Gilligan.*

It is unbelievable that in only their second season St. John's captured the Minor 'B' title at the expense of Parteen (7-2 to 2-2). Sean O'Gorman remembers, *"our juveniles had been beaten in their semi-final and we were more determined than ever to win this minor title, but of the 18 players selected only two had ever won a championship medal (Sean Spring and Pat Kirby), so when we took the field we were determined to win our first championship and win we did. Parteen led 2-2 to 1-2 at the interval but we made the necessary switches at half time. On the day our best players were Pat Kirby, Jack Daly and Sean Spring. I felt it was a great privilege to captain a winning team in only our second year in competition."*

The team was Brendan Considine, Joe Daly, Jim Cullinan, Sean O'Gorman, Sean Cleary, John Loftus, Sean Spring, Pat Kirby, Joe Noone, Bernie Guilfoyle, Raymond Molloy, Fred Ensko, Hugh Ensko, Jack Daly, Joe Guerin.

Adult Club

In 1955 St. John's invited a Cork selection, St. Mary's to play their adult team in an exhibition game at Ennis. St. John's, fielding a representative Ennis side with guest players Gerry Moroney, Larry Blake, Michael Dilger (Éire Og) and Sean Mounsey and Josie (Mc)Carthy (Rovers), overcame the Tony O'Shaughnessy led Cork side by 4-7 to 4-5. On the day their outstanding players were Josie (Mc)Carthy, Martin Linnane and Joe Daly. After the game the Cork and Ennis players retired to the Queen's Hotel for refreshments. The Cork group included Christy Ring.

Great Success

Incredibly Minor 'A' titles followed in 1955 and 1956 at the expense of Ennis DALS (6-5 to 1-1) and Tulla (10-4 to 2-0). The 1956 winning side included Jim Ball, Noel Gilligan, Brendan Doyle and Hugh Ensko. Following a 3-10 to 2-4 win over Ogonnelloe, St. John's qualified for their first adult final. By playing the wings St. John's accounted for Ballyea by 3-6 to 1-1 in the Junior 'B' Final. Then in 1957, following a facile win over Ruan in the minor semi-final, St. John's again contested an all Ennis Minor 'A' final; this time their opponents were the Rovers.

Rovers deny St. John's Three-in-a-Row

At half time St. John's led by the narrowest of margins, 4-0 to 2-5. Rovers had the wind advantage in the second period and Francie McMahon played himself to a standstill. Frank Cullinan at centre-back for Rovers had the game of his life, clearing ball after ball despite some heroic attempts by the St. John's half-forward line of Seán Micks, Liam Cahir and Martin Bradley to foil him. Most prominent for St. John's were Tony Lynch, Richard Kennedy, Aidan Tuttle and Seán Cooley, who bagged three goals.

A feature of the 1957 minor final was the part played by the Bradley brothers. John at right wing back marked his brother Martin who was at left half forward for St. John's. Also in 1957, St. John's contested the Juvenile 'A' final against the Blues. Playing fast, open hurling, Newmarket always had the edge winning by 10-5 to 8-3. Best for the Ennis side were Colum Flynn and Liam Cahir while Pat Cronin, Liam Danagher and Seamus Logue shone for the Blues.

Juvenile Champions 1959 – 1960

In 1959, St. John's, captained by Paddy Flynn, gained revenge by defeating the Blues in the final. By 1960 a new spirit was evident in Rovers and a strong juvenile team swept all before them to reach the County Final in which they met arch-rivals, St. John's.

During this era juvenile finals were always played as a curtain raiser to the senior final, but some controversy was created when the final was switched to Dr. Daly Park in Tulla, much to the annoyance of the Rovers' mentors. The smaller pitch they believed would suit St. John's. Though installed as favourites, Rovers were well beaten by a rampant St. John's team whose stars included Seamie Murphy (Goalie) Michael Flaherty, Ben Sheehan in defence and Peter and Paddy 'Bomb' Brigdale and Frankie Moloney in the attack.

By late 1957 St. John's had won a Junior 'A' Championship and at a committee meeting it was unanimously agreed to enter the Senior Championship and Clare Cup. The club also announced plans to field teams in Intermediate, Junior 'A' & 'B', Minor 'A' & 'B', thus fielding eight separate teams. A great achievement for one club!

Good Start in Clare Cup

A depleted outfit accounted for Ballyea in the first round of the Cup in 1957, by 3-4 to 1-1. This was followed by a massive 9-6 to 1-3 victory over Ogonnelloe with outstanding displays from John Tatton, Georgie Dilger, Brendan Doyle and Tony and Tom Cosgrove.

With further wins John's went on to contest the quarter final of the Clare Cup in 1957, where they gave a good account of themselves before fading in the final quarter, 3-11 to 3-4 to St. Joseph's. With great first half displays from Jack Daly and Johnny McCarthy, St. John's retired at the interval only one point in arrears, 1-4 to 1-3, but a series of unanswered points in the last quarter gave St. Joseph's a seven-point victory.

Co. Minor (A) Champions 1956, St. John's H.C., Ennis. Left to right: *Aidan Tuttle, Jack Daly, Patsy Malone, George Meehan, Noel Gilligan, Seamus McMahon, Ml. Guerin, Ml. Greene, Fintan Brennan.* ***Front row:*** *Micheál Casey, Tony Blake, Jim Ball, Paddy Kearney, Hugh Ensko, Brendan Doyle, Seán T. Keane, Richie Kennedy, Peadar McNamara.* *Courtesy of Esther Gilligan.*

St. John's Minor (B) Champions 1954. Back row, left to right: *Francis Tierney, Seán O'Donoghue, Joe Guerin, John Loftus, Jim Cullinan, Seán O'Gorman, Jack Daly, John O'Donoghue.* ***Middle row:*** *Bernie Guilfoyle, Seán Cleary, Seamus McMahon, M.J. Brennan, Martin Linnane, Raymond Molloy.* ***Front row:*** *'Brudsy' O'Halloran, Joe Daly, Pat Kirby, Brendan Considine.*

Controversy

In February 1957, the Champion reported on the wisdom of Ennis fielding a second senior hurling club. *"The wisdom of putting out a second team now, especially with Éire Og doing so well is questionable for there is a danger of inter-rivalry, coupled with a dissipation of the unified senior hurling strength in the town. Éire Og, 'the parent club' can oppose the move and cause the affiliation to be refused by the County Board, but it has been officially learnt that the club does not intend exercising its right. St. John's, however, have made a courageous decision and undertaken an unenviable task of fielding eight teams in one season."*

However, a couple of weeks later the Champion reporter contradicted this earlier article when he wrote: *"Éire Og withhold consent to St. John's fielding a second senior team at the second meeting of the Clare County Board in Ennis on Monday night, February 25th. It announced that a conference between the two clubs is to be held on Wednesday night and Rev. John Corry has agreed to act as chairman."*

At the meeting the Éire Og delegation asked if St. John's had produced the consent of the parent club when affiliating a senior team. Frank O'Gorman (St. John's) said that *"he believed if they were starting a new club the parent club could object but in the event of it being a club already in existence they could not do so. The Éire Og delegation replied that they had nothing against St. John's and appreciated the work being done for minors and juveniles. They could not see that the town could produce two senior clubs. Éire Og could not stand down and let another club take over senior affairs in the town just as they were getting fairly strong and had won the County Senior Championship for the first time in 15 years. Since 1941 there had been a lot of disunity in Ennis hurling and several teams were fielded under the names of Turnpike, Faughs, DALS, Commercials and Rovers, but when one club came along they saw what unity could do."* This meeting ended in stalemate.

Johnny McCarthy recalls, *"St. John's played in the Clare Cup and we had a reasonable record. It was felt within the club that we had the nucleus of a good senior team. What would have happened eventually I don't know. It was very likely that one club would have swallowed the other."*

Paddy Flynn accepts the Dr. Stuart Shield for U/16 Juvenile Championship, August 1959. Courtesy of Yvonne Flynn.

To make a long story short it's suffice to say that St. John's decision to play senior championship was blocked. The County Board felt it was an internal Ennis dispute and remained on the fence. Shortly afterwards four of the St. John's players were taken by Éire Og for the quarter-final replay with St. Joseph's in 1957. The mentors of St. John's were upset by it; Des McCullough in particular. They felt that Éire Óg were poaching from St. John's. There is also a school of thought that many St. John's players looked up to the Éire Óg senior players like Michael Blake, Michael Dilger and others that backboned the Éire Óg club and secretly wanted to line out with them.

In November 1995, I put it to Michael Nihill - was the Éire Óg club right to object? *"St. John's won Minor 'B', Minor 'A', Junior and Intermediate. They were entitled to go Senior but Éire Óg were also entitled to object. Then a number of players who had won intermediate medals with St. John's had no option but to transfer to Éire Óg, all of whom had come up through the ranks of St. John's, so St. John's then became known as a nursery for the Éire Óg senior team. I would put that down to the slow demise of St. John's because lads felt, what's the point of hurling from our youth if we can't represent our club at senior level. When we at St. John's started out we had players who couldn't get their place on the DALS Juvenile and Minor teams. We were just left on the sideline."*

Éire Og Retain Senior Championship

In 1957 Éire Óg went on to retain the championship and afterwards at a victory social at the Queen's Hotel they thanked St. John's for releasing four players for duty with Éire Óg.

By 1959 St. John's were reduced to Junior 'A' status where they reached the quarter final of that championship. Despite great displays from Sean Cooley and Noel Bane they lost to a Kilnamona side inspired by Joe Keane and Jimmy Heuston.

In 1961 a highly rated Newmarket side stopped St. John's, the favourites, in the Minor 'A' semi-final. However, the Blues gave way to Rovers in the final, losing by eight points. After the game Lewy Halpin congratulated the Rovers coach, Rev. Brother Jim Hennessy, adding, *"not alone*

Brendan Doyle, Seán Cooley.

had Rovers beaten Newmarket but they had beaten the best minor team ever to come out of the parish."

Sadly by 1962 St. John's ceased as a minor club and Rovers were then the sole organisers of minor hurling in town making Rovers extremely strong with many St. John's players transferring allegiance to them. This was a great era for Rovers. In the six years 1961 – 1966 they contested six Minor 'A' finals, winning five. The 1961 team coached by Brother Jim Hennessy, who also coached the successful CBS winning teams of 1961-'63 in the Rodgers and Harty Cup. Brother Hennessy instilled into those who came under his influence a burning desire to succeed, which was very evident, even in the years after he left town to go to Limerick CBS.

In 1964, St. John's had the unique distinction of fielding two juvenile teams, both of whom contested the County Final, with St. John's (No. 1) accounting for their 2nd string, a much younger side, played before the Newmarket-Clarecastle senior final. Some of the players who played that day and later became prominent included: - John McAllister, Terry Hurson, Joe Barry, Sean Lynch and Tommy Pilkington.

In 1965, a St. John's Minor Football Team trained by Seán Guinnane shocked the football world by reaching the Minor 'A' final. Along the way the Ennis club had wins over Lahinch, Miltown and Clohanes (Doonbeg). Playing against the wind in the first half the County Champions, Kilmurry-Ibrickane led by 1-2 to 0-1. After an even third quarter Kilmurry, despite the stiff breeze, were far from being on dry land with St. John's still within striking distance. However, a series of unanswered points saw the Quilty boys run riot in the final quarter. Best for St. John's were the hard working defence of Victor Greene (Goalie), Seán O'Driscoll, Vincent O'Shaughnessy, Donal Kenny with John McAllister and Derry Griffin the pick of the attack.

1966 was the climax of a golden era in Ennis hurling with Éire Og winning the Senior and Rovers winning the U-21 and Minor Championships. Surely a proud year for hurling in the town! Yet despite the triple coming to Ennis in 1966 it's ironic that Johnny McGann, one of the mainstays of St. John's, should pen the following lines in the Éire Og booklet. This is a brief synopsis: - *"Pages could be written about St. John's but suffice to say that it has now fallen into obscurity, not through lack of talent but through lack of interest by players and public. In its years of existence the club produced many notable hurlers who were to prove their prowess in the Clare minor teams and later on the Éire Og and County senior teams. Names which come to mind include Pat Kirby, Jack Daly, Hugh Ensko, Declan Ensko, Paddy Kearney, Johnny McCarthy, Martin Bradley, Paschal O'Brien, George Dilger, Sean Micks, John Tatton, Tony Blake, Aidan Lynch, Brendan Doyle, Paddy Flynn, Michael Guerin and many others who contributed in no small way to the exciting days of hurling in Ennis during the fifties. Although rivalry was keen in the town during those years let it be said it contributed to the well-being of the game and gave players an incentive to play."*

Notes:

The St. John's team that lined out in the quarter final of the Clare Cup in 1957 was: -

Tony Cosgrove

Seamie McMahon   Declan Ensko   Joe Daly

Brendan Doyle   Georgie Dilger   Noel Bane

Gerry Roche   John Tatton

Richard Kennedy   Hugh Ensko   Seán O'Gorman

Tom Cosgrove   Jack Daly   Johnny McCarthy

St. John's featuring guests from Éire Óg, Rovers and Turnpike pictured in 1955 vSt. Mary's, Cork at Cusack Park, Ennis. Back row, left to right: *Paddy McInerney, Michael Dilger, Gerry Moroney, Paddy Loftus, Francis Tierney, Seán Mounsey, Michael Hanrahan, Tony Conroy, Noel Bane, Christy Ring (Glen Rovers), Frank O'Gorman.* ***Front row:*** *Larry Blake Jnr., Paddy Duggan, Gerry Roche, Josie McCarthy, Joe Daly, martin Linnane, Paschal Brooks.* ***Both clubs fielded representative teams.*** *The Cork team was led by Tony O'Shaughnessy, St. John's won by 4-7 to 4-5. After the game the players headed to McKaigneys (The Queen's Hotel) where Christy Ring was heard to say jokingly to a St. John's selector "ye took them out of St. Flannan's today boy".*

The Long Hot Summers 1959 – 1971

"There are two main reasons for the resurgence of Ennis. The first is the town's proximity to Shannon Airport with its industry and tourism and the second is that new industries are attracted to Ennis by Government financial incentive."
Patrick Gallagher – Telefís Scoile- 1969

1966 was a memorable year in Ennis hurling. Éire Óg won the Canon Hamilton Cup after a series of near misses. I recall team captain John Dunne visiting the CBS primary school with the cup. The excitement, the pride and of course the inevitable half day. The decade had started on a high for Éire Óg. The senior club had captured the Clare Champion Cup in 1959 and St. John's and Rovers were dominant in minor and juvenile in the early sixties. Kyran Kennedy, a hurler and teacher in my time at the CBS, filled me in on the background of the Ennis of his youth. *"The GAA clubs in town from the late 1950s on were hurling clubs. They had no aspirations that one would get in a GAA rulebook. In all my time in committees, aspirations of Irishness, of language, of games even, didn't matter to us. What mattered was the game of hurling, and we were stone mad about it. If the game happened to be rugby then we'd have played rugby. Nobody got carried away with the folklore or the aims of the GAA. We were a hurling club, full stop. A few years later there was a feeling that we'd better participate in the other activities. Hurling was very healthy. Rovers, St. John's and Ennis CBS were all strong. The Rovers were the nearest thing to a rural club you could get. Meetings were held in the home of John and Ellen Kearney in Hermitage. John, or 'Dugger' as we called him, was the Chairman; he was the father figure of the club. The other prominent members included Peter Wilkie, Paschal Molloy, Jack Summerly, Gerry 'Stud' Moloney. Likewise, St. John's was very well run by Joe Daly and Seán O'Gorman. St. John's was winning everything. They were a credit to the town. They had the best of management, the best of gear and were financially very well off."*

Massey Dilger is one of four brothers from Connolly Villas to wear the saffron and blue of Clare. After finishing the Boys' National School, Massey attended Ennis CBS Secondary and the Technical School. Massey won a Munster Inter-Provincial medal with the Clare Vocational Schools.

Éire Óg, 1966 Senior Champions. Back row, left to right: *Paschal O'Brien, Vincent Loftus, Des Neylon, Noel Pyne, Tony Kinnevane, Martin Bradley, Des Loftus, Haulie Casey, Pat Brennan, Garry Stack.* ***Front row:*** *John Nevin, Johnny McCarthy, John Dunne (capt.), Dickie Pyne, Massey Dilger, Michael Hanrahan, James Ball, Pat Coffey, Seamus (Jimmo) Blake.* Courtesy of Clare Champion.

Trained by Kevin Marren and Seán O'Beacháin, Clare won two titles back to back. Massey featured on the winning team the second year. He recalled: *"We had an excellent team in Johnny Stack, Tony Butler, Paddy McNamara, Aidan Lynch, Pat McMahon, Liam Danagher, and Seán Kelly from Broadford played in goal. A feature of the 1958 Munster Vocational Schools final was that Milo Keane scored seven goals in the provincial decider against Cork. When I finished at minor, I found there was a big step up to senior as the Under 21 Grade was yet to be inaugurated. I played soccer with a very strong St. Michael's team. Then Paddy Gilligan approached me to go back hurling with the Éire Óg junior team. We contested the 1964 final but lost to Cratloe. Noel Pyne and Paschal O'Brien went from that junior team to the Clare Senior team before playing senior for Éire Óg. I got on the Éire Óg senior panel as a result of that junior team."*

Following Éire Óg's success of the 1955 – 1959 era it was inevitable that they should go into a slump, especially as so many of their players retired. The club drew with Sixmilebridge, 2-5 to 1-8 in the Senior Championship but lost the replay, 3-11 to 3-4. After this game the selectors came in for much criticism in the sports pages of the Clare Champion. The mentors were castigated for omitting Patsy O'Loughlin from the starting line up; - *"This is a game that the Éire Óg forwards will want to forget. They wasted chance after chance throughout the hour. Johnny McCarthy and Ollie Ball were the only forwards that looked dangerous. Patsy O'Loughlin made a great difference when introduced and the mentors must again be blamed for not having O'Loughlin on earlier in the game."*

Added to the retirement of so many key players, Michael Blake emigrated to England, while Jimmy Conroy, the Galway inter-county hurler, transferred to Whitegate. Conroy picked up a Senior Championship medal with Whitegate in 1961 and a Clare Cup with Feakle three years later. The loss of these, and other players, through premature retirement left a void, which wasn't filled until 1963.

During the early sixties the Éire Óg Club competed in several competitions and feiseanna - McKaigney Cup and Cusack Park tournaments. The former was then sponsored by the McKaigney family, the then owners of the Queen's Hotel and the McKaigney Cup was taken seriously by all participants. In the opening round, inspired by Limerick's Dermot Kelly, Éire Óg destroyed Sixmilebridge by 4-6 to 0-8, with John Dunne and Richie Kennedy also to the fore. Following this victory, Éire Óg beat Tulla by 2-8 to 0-6 but lost the McKaigney Cup Final to the Blues by 4-10 to 6-2.

An example of the hurling strength in the town was the fine crop of under-age talent coming through which was reflected on the Clare Minor Hurling panel. Aidan Lynch, Vincent Loftus, Paddy Flynn, Tony Maher and John Nevin were just some of the players who found favour with the minor selectors during 1960 and 1961.

In the 1961 Senior Championship, a young Éire Óg side was overwhelmed by a powerful Ruan side on the score of 8-6 to 1-5. By 1963, Éire Óg was beginning to put a useful senior team together. Having disposed of Feakle, 2-8 to 0-5 and St. Joseph's, 3-7 to 3-4, Éire Óg came up against Newmarket in the championship. The Clare Champion of August 17, 1963, reported, *"the Blues' play from the start was in keeping with their bouncy appearance on the pitch and after the first fifteen minutes the Newmarket supporters were in jubilant mood. Not since the days when Donal O'Grady was in his prime was there such a performance from a centre-back within the county as that given by Newmarket's Jimmy Cullinan on Sunday last. Newmarket won and deservedly so, but they themselves were first to admit that they got most of the breaks and were lucky to have gained a place in the final at the expense of a useful town team. The damage was done in the opening quarter when Newmarket led 2-5 to 0-2 with Pat Cronin causing havoc. By the time Paddy Flynn was moved on Cronin it was too late. The introduction of Bobby Burke was a good move, as his two goals brought Éire Óg back into it. Paddy McNamara was held by Vincent Loftus and later Pat Brennan. Other Éire Óg stalwarts included Des and Steve Loftus, Michael Guerin, Martin Bradley, Jim Blake. Paddy Flynn made some wonderful clearances with Aidan Lynch bringing off a number of master saves in goal. Michael Cullinan, Brendan Considine and Bobby Burke all did well when introduced."* The final score was 3-12 to 3-7. The Blues and Éire Óg met again in the 1964 semi-final. Éire Óg had earlier disposed of Scariff and St. Joseph's. The turning point in the St. Joseph's game came mid-way through the second half with decisive goals from Dick Pyne and Bobby Burke and an outstanding display by Des Neylon.

The semi-final clash with Newmarket lived up to all expectations with both sides producing skilled hurling. Played on a glorious day the Blues just about shaded it by 4-4 to 1-11. This game is recalled in the Newmarket History, *A Proud Past. "Once again Newmarket, the reigning champions can boast of dampening the spirits of their great rivals in the premier championship by yet another sweet victory. In glorious sunshine, and a well-trimmed and lively Fr. Murphy Memorial Park, the hurling lived up to all expectations, with hectic goalmouth clashes, brilliant midfield clashes and the fans provided with excellent entertainment."*

Michael Guerin was chairman of Éire Óg from 1963 to 1967. He recalls this year vividly: *"I played up to 1963. We were close enough every year but not good enough at the same time. Michael Blake was a terrible loss. Players looked up to him. His death in England was an awful waste of life. Michael Blake was great. It's quite possible he could have been part of the 1966 team. He was a naturally fit man. I remember Ned Henry, a native of Dundalk; he was a sergeant in the Gardaí. He was totally engrossed in Éire Óg, an out and out Éire Óg man. Gerry Blake from Clonroad was another. He was a Personnel Officer in Shannon and a great follower and enthusiast of hurling. Frank O'Gorman of St. John's was another staunch supporter. He lived in Francis Street. There were no side attractions then."*

In preparation for the 1965 Championship, Éire Óg played Galway kingpins, Turloughmore, in a rousing game played at championship pace and filled with wonderful scores and goalmouth action. Éire Óg came out on top by 7-7 to 6-9. This Ennis team included many inter-county hurlers. Such was the talent available to Éire Óg at this time that at least ten players played at one time for the county team in a league outing.

In the quarter final of the Championship Éire Óg disposed of Crusheen, 5-6 to 2-3 in a hard, robust game. The scoreline in this game is extremely flattering to the Ennismen. Éire Óg trailed 2-3 to 1-5 after fifty minutes, mainly thanks to the brilliance of Gerry O'Connell in the Crusheen goal. Following an opportunist goal from Des Loftus, Éire Óg hit a purple patch and began to open up Crusheen with their wide wing play. Further goals followed from Aidan Lynch, Michael Hanrahan and Paddy Kearney, ending Crusheen's strong challenge.

In the other group, Ruan, with Tony Meaney, Dessie and Paddy Crowe in fine form, ended Clarecastle's hopes with a 1-9 to 1-7 win, thus setting up a tilt with Éire Óg in the semi-final. Thanks to a great display from Noel Pyne and Garry Stack at centre-field, Ruan never found their true rhythm and were well beaten by 5-11 to 2-6. Éire Óg also qualified for the Clare Champion Cup Final, accounting for Whitegate by 4-4 to 2-6 in the semi-final.

Prior to the 1965 County Final meeting with the Blues the Clare Champion installed Newmarket as slight favourites because of their better blend of youth and experience. The sports correspondent with the Champion reported: *"The Newmarket and Éire Óg final should be a hectic one. The Ennismen haven't beaten the Blues in senior championship hurling for several years. Éire Óg and the Blues are both young sides but Newmarket have a number of strong experienced players in Jim Cullinan, whom I consider to be the best hurler in the County at present, Pat Halpin, Lewy Halpin, a survivor since the 1955 final, Gus Lohan, the Lissycasey-based Galway hurler, and Tom Melody, who always seems to reserve his best efforts for County Final day."* Though they trailed by 1-6 to 0-3 the Clare Champion's faith in the Blues was justified, as between the seventh and fifteenth minute of the second half, Pat Cronin struck two 21 yard frees to the net. Prior to Cronin's goals it looked like Éire Óg were about to break the Newmarket jinx when Noel Pyne scored a great goal just before the interval to put Éire Óg into a five-point lead. On the resumption John Dunne extended Éire Óg's lead with a point before the rally by Newmarket in the third quarter. The Blues held out to win by 2-6 to 1-6. It appears little separated Newmarket and Éire Óg in these years, yet Newmarket completed the three-in-a-row in 1965 with yet another narrow win. I asked several Éire Óg hurlers about the lack of success at senior level from 1960-65 and the amalgamation of the nurseries, St. John's and Rovers.

Massey Dilger recalls: *"The irony of it was you had a situation where the bulk of both Éire Óg and Newmarket senior teams were part of the Under-21 set up, but when it came to the additional three or four extra we couldn't master them. The addition of Pat Cronin, Jim Woods, Michael Arthur and Tom Melody made all the difference. Jim Woods was an exceptionally long striker of the ball. We were lucky to beat Newmarket in the quarter-final in Tulla in 1966."*

1966 Championship

In preparation for the senior championship, Éire Óg had wins over Mount Sion and Toomevara. Éire Óg opened their championship season with Tubber on 5th June. One moment of madness marred this overall sporting game, doing credit to neither club. Shortly before the interval an incident sparked off a violent row. The pitch at Ruan was invaded, hurleys were used and a Tubber player was seriously injured. The Tubber man left the pitch with a serious head wound and after being detained in the County Hospital he was later removed to the Richmond in Dublin. Tubber, who played with the wind in the first half, led at the interval by 1-3 to 0-4. In the second spell, the Ennismen added a further goal and eight points to win handsomely. While the Éire Óg/Tubber game was, for the most part, a clean game, the incident just before half time had a lasting effect later leading to a court case. In the meantime, Éire Óg disposed of the mid-Clare amalgamation Dalcassians by 5-9 to 1-6 and St. Joseph's by 2-10 to 2-7. In the quarter final with archrivals Newmarket, Ennis trailed by 5 points with 5 minutes remaining. The selectors then made a master move bringing Vincent Loftus to centre forward and Noel Pyne to mid-field. These moves had a telling effect with Brendan Considine and Pat Coffey scoring two late goals putting Éire Óg ahead by 2-8 to 1-10 at the finish.

Éire Óg/Clarecastle Marathon

John Nevin and Massey Dilger recalled the Clarecastle/Éire Óg marathon of 1966 with fondness to me one evening over a pint at James O'Keeffe's in Lifford. John remembered the 30 players lining up at the centre of the pitch. *"Paddy Russell looked over at Paschal O'Brien and said 'Ref, can you charge the goalkeeper?' Paschal got a fit of laughing. Patsy O'Loughlin didn't play in the last game. The 'Sparrow' was born that weekend. Patsy was a great hurler. He's related to the 'Gunner' and Paddy 'Cock' McMahon. You can see where the 'Sparrow' got the hurling from. The County Final was played on a bitterly cold November day; it was hard to get into the tempo of the game."*

Former Éire Óg hurler, Patsy O'Loughlin, wearing the magpie colours almost denied Éire Óg in the semi-final with a late goal from a goalmouth melee but Vincent Loftus responded for the equalising point to leave the sides level. The introduction of Tony Kinnevane proved a shrewd move in the replay when he subdued Christy 'Wax' Guinnane *"who was having the game of his life. Played before an exceptionally large attendance the sides again finished level in a thrill-a-minute battle royal."* – Clare Champion.

A decisive goal by Johnny McCarthy during a great second half rally helped Éire Óg dispose of the Magpies at the third attempt, 3-12 to 3-7, in a sporting game. Noel Pyne was one of the heroes of the hour notching 1-8 with Tony Kinnevane getting the other goal. This was hurling played as it should be played with Massey Dilger, Pat Brennan, John Nevin, Dick

Goalmouth action featuring Vincent Loftus and Martin Bradley (3) from the Éire Óg /Whitegate Final, 1966. Courtesy of Clare Champion.

Pyne and Martin Bradley standing out for Éire Óg while George Horan and Chris Hanrahan were prominent for the Magpies. The Ennis win was instigated by the powerhouse display of their halfbacks.

Éire Óg were back in the County Final, facing Whitegate, who accounted for Feakle on a score of 3-9 to 2-8 in the other semi-final.

The 1966 Championship was run on a Round Robin system with Whitegate losing their opening game by 7-6 to 5-7 to a Joe O'Halloran inspired St. Joseph's. 19 teams entered the Championship, including the amalgamations Eastern Gaels, and Dalcassians.

1966 County Final

On a bitter cold day, Whitegate boasting such players as Naoise Jordan, Tom Turner, Ned and Michael 'Danno' Doyle and their captain, Ned Cahill, a ground-hurling specialist brought big support from East Clare. After a bright start which yielded 1-1, Whitegate were overhauled in the second half with Éire Óg running out comfortable winners by 2-8 to 1-4. Prior to the game the captains, John Dunne and Ned Cahill, were introduced to Monsignor Michael Hamilton, former Chairman of the County Board. The teams then paraded behind the Ennis CBS Band.

Unlike the '65 decider the 1966 final never seemed to get off the ground with the hurling for the most part lacklustre. Whether this was down to the fact that Whitegate were an ageing team, or hot favourites Éire Óg being burned out after a long season, or the tension with the Tubber case hanging over members of the team, we'll never know.

The incident in the Éire Óg/Tubber game was most unfortunate and totally out of character with the rest of the game. It was a credit to Éire Óg that they won the championship in the face of the controversy. It took tremendous character from that group of players to finish the championship in winning style with what was hanging over the club at that time. The players hurled on in spite of personal problems. Players' jobs were in jeopardy. To bind together as a group and win the County Championship took some guts.

Late in 1966 a court case arising from the incident in the Tubber game was presided over by Justice Barra O'Briain. The referee's report read: *"that following a minor incident in the 29th minute between two players, a Tubber supporter ran onto the pitch with a hurley and struck the Éire Óg player in question. The Tubber officials did their best to calm the supporter but following the incursion by the supporter he was felled by a belt of a fist from another Éire Óg man. A row then developed involving 10 to 15 players, which lasted a couple of minutes. There is no evidence as to who struck whom, as it happened so fast". During the melee a Tubber player was seriously injured and taken to hospital. Apart from the Tubber man, it's unfortunate that one Ennis player suffered greatly because of this incident even though there is no evidence to link him with the incident. In his evidence the Tubber player stated, 'he did not know who hit him'. Michael Guerin, Chairman of Éire Óg said, 'he did not see the accused at all'. In his summing up the judge stated that 'the great game of hurling was debased by indiscipline'".* He then found the Ennis player not guilty of causing grievous bodily harm. The Éire Óg Club was then ordered to pay a sum of money in compensation to the Tubber man.

Shortly after the Tubber match, Éire Óg met Crusheen in the 1965 Cup Final, played September 1966. Fireworks were expected in this Cup Final and prior to the throw in Paddy McNamara of Ennis UDC visited the Éire Óg dressing room. He asked the players to remain calm despite any provocation, adding, *"in no circumstance should the Éire Óg players raise a hurley in anger against Crusheen, because the whole County is looking on."* Despite powerhouse displays from Michael Hanrahan and Brendan Considine, Éire Óg lost by the narrowest of margins, 5-4 to 4-6. The *Clare Champion* was scathing in its reporting of this match, under the heading *"Crusheen shock Éire Óg in an unruly Cup Final."* The reporter goes on to say the *"loss through injury of Vincent Loftus had an unsettling effect on the Éire Óg defence; however, wingback, Massey Dilger played another fine game and showed plenty of spirit. Pat Brennan was a tower of strength, in the final quarter. Undoubtedly it was a memorable occasion for the North Clare side to win their first ever senior trophy and to beat hot favourites Éire Óg into the bargain. This is a game that Éire Óg will not forget for a long time. They had to re-shuffle their side a lot and introduce substitutes."*

The following is a list of pen pictures of the 1966 Éire Óg winning championship team, as compiled by a member of the squad.

Paschal O'Brien: Made his senior inter-county debut before playing senior club in 1964. Ever present on county side up to 1971 when he also represented Munster. Agile, eagle eyed with superb reflexes, Paschal was one of the best ever custodians to guard the net in Clare. His wit both on and off the field won him many friends far beyond the boundaries of Ennis and Clare.

Jimmo Blake: Long serving, loyal servant of Éire Óg who got his just reward in '66 with championship success. Hard and sticky corner back who never gave ground to his opponents. Jimmo was tremendous in the games with Clarecastle. Was a sub on the successful '57 Éire Óg side.

Michael 'Haulie' Casey: Another ever reliable servant to the club during this period who gave of his all whenever called upon. A man with a great engine who had won minor and intermediate medals with St. John's, as well as playing football with the Faughs.

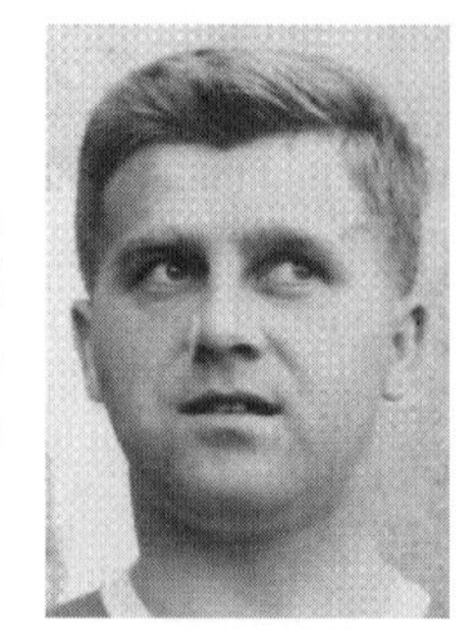

Martin Bradley: A product of St. John's juvenile club, where he won underage titles. Not known for his speed but kept a vigilant eye around the square, and used his strength to telling effect. An ever-present on the county side during the mid 60's after championship success in '66.

Des Neylon: Des came through the ranks of the Rovers winning 3 minor and 3 under-21 championship medals as well as the senior title in '66. Hard tackling and robust, was rarely found wanting even in 'backs and forwards'.

John Nevin: A hurler to his fingertips whose positional sense rarely let him down. Holder of 3 minor, 3 under-21, 1 junior football and senior championship medals. Played all grades from minor to senior for his county and matched the best of corner and wing forwards at county level with his silken skills. Also played minor football for the county. A born sportsman who would have been adept at any sport he chose.

Vincent Loftus: A leader through example whose 'exuberance' was not often appreciated by referees. Harty Cup Medal with CBS in 1962. Three minor and three under-21 championship along with the senior medal in '66. An adept footballer at juvenile level also. Ever present on the Clare team from 1964 to1974. Represented Munster in Railway Cup in 1967.

Pat Brennan: The athlete of the outfit, Pat had tremendous speed and agility, having won many juvenile sprint championships when he took to hurling and football. Represented the county at minor hurling and football, under-21 hurling and NHL. A founder member of Éire Óg Football Club and is still involved in coaching underage hurling at the turn of the millennium.

John Dunne: The fiery flame haired captain of the '66 winning team. A player with a great engine and rangy skills whose doubling on 'air balls' was a feature of his game. Midfielder cum centre back with a penchant for accurate free-taking, whose motivational skills were always apparent on the field. Played for Clare regularly during the '60s at midfield. John went on to give willingly of his time as a coach and many of his prodigies also left their mark on the game.

Massey Dilger: A stylish, crisp striker of the ball, with a good positional sense. One of four brothers to represent Éire Óg and Clare, Bernie, Michael ("Gruggy"), and George being the other three. Won Munster Vocational medal with Clare and juvenile titles with St. John's. Won senior championship medal in 1966. Favourite position was wing-back but campaigned at midfield to good effect also. Has many soccer awards being an outstanding player with the all-conquering St. Michael's FC.

Noel Pyne: Like Paschal O'Brien, played senior for his county before his club. Fleet-footed and elusive, showing a clear pair of heels to both club and county players from 1966 to 1970. Also a very fine footballer and represented Clare at minor level. Comfortable at both midfield and wing forward. Represented Munster in the Railway Cup in 1969. A superb all-round athlete who could turn his ability to any game as proved when he also represented Munster in golf. He also captained the province in successful campaigns in the latter part of the 1980s.

Brendan Considine: Another all-round sportsman, who won many juvenile, and junior titles with St. John's. A beautiful striker, who complemented John Dunne's style in the middle of the field. Also played at wing back or wing forward, and represented the county senior side. A golfer of some renown after retiring from the hurling fields.

Dickie Pyne: A playmaker rather than score getter, comfortable at centre or corner forward, with a fearsome left-hand drive. Represented St. Flannan's in Dean Ryan and Harty. Played inter-county for both Clare and Antrim and also represented Ulster in Railway Cup. During the '66 campaign had a round trip of some 400 miles to represent the club. Dickie was also an adept golfer and won many trophies in this sport.

Michael Hanrahan: First came to prominence with outstanding displays at centre forward for Ennis CBS Harty Cup winning side. Superb ground hurler with a deadly finish in front of goals. Has 2 minor, 3 under-21, 1 junior football and 1 senior championship medals. Has represented the county side through minor, under-21 and senior. Also a very fine footballer and soccer player, getting a trial for Limerick Utd.

Johnny McCarthy: Fast, elusive, teak tough, whose stature often belied his immense power in the pull. Has a full collection of juvenile titles with St. John's along with 2 senior medals with Éire Óg. A forward who could play in any of the scoring positions and often did to help bring the younger players around him into the game. Played in all grades for the county.

Tony Kinnevane: Joined the club from Cratloe in 1965 and immediately established himself as a robust, tough full forward, complementing the sweet hurlers around him. Won a junior championship medal with Cratloe before adding the senior medal with Éire Óg.

Des Loftus: Another member of the Loftus clan who represented Éire Óg with distinction. Probably the best ball player of the family and his skill in weaving his way goalwards often left opponents gasping in his wake. Has juvenile, minor and senior championship medals. Represented Clare at minor and senior.

Garry Stack: An underage player of great promise and skill, winning Dr. Rodger's and Harty medals with Ennis CBS and adding 2 minor and 3 under-21 titles and a senior medal with Rovers and Éire Óg respectively. A crisp striker with a tigerish instinct for possession never let the side down. Represented Clare at minor and under-21 and continues to give willingly of his time as Principal of the Ennis 'Nash' in promoting the game.

Pat Coffey: Another product of the successful CBS Harty team to make his mark at senior level. Fiery, forceful and very fast – a no nonsense style of centre cum corner-forward who scored regularly when introduced in the championship. Has represented Clare at minor and under-21. A very fast player whose later involvement with the club was curtailed by work commitments outside the county.

Maurice Carey: A garda based in town who has given loyal service throughout the 60s to Éire Óg. A hard sticky corner back who gave very little away, and was always capable of handling himself in the stickiest of situations.

James Ball: Elusive poacher of goals for many an Ennis side. Has 3 minor and 3 under-21 medals along with his senior title. James was an integral part of the team from juvenile level up and his ability to lift spirits when they were low and often lightened many an occasion with his singing ability.

Sean O'Driscoll: One of the youths of the '66 panel who went on to greater things later but his sole senior championship medal was won in '66. Won a minor and under-21 medal also with the town team. A player with great strength and fine stick work. Had the distinction of holding Christy Ring in a challenge match in 1967.

Terry Hurson: Another fiery hurling product of the CBS who cut his teeth through winning minor and under-21 titles with Rovers. Represented the Ennis CBS at Dean Ryan and Harty Cup level. A good solid, tough fullback who gave very little away to any opponent. Played minor and under 21 for the county.

Tom Glynn: Another of the youths of the side who later went on to represent the county side at senior level getting a NHL medal as understudy to Seamus Durack in the mid-70s. A fine footballer and soccer player, Tom won minor medals along with junior football titles with Éire Óg. Tom was also a fine soccer player during the 70s, representing Bohemians in the league while based in Dublin.

Aidan Lynch: A sporting prodigy from an early age, Aidan made his debut for the senior team in 1959. A wonderful all-round athlete. Represented his county at both hurling and football in both minor and u-21 as well as senior hurling. Holder of minor, u-21, Clare Cup and senior championship medals.

Munster Club Championship

The Munster Club Championship, comprising the County Champions from each of the province's six counties was introduced in 1964. The chance to represent one's county was a great honour.

As County Champions for 1966, Éire Óg represented Clare in the Munster Club Championship, where they drew with the Cork Champions Avondhu. Played at Cusack Park the game ended level. For the replay Éire Óg were forced to field at the Cork Athletic Grounds without Paschal O'Brien and newcomer Tom Ryan, who was cup tied. With Derry O'Connell rampant at centre field for the Cork regional team, Éire Óg's forwards were starved of possession and never got into the tempo of the game, with Avondhu going on to win by 3-13 to 2-4. The Clare Champion castigated the *"inept, couldn't care less, carefree attitude of the Éire Óg team"*. I put this to Massey Dilger: *"we had an excellent panel, nine of whom played on the Clare team against Cork in the league. We didn't really know what was involved in the Munster club at the time. On the other hand, Newmarket had great hunger; they were winners. They could have won the All-Ireland Club title. They had the killer instinct. Éire Óg had a lot of talent but lacked that killer instinct."*

To prove that Éire Óg had the stuff they bounced back to beat the rest of Clare by 3-7 to 4-2 in an exhibition match. They then took on Glen Rovers in a tournament game at Cusack Park. Unfortunately, the Ennismen were forced to field a weakened team as they had earlier played Newmarket in a Clare Cup match the same day.

Despite this, many patrons flocked to Cusack Park on May 7, 1967 to see an almost full-strength Blackpool team. A feature of this game was that Christy Ring was held to a solitary point from play by Seán O'Driscoll, though the Glen triumphed on a scoreline of 6-4 to 2-6.

Éire Óg's chances of retaining their status for 1967 were further enhanced by the arrival of Tipperary hurler, Tom Ryan to their ranks. Tom Ryan made his debut with Éire Óg in the 1967 championship against Dalcassians with Éire Óg romping home by a staggering margin of 54 points, 13-16 to 0-1. In this new look team, Michael Hanrahan partnered Vincent Loftus at centre field. However, Clarecastle were waiting around the corner and in a downpour they ended Éire Óg's aspirations for 1967 in a low scoring game by 2-4 to 1-3, with Michael Slattery majestic for the Magpies. At the annual dinner dance, December 1967, over 60 medals were presented to Éire Óg players for Senior, Minor and U-21. Michael Guerin welcomed all on a proud night and called on all to help in providing finances for playing facilities for the club.

Following the demise of the senior hurlers to Clarecastle, the Under-21s, featuring eight members of the senior squad, proved too strong for the Blues in the County Final. After a lacklustre first half, the introduction of Bonaventure McCullough brought much needed life to the Ennis side. A goal by James Ball after six minutes of the re-start set Éire Óg on their way. After the game, the Blake Memorial Cup was presented to Noel Pyne by John Hanly, who congratulated both teams on a fine sporting game.

1967 – AGM

Despite the successful Gala night at the Annual Dinner Dance more important issues were hammered out at the Éire Óg AGM on Sunday night, January 21, 1968. In a hard-hitting address the Club Secretary Michael Brennan spoke of the lack of commitment by some of their senior players. *"It is common knowledge that many of our players at all grades are playing other codes illegally and it is logical to conclude that at some stage a choice would have to be made between two codes, and somebody would suffer. This year we suffered by the action of irresponsibles and our lack of courage in not implementing discipline. 1967 has come and gone and what was looked forward to as a year of great impact by Éire Óg turned out to be a year of great frustration and definitely was one of the most disappointing for a number of years. For a club of senior status, the main concentration and effort is put into winning a senior championship title. Éire Óg achieved this in 1966, and with 14 of that side and the addition of Tom Ryan the club looked forward to 1967 as a year when Éire Óg would sweep the boards in Clare hurling. To say that defeat in the second round was to be our fate was akin to saying that Arkle would fall at the first fence in a race, but the unexpected happened and our neighbours, Clarecastle gained sweet*

Michael Brennan.

Éire Óg Juvenile Champions 1968, Under 16. Back row, left to right: *Seán Millar, Ml. Smythe, Noel Glynn, Ollie O'Regan, Ollie Piggott, Michael McNamara, Davy Connellan, Kieran Earlie, Colm O'Grady, Martin Fitzpatrick, Haulie O'Connell.* ***Inset Ml. Hanrahan. Front row:*** *Ml. Griffin, Jimmy Spellissy, Seamus O'Connell, Michael Quinn, Ml. Leahy, 'Archie' Meaney, Seán O'Grady, Kieran Gibbons, Don Ryan, Conor McCarthy.*
Courtesy of Clare Champion.

revenge for their 1966 defeat by gaining a four point win." Michael Brennan concluded that *"overall 1967 was a very disappointing year, especially so in the Munster Club, going out tamely in a replay to Avondhu of Cork."*

Talent at Under-age Level

Such was the talent at under-age level during the mid-sixties that by 1968 a sixth minor crown came to the town in the space of nine seasons. With players of the calibre of Tom Glynn, Noel Ryan, Joe Barry, Ollie O'Regan and Michael Carmody, the town minors defeated Newmarket in the County Final by 6-2 to 4-2. Ollie O'Regan recalled this year to me: *"I played with both St. John's and Rovers. I was a sub on the St. John's (A) team that beat St. John's (B) in the county juvenile final in 1964. In 1969 I was on the Éire Óg minor side which beat Sixmilebridge in the final. The 'Bridge led 4-5 to 1-2 at the interval; then Paddy Duggan gave a rousing speech. The selectors then made several positional switches – including putting Conor McCarthy into goal for the second half. They brought Martin Leahy to centre-back and put Noel Glynn in at fullback. We were a transformed team. Duggan and Paddy O'Halloran were great men to rise and motivate a team and without doubt they won matches for us through motivation. That '68 team included Michael Leahy, Bobby Stack, Francis White, Seán Lynch, Seán Neylon and Liam Pyne. Liam Pyne scored a fabulous goal in the semi-final replay against Newmarket at Tulla, by doubling on a long free to the net. He had great wrists. In the final we had a tremendous second half to win 6-6 to 5-6. Out of that '69 minor team only three went on to play senior on a regular basis; Noel Ryan, Seán Lynch and myself. That team had great potential, a team of great hurlers. A lot of them emigrated or went on to Third Level. We didn't win an under-21 title in my years playing. In 1973 Éire Óg got to the senior championship semi-final with a very good team – with Vincent Loftus, Pat Brennan, Jimmy Cullinan, Haulie O'Connell, etc. I'll always remember walking in and meeting Seanie Lynch (a spectator); he should have been automatic on the Éire Óg teams of those years. Soccer was going well; St. Michael's FC were doing well. Tony Roche, Michael Hanrahan, Sean Lynch and others were missing during those years. They*

Éire Óg U/15 Champions pictured at Cusack Park 29 Sept., 1968. Back row, left to right: Cha Kenny, Davy Connellan, Seán Daly, Brian Casey, Seamus Kelly, Paddy 'Cus' Kelly, John Molloy, Don Ryan, Jimmy Spellissy, Paddy 'Archie' Meaney, Haulie O'Connell. **Front row:** Eugene Judge, Mickie Guilfoyle, Dermot Kelly, Barry McGann, Paddy Kelly, Flan Morrissey, Paddy Neylon, Gerry O'Connell, Brendan Gilligan, Michael Skelly. **Missing:** Flan Hehir, Noel Pilkington, Seán O'Grady, Paddy Piggott, John O'Loughlin.

took up soccer in a big way. There's no particular reason; they were good hurlers who weren't playing hurling – they just opted for soccer."

Revival of the Town Leagues

By the late sixties the town leagues and inter-parish leagues involving Kilnamona and Ruan were organised to improve matters and to find new talent for teams in all grades. Apart from native Ennismen the town league was open to players living and working in Ennis, and seasoned hurlers such as Pat Henchy (Ruan), Naoise Jordan (Whitegate), Mick Kearns (Galway) and Tony Meaney (Ruan) all lined out with their respective areas. The chief movers behind the league were Paschal O'Brien, Tony Kinnevane, Pat Brennan and Jim (Seamus) Blake. A wonderful senior league was run off from February to September 1968 serving up many fine games, especially between the Town and Hermitage, who clashed on a number of occasions. Their first encounter was contested with fierce rivalry on a bitterly cold February Sunday morning before a large crowd at Cusack Park. I recall Paschal O'Brien being brought from goal to left-half forward, where he struck two fine goals before retiring nonchalantly to goal again for the second half. The 'Tage ran out winners in this tie by 6-2 to 2-9, with Gerry Moloney, James Ball and Naoise Jordan in fine form for the 'Tage. However, both Hermitage and the Town met in the final, which was played after a tense County Final between the Blues and the Magpies; serving up wonderful hurling, the teams finished level at 4-6 to 4-6. In the replay the Town had a 6 point win (7-6 to 4-9) with Tom Ryan, Peter Guinnane, Peadar Cosgrove and Jim McMahon (in goal) starring for the winners; while Hermitage had their best players in Aidan Guilfoyle, Donal Kenny, Pat Henchy and John Nevin. *"The hurling was tremendous as both sides fought for the initiative with the Town holding sway at centre-field where Derry Pyne and Pat Brennan laid on a plentiful supply of the ball to the forwards"*, wrote Seán King in the *Clare Champion*. Commenting afterwards to King many old-timers described the hurling as *"the best they had seen for many a long day."*

Certainly the leagues of '68 brought renewed spirit to Éire Óg, who disposed of Mount Sion 3-9 to 3-6 in a challenge and Sixmilebridge 2-8 to 1-3 in the quarter-final of the Championship. Once again the Magpies proved the stumbling block in the semi-final. Éire Óg lost to them 3-8 to 2-8, despite a great opening quarter. Ennis were also unfortunate in that a Paul Higgins goal was disallowed at a vital stage. Higgins was just one of many stars to come through the ranks of the Rovers. Captained by Noel Pyne and with Tom Ryan and Paul Glynn lording it at centre-field Éire Óg raced into a 1-3 to nil lead. But the Magpies, inspired by Dermot Fitzgerald and George Horan, stormed back into the game to qualify for

Clare team 1968 v Tipperary at Athletic Grounds, Cork. Back row, left to right: *Paschal O'Brien, Vincent Loftus, Mick Considine, Gus Lohan, Eamon Russell, Jackie O'Gorman, Tom Ryan, Ml. Arthur.* **Front row:** *Noel Pyne, Pat Cronin, Jimmy Cullinan, Liam Danagher, John Nevin, Paddy McNamara, Pat Henchy.*

another showdown with the Blues. Likewise, in the Clare Cup, Éire Óg went out to Newmarket in the semi-final stage by 2-14 to 2-4. The sides met again in a cracking Cup Final in 1969, played in biting frosty conditions. A disallowed Martin Bradley goal swung the game Newmarket's way. The *Champion* reporter castigated the Ennis selectors for moving Pat Brennan off Liam Danagher, *"particularly as Brennan was proving more than a match for Danagher, the 'Ebony Idol', with Derry Pyne excelling on the wing"*. However, the Blues pulled away in the end to win the 1969 Clare Champion Cup Final by 5-8 to 3-4.

Earlier in the cup semi-final, Éire Óg had confounded their critics when taking Clarecastle apart 6-9 to 4-4 with splendid displays from Tom Ryan, Massey Dilger and a rampant Martin Bradley. The game was over as a contest after the third quarter when they led the Magpies 5-9 to 0-3. However, a rejuvenated St. Joseph's caught Éire Óg napping in the quarter-final of the Championship in a tremendous game. *"Matt Nugent and Milo Keane tear Éire Óg defence to ribbons"*, reported the *Clare Champion*. *"Éire Óg's 'nonchalant' hurling couldn't care less attitude just won't do. The kid glove hurling which has become synonymous with Éire Óg proved their worst enemy, as the tiptoe coruscating movements of the forwards petered out in the face of rock solid defensive play of Anthony Corry, Oliver Clune and Christy 'Buddy' Reddan"*, wrote Seán King. This result was indeed a huge shock as a P. J. Purcell led St. Joseph's team emerged from the doldrums. I'll always remember this game for the magnificence of Matt Nugent's hurling artistry. St. Joseph's were unlucky to lose to Clarecastle by a narrow margin in a teak-tough championship semi-final at Cusack Park.

While not wishing this Ennis book to be in any way insular I spoke to as many hurlers who played against Ennis teams as possible. One player I greatly admired for his stickwork and sportsmanship was Liam Danagher. Liam recalled his sporting days with Newmarket, Clare and Munster and his memories of playing Éire Óg, St. John's and the Rovers with great fondness. *"Newmarket were very fit. Jimmy Halpin was our trainer. We trained most nights of the week, hail, rain or snow. If you didn't turn up on time you did extra rounds of the pitch before you were allowed train with the team. We always had a big turnout. Hurling wise, Éire Óg were on a par with us, no doubt about it. We were very lucky to beat them in the 1965 County Final. "Fagin" Cronin got a late goal from a 21-yard free. The Rovers and St. John's dominated minor and under-21 in the early to mid-sixties. We beat Rovers in the 1957 juvenile final. I played on "Lowry" (Tony) Maher. That was the first year we won it. Even if you look at the present moment, the teams that win at under-age level don't always come through at senior. It was the opposite in Newmarket. When we won the juvenile in 1957, it was the club's first title in years but the Blues had good senior teams in those years. The Ennis players I admired most in my time were John Dunne, Johnny McCarthy, Vincent Loftus, Paschal (O'Brien), John Nevin, the Pynes, Pat Brennan, Aidan Lynch was a fine hurler, the Dilgers were very respected. Tom Ryan was a big addition to Éire Óg and the county. A fine hurler, he got on great with us. He was great fun, very happy-go-lucky – but dedicated. That Clare team played tremendous hurling. If we had won only one Munster title, we could have gone on to great things, like the present team. Éire Óg and Newmarket played pure hurling. There was a great bond between the clubs."*

By 1969 the inter-parish league helped rejuvenate Ennis hurling. The Éire Óg Club fielded at least two teams in St. Michael's and Hermitage, while Kilnamona and Ruan also featured in this championship. Also a lot of much needed new blood came into the club in the form of Martin Linnane, who returned from England in the late sixties. He was a whole-hearted player and a great clubman, totally dedicated. Martin was only back a couple of months when he starred with the Clare intermediate team; needless to say he went straight into the Éire Óg senior team. Peter

Guinnane, a brother of 'Wax' and the late 'Tolly' also returned from England and set up home in the Turnpike. Other newcomers to the club at the time include Dan Fitzgerald and Pat Hyland, both members of the Ennis Christian Brothers and Galway native, Jim Kerins, a former St. Joseph's player. Also many young players were coming on stream from the under-21 grade, including Terry Hurson, Paul Higgins, Brian Higgins, Ollie O'Regan, P. J., Tommie and Noel Ryan.

In the latter stages of the inter-parish league (for 1970) St. Michael's/Boreen defeated a Jimmy Smyth led Ruan by 4-2 to 2-4 before accounting for Town/Hermitage 2-6 to 2-4 in a razor-sharp final. Best for the winners were Michael Smythe, Flan Howard and Eric Hanrahan. John Dunne took over the club as trainer of the senior team and he brought more professionalism into training.

In 1970, Éire Óg had wins 2-8 to 2-5 over Sixmilebridge and 3-13 to 2-4 over Ruan in the Clare Cup before drawing 3-8 to 3-8 with Feakle in the championship, with John Nevin outstanding at centre-back, while Derry Pyne, Sean Neylon, Ollie O'Regan and Seán O'Driscoll were others to impress. In the replay Éire Óg gave one of their best displays of these years, winning 3-15 to 3-6, with Massey Dilger outstanding at centre-field, assisted by fine displays from Martin Linnane, Georgie Dilger, Noel Pyne and Joe Barry. Éire Óg's performance was *"a breath of fresh air"* wrote Seán King in the *Champion*, with *"Tommie Ryan a shining light in defence"*. Every effort was also put in to fielding a full-strength team with Dublin-based players such as Michael Carmody, Tom Glynn and Terry Hurson being brought down at weekends for games.

Martin Linnane also praises the contribution made by Jim Cullinan when he transferred from Newmarket to Éire Óg in the early seventies. *"Jimmy Cullinan was dynamite, a great clubman. He always played his heart out for Éire Óg. He was worth his weight in gold. We trained indoors at Paddy Con's. Cullinan put everything into training and his enthusiasm rubbed off."*

Retirement of Paschal O'Brien

In April 1971, Paschal O'Brien announced his retirement from hurling. Ironically his last senior game was in the Munster colours on St. Patrick's Day in the Railway Cup Final. Throughout most of 1970, O'Brien was clubless. In the replayed Munster Championship tie versus Limerick on the 21st June 1970, O'Brien gave a wonderful display of goalkeeping in atrocious conditions at the Gaelic Grounds as the rain poured down. Such was the magnificence of O'Brien's goalkeeping that Seán King in his *Clare Champion* column immediately called for O'Brien's selection on the Munster Railway Cup team. I quote from that article: *"In a gloomy hour for Clare hurling, only a few defenders emerged from the game with untarnished reputations. These were goalkeeper Paschal O'Brien, who can wash his hands clean of the defeat with a truly outstanding game between the posts. O'Brien will undoubtedly go down in the annals of the game as the greatest goalkeeper of all time never to have represented his Province. That last remaining honour must surely be around the corner. Others to impress were Vincent Loftus, Jackie O'Gorman and Christy 'Wax' Guinnane when introduced to the attack."* High praise indeed from King! Paschal continued to assist Clare in the National Hurling League. His successor on the Clare team was Seamus Durack, while John Nevin and Michael Ball played between the posts for the club.

Summer Junior League

A very entertaining summer junior league was run off in 1971 with Éire Óg in top form accounting for St. Joseph's, 10-10 to 2-3. The senior team had a great run in the Clare Cup beating Clarecastle, 1-7 to 2-2 in a replay. The town teams were then brought back into the cup competition after the Blues beat Clarecastle by 3-5 to 2-6 in a stormy game.

The Clare Cup of 1971 was played on an experimental 13-a-side. Despite reaching the final, Éire Óg were well beaten by the Blues 8-5 to 1-5. The loss of centre-back Vincent Loftus through injury was a huge blow, though Peter Guinnane, Seán O'Driscoll and Michael 'Haulie' O'Connell did well.

Senior Championship

In the quarter-final of the senior championship, Éire Óg bowed out to a Sixmilebridge / O'Callaghan's Mills combination by 2-10 to 2-8. The Éire Óg team came in for scathing criticism in the *Clare Champion* with only Pat Hyland, Dan Fitzgerald and Ollie O'Regan escaping the wrath of the *Champion* journalist. *"The less said about this Éire Óg display the better. Rarely has a more insipid bunch of hurlers left the capital town in a long number of years. Éire Óg hit rock bottom. From and until such time that the Ennismen realise that nothing succeeds like hard, direct hurling, they will continue to remain the poor relations of Clare hurling. Weaving pretty patterns all over the field with fancy play is delightful to watch, but it does not win County Championships. Maybe that is something to remember for next year."*

Pat Brennan bemoaned the lack of young players coming through to the senior team from the successful minor teams. Pat recalled: *"Éire Óg always fielded young teams. This changed after 1968. Éire Óg were winning minor and under-21 titles but very few of these players progressed to senior. Davy Connellan, Jimmy Spellissy and Seanie Lynch should have been starring for us – Lynch came back later but he should have been an automatic choice much earlier."*

The senior championship game with Crusheen in 1970 was again shrouded in controversy according to Seán King in the *Clare Champion* – *"In what seemed like a crazy decision, a Martin Linnane goal was flagged as a point to the utter amazement of the Ennis faithful."* However, the North Clare club held out to win by 2-9 to 2-5.

Ennis Dalcassians

A special committee was formed in the late 1960s to look after the under-age hurling in town and, under the name The Dalcassians, proceeded to administer successfully and independently the affairs of juvenile hurling games. This group was formed with the assistance of a grant from Éire Óg – the senior body. Involved in this group were Don Ryan Snr., Brendan Spellissy, Bro. Clancy, and others. They did great work for juvenile hurling up until around 1973 and through a lack of flow of new officers, the group handed back the running of under-age affairs to Éire Óg, who at their Annual General Meeting of 1974 set up the Éire Óg Minor Club.

The winning 1966 u-21 team lined out as follows: -

Paschal O'Brien

Vincent Shaughnessy — Des Neylon — John Nevin

Seán O'Driscoll — Vincent Loftus — Pat Brennan

Paul Glynn — Noel Pyne

Brian Higgins — Tim McAllister — Michael Hanrahan

Paul Higgins — P. J. Ryan — James Ball

Sub: Bonaventure McCullough.

MARKET STREET, ENNIS

Newsagent, Tobacconist and

Fancy Goods

A landmark shop and meeting place in the Ennis of the 1960s and '70s.

1972 – 1979 Juvenile Successes and Adult Controversies

The Ennis I remember of the early 1970s was a great place to come of age. As a schoolboy at the CBS, I recall Brother Murphy, the Superior, almost always allowing us home for dinner at 12.15 rather than the usual time of 12.45. This added freedom allowed us slope home getting in just in time to tune into Liam Nolan's lunch time serendipity radio show, where the compere played the best of jazz. There was always something to do. We frequented the hops at the Friary Hall and at weekends went to the New Hall where Horslips or some such other group played. Jackie Hanrahan, the doorman, always gave us the beck when the coast was clear to enter. Jackie knew we were underage but it was only a mineral bar after all. Horslips, a wonderful group, fused rock with elements of Irish Traditional music tastefully presented would come on. No one danced, we just stood there and listened. We also frequented the Gaiety Cinema. Those of us who were mad for music scoured the advertisements page of the Champion to see when Woodstock, 'Gimme' Shelter, Easy Rider, or Let It Be were coming to the big screen.

For me the 1960s ended when, in April 1970, it was announced on the 1 o'clock news that the Beatles had officially broken up. The Liverpool group had more than anyone or anything else opened my eyes to the world. Brimful of talent and intelligence, the sum of the 4 parts no longer equalled the whole.

Sports Stars and Harvest Festivals

On the local entertainment scene Dan O'Driscoll, Tom Mannion and Michael Mulqueen, the then Chairman of the UDC, organised the Ennis Harvest Festival, which brought colour and a carnival type atmosphere to the town. Homecoming Queens and beauty pageants involving outdoor musical events were the order of the day. The 1972 Harvest Festival was especially memorable with the event officially launched by George Furness, Secretary for Economic Affairs in the American Embassy.

A contemporary festival was held in Ennistymon called the Family Festival. A feature of the Ennistymon festival was the annual Sports Star of the Year Awards. Some of the recipients in 1972 included Maureen

The St. Michael's/Lifford team that played in the Inter-Parish League 1971. Back row, left to right: *Paddy Flynn, Ml. Hanrahan, Gerry O'Connell, Denis Mulcaire, Ollie O'Regan, Dan Fitzgerald, Tony Kelly, Seán Lynch, Jack Murphy, Ml. Leahy, Massey Dilger.* ***Front row:*** *Paul Glynn, Eric Hanrahan, Tom Glynn, Pat Kirby, Tony Roche, Ml. Carmody, Noel Pilkington, Ml. Griffin, Seán O'Driscoll.* ***Seated:*** *George Dilger.* Courtesy of Ml. Leahy.

McEnery (Athletics), Ollie Markham (Boxing), Kevin Woods (Soccer) and Aidan Deegan (Rugby) with Jimmy Smyth picking up the Hall of Fame Award. Noel Pyne recalled this festival of 1969 to me: 'Jackie O'Gorman, Liam Danagher and I were nominated for the Hurler of the Year. We had a great night; Brendan O'Reilly of RTE interviewed us. The fact that I played Railway Cup for Munster that year probably swung it for me. Gordon Hurley was one of the interviewees. It was a stylish night and a great honour.'

Senior Championship

The 1972 hurling year began on a promising note with over 140 young hurlers taking part in the Dalcassian Juvenile League. Apart from the traditional areas, the parish of Doora Barefield also entered a team. The keen competition afforded the juveniles in the league gave them an added advantage over their rivals. The under 15s hurling with power, purpose and pattern went on a scoring spree when they trounced Ballyea by 9-10 to 2-2. The stars included Richie McAllister, Pat McInerney and Ollie O'Loughlin.

Intense rivalry existed between the Dals and Ruan, and following a fracas in Tulla, the U-16 final was abandoned when an altercation broke out along the sideline. Featuring many survivors from the winning minor team of 1971, the Dals defeated the Blues in the 1972 County Minor

Final. *"The Dals in their vivid red jerseys warming the corridors of memory swept forward in waves to defeat the Blues by 3-12 to 2-5. Paddy's Neylon's accuracy from placed balls was a revelation and once Tony Mahony and Leo Mannion took over at centre field it was all over for the Blues. Others to impress for the Dals were Michael Nugent, Noel Pilkington and Michael Griffin"* wrote Sean King in the Clare Champion.

The apathy that affected the seniors continued as Newmarket brushed them aside by 3-12 to 3-4. Later on, Éire Óg travelled to Blackrock and inflicted a 2 point win over 'the Rockies' in a tournament. Then with the introduction of new blood in Tony Kelly, Tony Roche and John McAllister, Éire Óg reached the semi-final of the 1973 championship where they lost by 1-15 to 3-7 to Clarecastle in an explosive game.

Under 21's

Since its inauguration in 1964, Ennis teams had always done well in the U-21 grade but in 1973 Éire Óg were destroyed by Whitegate. The following year, Michael Guerin was asked by the club to get involved. Michael didn't know the players but he asked the club for a list of names and where the players could be located. Many of those available for selection were into other activities. Michael Guerin enlisted the support of Paddy Gilligan and Jimmy McNamara. Under the guidance of the selectors much effort was put into training at the Fairgreen and featuring very young players like Eric Connellan, Denis Mulcaire and Martin

Éire Óg U/21 Champions 1974 pictured on a miserable day in Tulla. Back row, left to right: *Paddy Gilligan, Michael Guerin, Jimmy Spellissy, Seán Daly, Paddy Kelly, Pat Daly, John Coughlan, Michael Ryan, Seán Heaslip, Gerard O'Loughlin, Michael Griffin, Michael Skelly, Christy Glynn, Brendan Gilligan.* ***Front row:*** *Brian Stenson, Vinny Daly, Paddy Neylon, Seán O'Grady (capt.), Noel Pilkington, Gerry O'Connell, Ml. Griffin, Barry Smythe, Ml. Shanahan, Jimmy McNamara.* ***Seated:*** *Denis Mulcaire, Eric Connellan, Martin Nugent, Kieran Ryan.* Courtesy of Esther Gilligan.

Nugent, players in the 16-18 bracket who generally wouldn't get a look in at U-21 level, reached the County Final drawing with Whitegate 2-4 to 1-7. Because the replay was staged just 2 weeks before Christmas in arctic like conditions, the GAA came in for fair criticism for being detached from the feelings of supporters by playing such a prestigious game so late in the year. Featuring 8 players eligible for minor ranks, Éire Óg came to life in the second half after a goal by Brendan Gilligan was disallowed and a 21 yard free awarded instead. The resulting free was saved but the alert Jimmy Spellissy following through drove the rebound to the back of the net, setting Éire Óg up for a 3-5 to 1-2 win. It was Whitegate's third final appearance in as many years.

1974 Juvenile Leagues

Perhaps the most successful of all under-age leagues were the championships of 1974, played out over balmy summer evenings. Hermitage took the laurels in the Under 16 grade when they just about managed to hold out against a powerful Lifford rally. The 'Tage included Michael Chandler, Gerry Dilger, Michael Dilger, Declan Ryan and Brendan McEnery, while Lifford were best served by Johnny Mulcaire, Noel Cuddihy, Brian and Adrian Sheedy and Michael and Martin Dormer. The Dormer brothers are nephews of Kilkenny's Dick Carroll.

Amidst great jubilation, His Lordship, Dr. Michael Harty, Bishop of Killaloe, presented Pat Treacy with the Cup.

Though successful in the U-16, Hermitage gave way to the Turnpike in the Under-13 final. Afterwards the Éire Óg Cup was presented to Brian Toomey by John Hanly, Chairman of the Clare County Board.

Huge work was put into these juvenile leagues by Michael Rynne, Jimmy McNamara, Peter Guinnane, Paddy Ryan, Michael Carmody and others, bearing fruit at senior level within a few years.

Playing against the wind, Éire Óg defeated a gallant Ruan team in the 1974 Minor Final. Ruan led at the interval by 2-5 to no score. The Éire Óg selectors then brought Seán Heaslip to mid-field to act as a third mid-fielder. This move had a big bearing on the game with the Ennis lads dominating the second half to such an extent that they won by 3-5 to 2-5.

Those who impressed for Éire Óg were Pat McInerney, Michael Ryan, Peter Quinn and Joe Pilkington. Prior to the game John Glynn replaced Jim Collins at corner back.

Féile na nGael

Féile is a festival for youth. Inaugurated in the early 1970s. Féile was based on an idea by Seamus Ó'Riain, former President of the G.A.A. In the County U-14 Final of 1974, Éire Óg defeated Newmarket and so won

Éire Óg U/16 - Winners of Clarecastle Tournament 1974. Back row, left to right: *John Ryan, Pat Treacy, Johnny Moroney, Noel Cuddihy, Martin Dormer, Maurice Mann, Johnny Mulcaire, Joe Lyons, John Quinn.* ***Middle row:*** *Johnny Kearse, Martin Nugent, Pat O'Connell, Joe Downey.* ***Front row:*** *Michael Chandler, Jimmy Real, Gerard Dilger.* ***Missing from photo:*** *Tommy Coughlan, Dermot Meere, Adrian Sheedy, Brian Sheedy, Tom Pyne, Liam Lynch and Michael Dormer.*

the right to represent Clare at Féile na nGael. In the opening game, Éire Óg beat their host club, Kilmallock before losing out to Rapparees of Wexford. Éire Óg's leading marksman was Pat Lynch, who scored 23-8 in the U-14 grade. Tyrone Allard, who notched six goals, was the highest individual scorer in a single juvenile match.

Féile 1976/'77

In 1976, with star players such as J.J. Dormer, Jarlath O'Halloran, Tomás Mannion, and Seán Walzer, Éire Og, representing the Banner County, went all the way to the National Final before losing to Glen Rovers. Likewise in 1977, Éire Óg again reached the Féile Final after wins over Abbeyside, Doon and Cashel, before tasting defeat to a north Cork City side, Na Piarsaigh. Best for Éire Óg were Johnny Chandler and

County U-14 Champions and Clare representatives at Féile na nGael. Front row, left to right: *Albert Mounsey, Pat Lynch, Michael Dinan, Eamon Tuohy, Frank McEnery, Michael Chandler (capt.), Tony Nugent, Noel Purtill, Philip Markham, Jimmy Lane, Edward Casey.* ***Back row:*** *Oliver Hanrahan, Joe Hahessy, Brian Toomey, Frank Cosgrove, Tyrone Allard, Pat Hayes, Louis Galvin, Jarlath O'Halloran, Michael Lynch, Vincent O'Connor, Kevin Walzer, Michéal Glynn.*

Kieran Moroney. Such was the magnificence of the performance of goalkeeper Eoin McMahon that he was brought out to lead the attack.

Huge credit was due to trainers Paddy Duggan and Bro. Cusack, ably assisted by Jim Lordan, Leo English and Paddy O'Connell.

John O'Connor has great memories of those Féile days and recently he recalled to me, "I remember coming to Éire Óg through Willie Purtill. Up to then I had only played football at the CBS. Willie was in my class so he asked me to join Éire Óg. That was my introduction to the club. I played Féile in Abbeyside in Waterford. I stayed with a family called Hogan. Na Piarsaigh (Cork) were the masters that year. The mentors involved in those years in hurling and football were Denis Horgan, Liam Harvey, Paddy O'Halloran and Albert Lewis. I remember thinking back retrospectively about the time those men put into it. It's the same with any under-age set-up, everybody takes it for granted. The time these men put into it, putting their hands in their own pockets, spending their own money, bringing lads to matches. They gave us great nourishment and yet were taken for granted by parents".

Path to Féile na nGael Final 1976

Éire Óg	2-3	...	Mallow	1-1
Éire Óg	1-5	...	Nemo Rangers (Cork)	0-1
Éire Óg	4-4	...	Delaney Rovers (Cork)	Nil
Éire Óg	4-2	...	Erin's own (Dublin)	2-1

Returning briefly to 1973, Éire Óg seniors reached the final of the Clare Cup (played in late April 1974). Again pitted against Newmarket, Éire Óg lost by 3-5 to 1-5. This defeat seemed to demoralise the Ennismen who then lost to Tubber by 4-6 to 2-7 in the senior championship. Later in the final of the losers group, Brian Borus withstood a strong challenge from Éire Óg to win by 6-10 to 5-6, with Massey Dilger having a great hour, scoring 2-4. Joe Barry at centre-back, Dan Fitzgerald, Vincent Loftus and John Nevin also impressed. Brian Borus went on to account for Feakle before bowing out to Newmarket by 1-14 to 1-8 in the championship semi-final.

On the minor front, Denis Mulcaire, Vinny Daly and Seán Heaslip were selected on the Clare minor hurling team of 1974, while Leo Mannion and Gerard O'Loughlin were honoured by the football selectors. Gerard's brother, Ollie won the Éire Óg Under 18 Hurler of the Year Award with Alan Lewis claiming the Minor Footballer of the Year Award. Also around this time Joe Pilkington scored five goals in a league game against the 1973 Minor Champions, Kilmaley.

St. Flannan's

Kilnamona re-entered senior ranks in 1966 for the first time in many years. By 1972 they had amalgamated with Inagh and Kilmaley producing a very strong side with senior championship aspirations. This combination was known as St. Flannan's.

St. Flannan's were just one of many regional sides common in Clare hurling circles during the 1970s. Other sides included St. Senan's, Inis Cealtra and Sarsfields. The St. Flannan's selection featured county men in Michael and Milo Keane and Martin Commane. Other prominent men included Flan and Michael Hegarty, Tom Harvey, Tommy Keating, John Hehir and Christy and Michael Barry. In 1972, they reached the semi-final, running Newmarket close for 45 minutes before collapsing in the final moments to the splendour of the Blues power-packed play. Again in 1975, St. Flannan's reached the last four in the championship where they opposed Éire Óg.

St. Flannan's/Éire Óg

In the 1975 semi-final Éire Óg lined out without regular goalkeeper Tom Glynn, who was away on honeymoon. The goalkeeping position was filled by minor and Under-21 star, Martin Nugent, who acquitted himself very well. In a tense tie, a tremendous display by Tony Kelly was the difference between the sides leaving Éire Óg winners by 1-10 to 3-3.

So Éire Óg were back in the County Final for the first time in nine years. Their opponents, Brian Boru's were worthy opposition having disposed of Newmarket (it was Newmarket's first championship defeat in 5 years), and Sixmilebridge along the way. With the Blues and Clarecastle out of the way, Éire Óg were probably lulled into a false sense of security. Michael Carmody felt that *"deep down Éire Óg didn't expect to lose. In our own minds we were favourites. Subconsciously I thought we'd win it. Up to 1973, I was in Dublin so I came down at weekends. Éire Óg looked after us very well. They always paid our way down, or hired out a car for Tom Glynn, Terry Hurson and I. The dominant figure at senior level during my career was John Dunne and, though he didn't have success in terms of winning championships, he had success in that he had the respect of the vast majority of players. Dunne was a players' manager and above all a players' player.*

Before the final we had a get-together in the Queen's. The club management didn't want fellows hanging around the town before such an important match. I didn't agree with it."

Ollie O'Regan continues: *"the 1975 final with Brian Boru's was a huge disappointment. We had trained hard. On the morning of the match the panel was brought to the Queen's Hotel. We were cooped up together playing cards, etc. I didn't agree with it and I didn't go to the Queen's. I preferred to relax on my own. I feel it affected our performance."*

Brian Boru's entered the park sporting the famed claret and gold colours of Tulla. The East Clare side was installed as slight favourites, having broken the monopoly of Newmarket in the quarter-final by 1-12 to 1-8 and disposed of the 'Bridge (with Clonlara/Wolfe Tones assistance) by 2-7 to 2-6 in the semi-final. Brendan Vaughan and Andrew Curtin (Chairman of Clare Hurling Board) welcomed both teams to Cusack Park. Brendan Vaughan added: 'it's good for the game to see teams from our capital town and from East Clare contesting the final. For too long these areas, once the hub of Clare hurling, were unrepresented on final day. Let us hope that the presence of Éire Óg and Brian Boru's here today presages a real resurgence in these great traditional strongholds.'

Éire Óg made one change in personnel and several positional switches from the official programme. Michael Skelly wearing Number 16 started at centre-field with John McAllister going to the '40 and Brendan Gilligan to the wing. Noel Ryan started on the edge of the square with Paddy Kelly losing out. *'It was clear at a very early stage that*

Cumann Luthchleas Gael

COISTE CO. AN CHLAIR

CLÁR OIFIGIÚIL

14-9-75

CLARE COUNTY HURLING FINAL

Páirc an Ciosaghaigh Inis

EIRE Og V BRIAN BORU'S

Joe Barry

Réiteoir

MICHAEL SLATTERY

3.15 P.M.

Colm Wiley

Sgiath Na nÓgánach

Under 16 Hurling Final

Droichead Abhann Ui Cearnaigh

V

Droichead An Chláir

Réiteoir JOHN DUGGAN 1.45 P.M.

Runai, Coiste Iomana Contae.

LUACH 10p

Éire Óg were struggling in a number of sectors. At mid-field, Kevin Kennedy ruled the roost throughout the opening period blotting out inter-county player, Tony Kelly. Kelly came more into the game in the second half. Boru's were also on top in the half-forward line. Jimmy Walsh, leading the attack had the measure of Éire Óg's centre-back and Captain

Joe Barry, who, whilst getting in some clearances, failed to make a lasting impact on the game. His fellow teammates in the half-back line, Vinny Daly and Declan Coote were also put to the pin of their collars to control Jimmy Rochford and Joe Brady respectively.' – Clare Champion.

Most Impressive Performance

But by far the most impressive display, upon which Boru's victory was built, was that put in by the champions' centre-back, Pat Danaher. Danaher, on the day, was nothing less than unbeatable, no matter who took up the task of spearheading the Éire Óg attack. His reading of the ball played dividends, his quick deliveries up field played hell with Éire Óg.

Brian Boru's got off to a dream start; playing from the town end they were first to break away from the throw-in and in the first minute, wing-forward Joe Brady had registered his side's first score of the game with a goal. A sluggish Éire Óg trailed, 2-6 to 1-3 at the interval but a spirited second half fight back brought the town teams to within a point, 3-7 to 2-9 before Anthony Conlon sealed the issue with a goal in the dying

Seán O'Halloran about to clear, is challenged by Brendan Gilligan during the Brian Boru's/Éire Óg County Final, 1975.

seconds. The final score read Brian Boru's 4-7, Éire Óg 2-9. After the game, Pat Danaher received the Man of the Match Award.

Colm Wiley of Bodyke captained the winning Brian Boru's team of '75 from the corner-back position. The former St. Flannan's College and Dublin Faugh's man reminisced of his playing career. *"I played with Billy Quinn (Niall's father), Billy O'Dwyer, Jim Prior and Michael Lynch (Clarecastle). The Faugh's was comprised mostly of players from Tipperary, Laois and Clare. Later I captained the London team that won the Intermediate Championship. When I came back from England we put the Brian Boru's team together. We got a few from Tulla and a few from Killanena. We didn't have a morning get-together but we met in the Queen's Hotel about midday. We togged out there and after a light meal we walked down Francis Street to the park. I can still remember the noise of the cogs on the road. We did use the dressing rooms before going out though.*

It's hard to beat East Clare hurling when it's going well. The County Board allowed the amalgamations. I felt confident going in to the '75 County Final. We had beaten Newmarket and Sixmilebridge."

Seán O'Halloran added: *"Tulla and Bodyke were intermediate teams at this time and Killanena fielded a junior side. The purpose of this was to allow the stronger players in the three clubs to play senior hurling, to perform on a bigger stage. We reached the Clare Cup Final in 1974. Getting to the Cup final was a great beginning. That was the real bonding*

Kevin Kennedy in possession, as Noel Ryan closes in during the 1975 County Final. Courtesy of Clare Champion.

of the team, though we lost to Newmarket by 5-14 to 3-8, we learned a lot. We learned that letting the Newmarket forwards run loose got us into trouble. We tightened up after that. Having beaten the 'Bridge and Newmarket in the 1975 championship gave us great confidence. We felt if we could beat Newmarket we could beat anyone. We had a good lead coming up to the last quarter. Éire Óg pressed very strongly in the final ten minutes. We were lucky to keep them out at the finish."

Frankie McNamara partnered Kevin Kennedy for Brian Boru's. McNamara put much of their success down to Pat Kirby. *"In preparation for Éire Óg we played a few challenge matches and Pat Kirby gave us a fair going over in training. We had all East Clare behind us."* Kevin Kennedy recalled: *"After leaving the CBS, I joined the Gardaí. I was stationed for a while in Connemara and I missed hurling. Amalgamations became popular in Clare at this time. Brian Boru's had a very strong team. When you think of it, we beat Newmarket in the Championship, the 'Bridge with Shannon and Clonlara assistance in the form of Jim Corr, Richie Grace and Colm Honan. We then beat a good Éire Óg team in the final. We later won the Clare Champion Cup in 1977. The amalgamation broke up when Tulla went senior. I later played with Graney Rovers for a season. Being in the Gardaí my work took me to different parishes. I was later stationed in Ennis so I declared for Éire Óg. They (Éire Óg) were very organised and had little difficulty in getting challenge matches from Blackrock, Patrickwell and Middleton, etc. Colum Flynn's training methods were excellent."*

Because amalgamations are not permitted in the Munster Club Championship, Éire Óg, the defeated 1975 finalists represented the county but lost badly to Moneygall by 2-11 to 0-6.

Éire Óg suffered further defeats in 1976 at the hands of Inis Cealtra in the Clare Cup and Senior Championship. In the Cup they went under to the East Clare side by 1-10 to 1-5. Then after a 4-9 to 3-12 draw in the Championship, a rampant Inis Cealtra easily dismissed Éire Óg in the replay by 3-21 to 3-9. Inspired by Seanie Pearl from his full-back position, Inis Cealtra led by 14 points at the break, despite good displays from Massey Dilger, Michael Carmody, Noel Ryan and Brendan Gilligan.

Growing Population – New Club Grounds

In order to cater for the growing population, Éire Óg procured an 8 acre field from St. Flannan's College. This development, which preceded the major county grounds development at Cusack Park, was undertaken by Éire Óg to mark its 25 years in existence. The land, formerly known as 'Dillon's Field' was purchased by the club in 1976 at a cost of £20,000. The purchase of this field was instigated by forward thinking men like

At the gates of Éire Óg s new grounds. Left to right: Pat Daly, Christy Glynn, Fr. Seamus Gardiner, Kyran Kennedy, Albert Lewis, Joe Lynch, Jackie Browne, Michael Griffin. *Courtesy of Éire Óg Bulletin.*

Jackie Browne, Michael Howard, Christy Glynn, Kyran Kennedy, Ollie O'Regan, Miko McNamara, Rev. Fr. Seamus Gardiner and Denis Horgan, etc. The new grounds simply became known as the Éire Óg grounds. In the development of the new grounds the Club was supported by the 'Gunner McMahon and Miko Lyons.

In complete contrast, 1978 proved a great year for Éire Óg. The return of Seán Lynch to the game was much welcomed and with inter-county players, Noel Ryan and Brendan Gilligan playing great hurling, Éire Óg duly accounted for Clonlara Gaels (4-10 to 0-13) and Sarsfields (4-12 to 3-8). In the quarter-final St. Brendan's held the Ennismen to a 1-7 to 1-7 draw.

Éire Óg Dals (featuring a number of players from the newly formed Banner Club) produced an excellent display in the replay with Martin Leahy, Barry Smythe and Seán Lynch outstanding. Notching 3-2 from play, Seán Lynch's display was so impressive that he was called on to the Clare Senior team for the 1978/1979 season. The final score was Éire Óg 6-7, St. Brendan's 3-9.

After a poor opening half against Clarecastle in the Championship semi-final at Tulla, Éire Óg clawed their way back into the game in the second half. The move of Declan Coote to centre-field and Seán Lynch to centre-forward brought the Ennismen to life with Lynch hitting three great points before Heaslip goaled. With a couple of minutes to go, Éire Óg led the Magpies by 2-7 to 1-9. Then disaster struck with the sending off of a Clarecastle player; the pitch was invaded. Following this fracas, Éire Óg lost their composure and Paddy Quinn got through for a late goal.

The Under-21 team reached the County Final. Winners in 1974, 1977 and finalists in 1976, Éire Óg were fancied to take the Blake Memorial Cup in 1978. However, Ruan, playing wonderful ground hurling, prevailed by the narrowest of margins, 1-14 to 4-4. A feature of this final was the tremendous display of Cyril Lyons at centre-forward. Lyons, who scored two late points to snatch victory, hit a personal 1-8. Éire Óg were best served by Francis Heaslip, John Glynn, Johnny Kierce and Philip Markham in defence, while Pat Lynch, Michael Ryan and Tom Kelly caught the eye in the attack.

Club in Disarray – In-fighting in Éire Óg

Following a 2-8 to 1-4 defeat to Tubber in the opening round of the 1979 Senior Championship, Éire Óg was rocked by serious in-fighting. The controversy arose when John Dunne (the Éire Óg trainer) allowed

Éire Óg Under 21 Champions 1978. Back row, left to right: *Pat Treacy, Ml. Flaherty, Ml. Ryan, Joe Pilkington, Seán Heaslip, Joe Downey, Adrian Sheedy, Pat Daly, Vinny Daly, Peter Quinn, Pat Hayes, Pat McInerney, Oliver Hanrahan, Christy Glynn.* ***Middle row:*** *Paddy O'Halloran, Richard McAllister, Francis Heaslip, Martin Nugent, Declan Coote, Johnny Kearse, John Quinn, Brian Tuohy, John Glynn, Kevin Walzer.* ***Front row:*** *Donal Fitzpatrick, Tony Nugent, Pete Barry, Tom Russell, Denis O'Connor, Paddy Duggan.*

Courtesy of Clare Champion.

Pat Daly (3rd left) of John Daly Menswear making a presentation of sportswear to P.J. McMahon, vice-chairman of County Board. Also pictured are Flan Hynes, Ml. McTigue, Jimmy McNamara (Clare team captain), Tom Neylon.

three of his players, Martin and Tony Nugent and Tony Roche, assist St. Michaels A.F.C. in a Haughey Cup soccer match on the same day that Eire Og played Tubber in the championship. Sean Heaslip takes up the story: "We had six players on the St. Michael's soccer team and Dunne allowed three of them play for St. Michaels in their cup game. I don't know which way he divided them but the powers that be didn't like it. We, the players backed Dunne, but the club executive withdrew his membership. The Club Executive then appointed Paddy Duggan as team trainer. We trained in St. Flannan's, as we had no pitch, and 'Duggie' was in another pitch with another group of players".

A Committee meeting of Friday night, 22nd of June, saw heated exchanges between John Dunne and club officials. John Dunne then made his position clear when he told the Clare News (a then weekly County Newspaper), four days after his membership of the club had been withdrawn that his interest was only in hurling. "Only for the players' support I would not be here. Until the players say I am not wanted, I will stay despite what the club officials might think, because without players you have no club".

Some felt that the controversy flared up as a direct result of the so-called Mahon affair. Paschal Mahon played illegally with Éire Óg in an intermediate match against Whitegate, though he was still a member of the St. Joseph's club.

In fairness to Éire Óg club Chairman, Paddy O'Halloran, it was he who brought the matter before the County Board, probably the first time ever that a club officer came forward with such a confession. Though the intermediate team was reinstated as legal, Pat Daly, Club Secretary, Martin Linnane, Intermediate Team Manager and Christy Glynn, Board Delegate, were each suspended for three months. Meanwhile, the row became more entrenched when most of the players backed John Dunne. The Executive Committee then resigned en bloc making the club illegal for their losers group clash with Kilkishen.

To further complicate matters the newly signed Éire Óg goalkeeper, Seamus Durack took no side in the dispute. In hindsight, it was hard to blame Durack.

An Éire Óg XV, dubbed The Rebels lined out against Kilkishen in the losers group, with John Quinn replacing Seamus Durack. Previously beaten by Clonlara Gaels, Kilkishen with a number of big names in Sean Hehir, Michael O'Connor, Martin McKeogh and P.J. and Michael Deasy came from behind at the interval to win by 3-12 to 4-6, despite fine displays from Michael Carmody, Tony Roche and Joe Barry.

Éire Óg at Tulla 1979. Back row, left to right: *Pat Hayes, Declan Coote, Francis Heaslip, Michael Barry, Johnny Kearse, Tom Kelly, John Glynn, Paddy Kelly, Michael Carmody, John Quinn, Colm Mahon, Martin Nugent, Tony Nugent, Michael Griffin (Parnell Street).* ***Front row:*** *Michael Griffin, Gerard O'Loughlin, John Coughlan, Michael Skelly, Seán Heaslip, Noel Ryan, Tony Roche, Frank Molloy, Joe Barry, Martin Leahy.*

Courtesy of Clare News.

In terms of the dispute, the County Board Chairman, Andrew Curtin and Secretary Michael McTigue, intervened and brought the two groups together for a meeting. Things were later reconciled but John Dunne left. Nothing more was made of the controversy, but it was an unfortunate rift because very good relations had prevailed between club chairman and team manager.

Thankfully, success was just around the corner and the 1980's ushered in a great era for Éire Óg.

Notes:

Many amalgamations were formed in the sixties and seventies. Some clubs also sought assistance. These are some of the amalgamations mentioned in this section.

Inis Cealtra	Scariff/Whitegate.
St. Flannan's	Inagh/Kilnamona/Ennistymon.
St. Brendan's	Kilmaley/St. Joseph's/Our Lady's.
Eastern Gaels	Ogonnelloe/Clonlara/Meelick.
Brian Boru's	Tulla/Bodyke/Killanena.
Sarsfields	Killaloe/Broadford.
Dalcassians	Tulla/Clooney/O'Callaghan's Mills.
Donnachadha Rua's	Cratloe/Shannon.
***Graney Rovers**	Killanena/Scariff.

*Very short-lived combination obviously formed after the break-up of Inis Cealtra.

Some clubs also sought assistance in the mid-seventies; Sixmilebridge had assistance from Shannon and Clonlara, while Crusheen with Clooney assistance played under the name of **Crusheen Fenians**.

The **Éire Óg** team that played in the 1973 Clare Cup Final, losing to Newmarket 3-5 to 1-5, lined out as follows: -

Tom Glynn

Ollie O'Regan Vincent Loftus Michael Griffin *(Parnell St.)*

Jim Cullinan John McAllister Massey Dilger

Pat Kirby Tony Kelly

Paddy Neylon John Dunne Michael Hanrahan

Paddy Flynn Joe Barry Paddy Kelly

Subs used: Tommie Ryan, Georgie Dilger, Michael Skelly.

Brian Boru's – Winning County Championship Team 1975

Pat Kirby
(Bodyke)

Colm Wiley *(Bodyke)* | Jim Power *(Tulla)* | Denis Sammon *(Killanena)*

Joe Sammon *(Killanena)* | Pat Danaher *(Tulla)* | Seán O'Halloran *(Bodyke)*

Kevin Kennedy *(Killanena) (0-2)* | Frankie McNamara *(Bodyke)*

Joe Brady *(Killanena) (2-2)* | Jimmy Walsh *(Bodyke)* | Jim Rochford *(Bodyke)*

Michael McGrath *(Bodyke)* | Anthony Conlon *(Tulla) (1-0)* | Michael McNamara *(Tulla) (1-3)*

Subs: Paddy Brody, John Kirby, Monty Murphy - Used

Other Subs: Pat Tuohy, John O'Riordan, John Hunt, Michael Dinan.

Éire Óg – 1975 County Finalists

Tom Glynn

Ollie O'Regan | Enda Murphy | Seán O'Driscoll

Vinny Daly | Joe Barry | Declan Coote

Tony Kelly (0-4) | Michael Skelly (0-1)

Brendan Gilligan (1-0) | John McAllister (0-1) | Michael Carmody

Paddy Flynn | Noel Ryan (1-1) | Massey Dilger (0-2)

Subs: Dan Fitzgerald, Paddy Kelly

Other Subs: Martin Nugent, Pat Kirby, Michael Griffin, *(Parnell St.),* John Coughlan.

1979 Senior Championship

From the Éire Óg panel of 24 present at Tulla the 'Rebels' lined out as follows:

John Quinn

Tony Roche | Paddy Kelly | Michael Barry

Frannie Heaslip | Noel Ryan | John Glynn

Declan Coote | Tony Nugent

Martin Nugent | Seán Heaslip | Colm Mahon

Michael Skelly | Joe Barry | Michael Carmody

Subs used: Gerard O'Loughlin, Michael Griffin, *(Parnell St.),* Pat Hayes.

1980 – 2002

1980s

The decade began in style for Éire Óg; the controversies that had dogged the club faded away and, with the introduction of new blood, things began to go right.

Nothing brightens up a town as much as its senior team taking part in a County Final. In that era (1980 – 1985) the club contested four county finals, winning two. The excitement surrounding these games was palpable. On County Final day thousands of Ennis natives would flock to Cusack Park and the sense of excitement and solidarity amongst supporters was tremendous. For weeks beforehand the words Éire Óg would be on everyone's lips and homes and cars would be decked out in red and white flags and bunting. Not alone were these games great sporting spectacles but they provided townspeople with a sense of belonging.

All of these games, played against the Blues (1980), Kilmaley (1985) and the four with Sixmilebridge (two drawn finals) were of the highest quality. The replayed finals with Sixmilebridge in 1982 and 1983 were played over the October bank holiday weekend. Such was the quality and pulling power of the Éire Óg team that nobody would dream of missing a final and I can remember returning home early from the Cork Jazz Festivals to support Éire Óg.

St. Brendan's

The St. Brendan's team was formed in February 1978 at a meeting held in Our Lady's Hospital. The meeting was attended by Gerry Pyne and Martin Meehan, (Kilmaley), Paddy Ryan and Jim Costello, (Our Lady's), and Francis McNamara and Michael Carmody, (St. Joseph's). It was agreed three clubs should pool their resources and enter a team in the senior championship. The clubs that came together under the name of St. Brendan's were Kilmaley, St. Joseph's and Our Lady's Hospital. After a good run in 1978 they reached the quarter-final where they were eliminated by Éire Óg Dals in a replay. In 1979 St. Brendan's fared better, reaching the County Final. Though losing heavily to an in-form

Our Lady's Hospital team 1979. Back row, left to right: *Gerry Kelly (Mentor), Michael 'Milo' Keane, Gerry Heagney, Frank Moroney, John Joe Burns, Pat O'Driscoll, Michael O'Regan, Martin Fitzpatrick, John Queally, Kevin Barry.* ***Front row:*** *John Hogan, Frank Gavin, Tom McNamara, Declan Cummins, Bernie Gavin, James Costello, Andrew Callinan, John Ryan.*

Courtesy of James Costello.

Sixmilebridge selection, St. Brendan's featuring quality players in Martin Darcy, Gerry Pyne, Joe Griffey, Michael and Gerard McNamara, bounced back in 1980 to reach the semi-final.

One of their leading hurlers, P. J. Purcell feels they were unfortunate to lose to Éire Óg Dals in 1980. P. J. recalled to me, *"we were unlucky against Éire Óg in the semi-final. We were two points down with a couple of minutes to go. A ball came over to my corner and about six players fought for it. I took off for the far corner hoping someone would flick it over. And sure enough a spinning ball came over with just Durack to beat. I put my hand out, but it spun away from me. Had I got clean possession, we probably would have won it. I've been reminded about it a lot since."* Éire Óg Dals just did enough to hold out by 3-9 to 2-10. [In the other section Newmarket had wins over Sixmilebridge and Feakle before accounting for the 'Bridge again (2-9 to 1-10) to qualify for the County Final.]

Writing in his Clare Champion column, Seamus Hayes had this to say, *"In fairness St. Brendan's have reason to be disappointed as this was a game they could have won. One or two of their side played below form and it was most surprising that they didn't introduce a substitute during the hour. Over the hour Éire Óg were marginally the better side. Their attack looked that bit more dangerous in the second half when they notched 3-4. The difference between the sides was that the winners made some vital positional switches during the course of the game. The most notable of these was the move that brought Barry Smythe from centre-back to mid-field at the start of the second half. Here Smythe teamed up with Tony Nugent who had moved from the attack and they gave Éire Óg a vital pull here in the third quarter of the game.*

Seamus Durack again had a good game between the posts and his puck outs, particularly in the second half, proved invaluable. Colm Mahon, until injured, had a great game at wingback and he got good support from Declan Coote and Paddy Kelly. Up front, Noel Ryan and Michael Carmody always worried the losers' defence with Seán Heaslip and Seán Lynch also doing well. Once again Tommy Keane played his heart out for St. Brendan's. Paddy Hill, Noel McGuane and Con Haugh were also prominent in defence. Martin Meehan was good at mid-field while up front P. J. Purcell and Bernie Gavin were most dangerous."

Re-opening of Cusack Park

At a cost of £350,000 Cusack Park was re-opened on June 29th, 1980 when an impressive Clare display saw the home side defeat Galway by 2-15 to 0-13 in an entertaining game. Though the standard of hurling was good, the hurling lacked the competitive bite of championship. In the curtain raiser the Mayo footballers defeated Clare by 2-9 to 0-8.

The 1980 County Final between Éire Óg and the Blues was the first one staged at Cusack Park since Newmarket defeated Sixmilebridge in 1976.

Brendan Vaughan and others put their heart and soul into the re-development of the park. Through their hard work they ensured that we have a County Ground to be proud of. On St. Patrick's Day 1981, Central Council Representative, Tom Downes, was successful in having the Railway Cup Hurling Final staged at the park. With Ger Loughnane, Sean Hehir and John Callinan on duty, Munster defeated Leinster by 2-16 to 2-6.

Flynn and Nugent Honoured

Colum Flynn received long overdue recognition winning the Clare Champion Sports Star of the Year Award for 1980. Long associated with Clare hurling teams going back to 1966, Colum is also a former National boxing champion, he put many boxers through their paces, most notably greats like Michael Queally and Ollie Markham. Colum picked up the 1980 award for his excellent work with the Éire Óg senior hurlers and guiding them to win their first county title since 1966. Speaking at the presentation of the awards, Fr. Harry Bohan spoke highly of Colum's contribution to sport. "Since early last year Colum believed that Éire Óg had a team capable of winning the county title. The level of fitness which the team showed is evidence of his great ability and I could go as far as to say he is the best trainer in Ireland." Fr. Bohan went on to pay tribute to Colum's wife, Kay, for her assistance over the years.

Martin Nugent was honoured with the September award following his spectacular display in the County Final. Nugent, in a long and illustrious career in the Éire Óg colours gave one of his best ever displays in a great career scoring 3-3 from play.

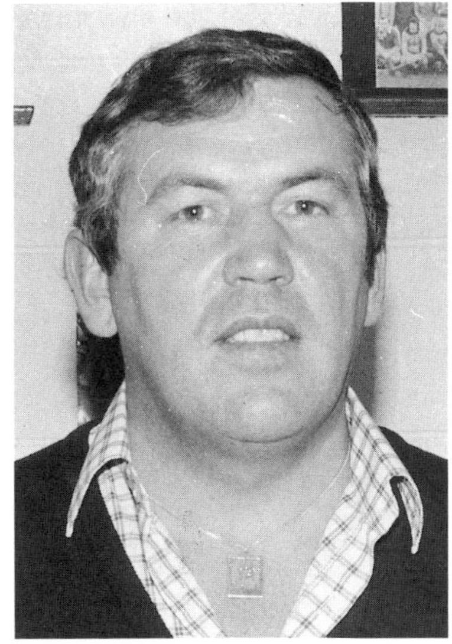

Colum Flynn has given a lifetime of service to the promotion of sport.

Town Leagues 1980 – 1984

It was no mere coincidence that the revival of the Town Leagues helped usher in one of the most successful era's in the story of Ennis hurling. The leagues, organised by Éire Óg and Banner clubs in March 1980, were thrown open to all hurlers in Ennis. The old traditional areas of Turnpike, Cloughleigh (Old Mill Street), Market areas (the Town), and Boreen were all represented. Newer areas such as Hermitage, St. Michael's Villas also entered teams. The Boreen team, now known as Lifford, included Marian Avenue, Corrovorrin and the New Road. The old Boreen disappeared around 1954 when the last remaining dwellings were demolished and in their stead a new housing estate, Marian Avenue, was erected. The contractors were Solon and Garvey, and a total of 64 houses were built at a cost of £96,000.

At least 120 hurlers took part in the league of 1980. Some of those who spring to mind include Brian Toomey, Tommy Coughlan, Brian Casey, Michael Fawl, Frank Garry, Simon Moroney, Philip Markham, Tony Coote, Pat Treacy, Harry Crowe, Flan Morrissey and Tony Quinn.

In the opening rounds the Town defeated Lifford by 4-10 to 2-6 while Cloughleigh shaded the issue by 3-8 to 3-5 over the Turnpike in a replay. The Town later defeated Lifford by 3-8 to 4-3. Cloughleigh, who were inspired by a host of prominent players in T. J. Scanlan, Seán Lynch and Francie Mahon easily accounted for the Town in a lack-lustre final, played before a crowd of 600.

The 'Pike Upset the Favourites

The 1984 Town League final drew an enormous crowd. Played on an immaculate pitch, the Turnpike and the Town/St. Michael's combination produced excellent fare in ideal playing conditions. Prior to referee, Jimmy McNamara, setting the game in motion, the pupils of the Boys National School Band led the teams around in a pre-match parade.

After early scores by Pat Lynch and Seán Heaslip, for the Town/St. Michael's, the 'Pike settled down. The switch of Joe Barry and Mike Skelly to centre-field and wing-forward respectively and the move of Tom Russell on to Pat Lynch helped matters greatly for the 'Pike who trailed by just two points at the change of ends. An amount of good ball from Skelly helped set up goals for Matthew Lernihan and Jim Costelloe (2) to put the 'Pike into a commanding position mid-way through the second half. In the end, St. Michael's were well beaten by 5-5 to 2-8. Best for Turnpike were John and Tom Russell, the Barrys, Tommy Pilkington and Pat Brennan. For a disappointing Town/St. Michael's, Tomás English, Brian O'Connell, Michael Griffin, Joe Hahessy and Johnny Guerin tried hardest.

The leagues of 1980/'84 were hugely successful as they exposed the enormous talent that existed in Ennis. Sponsored by Paddy Kelly, Tony Honan and others, players like Dermot Delaney, Johnny Kearse, Peadar Derrane and many others came to the attention of the senior selectors.

A Town/St. Michaels combination c. 1983 during the Ennis Town League. Back row, left to right: *Ml. Griffin, Brian O'Connell, Francis Heaslip, Dermot Delaney, Michael Dinan, Pat Lynch, Joe Hahessy, Peter Quinn, Pat Daly.* ***Front row:*** *Tomás English, Seán Heaslip, John Glynn, Johnny Guerin, John Quinn, Johnny Corbett, Eoin McMahon.*

Michael Lynch making a presentation to Joe Barry. Courtesy of Clare Champion.

The Éire Óg Bulletin

In March 1980, when the structures of the club were re-organised, Michael Brennan suggested putting together a monthly type magazine. A small group of people, including Ollie O'Regan, Gerry Slevin and Pat Brennan were the chief movers behind this innovative publication. The Bulletin was well received from the local enthusiast to the County Board, projecting Éire Óg in a proper light. Featuring match reports, news items, stars and photos of the past, player profiles, social outings and female personalities, the back page, which was compiled by 'Observer' was reserved for fair criticism with naturally a right of reply.

Initially only four pages, the Bulletin was expanded into a fine magazine, winning three McNamee awards, the first in May 1981, as the best club publication in Ireland.

A snippet taken from the *Irish Independent* in October 1980 read, "Very praiseworthy, indeed, is the Bulletin produced monthly by Éire Óg, Ennis. Selling at 20 pence and packed with useful bits of information, it boasts a sale of 400 copies, which – and not surprisingly in view of the sparkling content – topped the 1,200 sale mark for the recent County Final."

The Éire Óg Bulletin was sold throughout the town and ran regularly until the summer of 1984 and occasionally thereafter, when it sadly began to disappear.

Jack Heaslip making a presentation of jerseys to Declan Coote, winning captain 1980. Courtesy of Clare Champion.

1980 County Final

Newmarket entering their 31st senior final were installed as slight favourites to take the championship. *"Experienced Blues to shade it"* was the Champion headline. Paddy McNamara, the most experienced member of the Blues, played down the favourites tag when he spoke to Seamus Hayes. *"We have always had hard games with Éire Óg in which there was little between the sides. Some people are making us hot favourites but we know that it will be a tough contest."* McNamara sportingly added, *"if we are beaten then I will be happy that it will be Éire Óg, but we are going all out to take the title."* Gus Lohan added, *"we would love to have another crack at the Munster Club title as Clare champions. Furthermore, we're planning a trip to the United States and we'd love to go over as County champions."*

However, 1980 was not to be Newmarket's year. Éire Óg emerged deserved winners in the County Final, prompting the following headline in the club bulletin:

"Success is Ours – Silken Skills Blossom Forth in Glorious County Final – Martin Nugent Aspires to New Heights as he becomes Newmarket's Chief Executioner."

Éire Óg 3-10 . . . Newmarket 1-9

From the Pages of the Bulletin

"'I want 13 points from you – Remember what Blackrock did to us with points. Get out there now and win' – so said coach Bro. Cahill sending his fighting fit warriors down the tunnel and out to a tremendous reception from the crowd on Sunday, September 28, 1980 – a day that will for long be cherished and remembered by all who have the interest and love of Éire Óg at heart.

Bounding onto the field like hungry young lions ready to devour all in sight, our side's entrance was reminiscent of the great Down footballers of the early 1960s.

Newmarket made their entrance some 6 minutes later and both Captains, Declan Coote and Pat O'Leary were introduced to Clare President of the Association, Vincent Murphy. Red and White Banners seemed to take over behind the town goal as both sides lined up behind Ennis Brass Band in glorious sunshine before a huge attendance to set the parade in motion.

With the preliminaries out of the way, referee, John Nihill, Sixmile-bridge, threw in the ball to start the game in motion. Éire Óg were first to attack but John McMahon relieved and sent the ball up field. Pete Barry with the coolness of a veteran opened the scoring after two minutes with a point. Con Woods levelled soon after from a '65'.

Newmarket were playing the better hurling now and Paddy McNamara eluded Tony Roche after ten minutes to point after a brilliant save from Seamus Durack. Paddy Mac at this stage was looking very

1980 County Final. *Seán Heaslip with Pete Barry in support chased by Seanie McMahon and D.J. Meehan.* Courtesy of Clare Champion.

sharp and when after twelve minutes he rounded a cluster of backs and hit a shot which deceived 'the Duke' and ended up in the back of the net many people in the Park had visions of an easy win for the Blues. Sean Liddy added another point from a free but it was here that our backroom boys made the switch of the match when they exchanged Colm Mahon and Declan Coote. Coote was playing well but Jimmy McNamara was even better and controlled the area.

Colm Mahon's advent to midfield was a master stroke. Colm was also a big help to Tony Nugent and they combined to give a masterful display that has never been bettered by any Ennis pairing.

Seán Heaslip and Seán Liddy exchanged points to leave the score at 1-4 to 0-2 after 17 minutes. Our lads had more of the play now with the half backs and midfield playing well. Noel Ryan rounded his namesake for John Twoomey to bring off a fine save only for Martin Nugent to slap the rebound to the back of the net. Nugent was now seeing more of the ball and he was in sparkling form, "owning" his corner, his point in the 23rd minute was a beauty from out on the touchline. Seán Lynch evaded despairing tackles a minute later for another minor.

The Blues, finding the going rough, brought on Timmy Ryan at midfield, moved Con Woods to wing back with John McMahon going to the corner in a bid to curb Martin Nugent.

John McMahon had little time to get accustomed to his new surrounds when Martin Nugent had slipped behind him to goal again after a magnificent free from Seamus Durack taken just outside his own 30 yard line. Éire Óg were back in front and there to stay.

Adjectives couldn't describe the hurling at this stage – champagne stuff – free flowing up and down – heroics on both sides, no fouling, no stoppages of any kind.

Half time was reached and we couldn't believe the game was on for a half-hour, it went so fast. The score – Éire Óg 2-4 Newmarket 1-5.

At the interval we were entertained by the Boys' National School Band and as they marched and played we could see why they were recently crowned the top marching band in their class in Munster.

Éire Óg resumed with Pat Lynch substituting for Michael Skelly and was quick into his stride. After 30 seconds Seán Heaslip sent over a glorious point. Con Woods reduced our lead with a point and Timmy Ryan found 'the Duke' equal to the occasion when he tried a drop shot after seven minutes. Pat Lynch rounded his man and soloed up the wing, he passed to Martin Nugent and he sidestepping his man tapped over a beautiful point. Pat O'Leary and Noel Ryan exchanged points.

Éire Óg were now well on top and hurled with rare abandon but scores were still very hard to come by. Noel Ryan moved to corner

1980 Éire Óg Bench - *includes Michael Hanrahan, Bro. Cahill, Vinnie Daly, Dermot Delaney, John Glynn, Tom Russell, Ollie O'Regan (John Quinn and Frannie Heaslip partly hidden). It was a reaction to Martin Nugent's last goal.*
Courtesy of Liam McGrath, Clare Champion.

forward in an exchange with Sean Lynch. Fifteen minutes into the second half John Twoomey found himself bottled up after saving and the ball came to Martin Nugent, who promptly netted his hat trick.

Seven points up with 14 minutes to go there was no way we were going to be caught. Declan Coote pointed a free and Newmarket dug deep into their vast reservoir of experience and know how in an effort to combat defeat.

Jimmy McNamara and Timmy Ryan pointed cutting the lead to two goals. D. J. Meehan was injured, which resulted in Gus Lohan going to wingback and Martin Ryan coming into the forwards. Paddy McNamara roamed far and wide as if chasing his first rather than his thirteenth championship medal in an effort to motivate his colleagues.

The final score of the game fell to Éire Óg and Martin Nugent, a point, and so the long wait was at an end. With the long whistle came the release of a long flood of emotion and tears of joy from many of us who

The great Taoiseach (Jack Lynch) in full flight against Newmarket 1980. D.J. Meehan and Seán Heaslip are also pictured.

have waited and longed through the many bad years and our joy knew no bounds. We were joined in our ecstasies by young and old from all over town plus many country folk as well who willed us on to this great victory.

Essentially this was a team victory and the many long hours of training, dedication and sacrifice showed in the performance of all sixteen who played. Seamus Durack lived up to his glowing reputation and never put a foot wrong. Our full back line of Joe Barry, Paddy Kelly and Tony Roche, as I predicted last month, were equal to the occasion, after they got over the tenseness of the opening five minutes.

Half backs, Tony Kelly, Barry Smythe and Declan Coote with midfielders Tony Nugent and Colm Mahon all added to their reputations and it was here that the seed of victory was sown to be so successfully reaped in the forward line.

Martin Nugent may have been the executioner in chief but he got a plentiful supply from an in-form Seán Heaslip, Pete Barry and Pat Lynch. Seán Lynch, Noel Ryan and Michael Skelly have played better games for the club but in this game they lent their skills more to making scores for their colleagues around them.

Newmarket also had their heroes and as Andrew Curtin said at the presentation of the cup, 'It takes two teams to give an exhibition as we've seen today, and Newmarket even though staring defeat in the face never gave up hope, hurling with skill and determination to the finish never resorting to foul or mean tactics.' Players who enhanced their reputations for 'the Blues' were John Twoomey, John Ryan and John O'Leary, with Seanie McMahon starring in defence. Jimmy McNamara played well while up front Paddy McNamara and Dessie Hayes tried hardest.

To the public at large the sixteen who played on Sunday may seem the only heroes but this report would not be complete without a special commendation to the other fifteen members of the panel along with Bro. Cahill, Colum Flynn, Michael Hanrahan, and Paddy Duggan, who gave so much of their time, energy and skill over the long spring and summer months to bring us to our "Everest" and plant our pennant there. Also a

Jimmy McNamara in possession, as Tony Kelly closes in. Record County medalist Paddy McNamara is on the right - 1980 County Final. Courtesy of Ml. Arthur.

special word of praise to Christy Glynn who put in many hours banding hurleys and to Michael Brennan and Paddy O'Halloran who went out of their way arranging top class opposition, which in no small way helped the team peak for the county final. Last but definitely not least, we thank our faithful supporters who stuck with us through thick and thin and we know your continued support will be forthcoming."

After Match Comments:

Immediately after the County Final a number of interested parties and inter-county players spoke to the Bulletin reporter: -

Bro. J. F. Cahill*: "Many factors contributed to today's success. It has been a hard grind all year trying to blend together and I believe the 'Bulletin' played no small part in getting the team psyched up and the whole club together as a unit after our differences in the recent past."*

Declan Coote: *"It was a tremendous game to play in. Great credit is due to our full-back line."*

Colm Honan: (Clonlara) *"I really enjoyed the game. A good match. Éire Óg showed great commitment and fitness. They were not lacking in skill."*

Cyril Lyons: (Ruan) – *"Éire Óg's level of fitness and use of the big pitch were important factors in their win which on the day was a merited one."*

Gerry McInerney: ('Bridge) *"It was a great game to watch – tense and exciting. Éire Óg were fully deserving of their victory, being fitter and faster to the ball. Playing the open spaces was the decisive factor in their win."*

Seán Stack: ('Bridge) *"At vital stages in the game Éire Óg's full back line closed sharply on Michael Kilmartin and Company mainly due to Joe Barry's dedication to the fray. Éire Óg were faster and in no way overawed with the occasion."*

Jimmy McNamara and **Jim Woods** of Newmarket were also generous in their praise of Éire Óg. McNamara, one of Newmarket's most dangerous forwards of the era, stated, *"I thought we would win it even up to half time, but Éire Óg's fitness told in the end."* Jim Woods, the Newmarket Manager, concluded, *"People were saying it would be bad for Clare hurling if we won again but our reply was 'until a team capable of donning our mantle of success appeared on the scene we were still the best. Éire Óg could be that team if they maintain their present set up.'"* The Newmarket Manager then went to the Éire Óg dressing room where he paid tribute to the winning team.

Shortly after the County Final, Éire Óg played Ruan in the Clare Champion Cup. But they failed to repeat their champonship form.

Declan Coote raises the Canon Hamilton Cup after a memorable County Final with the Blues in 1980. Photo includes from left, Brendan Vaughan, Andrew Curtin, Declan Coote, Vincent Murphy, Des Crowe.
Courtesy of Pat Brennan, Clare Champion.

A Rude Awakening

The Bulletin reported, *"Fielding without Paddy Kelly, Noel Ryan and Seán Lynch of the Championship winning side and losing Martin Nugent after five minutes through injury we went under by a point to a hard hitting, no-nonsense Ruan side by 0-11 to 1-7, just six days after our championship success.*

Gone was the fluent open play we displayed in the County Final and our forwards proved a spendthrift lot wasting many chances throughout from play and placed balls. Ruan hit hard from the start and never let our forwards settle into any rhythm. Four points up after 10 minutes, mainly due to full forward Francie Mahon's contribution, Éire Óg seemed on course for a win but Ruan had other ideas. Picking off points from the half forward line, Donal Hassett had Ruan back in the game going in at half time with a score of 1-4 to 0-6. On the resumption Éire Óg hurled with more determination but the forwards lacked punch and finish wasting many scoreable chances. Ruan matched us point for point until five minutes to go when Cyril Lyons pointed from 50 yards out, to give the winners the lead for the first time. Try as we might Ennis could not break down the Ruan defence. Seamus Durack got little to do in goal as he received good cover from Tony Roche, Joe Barry and Dermot Delaney.

Colm Mahon and Tony Nugent played well at mid-field and Francie Mahon impressed at full forward. The other forwards never really hit it off on the day and though they made many openings their finishing was sadly lacking. It is easy to reason why there was such a drop in standard after a week of celebrations, but because of it we are now out of the Clare Champion Cup – a competition we have failed to capture since 1959."

1981 Season

Éire Óg opened their 1981 season with their usual careless approach to the Clare Cup. In a rather erratic campaign they beat 'the Mills' and Crusheen while they were hammered by Tubber and Feakle. Without doubt their best display in the Clare Cup was reserved for old rivals, the Blues. With Coote in devastating form at centre-back, Éire Óg triumphed by 2-9 to 0-7. In the County Grounds Tournament the town team annihilated St. Joseph's, 7-11 to 1-8 with Noel Ryan, Francie Mahon and Michael Barry in scoring form. A feature of these games were the performances of relative newcomers like Johnny Kearse, Michael Chandler, Michael Kenny and the free-scoring Francie Mahon, who proved himself a full-forward of note.

Pat Daly presents Joe Barry with the Man of the Match Award for one of the Town League Finals during the early 1980s, while Ml. Brennan and Des Neylon look on.

In the senior championship, Éire Óg accounted for Feakle (3-12 to 3-7) before overcoming the challenge of O'Callaghan's Mills in the quarter-final. In the lead up to their semi-final clash with Newmarket, Éire Óg didn't take anything for granted and had a fine workout with Castlegar in a friendly. Playing sparkling hurling, Éire Óg easily accounted for the Galway side by 5-14 to 2-6. In the quarter final of the County Championship, Newmarket struggled to beat a gallant Banner side. Watching this display, it is possible Éire Óg were lulled into a false sense of security and were looking at a County Final meeting with Tubber in September. Tubber and Sixmilebridge played a fabulous semi-final with the North Claremen shading the issue by 3-9 to 1-14.

Saturday Night Blues

The fast, open-wing play of the Castlegar challenge was quickly forgotten, as Éire Óg played right into the hands of a much-improved Newmarket team. Winning the throw in, Newmarket delivered a killer blow when Paddy MacNamara whipped a vicious incoming ball to the net after just five seconds. The rapid goal, instead of galvanising Éire Óg into the polished play they are capable of, but the town side fumbled their way through 60 minutes play giving their poorest championship display of the era. The team came in for scathing but fair criticism in the Bulletin. *"Hurling way below form, the Éire Óg senior hurlers surrendered their championship crown with their semi-final defeat by a moderate Newmarket side on Saturday evening. The question on many people's lips after the game was what happened to the flowing wing play that had been the main feature of the Éire Óg side? Bad and all as the team was playing it is hard to fathom why the mentors did not get involved and encourage the side to open up the play."*

The Bulletin scribe goes on to say, *"The feature of this was that in the final seven minutes we got eight scoreable frees within range, which were all lobbed into a crowded square in search of goals. Maybe when the bitter disappointment wears off the 'peacock attitude' of some of the players will go with it and we can again settle down to preparing for another tilt at the title next season. Colm Mahon tried exceptionally hard, scoring two fine points. Tony Kelly steadied up considerably after the interval and showed some nice touches. Pete Barry had a fine opening 20 minutes when the ball was played out the wings but thereafter faded with the closing up of the game. Martin Nugent was the only other player worthy of mention as he tried hard throughout but constant switching didn't give him much chance to settle down."*

Outstanding for the winners were John Ryan at fullback, getting great support from Gus Lohan. Johnny McMahon and Seanie McMahon dominated in defence while Dessie Hayes, Seán Liddy and Julian Crimmins contributed to the attack.

Éire Óg never regained the sharpness and commitment displayed in the 1980 season. All year the side struggled and it is surprising that at an early stage the selectors did not introduce younger players like Philip Markham, Tom Russell, John Glynn or Seán Cleary.

Breakthrough for Sixmilebridge

Hurling has been part of life in Sixmilebridge for over 100 years. They fielded parish teams in the early part of the 20th century but without much success. By the early 1930s, the 'Bridge were playing in the worst grade of junior. Ballycar beat them cricket score in 1936. In 1939 they won the Intermediate 'B'. In 1952 Sixmilebridge reached their first senior final, losing to Scariff. After the 1952 defeat, Jimmy Corry, former Club Secretary and Chairman, felt they were very close to a breakthrough. It took 25 years. *"Corry believes the 1962 team was as good a team as ever represented the parish. In the semi-final of '53, Scariff again beat us. In 1955 and '56 the 'Bridge went out at the quarter-final stage to Newmarket and Clarecastle respectively. In 1957 we lost at the semi-final stage to a classy Éire Óg. In 1961 and '62, we suffered at the hands of a powerful Ruan team. We drew the final of 1962 but lost the replay. We had the Barrons, Jimmy Mulready, Tommy Gorman. Paddy Quinn was a great clubman and a great 'Bridge supporter. Jimmy Mulready was so anxious to win a senior championship he brought Jimmy Carney to the club in 1956. Carney played with us for a couple of years before emigrating. About 1968 it was decided to set up a minor club and this decision proved very fruitful."*

After 1962 the club seniors declined for a number of years before reaching the semi-final in 1967 when they lost to Clarecastle. In 1969 with Cratloe assistance, they were beaten in the latter stages by the Blues. After many near misses, Sixmilebridge won their first senior championship in 1977, beating Kilkishen, 1-6 to 1-5, with Michael White scoring the winning point. From there the club reached the Munster Club Final with players of the calibre of Tommy and Pat Morey, Seán Stack, Leo Quinlan. They lost the provincial final replay to St. Finbarr's. Two years later the 'Bridge regained the senior club championship at the expense of St. Brendan's. In 1982, they were back in the final to face Éire Óg. The 1982 Championship was played on a league system of two sections with 7 teams. Sixmilebridge's only defeat was to Feakle when they lost on a score of 2-14 to 0-11. Éire Óg got off to a great start but then went through an indifferent patch losing two games before regaining their true form.

Éire Óg's path to County Final

	Éire Óg	2-15	...	Kilmaley	1-6
	Tubber	1-14	...	Éire Óg	2-9
	Ruan	3-8	...	Éire Óg	1-7
	Éire Óg	0-15	...	Clarecastle	1-9
	Éire Óg	1-14	...	Tulla	0-3
	Éire Óg	2-13	...	O'Callaghan's Mills	1-3
Semi-final	Éire Óg	1-13	...	Feakle	1-6

County Finals – 1982/1983

The drawn and replayed finals of 1982 and 1983 between Éire Óg and Sixmilebridge are amongst the best in modern times. The drawn final of 1982 produced some great scores. Noel Ryan's opening goal for Éire Óg, some good points from John Lynch of Sixmilebridge and Éire Óg's Seán and Pat Lynch, were amongst the highlights of the first half. The second period saw some fine hurling with both sides enjoying dominant spells before Pat Lynch's superb goal brought the crowd to its feet. Lynch gained possession on the wing and weaved his way past a couple of tackles before cutting inside on a 40-yard solo run through the middle, opening up the defence and sending a pile driver to the corner of the net. It looked like Éire Óg's day but a late goal from Peter Golden and a pointed free by Flan Quilligan gave Sixmilebridge a deserved draw. Pat Lynch was presented with the Man of the Match Award.

Late Rally saves Defiant 'Bridge

John Brennan of the *Irish Press* of the 30th August 1982 wrote the following: -

"Both teams squandered chances of victory in yesterday's very skilful and exciting Clare Senior Final in Cusack Park, Ennis. That must be the only real assessment of a game, which showed Clare club hurling at its best.

When the heat and tension of battle have died away, the teams will be aware that they each should, this morning, be admiring the county trophy.

Sixmilebridge came out for the second half with the scores level and a near gale in their favour. In the second half they met a resilient Éire Óg side who defied the elements to turn on some splendid hurling and lead by five points with just nine minutes remaining. Then with their followers already savouring success, the 'Bridge inspired by a rampant Gerry McInerney, got a goal and two points to send the game to a replay.

Most of the excitement and all the good hurling came in the second half. Sixmilebridge raced into a two-point lead with points from Danny

Chaplin and their hero of the first half, Pat Morey. Instead of building on that lead, Sixmilebridge were rocked by a wonderful Éire Óg comeback."

The replay took place in a downpour on 26th September, and Sixmilebridge raced into a 2-4 to nil lead before a late first half goal from Seán Lynch signalled an Éire Óg revival. Éire Óg came out for the second half a transformed side and, playing superb ground hurling, wore down Sixmilebridge. A Pat Lynch goal, almost a replica of the one in the drawn game, put paid to the 'Bridge on a score of 3-8 to 2-9. After the match, Pete Barry received the Man of the Match Award and Tony Nugent was presented with the Hamilton Cup, evoking memories for the more senior followers, who recollected his father, Matt, lifting the same cup in 1958 as a member of the great St. Joseph's team.

"Éire Óg's second half fire foils 'Bridge ambition, but hurling wins in thriller" wrote Gerry Slevin in the *Clare Champion. "The tonic of a goal just before the interval has often proved to be a cushion of inestimable worth in a side's quest for honours. It was a great moment that brought a ten point deficit down to more manageable proportions with the knowledge of wind assistance to come. Conversely, for Sixmilebridge it was a disaster moment because a shot which their splendid 'keeper seemed to have covered eased out of his reach and into the net, deflected on its way by one of his defenders. Pat Collins saved well from Martin Nugent but the ball came back in again and Seanie Lynch pulled strongly. Collins seemed to have it under control but the ball deflected off Jim Corbett's stick and into the net."*

Éire Óg began the game with Micheál Glynn at corner back. Tony Nugent was at centre-back. Seán Heaslip joined Declan Coote at centre-field. Kevin Kennedy started on the '40 with Michael Chandler losing out.

In the Munster Club Championship Éire Óg drew Ballyduff who defeated Dunhill in the Waterford final. A feature of this lively contest was that both clubs lined out in their county colours. After getting off to a good start, Éire Óg went to sleep and allowed their Waterford opponents back into the game in the second quarter, scoring 1-4 to go in front. Éire Óg responded well in the second half but curiously in a controversial decision the selectors replaced Michael Chandler in the 50th minute. Chandler was having a fine game on Mossy Walsh. In the end Ballyduff just about deserved to hold out by 3-8 to 1-13 in a heated final quarter.

Sportsmanship the Winner

As in 1982, the 1983 County Final ended in a draw between Éire Óg and Sixmilebridge. Trailing by 1-4 to 2 points at the half-way stage, the Ennismen battled their way back with a gutsy second half display. Goals by Noel Ryan and Martin Nugent kept Éire Óg in the game, 1-10 to 2-4

Tony Nugent captain of the winning Éire Óg team of 1982.
Courtesy of Liam McGrath, Clare Champion.

with the moments ticking away, Éire Óg were awarded a 21 yard free, which Tony Nugent dispatched to the net to leave the sides level, 3-4 to 1-10 after another stirring contest.

Controversy raged over the fixture for the replay as some 'Bridge players had arranged holidays and at least one or two were due to go on honeymoon, so the club refused to play before 6 November. *"Éire Óg to be awarded the Championship"*, headlined the *Clare Champion*. The County Board awarded the Cup to Éire Óg, but their Chairman, Michael Brennan, announced that Éire Óg would not accept the Hamilton Cup in this way. The championship was declared null and void.

However, sanity prevailed and the game went ahead on the Bank Holiday Monday, 31 October, with a sharper 'Bridge side winning the title by 1-10 to 1-7 in a sporting tie. Noel O'Gorman was awarded Man of the Match. Seán Stack says he got tremendous satisfaction from the defeat of Éire Óg, but the sporting attitude displayed by Éire Óg was praised by Christy Sheehan, the 'Bridge Chairman, who thanked Éire Óg for not accepting a walkover and playing their part in having the matter resolved. Gerry McInerney added that *"while 1983 will long be remembered in the 'Bridge as the year the senior team captured its third county title, it will never slip the mind of the sporting stance adopted by Éire Óg when the replay crux arose. When Éire Óg were awarded the title by default, they left no doubt in the minds of the hurling fraternity that regardless of the eventual outcome – sportsmanship was the winner."*

Sixmilebridge retained the Centenary title in 1984 by beating a gallant Clarecastle, 3-7 to 1-12, before going on to capture their first ever Munster Club title.

ÉIRE ÓG PEN PICTURES – 1980/'82

Compiled by a member of this team

Joe Barry: Colleges star with St. Flannan's. Holder of 3 minor, 2 senior and 1 u/21 championship. A member of a well-known sporting family. His brothers, Seán, Michael, Pete and Gerry, all played hurling for Éire Óg. Joe who began his playing career with Rovers in 1961 was a very loyal player whose love for the game was matched by few. He could play in any position and his high fielding of the ball was a feature of his play. Tough and rugged, his positional play was another strength. Favourite position centre-back.

Pete Barry: An all-round sportsman. Played hurling and Gaelic Football with Clare and Rugby with Ennis RFC. Harty Cup and All-Ireland Colleges medals with St. Flannan's in 1979 and Oireachtas medal with Clare. A very skilful under-age hurler who could play in any position. Eventually developed into an outstanding full-forward. Scored countless important goals for the town team. He managed Éire Óg to reach the County Final in 2000.

Michael Carmody: An excellent 'poacher' in the forward line and a very determined player who was always in the thick of it. Fleet footed and cheeky, he was always good for a goal. A link with the team of 1975, Michael has dedicated a lot of time to under-age hurling at the CBS Primary School, where he teaches.

Michael Chandler: A very successful under age captain with the club who developed into a wholehearted centre-fielder. Holder of two senior, 1 minor, 1 U/16. Not many could match 'Chief' in the 50/50 pull.

Declan Coote: Highly dedicated, confident and loyal hurler who led by example on the field. An elusive stylish attacking wing back who was astonishingly accurate from placed-balls. Could play centre-field and indeed finished his career very successfully in the forwards. A brilliant Harty Cup player. He played inter-county from 1981 – 1988.

Vinny Daly: A player of note with St. Flannan's whose career took him away from Ennis and so had less of an influence than he might. A tenacious wing back and a member of the 1975 team. Vinny captained UCG's successful Fitzgibbon Cup team of 1980. Favourite position wing-back.

Dermot Delaney: Strong full back player. Senior medallist in 1980. Didn't feature as much as he should have. A needless injury curtailed his hurling. Dermot represented the Banner Club in 1981.

Seamus Durack: First choice Munster Railway Cup goalkeeper for seven seasons 1973 – 1979 inclusive, equalling the record set by Tony Reddin of Tipperary (1950 – 1956). His transfer from Feakle was significant in giving confidence to the team in many ways. A dedicated motivated hurler whose shot-stopping was second to none, clearances immense and puck outs of the highest order. Could have played outfield if required. 2 National League, 2 Oireachtas and 2 All-Star Awards.

Donie Fitzpatrick: Stylish wing back with loads of hurling. Very prominent underage and Harty Cup level with CBS.

Louis Galvin: Very prominent dual player at under-age level. Won minor football medal in 1979. Played in the early rounds of the 1980 season. Favourite position centre-field. Member of the 1980 and '82 winning squads. Louis represented Clare at minor level in hurling.

John Glynn: Regular corner/back or wing for a number of years. Played at all levels for the club; was extremely competitive and sticky. Gave a lot of dedication to Éire Óg.

Micheál Glynn: A rangy defender was at his best coming forward. Won Kinnane and Corn Phadraig with CBS. Played for UCD in Fitzgibbon Cup – represented Clare at senior level for a number of years. Vital defender in the '86 championship. A member of a great sporting family. Micheál captained the winning team in 1990.

Pat Hayes: Very prominent at under age, Pat played senior championship for the club in 1979.

Francis Heaslip: Underrate him at your peril, Frannie had deceptive speed and a great engine. Intelligent and economical hurler who could always find a team-mate with a pass. Retired at a young age and is still remembered for his outstanding display in the 1982 County Final with Sixmilebridge.

Seán Heaslip: Came to prominence with the CBS nursery. A dual player for Clare at both senior hurling and football. A member of the CBS Leaving Cert. Class of 1973/74, Seán was unavailable for the Harty Cup team of that year. Had Heaslip been reinstated by the County Board, I have no doubt CBS would have contested the Harty Cup Final. Tall and speedy, great attitude, often first to the ball, always endeavoured to mark the centre-back tightly to keep him quiet. Gave great service to the club over a 20-year spell. Had a great season with the Clare hurlers in 1980/81. Winner of 3 senior medals.

Michael Kenny: Corn Phadraig medallist with CBS. Won honours at most levels at underage including Minor (A) football medal in 1979. Michael always played the game as it should be played. He was a big loss to the club when he emigrated to the United States.

Tony Kelly: Dr. Rodgers Cup medal winner with CBS. Represented Clare and Dublin at inter-county level. Much travelled player (and holder of three inter-county intermediate medals with Dublin) who graced the half-back line in the latter stages of his career. Has become a coach of much repute since.

Paddy Kelly: Tough, stylish hurler who could mix it if needed. Represented CBS and Vocational School and came up through the Éire Óg ranks with the successful under-age teams. Easy going, friendly off the field but not many of the opposition volunteered for full-forward duty when confronting Pat. He gave great service to the club from 1973 to 1985.

Kevin Kennedy: A great hurling man, Kevin possesses a deep love of the ancient game. He gave great service to CBS. A member of the Harty Cup teams of 1970, 71, 72. His career with the Gardaí took him to different parishes. Kevin holds a myriad list of medals with Killanena, Brian Borus and Éire Óg. Holder of 2 senior medals 1975, 1982. He also represented

Pat Lynch receives the Man of the Match award after a glorious display in the 1982 drawn County Final. Pa accepts the trophy from Roger Knightson and Matt O'Connor as Brendan Vaughan says a few words.

the combination Graney Rovers. Kevin managed the Clare Minors to All-Ireland success in 1997.

Johnny Kearse: Solid, hard pulling defender. As good as what was around. Shone in Town Leagues and Clare Cup. Deserved more runs.

Seán Lynch: Tremendous Colleges player with Ennis CBS. Represented Clare at minor, U/21 and senior. A tenacious carrier of the ball who was blessed with blistering pace. "Taoiseach" was always good for at least a couple of scores per match.

Pat Lynch: As swift as they come, the will o' the wisp of this team. Unstoppable in full flight, Pa scored many memorable goals for the Reds. Represented the Clare senior team from 1984-86. Injury cost him his place in the Munster Final of 1986.

Colm (Mc)Mahon: Colm was without doubt the most improved player over the years and not by accident. Training long and hard, developing all the skills, his love for the fray and the game drove him to success. A fearless hurler and a running back who could always manage a few scores. A role model for any under-age hurler who wishes to make it, Colm holds 3 senior medals.

Martin Nugent: One of three brothers to play senior hurling for Éire Óg. Martin made his senior debut at a very young age when he played in goal in the 1975 semi-final against St. Flannan's amalgamation. A very fit, stylish dedicated hurler who could out-fox opponents with delicate footwork and speed. Had an unbelievable county final in 1980 scoring at will. Martin holds 3 senior medals. A versatile sportsman. Selector with the 2001 Éire Óg team.

Tony Nugent: A strong, gifted, energetic hurler whose youthful enthusiasm was always to the fore. Didn't know the meaning of defeat. Tony made his senior inter-county championship debut when he partnered Declan Coote at centre-field in 1981. A regular on the county team until 1985 when he emigrated to the United States.

Brian O'Connell: Member of the successful Clare Minor Hurling team of 1981 (Munster Championship). Brian played at corner back though his favourite position was full back. Later played a goal-keeping role with the Faughs in senior football, served as Chairman of the Club c.1998-2002.

Jarlath O'Halloran: Star forward with Rice College, Corn Pádraig winning team of 1979. Probably best known as a natural footballer starring with Éire Óg and Faughs. Favourite position - wing forward.

Ollie O'Regan: A regular on the squad from 1972 to 1980 and a dedicated hurler who never missed a training session. A stylish back and close marker who came up through the juvenile and minor ranks.

John Quinn: Versatile all-round player, could play anywhere. Represented Éire Óg seniors in goal in 1979.

Tony Roche: A fearless defender and 'marker' whose influence on the training pitch and in the dressing rooms was vital and irreplaceable.

Starred in the 1980 final keeping a close eye on the great Paddy McNamara. 'Rochie' was the life and soul of the panel.

Tom Russell: Dual player who starred in the Gaelic football fields as well as hurling. A strong uncompromising player who was never found wanting when the going got tough. Tom later played a lot of football in County Monaghan before returning to Éire Óg. A brother of John.

Noel Ryan: A brilliant all-round sportsman. A polished hurler, Noel made his inter-county debut in 1973. A great target-man, he scored many vital goals on the March to success. A big man but could turn on a sixpence and elude his marker with ease. Noel Ryan was successful at any game he turned his hand to.

Michael Ryan: An extremely effective corner forward, Mikey came up through the ranks of the successful juveniles. A fine footballer, he later played for Shannon Gaels and Clare. Brother of P. J., Tommie, Noel and Pauline (Kilmartin).

Michael Skelly: A fantastic under-age star who played with the best. 'Wag' was at home at centre-field where he used his blistering pace to great effect. A stylish striker of the ball who could take the 'ball out of your eye', learned his hurling at the CBS nursery. Played Harty Cup 1971. Michael dedicated a lot of his time to Éire Óg – resodding the pitch and working in the club bar – a dedicated clubman.

Barry Smythe: Gave a power display for St. Flannan's in the Harty Cup Final of 1976 in Bansha. A member of a sporting family of the highest order. Injury cut short his career which without doubt would have been long and memorable. Any player who came up against 'Smythe' knew exactly where he stood with him. A Railway Cup player in 1982, Barry returned in 1990 to play storming hurling at full-back.

Michael Griffin: Parnell St. A very good underage career which saw him win minor junior A league, and u/21 Championship (1974). A rugged defender who trained hard. A product of CBS Harty Cup team 1971/72, 'Ganga' later played senior championship with the Banner Club in 1981.

Francie (Mc)Mahon: Rugged full-forward who revelled in the fray. Extremely hard to stop in full-flight. Powerful slap of a ball, Francie played a big role in the 1982 campaign. Holder of minor and senior medal. Favourite player Tony Doran of Wexford. In fact, all the Mahons hurled at some level for Ennis; Seán, Gerry, Noel, Colm, Michael and Paschal.

Paschal (Mc)Mahon: Another son of Seán's to wear the red of Éire Óg. A fine stylish wing-back, Paschal came to prominence with the Clare Vocational and Ennis Vocational School teams. Played with Éire Óg for a number of years before emigrating in his prime. Favourite player John Horgan of Blackrock.

1984 Opening of Éire Óg Clubhouse

Though a disappointing year on the championship front, going out to a Cyril Lyons inspired Ruan (0-12 to 0-10) in the quarter final, 1984 proved a historic year for the club with the opening of the new clubhouse at Clonroadmore. The official opening was performed by Brendan Vaughan, the Munster Council Chairman, who spoke of the 'long and glorious GAA tradition in Ennis'. The clubhouse was blessed by Most Rev. Dr. Michael Harty, Bishop of Killaloe.

In the Centenary Cup, Éire Óg lost to 'the Mills' by 1-12 to 2-5. Newcomers who came through to senior ranks around this time include John and Tom Russell, Gearóid Mannion, Bernie O'Brien, Michael Dinan, Tomás English, while John Glynn was recalled to the squad.

Michael Meagher (Kilkenny) and Michael O'Sullivan (Ballyea) joined the club with Tony Nugent transferring to Tulla.

Market Street - Town League Team c.1982. Back row, left to right: *Joe Downey, Joe Pilkington, Michael Quinn, Paddy Neylon, Colm Slattery, Paddy Kelly, Tom Kelly, Dermot Delaney, Seán Daly.* ***Front row:*** *Gerry McCullough, Seán Heaslip, Michael Griffin, Brenny Pyne, Peter Quinn, John Quinn, Francis Heaslip, James Kennedy, James Ball.*

Clare County Champions 1982. Back row, left to right: *Seán Lynch, Joe Barry, Declan Coote, Micheál Glynn, Ml. Chandler, Francis Heaslip, Seán Heaslip.* ***Front row:*** *Pete Barry, Paddy Kelly, Martin Nugent, Seamus Durack, Tony Nugent, Noel Ryan, Colm McMahon, Pat Lynch.* ***Mascot:*** *Barry Ryan.*
Courtesy of Clare Champion.

Kilmaley

Kilmaley is one of the oldest hurling parishes in Clare. In the early days, the clubs Michael Davitt's, Wolfe Tones and Smith O'Brien's, all represented the parish. It wasn't until 1938 that Kilmaley won the Intermediate 'B' title beating Ogonnelloe. In 1963 they were promoted to senior ranks without success. Later they would return to the intermediate grade, winning the Championship in 1980. The following year they captured the Clare Champion Cup.

Kilmaley made a historic breakthrough in 1985 by becoming the first team promoted from intermediate grade to win the senior championship in over 25 years. Their achievement is all the greater considering that they defeated the then Munster Club Champions, Sixmilebridge in a semi-final replay. Many felt that Kilmaley had lost their chance the first day, but they accounted for a very strong and experienced Éire Óg side in the final.

Éire Óg excelled in their semi-final win over Clarecastle.

Kilmaley were probably underestimated, though I don't know why, considering that their team included many of the defeated County finalists, St. Brendan's, of 1979. They also boasted leading inter-county players in

Tommy Keane, Martin Meehan and Seamus Fitzpatrick. The success of the team originated with the successful juvenile, minor and u/21's of the early to mid-1970s, whom I saw play a very attractive brand of hurling. I was also familiar with some of these players through their involvement with Colleges hurling at Ennis CBS and the Vocational School.

1985 Paths to County Final

Scariff	3-7	...	Éire Óg	1-11
Éire Óg	1-14	...	Tubber	3-4
Éire Óg	2-10	...	Sixmilebridge	1-13
Éire Óg	2-9	...	Tulla	0-8
Éire Óg	4-10	...	Clarecastle	2-7

As with Éire Óg, Kilmaley too lost their opening game when defeated by Feakle.

Rd. 2	Kilmaley	3-10	...	Newmarket	3-9
	Kilmaley	2-8	...	O'Callaghan's Mills	3-4
	Kilmaley	0-11	...	Sixmilebridge	1-8
	Kilmaley	1-11	...	Sixmilebridge	1-5

A crowd of 8,000 paid gate receipts of £12,282 to see Kilmaley win their first ever senior championship. The switch of Paddy Hill and Tommy Keane and the slight edge enjoyed by Eugene McMahon and Martin Cahill at centre-field swung it for Kilmaley, who absorbed tremendous pressure in the closing minutes, to win by 0-10 to 0-8. A Noel Ryan 'goal' was whistled back by the referee for a penalty. Kilmaley also claimed a goal when Johnsie Mungovan bundled John Russell over the goal line while in possession. Many felt Mungovan's shoulder charge was a fair one.

Anna Kennelly was the first lady secretary of Éire Óg in 1984.

"Mighty Kilmaley! The Hill/Keane switch proves decisive. Allied with astute positional switches and tremendous determination to win. These were the chief ingredients in Kilmaley's historic success in beating a favoured Éire Óg at Cusack Park", wrote Seamus Hayes in the Clare Champion.

Immediately after the game, P. J. Kennedy, accepted the Canon Hamilton Cup from Board Chairman Robert Frost. While Michael Leyden of Meaney & Leyden Insurance presented the 'Man of the Match' Award to Martin Cahill. The 17-year-old Kilmaley youth was certainly entitled to the honour after a great hour's hurling. Cahill emigrated to England and was a big loss to Clare hurling.

The Kilmaley 1985 winning team was:

P. J. Kennedy

Martin D'Arcy — Noel McGuane — Paddy Hill

Pat Keane — Tommy Keane — Niall Romer

Eugene McMahon — Martin Cahill

Seamus Fitzpatrick — Gerry Pyne — Martin Meehan

John Cahill — Johnsie Mungovan — Gerry Kennedy

Subs: Michael Murphy (used), Michael Killeen (used).

Team Manager: Michael Maher.

Trainer: Brian O'Reilly (Kilrush).

Coach: Jim McMahon.

Selectors: Johnny Hogan, Freddie Markham, Michael Griffin.

1985 Éire Óg County Finalists versus Kilmaley:

Seamus Durack

Michael Meagher — Paddy Kelly — Gerry Barry

John Russell — Micheál Glynn — Paschal Mahon

Declan Coote — Michael O'Sullivan

Pat Lynch — Seán Heaslip (Capt.) — Gearóid Mannion

Bernie O'Brien — Noel Ryan — Martin Nugent

Subs: Shaun McCarthy, Michael Ryan, Pete Barry (All Used).

Selectors: Massey Dilger, Michael Hanrahan, Barry Smythe.

WE LIVE IN HOPE

I've wandered far from the Banner County
Seen many's the city and many's the country,
But always and ever my mind's eye returns
To the old town of Ennis where my homefire burns.

I have feasted high, well above the salt,
But nothing compares to the old ball 'a malt
That I shared with friends up in Nuggy's bar
Where we laughed and sang and had many's the jar.

We spoke of hurlers and nineteen fourteen
And longed for the day when victory'd be seen,
When we won the League we all went berserk
Drank for week with no mention of work.

When in defeat we were often quite low
But come the next year, again we would go,
To wave our flags with partisan glee
In the hope that we'd beat the boys from the Lee.

At one time or another we have beaten them all
And just missed the Croker by the hop of a ball.
But again we'll go and always be there
For as long as the hurley's held in Clare.

Was it Biddy or was it ill-luck
That year after year our confidence shook?
In fairness Biddy isn't it time to scratch
That ancient curse that cost many's the match.

Haven't we paid our debt for slighting you?
Isn't it now the turn of the saffron and blue?
Or in Dante's Inferno will we evermore stroll
Never nearing nor reaching our sought after goal?

But forget the past lads and look to the fore,
We've had great hurlers and will have some more.
I hope I'm alive and there with the best
When Biddy at last lays the old curse to rest.

Then back from the Croker all happy and hoarse
And many's the pint will be lowered of course,
We'll drink to the boys at last victorious
And go to our Maker all mirthful and glorious.
Christy Murphy – Ennis and Denmark.

Éire Óg/Sixmilebridge

The rivalry continued unabated between these clubs when the Ennismen had two points to spare (1-10 to 2-5) over the 'Bridge in round two of the 1986 Championship. Éire Óg had earlier defeated 'The Mills' (1-13 to 3-3) when the town team came to life in the closing stages. However, following Éire Óg's defeat to Cooraclare in the Senior Football

Paddy Duggan with a group of Éire Óg hurlers pictured at Féile na nGael 1987.
Courtesy of Colm Keating.

Final, the hurling team seemed to lose heart and they lost to the Mills in the hurling semi-final. The hurling and football teams shared seven players in common. The other footballers were Enda Connolly, Seamus Flanagan (Fermanagh), Johnny Guerin, John O'Connor, Roibéard Lyne, David McCullough, Johnny Purtill, Patrick Walzer. The Sixmilebridge avenged the 1986 defeat when they had 4 points to spare over Éire Óg in '87. Little separated the sides, and Éire Óg bounced back to take the 'Bridge (2-12 to 2-11) in a cracker at Tulla. With the teams level on four occasions, Martin Nugent inspired Ennis when he moved to centre-field. A dominant half-back line of Micheál Glynn, John Russell and Shaun McCarthy wasn't enough to stop Feakle in the semi-final at Cusack Park. Though leading by three points at the interval, Feakle struck back when Val Donnellan blasted a 21-yard free to the net early in the second half. Feakle had greater hunger and with Ger Loughnane, Paul Callinan and the Guilfoyles in form, they held on to win 2-11 to 2-8. In the County Final, Feakle disposed of Ruan by 7 points. Feakle added the Clare Champion Cup to the championship, accounting for Broadford 2-15 to 1-7.

There is no doubt but 1990 was one of the greatest years for the Éire Óg senior team. They played with an abandon not seen for some time. From early on in the championship Éire Óg showed their hand. They demolished their old rivals, Newmarket, by 5-12 to 2-4. Martin Nugent and goal poacher supreme Pete Barry notched 4-8 between them in this rare one-sided win over the Blues. Barry had a great season. It was his goals that saw off the threat of 'the Mills' and the 'Bridge. In the semi-final of the County Championship, Éire Óg and Sixmilebridge served up wonderful fare. Éire Óg should have put away the 'Bridge the first day. The replay was a hot game with a player from both sides sent to the line.

Declan Coote and Michael Meagher in happy mood after the 1990 County Final.

It took a late goal from Pete Barry to see a highly motivated side through, with Declan Coote and Barry Smythe showing great leadership.

The County Final with 'the Mills' is now regarded as one of the poorest. It was a game O'Callaghan's Mills could have won but they didn't take their chances. It was a tense game for Éire Óg, and Paddy Duggan summed it up best when he told the gathering media, "We have had our share of disappointments and we really wanted to win this one. We especially wanted to win it as a contribution to the Ennis 750 celebrations. We have a good blend of youth and experience. We'll take a break and we'll get back in training early next week for the Munster Club." The founding father of Éire Óg then paid tribute to Seán Hehir and 'The Mills'. While the 1990 County Final produced few great displays, Barry Smythe at full-back excelled. As usual, Pete Barry took his goal chance well. For 'The Mills' Mike Deasy and Kevin McNamara were best.

Ennis Welcomes Home its Rovers (Ennis Rovers Reunion)

Like St. John's before them, Rovers HC regrouped for a weekend of nostalgia culminating at the Old Ground Hotel on April 28th, 1990. They came from all corners of the globe. The returned exiles included James

Declan Coote wins possession in the 1990 County Final (supported by Gearóid Mannion and Martin Nugent) against O'Callaghan Mills.
Courtesy of Clare Champion.

Mulqueen, George Summerly, Willie and Albert Molloy, Sean Coffey, Michael Leyden and the Murphy family. The Master of Ceremonies was Terry Hennigan and music was provided by Tony Neenan and the Dukes of Jazz, the very popular Cork band, who then held a residency at the Old Ground. The Champion reported: *"Revelries continued long into the early hours. It was a revelation to see people from their 30s to their 80s dancing the night away with intermittent renditions of songs from the 'floor' by Joe Shannon, Mary O'Loughlin, James Ball and Eileen Bradley, as the morning began to dawn. Des Loftus, who substituted for his brother, John, was the main after-dinner speaker and went on to recall joyful moments from the past and the closeness of community life."*

Drawn to the jazz, I was tempted to climb the stairs and mingle with the returned Rovers. Somehow I felt outside and I didn't proceed.

Éire Óg - Munster Club Championship

In the first round proper of the provincial championship of 1990, Éire Óg drew Roanmore of Waterford. Roanmore led at the half way stage by 1-11 to 1-4, having played with a stiff wind. The Ennismen resumed with John Russell outstanding at centre-back. Éire Óg scored seven points in quick succession to draw level entering the final quarter. The crucial goal came from Declan Coote in the closing minutes for Éire Óg to run our deserving winners by 2-16 to 1-14. Other prominent players included Pete Barry, Johnny Corbett and substitute, Tony McEnery, who scored a magnificent point from close to the end line.

Na Piarsaigh of Cork, founded in 1943, won their first ever senior championship in 1990 beating city rivals, St. Finbarr's (2-7 to 1-8) in a replay. The *Examiner* reported *"it was a long and lonely wait, punctuated with sorrow, heartbreak and bitter disappointment but all those sad and painful memories were banished into oblivion when Na Piarsaigh thrillingly overcame the marvellous challenge of St. Finbarr's at Pairc Uí Chaoimh to win their first Cork title in one of the great finals of the*

***Éire Óg Executive officers 1990. Back row, left to right:** Pat Daly (P.R.O.), Joe Nevin (joint Treasurer), Martin Brooks, Pat Fitzpatrick, Michael Skelly (Registrar), Jackie Browne, Michael Barry (joint Treasurer) and Paddy Neylon. **Front row:** Jack Heaslip (President), Liam Griffin (Secretary), Barry Smythe (Chairman), Fr. Willie Walsh (Vice-Chairman), Tony Honan and Christy Glynn. **Missing from picture:** John Bradley and Tom Flynn.*

modern era midst rapturous scenes of unbridled joy and emotion in a breathtaking duel that enthralled the attendance of 19,153."

Cork inter-county hurler Tony O'Sullivan, who played from 1982-1994, gave me some insight into their history. *"We were formed by a group of men, mostly, ex-North Mon. The club was formed in Redemption Road. The founders included Derry Terry, Liam Connery and Christy Twomey. Na Piarsaigh had tremendous success at juvenile level and in my time we didn't actually lose a game from juvenile until we reached u/21 level. The players from those years are basically the nucleus of our present senior team. We didn't make the breakthrough at senior level earlier because the Glen, the Rockies, the Barrs and Midleton were very strong, we had to wait until players matured."*

Micheál Glynn raises the Canon Hamilton Cup in 1990. Also included are Brendan Vaughan and Donal Carey T.D. seated.
Courtesy of Clare Champion.

Because of the victory over St. Finbarr's, Na Piarsaigh were installed as warm favourites to stop the progress of Éire Óg but they were unsuccessful and the following extract is taken in full from the *Cork Examiner* of Monday, 12th November 1990.

"Éire Óg stand firm in cracker - Éire Óg 2-5 . . . Na Piarsaigh 0-9"

"Displaying greater determination, Éire Óg from Clare caused a surprise when they scored a fully merited victory over Cork Champions, Na Piarsaigh in a tremendous Munster Club Senior Hurling semi-final at Cusack Park, Ennis on Saturday.

This was a magnificent game with many outstanding passages of play but in the end the newly crowned Cork Champions were unable to break

Éire Óg Senior team that defeated Na Piarsaigh (Cork) in the 1990 Club Championship. Back row, left to right: *Gerry Barry, Pete Barry, Micheál Glynn (capt.), Declan Tobin, Eoin McMahon, Tomás Corbett, Mick Meagher, Martin Nugent.* ***Front row:*** *Colm Mahon, Seán Heaslip, John Russell, Gearoid Mannion, Barry Smythe, Declan Coote, Shaun McCarthy.*

Courtesy of John Kelly, Clare Champion.

down a teak tough Éire Óg defence to get the vital scores and the Ennismen deservedly qualified for a final meeting with Limerick's Patrickswell on Sunday week. For Na Piarsaigh, John Whooley replaced the injured Seán Guiheen at corner back while John Twomey, a substitute during the Cork final for Mark Dineen, retained his place. Éire Óg were at full strength with both Micheál Glynn and centre-forward Gearóid Mannion back in the side having missed the first round win over Roanmore. Mannion opened the scoring for the home side but by the end of the first quarter Na Piarsaigh had opened a two-point gap following two good points from Mark Mullins and one from James O'Connor. At this stage, Éire Óg lost John Russell with a facial injury and this was certainly a blow to their hopes. Spurred on, however, by their followers in the attendance of 2,000, they fought back and went in front ten minutes from the interval with a fine goal. Full-forward Pete Barry caught a long drive from Declan Tobin and he got inside the defence to kick the ball low into the back of the net. This helped his team to lead at the interval 1-4 to 0-5 having played with the aid of the breeze.

Just before the half-time whistle the Ennismen were dealt what appeared to be another major blow when mid-fielder Colm Mahon was taken off on a stretcher with a leg injury. He was replaced by County Minor Colin Lynch.

Na Piarsaigh resumed with Gearóid Bailey in the attack in place of Liam O'Callaghan and points from Mark Mullins (free) and the skilful Tony O'Sullivan had the sides level after four minutes. A minute later Éire Óg struck a vital blow when Gerry Barry crashed a semi-penalty to the net.

The Ennismen never lost the lead after this as the remaining 25 minutes were dominated by the respective back lines.

Eleven minutes from time, Na Piarsaigh were awarded a semi-penalty following a foul on Michael Mullins but his namesake Mark was content to take his point. Despite their best efforts after this, they just could not break down the home team's back line in which Shaun McCarthy at wing back was outstanding with full-back Barry Smythe having a storming hour.

Full back Jim Hanifin played his heart out for the Cork representatives with Christy Connery and Leonard O'Sullivan battling bravely at mid-field but in the attack only Mark Mullins and James O'Connor threatened the Éire Óg defence."

Micheál Glynn wins possession supported by Tomás Corbett in the 1990 Munster Club Final v Patrickswell. Courtesy of Ollie O'Regan.

1990 path to Munster Club Final

Éire Óg	2-9	...	Kilmaley	2-5
Éire Óg	5-12	...	Newmarket-on-Fergus,	2-4
Éire Óg	1-10	...	Sixmilebridge	2-7
Éire Óg	2-10	...	Sixmilebridge	2-8
Éire Óg	1-5	...	O'Callaghan's Mills	1-3
Éire Óg	2-16	...	Roanmore (Waterford)	1-14
Éire Óg	2-5	...	Na Piarsaigh (Cork)	0-9

Provincial Final

While Éire Óg played against Na Piarsaigh in one semi-final, Patrickswell had overcome Holycross/Ballycahill in the other semi-final by 0-13 to 0-9. Some bad feeling crept into the game even before a ball was struck. The controversy began on 1st April, when Ciarán Carey was sent off against Doon for over robust play. He was suspended for two weeks. On 18th April he returned to the 'Well colours against Claughaun and was dismissed again for rough play. The minimum suspension is two weeks. If a player is sent off for a second time he is supposed to get double the minimum (i.e. 4 weeks) and the Limerick County Board only gave him the minimum. When Patrickswell played Holycross/Ballycahill, Ciarán Carey was sent to the line again. The Munster Council, unaware of his record, proposed to suspend him for two weeks. At an Officers' Meeting of the Éire Óg Club on the Monday prior to the provincial club final this saga never arose. An officer of the Éire Óg Club innocently told a Clare Munster Council delegate about the Carey affair. The Council delegate informed Donie Neylon, Secretary of the Munster Council, who called a special meeting on the matter. The facts were established and, on a vote of 10-4, Ciarán Carey was suspended for a month depriving him from lining out in the Munster Club Final. His place went to Ger Hayes. To be fair to Patrickswell, they felt hard done by. The Limerick club claimed that the rule is not enforced in most counties except in serious circumstances and they felt that Carey's offences were of a minor nature.

Patrickswell felt Éire Óg were meddling in their affairs. It got their blood up. The net result was that the tension affected the performances of both teams on the day.

A very experienced Patrickswell side opened well with points from Gary Kirby. Éire Óg got on top during the second quarter but were guilty of poor finishing. They had the winning of the game during this spell but let it slip. It is interesting to note that neither side scored in the final quarter. The full-time score of 0-8 to 0-6 is indicative of the tension that prevailed throughout the game played in ideal conditions, before a huge Clare crowd at Cusack Park. Éire Óg didn't play their usual game, and, with the exception of Colm Mahon, Tomás Corbett, Colin Lynch, and outstanding goalkeeper Eoin McMahon, the team in general disappointed.

The Éire Óg team was: -

Eoin McMahon
Michael Meagher Barry Smythe Gerry Barry
Tomás Corbett Micheál Glynn (Capt.) Shaun McCarthy
Declan Tobin Colm Mahon
Seán Heaslip Gearóid Mannion Colin Lynch
Martin Nugent Pete Barry Declan Coote
Subs: Johnny Corbett, Tony McEnery

I think it is fair to say that the Éire Óg teams of 1980 – 1990 must rank as some of the best to represent the town of Ennis. If any criticism could be levelled at the club, it is that they under-achieved. The nucleus of the team that beat Newmarket in 1980 was still intact. Long serving player Seán Heaslip recalled this era to me and agrees that this Éire Óg team did under-achieve in terms of championships won.

"We lost a lot; for instance, the 1981 semi-final loss to Newmarket, the 1985 final defeat by Kilmaley. We were over confident going in to the Newmarket game in 1981. The selectors took off (Declan) Coote. He was the scapegoat. In the 1984 championship we beat Kilmaley by 21 points, so in 1985 we were very confident going into the County Final. I got two points off Tommy Keane, then Paddy Hill came out on me. We missed several frees and I missed the penalty at the end. The longer you let a team hang on they'll beat you. Everything was going well in 1986 until the County Football Final. We never recovered after losing 2-5 to 1-5 to Cooraclare. In the hurling semi-final against 'The Mills' we started bickering amongst ourselves, players roaring at each other. We panicked. In the old teams of 1978 – 1982, we didn't have that. John Dunne wouldn't have tolerated it. It upsets teams. In the last few years the teams haven't gelled as well as they should and used to. There was a lot of bickering in Éire Óg. I didn't enjoy my hurling, so I pulled out of the county scene. 1990 was our best year, though the County Final was terrible, the worst ever. Nobody played well. The 'Mills' had the winning of it in the first half. The Roanmore (Waterford) game made up for it. We really expressed ourselves. It was the most satisfying game I ever played in. We gave a great display in the second half. I felt great coming off the field. Then we beat Na Piarsaigh of Cork. Shaun McCarthy and Tommy Corbett played 'blinders'. But we flopped in the Munster Club Final losing to Patrickswell. The controversy off the pitch didn't help us. The games with Roanmore and Na Piarsaigh made up for the poor County Final. We desperately wanted to win the County Championship in 1990

and promised the Ennis 750 Committee that we would win it. Which we did! But victory in the Provincial would have been the best thing to happen to us, especially the more senior players like Mahon, Smythe, Nugent, Coote and myself."

PEN PICTURES 1990

Compiled by a member of this team

Francis Corey: A brilliant minor with Clare and Colleges star with St. Flannan's, developed into a fine full-back with the club. Represented Clare at senior championship level 1994. Injury laid him low in 1990. A member of the defeated county final squad in 2000.

Eoin McMahon: Clare goalie 1985-1987, giving many memorable performances. Very competent, well prepared keeper who always seemed to play well. Rarely had an off day. Eoin succeeded 'the Duke'. A golfer of note.

Gerry Barry: Munster Minor medallist with Clare (1981) – a rare breed. Gerry favoured defence but could play anywhere – a utility player. Tough, crisp hurler – his strength was his ground striking. A regular since 1983.

Mick Meagher: An All-Ireland winning medallist with St. Kieran's College and Kilkenny Minors; came to Ennis to hurl with the Townies. As dedicated as they come, gentleman off the field but a very determined defender on it. Represented Clare at senior level 1984/1985. Most deserving of his county medal after years of endeavour with Éire Óg. Very popular with his team-mates.

John Russell: Wholehearted defender who never saw danger and so was quite injury-prone. On his day was unbeatable and played many memorable games at centre-back. "Rooskie" was as game as they come, very stylish and as hard as stone. Gave loyal service to the Banner County.

Declan Tobin: Tall, rangy mid-fielder who was used to great effect as a substitute in 1990. Never let the side down and scored many useful points in the championship. He played senior championship for Clare in 1993. Later captained Éire Óg in the County Final 2000.

Ger Cahill: Another Munster Minor Medal winner (1989), a very skilful underage hurler who played wholehearted hurling for the town. Never selfish, good to find a colleague. Scored two wonderful points in the All-Ireland Minor Final versus Offaly.

Seánie Lyne: A late developer as a hurler, whose wonderful pace was a huge threat to the opposition. Played well against no less a man than Anthony Daly in the semi-final.

Shaun McCarthy: "Bomb" was a hugely impressive defender – always stylish – a feature of his play would have been his tigerish forays into attack with his customary solo-runs. Had his greatest day ever against the Cork Champions Na Piarsaigh in the Munster Club Semi-Final 1990.

John Corbett: A very tenacious attacker whose strength was his ability to field the dropping ball. Used to run at defenders, using his tremendous strength to succeed.

Gearóid Mannion "Mannix" gave some great years to Éire Óg seniors and was a major influence in the 1990 team. Versatile provider who could play anywhere in the forwards. A soccer player of note with Avenue United.

Colin Lynch: Young when involved with this team but a product of very successful underage structures in Éire Óg whom he joined age 16. Represented Clare at all levels. Very quick and strong, broke on to the County Senior team in 1996.

Tommy Corbett: Outstanding wing back (age 17) on this team, contributing greatly to all the victories of the year. "Corbie" was unbeatable in every match. County senior panellist 1997 could have featured more. Defender turned forward in 2000. Brother of Johnny.

Stephen McNamara: Injured for final – was used as substitute in early round. Stephen scored many important goals in Clare's championship successes of 1995 to 1999. Could see the promise then.

Tony McEnery: Great hearted and energetic, fast player who scored a beauty against Roanmore from the wing. Thankfully still playing the game. Son of Jimmy and grandson of Charlie, who were involved with Rovers H.C.

Éire Óg Junior (A) Champions 1990. Back row, left to right: *Ml. Ryan, Ml. Griffin, Tadgh Lyne, Tony McEnery, Noel Ryan, Colin Lynch, Paul Nihill, Ml. Skelly.* ***Front row:*** *David McCarthy, Ger Curran, Pat O'Shea, Noel Kenny, Seamus Durack, Peter Kelly, Michael McCarthy.*

Michael McCarthy/David McCarthy: Valuable members of the panel. Much underrated brothers who would have walked on to most other club teams.

Other Panellists: Barry Smythe, Seamus Durack, Seán Heaslip, Martin Nugent, Pete Barry, Declan Coote, Peter Kelly, Cathal Kilcawley, Tadhg Lyne.

Back Room

Colum Flynn: A brilliant miracle-worker for Éire Óg, who has given years of dedication. A tremendous motivator and coach. The players down the years are indebted to him for all his effort and time – though he has other commitments – Boxing Coach/Healer/Galway Coach. A great witty friend who tells an excellent yarn.

Martin (Massey) Dilger: Intelligent "feel-good" motivator, whose invaluable experience and know-how was of great benefit to the team.

Fr. Willie Walsh: (Later Bishop of Killaloe) A very good coach and pragmatist who knows his hurling and could spot a change very early. Commanded great respect always – a gentleman who never offended – but not the eternal optimist.

Paddy Duggan: Mr. Éire Óg from 1952 until his untimely death. Each of the teams 1980, 1982, 1990 were trained at some stage by Paddy. Never minced his words and demanded attention and respect. It's highly unlikely that the 3 championships would have been won without "Dougie's" valuable contribution. His attention to detail was renowned and God help the fella who forgot to buy the new laces. It was well known that you never stood behind Paddy in the dressing room when he had a hurley in his hand. Paddy was well liked and hugely respected by all the club members and he may be gone now to his eternal reward but he is not forgotten. I'm sure his spirit was present in September 1995 when Clare captured the McCarthy Cup. Ar dheis Dé go raibh a anam Dhílis.

Junior (A) 1990

Éire Óg added the Junior 'A' title to their senior crown when they defeated Scariff, 2-7 to 1-9. The junior title was a sweet success as they

John Russell (18) supported by Pete Barry in the 1990 County Final.

Courtesy of Clare Champion.

lost the final of 1988 by two points to a John McKenna inspired Ogonnelloe. Amongst the stars for Éire Óg were Michael Skelly, Peter Kelly, Michael Griffin, Colin Lynch and Michael McCarthy. Tony McEnery scored a cracking goal just 20 seconds into the second half setting Éire Óg on their way.

Éire Óg just failed to add the Minor 'A' crown to their senior and junior when they went down, 1-11 to 2-7 to St. Joseph's, despite good displays from Declan Tobin, Peter Quinn and Stephen McNamara. In the following year, St. Joseph's again pipped Éire Óg, this time in the Intermediate Championship by 2-15 to 4-7. By 1993, St. Joseph's were back in the senior grade.

1991/1992 Senior Championships

Despite losing by 12 points to Sixmilebridge in a divisional match, Éire Óg progressed to the semi-final stage in the 1991 championship to meet old rivals Clarecastle. A rampant Clarecastle forward line featuring 'Sparrow' O'Loughlin, Alan Neville and Paschal Russell tore open the Éire Óg defence in the opening quarter. Noel Considine was outstanding in goal for 'the Magpies' as Éire Óg threatened a recovery. However, 'the Magpies' held on to win by 4-7 to 1-8.

A youthful Éire Óg featuring newcomers Gary Logue and Seán Lyne bounced back in 1992 to again reach the County Final. The biggest shock of the season was the defeat of holders Clarecastle to a lively Newmarket team. The Blues were stopped at the quarter-final stage in an excellent game, filled with passages of great ground hurling, by 1-10 to 1-8. Éire Óg, who had earlier accounted for Ruan, went on to take Kilmaley in the semi-final.

Awaiting Éire Óg in the final were their modern day rivals, Sixmilebridge. Prior to the start of the game, a minute's silence was observed for Pappy Callaghan of Bodyke/The Mills and Clare fame. The former great was laid to rest the previous day.

A controversial point by Eamon Healy was just one of many talking points in the 1992 final. Tempers flared a little after this when referee Kevin Walsh (Wolfe Tones) had to caution Éire Óg backroom officials. A superb goal by Gerry McInerney set the 'Bridge up for a good interval lead but good work by Barry Keating and John Russell saw Éire Óg fight back in the second half, with just one point separating the teams at the end. With victory going to Sixmilebridge and such an abundance of talent on the bench it was surprising that the Éire Óg mentors didn't introduce Seán Heaslip, or one of the up and coming stars in Stephen McNamara or Tony McEnery into the fray. It was the 12th championship meeting between theses modern day rivals in a decade.

Three first cousins pictured at the 1996 Sports Awards. *Photo shows the then Wexford hurling Manager Liam Griffin (centre) with Liam Griffin of Éire Óg and publican/County Councillor Peter Considine. Liam Griffin of Wexford hurled for Newmarket and Clare in 1968. Liam's father was Michael Griffin of Carrowmere, Maurices Mills. After joining the Gardaí he was posted to Rosslare, Co. Wexford.*

After the 1992 Championship Final John Chaplin received the Canon Hamilton Cup, while Gary Logue was presented with the ninth Annual County Express/Shannon Crystal Top Score Award. Gary Logue, who came up through the ranks of the Banner Club, notched 3-23 in four championship outings.

Results at a Glance

Sixmilebridge and Éire Óg clashed in a dozen senior championship games between 1982-1992. The 'Bridge won 4, Éire Óg won 4, and 4 were drawn.

These are the results: -

1982	**County Final**	Éire Óg	2-11	...	Sixmilebridge	2-11
	County Final replay	Éire Óg	3-8	...	Sixmilebridge	2-9
1983	**County Final**	Sixmilebridge	1-10	...	Éire Óg	3-4
	County Final replay	Sixmilebridge	1-10	...	Éire Óg	1-7
1985	**Rd. 3 – divisional**	Éire Óg	2-10	...	Sixmilebridge	1-13

1986	**Quarter-Final**	Éire Óg	1-10	... Sixmilebridge	2-5
1987	**Quarter-Final**	Sixmilebridge	2-10	... Éire Óg	0-12
1988	**Quarter-Final**	Éire Óg	2-12	... Sixmilebridge	2-11
1990	**Semi-Final**	Éire Óg	1-10	... Sixmilebridge	2-7
	Semi-Final replay	Éire Óg	2-10	... Sixmilebridge	2-8
1991	**Divisional game**	Sixmilebridge	1-14	... Éire Óg	0-5
1992	**County Final**	Sixmilebridge	1-11	... Éire Óg	1-10

After the highpoint of the 1990/1992 era, Éire Óg slipped back into a state of depression for a couple of years. In 1993 they lost 4-12 to 0-12 to an up and coming Wolfe Tones Na Sionna ably marshalled by Brian Lohan and John McPhilips. The following year despite the best intentions of Gary Logue and Stephen McNamara, Éire Óg lost at the semi-final stage to St. Joseph's (2-12 to 2-10). In 1995, Tubber/Ruan left it late scoring six unanswered points in the final quarter to defeat Éire Óg by 1-12 to 1-10. And in 1996 they lost out to a Scariff team inspired by Mark McKenna and the Murphys, going under by 1-16 to 0-16 in a fine game. The East Clare men were most unlucky to lose the 1995 decider in a

Éire Óg - County U/14 Champions 1998 and Féile na nGael (Clare) Champions. Back row, left to right: *Michael Craven (selector), Conor Considine, Stephen McNamara (selector), Brian Lynch, Jamie Deniffe, Stephen Skelly, David Gallagher, Gerard Keane, Tomás Craven, Ollie O'Regan, (mentor), Pat Brennan (mentor).* ***Middle row:*** *Paddy Guilfoyle, Andrew Darmody, Eoin O'Connell, Garry O'Connell, Enda McNamara, Ronan Keane, Rory Hally, Joe Treacy, John Brennan, Adrian Flaherty.* ***Front row:*** *Eoin Woulfe, Niall Daly, James Gallagher, Conor O'Brien, Colm O'Callaghan, David Grey, Ray Casey, Conor McNamara.*

showcase final by 2-10 to 0-15 to Sixmilebridge. The 'Bridge would go on to win the Munster and All-Ireland Club titles in flamboyant style. This Sixmilebridge success ushered in a great era in Clare club hurling with Wolfe Tones, Clarecastle, St. Joseph's (twice) and Sixmilebridge, again, taking further provincial senior honours. St. Joseph's added the All-Ireland to their Munster Club title beating Rathnure (2-14 to 0-8). 'The Magpies' and Wolfe Tones were unlucky not to win All-Ireland honours. Was this incredible success story brought on by the County team's success in 1995? Why did Éire Óg lose to Patrickswell in 1990 and why did Sixmilebridge throw away a big lead to Ballybrown the previous year?

Paddy Guilfoyle, Man of the Match in the 1993 County Minor Final. Paddy is pictured with his nephew Stephen.

Paddy Downey wasn't far wrong when he wrote in 1995: "With the barriers which imprisoned the County for so long now surmounted, Clare will be a major force for the foreseeable future." And, indeed they were. Further All-Ireland success at Senior (and Minor) level in 1997 and but for some amazing intervention in 1998, I've no doubt another All-Ireland could have been won. For me the 1998 Clare team was the best I've ever seen.

Féile Na nGael 1998/1999

After a great run in the 1998 Féile (Clare area), Éire Óg were crowned champions in style the following year, beating Sixmilebridge by 2-13 to 1-5. It was the club's first success in this competition since the great years of 1974/78, and their first final appearance since 1987. The scoreline is a bit flattering but it was a purple patch by Niall Daly between the 44 and 50 minute that put daylight between Éire Óg and the holders.

"Jubilant scenes as Éire Óg bridge 20 year gap," screamed the Clare Champion headlines. *"Now Éire Óg carry the fortunes of the Banner in Wexford."* And carry them they did, emerging from Group (1) with wins over St. Martin's, the hosts, by 3-13 to 0-3 and Faythe Harriers, 5-6 to 2-7. However, in their group they lost to Askeaton, 1-7 to 2-3, but by virtue of St. Martin's win over the Limerick representatives, it brought Éire Óg back into contention. The Ennis side then went out at the semi-final stage to Toomevarra.

The team that accounted for Sixmilebridge in the Clare final of Féile was as follows:

Ronan Keane

Stephen Skelly John Brennan Conor Considine

Conor McNamara Enda McNamara (Capt.) Rory Hally

Thomas Craven Eoin O'Connell

Colm O'Callaghan David Gallagher James Gallagher

Niall Daly Jamie Denieffe Eoin Woulfe

Subs: Ger Keane and Brian Lynch

Meanwhile in the domestic championship, Éire Óg were lucky to scrape a draw with Sixmilebridge when they fought back from a 13-point deficit. Goals by Eoin O'Connell (2), Jamie Denieffe and Colm O'Callaghan brought Éire Óg back into it, to force a draw Éire Óg 5-5, Sixmilebridge 4-8. The sides again drew before Éire Óg finally dispatched the 'Bridge by 1-15 to 1-4 to win a final meeting with Newmarket.

It would take two games to separate the sides.

Tremendous Fight Back by the Blues is Unrewarded – County u/14 Hurling Final

Éire Óg and Newmarket served up a tremendous standard of hurling in the replay of the u/14 final on Sunday, 27th September, 1999. Newmarket started well but it was Éire Óg who took complete control with three great goals from Niall Daly, Colm O'Callaghan and Thomas Craven, to lead at the interval by 3-6 to 0-4. Éire Óg added a point on the resumption to go 12 points up before 'the Blues' staged a tremendous rally.

Padraig Collins pointed magnificently on several occasions before blasting a 21-yard free to the net following a fierce onslaught. At this stage the 'Blues' were rampant having got on top in vital positions, and John McInerney, Gerard Hannon and David Guinnane prominent, they pressed hard for the equaliser with time running out. However, the Éire Óg backs, Stephen Skelly, Paddy Guilfoyle and John Brennan, stood up to the pressure and just about held out to add the County Championship to

Éire Óg - All Ireland Féile na nGael Champions 1999. Back row, left to right: *Barry Keane (selector), Eamon O'Reilly, Timmy Smythe, Conor Considine, Keith Dormer, Gary O'Connell, John O'Loughlin, Eric Kelly, Mark Brigdale, Bryan Guilfoyle, Seán O'Meara, Eamon Cagney (selector).* ***Middle row:*** *Michael Griffin (mentor), James Gallagher, John O'Driscoll, Brian Hehir, Joe Treacy, Eoin McNamara, Ronan Keane, Noel Whelan, Andrew Darmody, Gerry Kelly (Manager).* ***Front row:*** *John Quinn, Conor O'Brien, Killian Ryan, Damian Coleman, Fergal Brennan, Colin Heaslip. Adrian Flaherty and Colm O'Callaghan of the '98 team are in the background. Courtesy of Gerry Kelly.*

their (Clare) Féile title. In 1998, Éire Óg also won the Lenmac u/10 final from Clonlara. The stars included Eoin and Seosamh O'Loughlin, Chris Shannon, Stephen Guilfoyle and Liam Óg Murphy. A goal by Ian Mounsey proved the decisive score of the game.

In 1999, Éire Óg again earned the right to represent the Banner County in Féile na nGael when they had a hard earned 1 point victory over Clarecastle, 1-7 to 1-6, in the Clare Final.

Managed by Gerry Kelly, the team really took off from there and literally cakewalked the competition. In their five games in the finals they scored an incredible 24 goals and 47 points while conceding a mere 14 points. Amazing statistics considering the fact that they met Carrick Swans of Tipperary and Glen Rovers of Cork along the way.

In the decider Éire Óg had an easy 3-11 to 3 point win over one-time specialists Glen Rovers. Leading by 12 points at the half way stage, Seán O'Meara's third goal put the game out of the reach of The Glen.

Féile Facts 1999

Clare Final	Éire Óg	1-7	...	Clarecastle	1-6
	Éire Óg	5-4	...	Dufry Rovers	0-3
	Éire Óg	7-10	...	Carrick Swans	0-5
	Éire Óg	7-11	...	Ferns	0-2
	Éire Óg	2-11	...	St. Bridget's, Dublin	0-1
National Final	Éire Óg	3-11	...	Glen Rovers	0-3

Éire Óg Team v. Glen Rovers

Joe Treacy

Timmy Smythe Eamon O'Reilly Noel Whelan

John Quinn Keith Dormer Conor Considine

Ronan Keane (0-1) Damien Coleman

Gary O'Connell (0-1) Seán O'Meara (Capt.) (1-2) James Gallagher (1-3)

John O'Driscoll (0-3) John O'Loughlin Brian Hehir (1-1)

Subs: Mark Brigdale, Colin Heaslip, Eoin McNamara, Fergal Brennan, Eric Kelly, Andrew Darmody, Killian Ryan, Conor O'Brien, Brian Guilfoyle.

Back Room

Manager: Gerry Kelly.

Selectors: Michael Griffin, Barry Keane, Eamon Cagney.

Féile Officer: J. J. Considine.

Top Scorers: Brian Hehir (8-2) Seán O'Meara (5-8) James Gallagher (2-13).

The team showed a number of changes from the side that defeated 'the Magpies'. In the Juvenile County Final John O'Loughlin replaced Mark Brigdale at full-forward, while Colin Heaslip lost out to Brian Hehir for the Number 15 jersey. Damien Coleman went from corner forward to centre-field.

This win augurs well for the future of Éire Óg. It is also interesting to note the pedigree of those coming through the ranks. The names Brigdale, Brennan, Dormer, Heaslip, O'Connell, O'Loughlin, Guilfoyle and Smythe are all synonymous with the very best in Ennis hurling. Damien Coleman is a grandson of the late Flan Hynes of Faughs and St. Joseph's fame.

Success at senior level continues to elude Éire Óg for over a decade. In 1997 they threw away a 14-point lead to 'The Mills'. 1998 saw something of a revival when they defeated Clarecastle 1-10 to 0-9 in a replay. Two cracking games were served up by 'the Magpies' and Éire Óg. In the replay the town team got off to a storming opening, notching 1-2.

***Éire Óg Under 12s Division 1A Semi-Finalists. Back row, left to right:** Conor McDonagh, Keith Dormer, Mark Brigdale, Timothy Smythe, Conor Considine (capt.), Gary O'Connell, Joe Treacy, Colin Heaslip, David Molloy, David O'Dwyer. **Front row:** James Gallagher, Ronan Keane, Eamon O'Reilly, Richie Nealon, Darren Longe, Sean O'Meara, Noel Whelan, Eoin McNamara, Damian Coleman.*

Their full-back line of Michael Guerin, Tomás Corbett and Paddy Guilfoyle stood up to some great hurling from a star studded 'Magpie' side. But once again they flattered to deceive when going under by 1-10 to 1-7 to a good Scariff team at Miltown.

County Finalists 2000 - 'Bridge Burst the Double Bubble

After victory over Tulla, and a lucky, lucky, 4-9 to 4-8 win over Clonlara, Éire Óg faced Munster Club Champions, St. Joseph's, as complete underdogs in the County Championship semi-final at Cusack Park.

Writing in the Irish Examiner of Monday, 25 September 2000, Damien Irwin reported - *"In a shock of seismic proportions St. Joseph's were ejected from the Clare Championship by a highly motivated Éire Óg. In a game devoid of a goal and played in a steady drizzle of rain it did, however, hold the interest of all spectators right to the end because of the unlikely proceedings that were unfolding on the pitch. With the game a minute into injury time, Lorcan Hassett stole inside the Éire Óg defence but his shot for goal was courageously smothered by goalkeeper Michael Barry who prevented what would have been an ill-deserved draw for St. Joseph's."*

Played after the Sixmilebridge/Kilmaley tie, this was a gritty team performance from Éire Óg. St. Joseph's were never allowed play their usual game. Barry Keating had a good hour on Seán McMahon while Barry Nugent and Cathal Egan were impressive in the attack. Wing back Mark Fitzgerald was in tremendous form *"winning tackle after tackle by a combination of bravery and technique, he hurled an ocean of ball and blotted his opponents almost completely out of the game."* (Examiner)

Éire Óg - County Senior Finalists 2000. Back row, left to right: *Tadhg McNamara, Damian Barry, Ronan Cooney, Fergus Flynn, Mark Fitzgerald, Cathal Egan, Ronan O'Brien, Mark Kelly.* ***Front row:*** *Barry Keating, Tomás Corbett, Declan Tobin (captain), Michael Barry, Billy Piggott, Stephen McNamara, Barry Nugent. Courtesy of County Express.*

Coming from the pitch after the Éire Óg/St. Joseph's game, there was a great feeling of well being amongst the Ennis hurling followers who revelled in this unexpected but fully deserved victory. After tremendous displays in the earlier rounds Éire Óg failed to reproduce their true form in the County Final. Three good points just before half time brought the Ennismen back into contention by the half way stage. However, a devastating opening 10 minutes by the 'Bridge forwards saw Niall Gilligan, Brian Kennedy and Robert Conlon score three killer goals. Conlon's goal was excellently taken as he snapped up a breaking ball on the '40' to cut through for a great goal. *'Bridge Burst the Double Bubble'* (a reference to the possible football and hurling double) and *'Gilligan's Brilliance leaves Éire Óg reeling'* wrote the Clare Champion. It was indeed a fabulous team performance by the 'Bridge who went on to capture the Munster Crown.

For Éire Óg it was a disappointing day with only Fergus Flynn, Tomás Corbett and Michael Barry playing to form.

2001/2002 Championships

Overall the Michael Lynch Hotels 2001/2002 Senior Championships have been disappointing. Having got off to a disappointing start in 2002 (losing to Ogonnelloe by 2-10 to 1-9) Éire Óg bounced back to defeat

John Brennan, Barry Nugent, Ciarán and Niall Daly pictured in 1999. John Brennan is holding a hurley found in Michael Cusacks' Cottage, Carron, by Paddy McGann, John's grandfather while foddering cattle in the 1930s.

Scariff by 0-17 to 1-9. Played in ideal conditions in Scariff, the scoring was dominated by Cathal Egan and Barry Nugent, who contributed 16 points between them. Éire Óg then produced a spirited display to hold Sixmilebridge to a draw, 2-9 to 1-12. A late injury time goal by Barry Nugent kept Éire Óg's hopes of championship survival alive. Scariff then drew with Ogonnelloe to keep Éire Óg in the race. Again, superb play from Nugent (2-3) and Cathal Egan (1-10) swamped a disappointing Ogonnelloe by 3-21 to 4-4, putting Éire Óg through to the quarter-final where they dispatched Kilnamona by 2-12 to 0-12 at Cusack Park, the goals coming from Tomás Corbett and Stephen McNamara. A showdown with St. Joseph's ensued but the 'Parish' had too much power and on the night they crushed the town team by 5-16 to 1-5. 2002 has brought little joy for Éire Óg in senior hurling. Following a defeat to Sixmilebridge, a depleted Éire Óg were again unmercifully put to the sword by a great St. Joseph's team, 1-16 to 0-8 and with the exception of Ronan Lynch, few Ennismen played well. In Round 3, a revitalised Éire Óg beat O'Callaghan's Mills, 5-11 to 0-14. This was a hugely important game for the club, as defeat to the 'Mills' would have relegated Éire Óg to Senior (B) status for the coming season. Thankfully, a fired up Éire Óg, with Niall Daly, who notched 2-5, and Barry Nugent (2-1) in scoring form. Others to impress were Mark Fitzgerald and Eoin Bradley.

Mark Fitzgerald (capt.) Éire Óg, Seán McMahon (St. Josephs) and Referee Kevin Walsh pictured prior to the 2002 Championship clash. Courtesy of County Express.

However, great things are happening in Minor and Junior ranks. Managed by Des Neylon, who promoted many of the youngsters to Junior (A), his charges repaid his faith in them by annexing the County title. Captained by Cathal Kilcawley, the juniors had fine displays from Ronan Eade, a promising minor of some years back, making a welcome return to the Éire Óg colours. Brian McMahon and Tomás Corbett, an outstanding senior for many years, who regraded to junior ranks, proved too strong for a good Ennistymon team.

A few weeks later Éire Óg contested the Minor (A) final, but lost to Newmarket.

In reviewing any history, one has to ask what the future holds? In hurling, Éire Óg has had a chequered past with a senior championship or two coming their way almost every decade. Since 1990, when both Senior and Junior A Championships were won, until this year no adult title has rested on the sideboard of the capital town. Football has gained the ascendancy in the last decade of the century and titles have been won at all levels from U-12 to the club's first senior title in 2000. The constant stream of good talent to senior ranks (with good management) should ensure that more Gaelic football titles should come to the town.

The future of hurling, however, asks many questions. The Minor title was last won in 1994, with this title also coming to Éire Óg in 1991 and 1992. The transition of these players has not been seen in U-21 or senior ranks and very few of the players are now representing the club.

Further down the grades, an U-10 tournament was won in Kilmaley in 1993 and the final was again contested in 1994. The team of 1994 reached the U-12 County Final in 1996 but was defeated by Newmarket on a narrow margin. Since then this group of young lads has taken the U-14 Féile na nGael County title along with the county championship and reached the national semi-finals of Féile in 1998. The same boys have gone on to win the U-15 and U-16 titles in consecutive years. Reaching the Féile na nGael national semi-finals was to be climaxed in 1999 when, with the backbone of the team having gained experience the previous year, Éire Óg swept all before them in winning the Christy Ring Trophy to gain national honours for the club for the first time when they were crowned All-Ireland Champions at U-14 level.

In the year, 2002, the golden anniversary of the club's foundation, Éire Óg have already felt the influence of the above success when twelve

Éire Óg Executive Committee 2001. Front row, left to right: *Pat Daly (P.R.O.), Ted Finn (Secretary), Tom Flynn (President), Brian O'Connell (Chairman), Josie Nevin (Vice-Chairman).* ***Back row:*** *Martin Nugent, Pat McInerney (Treasurer), Liam Griffin (County Board Delegate), Pat Fitzpatrick, Tom Russell, Bobby Gray (Bar Treasurer), and J.J. Considine.* ***Missing:*** *Michael Skelly (Registrar), Larry Hally, Peter Moylan, Tommie Molloy and Gerry Kelly.*

Courtesy of Éire Óg.

Under-21s, seven of whom are minors were part of the finishing line up that defeated Ennistymon in the Junior (A) hurling final. A further five Under-21s and two minors participated in the senior championship. The youth that are now blossoming and breaking on the adult hurling scene should have deeper foundations by year's end, for at the time of writing, the U-14 and U-15(A) championships are already won.

Pictured is up and coming star forward Niall Daly who played for Clare in last years Munster Minor Hurling Championship against Cork in Thurles. He captained the Éire Óg Minor team that contested the 2002 County Championship Final. He is presently a student at University College Dublin.

Munster Junior Club

In the opening round of the Munster Junior Championship, Éire Óg lost to the Limerick champions, Kildimo, at the Claughaun grounds. Forced to play without six regulars, a seriously depleted Éire Óg lacked the resources to cope on the day, and with John Chawke in scoring form, Kildimo pulled away in extra time, to win by 2-13 to 2-5. On the day, Ronan Keane, Adrian Flaherty and Conor Considine were in action with St. Flannan's College in Dolla, while Colin O'Callaghan, Ciarán Daly and John Maher cried off the Éire Óg team because of flu.

The teams were evenly matched throughout normal time. Tomás Corbett and Fergal Brennan scored the goals for the Clare side but Richard McKeogh had two rapid goals in extra time sealed it for Kildimo.

St. Flannan's compensated by booking their place in the Harty Cup Final with a 1-13 to 1-6 win over St. Fintans CBS, Doon.

The loss in the Junior Championship was a blow to Éire Óg particularly in view of the hard work put in by manager Des Neylon. However, on a more serious note the transfers of Fergus Flynn, Colin Lynch and more recently Cathal Egan to Clooney from the senior club, is severe, at least in the short term.

Urban Board

The Urban G.A.A. Board was set up in 1998. Some of the original officers included Jimmy Cooney and Gerard Lynch. Ennis was surveyed in a geographical way to see where the appropriate divisions in the town could be made. Four distinct areas were identified. They being Ennis North (An Bóitherín), Ennis West (Na Fianna), Ennis South (Naomh Fhlannáin), and the town and market area (Dal gCais).

The current officers of the E.U.B. include Michael O'Brien, Bríd Dileen, Noel Mulhaire and Gerry O'Connor.

So, in a final summary one has to be optimistic about the future of hurling in Ennis. Good management will play a vital part in the progression of the talented groups coming through the club and the Urban Board and, if this is provided, then aother senior championship cannot be far away.

ENNIS

Stand at the height
To get a sight
Off all the crowd
As Dan stands proud.
Townies chatting
As the breeze they're batting.
Salutation rings,
'Well, how's things?'
'Ah, not too bad.'
And we are glad
To see familiar faces
And all the old places.
Peaked caps
And warm hand clasps
Courtesy great
Can't be bate
Child by the hand
Ah, isn't it great.
Abbey, O'Connell and Parnell
Know every inch really well.
Streets narrow
The true marrow
You will find
Kerbstones shined
By soft footfalls
Of women in shawls.
Now sad to say,
Shawls gone their way.
Mino the last
Tie with the past.
Auld stock were shocked

To see grainstores knocked.
Now the mills as well
Have heard the deathknell.
Bulldozer's roar
Has settled the score.
Now it's lounge bars,
Streets choked with cars.
Old ghosts walk
And whisper talk
Along the street
As they meet and greet,
'The lanes are gone
The cars have won,
Perhaps it had to be
But it's sad to see.'
In the lanes we lived,
We laughed and grieved.
Houses were tiny
But clean and shiny.
Families were big
But we'd dance a jig
At wedding or wake
And drink a rake
Of porter from bucket
We'd slug and sup it.
You'd get enough
And a pinch of snuff.
Corpse in shroud
Midst the crowd.
Many years ago
There wasn't much dough,
For a hearse to pay
So we'd shoulder the way
Up to Drumcliffe
To share the grief.
No women in bars,

Horses and cars,
Streets gas lit,
Films in the Pit.
Fourpenny hop
Dance till you drop.
Dark, bowed lanes,
Rainwater drains.
Kids hurling in the street,
Waring nothing but bare feet.
Sliotar of tied rags
Hurleys from the crags.
Raw Ash-plant
Heard the ceant.
'Hatten you a' sthor!'
Cried from the auld half door.
Scelp or clitter
Didn't make much differ.
Get the ball
No mercy at all.
If you can't take the tide
Then step aside.
'Jasus! Mind the window!
Or your mother 'll kill you!'
The auld wans smiled
Upon the child.
Blood on his knuckle
But in he'd buckle.
Never buckled under
Though torn asunder.
They scorned and shot us
But never got us.
Huge hearted people
Built the steeple.
And there she stands
Minding praying hands.
Unfinished

Christy Murphy

Ennis Boys National School 1996. Back row, left to right: *Neil Slattery, Enda McNamara, Stephen Skelly, Eamonn Concannon, Jamie Denieffe, Daniel Ryan, Ivan Kilbane, Ronan Keane, Niall Daly, Robert O'Riordan, Mark Brigdale.* ***Front row:*** *Gerard Keane, John Brennan, Thomas Craven, Colm O'Callaghan, Conor McNamara, Gary Collins, Adrian Flaherty, Ian Burns, James Gallagher.* Courtesy of Pat Brennan.

Cumann na mBratach CLG, Inis

The Banner Club was founded in January 1977 by an enthusiastic group, who felt a need for a second club in town. Many of the best known and respected names in Ennis hurling were involved. Genuine enthusiasts all! Johnny McGann and Seamie Murphy were previously involved with St. John's, while Paddy Gilligan and Tony Maher had strong links with Rovers. The founders wanted to pick a neutral name. The name Banner was chosen. Within a short time a couple of hundred members had joined the club, including newcomers to the game, quality players who had drifted away and others who felt disenchanted with the GAA scene in Ennis.

Tony Maher filled me in on the background. *"The basic idea behind the foundation of the Banner was to cater for young people who weren't getting games because there was only one club in Ennis, that being Éire Óg. Naturally, Éire Óg didn't have the personnel to look after numerous teams at various levels at one time. We certainly weren't formed to upset or go against Éire Óg. Can I read to you a section from the minutes of our very first meeting of January 23, 1977, at the Friary Hall? Johnny McGann presided as Chairman and in his address to the gathering he stressed 'that the Banner Club was not here to rival Éire Óg, but to supplement them. The aim of the club is to further underage hurling in town.' John Nevin then proposed that a letter be sent to the Clare Champion to that effect."*

Huge work went in with regular training sessions held twice or three times weekly under the guidance of Tony Blake and Paddy Gilligan. Big attendances were always present filling the ranks of the adult teams at Junior (A) and Junior (B). Apart from this, the big emphasis was on juvenile hurling. It is interesting to note that the Banner won the Under-14 Newmarket tournament in only its first year in existence. With players of the calibre of Jimmy Twomey, Tom Tuttle and Michael Guinnane they accounted for the Blues in their own tournament. Some of the juveniles I recall from this time include Chris Connery, Bernard Sheehan and Gary Logue. Other honours would follow quickly in U-12 hurling and U-16 football. By 1982 the club was catering for 12 teams at underage.

Much emphasis was put on travel. Trips were regularly organised for

***Under 15 Banner team 1978** - included are Colm and Ross O'Malley, Tom Tuttle, Paul Gormley, David McCullough, Mikie Ryan, Matthew Lernihan.*

the juveniles to Cork, Galway and Dublin. Sean 'Nobbers' Kelly was the chief mover behind this, and indeed it was he who organised the trip to Ruislip in London for the adult club for the weekend of October 26th to 29th 1979 to play the Desmonds.

Tom O'Grady, Ennis Furniture Centre, presenting hurleys to Banner officials Johnny McGann, Paddy O'Loughlin, Frank O'Malley and Kieran McNamara.

A strong Banner side featuring Barry Smythe, P. J. King and guests - Pat O'Connor (Tubber), Haulie Russell (Clarecastle), and Paddy Tom Malone (St. Joseph's) - defeated the Exiles, 7-6 to 4-13 in a fine game, Brenny Pyne's goals proving decisive in the end. The Desmonds featured many Claremen in Mickey Burke (Whitegate), Malachy Hehir, John King and Miko Cullinan of Ruan/Dysart and the Considine brothers, John and Michael, from Parnell Street, Ennis.

Afterwards, both teams were wined and dined at John Considine's pub in Hammersmith and later in the 'Spotted Dog' in Willesden. After a hugely enjoyable day the Banner contingent headed back to their headquarters at the Black Lion where singer, Liam Murphy, entertained the revellers. The following year the Desmonds Club was invited to Ennis. Again in 1981 the Banner returned to London for another memorable weekend.

Liam Murphy pictured in London about 1979. He was then a member of the traditional group Crusheen. Liam later sang with The Irish Brigade in New York. Currently a member of Moher, he released the C.D. "The Full Circle" in late 2002. Liam is a grand nephew of Brendan 'Barcelona' Moroney who played an active part in the Spanish Civil War - 1936-1939.

Junior A Championship

In 1979 the club reached the latter stages of the Junior A Championship, but after a disastrous start they were badly beaten by a fired up Ballyea by 4-9 to 0-6, with only Seamus O'Connell, Dermot Delaney and Brenny Pyne playing to their true form.

The following year Paddy Gilligan proposed that the Banner again assist Éire Óg in the senior championship. Playing under the name of Éire Óg Dal gCais, Ennis captured their first senior championship since 1966. Sean Lynch and Barry Smythe played leading roles with Dermot Delaney, Johnny Kearse and Francie Mahon featuring to a lesser extent. Without winning a junior or intermediate title, the Banner now made the ambitious move to play senior hurling in 1981. This might seem a ludicrous decision but it must be remembered that Éire Óg made the same decision in 1953. Perhaps the Banner was also hoping to entice more players to its ranks by taking this gamble.

Favoured by a series of lucky draws the club found themselves in the quarter final of the championship facing the Blues. Newmarket had, on

The Banner team that lost to Newmarket (the eventual winners) in the 1981 senior championship. Back row, left to right: *Dermot Delaney, Jim Collins, Brenny Pyne, P.J. King, Ml. Griffin, Barry Smythe, Seamus O'Connell, Kieran McNamara.* **Front row:** *Seán Dixon, James Kennedy, Denis Mulcaire Gerard McCullough, Pat Kirby, Haulie Russell, Pat Flynn.*

the other hand, reached the same stage through the losers' group. Few gave the Banner a chance of beating Newmarket but a shock seemed likely midway through the second half. An accidental injury to Sean Dixon proved costly for the Banner. After Dixon left the pitch, Newmarket introduced Timmy Ryan and the game was won and lost in the blink of an eye. A late goal sealed the game for the Blues on a rather flattering score of 2-11 to 1-8. For the Ennismen, Kieran McNamara, Gerry McCullough, Jim Collins, Denis Mulcaire, and Dermot Delaney were amongst the best players on view.

Tony Maher feels – *"Had we beaten Newmarket we would have been fired up against Éire Óg. The Banner should have gone and picked up a few more quality players for senior ranks. After all, we had lost Seán Lynch and Francie Mahon to Éire Óg. Over the years we continued to lose key players in Gary Logue, Paul Nihill, Declan Flynn and Tony Moroney – we could have won a Junior (A) title with those guys."*

The mid-1980s would prove the high point. The club continued to do well at juvenile level. By 1986 several of its players had represented Clare at U-16 and minor including Brian Pyne, Paul Nihill, Roddy and David McCullough, John McEnery and Paul Gormley. The latter was a promising goalkeeper. Other fine hurlers included the brothers, David, Ross and Colm O'Malley. By 1986/'87 the club was performing well in Minor (B) ranks. Anchored by David O'Malley at centre-back they lost narrowly to Kilnamona and Scariff. In 1987 the club reached the final of the Minor (B) League and Championship. A tremendous fight-back orchestrated by David O'Malley at centre-back brought the Banner back into the game. Michael O'Loughlin notched the winning point for Kilnamona to take the league title by 4-6 to 4-5. In the Minor (B) championship the Banner lost to Scariff by 1-8 to 1-3 with Sean McEnery outstanding in goal for the Ennismen. After the game, John Brett, Treasurer of Bord na nÓg presented the cup to Mark McKenna.

The previous year saw the Banner take the ambitious and brave step of developing their own grounds at Kilnacally, just a mile off the Lahinch Road. The club purchased 37 acres for £62,000. PRO, Tony Maher, announced *"the new site will be a great asset to the young people of the town."* The site contained an unoccupied dwelling house, which the club renovated and turned into dressing rooms. This was to be a temporary arrangement and plans were going to be put into place to construct a proper clubhouse. The initial success that the Banner enjoyed could not be sustained and the proposed development did not materialise. The club paid off the debt incurred in buying the site by selling a parcel of land to local builders.

The same year the club annexed the Under-21 (C) in a very entertaining game at Cusack Park. Due to the tremendous goal-scoring ability of Gary Logue (4 goals) and the accuracy of Brian Pyne the Banner led by six points at the interval. Others to impress were Ger Miniter, David O'Malley, Ruairí MacMathúna and John McInerney (in goal). Liam O'Doherty and Niall O'Connor had the upper hand at centre-field. In a Puc Fada competition run at this time the club was represented by Donal O'Halloran, Gerard Miniter, David Considine and Gary Logue.

In 1991 a major row broke out in Ennis hurling. The County Board Chairman refused the application to allow seven underage players to transfer to Éire Óg. Brendan Vaughan told the meeting – *"The Banner is being threatened with extinction and I cannot allow clubs to be forced out of existence."* Many heated exchanges took place between the clubs.

In March 1993, Jim Costello of the Banner claimed at a board meeting that *"Éire Óg are destroying us"*. The Roscommon native was quoted in the Clare Champion as follows: - *"All our officers work hard to promote hurling and football. There are many players in the town who could be brought into the fold if the right approach from all was there. Why have so many stopped playing Gaelic games in the town? How many county players are coming out of Ennis? The Board will have to stand up and support clubs like the Banner, who are struggling to survive. Éire Óg have a monopoly in the schools. We in the Banner could join other clubs and be associated with successful teams every year. We don't want that. We feel we have a purpose to develop the games in the town. Éire Óg's purpose should be the same as ours but their primary aim is to*

Banner Officers and Committee 1986. Standing, left to right: *Frank O'Malley (Vice-Chairman), Eamon O'Loughlin, Paddy Gilligan (Vice-President), Bernard Keane, Ross O'Malley, Robert O'Mahony (Asst. Sec.), Kieran Shanahan, Noel Pilkington.* **Front row:** *Tony Maher, Michael Considine (Chairman), Aidan O Murchadha, Tommy Pilkington. Missing - Flan Hynes, Dan O'Connor, Seán Nihill.*

Banner selection that played London Desmonds in 1980. Back row, left to right: *Tony Blake, Jimmy McNamara, Seán Dixon, Michael Considine, Brenny Pyne, P.J. King, Dermot Delaney, Francie McMahon, Kieran McNamara, Haulie Russell, Paddy Gilligan, Joe Nevin, Flan Hynes.* **Middle row:** *Barry Smythe, Simon Moroney, Seamus O'Connell, Tommy Pilkington, Pat Kirby, Ollie Byrnes, Jackie Hynes, Eric Hanrahan, Seán 'Nobbers' Kelly.* **Seated:** *Tommy Coughlan, Paschal McMahon, Martin Gardiner. Courtesy of Clare Champion.*

Banner players pictured after Junior 'B' Football success 1990. Back row, left to right: *Bernard Keane, Tony McDonagh, Seán Kennelly, P.J. Phillips (captain), James Costello (manager), Aidan Ó Murchadha (secretary), John Burke, present club chairman.* ***Front row:*** *M.J. Mathers, Martin Moloney, Pádraig Kerins.*

bury the Banner. It's your duty to respond and help us." he told the County Board.

Liam Griffin, secretary of Éire Óg didn't concur with Costello's remarks. *"We are too busy in Éire Óg to have time to be bothered about the destiny of the Banner. We have no reason to knock the Banner."*

Regardless of club politics players are suffering. Most players just want to go out and play the game. The Banner felt that the stronger senior club was poaching from them. At that time the club was having difficulty retaining players. To be fair to Éire Óg, they claim that the only players they acquired from the Banner were Gary Logue and John Mulcahy, a then member of both county minor panels.

This problem continued for a number of years but in May 2000, a historic agreement was signed, under the auspices of the County Board, giving each club in the town the right to retain players until after minor grade. This would now ensure that the best players would be retained and should ensure that the Banner participation in competitions would be more fruitful than before.

On the ladies football front the club has had great success. Last year, 2001, the Ladies captained by Eimhear Griffin, a daughter of the aforementioned Liam, captured the Féile National title. An outstanding achievement given the high level ladies football has attained!

The Banner, founded 25 years ago, has survived mainly thanks to an extraordinary group of people – the likes of John Burke, Michael Fawl, Domhnall O'Loingsigh and Jim Costello. Frank O'Malley really kept the

Successful Banner Junior 'B' team 1990. Back row, left to right: *Bernard Keane, Martin Moloney, Michael O'Connor, Seán Kennelly, Anthony Miniter, Martin Meehan, Pádraig Folan, John Burke, James Costello, Manager.* ***Front row:*** *Pat Keane, Seán Nihill, Brian Pyne, P.J. Phillips (capt.), John Queally, M.J. Mathers, Flan Markham.* ***Front:*** *Damien Keane.*

Banner Under 16 Ladies Football team of 1997. Back row, left to right: *Denise McMahon, Marie McNamara, Caroline Gardiner, Catherine Mulcahy, Ann O'Regan, Sinéad Hallissey, Louise Henchy, Dearbhla Rice, James Costello (Manager), Ciara McMahon, Donna Courtney.* ***Front row:*** *Leona Moylan, Sharon O'Flaherty, Carol Meere, Chorlene Reynolds, Selina Moylan, Laura Brennan, Claire Kilmartin (capt.), Lillian Finnucane, Joanne Creehan.*

club together during lean times before stepping down as chairman in 1996; Pat Crotty, Michael McInerney and Donny Martin have done tremendous work. On a positive note John Burke feels that the Banner has a great future and is now very confident because of the current good relationship between the Banner and Éire Óg and also due to a good stream of players coming through from the U-12 Town Board.

NOTES
The Banner GAA Club

Founder Members

Seamie Murphy	Seán Daly	Tony Maher
Fintan Quinn	P. J. Summerly	Paddy O'Loughlin
Paddy Gilligan	Johnny McGann	Frank O'Malley
Josie Nevin	Michael Considine	Seán 'Nobbers' Kelly
Tony Blake		
Patrons:	Tull Considine	Ralphie Burns

A Brief Summary of some Achievements

Hurling

1981 Under 12 (B) County Champions
1983 Under 14 (B) County Champions
1986 Under 21 (C) County Champions

Football

1979 Under 16 County Champions
1980 Under 16 County Champions

2001 All-Ireland Ladies Football Féile Champions

	Banner 2-4	...	Cappawhite 0-2
	Banner 0-5	...	Cahir (Tipp) 0-3
	Banner 1-2	...	Carbury (Kildare) 0-1
	Banner 2-1	...	Naomh Errigal (Tyrone) 0-6
Final	Banner 1-4	...	Lurgan Gaels (Cavan) 0-6

Banner Panel Féile 2001: Miriam Darcy, Sarah Hoey, Kate Keohane, Aoife Kavanagh, Ciara Normoyle, Lorraine O'Hanlon, Maria Hennessy, Caoimhe McNamara, Edel Griffin, Louise Skelly, Ann Marie McGann, Eimhear Griffin, Linda Cahir, Aisling Murphy, Siobhán Reidy, Edel Meere, Emma Gaynor, Harriett Hamilton, Claire Ann Neylon, Patricia Lynch.
Management: Jim Costello, Joe Reidy, Pat O'Driscoll, Geraldine Reidy.

Camogie

Camogie was first organised in 1904 when the association was founded, but went into decline during the turbulent years 1917 – 1923. It was popular in Clare during the 1920s but records are very sketchy. A County Board was formed in 1934 and clubs came into existence in places like Kilshanny, Doolin and Ballynacally, plus hurling strongholds like Newmarket-on-Fergus, Tulla, Ennis and Clooney. Clooney, trained by Paddy Carmody, was a dominant force in the 1930s. Some of their most notable players included Babs (Mary Catherine) Clune, Chris Markham and Annie Conheady. Annie Conheady (later O'Loughlin) told me about those times. *"We were very strong in Clooney and we won the County Championship two or three times before Kilshanny took it from us. Later there was a separation in Clooney and Creevagh formed a team; we beat them in a County Final replay."*

The county team met with little success, losing to Kerry at the Showgrounds in 1934 and to the all-conquering Cork team in 1935. Clare then withdrew until about 1944. In that year they created history by winning the Munster Senior Championship, beating Cork and later Waterford by 3-1 to 3-0. Chris Markham scored Clare's entire tally of 3-1 and the side also included Carmel Waterstone, Dympna Davis and the Captain, Theresa McNamara.

At her home in Clonroad, Theresa Blake (nee McNamara) filled me in on her playing days: *"Clooney Camogie Club was founded by Mick Hennessy, a native of the parish and a prominent Clare and Munster hurler of the 1930s. He was also an outstanding referee and was in control of one or two senior All-Ireland hurling finals. Clooney had a great hurling team then. I started playing camogie when I was about 14. By then the game had really become popular in Clare with teams starting up in Mountshannon, Tulla, Meelick, Ennis, Kildysart and Liscannor, but Clooney dominated all competitions in Clare. It was great. Our mothers didn't have to worry about us. All we did was play camogie. We were gone every Sunday. We went to Kilshanny, Whitegate. It was great fun."*

A native of Ennis, one of Clare's greatest players was Marjorie Griffin. *"A class wing-back, she matched style with reliability. Marjorie won 3 senior All-Ireland medals with Antrim in 1945, 1946 and 1947. She captained the All-Ireland winning team of 1946".* (From the Book, Camogie Champions).

The 1944 Munster Championship win was the highlight of Clare's achievement in camogie at this time. It went into a decline in the late 1940s, mainly due to emigration, and girls getting married, and it wasn't until 1958 that the game was revived following a meeting in Ennistymon. Several teams were formed including Liscannor, Spanish Point, Bodyke and Coláiste Muire (Ennis). Many friendlies were organised before a championship proper was played in 1959.

Feakle had a strong team in the late 1950s, which included Claire Harrington, Eva Bane and Liz Howard. The Killanena club was founded in 1959. The dominant clubs at the time were Cliffs of Moher, Coláiste Muire, with Killanena capturing both league and championship in 1959.

1968/69 Significant Season

Throughout the 1950s and 1960s, the inter-county championship was dominated by Dublin and Antrim. Dublin camogie was so well organised that they literally swept the boards year after year with only Antrim and later Wexford offering strong resistance.

1969 was a significant year in that Colleges camogie was introduced. Corn Sceilge was presented in memory of Seán Ó Ceallaigh, one of the men who helped draw up the rules in 1904. Coláiste Muire, Ennis entered a talented team. Trained by Sr. Angela, the side reached the provincial final only to lose by two points to St. Aloysius, Cork. The Ennis team included Mary O'Dea, Ann Brassil, Betty McMahon, Mary O'Brien and Louise O'Connor. Later Sr. Angela organised a team called Dal gCais featuring many former Coláiste girls.

Colleges Camogie

Well-known hurling and camogie coach, Mary Hanly praises the contribution made by Sr. Angela at Coláiste Muire. *"Sr. Angela was fantastic. We reached the Munster Colleges (A) Final in 1969. The team was put together by Sr. Angela. We had a great team. Later Louise O'Connor and I went to UCC. We won a couple of Ashbourne Cups in 1972 and 1973."* Later, coaching at Coláiste Muire was carried on by Catherine McNicholas.

In the early 1980s, Ennis Vocational School also became a major force in Colleges competition, contesting a couple of deciders and eventually defeating Thomastown of Kilkenny at Banagher in the 1983 final. Ennis Vocational School led by four points at half time thanks to goals from Patricia Rynne, plus top class displays by Jackie Moloney in goal, Mary Naughton, Marie Gormley, Bridie Roche and Monica Morgan.

Coláiste Muire, Munster Colleges Senior Finalists 1968. Back row, left to right: *Mary O'Dea (Ennis), Mary O'Brien (Newmarket-on-Fergus), Catherine Hanrahan (Ennis), capt., Sr. Angela (trainer), Pauline Ryan (Broadford), Ann Brassil (Newmarket-on-Fergus), Marie Kennedy (Ennis), Marian Garry (Ennis), Kitty Purcell (Feakle.* ***Front row:*** *Síle Harrington (Feakle), Ann Cody (Kilkenny), Ann Field (Cork), Bridie Clancy (Doonbeg), Louise O'Connor (Tubber), Kay Kinnevane (Cratloe), Betty McMahon (Newmarket-on-Fergus). Courtesy of Mary Hanly.*

Éire Óg Dominant

In March 1968, the Clare Champion reported an upsurge in Camogie affairs under the heading of *"Trying to revive Camogie." "For some time past, numerous females have been seen swinging the camán around town and their knowledge of the game amazed many onlookers at the final of the newly revived sport in the capital town."* With well over 50 girls signifying their intention to play in a town league, four teams were fielded with the Mods defeating the Minis by two goals in a closely contested final. Camogie was reformed under the auspices of the Éire Óg Hurling Club, but within a couple of years, the game became self-supporting. In 1969, Éire Óg won the league and championship double. Highly organised, the club members met regularly at the Forresters Club where detailed accounts of club minutes were kept in journals. Amongst the prime movers at this time were Eileen O'Loughlin, Rose Gilligan, Mary Griffin, Mai McGann, and a very young Therese Lynch. The 1969 victory was followed by a championship final win over Killanena in 1970 – *"played in a welter of excitement before an enthusiastic band of*

Éire Óg, County Champions 1970. Back row, left to right: *Liz Scanlan, Martina O'Grady, Patricia O'Grady, Pauline Ryan, Catherine Glynn, Eilish Burke, Catherine Collins, Stephanie McCarthy, Eileen O'Sullivan.* **Front row:** *Mairéad Collins, Mary Ballinger, Betty Ryan, Therése McDonagh, Freda Ryan, Marian Garry.* **Missing from photo:** *Margaret Glynn.* Courtesy of Catherine Glynn.

supporters." In 1970 they retained the championship when they beat Killanena at Tulla by 2-2 to 1-1. The game was played at a cracking pace, with Pauline Ryan and Catherine Glynn on top at centre-field. Catherine Collins was basically the difference between the sides, scoring all of Éire Óg's 2-2. After the game Fr. O'Keeffe, Chairman of the Camogie Board, presented the cup to Liz Scanlan. Éire Óg retained the title in 1971 when they had a big win over Kilmaley at Cusack Park before a large attendance. In 1971 the club decided to accept non-Ennis girls making Éire Óg even more dominant.

Brave Shannon Bid

Wolfe Tones, playing the pick of Newmarket, put up a brave bid in 1972 but failed to stop Éire Óg winning their fourth in a row on a scoreline of 5-8 to 3-1. The 'Champion' reported – *"The scoreline for once does an injustice to a game which was memorable and throbbed with tension, as underdogs Shannon rose to new heights before eventually failing to the might of Éire Óg. This was a game which gave new dimensions to camogie in Clare and proved wonderful value to those lucky enough to see it. Quicker to the ball and playing a more determined brand of camogie, the challengers strode into a quick lead with a goal from Jenny Downes and kept the pressure on the Ennis back line with continued attacks on the home goal. Wing to wing play gave*

Catherine Glynn (right) and Freda Ryan in action in the 1970 County Final against Killanena. Courtesy of Clare Champion.

Stephanie McCarthy the opening for a point for the defending champions but a beautiful opportunist goal from Eleese Fitzgibbon put Shannon five points up. This was a wonderful score as a cross ball hopped behind Margaret O'Toole, and the Shannon forward running in doubled first time to give Maureen Kelly no chance of saving. Inspiring Ennis captain, Catherine Glynn, pointed a 30 and then Theresa McDonagh pointed from play to leave just one goal between the sides after 18 minutes play. Betty Ryan at mid-field came into her own and set up many dangerous raids with her quick ground play, and it was rewarding to her efforts when she pounced on a hasty clearance to send a rasper to the net after 20 minutes. Two minutes later, Margaret Glynn goaled to put the Ennis side ahead for the first time. Shannon did come again mid-way through the second half and a goal from Mary O'Brien, followed by a point by Mary Dolan put the game back in the melting pot." However, the experience of Catherine Collins, Stephanie McCarthy, Mary Griffin, and the dynamic Betty Ryan, held out to win by a flattering margin.

1974 All-Ireland Junior Champions

In 1964, Clare's fortunes improved greatly when they won a four-county tournament involving Cork, Limerick and Waterford. The formation of Éire Óg and Wolfe Tones in the late 1960s improved standards and, by 1974, County Board Treasurer, Michael Brennan was appointed team trainer, ushering in a new era. Michael drew up a panel of 25 and, though defeated by Limerick in this opening league game, they improved greatly. They trounced Tipperary and had a big margin to spare over Kerry.

The Munster Final against Limerick attracted huge interest and was heavily featured in the Clare Champion at the time. It was played at the Fairgreen, Ennis and Clare got off to a great start with a Maureen Davoren goal, to win by 4-0 to 3-1.

The 1974 All-Ireland against Dublin at Croke Park produced a high standard of play and some delightful ground hurling. In a tight game, Mary Griffin scored the winning goal to leave the final score Clare 3-2 Dublin 3-0. In her acceptance speech, which was entirely in Irish, team captain Margaret O'Toole felt that the introduction of Mary Griffin won the match for Clare.

Margaret told me how she became interested in camogie. *"I got my first hurley from my father when I was four and this sparked my interest. Later I played Munster Colleges with Salesian Convent, Cahercon. In second year I wrote an essay saying that my biggest wish in life would be to captain Clare to an All-Ireland victory. The club in Ballynacally had gone into a decline because of emigration, so Michael Brennan asked me to sign for Éire Óg in 1972. At that time Shannon and Éire Óg were the dominant clubs and supplied most of the players. Claire Harrington, Anne Harrington and Anne Marie O'Loughlin came back from Dublin and provided a big boost. We had some very dedicated people working behind the scenes, like Michael Brennan, Jim and Kitty McNicholas, Mary O'Halloran and Paddy Duggan. It was a great outlet for me and a great social scene. There is a huge commitment involved if you want to compete at the highest level; we trained three nights a week and some of us used to travel down from Dublin for matches. Éire Óg lost several Munster club games by a point including a Munster Final; these were bitterly disappointing defeats. I remember one night at the Fairgreen when we lost a game. There was no net and the November darkness had descended. A Stephanie McCarthy goal was flagged as a point. We were convinced that the ball had gone under the bar for a goal. Stephanie thought it was a goal. The Clare Champion reporter felt it was a goal, but the white flag went up. Ahane won 3-4 to 3-3. I remember going back to Dublin totally distraught and very disappointed. We never expected anything like the reception we got having won the All-Ireland; the roads were lined from Ballycasey Cross to Shannon. We were put up on the back of a lorry and brought to Shannon, Newmarket, Clarecastle and*

Ennis. The Square in Ennis was thronged; it was beyond our wildest dreams. A lot of time and effort went into preparing for the All-Ireland but winning made everything worthwhile."

The fact that Éire Óg had so many girls that had played Munster Club and Inter-county competition and because of players of the calibre of Catherine McNicholas, Anne Marie Russell, and Therese McDonagh, they continued to dominate the domestic club scene, winning the Championship for the seventh consecutive time in 1975. Another important factor in the development of Clare camogie during the late 1970s was the inauguration of a very successful primary schools competition. As many as eight teams took part, with the Flan Garvey-coached Inagh team proving successful.

Successful Visit to Boston

Around this time, late 1970s or so, Éire Óg embarked on a successful trip to Boston and Philadelphia. The trip came about as the result of an invitation from the President of the Éire Óg Club in Boston, Mary O'Dea, who had earlier visited Ennis. Included in the Ennis party who made the trip were Margaret O'Toole (Ballynacally), Maureen and Kay Saunders (Kilmihil), Pauline Ryan, Eilish and Catherine Glynn, Catherine McNicholas, Martina O'Grady, Joan McCarthy (Lissycasey), Ann Daly (Clarecastle), Carmel Kenny, and Theresa Reidy (Connolly).

1981 All-Ireland Junior Champions

After a lapse of seven years Clare regained the Junior Championship in 1981. Along the way they were held to a draw by Limerick in the Munster Final at Shannon (Clare 1-1 Limerick 0-4) with Claire Jones getting both the Banner County's scores. A much-improved Clare defeated Limerick by 4-4 to 2-3 at Adare. Limerick looked in control, with goals by Agnes Sheedy, but Clare came back into the game. Mary Howard was in great form at centre-back and gave the forwards a plentiful supply of the ball. Goals from Carmel Wall (2) and Lourda Fox saw Clare to victory. Clare had the narrowest of victories over Kildare in the All-Ireland semi-final at Clane by 1-5 to 1-4. *"Lourda points Clare into another All-Ireland Final"* was the Clare Champion headline the following week. Others to do well were Mary Carey in goal, Carmel Wall, Martina Beegan and Claire Jones.

In the All-Ireland Final against Antrim Clare got off to a great start with a goal in the opening minute. Veronica Casey sent a long clearance, which was gathered by Lourda Fox, who drove a great shot to the net past Karen Coyles; Fox had an outstanding game with a personal tally of 2-1. Antrim came back strongly in the second half and reduced the deficit to two points but Clare finished strongly; this was a feature of their 1981 campaign. The management and team had put in a huge effort under Fr. McNamara and mentor, Catherine McNicholas, with over 40 training sessions held over the season. At a reception held in Ennis for the victorious team, organised by Clare County Council, Haulie Daly, Tadhg McNamara and Michael Guerin paid tribute to all concerned.

1986 All-Ireland Junior Champions

Clare won their second junior title of the decade in style, beating Limerick by nine points in a replay, then Cork and Roscommon to qualify for the final. This campaign produced splendid performances from Patricia Ryan, Helen Cusack and Pauline O'Brien amongst others. In the final at Croke Park, inspirational performances from Catherine O'Loughlin and team captain, Maura McNicholas, led them to victory over a strong Kildare team by 1-13 to 3-4. An interesting feature of the game was that Maura McNicholas with 1-7 and Catherine O'Loughlin 0-6 were the only players to score for Clare. The New Ireland Cup was presented to Maura McNicholas. In her acceptance speech she paid tribute to the work done over the season by team coach, Kevin 'Trixie' Twomey. In the senior final played afterwards, former Clare star, Claire Jones, won a senior medal with Kilkenny in their victory over Dublin.

Maura McNicholas.

In 1987, Catherine Molloy, Patricia O'Grady and Catherine O'Loughlin were honoured with selection on the Munster team, the latter receiving the Cork Examiner Sports Award for camogie. Other highlights included Anne O'Dwyer of Bodyke winning the skills competition at Féile na nGael and Kitty McNicholas refereeing the junior final between Armagh and Kildare. In 1990, Wolfe Tones swept the board at underage level with star player Debbie McDonagh honoured with selection on the Clare team at U-16, minor, junior and senior level.

Intermediate Titles

The strength in camogie at the moment is evident in the fact that the county won two intermediate titles in the 1990s. The first of these came in 1993 when the Banner overcame Dublin at Ennis by 1-8 to 1-5. Clare were rocked early on by a Ruth Lyons goal but, inspired by Moira McMahon and Debbie McDonagh, they fought back to win the day. After the game, camogie board president, Bridín Ní Mhaolagáin presented Corn Úna Ní Phuirséal to the Clare Captain, Frances Phelan. At least seven survivors from 1993 featured in the 1995 team when Clare regained the title by beating Tipperary at Toomevara. The marksmanship of Catherine O'Loughlin plus Patricia Moloney's goal and the skill of substitute Edel Arthur were the highlights of this game. A feature of these intermediate successes has been the large number of players from the Wolfe Tones Club.

Coláiste Muire, Ennis Make History

The Clare hurling success story continued at windy Ballinasloe when Coláiste Muire, Ennis, became the first ever winners of the All-Ireland Colleges U-16 (B) Championship. The team, mainly comprised of Junior Certificate and Second Year students, has been together for a couple of years and their commitment to the school team was never more evident. Under the guidance of Corkman, Aidan Lawton and former Clare hurler, Leo Quinlan, the Coláiste Muire girls were clearly aware of the honour attached to the wearing of the school colours on such an auspicious occasion. Quinlan last tasted success at College level as captain of St. Flannan's All-Ireland winning team in 1976, following an eighteen-year barren spell.

In reaching the latter stages of the competition, Coláiste Muire overcame the better intentions of Laurel Hill, St. John Bosco, and Kilmacthomas. In the quarter final they held St. Aidan's, Cork scoreless before travelling to Castlewellan, Co. Down for a semi-final meeting with St. Malachy's emerging victorious 1-7 to 0-2.

Though the Ennis college eventually proved themselves too strong for their Mullingar opponents, the final played at the Patrick Pearse Grounds in Ballinasloe proved to be a much harder battle than that suggested by the final scoreline.

After playing with the aid of the breeze, Coláiste Muire, Ennis led by 0-7 to 0-1 at the break. Things looked precarious enough at the midway stage. A well taken goal two minutes into the second half settled the Clare team. Two minutes later Loreto Martin replied with a similar score for Westmeath. From then on it was nip and tuck until Aisling Kelleher sealed the final outcome with a late goal. The second All-Ireland title to travel to Clare in the space of four days equally reflected the quality of hurling now apparent in the new found belief of the tradition of the game in the county. Many of the Coláiste players' backgrounds are deeply rooted in the backdrop of Clare hurling. Corner-back Aoife Ryan is a niece of All-Ireland medallist Pauline Ryan; Sharon O'Loughlin and Deirdre Hegarty, being sisters of inter-county hurlers Fergal, David and the 'Sparrow' O'Loughlin and Mairead Keane is a daughter of former 1960s Banner stalwart Milo Keane.

As Michael McMahon, Chairman of St. Joseph's told the homecoming

Coláiste Muire Senior Camogie team 1999. Back row, left to right: *Ruth O'Gorman, Marie Whelan, Linda McMahon, Ciara McMahon, Anne O'Regan, Louise Henchy, Donna Courtney.* ***Middle row:*** *Jane Scanlan, Marie Lynch, Zelma Power, Aislinn Kelleher, Caroline Brigdale, Dervilla Rice, Orla Doolaghty.* ***Front row:*** *Denise Lynch, Niamh Keogh, Sharon O'Loughlin, Mairéad Keane, Aoife Ryan (capt.), Marie O'Halloran, Karen Moore. Courtesy of Coláiste Muire.*

crowd last St. Patrick's night: *"the cost of success doesn't come cheap."* Leo Quinlan echoed these sentiments in the aftermath of Coláiste Muire's victory by thanking sponsors whose contributions to their campaign were invaluable. The cost of travelling to Castlewellan alone for the semi-final was in excess of £1,500.

The All-Ireland success continues to be built on. In 2002 the First Years and the Juniors captured the county double for the Coláiste. The First Years, coached by Aidan Lawton and Anne Madden, overcame Scariff Community College in a tense game by 4-2 to 4-0. Coláiste had excellent sharpshooters in Fiona Lafferty, Christina Tierney and J. J. Howard, who contributed all their scores. Niamh Casey, Mary Tierney and Ruth Lillis were the pick of the team playing in more defensive roles. Likewise the Juniors defeated Scariff by 2-5 to 1-4 in their county decider. Coached by Tom Ward, Coláiste Muire's outstanding players included Cathriona Power, Sarah O'Gorman, Niamh Shannon, Ciara Cullinan,

Coláiste Junior team 1999. *Niamh Ní Mhuirí (trainer).* ***Back row, left to right:*** *Linda Moloney, Martha Griffin, Antoinette Carey, Siobhán Lafferty, Eileen O'Sullivan, Roisín Bhamjee, Helen McMahon, Michelle Carolan.* ***Middle row:*** *Deirdre Griffin, Emma O'Driscoll, Deirdre Hegarty, Aislinn Kelleher, Jane Scanlan, Caitríona Donnellan, Edel Malone.* ***Front row:*** *Priscilla O'Connor, Sinéad Gavin, Denise Lynch (captain), Sharon O'Loughlin, Mairéad Keane, Joanne O'Malley, Aida Griffey.* Courtesy of Coláiste Muire.

Christina Colleran and Siobhan Commane was outstanding in goal. Now with top class facilities and coaches at their disposal, it should only be a matter of time before Coláiste Muire become a major force in Senior Colleges camogie.

Hopefully, Coláiste Muire will go on to become the force they were in the late sixties when they came close to winning the Senior Championship, with players of the calibre of Mary O'Brien, Ann Field, and Catherine Hanrahan. This team, trained by Sr. Angela, was defeated by St. Al's, Cork in the 1969 provincial final. Following this, past pupils from the college went on to form the club Dal gCais.

Jim and Catherine McNicholas have been involved in camogie since they came to Clare 30 years ago, Jim from Mayo and Kitty from Galway. They spoke to me about how the game has developed during the years of their involvement. Kitty played at mid-field on the All-Ireland winning team of 1974. *"We had huge crowds following us in the mid-1970s and we had a belief in ourselves. We went senior in 1975 and drew with Wexford, but they beat us in the replay; there's a big gap between junior and senior. Cork and Kilkenny were a couple of steps above us and we didn't have their pool to gather from as we had only eight clubs; today* (speaking in 1996) *we have 25. Never before have we had so much skill; now we have skill all over the team because they are starting earlier. There are a lot of girls who want to play but there is a lack of personnel at the organisation end of things. However, the future is very bright from the point of view of the numbers playing. Recently three new clubs were formed in Parteen, Broadford and Meelick and we're working on clubs in Bridgetown and Ballynacally."*

CAMOGIE NOTES

Éire Óg won 7 County Senior titles in a row from 1969 – 1975. These are just some of their winning teams: -

1969 - Mary Carey (goal), Mary Strand, Catherine Glynn, Maria Kennedy, Ann Hurley (Captain), Freda Ryan, Margaret Glynn, Catherine Collins, Mary Pyne, Pat Dinan, Beatrice Foley. **Subs:** Pauline Ryan and Mary Griffin (used). **Other reserves** included – Theresa Heaslip, Marie Glynn, Connie O'Driscoll, Eilish Burke.

1970 – Éire Óg County Senior Champions
Éire Óg 2-2 . . . Killanena 1-1

Marian Garry (goal), Eilish Burke, Patricia O'Grady, Liz Scanlan (Captain), Theresa McDonagh, Pauline Ryan, Freda Ryan, Catherine Glynn, Catherine Collins (2-2), Betty Ryan, Stephanie McCarthy, Mary Ballinger. **Subs:** Eileen O'Sullivan, Martina O'Grady, (used). **Other reserves:** Margaret Glynn, Mairéad Collins.

1971 – Team that overcame Kilmaley

Maureen Kelly, Margaret O'Toole, Patricia O'Grady, Liz Scanlan, Catherine Glynn, Maureen Saunders, Ann Hurley, Pauline Ryan, Stephanie McCarthy, Mary Griffin, Catherine Collins, Mary Strand. **Subs:** Betty Ryan, Marian Garry, Maureen Saunders (all used).

1972 – Éire Óg 5-8 . . . Wolfe Tones, Shannon 3-1

Maureen Kelly, Margaret O'Toole, Patricia O'Grady, Maureen Saunders, Catherine Glynn, Betty Ryan, Mary Griffin, Pauline Ryan, Stephanie McCarthy, Theresa McDonagh, Catherine Collins, Margaret Glynn. **Sub:** Mary Strand (used). **Other reserves:** Geraldine Crowe, Nora Coote, Claire Nugent, Marion McDonagh.

1974 – Clare All-Ireland Junior Champions v. Dublin
Clare 3-2 . . . Dublin 3-0

Maureen Kelly (Éire Óg), Anne Marie O'Loughlin (Dal gCais), Rose Kelleher (Shannon) Margaret O'Toole (Éire Óg), Claire Harrington (Celtic,

Scoil Chríost Rí, Cloughleigh beaten in extra time by Scariff in Div. II Final 1990. Back row, left to right: *Niamh Brennan, Shauna Keane, Patrice Skerritt, Andrea Casey, Rita Queally, Michelle Keavey, Anne Marie Kinsella, Suzanne King, Gráinne Malone.* ***Front row:*** *Bríd Mulqueen, Sinéad Malone, Elaine Kelly, Janette O'Shea, Tracey Hayes, Antoinette Baker.* Courtesy of Clare Champion.

Dublin), Theresa McDonagh (Éire Óg), Catherine McNicholas (Éire Óg), Maureen Davoren (Celtic, Dublin), Mary Dolan (Shannon, Mary Mahon (Muskerry, Cork), Pauline Ryan (Éire Óg), Eleece Fitzgibbon (Shannon). **Subs:** Maureen Saunders (Éire Óg), Catherine Glynn (Éire Óg), Mary Griffin (Éire Óg), Theresa Daly (Shannon), Anne Marie Russell (Éire Óg), Bridie McGirl (Shannon), Geraldine Crowe (Éire Óg), Martina O'Grady (Éire Óg).

1986 – Clare Junior Champions v. Kildare
Clare 1-13 . . . Kildare 3-4

Pauline O'Brien, Helen Cusack, Patricia Ryan, Noeleen Quinn, Siobhán Reidy, Patricia Rynne, Sheila O'Halloran, Noelle Comyns, Catherine O'Loughlin, Maura McNicholas (Captain), Catherine Molloy, Carmel Wall. **Reserves:** Shelley Hegarty, Elaine McTaggart, Claire Bracken, Josephine Conlon.

Coláiste Muire – All Ireland Colleges u-16 (B) Championship 1999

Paula McCarthy, Ruth O'Gorman, Jane Scanlan, Mairead Keane, Aoife Ryan, Marie Lynch, Denise Lynch (0-4), Marie O'Halloran (0-4), Deirdre Hegarty, Sharon O'Loughlin (0-2), Aisling Kelleher (1-0), Marie Whelan (1-0). **Subs:** Niamh Keogh, Martha Courtney, Karen Moore (all played).

PART TWO

"The Days of the Old Schoolyard"

Hurling at Ennis CBS

"Eggs and Rashers for the Boreen slashers,
The lickings of the pan for the Market gang."
John Leyden

"The passage of time seems to illuminate rather than dim the memory of my schooldays and of the legion of stories that I can recall. Very few, unfortunately, would pass a parent-teacher censorship board as being the ideal recipe for students' behaviour."
Aidan Tuttle

The Christian Brother's have been part of the fabric of Ennis life since 1827. The Religious Order's founder, Edmund Rice was born to a well-to-do couple, Laurence Rice and Margaret (Tierney) near Callan, Co. Kilkenny in 1762. The young Rice followed his father into the family business during which time he married. But, after the death of his young wife he decided to devote his life to the Christian education of Catholic boys. In 1827, he sent Bro. Jerome O'Connor and Bro. Ignatius Barry to Ennis to establish a school.

Ennis was described in the official 1827 report as *"having very little trade, no manufacturers, no municipal police, no charities, no lamps and no scavengers"*. Soon the word was out that a new school was to be opened for the education of poor Catholic boys. *On the first day at school *"the two brothers were confronted by a milling crowd of about 400 urchins, all eager to taste the novelty of school life. Their dress spoke eloquently of the perpetual squalor in which they were reared. Ragged, unkempt, some ill-mannered, others decidedly vicious, they flocked in as to a circus"*.

The great English novelist Charles Dickens (1812-1870) could well have penned the above description. A keen observer of life, Dickens would have witnessed several such scenes in his day in London. The so-called "common people" were hungry and oppressed and were denied educational opportunities for their children. Bro. Edmund Rice opened schools not only in Ireland but in industrial England as well, in such cities as Liverpool, Preston and Manchester.

Due to a difference of opinion with the National Board of Education over the teaching of religion, the Christian Brothers left Ennis in 1840, but thankfully they returned in 1854 to continue their work.

Colleges GAA

Ennis CBS entered teams in Colleges competitions at least as early as 1927 by fielding three teams in the western league. The other colleges in the competition included Kilrush CBS, Ennistymon CBS, Tuam and Ballinrobe. Initially, Ennis fielded teams in senior and junior football and senior hurling. The junior footballers and senior hurlers were successful. A Gaelic football enthusiast Bro. Moloney spent two terms in Ennis. He was appointed superior in 1932 having been at the school since 1923. During Bro. Moloney's stay huge emphasis was placed on football and athletics. In 1929 the senior team reached the Munster provincial final only to lose to St. Brendan's, Killarney. Prominent players on the 1929

C.B.S. Dr. Harty Team 1939/1940. Back row, left to right: *Gerry McNamara (Newmarket), Willie McAllister (Clarecastle), Kevin O'Shaughnessy (Tubber), Raymond McNamara (Newmarket), Amby McMahon (Corofin), Kevin Griffin (Kilmaley), Michael Eustace (Kilmaley), Reggie Connellan (Ennis).* ***Front row:*** *Séamus Reddan (Clooney), Jimmy Kelly (Clooney), Joe O'Halloran (Clooney), Paul Brohan (Spancilhill), Pat Kearney (Tubber), Paddy 'Whackey' Murphy (Tulla), Paddy Floyd (Tulla).*

side included Stephen Tuohy, George Tuohy, Christy Coleman, Leo Connellan and John Browne. Connellan was selected on the successful Clare minor football team of 1929 that won the All Ireland while John Browne starred for the Dals and later the Clare senior team.

Bro. Moloney also introduced drill as an extra curricular activity in both schools and had a special drill inspector to prepare the boys. These events, held in the Showgrounds and later Cusack Park, included Flag and Pole displays and Bolasses. The Bolasses which resembled a German grenade or miniature bowling pins were attached to heavy string and swung over the head. In full flow these displays looked magnificent and they continued well into the late 1960s.

In the 1936/37 school year Ennis reached the Munster Colleges football final having disposed of Ennistymon, St. Flannan's and Rockwell College. Again pitted against St. Brendan's, the teams were paraded onto the Deerpark enclosure in Charleville by the local confraternity band. Bad conditions mitigated against both teams with snow falling throughout. The Kerry footballers adapted better to the conditions and emerged victorious by 1-8 to 1-1.

Brother Irwin and Willie McAllister

Bro. Irwin arrived as Superior to Ennis from Mount Sion in September 1937 and held the position until 1942. John Leyden and Mick Leahy were students there at this time. John Leyden recalled his school days at the CBS. *"They were harsh, yet beautiful times. Willie McAllister was an excellent chap. My first encounter with Willie was when the late Tom Slattery introduced him to 'Crusty' Irwin. The new CBS had not been open long. Bro. Irwin had ideas of the school being not only a seat of learning – but also a bastion of hurling and football. The Dean Ryan Cup was first introduced in 1936. 'Crusty' realised he did not have enough hurling material on the rolls in class to win the competition. However, he had his mind set on winning the cup, be it by fair or foul means. Unfortunately, the method had to be the latter. Enter an unholy conspiracy with students such as Tom Slattery, Mick Leahy, Martin Power and I. We were to introduce to 'Crusty' a handful of capable hurlers with under 16 looks and who were on no other school roll. The strictest secrecy was entered into. The first player engaged was Willie McAllister. As the competition progressed, it became more difficult winning each game. For various games – various other 'foreigners' were introduced, but not at the same time. These included Matt Nugent, Paddy O'Loughlin, Joe McDonald, James 'Dutcher' Moloney, Haulie Daly, and 'Blondie' Keane. Bro. Irwin had achieved his great ambition – but the smile on his face was not to last long, as Ennis accounted for Midleton CBS in the final by 6-5 to 3-2. Someone – somewhere spilled the beans on 'Crusty's' activities. There is a school of thought which suggested that the information came from within the Christian Brotherhood. The more likely source seemed to be another seat of education within the Ennis area – who had already been engaged in poaching 'Crusty's' academically better students and staff. The net result is that Ennis CBS teams were debarred for some time from the Dean Ryan Cup. Bro. Irwin and his hurlers were referred to by a member of the Munster Colleges Council, Bro. Quinlivan, as Clare's renegades. Tom Walsh, CBS Ennis Delegate to the Munster Council retorted: 'Better a Clare renegade than a Cork rebel.'"* Certainly the winners didn't compete in 1942. Willie McAllister also represented Ennis at Harty Cup level in 1939/40. It is highly unlikely that the great Magpie was illegal. Though John Leyden added: *"Willie McAllister was brought in to tend the gardens with John Joe Crowe. Irwin suggested that Willie looked boyish enough to be on the school roll. God grant you eternal rest, Willie McAllister, you were cherished and loved by all whom it was their privilege to befriend you."*

Mick Leahy, one of the stars of 1941 and a contemporary of John Leyden, has slightly different memories of the Dean Ryan Cup. *"It was a grey area. Some of the lads worked part-time and went to school as well. It wasn't as it seemed. Bro. Irwin had a tremendous love of hurling and he made lads hurl as it should be played. He made ground hurlers out of a lot of the players. He lived for hurling and if he got carried away a little, it was due to the fact that he loved the game."* The one positive thing about the whole episode of 1941 is that Ennis CBS are in the record books as champions.

Harty Cup 1939/40

It is unclear when Ennis CBS first entered the Harty Cup but they certainly fielded a team in the 1939/40 season, losing to Limerick CBS by 7-2 to 3-2 before a big home crowd at Cusack Park. Though well beaten in the end, Bro. Irwin told the Clare Champion on Thursday, March 14th, 1940 *"that he was delighted with this fine exhibition of hurling"*. Bro. Irwin instilled great zip and enthusiasm into hurling in those years. The 1940 team consisted of players from Newmarket, Tulla and Clooney. They started well against Limerick with one of their star players, the great Willie McAllister, later of Clarecastle and Munster fame, finding the net in the opening minute. This talented side included Raymond McNamara, Paddy Floyd, Joe Halloran, Jimmy Kelly and Reggie Connellan. Many of these hurlers would play a leading part in club hurling throughout the 1940s.

I'm not sure when Ennis CBS returned to competitive fare but they definitely fielded useful Dean Ryan teams throughout the mid to late

Larry Blake congratulates Hugh O'Donnell (with cup) after Boreen's win over Turnpike in the 1947 CBS Town League Final. *Other hurlers in photo include,* ***left to right:*** *Seán Shanahan, Mikey Coffey, Denis McInerney, Noel Bane (with hurley), Tommy Keane, Georgie Guilfoyle, Ml. O'Loughlin, Andy Carmody.* *Courtesy of Cyril Brennan.*

1940s, as Michael Doherty testifies to but, possibly because of lack of numbers, the school didn't compete in the Senior (Harty Cup) competition. In 1951 a fine CBS side, which featured Michael Blake, Val McGann, Cyril Brennan and Michael Garry, accounted for Limerick CBS (7-4 to 4-1) before bowing out to Thurles CBS (3-5 to 2-3) in controversial circumstances in the Dean Ryan competition at Newport.

George Dilger paints an idyllic picture postcard of growing up in Ennis in the 1950s. *"We did a lot of swimming in the 'cut' during those scorching summers. Hurling was part of life. We hurled in the summer time and played soccer in the winter. We hurled on the roads. We didn't need organised games. Bernie, Michael and I didn't play juvenile with Ennis. We played in our ordinary clothes, 15 or 20 a side in small confined areas. We honed our skills. Everything was geared towards hurling. I can't remember a time when I didn't play. After leaving the Boys' National School, I went to the CBS. I played on a fine Harty Cup team in 1955/56. We had full-time training with Bro. Burke and Bro.*

Boreen (CBS League Champions 1947). Seated left to right: *Bernie O'Connor, Paddy Hewitt, Hugh O'Donnell, Josie White, Tommy Grannell.* ***Middle row:*** *Bobby Burke, Noel Bane, Ml. 'Brack' Halloran, Seán Shanahan, Ml. 'Acum' Hanrahan.* ***Back row:*** *Jack Lynch, Frankie Cassidy, Paddy McMahon (Spancilhill), Tommy McMahon, Mikey Coffey, Denis McInerney, Cyril Brennan.* *Courtesy of Cyril Brennan.*

Fegan. The players were treated like kings. We always had soup and sandwiches after training. The Harty team included Brendan Doyle, a fine wingback; you wouldn't get much change there. Pat Henchy, Sean O'Gorman, Hughie Ensko and Johnny McCarthy were other members of the team. Hughie Ensko and Sean Madigan played Inter-Provincial Colleges with Munster. After a great run in the Harty, we were beaten by two points by the North Monastery (North Mon) on an atrocious day at the Gaelic Grounds. I remember flicking a ball into the net. It was scooped out by their goalkeeper (Seanie O'Brien). The umpire turned a blind eye. Many of the CBS players played for St. John's, including the entire half-back line. Joe Daly and Frank O'Gorman, dedicated clubmen, ran a great club. St. John's fielded players who never saw an Éire Óg jersey. The biggest mistake was that St. John's didn't play senior championship. The success of hurling in Ennis was also the ruination of it. Ennis had plenty quality players to field two senior clubs. When St. John's were prevented from playing senior championship, players fell away. Some of the mentors also went little by little. It's amazing how things can topple. On a more positive note, we had a huge amount of games then. We had great games with St. Flannan's. We loved playing Flannan's. We'd be thinking of the game all week. St. Flannan's were great opposition because of their constant training, great playing pitches and facilities. There is no substitute for playing the game. The pace dictates the play."

Bro. Fegan, a native of Dublin City, was appointed as superior from 1955 to 1961. He took a keen interest in hurling and, along with Bro. Burke, recognised that sufficient talent existed in the school for an assault

Ennis Vocational School team 1945. Back row, left to right: *– –, Seán Brody (Clare Road), Charlie Considine (Lifford), Batt Dillon (Clarecastle), Seán O'Brien (Turnpike), B. Purcell.* ***Centre row:*** *Seán O'Ceallaigh (Irish Teacher, R.I.P.), Stanley Culligan (Spancilhill), Michael Broderick (Broderick's Garage), Des McMahon (Spancilhill), M. Galvin, Jackie Moroney (Turnpike), Michael Lyons (Ruan).* ***Front row:*** *John Joe McInerney (Cahercalla, Rockmount), C. Ryan (Clare Rd.), Seán Dinan (Kilrush Rd.), George O'Halloran (Corrovorrin), Seán Clohessy (Clare Rd.), Joe O'Halloran (Knockanean). Courtesy of George O'Halloran.*

A group of CBS schoolboys c.1953. Included are: Paddy Coughlan in front with football, Paddy Ferrigan (with cup), Aidan Tuttle, Johnny Pickford, Seán Murphy, John Carroll, Michael Quinn. Courtesy of Paddy Molony (R.I.P.).

on the Harty cup. On October 22nd, 1955, Ennis CBS re-entered the Harty cup on a winning note when they trounced Charleville by 11-10 to 2-1. *"Speed, weight and teamwork were in abundance on the winning side and for these assets Charleville had no answer. A special train carried 400 supporters from Ennis and their heroes were not wanting in vocal support on the field. On their return the schoolboys marched in triumph from the railway station chanting the resounding team ditties '2 – 4 – 6 – 8 who do we appreciate E N N I S C B S.'"*

With Pat Henchy in devastating form on the '40' (centre-forward), Dungarvan proved no match for Ennis on a scoreline of 6-11 to 2-1 to reach the quarter final. Georgie Dilger came in for special praise in the pages of the Clare Champion – *"Dilger came on as a sub in the second half and his influence was such that one wonders how much greater would have been the superiority of the Ennis boys had he been on the field for the full hour. Dilger proved a tonic tearing the Waterford defence to shreds. The final score read Ennis CBS 5-9, De La Salle 2 goals. With resounding victories to date, I eagerly await the big semi-final with North Monastery. The promise shown by last year's Dean Ryan Cup team is being fulfilled and I sincerely trust that success will crown their valiant endeavour in the bid to ultimate victory. Unless the "Mon" can sufficiently remedy evident weaknesses, this promising young Ennis team should crash their way into the final against Thurles. The Mon are great crowd pullers and everything points to the existing gate receipts for a colleges match being broken on Sunday week."*

As predicted, the semi-final meeting with North Monastery was a different affair played in terrible conditions. The Mon, assisted by a gale, built up a big interval lead of 6-1 to 0-2. On the changeover, the Ennis mentors made a terrific switch by bringing Jack Daly to full forward and Sean O'Gorman to full-back. Daly immediately signalled his arrival on the edge of the square with a powerful goal. Sean O'Gorman gave an exhibition at full-back mopping up everything with his fine relieving clearances. The rally continued with two well taken goals by Colm Madigan reducing the deficit to just 5 points when a row broke out culminating in a pitch invasion which held up play for several moments. A fourth goal from Hughie Ensko following a melee after the North Mon goalie, Seanie O'Brien, was warned by the referee for time wasting. Ensko's goal proved the final score, as Ennis pressed forward for the winner, the referee sounded the final whistle - a bit prematurely in the opinion of some irate Ennis supporters.

The Champion reporter continues: *"On an ordinary day, Ennis should have won, but in the freak conditions that prevailed, it was a matter of 'ifs'. If the team had played with the wind in the first half, if those two*

Hermitage (CBS Town League Senior winners) U-13, 1957. Back row, left to right: *Michael Considine, Stephen Donovan, John O'Brien, Naoise 'Nazzer' Fitzpatrick, Tony Meere, Paschal O'Brien, Padraigh Ryan, Seán Cullinan, James Ball.* **Front row:** *John Nevin, Gerard Feely, Brian Higgins, Frank Rice, Vincent Loftus, Michael Ball, Haulie Molloy, Seán Coffey.*

blinding showers of hail had not swept with cutting force into the Ennis boys' faces and if the breeze did not die down somewhat in the second half. The final score read North Mon. 6-2, Ennis 4-6. For Ennis, Daly, O'Gorman, McCarthy and Madigan excelled when the going got tough". To this day, Ennis feel they were robbed of a final appearance but, despite defeat, it can be argued that the 1956 team laid the foundation for success in 1962. In the 1956/57 school year, CBS, inspired by a superb performance from Pat Henchy, defeated De La Salle by 5-9 to 2 goals, but went out in the second round to a great Thurles side by 3-10 to 1-3. The late Michael Gallagher (Sports Reporter with Clare FM) recalled: *"the teams then were about 50/50 town and country. Rockwell College beat us by one point in 1958, 4-5 to 4-4. Aidan Tuttle, Noel Carmody, Des Loftus and Jim Blake were prominent members of the team. Tuttle was good, strong and tough. He was gifted; a great wit and raconteur. He once got £5.00 from his mother for school expenses but he put the fiver on a horse and won £100.00. He brought us all to T. V. Honan's pub in the Square for a mineral; he had a pint of Guinness himself, of course".* The 'Tut' himself recalled his schooldays with great fondness when he wrote in 1977: *"the passage of time seems to illuminate rather that dim the memory of my schooldays and the legion of stories that I can recall, very few unfortunately would pass a parent/teacher censorship board as*

Turnpike team (CBS Leagues) 1959. The picture features many from St. Michael's Villas. Front row, left to right: *Francis Guilfoyle, John O'Donoghue, Eric Hanrahan, Dermot Cunningham, James Bradley, Sean Queally, Sean Feaney, Tony Corry, Francis Shanahan, Martin Shanahan.* ***Back row:*** *Jimmy O'Loughlin, Tony Hahessy, J.J. Corry, John McKeown, Val Bredin, Gearoid White, Rory Flynn, S. O'Connor, Kieran O'Connor and Niall Matthews.*

being the ideal recipe for student behaviour. The absence of exaggeration in my last sentence can be verified by "other graduates" of what we can call the class of '57".

In 1958, Bro. Bridges, a native of Wexford, arrived from the North Monastery. He set about organising hurling in the primary schools competitions. His team inflicted victories on St. Munchin's (Limerick), Clonmel and Limerick CBS. A sight of young hurlers were present at the primary school then, including Michael Flynn, P. J. Kelly, Willie Kelly, Tony Coote, Frank Molloy, Anthony and J. J. Corry and John McKeown. Many of these youngsters would backbone the winning Rice Cup team of 1962. The Dr. Rodgers Cup was inaugurated in the late 1950s. Ennis CBS had traditionally performed well in the competition. In February 1961, they opened their campaign with a 6-8 to 3-1 victory over Nenagh CBS. Featuring six or seven members of the Harty Cup team, they went on to destroy Clonmel CBS by 9-5 to 3-1 to coast into the semi-final. A classical centre-field display by Garry Stack and Sean Coffey laid the foundation for a 9-3 to 4-3 win over Rockwell (Cashel) to qualify for the final with Coláiste Iognaid Rís from Sullivan's Quay. With ten members of their Harty Cup team on duty, Sullivan's Quay were installed as favourites to take the cup but, by sheer determination and crisp ground hurling, Ennis raced into a 4 goal lead early in the second period. Nevertheless, they

Ennis CBS Dr. Rodgers Munster Colleges Champions 1961. Back row, left to right: *Bro. Jim Hennessy (coach), P.J. Moloney, Pat O'Connor, Seán Coffey, Vincent Hogan, Vincent Loftus, Jim McMahon, Tony Vaughan, Garry Stack, Ml. Hanrahan.* ***Front row, left to right:*** *Des Shanahan, Hughie Malone, Pat Brennan, Toddy O'Loughlin, Paddy Flynn, Paschal O'Brien, Bill Murphy, Derry Dinan, Senan Donoghue.* ***Seated:*** *Tony Kelly, Pat Coffey. Eleven of the panel were part of the winning Harty Cup team of 1962.*

had to withstand a grandstand rally led by Spencer to just about hold out by 8-4 to 8-3 to take their first trophy back to Ennis CBS since 1941. Some of the stars of the competition included Hughie Malone, Toddy O'Loughlin, Derry Dinan, and Senan O'Donoghue.

Bro. Jim Hennessy

Waterford native, Bro. Jim Hennessy came to Ennis primary school in 1960 and for the next four years Ennis CBS hurling enjoyed its greatest ever spell. To this day, Jim Hennessy is held in the highest esteem by all who knew him. Pat Brennan recalls: *"I left school after Inter-Cert. It was a huge disappointment to miss the Harty Cup Finals of 1962 and 1963. Ennis CBS declined somewhat when Jim Hennessy moved to Limerick CBS, and they turned the tables on us. Bro. Hennessy was the greatest influence on hurling in Ennis at that time. He gave the players great belief in themselves. Not only did he motivate the CBS but he also took control of the Rovers minor club. St. John's were considered to be much stronger with players of the calibre of Aidan Lynch, Paddy Flynn, Richard (Dickie) and Noel Pyne and Jimmy Lillis. The Rovers minor team of 1961 was very young but Hennessy had us fired up. Rovers went on to win five minor and three Under-21 titles and provided eleven of the side that won the senior championship for Éire Óg in 1966."*

Ennis CBS opened their Harty Cup campaign of 1960-61 against Coláiste Chríost Rí (Cork) at Kilmallock and, after trailing by 3-1 to 0-5, the Ennis lads hit 'a purple patch' in a ten-minute spell early in the second half with Michael Hanrahan and Johnny Cullinan outstanding. *"Cork hurlers overwhelmed by team spirit"* wrote the Clare Champion as Ennis triumphed over their more fancied rivals by 4-10 to 4-1.

Few Colleges games at this time caught the public imagination more than the re-match between Ennis and St. Finbarr's at the Gaelic Grounds.

St. Finbarr's/Ennis CBS Rivalry

The St. Finbarr's Farranferris hurling story goes back to the turn of the 20th century, but it wasn't until 1952 that they reached their first Harty Cup Final losing to St. Flannan's.

Fr. Carthach McCarthy became coach to St. Finbarr's about 1950 and he set about building strong Colleges teams. In 1960, Farranferris met Ennis CBS in the quarterfinal of the 1960/1961 Harty Cup.

Played in Buttevant in atrocious conditions, the game ended in a blaze of controversy. *"Controversial finish to Harty Cup match. Bewildered Ennis CBS supporters were talking about the mystery of the*

The CBS team that defeated St. Finbarrs in the 1961 Harty Cup Quarter Final replay at the Gaelic Grounds. Back row, left to right: *Ml. Maher, Tony Vaughan, Vincent Hogan, Paddy Flynn, Vincent Loftus, Tony Maher, Joe Hehir, Frankie Hassett, Michael Hayes, Johnny Pickford, Seán Coffey.* ***Front row:*** *Kyran Kennedy, Dessie Guerin, Chris Considine, Michael Hanrahan, Johnny Cullinan (capt.), Ml. Cullinan, Seán O'Connor, Derry Dinan, Tom Quinn.*

extra four minutes. At the end of the hour they had 'won' by two points only to lose four minutes later" wrote the Cork Examiner.

Tim Horgan, a pupil at Farranferris, wrote many years later in Farna's Hurling Story – *"It rained and rained all through the match as we juniors huddled for shelter beneath the crumbling army barrack walls that surrounded the Buttevant pitch. At the end of the hour Farna looked beaten. We waited anxiously for the Ref. to blow the whistle so that we could rush to the shelter of our single-decker (Canny's) bus. But no whistle sounded. Two minutes later Farna scored a goal and we were suddenly in front. 'Blow the whistle now Ref.', we pleaded as we shivered but still no whistle. Two minutes later we were still a point in front and finally the referee blew full-time. We were ecstatic. Then something remarkable happened. A swarm of irate Christian Brothers descended on the referee, roaring, shouting, gesticulating and threatening. We'd never seen clergymen acting like this before. It was a startling revelation. They were pointing at their watches and wagging their fingers at the referee and we couldn't quite hear what they were saying. We knew that the language they were using didn't come from the Book of Kells. The 34 minute second half came as a surprise to the referee."*

Stephen Gleeson felt he'd played the standard 30 minutes in the second half. Apparently, because of the atrocious weather, he'd changed

Action from the 1962 Harty Cup Final - Paddy Corbett (CBS) about to win possession, supported by Tony Vaughan, John Nevin of St. Flannan's is on the extreme left.

Paddy Flynn (captain of Ennis CBS) is carried from Cusack Park by James Moore and Raymond Duggan, a brother of Paddy Duggan, following CBS victory over St. Flannan's. The other CBS player carried shoulder high is Tony Vaughan (Clooney). Paddy Flynn was a highly rated Ennis hurler - a contemporary of his described him to me as follows - "Paddy Flynn was never beaten. He always reminded me of Michael Blake. He had the same temperment and determination as Blake". Conor McCarthy (O'Connell Street), is the young boy in front. Courtesy of Brooks Studios.

his jersey at the interval and put on a short sleeved gansey and it's quite possible that the heavy rain affected his timepiece. When he realised his mistake he immediately phoned the Munster Colleges Council, who ordered a replay.

St. Finbarr's had no problem with the replay and sportingly agreed to a re-fixture. Stephen Gleeson was again appointed to take charge. *"Spurred on by a large number of wildly excited supporters Ennis made no mistake in the replay. Playing their usual brand of fast stylish ground hurling they came to life after Des Guerin's goal in the 19th minute. This inspired Tony Maher and Seán O'Connor at centre-field where prior to this Derry Scully and Tom Murphy were holding sway. The selection of Des Guerin at centre-forward also proved a master move as he dominated St. Finbarr's star centre-back of the 'drawn' game, Charlie Nyhan. The brilliance of St. Finbarr's goalie, John O'Callaghan, kept 'Farna' in touch up to the final minutes when Vincent Loftus sealed the game with a goal to leave the score at 2-5 to 1-2"* wrote the Clare Champion reporter.

Despite a great run in the Harty Cup, Ennis went out to the eventual winners, the North Monastery, by 5-6 to 3-3 in the semi-final. At least seven of the successful Rodgers team were selected for the Harty team in 1961-1962.

Beginning of Ennis CBS/Limerick CBS Rivalry

In preparation for the 1961/62 Harty Cup campaign, Ennis CBS went into serious training. Challenge games were organised with Kilkenny CBS and St. Molaisse's of Portumna. Many players were tried and tested such as Johnny Pickford, Senan O'Donoghue, Gerard Bergin and Liam Murphy. For their opening game with Limerick CBS, Johnny Pickford *"an accurate wing forward"*, was selected in the attack. A powerful Limerick side, featuring Mick and Eamon Cregan and Bernie Hartigan, began in devastating form notching 1-2 in the opening minutes by carving holes in the Ennis defence. Having pulled back the deficit to one point at the interval, Limerick again upped a gear before Ennis came to life in the final quarter playing 'text book' hurling to win by 7-8 to 6-5 in a cracking game. Vincent Loftus, Pat Coffey and Michael Hanrahan opened the Limerick defence while 'Dashie' Maher subdued Bernie Hartigan at centre field. In spite of scoring 7-8 the Clare Champion reporter wrote: *"This was a game that Ennis deserved to win. Taken all around they were a better equipped side which showed signs of a strenuous training programme, however, an improvement is needed and their sometimes lackadaisical approach won't do against the North Monastery or Coláiste Chríost Rí."* Featuring six of their winning team of 1961, the 'Mon' overcame their Cork City rivals by 4-9 to 2-4 but proved no match for a much-improved Ennis CBS side. Played at Kilmallock before 9,000 spectators a stylish Ennis team destroyed the 'Mon' by 6-8 to 2-3. *"Playing as a unit, Ennis CBS' trademark ground hurling paid off. The spectacular 'blackboard' play of the Ennis forwards was the highlight of the game. Rarely did they attack down the centre as the ball flashed from wing to wing, giving the Mon defenders what must have been their most trying 60 minutes to-date"*. The typical Cork comeback never materialised even though the winners rested on their oars for the latter

The Ennis CBS team of 1963 that beat Limerick CBS in the Harty Cup. This side eventually lost the final to St. Finbarrs. Back row, left to right: *Ml. Hanrahan, P.J. Ryan, Brian Fitzgerald, Vincent Loftus, Jim McMahon, Vincent Hogan, Seán Coffey, Jimmy Quinn, Raymond Shannon.* ***Front row:*** *Conor Smythe, Paschal O'Brien, Pat Coffey, Gary Stack, Seán O'Leary, Tony Vaughan.* *Courtesy of Yvonne Flynn.*

stages. With eight players getting on the scoreboard, Ennis gave possibly their greatest team performance of the 1961/64 era.

Unique Final

Following big wins in their section and allowing for their tradition and big time experience, St. Flannan's were installed by most as slight favourites to win their 9th senior championship. Michael Hanrahan of St. Michael's Villas, a star of the CBS team, recalls: *"It was very exciting. The closest I can come to it would be the euphoria surrounding Clare's win in 1995. The weeks leading up to the final were unbelievable. Being stopped in the street by well-wishers looking for a progress report on the team. Everybody in the Villas was interested in it because of the fact that Des Guerin and I were on the team. Mrs. Leahy made blue and yellow caps and scarves for the CBS. She was a great woman. You couldn't walk 10 or 15 yards without being stopped by Flan Hynes, Con Ryan, Tommy Pilkington or Tommy Coote. Practically everywhere you went you were treated as a celebrity. Andy Warhol said, 'everyone is famous for 15 minutes'. Well that was my 15 minutes. The 1962 team was regarded as a springboard for hurling in Clare. It never materialised. Only Vincent Loftus went on to bigger and better things. He actually played for Munster."*

A record crowd of over 9,000 paying patrons swarmed into Cusack Park to witness one of the tensest ever finals. After much 'fumbling and messing' the CBS only got into their stride in the second quarter building up a reasonable lead by the interval. *"Rarely, if ever, have such scenes been witnessed as were in the dying minutes when St. Flannan's gradually whittled down their opponents lead to the minimum. Dickie Pyne and Tony Loughnane, the Flannan's danger men were 'competently handled' by the CBS defence but it was the quick thinking of Paddy Flynn that denied Flannan's two goals in the second half. Withstanding onslaught after onslaught, the CBS defence stood up to a constant buffeting from Flannan's and it took a brilliant save two minutes from time by Michael Hayes (Clooney) to give a deserving victory to the CBS after some desperate efforts since 1955 to enter the final."* (Clare Champion).

In the All-Ireland series, St. Peter's of Wexford overcame the challenge of Connaught Champions, St. Molaisse's, with Ennis CBS receiving a bye, setting up a final pairing of Ennis and Wexford. Was it nerves that cost the CBS a possible Colleges All-Ireland in 1962? Colleges' correspondent, Peadar O'Brien, writing at the time had this to say: *"For once this St. Peter's team was held. Their forwards never got away from the vigilant Ennis defence, which had stars in goalkeeper, Michael Hayes, Paddy Flynn, a truly great right fullback, Tony Vaughan at fullback and Chris 'Gus' Considine in the half line. Most of the Peters' 10 points in the drawn game came from outfield. Again Eamon Doyle was playing magnificently and notched some nice long-range points. And when Ennis CBS, slow starters that they were, held their rivals to a 1-2 to 0-5 score at the interval, it looked as if their more stylish hurling might just bring them through. The last five minutes of the game were tension packed. St. Peter's, in an effort to make up for a goodly number of lost chances, threw everything into a last ditch onslaught, but Ennis lived to fight another day. On now to May 6, with Croke Park as the venue, and when it was found that at least five of the Ennis side had never seen Croke Park, let alone play in it, St. Peter's were immediately installed as favourites. If ever there was a case of Croke Park nerves affecting a team, it happened that day, when nothing went right for the Clare side, and in turn nothing seemed to go wrong for the Wexford school.* [Played as a curtain raiser to the Kilkenny/Cork National Hurling League Final before a crowd of approx. 45,000.] *St. Peter's played high-powered hurling. They charged into a 1-2 to nil lead after 8 minutes, and thereafter were never caught. The final result, St. Peters 4-11, Ennis 2-4, was a just reflection of the game that did not live up to the previous tie. The win brought Wexford its first Colleges All-Ireland title, and no man could be more proud than centre-back, Mick Kinsella, who played storming games right through the championship. I single out Kinsella, the big Wexford lad, because he seemed to typify all that is great in Wexford hurling."*

Despite being well beaten in the replay, the Clare Champion singled out full-back Tony Vaughan for special praise: *"Tony Vaughan played a glorious hour. Roving far out field to make his clearances, Vaughan brought the ball from danger zone amidst a ruck of players on several occasions and Peter's would surely have added further to their total were it not for his stout hearted efforts. Vincent Hogan also shone at centre-back and did a lot of covering."* As a matter of interest, St. Peter's won four All-Ireland Colleges titles between 1962 and 1974; all were won at the second attempt against Ennis CBS, Limerick CBS, Coláiste Chríost Rí and Our Lady's, Gort.

1963 Harty Cup Season

Again with Bro. Jim Hennessy in charge, Ennis defended their Harty Cup title in the second round against Limerick CBS at Newmarket on Thursday, November 1st 1962. Inspired by Garry Stack they led 3-5 to 1-3 at the interval. With exchanges hotting up and tempers becoming frayed in the opening minutes of the second half, Limerick, thanks to the efforts of Mick and Eamon Cregan, Pat Nash and Donal Russell thundered back into the game. It took a magnificent last quarter by Ennis to hold out. At the end of play Ennis had eight points to spare (5-6 to 3-4). *"It will take a powerful team to take the Cup from Ennis"* wrote the Clare Champion. And a powerful side it took in the form of St. Finbarr's. Participating in the other side of the draw, Finbarr's defied the odds to beat St. Flannan's (5-7 to 4-6) in the second round. Following the terrific display against Limerick in the 1962/1963 season, the form of Ennis CBS declined a little, partly due to the loss of their outstanding full-back, Tony Vaughan, who discontinued his studies prior to the semi-final against St. Colman's Fermoy. The departure of Vaughan unsettled the forwards, as Vincent Loftus was moved from the attack to the full-back position. With Tim Field, Sean Murphy and Eamon Barry in form, St. Colman's went into an early lead before P. J. Ryan and Vincent Hogan began dominating central positions. Two well taken goals by Michael Hanrahan brought Ennis back into the game, but it was in the last few minutes of the first half when the intelligent play of Flan Quigney and Pat Coffey shattered the Fermoy defence. Four goals in four minutes by Pat Coffey sealed the outcome. Flan Quigney, operating at corner forward, made at least two of the goals with his well-timed crosses, putting Ennis into a fourteen point interval lead. Regardless of the best efforts of Fermoy in the second half, they had no answer to the strength of the Ennis defence. The final score read Ennis 6-2, St. Colman's 1-8. In the other semi-final, St. Finbarr's brushed aside the challenge of Thurles CBS by 5-12 to 3-4. In preparation for the Harty Cup final, Thurles sportingly gave Ennis a good workout with the latter winning by seven points.

1963 Harty Cup Final

Following St. Finbarr's heavy defeat to St. Flannan's in the 1962 Dean Ryan final, it was proposed that the Farranferris school teams would in future travel to games in cars rather than by bus. This they felt would prevent sickness. For the 1963 Harty Cup season Farna put in huge preparation travelling to Kilkenny on a black winter's day to play St. Kieran's in a challenge. Christy Ring came in as advisor to the team, giving the players huge confidence and belief in themselves.

In round one, Farna overcame Coláiste Iognaid Rís, before accounting for one of the favourites, St. Flannan's. They reserved their best hurling until the semi-final when disposing of Thurles CBS. *"It was always nice to beat the two Ennis Colleges,"* said Fr. Carthach McCarthy in Farna's Hurling Story. *"I remember a day when we surprised a great CBS team in the final."*

It seems Seán Barry, having scored 4-11 in the games with Flannan's and Thurles, was a marked man coming into the final. Christy Ring had instilled every skill in the game to his charges but, because of his involvement with the Munster Railway Cup team, he couldn't be in Thurles for the Harty game with Ennis CBS on St. Patrick's Day 1963. However, Fr. McCarthy pulled a stroke of genius to master Ennis. As Farranferris didn't have numbers on their jerseys at that point, they played Denis Harrington in Seanie Barry's position.

Harrington recalled: *"Seán Barry and I had much the same build but his crew cut made him easy to recognise. So I was ordered to get a crew cut and then the selectors placed me in Seán's wing-forward position. The Ennis backs beat the sugar out of me in the first ten minutes, thinking I was Seán Barry but, when he scored a quick goal and a point, they got the message. After that, I was told to revert to my normal position."*

Fielding about ten members of the 1962 winning panel, the CBS were installed as slight favourites to retain the cup. Undeterred by conceding a goal in the opening minute, St. Finbarr's just about deserved to win their first ever Harty Cup when defeating Ennis by 6 points on a heavy sod. The soft underfoot conditions didn't suit the Ennis style of ground hurling and they simply weren't let express themselves. A fine goal by Conor

Smythe got Ennis off to a dream start but the bigger Farranferris lads gradually took control and built a good lead by the interval.

The move of Vincent Loftus to centre field with P. J. Ryan going to centre forward and Raymond Shannon to full-back brought Ennis back into the game. A tremendous spell saw Michael Hanrahan score 2-2 closing the gap considerably. But it was too late, as a Seanie Barry inspired Cork side had done enough to capture the title by 4-9 to 4-3 amidst unbridled scenes of joy from the Cork supporters on a miserable, wet day at Semple Stadium, Thurles.

St. Finbarr's continued as a major force in Colleges competition. In 1969 they regained the Harty Cup. This was but a prelude to a long reign, when coached by Fr. Michael O'Brien, they won five Harty Cups up to 1974, 1970 being the only year to spoil the six-in-a-row.

1964 Colleges Season

The White Cup was inaugurated in 1964 for Under-15½ competition. Ennis defeated Thurles, 5-1 to 2-4 in their opening game. Meanwhile, their Dean Ryan team accounted for St. Flannan's, 3-8 to 2-3 at Newmarket. For the forthcoming clash with Limerick CBS in the Harty Cup, the selectors promoted goalkeeper Jim Bradley and fullback Paddy O'Brien from the Dean Ryan side. The team also included P. J. Ryan and Jimmy Quinn from the 1963 team and Eddie Lough at corner back. By 1964 Bro. Hennessy was transferred to Limerick and he set about moulding a powerful side from the considerable talent that was at his disposal. Playing fabulous ground hurling, Ennis raced into a nine point lead, thanks to a strong mid-field and a rampant forward line that included Michael Hanrahan, who hit a personal 3-2 and the stylish Paschal O'Brien operating at wing forward.

Limerick CBS had News for Ennis

"With Eamon Cregan picking off second half points with almost monotonous regularity, Limerick CBS came, saw and conquered at their former 'burial ground', Newmarket-on-Fergus, when coming from a 3-goal disadvantage to eliminate red hot favourites, Ennis CBS, from the Harty Cup. What with all the behind the scenes bickering, Limerick's reluctance to play in Newmarket, and the natural rivalry between the sides – remember Ennis had given Limerick the 'hammer' for the two previous years", wrote Cormac Liddy in the Limerick Leader.

Trailing by 4-2 to 1-2 at the interval, Cregan immediately cut the deficit with a point. Then following a melee, Limerick were awarded a 21 yard free, with Cregan burying the ball in the net. Pat Nash and Jack Kennedy added points to close the gap further. By the 54th minute

Cregan levelled the scores at 2-8 to 4-2, building up to a final six minutes culminating in fierce goalmouth tussles, before Jim Bradley (the Ennis goalie) was bundled over the goal line by the combined strength of Donie Leonard and Jack Kennedy. Limerick won by 3-9 to 4-2. Ironically Br. Jim Hennessy had worked the oracle against his old school. Limerick went all the way to Colleges success in 1964 culminating in a 6-7 to 4-5 victory over St. Peter's of Wexford. It was the beginning of a great era for Limerick.

In the 1965 Harty Cup, Ennis CBS went out to Limerick after a spirited display, from players of the calibre of Pat Coffey, Eric Hanrahan, Terry Hurson, Brian Higgins, Jimmy McNamara and Anthony Corry.

Peadar O'Brien takes up the story: *"Limerick go marching on in quest of their second Munster Colleges crown in a row. But the scoreline barely does justice to the heroic fight that Ennis put into this anything but one-sided quarter-final. Indeed for 33 minutes the unfancied Ennis boys held them to a single point, but thereafter Limerick's experience, super hurling skill and power pulled them through. Up to the midway stage, Ennis, playing against a crosswind, had hurled them stroke for stroke, and it was a tribute to the great Ennis defence more than the Limerick top class forward line that the city side led by only three points to two at half time."*

Harty Cup 1966/67

On Sunday October 16th 1966, Ennis CBS supporters travelled to Tipperary town to cheer on their favourites against Mount Sion of Waterford. *"Played in atrocious ground conditions, the game produced close exciting exchanges. Playing against the wind, Ennis trailed at the interval, before going out of the competition on a score line of 5-4 to 4-3. Best for the Clare side were Frank Burns, Joe Corbett, Michael Cullinan and Flan Hegarty in defence, while Jimmy McNamara, Martin Linnane, Liam (Willie) Griffin and the free scoring Michael Kilmartin impressed in the attack."*

Ennis gained revenge the following year when again at Sean Treacy Park, Tipperary Town, they easily accounted for Mount Sion. *"Captained by Niall McInerney, the team showed great fighting spirit. Michael Cullinan and Tim Hannon had a decisive pull at mid-field while up front Michael Galvin, Sean Lynch and Michael O'Regan caught the eye. Though Ennis won by 5-12 to 2-6 the score line could easily have been much greater in favour of the Clare boys"* wrote the Clare Champion reporter. In the following round, this young Ennis team was unlucky to come up against a seasoned Limerick CBS combination going for a record five Harty Cups in a row. Played at the Gaelic Grounds, Limerick, Ennis CBS were trounced.

Tim Hannon

At just seventeen Tim Hannon was a member of the Newmarket Club and an automatic choice on the Ennis Harty Cup teams of 1967/68. Contemporaries of his at the CBS, Michael Leahy and Noel Ryan, spoke to me in glowing terms of the Newmarket youth. Michael Leahy recalled: *"I was in the year behind Tim, we all looked up to him. Even then he was inter-county material and without doubt the best hurler in the school. He had a great attitude to the game. He was strong, well-built, a great all round athlete. Tim was part of the school team that performed very well at the North Munster sports in Charleville that school year. He was a gentleman on and off the field and was greatly admired by all his school friends".* On August 4th 1968, while swimming with a number of friends at Finlough Lake, he got into difficulties while under water. When he failed to surface, his friends raised the alarm. His body was later recovered from the water. His death was a terrible shock to all his school friends at the CBS.

Athletics

Apart from hurling, emphasis was also put on athletics in the late 1960s and early 1970s. The school produced top athletes in Sean Lynch, Paddy Firth and Fiachra Hensey. Fiachra won Munster U/15 at the Mardyke in Cork in 1967, breaking the existing record. He later came second in the national competition in Dublin. Others that competed at the highest level included Frank Chandler, David Barry and Niall Matthews. Later in 1971, Barry Smythe won the All-Ireland U/14 pole vault, while Frank Sweeney claimed the U/12 high jump. Gerard McGann was the most successful athlete in the CBS Sports in 1972. Rice College also produced two outstanding swimmers in Greg Scanlan and Kieran McGrath. In 1973, while still a mere schoolboy, Kieran McGrath won the Richard Harris and Watney-Murphy Cups for the Kilkee and Carrigaholt Bay Swims. These competitions were open to adults, which makes McGrath's achievement all the greater.

Revival of Gaelic Football

Bro. Power revived football about 1966, but not at the expense of hurling. He ran a great league for fifth and sixth classes (primary standard). The six teams were called after tribes in Irish mythology. The sides included Na Clanna Míle, Fir Bolg, and Tuatha De Danann. The team I played for, the Tuatha De Danann, reached the final. Captained by Paddy Kelly with Vice-Captain Alan Lewis, the side also included Eric Connellan and Pádraig Quinn. Unfortunately, our brand of magic cut little ice with Johnny Ryan's (Na Fianna) team in the decider; we were well beaten.

Later in 1968/'69, Bro. Power organised an Under-16 league open to all of Ennis. The idea was to get six panels of 20 and select the best U/16 and U/14 teams to represent the town. The winning league team was captained by Davy Connellan. At rain-lashed Cusack Park, his side ran out comprehensive winners against the favourites, Haulie O'Connell's team. At a gala occasion at the West County Inn, we were presented with beautiful plaques. Some of the other stars from these leagues included Gerry Bredin, Michael Fahy, Kieran Gibbons and Johnny Griffin. Bro. Power was the main mover behind all of this. Jack Murphy was also involved.

School Leagues

In 1954, Turnpike was going for 3-in-a-row. The players believed the cup was theirs to keep if they won it. Such was the strength of the 'Pike that the 'powers that be' divided the area. Regardless, Turnpike was always a haven of hurling. In the late 1940s the area produced George Browne and Georgie O'Neill. Later on it produced the likes of P. J. Heffernan, Pat and Bernard Dilger, Christy and John Brigdale and Peter 'Swift' Maher. Hurling matches were decided in Kelly's field and 'the plots' and there Don Kelleher, Sean Micks, Gerry Commane, Tommy Fitzpatrick, Pat and Denis Hennigan and John Joe and Tommy Geoghegan all displayed their considerable skills. The 1954 CBS final between the 'Pike and Ard na Gréine was a thriller. Played on a scorching summer's day, the 'Pike, captained by Patsy O'Loughlin, sporting their green and white jerseys, were first on the pitch. The other stalwarts included vice-captain Eddie Browne, Michael Casey and 'Spinky' Meehan. Ard na Gréine, who were led out by Fintan Quinn, pipped the 'Pike by 8-6 to 8-4. No shortage of marksmen there! Sean Micks came in for high praise when the Clare Champion described him *"as a coming Jimmy Smyth with his unerring left hand"*. Likewise Patsy O'Loughlin, *"a most promising young hurler, possessing the guile of Ring"*. After the final whistle sounded, Bro. O'Cinnéide presented the cup and medals to the Ard na Gréine team amidst great enthusiasm.

Jumping a few years, in 1959 the Past Pupils Union presented the cup for Comórtas na nÓg. The competition was possibly open to all youths in town, with the 'Pike, Boreen, Market, Old Millstreet all entering teams.

The Boreen who were blessed with proximity to the Fairgreen sported Brian Considine, noted for his spectacular solo runs, Liam Donnellan and David Keane were led out by Tony Kelly to face the 'Pike. A ding-dong game ensued with little to choose between the sides, save for the cool determination of the young red-headed Jim Bradley in the 'Pike goal. Bradley proved the difference, denying the fiery hurling of Tony Kelly and the sweeping solo play of Brendan Considine. The final score read Turnpike 4-3, Boreen 3-4. At the final whistle, Frank Burns, NT, presented Corn Iarscolairí to the winning team and Des McCullough presented Corn Eoin Naofa to the respective captains.

1968 was a particularly good year with the CBS U/14s reaching the Rice Cup final for the second year in a row, defeating Templemore by 11-3 to 4-2 in the semi-final at Newport. Much work was put into these Rice Cup teams by Bro. Power, Bro. Bridges and Bro. McGrath. Training usually took place in the Fairgreen or occasionally at Cusack Park when an extended panel would be brought to the Park to play 'possibles' versus 'probables'. As a fringe school player it was always a great thrill to run out on the turf of Cusack Park.

Town Leagues

There was a huge push in Ennis hurling about 1968 with leagues organised at all levels. Though the CBS was very much behind the juvenile leagues they were open to everyone. I vividly recall the U/15 town final played at Cusack Park on Sunday, September 15th, 1968, with the Boreen holding out for the narrowest of wins over the Town by 4-3 to 4-2 in a cracking decider. Jimmy Spellissy recalls: *"The Christian Brothers encouraged us to play hurling. We lived for it and there was nothing else. St. Michael's and the Town were very strong in the leagues. St. Michael's always had great hurlers. But the Boreen won the U/15 and U/16 Finals in 1968, winning a trip to Croke Park in the process. I played Rice Cup with the CBS in 1966 and 1967. We were beaten in the final by Thurles in 1967 (8-4 to 4-2) but 1966 was the beginning of it, as we had a good group of players. Paddy Neylon played a stormer at wingback in 1967. He was a great bit of stuff. Around this time, Éire Óg were beaten by the 'Bridge in the U/15 final but Don Ryan (Snr.), Brendan Spellissy, Michael Brennan and Des McCullough played a very important role as did Bro. Bridges. I liked Bro. Bridges; he encouraged us to play and he always had a word of praise. I remember playing Dean Ryan in 1968/'69. We drew with Coláiste Chríost Rí, Cork (6-1 to 5-4), Haulie O'Connell roasted Martin O'Doherty the same day; Frank Coffey also had a blinder. I was a sub on the 1969/70 Harty Cup team but I left after middle-grade. The World Cup of 1966 had a big influence. We became aware of a bigger world and we were attracted to it. One of the attractions of soccer was the fact that it was forbidden by the GAA's ban on foreign games. Michael Kenny formed an Under-16 soccer team called United."*

Like the Under-15 final of 1968, the U/16 decider attracted a big attendance to Cusack Park. St. Michael's, the most impressive in the earlier rounds, were installed as favourites. But the Boreen (playing the pick of Gaurus and Lifford) with Joe Corry, Tony Garry, Kieran Gibbons and Seán Mahon rose to it, winning by 2-5 to 1-5 in a tense game. After the final whistle the Jack Heaslip Cup was presented to Noel Glynn by Jack Daly.

Much effort and thought was put into these leagues. After each series of games the Clare Champion honoured a star player in their column, Sports Star of the Week. Among the recipients of this honour were Noel Ryan, Seán Lynch and Frankie Gilligan.

Apart from the schoolyard, great innovations were happening in primary education on a national level. On 30th November 1966, Donagh O'Malley, T.D. and Minister for Education, and the Taoiseach Jack Lynch, announced revolutionary proposals for post-primary education. O'Malley, who had earlier seen his 'free school transport' plan become reality told R.T.E.'s 7-Days programme that he would resign from the cabinet if his 'free education for all' plan was not accepted. What it meant was that the sixth class of 1967/1968 became the first group of primary school students not to sit the scholarship or primary exams. We were jubilant that we didn't have to face those examinations. It freed us up. School became more enjoyable, as less emphasis was put on cramming. We loved the outdoors, exploring the Rocky and Cornhill. We played hurling, rawked orchards. We picked 'blacky-tops' in the marshlands off the Watery Road, come rain or come shine.

The Brothers also screened films in the C.B.S. auditorium on wintry Friday afternoons. For a mere 6d, we watched a full length feature and several shorts. 'The Rajah of Rajakpore' was the operetta staged that year. Frankie Tuohy played the Rajah while his subjects included Gabriel Dillon, Mike McDonogh, Val Real, Seán Dinan and Seán Howard. "Guns in the Heather", a film produced by Walt Disney and starring Kurt Russell, was shot mostly in Clare and the opening scenes were filmed on the grounds of St. Flannan's. Russell, who had starred in several episodes of the Cult television classic, "The Fugitive", played a hurler caught up in intrigue. I recall the film extras and crew borrowing our hurleys during a break in filming. They gave us 'a few bob' each and proceeded to play a 7 a side game. "Guns in the Heather" cost £500,000 to make and was typical Disney good clean fun.

To prepare us for secondary school Bro. Bridges kept us back every Friday afternoon from Spring to early Summer. A Wexford man, he introduced us to Civil War politics, world geography, Latin and Mathematics. To say we were well prepared for second level was an understatement. There is no doubt that the introduction of free education allowed for access to second and third level for many young people, bringing with it an increased social confidence. Unfortunately, Donogh

Kurt Russell, on left with Patrick Dawson during the making of the film "Guns in the Heather" (1968) (Walt Disney). This still was shot in the grounds of St. Flannan's. Courtesy of Michael Mulcaire.

O'Malley didn't live to see the fruits of his work. He died on 10th March 1968 while addressing a Fianna Fáil meeting outside Sixmilebridge Church. He was only 47 years old.

By 1971, the once proud name of Ennis Dalcassians was revived in Ennis for minor and juvenile levels. I'm not sure of the exact reason for this but it certainly gave everyone involved a great sense of pride in the name. During pre-match meetings our mentors would talk with pride of the great men who had worn the Dals jersey. The U/16 juveniles won the league easily but were knocked out in the first round of the championship by arch-rivals, Ruan. The minor team went on to take the championship at the expense of Sixmilebridge, 4-4 to 2-1. The Champion of September 25th 1971 takes up the story: *"Shades of other days were conjured up at Dr. Daly Memorial Park, Tulla, on Sunday, when a skilful and highly spirited Ennis Dalcassian side blazed its way to a convincing victory over defending champions, Sixmilebridge, to win the Clare Minor Hurling Championship. Ahead by 2-3 to 1-1 at half time, the Dals survived a tremendous buffeting for a brief period after the change over but, apart from conceding a goal, the Ennismen emerged from the exchanges with glowing reputations. Although confronted by such up and coming hurling giants as Seán Stack and Tim Crowe, the Dals partnership of David*

Connellan and Jimmy Spellissy held the whip hand at centre-field in the first half. The Ennis pair, using a quota of spirit and skill, held the stage in the opening period and it was from their almost vice-like control that Seán Daly crashed home two well taken goals. Haulie O'Connell, the captain of the side, scored all four points. Michael Nugent played a sound game in goal, while in front of him, Seán O'Grady, Dermot Kelly, a tough tackling full-back, and Kieran Gibbons formed a rock solid full back line. The half-back line was anchored by Michael Skelly, a stylish and non-stop performer, and the brothers, Kieran and Don Ryan. Spellissy and Connellan played their hearts out at centre-field, while Brendan Gilligan led the attack with rare determination. Flanked by Seamus Kelly and Haulie O'Connell, this line packed loads of potential, while inside them Seán Daly, Paddy Kelly and Paddy Neylon saw to it that every chance was turned into valuable account." Despite all the talent in Ennis at this time, very few of these players were picked up on. Jimmy Spellissy has very positive memories of his playing days – but none-theless he had this to say – *"despite all our success at under-age hurling very few of us were ever approached to play for the county.*

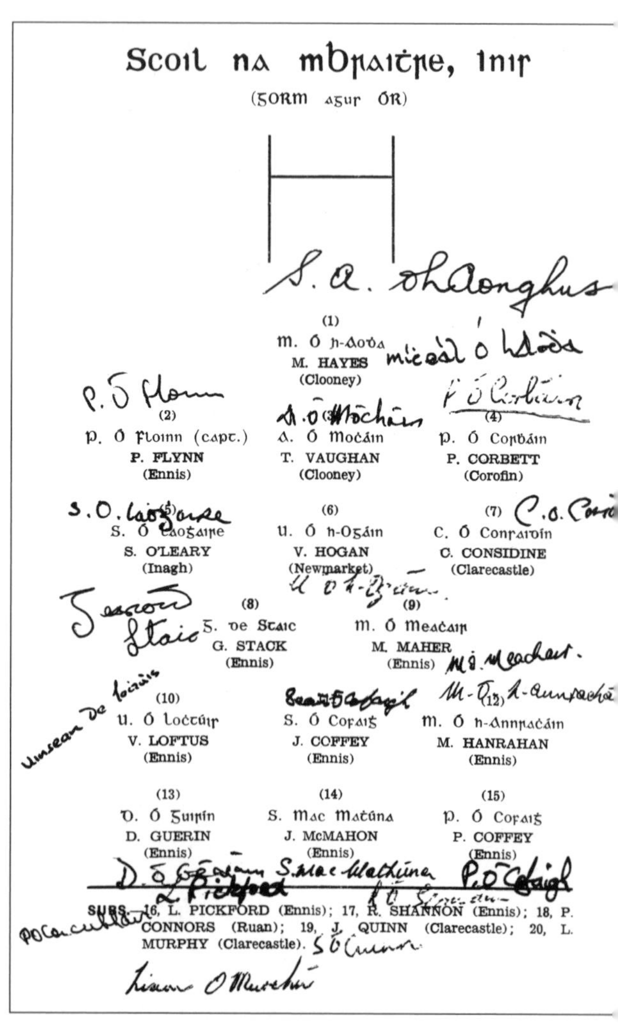

Scoil na mBráithre, Inis
(Gorm agus Ór)

(1) M. Ó h-Aodha — M. HAYES (Clooney)

(2) P. Ó Floinn (capt.) — P. FLYNN (Ennis)
(3) A. Ó Mocháin — T. VAUGHAN (Clooney)
(4) P. Ó Corbáin — P. CORBETT (Corofin)

(5) S. Ó Laoghaire — S. O'LEARY (Inagh)
(6) U. Ó h-Ogáin — V. HOGAN (Newmarket)
(7) C. Ó Conraoidín — C. CONSIDINE (Clarecastle)

(8) G. de Stac — G. STACK (Ennis)
(9) M. Ó Meachair — M. MAHER (Ennis)

(10) U. Ó Lochtúir — V. LOFTUS (Ennis)
S. Ó Cofaig — J. COFFEY (Ennis)
(12) M. Ó h-Annracháin — M. HANRAHAN (Ennis)

(13) D. Ó Guirín — D. GUERIN (Ennis)
(14) S. Mac Mathúna — J. McMAHON (Ennis)
(15) P. Ó Cofaig — P. COFFEY (Ennis)

SUBS.—16, L. PICKFORD (Ennis); 17, R. SHANNON (Ennis); 18, P. CONNORS (Ruan); 19, J. QUINN (Clarecastle); 20, L. MURPHY (Clarecastle).

Townie hurling is a different type of hurling. It's more skilful. I felt it was them versus us. I never met anyone in the town to congratulate us on winning. If we won a canoe race in the Fergus, people would have known more about it. If Sixmilebridge or Tulla won they'd be singing their praises, even writing songs about them. Then we didn't have the parish mentality in Ennis. My generation didn't tune in to the pride and passion

Ennis Vocational School 1971. Back row, left to right: *Tom Harvey, John Barrett, Paddy Kelly, James Meehan, Brendan Gilligan, Tom Casey, John Mullins, Oliver Gallagher, Gerry O'Connor, Flan Morrissey, Joe Hehir, Christy Ryan.* ***Front row:*** *Kieran Devanney, Martin King, Paddy Meere, Seamus McGann (capt), John Coughlan, Eugene Pewter, Gerry Daffy, Michael Shanahan, Martin Ryan. Courtesy of Clare Champion.*

that the Rovers had. We lost it somewhere. By 1974 I had drifted away from hurling when Michael Guerin and Paddy Gilligan asked me to go back for the U/21 championship. It was a totally different team. Some of the lads like Denis Mulcaire, Martin Nugent and Eric Connellan were very young. Generally speaking, players of that age wouldn't get a look in at U/21 level in Ennis."

Ennis CBS Smoked Out

In February, 1969, 2,000 Clare pupils were affected by the secondary school teachers' strike. The dispute by the nation's teachers affiliated to ASTI lasted three full weeks. All schools affected by the strike were re-opened on Tuesday, 25th February. Within two months, the Leaving Certificate students of Ennis CBS were affected by another dispute when 18 pupils from 6B were dismissed from attending classes. The controversy arose when one or more of the students lit up a cigarette in the classroom. When the guilty parties failed to own up, the class was suspended by the headmaster, Bro. Clancy. Consequently, the students spent a couple of weeks walking the streets in an attempt to find a solution. The quarrel was finally settled when Rev. Fr. Ryan was asked to intervene. The boys returned to class without losing face and Bro. Clancy informed the Clare Champion, who had carried the front page story, that the matter was now closed.

Bro. Clancy

A Limerick man, Bro. Clancy was appointed superior for the years 1967/72. A celebrated mathematics teacher, he kept hurling very robust in the school. He was a difficult taskmaster on those he considered promising hurlers and he kept a keen eye on the talent coming through the ranks. However, his bark was worse than his bite and there was never any doubt that he bore a great love for the game.

In 1968, Ennis shocked North Monastery in the Harty Cup. The Mon raced into an early 1-2 to nil lead, but a switch between Noel Glynn and Michael Smythe helped steady the defence, and with Noel Ryan and Paddy Firth dominating mid-field the Ennis lads recovered to level the score (0-6 to 1-3) at the interval. Ennis gave a powerful second half performance to win 2-11 to 3-4. Following this victory over the Mon, the Ennis lads were pitted against Coláiste Iognaid Rís. Featuring a revamped forward line, Ennis got off to a dream start and with a rampant attack raced into a seven point lead. Then disaster struck when one of their players was sent to the line for a harmless tackle. Ennis lost their way and Sullivan's Quay took control to win by 5-5 to 2-4 with only Seamus O'Connell, Sean Lynch and Ollie O'Regan playing up to form for Ennis.

North Mon. Again

The following season the North Mon made no mistake when the teams again clashed in Charleville. Level after 40 minutes with little to choose between the sides (4-1 to 3-4) the Mon pulled away in the final quarter giving an exhibition of power hurling. A final scoreline of 7-11 to 4-1 tells its own tale.

Davy Connellan takes up the story: *"I was part of the extended panel for the 1968/'69 season. Haulie O'Connell and possibly Jimmy Hehir, two classmates of mine, made the panel. We fancied ourselves to beat the North Mon as we had a fine team in Michael Smythe, Seán Neylon, the O'Connells, Noel Glynn, Michael ('Taidgh') McNamara and Michael Leahy, but we collapsed in the second half following wave after wave of pressure. I was at wing-back on a fellow called Stephen Greene. He was switched to the other wing and Bro. James told me to follow him. In spite of the heavy beating we had a fine team; about six of them made the Clare Minor team in 1970. Recently I was trying to piece together the team of 1969/'70. I think Clem Ryan and Conor McCarthy may have been in the corners with Jimmy Hehir at centre-forward, flanked by Seamus and Haulie O'Connell. Haulie was outstanding at Colleges level; he could do anything with a ball."*

The inaugural 13-a-side All-Ireland Colleges Championship of 1970 was won by the North Mon. The team, which included Des O'Grady,

Frankie Coughlan and Seamus O'Connell (not to be confused with the other O'Connells), was one of the finest Colleges sides I've ever seen. Ennis CBS opened their 1970/71 campaign against Limerick CBS at Newmarket. Played on a greasy surface, Ennis led by 1-4 to 1-1 at the interval but a goal by Chris Naughton and a Martin McKeogh point put Sexton Street ahead. These scores were cancelled out by points from John Hehir and Fintan Quinn before Naughton again found the net. However, this was Limerick's last throw of the dice before Ennis took over completely with further goals from Haulie O'Connell and Fintan Quinn. Following an off-the-ball incident, the pitch was invaded by rival groups of supporters and, when order was restored by the referee, Haulie O'Connell calmly sent the resulting free over the bar to leave the final score 3-9 to 3-2. This was one of Ennis CBS's finest displays in the Harty Cup with Kevin Kennedy and John Johnson on top at centre-field. In the other section, St. Flannan's hammered a very fancied St. Colman's, Fermoy by 4-9 to 2-2 at Kilmallock with John (Jack) Treacy at centre-forward scoring 3-3. Davy Connellan remembers: *"I was unavailable for the first round game with Limerick and the wing-back position was filled by Cha Kenny. Martin Fitzpatrick also played a wonderful game and he possibly should have been accommodated in the starting line up against Flannan's. Jimmy Hehir (Ruan) and Jimmy Spellissy both left after middle-grade. They were a huge loss to the Harty Cup team. Jimmy Spellissy could easily have been brought in again as he lived beside the school."*

Though St. Flannan's were considered favourites to reach the final and possibly win the competition, Clare Champion reporter, Seán King didn't rule out the possibility of a shock. *"Ennis CBS are hurling with fire and brimstone spirit, and lashings of devil; in a recent challenge they overcame Kilkenny CBS. Over the years Ennis CBS teams have thrived in the role of the underdog, invariably backboned by a strong nucleus of town and country, they have the happy knack of rising from the ashes and proving a match for the best."*

Without doubt this meeting of CBS and Flannan's, the first in senior hurling in nine years caught the imagination of the public. Little else was spoken about, as hurling fever took over at lunch times in the CBS schoolyard. For the semi-final both Noel Glynn and Davy Connellan were recalled to the CBS team. Tulla was bedlam on the 21st February 1971 with deafening rival school songs being sung as the teams ran out on to the pitch. Noel Glynn drew first blood for Ennis CBS, when he drove an unstoppable ground shot to the net following constant pressure. From my perch right behind a packed Flannan's goal, I watched Gerry Ryan making several outstanding saves. Seán King takes up the story: *"The costly number of easy scoring chances which went a-begging in the first half for the CBS was unbelievable. Strong in the backs, where Michael McNamara and John Sheehan reigned supreme, the CBS boys should have built up a considerable lead, especially from placed balls, but a tendency to opt for goals when points were there for the taking, robbed the blue and gold brigade of a possible victory. The story of a game that promised a feast of hurling could be wrapped up in one word – tension. The atmosphere was electric and the players, not used to the big occasion, were obviously overawed by the magnitude of it all."* Walking away from what was a far from distinguished game on that beautiful sunny afternoon, I felt completely empty. Maybe it was because the 13-a-side competition, which had recently been inaugurated by the Munster Colleges, wasn't all it was cracked up to be. The 13-a-side competition, run from 1969 to 1975, was intended, I'm sure, to open up the game, play the wings a bit more. Instead all we got was bunching and goalmouth melees with little open wing play. The corner-forwards didn't seem to know what to do with the ball when in possession, as they had no visible or recognisable full-forward to play it to. Personally, I was delighted when the Colleges Council reverted to the traditional 15-a-side game in 1975/76, with St. Flannan's winning the Cup on a glorious day in the beautiful setting of Bansha.

1972 Harty Cup

Following the reversal to St. Flannan's, Ennis CBS (fielding four survivors in Kevin Kennedy, Haulie O'Connell, Tony O'Donnell and Cha Kenny) defeated Limerick CBS by 2-7 to 3-3 in a fine game at Tulla with Michael Griffin bagging both goals. St. Flannan's again accounted for St. Colman's, Fermoy to set up another encounter with their local rivals. Once again, played at Tulla, this is a game best forgotten from a CBS perspective. St. Flannan's, fielding eight locals, gave an exhibition of hurling and in the process a lesson to the CBS. Though Tony O'Donnell and Michael (Ganga) Griffin excelled in the full-back line and with Michael Nugent blameless for the shots that beat him, very few of the CBS players came away with their reputations intact. Paddy Neylon and Brian Stenson ran themselves into the ground and Haulie O'Connell took the bare look off the scoreboard with two well-taken goals.

Rice College

Due to the humiliation of the 1972 semi-final defeat by Flannan's and because of lack of facilities (both the Fairgreen and Cusack Park were out of bounds) Ennis CBS didn't compete in the Harty Cup of 1972/73. For those of us interested in hurling this was a terrible shock to the system, as the material was in the school, particularly in middle grade. Bro. Gerard

Murphy was appointed headmaster in September 1972, becoming one of the most popular headmasters ever. An extremely placid man, a lover of the arts and music, he introduced many of the finer things of life to the school during his term of office. He had earlier served in the school during the great Harty Cup years of 1961/63 and often recalled these halcyon days during class. An outstanding Maths and Irish teacher, it was Bro. Murphy who changed the name of the school to Rice College in September 1972. I recall him telling the Leaving Certificate class *"It is very hard to break with tradition, but we have decided to do so. The school for over one hundred years has been known as Ennis CBS, however, we have now decided to change the name to Rice College or Coláiste an Risigh"*. With the Fairgreen redeveloped by the UDC, a more than useful Harty Cup team was fielded in the 1973/74 season. About 40 hurlers were looked at by Bro. Miniter and Bro. Donnellan before the panel was pruned to 19. A huge effort was put in by the two men in charge and if you didn't train, you didn't get on. Training took place at the top pitch in the Fairgreen or occasionally at Roslevan. Bro. Miniter instilled a lot of confidence into the panel. Several challenge matches were organised with wins over Our Lady's (Gort), Roscrea CBS, Limerick CBS (finalists) and Nenagh. Thurles CBS were pitted against Ennis in the first round of the competition.

CBS fielded nine players from the town of Ennis in the starting thirteen. Thurles raced into an early 1-3 to nil lead. Ennis fought back when Ollie O'Loughlin opened the Ennis account with a point. This score was followed by a superb point from an acute angle by his brother, Gerard. Having reduced the arrears to three points by half time, Ennis found themselves level after a great goal by Denis O'Connor to leave the sides at 2-6 to 1-9. A bizarre incident followed when a well-struck goal by Ollie O'Loughlin, after great play by Peter O'Loughlin, was waved wide (the ball went through the back of the net). Following a consultation with the referee and umpires the goal was disallowed. In the 22nd minute of the second half David Sheedy was sent to the line for what the referee considered over robust play, forcing Ollie O'Loughlin to revert to the backs with Ennis losing their edge at centre-field. The Ennis backs played magnificently, especially Declan Coote and Michael (Milo) Keane in the corner. Thurles held out to win by the narrowest of margins, 3-10 to 3-9. To this day everyone involved with this Ennis CBS team feels they could have gone places. Still the finger can be pointed at no-one, as this was one of the best prepared teams to represent the school. Despite the failure to convert a late close-in free after a foul on Patsy Hehir, Ennis should have won by at least a few points. *"Spirited CBS go out at Emly. Ennis CBS should be proud of a great display, as many of the members of the team showed a lot of promise for the future"*, wrote the Champion reporter. And a promising side it was, as the majority of this team went on to play senior club hurling with a few representing the county at senior level.

Other players I recall from this panel include Declan Cummins and Gabriel Dillon. Dillon, a versatile hurler, returned to CBS after a number of years at Good Counsel of New Ross. In the 1974/75 school year, the CBS went out of the Harty cup in the first round losing to North Monastery, prompting the school selectors to enter the senior 'B' competition. This was the first time in more than 20 years, with the exception of 1972/73, that Ennis CBS didn't compete in the Harty Cup. The decision taken by the selectors was justified, as the senior team was knocked out by Causeway Comprehensive in a first round replay by 6-0 to 3-4 despite the best efforts of Michael Clohessy, Pat Hayes, Michael and Kieran Hanrahan. By the mid 1970s soccer and rugby were introduced. A talented group of soccer players were present in the school. I recall the likes of Adrian Sheedy, a superb goal-keeper, Jimmy Real and Joe Downey from the Lifford club and Bernard Collins of Newmarket Celtic. Collins later became one of the leading players in the Newmarket Club

Ennis Vocational School All Ireland Cross Country post Primary Schools Champions c.1982. Back row, left to right: *Marie Gormley, Fiona Broderick, Bridie Roche, Patricia Rynne.* **Front row:** *Mary Lyons, Deirdre Daly, Brenda Daffy.*

during a great spell. Other top players at Rice College included Michael Hensey, Ray Hennessy, Tom and Tim Murphy, and Noel Purtill. It is very possible the players entered the team themselves in the Munster Senior Cup with Bro. Murphy's blessing. In May 1977, Rice College reached the Munster Cup final with wins over Tulla (5-0), Salesian (2-1), Crescent Comprehensive (2-0) and Nenagh (4-2) in the North Munster area final. In the final proper, they were beaten by Coláiste An Spioraid Naomh. Rugby too was becoming popular and in 1978 a strong XV, coached by the all round sports follower, Jack Keane, defeated Water Park College by 12 points to 4.

Throughout these years hurling hadn't taken a back seat and a useful Dean Ryan team defeated Limerick CBS by 6-6 to 2-0 at St. Flannan's grounds in November 1976. Those prominent included, Ger Hickey, Vincent O'Connor, Seanie Lyons and Michael Kenny, a rock solid full-back. Relative success in the Junior A grade was built on and in the following year the seniors reached the final of the Corn Phadraig (Senior B) losing to Causeway Comprehensive of Kerry by 5-12 to 7-1. An incredible scoreline, it seemed every time Ennis got a goal the Kerry lads hit back with a series of points. Maybe Ennis didn't have the quantity but they certainly had the quality in Pat Lynch, Jarlath O'Halloran, Michael Dinan and Louis Galvin at this time.

Success Again

1979 was a great year in Clare Colleges hurling. At Rice College, a huge drive was put in by Pat Flynn and Paddy Duggan. Their traditional first-time, ground hurling proved a match winning formula in both the Dr. Kinnane and Corn Phadraig competitions. The senior championship was built on by the excellence of the defence as a unit, especially Michael Kenny at full-back and Ray Casey on the wing giving a plentiful supply to the in-form Jarlath O'Halloran and Pat Hanrahan in the attack. Rice College recorded a double when they again overcame Cashel by 6-5 to 1-4 in the final. Again it was the backs, especially the half line of Pat Ryan, Micheál Glynn and Paul Hogan that helped fashion the victory plus the free-scoring Jarlath O'Halloran and Seanie Cleary who notched 4-3 between them. In the All-Ireland semi-final, Rice College was shocked by a good Roscommon CBS team, with only Peadar Derrane playing to form.

Alas, little has been heard of Rice College since but, thankfully, a steady stream of players including greats like Colin Lynch, Seán McMahon and Stephen McNamara, all of them All-Ireland medal winners, have come through. Gerry Quinn, Tony Griffin and Shane O'Neill were part of the Dr. Kinnane Cup team of around 1997. Many of the successful St. Joseph's club team, the likes of Donal Cahill and Phelim

Barry Keating accepts the cup. Photo also includes from left of Barry, Michael Watson, Tony McInerney and Donal Cahill. *Courtesy of Colm Keating.*

Presentation to Éire Óg juveniles at Cusack Park 1985. Left to right: *Barry Keating, Brian McAllister, Gordon McCullough, David O'Brien.*

Courtesy of Colm Keating.

Some pupils of Rice College Class of 1973 photographed in 1998 at a school reunion at the Old Ground. Back row, left to right: *Michael Dillon, Simon Moroney, Greg Scanlan, Jackie Hynes, Frankie O'Gorman, Gerry O'Malley, Ml. Moloney, Michael Woods, Christy Murphy, Johnny Griffin, Martin Murphy, Ollie Byrnes.* ***Middle row:*** *Michael McNamara, Seán Howard (Newbridge Road), Joe Waters, Paddy Hill, Brian Burke, Michael Browne, Michael Talty, Marty O'Halloran, Joe Hanrahan, Flan Clune, Seán Howard, Michael O'Loughlin, Michael McDonagh, Gerry Tierney, Pat Brohan, Paddy Clohessy, Michael Skelly, Brendan Burke.* ***Front row:*** *Seamus Cahir, Brian Stenson, Mr. Mannix Berry (English/History), Mr. Seamus Meade (Irish), Mr. Tom Clohessy (Present Headmaster), Mr. Brendan Madigan (Physics/Chemistry), Mr. Seán O'Brien (History/Latin/English), Mr. Seán Dolan (Economics/Business Organisation). Frankie Tuohy is missing from photo.*

Courtesy of Martin Murphy.

Collins, are also products of Rice College. Kenneth Kennedy and Martin Brooks played on the successful Clare minor team of 1997. A fine strong physical side with loads of skill won Clare's only All Ireland in that grade to-date. Much has been done at primary school by Tom Lynch, Nuala Lynch, Michael Carmody, Seán Heaslip and Bro. Moloughney (now retired) with a fair amount of success achieved at Cumann Na mBunscoile. In Rice College, Gerry Queally and Norma Murphy have put a lot of their time into the game. Gerry Queally's team had considerable success in the White Cup in 1998 reaching the semi-final with wins over Midleton (2-14 to 2-2) and North Monastery (8-5 to 1-2). In 1999, Rice College lost to Scariff Community College (2-9 to 0-10) in the preliminary round of the Corn Phádraig at Tulla, despite great displays from John Mulcahy, and their top scorer, Micheál Brennan.

Rice Cup 2000

A useful Rice Cup team, trained by Martin Nolan and Norma Cahill (nee Murphy), reached the final of the 2000 competition. Played at the well-appointed GAA grounds at Newport, Rice College was well in contention at half-time, having played against the wind in the opening period. But several missed chances in the opening minutes of the second half proved their undoing. Templemore CBS flashed over two quick points to go 2-6 to 0-4 ahead. A superb goal by Jody Ryan from the Seán Treacy's Club put the Tipperary boys further ahead. Getting inside the defence, Ryan flicked the ball to the net for the stylish Templemore side. The final scoreline read 5-9 to 1-7. Fair play to Rice College, they battled to the end. They had impressive performers in Greg Lyons, Colin Heaslip and Eric Kelly.

Rice College and St. Flannan's clashed in the second round of the Whyte Cup, played at Cusack Park in the Spring of 2002. Rice College had no answer to the superb hurling of Flannan's in the first half with Flannan's hitting a staggering 1-16. Many of the Flannan's scores were superbly taken by Kevin Raftery and Francis O'Reilly. In the second half, Rice College put up a strong challenge, but failed to St. Flannan's (captained by the impressive James McInerney) the eventual winners of the competition. Nevertheless, Rice College should learn from this defeat. Hopefully, we'll hear more from these and other CBS players in the future.

Clare Senior hurlers: *Seán McMahon and Stephen McNamara pictured with Kyran Kennedy and the Liam McCarthy Cup on the grounds of Rice College, 1995.*

ENNIS CBS NOTES & RECORDS
Some Ennis CBS Teams

1936/37 – Munster College (A) – Football Runners Up
St. Brendan's 1-8 . . . Ennis CBS 1-1

They beat Ennistymon CBS, St. Flannan's and Rockwell College, but lost the final to St. Brendan's Killarney.

Frank Neylon, Larry O'Donoghue, Peter O'Loughlin, Frank Burns, P. Moloney, M. Collins, Anthony Guilfoyle, Gerard Commane, Michael F. Ryan, Michael Keane, P. Kelly, Joe Barry, Tom Woodgate, Michael Daly, Michael Clune.

1940 – Harty Cup (A) v. Limerick CBS – March 1940
Limerick 7-2 . . . Ennis CBS 3-2

Paul Brohan (Spancilhill), Raymond McNamara (Newmarket), Paddy 'Whackey' Murphy (Tulla), Kevin Griffin (Kilmaley), Reggie Connellan (Ennis Dals), Jimmy Kelly (Clooney), Pat Kearney (Tubber), Kevin O'Shaughnessy (Tubber), Michael Eustace (Kilmaley), Paddy Floyd (Tulla), Willie McAllister (Clarecastle), Seamus Reddan (Clooney), Joe O'Halloran (Clooney), Andy McMahon (Corofin), Gerry McNamara (Newmarket).

1941 – Dean Ryan Winners
Ennis CBS 6-5 . . . Midleton CBS 3-2

The team included Gerry McNamara (Capt.), John Leyden, Willie McAllister (Clarecastle), James 'Dutcher' Moloney (Clarecastle), Joe O'Halloran, Jackie and Joe Cullinan, Austin Hannon, Reggie Connellan, Mick Leahy (Ruan), Tom Slattery, Seán McCormack.

1955/56 – Semi-final v. The Mon
North Monastery 6-2 . . . Ennis CBS 4-6

Larry Walsh (Newmarket), Jack Daly, Martin Sheedy (St. Joseph's), Albert Costelloe (Ballyea), Brendan Doyle, Seamus McMahon, Tony Blake, Colm Madigan (Capt.), Jimmy Hassett (St. Joseph's), George Dilger, Hugh Ensko, Pat Henchy (Ruan), Michael Greene, Seán O'Gorman, Johnny McCarthy. Other panel members included Gerry Barrett (Ennis), P. J. Commane (Ballyea).

1961/1962 – Winning Harty Cup Team Line Out v. St. Flannan's
4-2 . . . 2-7 (all Ennis unless otherwise stated)

Michael Hayes (Clooney), Paddy Flynn, Tony Vaughan (Clooney), Paddy Corbett (Corofin), Sean O'Leary (Inagh), Vincent Hogan

(Newmarket), Chris 'Gus' Considine (Clarecastle), Gary Stack, Michael 'Dashie' Maher, Vincent Loftus, Seán Coffey, Michael Hanrahan, Des Guerin, Jim McMahon, Pat Coffey.

Subs: Johnny Pickford, Raymond Shannon (Coolmeen), Pat O'Connor (Ruan), Jimmy Quinn (Clarecastle), Liam (Bill) Murphy (Clarecastle).

Johnny Pickford played in the win over Limerick CBS. Jimmy Quinn was introduced during the course of the All-Ireland Colleges Final replay.

1962/1963 – Beaten Harty Cup Finalists
St. Finbarr's 4-9 . . . Ennis CBS 4-3

Paschal O'Brien, Jimmy Quinn (Clarecastle), Vincent Loftus , Brian Fitzgerald, Raymond Shannon (Coolmeen), Vincent Hogan (Newmarket), Seán O'Leary (Inagh), Gary Stack, P. J. Ryan, Paddy Murphy, Seán Coffey, Michael Hanrahan, Conor Smythe, Jim McMahon, Pat Coffey.

Sub: Flan Quigney (was introduced). Flan Quigney played a stormer in the semi-final versus St. Colman's.

Tony Vaughan (Clooney) played in opening round win over Limerick CBS.

1963/64 – Harty Cup Team – lost 3-9 to 4-2 to the future Harty and All-Ireland Colleges Champions, Limerick CBS

James Bradley, Eddie Lough, Paddy O'Brien, Brian Fitzgerald, Michael O'Driscoll, Vincent Loftus, Seán O'Leary (Inagh), P. J. Ryan, Jimmy Quinn (Clarecastle), Paschal O'Brien, Michael Hanrahan, Eric Hanrahan, Michael Waters, Conor Smythe, Pat Coffey.

Sub: Paddy Murphy (used).

1967/'68 Harty Team v. Mount Sion
Ennis 5-12 . . . Mount Sion 2-6 at Seán Treacy Park, Tipperary Town

Noel Ryan, Martin Leahy, Joe Corbett (Corofin), Flan Hegarty (Kilnamona), Nicholas Neylon (Kilnamona), Niall McInerney (Sixmilebridge), Frank Burns, Michael Cullinan (Crusheen), Tim Hannon (Newmarket), Seán Lynch, Martin Linnane (Corofin), Michael Galvin, Kevin Hoban (Sixmilebridge), Michael O'Regan, Michael O'Loughlin.

J. J. Corry played at corner back versus Limerick CBS and Martin Leahy went to corner forward in place of Kevin Hoban.

1968/69
Ennis CBS 2-11 . . . North Mon 3-4 – Emly

*Line out that lost to Coláiste Iognaid Rís.
Mike McCormack (Newmarket), Seán Liddy (Newmarket), Martin Leahy,

Michael Purcell (Sixmilebridge), Ollie O'Regan, Nicholas Neylon (Kilnamona), Noel Glynn, Noel Ryan, Paddy Firth (Tulla), Seamus O'Connell, Seán Lynch, Joe Pilkington (Kilnamona), Michael Galvin, Michael Smythe, Haulie O'Connell.

Frank Coffey and A. Barry played versus North Mon. Other subs possibly included Jimmy Hehir (Ruan), Tony Lynch (Clooney) and Clem Ryan.

***Note:* 13 a side was introduced in 1970 and continued until 1975.**

1970/'71 – lost to St. Flannan's 2-7 to 1-4 at semi-final stage in Tulla

Michael Skelly, Michael McNamara (Tulla), Tony O'Donnell (Crusheen), David Barry (Newmarket), John Sheehan (Ballyea), Davy Connellan, Johnny Johnson (Kerry), Kevin Kennedy (Killanena), Kieran McNamara (Newmarket), Noel Glynn, Haulie O'Connell, Cha Kenny, Gerard McNamara (St. Joseph's).

Subs: Fintan Quinn* (used), Martin Fitzpatrick*, Michael Griffin, Don Ryan, Noel Pilkington, Paddy 'Cuss' Kelly, Seán O'Grady, Paddy Neylon, John Hehir* (Kilnamona).

** Played v. Limerick CBS.*

The 1971/72 Harty Cup team that lost at the semi-final stages to St. Flannan's was: -

Michael Nugent, Michael 'Ganga' Griffin, Tony O'Donnell (Crusheen), Paddy 'Cuss' Kelly, Paddy Hill (Ballyea), Domhnaill Ó Loinsigh (Kilmaley), Kevin Kennedy (Killanena) (Capt.), Haulie O'Connell, Paddy Neylon, Michael Cooney (Quin), Brian Stenson, Pat McNamara (Tulla), Michael Griffin.

Subs: Cha Kenny, Denis Mulcaire, both introduced.

In the school year **1972/1973**, Rice College for the first time in more than 20 years failed to enter a team in the Harty Cup. The problem was two-fold, the Fairgreen, our natural training ground and Cusack Park were unavailable. The U.D.C. had begun to re-develop the fairgreen so the CBS lacked facilities.

The second problem was pride. In the previous Harty Cup of 1971/1972, Ennis CBS had lost heavily to St. Flannan's at the semi-final stage and school pride was dented. The College Management decided not to enter a team. It was a bad blow to all who played the game. The introduction of basketball at games time was a poor substitute to the cut and thrust of hurling.

The following hurlers were available for selection. Michael Cooney, Seán Hahessy, Paddy Hill, Jackie Hynes, Simon Moroney, Michael

McEnery, Michael McNamara, Frankie O'Gorman, Liam Ryan, Christy Murphy, Martin Murphy, Michael Talty, Michael O'Loughlin, Brian Stenson, Eddie Scanlan, Frankie Tuohy, Joe Waters, plus almost all the panel of 1973/1974.

1973/'74 – Harty Team lost 3-10 to 3-9 to Thurles CBS at Emly

Michael Clohessy (St. Joseph's), Michael (Milo) Keane, David Sheedy, Declan Coote, Denis Mulcaire, Donal Fitzpatrick, Ollie O'Loughlin, Gerry Pyne (Kilmaley), Peter O'Loughlin (Ballyea), Patsy Hehir (Ruan), Richard McAllister, Denis O'Connor, Gerard O'Loughlin.

Other panel members who played that year: -

Declan Cummins (Turloughmore), Eddie Fitzgibbon (Crusheen), Joe Pilkington, Seán Heaslip, Ollie Byrnes, Gabriel Dillon, Liam Ryan.

The 1974/'75 Harty Cup panel

Martin Chambers (goal), Michael Clohessy, Declan Cummins, Gerard Dilger, Gerry Daly, Tom Duggan, Pat Griffin, Tony Guilfoyle, Pat Hayes, Richard McAllister, Pat McInerney, Ollie O'Loughlin, Naoise Pyne, Seamus O'Reilly, Clem Ryan (Parnell St.), John Eugene Ryan, Adrian Sheedy, Pat Treacy, Gerry Queally.

Rice College 1979 Corn Padraig Winners – Munster Senior Hurling (B)

Gerry Browne (Banner), Pat Kilker, Michael Kenny, Seán English, Ray Casey, Pat Ryan, Conor Lynch, Micheál Glynn (Capt.), Fintan Ryan, Pat Lynch, Pat Hanrahan (Clarecastle), Jarlath O'Halloran. Seanie Cleary, Tony McInerney (St. Joseph's), Noel Galvin.

1979 Dr. Kinnane Cup Winners at Caherconlish
Munster Colleges u/17 (B) – Rice College CBS 6-5 . . . Cashel 1-4

Gerry Browne, Eoin O'Ceallaigh (Kilmaley), Paddy Kilker, Seán English, Pat Ryan (Quin), Micheál Glynn (1-0), Paul Hogan, Conor Lynch, George Guilfoyle (0-1), Seán Cleary (2-0), Tony McInerney (0-1), (St. Joseph's), Kieran Moroney (1-0), John O'Connor, Jarlath O'Halloran (2-3), Seán Cahir (St. Joseph's).

Sub: Noel Galvin for Pat Ryan (injured).

Rice Cup under 14 All-Ireland Competition for CBS Schools

Ennis CBS won the competition in 1962. They subsequently lost the finals of: **1967 to Thurles; 1968 to Callan; 1970 to Limerick; 2000 to Our Lady's Templemore.**

The 1968 team that qualified for the final was: -

Paddy Piggott, Paddy 'Cuss' Kelly, Brendan Gilligan, Noel Pilkington,

Michael McEnery, Seamus McGann (Kilmaley), Tony Piggott, Michael Skelly, Gerry O'Connell*, Cha Kenny, Paddy Neylon, Paul McNamara, Michael Nugent, Paddy Kelly, Frankie Tuohy.

** Didn't play in the final v. Callan CBS. His position possibly went to Tom Harvey (Inagh).*

I attended Ennis CBS Secondary School from 1968 - 1974. During those years, many good Harty Cup teams were fielded. The following team, picked for a little diversion, is my best 15 from those years: -

Michael Nugent

Seán Liddy *(Newmarket)* — Michael McNamara *(Tulla)* — Tony O'Donnell *(Crusheen)*

Martin Leahy — Noel Ryan — Davy Connellan

Kevin Kennedy *(Killanena)* — Declan Coote

Patsy Hehir *(Ruan)* — Seán Lynch — Haulie O'Connell

Seamus O'Connell — Seán Heaslip — Peter O'Loughlin *(Ballyea)*

As usual, a good mix of town and country. I picked Noel Ryan in his favourite position at centre-back. Though Michael Nugent played in goal for the CBS, he could play in most positions outfield. Kevin Kennedy also played in goal but he is better recognised as a mid-field player. Seán Liddy mostly played in the attack for the 'Blues' but it was as a defender that he played for CBS. Likewise, big Michael McNamara played full-forward for Brian Borus, but it was as a full-back I remember his during his time in the CBS.

During much of this time, Colleges hurling was played as a 13-a-side experiment. I selected the traditional 15-a-side. Apologies to all the other good hurlers who represented the CBS during those years.

The following team represented Rice College CBS in the Rice Cup of 1986: -

Matthew Arkett

Declan Fitzpatrick — Martin Clohessy — Lorcan Hassett

Patrick Burke — Seán McMahon — Oliver Nagle

Colin Lynch — Donal Cahill

Stephen McNamara — Derek Ryan — Barry Keating

Phelim Collins — Frank Landy — Michael Watson

Subs used in their win over Ard Scoil Rís: Colm Kerins, L. O'Reilly, Darragh Hassett. In hindsight, this has to be considered a great team.

HARTY CUP RECORD 1955 - 1974 AT A GLANCE

1955/'56	Ennis CBS	11-10	...	Charleville CBS	2-1
	Ennis CBS	5-9	...	De La Salle, W/rford	2-0
	Ennis CBS	6-11	...	Dungarvan CBS	2-0
Semi-final	Nth Monastery CBS	6-2	...	Ennis CBS	4-6
1956/'57	Ennis CBS	5-9	...	De La Salle	2-0
2nd Rd	Thurles CBS	3-10	...	Ennis CBS	1-3
1957/'58	Rockwell College	4-5	...	Ennis CBS	4-4
1958/'59					
1st Rd	Tipp CBS (winners)	6-5	...	Ennis CBS	2-6
1959/'60	*Lost to Charleville CBS - early stages.*				
1960/'61	Ennis CBS	4-10	...	Coláiste Chríost Rí	4-1
Replay	Ennis CBS	2-5	...	St. Finbarr's F/ferris	1-2
Semi-final	Nth Monastery	5-6	...	Ennis CBS	3-3
1961/'62	Ennis CBS	7-8	...	Limerick CBS	6-5
	Ennis CBS	6-8	...	North Monastery	2-3
Final	Ennis CBS	4-2	...	St. Flannan's	2-7

ALL-IRELAND COLLEGES FINAL

Draw	St. Peter's Wexford	0-10	...	Ennis CBS	2-4
Replay	St. Peter's Wexford	4-11	...	Ennis CBS	2-4
Croke Pk					
1962/'63	Ennis CBS	5-6	...	Limerick CBS	3-4
	Ennis CBS	6-2	...	St. Colman's Fermoy	1-8
Final	St. Finbarr's	4-9	...	Ennis CBS	4-3
Semple Stadium					
1963/'64	Limerick CBS				
1st Rd	(All-Irl Champions)	3-9	...	Ennis CBS	4-2
1964/'65	Limerick CBS	5-3	...	Ennis CBS	0-3
1965/'66	Limerick CBS	3-11	...	Ennis CBS	3-2

1966/'67					
1st Rd	Mount Sion	5-4	...	Ennis CBS	4-3
1967/'68	Ennis CBS	5-12	...	Mount Sion	2-6
	Limerick CBS	11-10	...	Ennis CBS	2-2
1968/'69	Ennis CBS	2-11	...	Nth Monastery	3-4
	Coláiste Iognáid Rís	5-5	...	Ennis CBS	2-4
1969/'70	Nth Mon (winners)	7-11	...	Ennis CBS	4-1
1970/'71	Ennis CBS	3-9	...	Limerick CBS	3-2
	St. Flannan's	2-7	...	Ennis CBS	1-4
1971/'72	Ennis CBS	2-7	...	Limerick CBS	3-3
	St. Flannan's	7-9	...	Ennis CBS	2-2
1972/'73	*Didn't compete - no facilities to train - Fairgreen was redeveloped - Cusack Park out of bounds.*				
1973/'74	Thurles CBS	3-10	...	Ennis CBS	3-9
1974/'75	Lost to North Monastery at Bansha.				

COLLEGES COMPETITIONS

Harty Cup (Senior A)

St. Flannan's and the North Monastery share the top spot of the Harty Cup with 19 titles. Limerick CBS are next with 10. St. Colman's, Fermoy have now moved to 4th spot with nine victories, two ahead of St. Finbarr's.

The complete list of Harty Cup Final results is as follows: -

Dr. Harty Cup Finals - Corn an Artaigh

1918	Rockwell College	5-5	...	Christian College, Cork	3-1
1919	North Monastery	3-2	...	Mt St. Joseph (Cistercian College, Roscrea)*	3-1
1920	Limerick CBS	7-0	...	St. Colman's, Fermoy	5-0
1921	*No competition*				
1922	St. Munchin's, Limerick	4-1	...	Rockwell College, Cashel	3-3
1923	Rockwell College	5-2	...	Limerick CBS	2-1
1924	Rockwell College	8-0	...	Limerick CBS	4-2
1925	Limerick CBS	4-0	...	Rockwell	1-1
1926	Limerick CBS	3-3	...	Rockwell	1-3

1927*	Limerick CBS	4-3	...	St. Flannan's	1-1
1928	*No competition*				
1929*	North Monastery	1-9	...	Limerick CBS	1-7
1930	Rockwell	9-2	...	Mount Sion	1-1
1931	Rockwell	6-2	...	Doon CBS	1-1
1932	Limerick CBS	4-2	...	Thurles CBS	2-2
1933	Thurles CBS	3-3	...	North Monastery	1-3
1934	North Monastery	4-2	...	Rockwell	4-2
Replay	North Monastery	7-1	...	Rockwell	3-3
1935	North Monastery	4-8	...	Rockwell	3-2
1936	North Monastery	4-3	...	Coláiste na Mumhan, Mellary	2-6
1937*	North Monastery	6-2	...	Mount Sion	4-4
1938	Thurles CBS	7-7	...	Charleville CBS	3-2
1939	Thurles CBS	7-4	...	North Monastery	4-4
1940	North Monastery	6-3	...	Limerick CBS	4-2
1941	North Monastery	4-2	...	Limerick CBS	1-3
1942	North Monastery	7-0	...	Thurles CBS	3-3
1943	North Monastery	8-7	...	Thurles CBS	3-1
1944					
Draw	St. Flannan's	1-10	...	Midleton CBS	3-4
Replay	St. Flannan's	4-5	...	Midleton CBS	2-2
1945	St. Flannan's	2-6	...	North Monastery	3-2
1946	St. Flannan's	4-5	...	North Monastery	2-1
1947	St. Flannan's	4-5	...	St. Colman's	3-6
1948					
Draw	St. Colman's	2-9	...	St. Flannan's	5-0
Draw	St. Colman's	3-6	...	St. Flannan's	4-3
2nd Replay	St. Colman's	6-4	...	St. Flannan's	4-6
1949	St. Colman's	4-6	...	St. Flannan's	1-3
1950	Thurles CBS	7-3	...	Midleton CBS	2-0
1951	Thurles CBS	3-5	...	Coláiste Iognáid Rís	1-3
1952	St. Flannan's	1-5	...	St. Finbarr's, F/ferris	1-3
1953	Mt Sion CBS	3-2	...	St. Flannan's	1-7
1954	St. Flannan's	2-11	...	Thurles CBS	3-5
1955	Nth Monastery	4-7	...	Limerick CBS	2-2
1956	Thurles CBS	2-5	...	North Monastery	2-3
1957	St. Flannan's	7-7	...	North Monastery	3-3
1958	St. Flannan's	6-2	...	Limerick CBS	3-7
1959	Tipperary CBS	1-9	...	St. Flannan's	2-4
1960	North Monastery	0-10	...	Limerick CBS	1-4

1961*	North Monastery	1-11	...	Thurles CBS	1-9
1962	Ennis CBS	4-2	...	St. Flannan's	2-7
1963	St. Finbarr's	4-9	...	Ennis CBS	4-3
1964	Limerick CBS	6-10	...	St. Flannan's	4-7
1965	Limerick CBS	4-6	...	De La Salle, Waterford	1-5
1966	Limerick CBS	6-5	...	Thurles CBS	5-3
1967	Limerick CBS	4-9	...	St. Finbarr's	1-5
1968	Coláiste Chríost Rí	5-9	...	Limerick CBS	5-4
1969	St. Finbarr's	6-6	...	Coláiste Chríost Rí	3-7
1970	North Monastery	6-5	...	Limerick CBS	4-7
1971	St. Finbarr's	4-12	...	St. Flannan's	2-4
1972	St. Finbarr's	6-11	...	St. Flannan's	2-7
1973	St. Finbarr's	5-14	...	Cashel CBS	2-5
1974	St. Finbarr's	10-11	...	Limerick CBS	2-2

A celebrated group of St. Flannan's hurlers together at the launch of 'Blue is the Colour', Christmas 2001 - Dermot Gleeson, Conor Plunkett, Gerard O'Loughlin, Niall Moran, Garrett Howard. Courtesy of Michael Mulcaire.

1975	Coláiste Iognáid Rís	5-6	...	Limerick CBS	2-4
1976*	St. Flannan's	2-9	...	De La Salle, Waterford	3-4
1977	St. Colman's	0-7	...	St. Flannan's	0-3
1978	Templemore CBS	3-5	...	St. Flannan's	2-6
1979	St. Flannan's	2-11	...	North Monastery	1-3
1980					
Draw	North Monastery	3-6	...	St. Colman's	2-9
Replay	North Monastery	2-10	...	St. Colman's	2-5

1981	North Monastery	2-6	...	Coláiste Chríost Rí	1-7
1982	St. Flannan's	2-7	...	North Monastery	1-7
1983					
Draw	St. Flannan's	0-9	...	North Monastery	0-9
Replay	St. Flannan's	1-6	...	North Monastery	0-7
1984	St. Finbarr's	4-9	...	Limerick CBS	1-7
1985	North Monastery	5-6	...	St. Flannan's	1-7
1986	North Monastery	1-12	...	Midleton CBS	0-9
1987	St. Flannan's	3-12	...	Midleton CBS	2-6
1988	Midleton CBS	2-7	...	Thurles CBS	2-3
1989	St. Flannan's	0-9	...	St. Patrick's, Shannon	0-5
1990	St. Flannan's	0-10	...	Nenagh CBS	0-3
1991	St. Flannan's	4-16	...	North Monastery	1-7
1992	St. Colman's	3-13	...	St. Flannan's	3-11
1993	Limerick CBS	5-5	...	St. Flannan's	1-12
1994	North Monastery	1-9	...	Midleton CBS	0-4
1995	Midleton CBS	3-18	...	Lismore CBS	3-5
1996	St. Colman's	3-19	...	Nenagh CBS	1-4
1997	St. Colman's	1-17	...	Nenagh CBS	0-8

The winning St. Flannan's All Ireland Colleges team of 1999. Back row, left to right: *Dermot Gleeson, Ronan O'Looney, Fergal Lynch, Tony Carmody, Tony Griffin, Justin McMahon, Conor Plunkett.* ***Front row:*** *Brendan Dunne, Brendan Gantley, Damien Kennedy, Gary Farmer, Seán Hawes, Robert Conlon, Andrew Quinn, Tom McNamara.*

1998	St. Flannan's	0-12	...	Limerick CBS	0-5
1999	St. Flannan's	1-14	...	St. Finbarr's	1-8
2000	St. Flannan's	3-14	...	Our Lady's T/more CBS	2-8
2001	St. Colman's	2-12	...	St. Flannan's	0-15
2002	St. Colman's	2-18	...	Our Lady's T/more CBS	0-6
2003	St. Colman's	1-6	...	St. Flannan's	1-6
Replay	St. Colman's	2-13	...	St. Flannan's	0-8

Munster Cup - Canon O'Kennedy Shield

The Munster Cup was inaugurated about 1929 as a Senior Colleges (A) competition. It was run separately from the Harty Cup.

In September 1943, St. Flannan's re-entered the Harty Cup but they continued to play in both competitions well into the early 1950s. I'm not sure when the Canon O'Kennedy Shield was dropped from the Colleges calendar. St. Flannan's contested the Munster Cup Final numerous times. They won it at least eight times.

St. Flannan's captain James McInerney - a player to watch for in the future.

1931	St. Flannan's	9-1	...	St. Finbarr's	3-2
1932	St. Flannan's	6-5	...	St. Colman's	5-3
1933	St. Flannan's	6-5	...	St. Colman's	2-4
1934	St. Flannan's *(winners)*				
1936	St. Finbarr's	4-2	...	St. Flannan's	1-1
1941	St. Flannan's *(lost final)*				
1945	St. Flannan's	8-3	...	St. Colman's	3-3
1946	St. Flannan's	2-6	...	St. Colman's	2-4
1947	St. Flannan's	7-11	...	Rockwell College	4-1
1951	St. Flannan's *(winners)*				

The following is a list of CBS players who went on to play senior hurling for Clare. I'm sure there are others: -

Michael Blake	Larry Blake (Jnr.)	Pat Brennan
Bobby Burke	Donal Cahill	Declan Coote
Phelim Collins	Reggie Connellan	Michael Dilger
Georgie Dilger	Massey Dilger	Micheál Glynn
Tom Glynn	Austin Hannon	Michael Hanrahan
Lorcan Hassett	Seán Heaslip	Patsy Hehir
Pat Henchy	Kenneth Kennedy	Kevin Kennedy
Michael Kilmartin	Mick Leahy	Seán Liddy

Des Loftus
Steve Loftus
Vincent Loftus
Pat Lynch
Seán Lynch
Seán Madigan
Colm Madigan
John McAllister
Willie McAllister
Johnny McCarthy
Niall McInerney
Seán McMahon (St. Joseph's)
Jimmy McNamara (Newmarket)
Michael McNamara (Tulla)
Stephen McNamara
Des Neylon
Matt Nugent
Paschal O'Brien
John O'Donnell
Joe O'Halloran
Noel Ryan

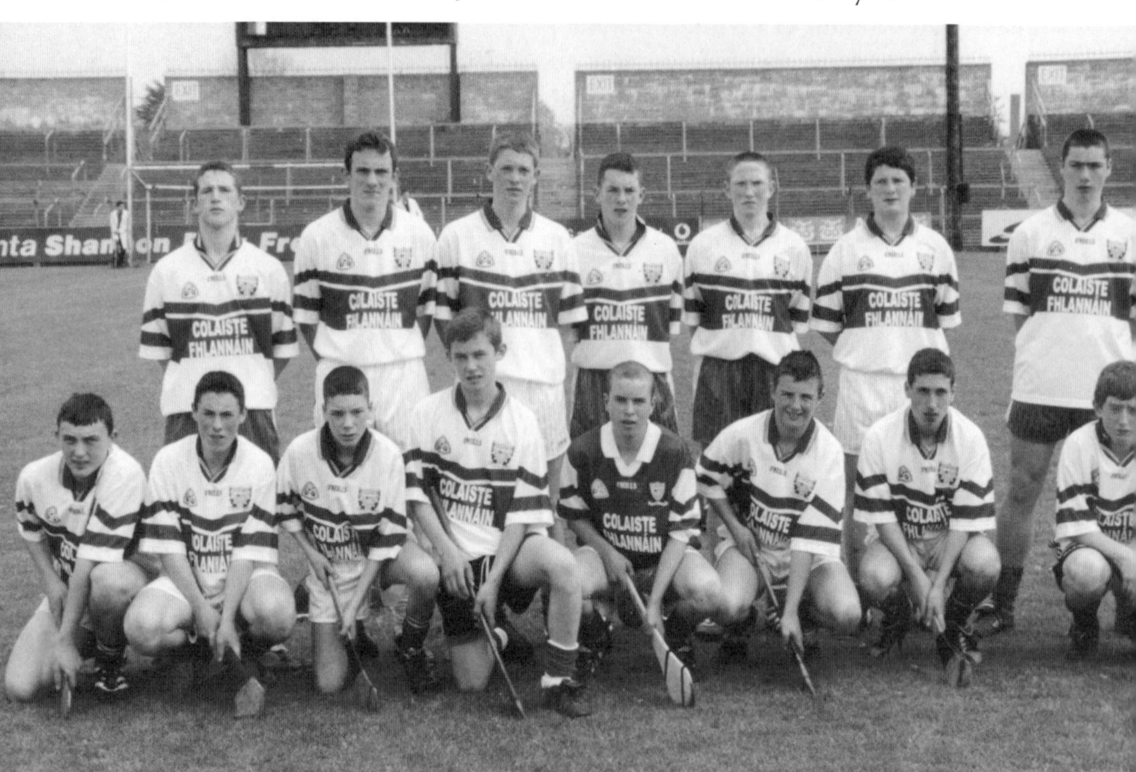

The St. Flannan's team that beat Rice College in the quarter final of the Whyte Cup 2001. Flannan's went on to win the cup. Back row, left to right: *Donnchadh Kelliher, James McInerney, George Hannigan, Derek Ryan, Seamus Hickey, Kevin Raftery, Bernard Gaffney.* ***Front row:*** *John Moloney, Francis O'Reilly, Conor Tierney, Seán Talty, Damien O'Halloran, Gerard Arthur, Conor Neylon, Seán Flynn.*

Townies on the Ball

Brian Dinan

Brian Dinan.

Young boys growing up in the fifties in the town of Ennis had very little organised recreation available to them, except hurling. If you didn't hurl, well you had better be good at your books, and that was that!

Most of us started out as street hurlers, i.e. pucking a ball up and down the street to each other, or against a wall if you were waiting for someone to show up. You could do that in those days because motorised traffic was sparse and slow moving.

Street hurling games took the form of: - (1) a pucking match; (2) three or maybe five-a-side; (3) scoring in the gate. For a pucking match all you needed was a pal whom you hit the ball to about fifty yards away. This game developed such skills as long striking, fielding and goalkeeping. The five-a-side games were little more than furiously-contested scrambles to hurl the ball in confined alleyways or squares. Maybe they developed the close quarter skills of pulling, jostling, hooking, and ball-fighting instincts. For the third format, 'scoring in the gate', all that was needed was a goalkeeper with two backs and two forwards to produce a fiery encounter.

The type of balls favoured for street hurling were made of rubber. It was unusual for individuals, other than clubs, to possess a sliother then. Anyway, hurling on streets was rough on sliothers. We had a choice of three types of rubber balls. First was the all rubber or sponge ball. It was not a favourite because it bounced too high and behaved erratically. Rubber balls for street hurling which gave performance more like the sliother on field, were made of hollow rubber and had a smooth outer layer. Best of all was the tennis ball, beloved of the purist, but a tennis ball was hard to come by, and didn't last long during hard clashing!

For serious games we progressed to a nearby field. O'Donahues and The Car Road field were well used down by the 'Back Cottages'. A match was put in progress with one of the stronger lads saying, 'Cuirim ort' (Irish for, I put it to you). The answer was 'Tuigim', which was the accepted signal to start the selection process. Each captain in alternate turn picked

Canon Hamilton Cup presented to Gerry Cronin captain of 1957 team with Bernie Dilger and Fr. Corry. Also included are Anthony 'Cato' O'Loughlin, Joe Madigan, Vincent Murphy, Peadar Kelly, Paddy Carney, and Joe Daly.

the best player in descending order of merit as he saw it. It was then the cries came from those already selected, "What did you pick that fella for? He's useless." No place for mushy sentiment there. You just hoped you weren't the last one selected, there was a certain shame in it. It might even get you put into goal. We were learning our trade in those pre-teen years, yet even then, Sean Kelly had perfected the slow motion solo run – and that was long before the advent of the 'slow-mo action replay' of today's television.

In fields near to home, with limited talent on view, some of us found it fairly easy to cope with the standard of play. Problem was, we often got chased out of those grazing fields by the owner. It seems hurling was not conducive to the growing of grass. Moving on to fields farther away meant we encountered progressively higher and tougher standards of play. Down in the Car Road Field we found the Dilgers (Michael, Bernie, George and Massey) well advanced in their chosen craft. There they played spirited matches with the likes of Haulie Casey, the elegant Ollie Ball, and injecting a touch of impassioned play, one Sean Cooley. No doubt the Blakes and Considines of the Turnpike were playing in St. Flannan's fields; the O'Briens, Molloys and Summerleys of Hermitage tussled in the Drumbiggle field behind Hassett's house; the Loftus and Cullinan brothers in the Butter Market; the Old Mill Street gang in the Cornmarket (not the corn field); while no doubt, the Brennans were lacing it up and down the streets of the town. For all we knew the Bohereen lads were playing similar games in the Fair Green, but that was far away and they were the 'enemy'.

Probably the best nursery of youthful hurling was Ennis CBS. From first class to sixth class leagues were in progress right through the year. For this, thanks must go to the Christian Brothers themselves, as well as the lay teachers Mick Hayes, Cyril Brennan, Bobby Burke and others. The school leagues generated huge interest, especially when it came to the final stages. A week before the final, pen-pictures of the players, the medals and cup, went on display in one of the O'Connell Street shops. Finals were played on Thursday afternoons, when the town shops had closed for their half-day. The school owned two sets of jerseys, an all green, and white with blue hoops. To be thrown a jersey in the classroom was the greatest thrill of all. The Pike usually got the green jerseys, and the Boreen mostly donned the blue-and-white.

Looking back on a school publication of the time, called the Topix, we take the following report on the primary league (by an unrecorded, but special correspondent): -

"Once again it's Primary League time and what a promising lot of players will be on view. Let's first examine the Senior League, which consists of three teams: -

1) Boreen; 2) The Market; 3) The Pike.

All striving for the "Corn Ui Shil". Boreen who are the leaders after the initial stages must attribute their position mainly to the fine centrefield partnership of Richard Pyne and Frank Hassett – a steady fullback line in which Paddy Flynn is most conspicuous and a number of roving utility players like Aiden Lynch and Pat Meere. Yet they will have to fight hard if they are to win the Cup. The Pike are at present in second position and they play more as a team than as individuals. However, goalkeeper Sean O'Callaghan must be singled out for special mention, as he is one of the best netminders in the Primary School. Other outstanding players are the Dinan Brothers – Brian and Derry; and Ernie Fahy who is at home either when attacking or defending. Now to the Market, who on paper appear to be the strongest side of all three, although they have not yet scored a win. Don't underrate them though, as the Boreen were very lucky to escape with a point in their last meeting. They possess more outstanding individuals than either of the other two teams put together. In full back Ben McAllister, Market have a player who can vie with the best. The purple patch of the team, however, is their half-back line of Murphy,

Commane and Cullinane. Time out of number the hard-working Murphy and clever Cullinane clear the lines while Commane often makes sudden dangerous solo efforts upfield, which oftentimes prove very costly to the opposition. Garry Stack, although he is in 5th class is a delightful player too. Anyway I'll stick my neck out and say that the Market will take the trophy in the end. They have the material and once they combine properly – look out!

The Teams:

Boreen: *Richard Pyne (Capt.); Frank Hassett (Vice Capt.); S. Shanahan; F. Cahir; J. Hickey; M. Maher; P. Micks; P. Flynn; C. Liddy; P. Shanahan; A. Lynch; C. MacInerney; P. MacAlle; J. O'Keefe; M.Brennan.*

The Pike: *D. Guerin; B. Dinan; P. Sheedy; S. MacCoillta; C. Fahy; P. MacMahon; D. Dinan; T. Cuinn; A. Sheehan; S. MacNamara; J. Kelly; P. Hickey; M. O'Neill; A. Moylan; P. Moylan.*

The Market: *J. Commane; B. MacAllister; P. Linnane; C. Purcell; B. Murphy; M. Cullinane; S. Lillis; M. Cahir; S. McEnri; M. Rahilly; G. Dooley; J. Callaghan; T. MacNamara; G. Stack; M. Fawl.*

It is interesting to note that the boys are now referreeing the matches themselves. This no doubt will help to produce future competent referees, of whom there is a considerable shortage. P. J. Linnane (Market), T. Quinn and S. Commane (Pike), R. Pyne (Boreen) are the four referees at present and they are doing a fine job indeed."

(End of *verbatim* report from the 'Topix' of 1956).

Meanwhile, away from school I remember Patsy O'Loughlin (later of Éire Og and Magpies fame, and father of the current 'Sparrow') calling to my house for a game of 'pulling', as he called it. This meant crossing the road to Donahue's field where we ran to a dead ball and both pulled together. The ball was flicked away, again we both ran shoulder-to-shoulder and pulled on it. This continued down to the crag, over Johnny MacInerney's field, across the Clare Road and into the College (St. Flannan's), and up the College fields as far as the Turnpike wall. We paused there for a while to get out breaths back. The pulling started up again, going back the way we had come. Patsy's hurley was a particularly rigid square-headed block that did not yield under any force (I think he made it himself), sending many a sting up through my hands. We would part at Captain Mac's Cross, him with a cavalier grin, me with skinned knuckles, as he remarked, "I'll call for you another day." I always hoped he might find someone more suitable to inflict his skills on.

We must have been doing something right, for next we came to the attentions of the emerging Ennis Rovers under-age mentors. My first away

County Final Day - Éire Óg 1959 - *Clare Cup Champions and beaten County Finalists.*

representative match was against a Newmarket team (probably under twelve) in the old Clarecastle field by the bridge. An unforgettable encounter! My first clash-of-the-ash against a country opponent was so intense that it almost splintered my arms, dislocated by bones, loosened my teeth, and I'm sure, rattled the delf on my mother's dresser at home. Thank God Patsy O'Loughlin had prepared me well, otherwise I wouldn't have been able for it.

Looking to our heroes of that time we found that Éire Og were reformulating with a new style of fast hurling. Young skilful players were making the headlines. When we gathered to watch their practice matches at St. Flannan's College we felt honoured if the players asked us to 'mind' their watches while they played. To us youngsters this was the big time. And the big time was in evidence when we travelled to see them in action in county championship matches, and to know the Blake family well enough to be in their home for after-match discussions.

But we had our own job of hurling to do. When the call came from the newly revitalised Ennis Rovers we were dropped into juvenile championship games. These were no timid affairs. When we ventured outside the town to play a match we were 'open season' for the hardy country boys.

We tested each other with taunts of: 'If you think our last match was hard, wait 'til you meet Crusheen!' Of course, all country teams provided us with testing encounters, particularly Tubber, Crusheen, Ogonnelloe, Broadford, Clarecastle and Newmarket. Hurling outside of the town meant we literally had to be on our toes at all times. Anything in the vicinity of the ball was fair game in those days! Rows were common enough. Sometimes matches didn't get finished because of rows. Referees were nearly always blamed – not too difficult to understand, since they were often selected from an 'innocent' bystander, whom the opposition assured us wasn't really related to half their own parish at all! In one Tulla encounter, just as we were about to draw level with a minute to go, the referee blew to stop the match to say the Angelus (the ball at that moment was sailing over the bar). The Angelus was said, the score duly disallowed, and then of course the row broke out.

In the town there was a deadly rivalry between St. John's and Ennis Rovers, although they rarely encountered each other in juvenile or minor championship games. Some players transferred between the clubs, more than once, especially juveniles who were searching for their real identities. The cross-channel soccer clubs had nothing on us in those days. Such was the rivalry built up by pride of place in both clubs that spirited displays were always guaranteed from both clubs. With plenty of teams available to the players, it was no wonder that town hurling was in a healthy and winning state in the fifties and early sixties. St. John's and Ennis Rovers had many county championships to their credit considering their relatively brief existences. They were disbanded in the mid-sixties when taken over by Éire Og. So ended a golden era of underage hurling in Ennis.

★ With the Compliments of the latest and Greatest Showband—THE

COASTERS COMBO

With Four Star Vocalists **(ENNIS)**

(SEVEN-PIECE—AVERAGE AGE 20 YEARS)

NEW MUSICAL SENSATION TO SUIT ALL TASTES

High Quality Amplification ***Punctual***

★ **Acclaimed by 450 Dancers who heard them on their Debut at the Queen's Hotel Ballroom, Ennis, on Wednesday Night, 9th November, as THE GREATEST EVER!**

Hoping to have the pleasure of playing for you

Apply: MANAGER, 23 Parnell Street, ENNIS - Telephone 153

A business card promoting the Coasters Combo, one of the best live acts to perform in the west of Ireland, during the heyday of the showband era.

Recollections of Ennis Hurling and Football

Jimmy Smyth

Larry Blake, Sr. one of the great Trojans of Ennis hurling was accustomed to tell the players on any bus travelling eastwards from Ennis that when they passed Corrovorrin they were on their own. To the country man, Ennis players were dapper, better dressed, tidier and smarter, hair was fashioned in the latest style, suits were well creased, they looked independent with a strut and a cockiness in everything they did. They seemed to be more advanced, were neat hurlers with tricks in abundance and always seemed to be so self-assured. We envied their clothes, style, environment, their questioning of events and opinions, their conversations and their cheekiness on the field of play. They had more opportunities for entertainment. They had the Cinema, and the dance halls, bigger shops, a bigger choice, electricity, tar roads, bigger schools and colleges. Country fellows were not always at ease in their company.

Jimmy Smyth.

It wasn't that Ennis players looked down on the culchie but rather that the culchie had this perception. We envied what they had and what they did. We felt a bit inferior I suppose and inferiority breeds resentment. Ennis don't get the rural support in the same way that The Dubs haven't support outside their own county. We hadn't come to grips with the town mentality. It was for such reasons that they were on their own when they passed Corrovorrin. We didn't fully appreciate the noble throb that thumps in the heart of a genuine Ennis man.

The weakness of the twopence halfpenny looking down on twopence is eternal in humanity. We have it in rural areas and we have it in big towns. There is always a fringe element that frowns on a perceived difference, the difference for instance between those who play gaelic games, play Irish music and sing Irish songs and those who feel that they

Éire Óg County Finalists 1955. Back row, left to right: *Tony Conroy, Gerry Moroney, Tony Keaty, Gerry Cronin, Dermot Leahy, Paddy Kerin, Paschal Brooks.* ***Front row:*** *Seán Madigan, Jimmy Cronin, Mick Morrissey, Larry Blake, Ml. Blake, Paddy Duggan, Pat Kirby, Bernie Dilger.* Courtesy of Larry Blake.

are distinct from the world of everyday experience. There are those of course, who have a genuine interest in other pursuits and games, but for those others there is no purification in the GAA. For such, there is no perception of reality in participation.

They do not belong and they want to exclude. There is no rubbing shoulders with the elite, no power, no prospect for improvement, no personal satisfaction from association with the masses. And then there is a residue that fawns on this fringe and who seek a universality on the crumbs that fall from the rich man's table. For such, hurling and football is a no man's land and a downer. But as Flan Hynes said to me at Purcell's pub in Ruan one night during a rendering of a beautiful Irish song, "They'll never drive the Irish out of this country".

Ennis have played, administered and followed our games from the beginning. They know that our games are a special ingredient in the make up of our nation, have the capacity to give the nation an individuality and a self-consciousness and point to a specific entity different from other nations. They are aware of the contentment, independence, satisfaction, special value and identity that hurling and football bring into their own lives and the lives of Irish people at home and abroad and that they ring out a sophistication of their own. They have a contentment in the knowledge that they have great games, great heroes, great people and great places. They know that through our games there is a deeper understanding of the nature of Irish society, and our national personality. And in this knowing they have participated and continue to participate. This is their reality.

And in my time Ennis, had great heroes and characters. I have mentioned Larry Blake, Sr., one of the most respected hurlers ever to play with the county. Mick Mackey always found him a difficult opponent. I met him socially at the Forester's Club on many occasions. And I remember Tull Considine, one of Ireland's greatest. We had him as manager of the St. Flannan's team in the early forties. He knew more about hurling than any man I have met since or before. One of his clearest instructions to forwards was that it was alright to sacrifice a goal in order to get the machine working. This was over fifty years ago and it was only in the present successful years that combination and team work surfaced in Clare teams.

And I remember Ralphie Burns and Aonar Sheridan, two of the niftiest and most skilled hurlers ever to don the Ennis and Clare jerseys. And it was in 1945 that I came across Peter (Slavery) Guilfoyle in full regalia of trousers and flowing shirt at Corofin. And of course Mickie White, a man with a fine flowing stroke and the greatest talker in the game. He was the barber in St. Flannan's in our time and we often had sore heads as he jerked with the machine when he spoke about the games of yore. Sean Guinnane, also comes to mind for his contribution to hurling and football. He was an able and fluent player in both codes and served for many years as Secretary of the County Board. At this time we were well grounded in the technological age but Sean always resisted the demands to install a telephone.

And in this account I cannot forget the one and only Sean McMahon from Corrovorrin. Mahon as he was popularly known was well able to swing the ash. He was a good friend of mine and we worked together at the clinic in the early 60's. He was one of my umpires at two Munster finals. One time, when we retired to the Catholic Commercial Club, Dublin, now extinct, for the usual few drinks after an Oireachtas final there was a great sing song in full swing. A Dublin lady, during the course of rendering a beautiful and strange song, kissed each one of the audience in turn. When it came to Sean's turn to partake of this unusual and delicate menu, the occasion inspired him to lift this enchanting willow into his arms and to waltz around the floor. Unfortunately he tripped over something, fell, and was out of commission with an injury for many weeks: an injury he never got during the toughest times in Clare hurling. But I remember Sean particularly for his great loyalty, sense of humour, enthusiasm and big heart.

Gerry Moroney, was one of the recognised stalwarts of the game. He played in both codes, for Faughs in football and for Ennis in the form of Ennis Rovers, The Faughs, The Dals or Éire Óg in hurling. Apart from his ability as a player and he was a good one, I always admired him for his leadership qualities. He was an all-rounder and he saw good in everything and in everybody. He was respected in the country and in the town. He attracted to his pub the core and worth of young and old. When we saw him walking his greyhounds or playing the games, he exuded this rare aura of dependability, and decency. He had no sides, like it or lump it, honesty had to prevail.

The late Fr. Michael Considine, who played hurling and football, was a man who never got the full opportunity of fulfilling his worth. In my opinion, he was one of the best centre-field men ever to don the saffron and the blue. He was a hard, unrelenting player, feared nothing, fought for every ball with a tigerish intensity and was rarely, if ever, beaten. He had this thundering approach to the game, not too unlike the present approach of Colin Lynch. Colin was a revelation in 1997; a ferocious tackler and ball-player. I find it very difficult to separate Colin, Jamesey, Brian Lohan and Anthony Daly as the Clare man of the '97 campaign. But Lohan, I suppose, is the best fullback that I have ever seen.

Christy Glynn was another that I feared and admired. I remember him playing at fullback and I was never too happy when I had to face him. He knew what he wanted and he always got there. There are always men who can dominate a situation with personality alone and Christy was in this category. On and off the field, he was a worker, a man with a great sense of loyalty to his club and his county and he contributed more than most to the promotion of hurling and football in the town. A countryman always admires courage and sincerity and Christy had such attributes.

Others that come to mind during this early period were Reggie Connellan, who worked at Kennedy's at the Square, Johnny Fleming, with whom I worked in the Fire Brigade, Sean Dinan, who probably was the best minor in those years, Michael Doherty, Turnpike, Josie Doherty, Turnpike (brothers), John Joe Keane, The Market, Monty Keane, Clare Road, Paddy Markham, Ballyea, P. J. O'Dea, Kilrush and Tony Strand. Markham always played with a feather in his mouth and O'Dea, who played with Ennis Rovers in the 1948 championship, was a hard nut to crack. Faughs, who won the football championship in 1947 had many well known hurlers with them, including Matt Nugent, probably the finest hurling stylist and forward ever to grace the game, Johnny Fleming, Ralphie Burns, Sean Guinnane and Gerry Moroney. The Moloneys were also to the fore in football in those early years.

Mick Murphy, Kilmaley, who won an All-Ireland final with Tipperary in 1945, played with Faughs in the Clare Championship around 1950, a team which included Paddy Duggan, a man who gave so much to his club, and his county. Paddy had an extraordinary way with young people. He radiated sincerity, wasn't afraid to call a spade a spade, and gave a lot of his time to organisation.

In the early 50's also emerged the nucleus of what was to be one of the finest club teams ever to represent the town. Into the side came Tony Conroy, Bernie Dilger, a real dynamo, Michael Dilger, Michael Blake, who later died tragically in a motorcycle accident. I remember Michael specifically for his eclipsing of Christy Ring in a Munster Championship game at Thurles. And I can bring to mind names such as Tony Keaty, Eugene Ryan, Larry Blake, Jr., Bobby Burke, Sean Madigan and Hugh O'Donnell. It was around this time, 1952, I think that the Éire Óg team was founded. It was the brainchild of either Larry Blake, Jr. or Sean Madigan or both, with the additional help of Jimmy and Gerry Cronin, two great hurling brothers, Pat Kirby, later to become World Handball Champion, Paschal Brooks, whom I found to be a very formidable opponent, Paddy Kerin, a colleague of mine at the Courthouse, and Paddy Loftus. Éire Óg were a powerful hurling force.

Mick Morrissey was also around and Jack Daly and Colm Madigan were introduced around 1956. Aidan Tuttle, one of the great personalities of the town, a natural wit, was playing minors with St. John's in this year. "You're so mean" he said to a very important man, "that you'd buy out Onassis with threepenny bits." And he did annoy Nuggie (Michael Nihill), who had purchased T. V. Honan's from Derry and Treas Honan. He always called in to rise the hackles. And speaking of St. John's always reminds me of the fact that it was St. John's who, in my opinion, were responsible for the official recognition of set dancing in this country. The GAA and Comhaltas did not recognise set dancing at this time and considered it to be of foreign origin and so was not racial of the soil or the people. But Joe Daly and Des McCullough thought otherwise.

They organised a set dancing competition at Paddy Con's Hall with a bullock as first prize. The hall was packed. Mickie Reddan and Monty Casey and their partners were the winners. It was the talk of the county. It was highly unlikely that St. John's would be penalised for holding a dance popular in every corner of the county. Eventually, the popularity of the set and the non-enforcement of the rules was discrediting the Association and so the dance was legitimised and recognised by the GAA at top level. Comhaltas followed suit later on. And during all this time, Gerry Moroney was still hurling away, fitting in with the new blood, advising and guiding.

Bringing to mind all these names and thinking over the vagaries of the games reminds me of the Gold Watches Tournament. There was great rivalry between St. Joseph's and Éire Óg as there is always between neighbouring teams. They were played at evening and were tough. When a player fell to the ground he was injured. No shamming. The players were all decent men who mercilessly followed the ball to the bitter end. The honour of the little parish was at stake. I refereed one of these games. I gave a free to Éire Óg and Pat Kirby went up to take it. He delayed and as I thought strutted too long about the ball and so I decided to hop the ball. Míle murder broke out and every Ennis man at the Park was howling for my blood.

The whole world revolved around the face of Joe Madigan (Juliar). I went to the sideline and pushed him over the concrete steps. He could have been seriously injured. The *Clare Champion* went to town on this. Afterwards I went back to Kilgobbin, Clooney where I was on holiday and had to account to my uncle who was an old Clooney hurler, who had heard of the incident. "Do you know young man", he said, "that you will never live to see the day when you have as much done for hurling and for your parish as Joe Madigan." It was a bad moment. He was right. Joe was the heart and soul of Ennis hurling. It took me some time to apologise but I did. We remained great friends.

And around 1957, Joe Ensko, Brendan Doyle, Jack Daly and Johnny McCarthy were introduced to the team. Jack Daly was later to become the Chairman of the County Board, member of the County Council, and Chairman of the University of Limerick. Michael Doherty (The Doc and no relation to Michael Doherty, Turnpike) was also to the fore here and got five goals against Kilkenny on one occasion. I remember Johnny McCarthy not alone for his hurling ability but also for his playing on the box. Occasionally in hurling we have that great accompaniment of hurling, traditional music and song. They blend so well together. Michael Dilger also came more into the picture at this time. Gruggy, as we used to call him, had marvellous talent. Fast, fit, intelligent and skilled, he was more than a match for the best in the country. All the Dilgers gave good service to the town. Gruggy was everyplace, Bernie at right half-back and Georgie of later camera fame and Massey.

Eventually, Ruan met Éire Óg in the famous final of 1959. Éire Óg had three new faces for this game. Steve Loftus, against whom I had many an anxious moment, Pat Tynan, a Kilkenny man living in Ennis (Pat broke his glasses in the 1959 final) and Michael Guerin. Ruan were the outsiders.

For most of the game, Éire Óg were superior but Frank Custy in the goal for Ruan didn't allow them to score. We had a custom in Ruan, to make all the changes possible before a game because we felt that the excitement of a game didn't allow a proper immediate decision to be taken by excited selectors. This custom allowed us to make the changes to overcome Éire Óg's early superiority, changes which eventually won the game.

Other Ennis names that I remember would be Denny Rice, who played with the Rovers in 1929. I never saw him play but remember him as a big genial man in a big truck, when he was working with the Council. Vincent Loftus, a hurler to his fingertips, John Dunne, who now devotes his life to the service of the people, Paschal O'Brien, a top class goalkeeper. As I write this I hear that Paschal has passed away. Ar dheis Dé go raibh a anam. He has etched his name forever in the consciousness of every true Gael in the town and in the county.

Vincent Loftus (on left) in action for Clare in the Munster Championship clash with Limerick in 1972. Loftus is supported by the Newmarket players D.J. Meehan and Gus Lohan.

Maura Keane (nee Reidy) and Ambie O'Connell (nee Costelloe).

I also recall Des Loftus, another member of that famous Loftus hurling family, Richie Pyne, Garry Stack, Michael Hanrahan, Noel Pyne, a flier on the wing and a noted golfer, Paddy Flynn, an immaculate corner-back, Martin Bradley of Bord Fáilte fame, John Nevin, a hurler with great hands, Declan Coote, who must be a relation of the famous Joker Coote, Tony Kelly, who afterwards devoted his services to management, Sean Heaslip, a nephew of a famous Kilkenny hurler, Brendan Gilligan, Noel Ryan, also a noted footballer, Barry Smythe, one of the great full-backs. We had Michael Glynn, a son of Francie and nephew of Miko: Martin Nugent, who had to follow in the footsteps of a famous father, Tony Nugent his brother, Francis Corey, Colm McMahon, Peter Barry, Eoin McMahon and of course Stephen McNamara of rare hurling and football progeny, the Cootes and the Powers. From St. Flannan's I have memories of Mick Neylon, who played full-back and Senan Bourke, nephew of Larry Blake, corner back, both of whom won a Colleges All-Ireland.

From a very young age I probed and poked through the streets of Ennis. I had heard tales of Sham Spellissy running on the battlements of the Fergus, on the club bridge side of Steele's Rock, with the ball stuck to his hurley. I remember Power's Yard as the Mecca of all country people. I remember John Leyden, a great Ennis supporter, with his horse and long car providing minerals and other drinks for the community. I remember Steele's Terrace, the home of Paddy Mac, who was the voice of Ennis GAA activity for many years. I remember M. J. Baker, who won a Junior All-Ireland with Clare in 1914 and the medal always proudly hanging from his waistcoat. And there are those who say that he tried to get the Council to build a bridge from the Park to join up with Steele's Rock, I remember the Ennis accent. In Clare there are at least five different accents that I can distinguish but the Ennis accent stands on its own. Ennis is a home for me and I still get great comfort reconstructing from the very modern Ennis the homes and businesses of days gone by.

I think of Considines, where as a boy I got the long Craven A butts

Éire Óg County Champions 1990. Back row, left to right: *Francis Corey, Ml. Meagher, Pete Barry, Eoin McMahon, Tomás Corbett, Micheál Glynn, Johnny Corbett, Gerry Barry, Martin Nugent.* ***Front row:*** *Seán Heaslip, Barry Smythe, Gearóid Mannion, Declan Coote, Colm Mahon, Ger Cahill, Shaun McCarthy.* ***Mascots:*** *Colin Heaslip, Mark Coote, Ian McMahon.*

from the ladies' toilets. Darcy's forge where I stood and gazed longingly at turf fires blazing around the horse car wheels: Guiton's, the Market, who supplied me with the Players' Weights in tough times: McPartland's, Parnell Street, who never failed to give a young lad his shilling's worth of fags: Miss McKenna, who gave music lessons at the Kilrush Road, where at eleven years of age I lost my heart to Nancy Collins. I never told Ted. And I recall Amby Costelloe and her singing: Della and her dancing: Frank their brother, who had one of the finest hurling hands in the hurling game. The market on the Saturdays, with the bonhams, the squealing, the calves and the haggling. Vincie Neylon, my cousin, who never lost his humour but still was a local historian in his own right: Dunkirk, where we sometimes went before a game but to which we never failed to retreat afterwards and Pakie Malone, his forge and his chat. And I have to think of Sam Lewin, who worked at Knox's and was later manager of the Forester's Club. He told Jack Deignan, a local reporter, that when he went to the Gaiety, he wore elastic bands around the ends of his trousers in order to stop the fleas getting through. Jack made hay with this story and it flourished in the *Evening Herald* for many evenings.

And so when I talk of the GAA in Ennis, I speak about the real grass roots, who are proud of their town, and their identity. I don't speak about the high and mighty and the rich. I speak about people who are themselves and nothing more. When I think of the GAA in Ennis, I am reminded of John M. Feehan's book, *The Wind that Round the Fastnet Sweeps,* and the old folktale which he recites: "The Lord was walking in the Garden of Paradise and he came to a little forget-me-not growing at the foot of a massive oak tree. The little flower spoke to the Lord and said, 'I wish I were like the old oak tree here, strong, powerful and majestic. Then I could be of some use to the world.' And the Lord answered: 'If you tried to be an oak you would end up revolting and ugly. Your beauty lies in being what your are – a simple lovely flower that has brought so much happiness to the hearts of young lovers than any oak tree. Your simplicity and your loveliness is yourself."

Kilkenny native and former Éire Óg hurler, Jack Heaslip continues to run a thriving business in O'Connell Street, Ennis.

Family Ties

The story of hurling in the capital town is littered with sets of brothers, two or more, who played hurling for Ennis. Since earliest records in the 1880s when the game was played under the auspices of 'The Alexander Martin Sullivan Club', there have been many families whose names have been synonymous with hurling in the town. When Clare won its first senior hurling title in 1914, the Dals had four representatives on the team on Final day. The Considines were well represented with Willie ('Dodger') and Brendan, members of perhaps one of the most famous sporting families in town.

'Dodger' captained The Ennis Hurling Club to championship success in 1911. He was also a member of the victorious sides of 1914 and 1915. His brother, Brendan is reputed to be the youngest man ever to win an All-Ireland Senior Medal. Even more surprising is the fact that Brendan was a member of the winning 1911 Ennis team when he was only 14 years old. In 1917 Brendan added a second championship medal to his collection, in the service of Dublin. His career in the bank later took him to Cork with whom he won a Munster Championship Medal. Amazingly he also played senior hurling for Waterford.

Though there is no denying the greatness of Brendan and 'Dodger', but the most famous of the Considines is the legendary Tull. Equally at home with football or hurling, his first experience of the big time was as a member of the Clare Senior Football team that contested the final with Wexford. An automatic choice on the Munster Railway Cup team of the 1927 – 1933 era, Tull's greatest hour was possibly the championship semi-final of 1932 against Galway when he scored 7 goals. His senior career with the Dals lasted from 1915 to 1935. Even when he had retired from the playing fields, Tull was still playing a big role in hurling. He, along with Fr. Jimmy Madden trained the St. Flannan's Harty Cup teams during their historic four in a row – 1944 – 1947. Tull also coached the last Dals team to win senior championship in 1941.

James 'Sham' Spellissy was a member of the 1914 Clare team. Like the Considines, he also won senior hurling and football medals and was undoubtedly one of the stalwarts of the Dals winning team during the years 1911 – 1924. His brother, Jack, also made a worthy contribution to GAA affairs. Jack won junior All-Ireland honours with the Banner County in 1914. A third member of the family, Michael, known as 'Beezer', also played hurling in the early days before emigrating. Beezer was involved in Land League activities and it was considered prudent if he departed before the British Police (RIC) came after him. He just got out one jump ahead of the law. 'Beezer' went to the historic Bay State of Massachusetts, home to the revolutionary war in 1775. His grandson, Bernie Spellissy is a native of the city of Lowell and a regular visitor to Ennis.

Joe Madigan was a regular member of the Dals team from 1924 to 1941. During those years he won five senior hurling championships. A dual player, Joe also won a senior football medal in 1929. Joe Madigan played regularly for the Clare seniors during the 1927 – 1932 era. He was a sub on the 1932 team that contested the All-Ireland Final. Though it is not generally known, he was also a popular referee, and had the distinction of refereeing Railway Cup and junior championship games in the mid-thirties. Apart from giving a lifetime of service to the games in Ennis at club and schools level, Joe has also the distinction of giving three sons to the game of hurling. Brendan played minor hurling and football with Clare and won two senior football titles with Faughs in 1952 and 1954. Seán had many fine hurling hours with Éire Óg in their great years from 1955 to 1958 and was one of their chief scoring forwards in that era. Colm, the youngest of the family, captained the Ennis CBS 1956 Harty Cup team. That year he was selected on the Munster Colleges team and won a senior championship with Éire Óg. Colm also gave some fine displays for his county, both minor and senior.

Bridie Byrnes (nee Mac Mahon), mother of the author, pictured in Kilkee by a local cameraman in the summer of 1958.

Larry Blake is acknowledged as one of the finest wingbacks that Clare has ever produced. He first played for Clare in the minor grade in 1928. Larry Blake was never off the Munster Railway Cup team during the 1930s. His brother, Tom, played regularly in goal for the Dals. He played junior for Clare many times and was sub goalie to Georgie O'Dea on the Clare Senior Team for some time. All five of Larry's sons played hurling at some level. The most prominent were Michael and Larry (Jnr). Michael, a regular county hurler, is regarded as one of the best centre-backs Ennis ever had. Likewise Larry (Jnr) was very prominent in the formation of Éire

Óg and a constant part of the team until his retirement in 1959. Tony represented St. John's and made a big contribution to the Banner Club some 20 years later. The Blakes and Madigans are first cousins.

When Éire Óg won the Senior Championships of 1956 and 1957, the Cronin brothers – Jimmy and Gerry – were part of the team. Gerry played at centre-forward in the 1956 final, though some of his most memorable games were from the centre-field position in the 1957 decider versus Whitegate. He played junior and senior for Clare during his career. Their father, Gerry Cronin (Snr), won senior titles with the Dals in 1924, 1929 and 1934. He also played senior for Clare on many occasions and made a big contribution to hurling, both on the field of play and in administration.

When the Dals won the championship in 1924, the Fahys filled over a quarter of the places on the team; Bill ('Botch') and Eddie Fahy had a big hand in re-organising hurling in the town. Mickey and Wally were the other two brothers on the team in 1924. Both Billy, who emigrated to the United States in 1925, and Eddie, who won a senior championship with Dublin in 1927, were gone for the next Dals victory in 1928.

St. Flannan's has always been a nursery for Ennis hurlers and nowhere is this more evident than in the case of the Quirkes. Jack played Canon O'Kennedy Shield. He graduated from there to play minor and senior for Clare. He was a regular on the Clare team from 1930 to 1938, and won County Championships with the Dals in 1934 and 1941. Tadhg Quirke won Munster Cup Medals with Flannan's in 1931, 1932 and 1933. He was a regular on the Dals team until 1940.

Many first cousins have represented Ennis. A prime example is the relationship between Aoner Sheridan, Jackie Duffy and Freddie and John Garrihy. The Garrihy brothers were first cousins of Jackie Duffy and Aoner Sheridan. They were connected through the sisters, Dotie, Honor, Georgina and Annie O'Loughlin. Georgina, later Mrs. O'Connor lived in Francis Street and when Eamon DeValera came to Ennis, although usually booked into Carmody's Hotel, he often stayed overnight with the O'Connor's in Francis Street to get some peace and quiet. Freddie Garrihy who won an All-Ireland junior medal in 1914 won county senior championships in 1911, 1915 and 1924. Jackie Duffy was on the winning teams of 1924, 1928 and 1929, while Aoner Sheridan picked up senior medals in 1934 and 1941. Their uncles, the O'Loughlin brothers, Anthony, Michael and Paul were other noted hurlers representing the Dals. They originally hailed from Upper Market Street, where the family ran a public house. Aoner Sheridan's father,Tom hurled for the Faughs way back in the early years of the 20th century. The Sheridan/Garrihy/ Duffy/O'Loughlin contribution is surely a proud one.

Many sons follow in their fathers' footsteps in representing the town team. Mick Linnane, a stalwart with Rovers in 1927, represented the Dals in the 1934 winning squad. His son, Martin, represented St. John's. After returning from a long stay in England, Martin played a leading role with Éire Óg in the late sixties and early 1970s. Likewise the McCarthys have links with town teams over the years. (John) Brudsy McCarthy was a member of the Dals winning team in 1941. His son, Johnny represented Éire Óg from 1957 – 1971 giving many sterling displays. Miko Ball won a winner's medal in 1941. His son, James was part of the winning combination of 1966. Another son, Chris was involved with Rovers. Tom Neylon played on the 1941 winning team. His sons, Des and Paddy were good. Des represented Rovers during a great spell at underage. He won senior championship in 1966. Paddy was a very prominent colleges player at Ennis CBS, playing all grades for the school. He represented Éire Óg at all levels, winning under-21 in 1974.

The St. Michael's and Connolly Villas area always produced the best of hurlers. They had a style of their own. A host of St. Michael's lads represented the CBS. The Green in St. Michael's was a haven for hurling on Sunday afternoons. The Leahys, Dinans, Lynchs, Piggotts, Hanrahans, O'Connells, O'Regans, and Tony Roche were all top class. Many of these lads represented Clare at minor level. Anthony and Ollie Piggott were prominent. Their cousins, Michael, Tony and Paddy, were classy players. Paddy could play anywhere, centre-back or in goal.

Michael Nugent and Martin Leahy.

The O'Connells, Seamie and Haulie, stood out at Colleges level. Haulie played four years Harty Cup for CBS. They both played county minor. Haulie went on to play senior for Éire Óg, but work commitments took him overseas, curtailing his hurling. Michael and Eric Hanrahan both played senior for Éire Óg. The Leahys, Michael and Martin, sons of Seán, were also to the fore. Michael and Seán Dinan were good too. Michael played at senior level for the town. He should have played more. They are sons of the late Seán Dinan (Snr), who represented the Turnpike. Sean starred for the Clare minors in 1948 when they went under to Waterford. Such was Dinan's display that the Clare Champion carried the headline 'Only Dinan and Smyth impress.' Sean's brother Frank was also a noted hurler in his young days. It's through Sean and Frank that their nephews Paddy and Tom Kelly got their hurling. Paddy played full-back for Éire Óg for many years.

The Dilger brothers, Michael (Gruggy), Bernie (Champ), Georgie and Massey came from Connolly Villas. The Dilgers all played inter-county, and are counted amongst the best hurlers to come out of Ennis. In the late 1960s, St. Michael's had so much talent they could have fielded a good Junior (A) or Intermediate team. They fielded a good side in the Inter-Parish Club League.

George Dilger.

Anthony's sons (Liam) Billy and Anthony Piggott junior have played regularly for Eire Og. They are nephews of Frankie Guilfoyle. The Guilfoyles are another prominent town family. Originally from The Market, Paddy (Polo) played for the Market in the famous Town League final of 1948. His first cousins were the brothers John 'Glory', and Peter 'Slavery' Guilfoyle. Frankie Guilfoyle is a son of Polo. In fact no fewer than 5 grandsons of Polo Guilfoyle have played for Eire Og. They are Paddy and Frankie (Jnr), Paddy Guilfoyle, a son of Paddy, and Liam and Anthony Piggott (Jnr.), while Stephen Guilfoyle is a great grandson of Paddy 'Polo'Guilfoyle. Polo was an uncle of Mickie Guilfoyle the councillor. Paddy Guilfoyle (Frankie's son) won a Tony Forrestal cup medal in 1990. Four years later he captained the Clare Minor hurling team. He played county u/21 in 1995 and 1996. Paddy Guilfoyle also represented the county seniors in national League and Oireachtas about 1996. Paddy Guilfoyle and Liam Piggott are first cousins.

Aidan Guilfoyle who played in defence with the county minors in 1958 is also connected. His brother Vinny is well known in swimming.

Eddie 'Bucky' Flynn won senior championship with the Dals in 1941. His son Pat likewise represented the town in senior hurling. Pat's son Fergus carries on the tradition. Fergus is one of the finest centre half backs to play for Eire Og in some time. Fergus Flynn represented both Clare and Galway in senior inter-county hurling.

Colum and Paddy Flynn are nephews of Eddie. Paddy was an outstanding colleges hurler with Ennis CBS. He played senior club hurling with Eire Og for many years. Colum is involved in training Ennis and Clare teams for over three decades. A top class boxer, he represented Ireland in the heavy weight division.

Hurlers and fishermen all - Michael "Paddence' O'Loughlin, Frankie Guilfoyle and Bernie Dilger. *Courtesy of George Dilger.*

Clem Ryan of Hermitage played hurling at all levels for Clarecastle. A product of Ennis CBS and a member of their 1970 Harty cup team, Clem is a grandson of Pa Corry of Clarecastle. Clem's brothers Liam and Vinny (Fintan) were also prominent. Liam represented Clonbony hurlers. Their sisters Betty and Freda played camogie with Eire Og. A young and coming skills champion Clooney's Derek Ryan is also a family member. Derek represented Clare in the national skills final in Summer 2002.

Like the Éire Óg team of the early 1980s, their counterparts in the 1950s also produced several sets of brothers to represent Ennis. Declan and Joe (Hugh) Ensko played for Ennis, be it Éire Óg or St. John's. As did Joe and Jack Daly. Turnpike produced the Cosgroves and Dohertys. Paddy, Josie and Michael Doherty played for the 'Pike in the 1948 league final. They are nephews of Rob Doherty of Newmarket and 1914 fame. Tom, Tony and Ger Cosgrove were also prominent hurlers with Turnpike and St. John's. To the best of my knowledge another brother, Patsy, didn't hurl at representative level. Their cousins Vince and Frank were also involved in the game. Johnny and Michael Guerin were also to the fore in the late 1950s. Michael played for Éire Óg well into the sixties. He later served as chairman of the club. A first cousin of theirs, Joe Guerin also played with distinction.

The excellent Éire Óg team of the early 1980s featured several sets of brothers in the Barrys, Heaslips, Lynchs, Mahons, Nugents, Russells and Ryans. The Heaslips – Seán and Frannie – gave great service as did the Lynchs, Seán and Pat. Pat possessed tremendous speed and was a joy to witness in full flight. The Lynch's are nephews of Jim, Barney, Michael and Tony Lynch of Clarecastle. John, father of Sean and Pat also played for the magpies. The Russells too were good. John played for many years with the county senior team. Tom was possibly better known as a footballer, and many of his best years were spent playing in Co. Monaghan. Tom made a big contribution when he returned to Éire Óg. The Mahons are sons of Seán, who played for Éire Óg in the early years of the club. All his sons hurled, but Colm, Francie and Paschal stood out. Paschal won an All-Ireland Vocational Schools medal for the Banner County in 1979. He later spent many years in the United States and his presence was greatly missed. Now, Seán, a son of Francie carries on the tradition.

The Barrys gave wonderful service to Éire Óg. Michael's sons, Damien and Michael (Jnr), were part of the town team that played in the County Final of 2000. Michael (Snr) played as did his brothers, Joe, Gerry and Pete. Joe gave great leadership to his club over the years. He and Pete were part of the successful team of the early 1980s. The Mannions are another family with strong hurling links. Tomás was outstanding at juvenile and minor level. In 1977, he won the under 15 BLOE pole vault championship of Ireland. Gearoid represented Clare at under 21 level in the 1985 Munster Championship. Leo also played for the county at minor level. Gearoid recalled to me *"My father (Tom) encouraged Leo, Tomas and I to play hurling., often driving car loads of us to matches. At the time I didn't know that he was a hurler in his day. The other mentors I remember are Paddy Duggan, Bro. Cusack and Gearóid Ó hEarcáin. Later on, Seamus Flanagan, Paddy O'Halloran, Liam Harvey and Sean (Tora) Kelly put their time into it."* Like the Barrys, Ryans and Nugents, etc. the Mannions were all round sportsmen. The Corbetts of Éire Óg, Tomás and Johnny played for club and college. Tomás captained the 1991 winning St. Flannan's team. Johnny normally played in attack, while Tomás excelled in defence before moving to the forward line where he too proved useful.

Tomás and Johnny Corbett. Courtesy of Ml. Mulcai

Like the Dilgers, the Loftus family contributed at least four hurlers for club and county - Paddy at full back, Stevie, Des and Vincent. Another brother, John was involved with Rovers at administration level. Vincent captained the county team to the 1967 Munster Final. He was regarded as one of the best defenders in the game at that time. Stevie too played senior championship with a good Clare team in 1960. The Pynes of Abbey Street are a noted sporting family, but Noel, Dick and Derry excelled at hurling. Brenny too was a fine hurler and he represented a good Banner Hurling team in the 1981 championship. All the Pynes, Louis, Liam, Tom are fine golfers. Noel's sons David and John hurl. David plays with Eire Og and John with Clarecastle. This might seem strange, but it happened naturally. When the Pyne's moved to Clarecastle in 1983, David was involved as a ten year old with Eire Og. John, then only 5 years gravitated towards Clarecastle. John Pyne played a leading role in Clarecastle's Munster Club Championship win a couple of years back, scoring one goal and fifteen points in their campaign.

The Gilligans, Noel, Paddy and Brendan, all represented town and county. Noel played for Éire Óg in the late 1950s while younger brother, Brendan, played minor, U/21 and senior for Clare during the years 1972–1979. Brendan later moved to London and represented Brian Borus and Desmonds. He also has the distinction of playing college hurling with CBS, St. Flannan's and the Vocational School. Brendan has long resided in the USA. Their sister, Margaret Lacheiner, excelled at squash. She was ladies champion in 1977 and 1978 and was honoured in the Clare Sports Star awards. Noel, Brendan and Paddy got a great love of hurling from their mother, the former Esther McGee, of Gowran, Co. Kilkenny. A first cousin of Paddy's is Frankie Gilligan, who possessed every skill in the game. Unfortunately, he left the game at a young age and was a considerable loss to hurling in the town.

Brendan Gilligan.

The Glynns of the Causeway have strong links with the ancient game. Micheál captained Éire Óg to senior championship success in 1990, a most appropriate year for Ennis to win senior honours. Tom and Noel also

Mrs. Esther Gilligan (nee McGee) of Gowran and Ennis, pictured with the Black and Amber and Saffron and Blue in the lead up to Kilkenny/Clare All-Ireland Final of 2002. Remarkably, Esther was present at the All-Ireland Finals of 1932 and 2002. Courtesy of Mike Mulcaire.

represented Éire Óg at all levels while Catherine, Margaret, Gráinne and Eilish were all associated with camogie.

Their namesakes in Clonroad, too, were involved in hurling. Paul was very prominent with Éire Óg in the late 1960s. He would have represented Clare in some grades, at least, in the inter-county arena. John was a good solid cornerback. Michael ('Hooper') was possibly on the Éire Óg winning Minor (A) football team in 1979. 'Hooper' was also a useful hurler. Their sister, Edel, was also involved with the Éire Óg club. Their late father, Christy, is featured elsewhere in this publication.

Ben, Tim, John and Richard McAllister all hurled. Tim and John played senior for the club during 1972 – 1975 or so. Richard was part of a very good CBS Harty Cup team in the 1973/1974 school year – a team that included Declan Coote, Dinny Mulcaire, and Michael (Milo) Keane. The Lynes from Abbey Street played both codes. Seanie, Roibéard (Bob), Taidgie and Donie are better known in football circles, but all wielded the camán as well. Seanie Lyne captained the Faughs to senior football success in 1994. Cathal Shannon too is a fine dual player. Cathal represented the town in both sports. His

John McAllister.

father, Tony ('Beef') played football for the Faughs in the 1960s. Tony's brothers, Paddy (R.I.P.), Frankie, Dermot, Joe, etc. come from a sporting family. They are involved in athletics, swimming, GAA, soccer, and they continue to follow all Ennis teams. Paddy's sons, Adrian and Colin were talented hurlers with the Banner club.

The Brennans and Stacks are just some of the many other families to play for the town. Pat Brennan played hurling for Éire Óg throughout the 1960s. His brother, Michael, who later served as chairman was also a noted hurler. Garry Stack, a contemporary of Pat Brennan's also played senior for Éire Óg in the mid-1960s. His younger brother, Bobby, starred at minor and U-21 level. The Ryans of Summerhill are also steeped in it. Don (Snr), a brother of Eugene was very involved in the re-formation of the Dalcassian Club in the 1970s. His sons, Padraig, Don and Kieran all played colleges for the CBS. Kieran, a good solid defender, played for the Clare Minors in 1972. His uncle, Eugene, played for Éire Óg in the formative years of the club. Seán and Pat Daly also turned out for the town at various grades. Both represented St. Flannan's also.

Tony McEnery, one of the stars of the 1990 Munster Club Championship.

The O'Connors of Clonroad also come to mind. Denis, an excellent Harty Cup hurler in 1973/1974, later played senior hurling for Éire Óg. His younger brother, John, excelled at Gaelic football.

Davy and Eric Connellan of Steele's Terrace were good at under-age. Work commitments took them both from home. A younger brother, Trevor, played soccer with Avenue United. Their cousin, Michael Connellan, is a son of Reggie, who played for the Dals and the Faughs with distinction. Their neighbour, Seán Millar, played juvenile for Éire Óg. Seán's late father, Terry, played for St. Joseph's. Terry's uncle was Martin 'Handsome' Moloney, one of the heroes of 1914, which is as good a place as any to end this short essay on some Ennis hurling families.

The Non Native

Ennis hurling has featured many 'non native' players over the years. Usually they moved to the town for work reasons, but they have always received a warm welcome, with many going on to wear the saffron and blue.

In the following article I've listed about 50 hurlers but I'm sure there must be others.

Sean Harrington came to the Dalcassian club from Templederry, Co. Tipperary. Sean won a senior championship with the DALS in 1934 before joining the powerful Feakle team of that era, which went on to dominate Clare club hurling. Sean was one of three Clare hurlers selected on the Railway Cup team of 1935 – the other two were Larry Blake and Mick Hennessy (Clooney). Sean Harrington also played at wing back on the Clare team that beat Cork by 19 points in the 1936 championship replay.

Peadar Dervan from Galway was a contemporary of Harrington. He was a member of the 1934 DALS team, though I believe he didn't play in the final. Dervan was selected at corner-back on the Clare team, which contested the controversial Munster championship semi-final in 1938, which led to what became known as the 'Cooney Case'. Sean Harrington played outside Dervan at wing back in 1938. Both players assisted the Boreen in the popular town leagues of that era.

Gerry Cronin played for the DALS and Clare in the late 1920's. His sons Jimmy and Gerry continued the tradition with Éire Og.

Tom Neylon of Kilmaley joined the DALS about 1940. He was part of the successful team of 1941. Earlier Tom Neylon played senior championship with the Éire Og amalgamation. Tom made a comeback to Kilmaley in 1962, when he coached their junior team to championship success.

Jim Quinlivan of Tulla played on the successful 1941 team at full-back. Jim had earlier represented St. Flannan's during a great spell from 1931-1934. Another product of Flannan's, Peadar Flanagan of Tipperary won a senior medal in 1934. Flanagan was highly rated by his team-mates. During the 1940's a lot of outsiders working in Ennis played in the town leagues. Those who threw in their lot with the DALS for a time included Dermot Solon of Whitegate, Paddy Markham (Ballyea) and P. J. O'Dea (Kilrush).

The 1950's conjure up an era when Éire Og always seemed to have an official waiting at the Railway Station, to view incoming talent, complete with hurley and gear in hand. This image is probably very unfair and exaggerated. Tony Keaty, Aidan Raleigh, Tom Murray, Jimmy Walker, Tom Mannion all played for the town at this time. Tom Mannion from Mulcaire Rovers hurled senior for the Faughs in 1950, as did Mick Murphy of Kilmaley. Murphy hurled for what Thomas Davis called *"the matchless men of Tipperary"*. Murphy, then playing his club hurling with Thurles Sarsfields, was called on at number five for Tipperary in 1945. He later returned to the saffron and blue and hurled senior for Ennis Faughs. Speaking of Tipperary hurling, Paddy 'Sweeper' Ryan was part of a fast moving forward line in the same All-Ireland final. Interestingly, his daughter Sadie is married to John Quinn of Paddy Quinn's pub in Ennis. Tom Murray of Loughrea was a strong, determined forward with Éire Og. Jack Heaslip from Kilkenny joined Éire Og in 1953 and, during the formative years of the club, Jack often supplied transport. A product of Kilkenny CBS, Jack played in the Leinster Colleges Final of 1945 losing to Marino CBS. Before coming to Ennis, Jack played senior championship for his club, Carrickshock.

Kilkennyman Pat Tynan played on the winning Cup team of 1959. He was also part of the side which lost to Ruan in the county final. Michael Grogan, also of Kilkenny, played juvenile with St. John's about 1963. Tony Keaty (Tipp.) is considered by many to be the best full-forward ever to hurl for Éire Og. A team mate Bernie Dilger called him a *'real Ennisman, he was fearless.'* Great praise from the late champ. Bernie also had great respect for Mick Morrissey (Adare) and Dermot Leahy – *'they had great strength and presence'. 'Aidan Raleigh (Bruff) was a stylist, a ball player.'* A member of the Limerick panel of 1955, Aidan played senior championship for the Banner County the following year. His stay was short. Speaking of 1955 Dermot Kelly also had a spell with Éire Og around 1960, turning in many good displays. Munster Railway Cup player Liam Moloney of Limerick was another to represent the club. Moloney was highly rated. The outstanding Galway hurler Jimmy Conroy joined Éire Óg about 1960. He was transferred to Whitegate in 1961 and played a huge role in their championship win over the Blues'. Conroy later won a Clare Cup medal with Feakle in1964. His position in the Gardaí later brought him to Toomevara. Pat Kirby could play anywhere, outstanding in goal and centre-field. He made a massive contribution to Éire Óg in 1956 and 1957. He represented Clare at senior level in the

Wembley Cup Tournament of 1958. Ironically he helped Brian Borus defeat his old club in 1975. His namesake, Pat Kirby, also from East Clare was part of the Éire Óg set-up at this time.

Though Ennis boasted a sight of good hurlers in the mid 1960's, Tony Kinnevane of Cratloe was still good enough to get his place in the 1966 team. The late Tony Kinnevane was a forceful full forward and prolific goal getter.

Peter Guinnane, a brother of Christy (Wax) and the late Michael 'Tolly', joined Éire Og after returning from England to live in the Turnpike. Peter was a popular club man during the late sixties and early 1970's.

Éire Óg goalkeeper of renown and world class handballer - Pat Kirby.

Founded in 1977, the Banner Hurling Club went senior for a time. It was an ambitious step. In 1981 they gave a good game to Newmarket in the quarter final of the championship. P.J. King (Dysart) played in goal while Sean Dixon of Inagh was outstanding at centre-field before retiring with an injury. Haulie Russell, captain of Clarecastle in 1978, was prominent on this Banner team as was Seamus O'Connell. A native of Cork, O'Connell won Harty Cup with the North Mon. in 1970.

Gerry Gleeson of Limerick was introduced at centre-field, the 'Blues' won 2-11 to 1-8 and went on to win the championship. Others to play for the Banner at that time include Robert O'Mahony (Cork) and Martin Gardiner from Ballinakill/Woodford. This parish in Galway now play under the name of Tommy Larkins.

Tom Ryan of Tipperary was a huge addition to Éire Óg and a big loss to Tipperary, as Michael Keating told Donal Keenan in the Book 'Babs – (the Michael Keating story)'. *"Tom Ryan was the one that got away. He had everything it took to make a major contribution to the Tipperary team. In the set up at the time he needed to be looked after and, as that didn't happen, he went off to play with Clare. He was an outstanding hurler and we badly missed his skill when we needed it, especially in the All-Ireland final of 1967. My reaction was two-fold. I was sorry Tom hadn't stuck it out with Tipperary but I was happy he was getting his chance to play on a stage he deserved, in a Munster Final with Clare."*

Tom Ryan in the Tipperary colours in 1961. The Pa Howard collection tells us Tom represented Éire Óg and Clare from May 1967 to March 1970.

The Christian Brothers order gave great commitment to hurling as mentors. Two members of their order, Dan Fitzgerald and Pat Hyland, represented the Éire Og Club during the early to mid 1970's.

One of the greatest Clare hurlers of all time, Jimmy Cullinan joined Éire Og from Newmarket. Cullinan played with Éire Óg during a lean spell. He could have remained with the Blues and added to his medal collection. Master of every skill in the game, Cullinan joined the County set-up in 1961. He played at least four years for the Munster Railway Cup team. He retired from inter-county fare in March 1977. At a gala occasion at the West County Inn, Fr. Harry Bohan and the Clare panel turned out to pay tribute to him on the

Jimmy Cullinan, one of Clare's all time greats wins possession against Wexford, Croke Park Grounds Tournament Final 1968. Jimmy represented Éire Óg 1972-'74.

occasion of his retirement from inter-county competition. Fr. Bohan said: *"Jimmy was always an inspiration to his colleagues and he was most reliable whether it was for training or challenge games. His contribution will not be forgotten."*

Wexford man Enda Murphy joined Éire Og in 1975. He was well known in colleges hurling, playing on the St. Peter's team of 1966, which included Dave Bernie and John Quigley. He represented Éire Og at full-back in the 1975 county final. Enda, who was then manager of the Agricultural Credit Corporation in Ennis, won minor and u/21 medals with Wexford. He played for Clare in the early rounds of the 1975/76 league.

Kevin Kennedy of Brian Borus joined Éire Og in 1982. A member of the Garda Siochana, Kevin's career took him to a lot of clubs. His sons, Kenneth and Damien are fine hurlers with St. Joseph's. The outstanding Clare goalkeeper Seamus Durack gave many years to Éire Og during a great spell. Durack was automatic choice as goalkeeper on the Munster team. He earlier represented his native Feakle

Mick Meagher of Kilkenny joined Clare in 1984 and played at centre-back on the team that reached the League Final of 1985. Mick was a loyal clubman, winning a county championship in 1990. Mick won an All-Ireland Colleges medal with St. Kieran's. Two years later he won minor championship with the 'Cats'.

Michael O'Sullivan played at centrefield for Éire Og in the 1985 County Final when he partnered

Seamus Durack - outstanding goalkeeper of the 1970s and 1980s. Durack proudly maintained a great Clare goalkeeping tradition.

Declan Coote. Mickie earlier won senior football and Cusack Cup medals with Shannon Gaels. He also represented Ballyea in hurling.

James Seymour played for Éire Og in the late 1980's, mostly at corner-forward. He had earlier represented the Tipperary minors in goal and this was the position he filled for Clare in the 1989 senior championship. Noel Considine, the highly rated Clarecastle goalkeeper of the late 1980s later represented Éire Og in goal. Noel played for the town team in 1996 and 1998. Considine will always be remembered for his great save from Alan Neville in the 1998 championship. There is a school of thought that he went from club to club, but this is not the case. In 1997, he was working in Limerick and Tom Ryan approached him to play with Ballybrown. A fantastic shot-stopper, Noel was in inspiring form in the 1993 All-Ireland Junior Final, so much so that a Kilkenny mentor was heard to say *"If Clare have a better goalkeeper, he must be a great one."* Noel is a son of the late Joe Considine, who kept goal for the County minors from 1958/1960. Joe and Noel Considine are probably the only father and son combination to play in goal for the Banner County.

From Tipperary, Cathal Egan was with the club for a number of years. Egan is a prominent marksman. He is now with Clooney.

Lastly and certainly not least is Colin Lynch of Lissycasey. A product of the CBS, Lynch gave the best part of 10 years to Éire Og, before joining Kilmaley who have an arrangement with Lissycasey concerning dual players. Lynch has had wonderful games for the county.

Without doubt the involvement of these men has enriched Ennis hurling over the years, whatever the duration of their stay.

Ennis All-Star teams

The following team selected from the teams of 1924-1942 was selected by Dál gCais. This team was first published in the Bulletin Magazine circa 1982.

Tom Blake

Freddie Garrihy | John Coote | John O'Leary

Sean Harrington | Tull Considine | Larry Blake

Jack Quirke | Peadar Dervan

Mickey White | Gerry Cronin | James Spellissy

Michael Malone | Eddie Fahy | Jackie Duffy

Subs: Jacksie Darcy, Billy Fahy, Joe Madigan, Tony 'Topper' Morrissey, Vinnie Considine, Paddy Kenny.

Dál gCais feels it would take some line up to compare with his team. The free-scoring Tull Considine is selected in his later defensive role, making space for the vigorous full-forward, Eddie Fahy, whom he selects on the edge of the square.

1952-1967

In 1967 John McCarthy and Michael Brennan published the book **Éire Óg 1952 - 1967.** Apart from being then a comprehensive history of Éire Óg, the book also included passages on The Dalcassians, Rovers and St. John's. To coincide with this publication the following team was selected by past and then present selectors to represent the best Éire Óg XV to play for the Club during the years 1952-1967.:-

Paschal O'Brien

Vincent Loftus | Paddy Loftus | Bobby Burke

Bernie Dilger | Michael Blake | John Nevin

Pat Kirby | John Dunne

Noel Pyne | Gerry Cronin (Jnr.) | Michael Dilger

Sean Madigan | Tony Keaty | Johnny McCarthy

Subs: Dermot Leahy, Jimmy Cronin, Colm Madigan.

1968-1979 by 'Onlooker'

Paschal O'Brien
Martin Leahy Vincent Loftus Ollie O'Regan
Jimmy Cullinan Joe Barry Sean O'Driscoll
Pat Brennan Tony Kelly
Noel Ryan Brendan Gilligan Massey Dilger
Sean Lynch Martin Linnane Paddy Kelly
Subs: Tom Glynn, Peter Guinnane, Declan Coote, Michael Barry, Paul Glynn, Michael Carmody.

This was kind of a hangover period from the late 1960s. Vincent Loftus, who played for the county up to 1974, has to be selected at full-back. Paddy Kelly, himself a fine full-back, is selected at corner-forward, a position he held down as a youth. Joe Barry, gets the centre-back position. The presence of goal-scorer, Martin Linnane at full-forward adds greatly to this team. Surrounded by Lynch, Gilligan, Dilger, Ryan and Kelly, bringing a mixture of strength, courage and skill to the attack. A formidable team!

1980-2002 selected by 'An t-Iománaí ar an gClaí

Seamus Durack
Barry Smythe Michael Meagher John Russell
Tomás Corbett Tony Nugent Colm Mahon
Declan Coote Colin Lynch
Pat Lynch Seán Heaslip Pete Barry
Stephen McNamara Noel Ryan Martin Nugent
Subs: Eoin McMahon, Micheál Glynn, Shaun McCarthy, Seanie Lynch, Gearóid Mannion.

Our correspondent would have liked to have selected Joe Barry and Tony Kelly but he felt they belonged to an earlier era. Seán Lynch is another he rated highly for his strength and ball-carrying ability. 'An t-Iománaí ar an gClaí' selects Seán in the subs.

Larry Blake

Dals, Clare, Munster

"Blake was a brilliant stylist; he often dominated and always held his own. He was one of the hardest and fastest pullers I met in a long career."
Tommy Doyle (Tipperary hurler – 1937 – 1950)

The above quote is one of numerous tributes paid to Larry Blake over a long and illustrious career. Larry Blake made his debut with the Dals in 1926 and continued to assist the senior club for the following 15 years.

Larry Blake.

After his retirement he served as a selector for the county team, but later declined the position when his sons came of age. Larry Blake hurled the best of them including Phil Cahill, John and Mick Mackey and Mick King. Blake's wonderful touch and sense of position are said to be the reasons why Clare defeated the great Cork team in the Munster Final of 1932. Jim Dermody played in goal for Kilkenny. He held the Clare team in high regard. Dermody recalled 1932, *"at midfield, Mick Falvey and Jack Gleeson played particularly well, while in the defence, Larry Blake and John Joe Doyle were tremendous. Larry played like two men that day. He was one of the youngest of the side. Actually, it was an old Clare team. That probably explains why they didn't come again."*

Many appraisals were paid to Larry Blake but none more generous than the comments of Tommy Doyle. Doyle is regarded as one of the greatest men to pull on the blue and gold jersey of Tipperary. In 1955 he told his story to Raymond Smith and in the process recalled the great men of his era.

The Thurles Sarsfields stalwart recalled the controversial Munster Championship of 1938, the so-called Cooney case. He spoke of Larry Blake's sportsmanship, before, during and after the game.

"Our team was brilliant that day in many positions, weak in none and dependable in all. I was pitted against the renowned Larry Blake and must say in all fairness that I came out second best in my duel with the Ennisman. Only once did I slip him to notch a point. A brilliant stylist, he

often dominated and always held his own. He was one of the hardest and fastest pullers I met in a long career. Equally good left or right. A terrier to the tackle, quick and tenacious to every ball. Though past his best in 1938, Larry Blake was still considered good enough to keep men like Johnny Ryan and John Maher off the Munster Railway Cup team. Blake was a great player."

Larry Blake – selected honours

4 Railway Cup Medals	1934, 1935, 1937, 1938
4 County Senior Championships	1928, 1929, 1934, 1941
3 Clare Cups	1928, 1929, 1937
1 County Senior Football	1929
1 Cusack Cup Senior Football	1929

Larry Blake made his senior club debut with the Dals in 1926. The team that defeated Clarecastle in the quarter final consisted of: Tull Considine (captain), Tom Blake, Larry Blake, Willie Considine, Joker Coote, Gerry Cronin, Joe Doherty, Paddy 'Boo' Doherty, Jackie Duffy, Michael Ensko, Joe Madigan, P. O'Donnell, John Sullivan, Mickie White, P. Walsh.

Larry Blake was first selected on the Munster team in 1932. He was never off the team from 1932 – 1938, playing seven consecutive seasons.

Larry Blake played at centre-back for Clare in the 1936 Senior Championship. Clare disposed of Waterford in Round I but were held to a draw by Cork (3-7 to Clare's 4-4). The Corkmen suffered a rare defeat in a replay when Clare had 19 points to spare. Paddy Loughnane's early goals kept Clare in front at the interval. However it was Mick Hennessy's three goal spree midway through the second half that swamped Cork who battled to the end, Clare 9-1 Cork 2-3. It was the Bannermen's biggest ever championship victory over Cork.

Clare - Paddy Callaghan, Michael Griffin, Flan Purcell, Paddy McGrath, Mick O'Halloran, Larry Blake, Seán Harrington, Mick Hennessy (3-0), John Jones, Jim Houlihan, Jim Mullane, Jack Quirke (1-1), Paddy Loughnane (4-0), Michael Power (1-0), P.J. Quaine.

'A Lifetime in Hurling' – the Tommy Doyle Story was written by Raymond Smith and published by Hutchinsons, in 1955. In the foreword, Phil Purcell wrote, *"Few players have worn the Tipperary colours with greater distinction. He is a model for all young players to reach the top."*

Michael Blake

Éire Óg and Clare

"I remember Michael specifically for his eclipsing of Christy Ring in a Munster championship game at Thurles".
Jimmy Smyth

When one looks back over Éire Óg's 50 eventful years, the figure of Michael Blake who died tragically at the young age of 28 seems to tower above most others.

Michael Blake.

He is regarded by purists of the game as one of the finest half backs that ever played for Éire Óg. Fellow players looked up to him. He held a special place in the affection of the people of Ennis. On a personal note, I remember my father Martin Byrnes, pointing him out to me one day at Cusack Park with the words *"that's Michael Blake, the great Clare hurler."* A club and county contemporary described Michael thus *"A natural leader, friendly and at ease in every company. His relaxed, quiet almost shy manner made it easy to like him. Of his hurling ability we need only say that, endowed with fine physique, he seldom used it and never against a weaker opponent, preferring to hurl with his wrists, his speed and intelligence. Who can forget his great duels with Matt Nugent in the middle 1950's which were the highlights of some of the greatest run of success in Éire Óg history."*

Michael Blake learned his hurling at the CBS. He was with Éire Óg from the beginning. In 1956 he made his senior inter-county debut with Clare and was a constant member of the team for a number of seasons.

In the 1958 championship he formed part of the half back line with Bernie Dilger and Michael Lynch. At the interval Clare led Cork by 3-7 to 1-3. The Clare Champion reported *"Bernie Dilger did valiant work on a masterful half back line from which nothing serious fell to the full back line from Michael Blake's berth."*

Michael Blake was also a star footballer with Faughs. After the halcyon days of 1946-1954, the Faughs form began to dip, though they captured the Cusack Cup in 1955, featuring evergreens like Murt O'Shea and Peadar O'Brien. The year 1960 was possibly the end of the line at senior level for the Faughs for many years. That year they defeated Clarecastle in the Cusack Cup but lost in the same competition to Kilmihil. I vaguely remember the pitch being invaded at Cusack Park after the referee awarded a late penalty to Faughs. The Clare Champion reported *"Faughs seemed to have the edge over their opponents and they were doing everything except scoring. Just before the interval, Aidan Lynch fisted the ball onto Colm Keating's path with Keating knocking the ball first time to the net."*

Michael emigrated to England about 1961. Four years later, in late January 1965 he was killed in a traffic accident, ending at 28 the short life of one of the most popular and respected Ennis hurlers of them all. He commanded huge respect from team mates and opponents and this was reflected in the massive funeral that took place in Ennis.

It is widely believed that Michael Blake intended to return home to assist Éire Óg in 1965. Had he done so, it is reasonable to assume that Éire Óg could have gone on to dominate the local championships for a number of years.

At a meeting of the Rovers hurling club at this time, it was decided to present a cup to the County Board for the Clare Under 21 championship and after much discussion as to what the cup should be called, it was decided to name it after a family who had given great service to the game in Clare – the Blakes, the tragic death of Michael being very much uppermost on the minds of all hurling followers in Clare at that time. Michael's father, Larry, was an outstanding Dals, Clare and Munster hurler of the years 1926-1941, as was Larry Jnr. with Éire Óg in the 1953-1959 era.

The Blake Memorial Cup is still the Under 21 Championship trophy and one of the finest and most coveted sought. The Blake Cup cost £64, a huge sum of money in 1965 and was bought through Nicholas Fine, jeweller, Limerick. The following inscription reads on the magnificent trophy *"Corn Cuimhneachain De Blaca – A bhronnadh ag Cumann Iomana Fanaithe na hInse."*

The Faughs team that played Clarecastle in the Cusack Cup in 1960 was:

Flan Griffin, Jim Curran, Michael Blake, Murt O'Shea, Hugh O'Donnell, Frank Corey, Brian Malone, Anthony Lynch, Kieran Crowe, B. Killoran, Tom Lillis, Colm Keating, Michael Dilger, Paddy Kerin, Aidan Lynch

*Eddie George also played in goal in this season.

Pat Brennan

Ennis CBS, Rovers, Éire Óg and Clare

"Pat Brennan was very sticky. He was my bogeyman, I couldn't hurl him."
Liam Danagher (Newmarket)

A member of the CBS Dr. Rodgers Munster Colleges winning team of 1961, Pat made his senior club debut at 16 with Éire Óg. A product of Rovers, Pat attributes much of his hurling development to two men, John 'Dugger' Kearney and Bro. Jim Hennessy. Of Bro. Hennessy, Pat remarked. *"Nobody ever had the same influence on me as Bro. Hennessy. He taught at the primary school, but when he came to the secondary to pick the teams he was totally detached. He looked at everyone. He brought the best talent from the school. He was the single greatest influence on hurling in Ennis in the early 1960's."*

Pat Brennan (centre) receives McNamee Award for his work on the Bulletin. Also present are Paddy McFlynn (President G.A.A.), Liam Mulvihill (General Secretary of G.A.A.).

Like 'Dugger' Kearney, Hennessy was involved with the all conquering Rovers minor teams, the bulk of which swelled the Éire Óg senior ranks from 1964 to 1966. A great Éire Óg team, but they never reached their peak. Pat agrees with this, *"After the incidents with Tubber and Crusheen in 1966, things weren't the same in Éire Óg. Apathy crept in. The same determination wasn't there. Players were coming and going, Johnny McCarthy, Brendan Considine and Gary Stack retired. Dick Pyne went to Antrim and Vincent Loftus was playing in Dublin with Faughs. The pride went out of it for a couple of years."*

Pat Brennan played off and on the Clare team during the years 1964 to 1971. He made his inter-county debut in November 1964, as part of an experimental Clare team that played hosts to Kilkenny at Cusack Park. The Leinster champions were powered by all the big names - Seamus Cleere, Ted Carroll and Paddy Moran. At half time both teams gathered in groups on the pitch, rather than going to the dressing rooms. Youngsters hovered around getting their autographs. It was all very relaxed. Some of us enjoyed a puck around, revelling in belting the sliotar into the net.

Kilkenny resumed the second half where they had left off, giving an exhibition of class hurling. The blond Tommy Walsh was a joy to watch, but Eddie Keher was held to one point by Pat Brennan.

Liam Danagher (former Newmarket, Clare and Munster hurler) has high praise for Brennan. Danagher's comments are always positive. Liam recalled great memories of Newmarket/Éire Óg games. He spoke of the greatness of Rovers and St. John's at under-age level. - *"There was a great bond between Newmarket and Éire Óg. Two hurling teams - pure hurling. Pat Brennan was very sticky. He was my bogeyman, I couldn't hurl him."*

The Éire Óg/Newmarket Clare Cup final of 1969 bears this out. Munster club champions, the Blues, were going for three consecutive championship/cup doubles. They met a fired up Éire Óg. *"It was a cracking cup final, played in bitterly cold conditions. The move of Pat Brennan off Liam Danagher was a big mistake. Brennan was proving more than a match for Danagher - 'The Ebony Idol'. The Blues deservedly triumphed, though on a flattering scoreline of 5-8 to 3-4"* wrote the Clare Champion.

Pat recalls that the Inter-parish league, played on the off season, was a big help in getting players fit. He recalled that *"John Dunne brought professionalism back into it. Jack Heaslip, too, was a great servant to the club. Around this time Martin Linnane returned from England. He was a whole-hearted player and a great club man, totally dedicated. Linnane was only back a few weeks when he scored four goals for the Clare Intermediate team in the championship against Limerick. Also Peter Guinnane came back from England and set up home in the Turnpike. Peter played for us. Martin and Peter gave great stability to the club."*

On the negative side Pat feels many young players were lost at this time. He feels players like Jimmy Spellissy, Davy Connellan and Seanie Lynch should have been starring. Lynch did, of course, return a few years later and made a big contribution.

Pat is still involved in the game, coaching at juvenile level. He has strong views on training and feels that the minors, under 21's and seniors should all train together. *"In my time they did train together. It meant that the senior selectors were viewing every bit of talent. If you were able to hurl a senior player they realised you were good enough for the senior panel. Now they all train separately. The younger lads aren't getting the hardening we got. I believe in good solid training. It has to be done on a professional basis. I've never agreed with haphazard training, hoping things will go right on the day."*

Path to the 1966 Championship

Éire Óg 2-11 ... ... Tubber 1-3
Éire Óg 5-9 ... ... Dalcassians 1-6
Éire Óg 2-10 ... ... St. Joseph's 2-7
Éire Óg 2-8 ... ... Newmarket 1-10 (Quarter Final)
Éire Óg 1-7 ... ... Clarecastle 3-1 Semi-Final (draw)
Éire Óg 2-7 ... ... Clarecastle 3-4 (draw)
Éire Óg 3-12 ... ... Clarecastle 3-7
Éire Óg 2-8 ... ... Whitegate 1-4 (Final)

Tull Considine

Dalcassians, Clare, Munster, Ireland.

"Tull Considine rarely shot at the goalkeeper. He picked a spot about five yards from goal and ricochetted the ball off it. Tull was a master at this tactic."
Jim Dermody, (Kilkenny goalkeeper, 1931/1932)

To quote newspaper reports of his time, Tull Considine 'is a brilliant sticksman, possessor of a deadly body swerve, when on the move he is fast and clever, a genius at converting the half chance into a score. Right or left, in the air or on the ground it doesn't matter to Tull as he can split a defence wide open with a darting weaving run.'

Tull Considine.

Turlough Owen Considine was one of a family of eleven, seven boys and four girls born to Patrick and Mary Considine, nee Lett, from the Turnpike. All the boys played hurling, but Willie 'Dodger', Brendan and Turlough excelled. Between them they played senior inter-county hurling for something like 45 years. Incredible but true. Tull learned his hurling in the CBS school leagues and playing in the streets, perfecting the delicate skills. Bro. Cronin was an early influence on him.

In 1917, Tull was selected on the Clare senior football team, the only team so far to contest the senior final.

I take the liberty of quoting Raymond Smith in the Football Immortals in 1967."Wexford had two titles in the bag and in their bid for the three timer in 1917 when opposed by Clare. Clare did two weeks collective training in Kilkee under Sham Spellissy but lacked experience of playing the parallelogram on the big occasion. They had a goal and a point disallowed for 'square infringements' - and they were only beaten in the end by four points.

Eamon DeValera had been elected Sinn Fein M.P. for Clare. There was a surge of nationalistic feeling and Aiden Doyle of Wexford recalled that 'neutrals were behind Clare to a man. Harry Boland carried the Sinn Fein flag at the head of the parade - and to the crowd the Claremen were patriots all and they wanted it very much to be the Banner county's day'. It wasn't to be and Wexford held out to win by 0-9 to 0-5."

Throughout the 1920's Tull was a dual star for the Banner county. In 1927 he partnered Mickie White at centre-field when Clare went under to Cork by 5-3 to 3-4 in the Munster final. Clare again tasted defeat at the hands of the rebel county in the 1928 provincial final. Other Ennismen to play in these finals include Joe Madigan (1927), Brendan Considine, Eddie Fahy and Jackie Duffy, in 1928.

United States and Tailteann Cup

In 1928 the U.S.A. hurling team toured Ireland. They lost 5-9 to 4-3 to an Ireland selection (including the Claremen Tull Considine and Tommy Daly (Dublin). The exiles team then visited the Ennis showgrounds and were greeted on arrival at the station by the Ennis brass band. Amongst the welcoming committee to greet James O'Duffy and the exiles team were Tull Considine and Fr. Michael Hamilton, chairman of the County Board. Before 9,000 paying patrons the U.S.A. triumphed over Clare by 4-7 to 2-6.

Regarding the lead-up to the 1932 championship, Michael J. Crimmins left us the following account in the Limerick Leader. *"Fanned by a stiff breeze, the tricolour and the stars and stripes waved side by side over a great throng of Gaels from all parts of the Banner County in the Showgrounds, to witness a friendly match between the American hurlers and those of the Clare senior hurling team. It was a splendid game and a significant reminder that Ireland has sown in every land, true to their racial games and to the land of their sires."*

"Throughout the globe, on every soil,
Where human foot has trod,
You'll find the hardy sons of toil,
From this old verdant sod,
And when the country calls for men,
Again, her cause to save,
They'll come with zeal and hearts of steel -
the Gaels beyond the wave."

Considine Genius – All-Ireland Semi-Final 1932

The 1932 semi-final between Clare, the favourites and Galway is considered one of the most amazing games in the history of Championship hurling. At half time a rampant Galway team led by 4-7 to 2-0. The Clare players remained on the pitch during the interval. A leader was needed. Jim Houlihan took charge. He gave his fellow players a pep talk. He consulted team captain John Joe Doyle and selector Fr. Eddie Murphy. Jim Houlihan suggested that Doyle go to centre-back in a direct switch with Jimmy Hogan and made several other significant switches, including the switch of himself to centre-field from wing-back. Galway opened the second half with a brace of points. Then Mick Gill drove through the Clare defence to make it 4-10 to 2-0 for Galway. The big Clare crowd began to head for the exits. Suddenly Clare flashed in two quick goals. Many of the spectators, who had been on the way home ran back excitedly, to see Jim Houlihan drive the ball over for Clare's first point. The score was now 4-10 to 4-1. The ball wasn't returned and Fr. Michael Hamilton threw in a spanking new white ball. However, Mick King and Mick Gill added a further three points to put Galway back into a commanding lead of 4-13 to 4-1. So after nineteen minutes of the second half, nothing had really changed. *"Streams of spectators hurried to the exits. A Tull Considine goal didn't stop the flow".* A minute later, Considine found the net again, making it 4-14 to 6-2, with nine minutes to go. *"Time ticked on and somehow Considine was in possession again. Once more, he turned, weaved in a deadly body swerve, splitting the defence wide open with a darting weaving run, shaking the net again."* Tom O'Rourke and Mick King exchanged points. Then the amazing genius that is Tull Considine goaled again and then the unbelievable – Considine rattled the net for the fifth time in less than 10 minutes. Larry Blake was fouled recalled Jim Houlihan - *"as I was standing over the ball near the sideline, someone shouted frantically – go for a point, while others shouted excitedly - no, you must go for a goal. Tull ran out and indicated to me to lob it in the square. I lifted and every Clare forward threw what remained of their ebbing strength in search for the winning scores."* In the dying minutes, Tull Considine added another goal and Jim Houlihan notched a point to clinch this sensational game by 9-4 to 4-14. In an eleven minute spell, Clare scored 5-3 to a solitary point from Galway.

Between the Cork and Galway games of the 1932 championship, Tull Considine scored eleven goals and it was this prolific goal scoring ability that set him apart from other forwards of his day. Jim Dermody, the Kilkenny goalkeeper studied Considine's style of play. He had a birds-eye view of Tull in the 1932 All-Ireland Final. Dermody recalled his unique style of forward play some thirty years later and spoke of the tension as Kilkenny clung on to a two point lead in the closing minutes of the 1932 final. *"Mick Falvey sent in a high ball. It dropped about 30 yards out, slightly to the left of the goal. In a flash, Tull was on it. He kicked the ball forward, thereby getting room to pick it. Then he had it in his hand and we were in real trouble. I knew that he would strike low and hard, making the ball hop about five or six yards in front of the goal. This was his gambit. I rarely saw him to hit the ball directly at a goalkeeper. He picked a spot and ricochetted the ball off it. You could well imagine how difficult it was for a goalman to cover such a ball. It could come at you any way and usually the way you wouldn't expect. Tull was a master at it. Tull was steadying himself to strike and Podge Byrne was closing in. Tull swung, Byrne hooked from behind and Paddy Phelan and Paddy Larkin came between the great Clare man and the goal. The door was shut. What I'm trying to say is that Tull Considine did not lose the All-Ireland for Clare. He got the type of chance that presents itself thirty times in an average match."* But perhaps, too much was expected by the public from the great man. About two months later, the Kilkenny team visited Ennis. They attended a dinner given in their honour by the Clare County Board. The Kilkenny and Clare players mingled and enjoyed themselves in a sporting and magnanimous fashion.

Tull Considine went on to assist Clare until their league campaign of 1934/1935, before concentrating his efforts in coaching the DALS and St. Flannan's to success. Its interesting to note that Tull Considine was involved in seven of the DALS eight championship hurling successes.

In 2000, Considine was selected posthumously by genuine Clare hurling followers, at full-forward on the greatest Clare fifteen of all time.

Honours Won

6 Senior hurling (Ennis DALS) 1914, 1915, 1924, 1928, 1929, 1934
1 Senior Football (Ennis DALS) 1929
2 Clare Cup, 1928, 1929
1 Cusack Cup, 1929
1 Tailteann (Ireland) 1928
4 Railway Cups (Munster) 1928, 1929, 1930, 1931
1 Munster Senior hurling, 1932
1 Munster Senior football 1917

Regarding the All-Ireland semi-final of 1932, played on the 14th August, the scorers for Clare were:

Tull Considine	7 goals
Jim Mullane	1 goal
Mick O'Rourke	1 goal
Jim Houlihan	2 points
Tom O'Rourke	1 point
Michael Connery (Conroy)	1 point

* Other sources credit Jim Houlihan with 1-2, Tom Burnell 1-0 and Tull with 5 goals.

The Clare Team that contested the 1917 football final possibly lined out as follows:

Mick Conole (Kilfenora), Paddy Hennessy (Miltown), Big Jim Foran (Kilkee Blues), Michael McNamara (Ballykett), Michael McMahon (Kilrush Shamrocks), Paddy (Pana) O'Brien (Cooraclare), Jim Fitzgerald (Miltown), Tull Considine (Ennis Dals), Jim Marrinan (Kilkee Blues), Sham Spellissy (Ennis Dals), Martin McNamara (Ballykett), Ned Carroll (Miltown), Michael Malone (Miltown), Ned Roche (Miltown), Paddy O'Donoghue (Ballyvaughan).

Subs: Paddy Haugh (Bealaha); Noel McNamara (Kilrush); Jack Carmody (Kilrush); Paddy J. Killeen (Miltown); Michael O'Loughlin (Ballyvaughan)

Acknowledgements

This Match I will Always Remember – John Joe Doyle (Irish Independent, January 4th, 1956 as told to John D. Hickey)

Jim Houlihan interviewed by John D. Hickey

Memorable Year for the Banner County – Gaelic Sport, August 1963

How We Beat Clare in the 1932 Final by Jim Dermody as told to Tomás O'Faolain, Gaelic Sport, February 1964.

The Football Immortals by Raymond Smith, 1967.

Down Memory Lane by Padraig Puirseál

Niall Cahill – Gaelic Weekly

Irish Press, 1932

Irish Independent, 1932

Bernie Dilger

Éire Óg and Clare

"I came expecting to see hockey without rules, but what I did see was tremendous. The discipline of the players is terrific. It is hard to believe they do not have full-time professional training. Their stamina and speed are just incredible."
Kenneth Wolstenholme B.B.C. Sports Commentator

The Connolly Villas estate was completed in 1935. The Dilger brothers grew up there. Connolly Villas was then in the outskirts of the town and youngsters growing up hurled on the roads and fields. They didn't need organised hurling to express themselves.

Bernie Dilger.

Hurling in Ennis in the early 1950's was in a depressing state. The DALS hadn't competed at senior level for a number of years. For a short time the Faughs represented the town in the senior grade. Success had eluded Ennis since 1941. Turnpike fielded a team in the Intermediate grade and Éire Óg initially fielded in Junior (B).

Bernie recalled to me *"We didn't come from a hurling background yet, all four of us hurled. It didn't have to come from your parents. We played in the fields (now St. Michael's). I went to various games to see Ruan, Newmarket and Clarecastle. But the question didn't dawn on me why isn't an Ennis team competing at the highest level. If Clarecastle or Scariff were playing in the park you'd go over. Paddy Duggan, Val McGann, Larry and Michael Blake, they went out and did it. They disassociated themselves from the DALS. Paddy Duggan was a driving force behind Éire Óg. A good hurler. He had great guts and courage. He was a bit older and a chief organiser and one of the founding members of the club. We had great supporters in Florrie Malone - she washed our jerseys by hand in her bath. Mrs. Loftus was fanatical. Esther Gilligan, Christina Kelly and Mrs. Callaghan. These women were real supporters. The banter was great. They were vocal. They were part of it. They just weren't going to matches as spectators. Some people go to games now and they don't open their mouths. These women knew their hurling."*

By 1955, Éire Óg had become a major force in Clare Cup and Championship. New players came to the club like Mick Morrissey and Donal Leahy who had great strength and presence recalled Bernie. *"Tony Keaty was one of the best full forwards we ever had, but he was often left off. He was from Tipperary, but his people were from Ennis. He was a real Ennisman. A great man to break a ball. Keaty was fearless. There were a lot of players who shone in the leagues and with the Rovers who didn't get a game with Éire Óg. The likes of Tom Cosgrove and Sean Mounsey, good players to read the game. Sean Mounsey played with the Rovers. The Rovers were very sticky. There was a lot of class distinction. My brother Michael was left off the team for the county final in 1955 v. Newmarket. Now, he didn't always put the full hour in, but when he got possession he scored and that's what counts."*

Bernie was a highly valued member of the Éire Óg teams of 1954/1959. Regarded by many as one of the best wing backs in the game at this time. The Clare/Kilkenny Wembley Cup final received glowing reviews in the British press. Graham Selkirk writing in the Daily Telegraph described the game as follows: "No holds barred. Hockey with the lid off." Also in May 1958, the Daily Mail sports correspondent wrote of hurling: "To every soccer man who has shirked a tackle, heavy-weight who has ducked a fight, batsman who has sulked over a decision, I commend the spirit, sportsmanship and guts of the 30 hurlers who took part in Saturday's tournament final at Wembley stadium."

The 1958 Clare team that played in Wembley included a large contingent of Éire Óg and St. Joseph's players. The advent of television in the 1960's brought this most attractive of tournaments into the home, and it became a major event in the G.A.A. calendar.

I asked Bernie about his technique, the players he admired and the Wembley Tournament.

"I never stayed with my opponent for the puck out. I retreated six or seven paces and when the ball was pucked out, I'd be running and jumping so I could get over my opponent who was then left flat footed. As regards the Wembley Tournament, Kilkenny and Waterford had met in the 1957 championship final. They expected a repeat of this. It wasn't expected we'd beat Waterford in the semi-final because we had many new players. Dan McInerney, Donal O'Grady, Haulie Donnellan were all gone. O'Grady was one of the best centre-backs in the game. We had many new players from Éire Óg and St. Joseph's. In the absence of Michael Blake, I was made captain for the Wembley final. No thought was put into it, Smyth or Nugent should have been captain. It was a great occasion though. When I ran out on the pitch I thought of Stanley Matthews. The only time I'd seen soccer was in the Pathe Newsreels at

the Gaiety Cinema. The GAA was very strong and well organised in London. Fanatical in the best sense. Look at what the Irish have achieved in the United States. Naturally they had the soccer nets up and one of their points was given as a goal. We gave Kilkenny a good game even though they were All-Ireland champions.

Ruan beat us in the county final in 1959 in a tense and low scoring game. Their backs were on top of our forwards. We got few chances and were well beaten by Ruan. Jimmy Smyth was like Ring, he would make three or four decisive moves which won games. He was very strong and when he played for Ruan he knew they depended on him. Michael (Dilger) had a great body swerve when on the run. He had great hands, was a bit like Smyth. Our games with St. Joseph's in the O'Doherty Cup and gold watches were great. They drew great crowds because we weren't into the television era."

Bernie Dilger retired from the game about 1960., though he did return to assist the junior team in 1964. This great Éire Óg team gradually disbanded. The 1959 Clare Cup win was the last hurrah. It's important to remember they had done a lot of hurling in championship, Clare Cup, O'Doherty Cup, McKaigney Cup, Winter League, Feiseanna and Tourneys, that a burn out factor was inevitable.

Notes

1958 Wembley Tournament, Kilkenny 6-10 . . . Clare 5-7

The score is recorded in other accounts as 5-11 to 5-7 as one of the Kilkenny points was recorded as a goal. Attendance: 33,240.

The late Mrs Loftus was formerly Bridget Caffrey. A Native of County Westmeath. Four of her sons played senior hurling for Clare - Paddy, Steve, Des, Vincent.

Mrs. Esther Gilligan was formerly Esther McGee. A Native of Gowran, Co. Kilkenny. Her sons, Noel and Brendan played senior for Clare. Paddy played for Éire Óg.

Eddie Fahy

Dalcassians, Army Metro, Garda Club
Clare, Dublin and Leinster

Eddie Fahy.

The Fahy brothers were amongst the prime movers behind the re-organisation of Ennis hurling in 1924, after the War of Independence and Civil War. Billy (Botch), Eddie, Mickie and Wally were part of the winning DALS team of 1924. A younger brother, Vincent represented the CBS in senior Colleges during this time. Eddie Fahy was one of several Ennismen to find favour with the Clare selectors during the 1925/26 season. In 1927, he moved to Dublin and quickly won his place on the Metropolitan team of 1927, regarded by many as one of the best combinations of all time. That same year he was back in the Showgrounds representing the Dublin hurlers against Clare. In fact, five other Claremen lined out for Dublin on that occasion.

With the change in rules regarding non-residents in 1928, Eddie Fahy was again back in the Clare colours. Eddie Fahy was highly rated amongst the best of his day. He was just one of a number of top GAA players honoured by Wills cigarettes – as "All Stars". – His pen-picture read – *"judged from a classic stand-point, Ned's methods do not suggest greatness, but though sticklers for science may find fault with this vigorous leader of the Garda attack, in the all important art of goalgetting he has repeatedly demonstrated his worth. He played for his native Clare, for the Dalcassians, and also for the victorious Leinster selection in the inter-provincial final. This vigorous and gritty forward came to the Garda Club via the National Army with whom he enjoyed a big reputation as a marksman. Height 5-10, Weight 12-4."*

U.S.A. in Showgrounds – The Tailteann Games

On September 22nd, 1928, the United States team received a tumultuous welcome as they arrived at the Railway Station. The Brass Band was part of this warm welcome as they led the exiles from the station to their hotel. A crowd estimated at 9,000 turned out at the

Showgrounds to witness the U.S.A. defeat Clare, the Munster finalists, by seven points. The USA team included natives from the following counties – Kilkenny, Laois, Offaly, Cork, Clare, and Tipperary.

United States – 1928 team

Jim Dermody (goal), J. Keoghan, H. Meagher, S. Fitzpatrick, J. Grey, P. Fitzgibbon, P. Delany, C. Clohane, J. Galvin, J. Halligan, J. Horan, A. Cordial, W. Ryan, Big Jim Burke (Tulla), T. Hickey.

Pen Picture text – courtesy of W.D. and H.O. Wills cigarettes No. 12 in a series of 50.

Photo and text supplied by Seamus O'Reilly, Clare County Express

Eddie Fahy - Honours Won

1 All-Ireland Senior – Dublin 1927
1 Leinster Championship – Dublin – 1927
1 Railway Cup Medal – Leinster – 1927
1 County (Clare) Senior – 1924 Dals

1927 – Railway Cup –Leinster 1-11, Munster 2-6
1927 - Leinster Final Dublin 7-7, Kilkenny 4-6
1927 – All Ireland Final Dublin 4-8, Cork 1-3
1928 – United States 4-7 Clare 2-6 Showgrounds

Dublin 1927 - All-Ireland Champions

Mick Gill (Capt.) *Pa 'Fowler' McInerney, W. Phelan, E. Tobin, *Jack Gleeson, *Tom O'Rourke, Garret Howard, Mattie Power, *Eddie Fahy, *Tommy Daly (Goalie), T. Barry, J Walsh, D. O'Neill, J. Bannon, M. Hayes *Tom Burnell (Tubber) was also on the panel.

***Claremen**

This Dublin team of 1927 was described by 'Pato' in The Irish Times as "probably the best fifteen who have ever contested a championship final".

Christy Glynn

Ennis Dals, Faughs

Christy Glynn gave a lifetime to GAA affairs be it with the Dalcassians, Faughs or Éire Óg. Christy played minor for the Dals in 1935 before making his senior debut in 1937. Four years later he was part of the successful team that won the senior championship.

Christy Glynn embraces Tony Nugent after the 1982 County Final win.

In June 1997, I spoke to him on a couple of occasions at his home in Clonroad. Christy recalled the town leagues, the controversial final of 1941 and the demise of the Dals. *"The standard of hurling in the leagues was very high. Many inter-County men who worked in Ennis played, the likes of Mick Hennessy and Seán Harrington. At that time I lived in O'Connell Street so I played for the Turnpike. Joe Madigan did a lot of good work with the Minors and Juveniles, and Tull Considine was an exceptional coach. We met Clooney in the 1941 final. Clooney were hot favourites for the Championship. They had big names in Mick Halloran, Mick Hennessy and the Kilmartins. We trailed at half time but the selectors made a master switch early in the second half when they brought on Jack Quirke, Joe Madigan and Miko Ball, and they all clicked."* The rumour of the Dals using several subs has persisted in folklore amongst not just Clooney hurlers but many Ennis hurlers of the time as well. Christy was quick to dispel this rumour and was adamant that the Dals only used 3 subs and that the management pulled no stroke whatsoever in the course of this final.

A few days later I checked this out. The old dusty match report read:

"Shortly after play resumed, Sean Guinnane retired as a result of an injury he received in the first half. His place was taken by Jack Quirke, who proved to be an excellent sub. Edward 'Bucky' Flynn was replaced by Joe Madigan who, like White, displayed the old form. Mickey White played to great advantage, and displayed some of his best form. Although handicapped by an injury in the opening stages, he played a dogged game until he eventually had to retire. He was replaced by Miko Ball who played a wonderful game. Then Aoner Sheridan broke the deadlock with a goal. After the final whistle, the Ennis players were loudly cheered, and amongst the first to congratulate them were the Clooney players and supporters. It indeed was an epic battle, which lived up to all expectations. The old timers who spoke to the Clare Champion afterwards enjoyed Sunday's game 'to their hearts content.'" There it was in black and white, just three subs.

Silver Jubilee 1952-1977. Christy Glynn, chairman that year and Paddy Duggan, first captain in 1952 cut the cake.

The Dals went into a decline after this championship. They drew twice with Clarecastle but lost the replays. Then the Faughs formed a new hurling club and they won the Intermediate Championship in 1945; Christy's brother, Tony, played with them. Christy later won a Senior Football medal with the Faughs and he finished his hurling days with them in 1950 when they took over the affairs of senior hurling in town. This was before Éire Óg was formed.

After his retirement from the playing pitches in the early 1950s, Christy joined Éire Óg. He served as chairman of Éire Óg in the 1970s and later acted in the honorary role as President.

His sons, Paul, John, Michael 'Hooper' all represented Éire Óg. His daughter, Edel, was also involved with the club.

Honours Won

1 Clare Champion Cup 1937
1 County Championship 1941
1 County Championship Football ... 1947

Sean Guinnane

Dalcassians, Faughs, and Clare

By Seamus O'Ceallaigh (written 1952)

Sean Guinnane.

Clare make the journey to Tralee to-day intent on proving the worth of the great county-wide drive to improve the standard of minor hurling and football, which has been the big feature of Banner County activities this season.

In charge as County Secretary is all-round sportsman Sean Guinnane, who is an accomplished hurler, footballer, golfer, handballer and tennis player.

Five years ago, when he was 30, Sean was forced to retire from the active Gaelic arena because of a knee injury.

He was then laden with honours he started gathering as a schoolboy at St. Flannan's. He won with them the Munster Hurling Cup for 1933 and 1934, supplemented by the Clare County Minor Hurling Championship in 1934.

With The Dals Club he won the Minor Football Championships of 1933 and 1934, and followed up by registering championship successes with three other clubs.

In Ennis Dalcassian colours he secured senior hurling and junior football honours. With Ennis Faughs he won an intermediate and two senior football titles, and he also has a senior football championship to his credit, got with Kilfenora.

Standing five feet, ten inches and weighing twelve and a half stones, Sean Guinnane, in his heyday played against some of Ireland's greatest hurlers and was able to hold his own with the best of them.

He takes a particular pride in having played on the same team as Larry Blake, whom he considers one of the best hurlers of his time.

Other players ranking high in Sean's estimation include footballers, Paddy Kennedy, of Kerry, and Bobby Beggs of Galway and hurlers Con Cottrell of Cork, Jackie Power and Paddy Clohessy of Limerick.

Sean Guinnane first donned the Saffron and Blue of the Dalcassian territory in 1933, when he campaigned in both minor hurling and football. He repeated the double appearance in the two following years.

In 1936 he was a member of the Clare Junior team in both codes, and that same season earned dual promotion to senior ranks. He continued in hurling until 1942 and in football for five further years, excepting the years 1944 and 1945.

His most exciting game was the Munster Hurling Final of 1938, in which Waterford beat the Banner County lads, and another memorable match for him was the National Football League Final of 1946, which Derry won from the Claremen. His only important inter-county success was in the Cusack Shield hurling competition in 1937, in which Clare proved best.

Sean's favourite football position was at midfield, while in hurling he preferred the left half-forward berth.

He admitted having no special training method, except to play handball, which he considers ideal preparation for hurling or football and an excellent means of keeping one's "eye-in".

Sean Guinnane – Honours Won

3 Senior Football Championships *1941, 1947, 1948 (Faughs)
2 Senior Hurling Championships 1934, 1941 (Dalcassians)
1 Intermediate Football 1946, Faughs
1 Junior Football 1943, Ennis Dals
2 Munster Cup (St. Flannan's) 1933, 1934 (Canon O'Kennedy Shield)
1 Cusack Shield (Clare) - 1937.

In 1941, Four Ennis men played legally for Kilfenora. They were Sean Clohessy, Ralphie Burns, Pat McMahon and Sean Guinnane. Kilfenora won the senior football crown in 1941.

Sean Guinnane represented Clare at both codes in minor, junior and senior. He was involved as coach/selector to the Clare senior hurlers in 1965. He coached the St. John's team which reached the minor 'A' football final of 1965. After good wins over Lahinch, Miltown, Clohanes (Doonbeg), they lost to the favourites Kilmurry Ibrickane.

Sean Heaslip

Eire Óg and Clare

Sean Heaslip, a contemporary of mine at Rice College and a native of O'Connell Street, is steeped in hurling. His uncle, Denis Heaslip won All-Ireland senior medals with Kilkenny in 1957 and 1963. Sean learned his hurling in the CBS School leagues and made his senior club debut in 1975.

I asked Sean about his background and the influences that helped shape him - *"My father Jack introduced me to hurling. We went to Croke Park for All-Ireland finals. My parents came from Kilkenny. My late mother Eilish[1] came from Ballyhale and my father from Knocktopher. In later years the two clubs came together to form Ballyhale Shamrocks[2]. An uncle of mine, a priest (Fr. Anthony Heaslip) was the main man in getting the clubs together. That's where my hurling came from."*

Sean's earliest memory is captaining the Town against Hermitage in the third and fourth class CBS final. Declan Coote captained Hermitage. Later Heaslip played on the Rice Cup team beaten by Limerick CBS in the 1970 final, but missed out on the Harty Cup through suspension. Heaslip received six months for allegedly abusing a referee. Bro. Miniter and Bro. Donnellan brought him to a county board meeting to appeal the decision. Unfortunately, Heaslip's suspension wasn't lifted. A lot of work went into training the team in 1973/1974 and despite good wins over Cashel, Limerick and Our Lady's, Gort, in challenge outings, the Ennis CBS team went under to Thurles CBS by 3-10 to 3-9, at Emly. A crucial disallowed goal by Ennis CBS was waved wide. Heaslip agrees that *"our team could have gone places"*.

Because Brian Borus couldn't compete in the 1975 Munster club championship, Éire Óg, the defeated county finalists, was nominated to play. Heaslip made his senior club debut against Moneygall.

This was a very unsettled period in the club, a lot was promised but little was delivered. In 1978, a silly incident in their semi-final with Clarecastle possibly cost them the game. Éire Óg Dals became disorganised after the row. In 1979, there was a split in the club. Thankfully the rift was healed. This reconciliation led to one of the best eras in town hurling.

Seán Heaslip and Leo Quinlan in action during one of the many memorable Éire Óg/Sixmilebridge clashes.

Vincent Loftus came on board early in 1980 with Éire Óg and set a trend of no messing - play well and keep your place - play badly - lose it - which was crucial at the time. A lot of what Loftus did set a trend for the year.

Heaslip recalls: *"Michael Hanrahan took over the team in 1980. Duggie (Paddy Duggan) came in as motivator and Bro. Cahill was coach. Colum Flynn trained us. We had never trained under Colum before, and when you get a group of lads who could hurl allied to the experience of Flynn's training, we were flying it. We were the fittest club team around.*

You could take Colum Flynn's training for four or five nights but after that you began to feel its benefit. I hold Flynn in the highest regard. It was hard going. We beat Newmarket in a good county final. Newmarket had beaten us in a tournament final a few weeks previously and I'm sure they felt they could beat us again. I was teaching with Michael Kilmartin in Shannon and I'd say they were confident. Fr. Harry Bohan gave us a great 'pep talk' in the Forresters' Club a few days earlier. It was a fine team performance. Martin Nugent with 3-3 had a terrific game".

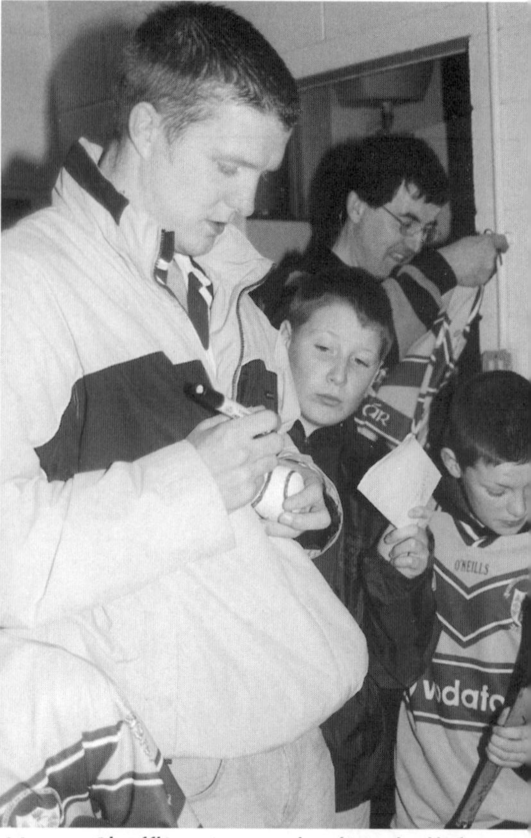

Henry Shefflin signs a hurling ball for Cormac O'Regan and Aaron Fitzgerald, former Éire Óg and Clare hurler Seán Heaslip is pictured in the background.

After the championship win in 1980 a lot of Éire Óg players were brought in to the county squad. Heaslip, operating at full-forward, scored 14-14 in that league campaign. Waterford eliminated Clare at the quarter-final stage of the N.H.L. at Thurles (3-15 to 1-14).

"I wasn't picked for the championship. I lost confidence. But on the way down I was told I was on. Sean Hehir was ill and Martin Meehan went to the backs. I was tight on my opponent and he wasn't playing well. I was used to playing on Sean Stack and, if you weren't tight on him, he'd disgrace you. Jackie O'Gorman (selector) felt I was tiring. I should have told him I was OK. I was taken off and Colm Mahon came on. Colm got very few runs on the County scene. He deserved more. In the semi-final against Cork they went back to the old team. Clare played with great spirit against Cork. I didn't play championship after that. There was a lot of bickering in Éire Óg. I wasn't enjoying my hurling so I pulled out of the county scene. We were overconfident against Newmarket in 1981. They took off Coote; he was the scapegoat. We had mighty county finals against Sixmilebridge in 1982 and 1983. In 1985 against Kilmaley we were overconfident. We had beaten them 21 points the previous year.

We missed several frees. I missed the penalty in the end. The longer you allow a team hang on, they'll beat you."

Sean Heaslip returned to the Clare team for the league in 1987/1988. In 1990 he collected another senior club championship medal. A just reward for great loyalty to his club.

Honours Won

3 Senior Club Championship 1980, 1982, 1990
2 Under 21 - 1974, 1977
Minor - 1974
1 National League Division II 1980/1981
1 Under 21 Dublin Football Championship (1975) - Erin's Hope
1 Under 21 Dublin Hurling Championship (1977) Erin's Hope.

The Éire Óg team that drew with St. Brendan's in the 1978 quarter final championship was: -

Tony Nugent, Ollie O'Regan, Paddy Kelly, Michael Barry, Martin Leahy, Barry Smythe, Tony Roche, Declan Coote, Denis O'Connor, Sean Heaslip, Brendan Gilligan, Michael Skelly, Sean Lynch, Noel Ryan, Michael Nugent.
Subs: Joe Barry/Michael Carmody.

Éire Óg won the replay fairly convincingly by 6-7 to 3-9.

1 Eilish Heaslip was formerly Eilish Long from Ballyhale, Co. Kilkenny.
2 Ballyhale Shamrocks have won 9 Kilkenny Senior Championships to date – 1978, 1979, 1980, 1982, 1983, 1985, 1988, 1989, 1991.
3 Seán Heaslip holds Under 21 Hurling and Football medals with Erin's Hope - St. Patrick's Training College team. He was quite legal to play both Dublin and Clare Championships, once transferred back.

Records for Everybody at Records Dept.

RANALOW &
O'BRIEN LTD

12 O'Connell Street, Ennis

Eric and Frank Ranalow, and Tim O'Brien's premises was a haven for all record collectors and music enthusiasts, in the Ennis of the 1960s and '70s.

Flan Hynes

Fermoy, DALS, Ennis Faughs, Avondhu (Cork), St. Joseph's

***"St. Joseph's were a leading team.
You had to be at your best to beat St. Joseph's"***

"My earliest memory of hurling is when the United States team came to the showgrounds to play Clare in 1932. In the 1950's, hurling was hard. We had great clubs in Ruan, Scariff, Newmarket 'the Mills', and Clarecastle. Whitegate had a style of their own, lovely strikers and great ball players. The Eire Og teams of 1955/59, I hold in the highest regard. They were beautiful hurlers. All the clubs were in contention. We, St. Joseph's, won two county titles and two Clare Champion Cups, but we lost more than we won."
Flan Hynes

The above comments came from the lips of Flan Hynes who passed away in February 2001. Flan's door in St. Michael's Villas was always open and he was a great help in my research for 'Against the Wind'. Flan learned his hurling at Ennis CBS. He was well known and respected through out the county, lining out with the DALS, Faughs and later St. Joseph's. His brother Paudge belonged to an earlier era, winning senior championship honours with the DALS in 1934.

While serving with the army in Kilworth, Flan lined out with Fermoy in junior while representing Avondhu in the senior championship. Up to 1941, Fermoy had never won a Cork hurling title. But with the large military presence in the town, the club was greatly strengthened. In their line-out, they had inter-county men in Paddy McCarthy of Limerick and Joe Kenny of Tipperary. The club that year also had the assistance of a couple of players from Castlelyons. Also playing for Fermoy in 1941 was Ruby Walsh, who later became better known in Horse Racing circles. In 1945 Flan returned to Ennis and joined the newly formed Faughs. The Faughs won the Intermediate championship of 1945, playing against Broadford.

About 1949 the newly formed St. Joseph's hurling team came into being and Flan threw in his lot with them. The St. Joseph's team of this era was a powerful combination, featuring several county men. In 1958, they contested five finals in all, Championship, Clare Cup, Fleadh

St. Joseph's, 1958 Clare Senior Champions. Front row, left to right: *Joe O'Halloran, Flan Hynes, Tommy Sheedy, Matt Nugent (capt.), Paschal Sheridan, Seamus Conlon, Raymond Greene.* ***Back row:*** *Gerry Browne, Justin Gleeson, Francie Keane, Pat Hynes, Sean Howard, Paddy Hassett, Michael Hayes and Johnny Purcell.*

tournament, Winter League and gold Watches. The latter tournament sponsored by Cusack Park, holds a special place in the affection of hurlers of this era. The 1958 'Joseph's' team lost to Eire Og after three games, but they won the senior championship. In a devastating spell, goals from Tommy Sheedy, Pat Hynes and Joe Halloran paved the way in their 3-10 to 2-5 win over Newmarket at the semi-final stage. In the final, their greater association with high tension games and their greater team work proved too much for Feakle who went down by 3-6 to 2-2.

Flan hung up his boots when 'The Blues' defeated St. Joseph's in the 1963 Clare Champion Cup Final. I asked Flan to name some of the great hurlers he played with or against.

"With the Faughs I remember Reggie Connellan, Johnny Fleming and Tony Strand. Matt Nugent and Jimmy Smyth were amongst the greats of all time. Donal O'Grady was the sweetest of all at centreback. Pat and Jackie Greene of Newmarket, Des Carroll, Jimmy Fennessy, Vinny Henchy, Paddy Jordan, Johnny Purcell and Paddy Russell were good ones. We had great games with Eire Og. Pat Kirby had a great eye for the

ball. Paddy Loftus, Paddy Kerin and the Dilgers. Sean Madigan was a beautiful hurler. Michael Blake, Johnny McCarthy, Paddy Duggan, Bobby Burke. Bernie Dilger was a prince amongst wingbacks. His brother Michael was one of the finest forwards that was in Munster. Willie McAllister (Clarecastle) was 'something else', a purest. The Wexford team of 1954-56 was a fine selection of men. I played against Mattie Foudy and Willie John Daly in Cork. They blew us away. Cork club hurling is great."

Flan Hynes later served as Treasurer of the Clare County Board, giving great loyalty to the game. It was always a pleasure to talk hurling with Flan. His memories of the game were always positive when he spoke of St. Joseph's many clashes.

Honours

2 County Senior Championship (St. Joseph's) 1954, 1958
2 Clare Cups (St. Joseph's) 1953, 1957
1 Intermediate (Faughs) 1945
1 North Cork Junior (A) 1941 – Fermoy

Fermoy subsequently lost to Carrigtowhill in the county championship semi-final proper.

The 1958 St. Joseph's team that defeated Newmarket in the championship semi-final was: -

Michael Hayes, Sean Howard, Justin Gleeson, Paddy Hassett, Flan Hynes, Johnny Purcell, Paschal Sheridan. Seamus Conlon, Gerry Browne, Tommy Sheedy, Matt Nugent, Raymond Greene, Joe Halloran, Frank Keane, Pat Hynes.

Colin Lynch

Éire Óg, Lissycasey, Kilmaley, Clare and Munster

"Colin Lynch turned the wheels all day long. He was awesome. He set up a goal, scored 0-2 himself and played like a Gladiator all through. Yesterday was perhaps his finest hour".
The Star, May 19, 2003.

Like all great sportsmen, Colin Lynch craves excellence. He doesn't accept second best lightly. Colin grew up in Caherea, Lissycasey, where traditionally hurlers gravitated towards Kilmaley or Ballyea.

Colin Lynch.

At Under-14, Colin represented Ballyea. While training with the county juvenile teams he came under the guidance of Paddy Duggan. Colin always wanted to play at the highest level. Stephen McNamara, a school friend at Rice College, suggested he join Éire Óg as an isolated player.

Colin has the distinction of playing inter-county hurling and football at all levels for the county. His hurling comes from both sides of his family. *"My father Johnny Lynch and his brothers, Jimmy, *Oliver and Christopher all played for Feakle, while my grandfather Jackie Clohessy was involved all his life in the game, he hurled with Kilmaley. Growing up I spent a lot of time in Feakle where I greatly admired the skills of Val Donnellan and Michael and Tommy Guilfoyle. I joined Éire Óg in 1990 playing on the successful Junior (A) and minor teams. I actually played Munster Club before playing county championship. After we won the county senior title in 1990, Paddy Duggan introduced me to the senior panel for the games with Roanmore, Na Piarsaigh and Patrickswell. That was my introduction to senior hurling."*

Colin Lynch broke on to the county Under-21 team in 1992, and was part of the excellent junior panel of 1993 that claimed the All-Ireland title from Kilkenny. In 1995, he was described as *'the find of the season'* but illness kept him from claiming a place on the All-Ireland winning Clare senior team. Again, 1996 proved disappointing for Lynch because of Clare's early championship exit.

Colin Lynch one of Clare's finest players of the modern era in action v Kilkenny in the All-Ireland final 2002.

Following a fabulous inter-county season in 1996/1997, everything came right. A tremendous final display in the 1997 All-Ireland final saw Lynch set up James O'Connor for the wining point in a nail-biting finish. An All-Star Award followed, just one of six Clare awards that year. Just desserts for a great group of men.

Apart from his Munster and All-Ireland medals, Colin is justifiably proud of his Oireachtas medal. He spoke of the hard work put into winning the Oireachtas in late 1996 and the part it played in getting players right for the rigours of the following year's championship. Colin also paid tribute to the commitment put in by the fringe players – *"The training is intense. Some players want it more that others."*

After many memorable displays in the Éire Óg colours, Lynch returned to assist Kilmaley and Lissycasey because of the great bond that exists between the clubs. Lissycasey hurlers always assisted Kilmaley hurlers in a verbal agreement but it was only in recent years that this agreement was validated. Of this agreement Colin states – *"I wanted to give something back to Kilmaley mainly because of my roots, but also because of the contribution and commitment of the likes of Conor Clancy and Alan Markham."*

Colin Lynch – Fact File
1 All-Ireland Senior Hurling – 1997
2 Munster Championship – 1997, 1998
1 Oireachtas – 1996
1 Railway Cup Medal – 1997 with Munster
1 All-Ireland Junior – 1993
1 Munster Junior – 1993
2 All-Star Award – 1997, 2002
1 Senior County Championship – Éire Óg – 1990
Waterford Crystal Man of the Match v Tipperary 2003 Championship
Vodafone Hurling Star of May 2003
1 Junior (A) Championship Éire Óg – 1990
1 Minor (A) Championship Éire Óg – 1990
1 Minor (A) League Éire Óg – 1990
1 Under-14 (B) Championship – Ballyea
1 Under-16 (B) League/Championship – Ballyea
1 Clare Hurler of the Year award - 2002
+ Numerous titles with Lissycasey Footballers.

Favourite Players – Joe Cooney (Galway), John Russell and Val Donnellan.

*Oliver Lynch played minor hurling for Clare in 1959 and 1960

Clare All-Star Recipients – 1997

Brian Lohan, Liam Doyle, Sean McMahon, Colin Lynch, James O'Connor, Gerard O'Loughlin.

Regarding Clare's All-Ireland Championship success in 1997, 12 players played in all 5 games; only 10 players started in all 5 games. 23 players played a part in the championship while 42 players were looked at in competitive hurling in 1997 (not including challenge games).

Sean Lynch

The Banner, Éire Óg and Clare

A product of the St. John's nursery, Sean Lynch came from a sporting background. His Uncle Michael played for Clare (1953-1960), while Sean's younger brother, Pat was a class hurler with Éire Óg and Clare in the 1980s.

Seanie came to prominence with Ennis CBS, starring on their Harty Cup teams of 1968 and 1969. These were fine sides that scored wins over Mount Sion and North Monastery in the Munster Senior Harty Cup Competition. Teammates of his in these years included Niall McInerney, Kevin Hoban (Sixmilebridge), Tim Hannon (Newmarket), Martin Linnane (Corofin) and Seamus and Haulie O'Connell (Éire Óg).

As a young first year student in 1968/1969, I recall the euphoria of setting off from Lifford on beautiful autumn and spring days. These matches conjure up an era when to support the CBS not only meant an hour's hurling but, more importantly, it spelt freedom and a half day, a bus or train trip to such exotic locations as Tipperary Town, Bansha, Emly or Kilmallock.

The Leaving Certificate students of 1968/69, a colourful lot, led 'the choir' on the buses as we headed off. 'Dicey Riley' by Sweeney's Men[1] was a popular folk song of the day and this was directed at the good-humoured Latin teacher, Bro. Frank O'Reilly.

"Poor old Dicey Riley she has taken to the sup,
Poor old Dicey Riley she will never give it up,
She's off each morning to the pub
Where she drops in for another little one,
Sure the heart of the Rowl is Dicey Riley"

Though a young side featuring a number of players from the Dean Ryan team, they shocked North Monastery CBS by 2-11 to 3-4. Inspired by Sean Lynch at centre-forward, Ennis gave a powerful second half performance to come from behind. On our way home, the bus drivers, prompted by the leaving certificate students, drove into the grounds of St. Flannan's, flags and banners waving and victory songs in full voice.

"The Clash of the Ash" *A tremendous shot captured by the Clare Champion during the 1983 County Final involving James Keogh (Sixmilebridge) and Michael Chandler and Seán Lynch.* Courtesy of Liam McGrath.

Needless to say, the presence of 300 raving students from the CBS disrupting study wasn't appreciated by the teaching staff of St. Flannan's and we were politely asked to leave.[2]

Following this victory over the 'Mon', Ennis were pitted against Coláiste Iognaid Rís (Sullivan's Quay) in the next round. Ennis CBS got off to a great start when a rampant forward line of Michael Smythe, Sean Lynch and Seamus O'Connell raced into a 2-4 to 1-0 lead. Then disaster struck when Paddy Firth was sent off for a harmless looking tackle. Ennis completely lost their way and the Cork City school took control to win by 5-5 to 2-4. Needless to say, there was little or no singing or jibing on the solemn journey home.

"Ennis CBS go out in a blaze of controversy" was the Champion headline. *"Ennis supporters arrived home on Sunday night sore and disgruntled contriving what might have been had not one of their players been erroneously sent to the line."* This side was one of the best to represent the school since the great days of the early sixties.

An outstanding athlete, Sean was Munster Colleges sprint champion. After leaving CBS he starred for two years with the Clare u/21 team, but later disappeared from the scene, concentrating his efforts with Braids Utd. and St. Michael's AFC. With the formation of the Banner GAA Club in 1977, he returned to the game and was quickly called up to the Éire Óg DALS senior team in 1978. It was here he proved his worth scoring 3-2 from play in their victory over St. Brendan's. He was then called into the Clare panel and played a number of times during the 1978/79 season. This team was beaten by Tipperary at the semi-final stage of the National League on a score of 2-13 to 2-12.

After dropping out of the county scene, Sean continued to assist Éire Óg until 1984. A great man to carry or break the ball, Sean Lynch always used his strength fairly and with telling effect, creating openings for those around him. After retiring from the game he continued to take an active interest in the fortunes of Éire Óg and Clare.

Honours Won

2 Senior Championship 1980, 1982
1 U/16
1 Minor (1969)
1 Munster Junior Inter-firm (Syntex)
1 Munster College Sprint Champion (Ennis CBS)
Munster Schools record (Ennis CBS)
Sean represented Clare at minor level for 2 years and 2 years at u/21 grade.

The Éire Óg team that lost to Ballyduff (Waterford) by 3-8 to 1-13 in the Munster club championship of 1982 was: -

Seamus Durack, Colm Mahon, Paddy Kelly, Joe Barry, Declan Coote (0-2), Micheál Glynn, Frannie Heaslip, Michael Chandler (0-1) Tony Nugent (0-4), Pat Lynch (0-1) Sean Heaslip, Martin Nugent (1-2), Sean Lynch (0-2), Pete Barry (0-1), Noel Ryan.

Subs: Michael Ryan; Francie Mahon; Gerry Barry (used).

1 Sweeney's Men consisted of Andy Irvine, Terry Woods and Johnny Moynihan. They paved the way for groups like Planxty and the Bothy Band. Sweeney's Men recorded 2 LPs for the Transatlantic Label – "1968" and "The Tracks of Sweeney". Their repertoire consisted of Irish, British and American Folk Songs and Sea Shanties. Sean Lynch had a great love of all music, especially Irish traditional music.
2 Coláiste Chríost Rí had earlier beaten St. Flannan's in the Harty Cup. After beating the North Mon, Ennis CBS supporters arrived into St. Flannan's to rub salt in their wounds. All good humoured fun of course.

Johnny McCarthy

St. John's, Éire Óg and Clare

Johnny McCarthy began his competitive playing days with Ennis Dals juvenile club. The club was run by Joe Madigan and Frank Burns, but the adult club, at this stage, was practically defunct. Johnny who attended the CBS from 1951-1956, was steeped in hurling. His father, John (Brudsy) won a senior hurling championship with Dalcassians in 1941, and his family also had links with Rovers H.C. Johnny's brother Frankie played Minor Championship with St. John's before concentrating on Rugby.

Johnny recalled: *"I learned my hurling at the CBS, where there was tremendous interest in the primary school leagues, and final day in the Fairgreen was a big day in Ennis hurling. But it was on a piece of waste ground in Hermitage, that I learned hurling's facts of life. I learned, like the pioneers of the west - to pull first and ask questions after. The solo run was never used except by some unfortunate newcomer, and he was quickly brought down to earth in more ways than one. St. John's had a solid nucleus. They had great mentors in Frank O'Gorman, Paddy McInerney, Des McCullough, Joe Daly and Sean O'Gorman. The club was based around the Causeway. They were the coming force in under-age hurling whereas we in the DALS were beginning to fade. The Dals juvenile and minor club soon collapsed and many of us joined St. John's."*

After good displays with Ennis CBS Harty Cup team (1955/56) Johnny was called on to the St. John's adult team. *"St. John's played in the Clare Champion Cup and we had a reasonable record. We played a good few senior teams. It was felt that St. John's had the nucleus of a good senior team. What would have happened eventually I don't know! It was very likely that one would have swallowed the other. As it turned out St. John's weren't allowed play senior championship and Éire Óg went on to retain the championship in 1957. Sixmilebridge were extremely good and they had Jimmy Carney playing for them. He was expected to swing it for the 'Bridge. Michael Blake was injured in training before the 'Bridge game and they expected that the absence of Blake would be enough to swing the game in favour of Sixmilebridge. Blake was automatic on the Clare*

Johnny McCarthy. "I remember Johnny McCarthy not alone for his hurling ability but also for his playing on the accordion. Occasionally in hurling we have that great accompaniment of hurling, traditional music and song. They blend so well together," Jimmy Smyth.

team. His importance to Éire Óg could hardly be overestimated. Michael 'Doc' Doherty was a great talent. Tony Keaty was a tremendous full-forward. Keaty was dropped for the County Final in 1956. It was a bombshell. I don't know why he was dropped. He still figured with the club though and played on until 1959. He was terrific in the 'watches' tournament of 1958. He was a major name. Keaty created chances for his corner-forwards. Jimmy Conroy played for us about 1959/60. He played at centre-forward. Our team at this time wasn't very successful. He went to Whitegate soon afterwards and starred at centre-back on their winning team of 1961. Whitegate hurlers were fast, strong and skilful."

After a few years in the doldrums, Éire Óg began building a fine team in the mid-60s. Johnny considers the county final defeat to Newmarket in 1965 as the biggest disappointment of his playing days. *"They only scored two points from play, yet we allowed them to steal the championship from under our noses. The Éire Óg victory of 1966 was extraordinary. That team never got real credit for winning the title. We had three great games with Clarecastle along the way. I loved playing against Clarecastle. I also liked playing Whitegate. There was always a great atmosphere. Newmarket and Éire Óg always produced a different type of hurling. When Newmarket were good, they were very good. I enjoyed a couple of great games with Newmarket. I played on Jimmy Cullinan a couple of times. I never hurled him, but I tried to prevent him hurling. He was a fantastic player. I tried to prevent him from hurling in the 1965 County Final. If I did that I'd consider it a job well done."*

Johnny who made his senior inter-county championship debut with Clare in 1961 (against Galway) also admired Matt Nugent, Jimmy Smyth, Naoise Jordan, Sean Custy, Liam Devanney (Tipperary) and Joe Salmon (Galway).

The Music

Johnny McCarthy's roots in Ennis go back several generations. His forebears came from the Circular Road and the Cornmarket. His grandfather, John McCarthy, played concertina. His father, Brudsy, played drums and accordion with the Fergus Ceili Band. Brudsy also played with the Fiach Roe. That celebrated band included in their ranks Tom Eustace, Paddy Murphy and Peter O'Loughlin. Music is in the blood. Johnny recalled: *"Most of my earliest memories seem to be about some member of the family either playing music or hurling. My uncles, Billy and P. J. Murphy, played with the brass band. I recall running after another uncle, Vincent, as he paraded with the rest of the victorious Rovers team. P. J. and Anthony – the youngest of the Murphy family – were lifelong traditional musicians and a continuing influence until their untimely deaths."*

Johnny taught music at Ballynacally National School. He introduced instrumental music in 1961 and, in the process, started a sight of young musicians on their way. His own particular influences include – Joe Ryan from Inagh and the late Paddy Murphy, Kilmaley. These men were lifelong friends of his late father and so he had the best of musical advice from an early age. Paddy Canny's fiddle playing is another influence on his music. I think it's fair to say that Johnny McCarthy is one of the finest exponents of the accordeon. His interpretations of slow airs for me is without equal. Last year Johnny released his first recording titled 'Solo Run'. A unique recording in that it explores the affinity between two of our national treasures – hurling and traditional Irish music and song. The tunes on the CD come from a wide and diverse repertoire. His playing of slow airs is especially beautiful. On the CD Johnny is accompanied by Mike Fitzgerald (fiddle), Anne Marie McCormack (fiddle), Alph Duggan (guitar), while Terry Moorehead (guitar) and Conor McCarthy also guest.

Johnny McCarthy's sons, Conor, Fergus and John, have carried on the musical heritage. Fergus and John are better known in the rock field. John was a member of one of Ennis' best groups, Twilight Zone. Fergus earlier won All-Ireland honours in Slogadh on concertina. Conor is himself a widely respected accordeon player and has recorded with his wife, Anne Marie McCormack.

Honours Won

2 Senior County Championship 1957, 1966
1 Intermediate (St. John's)
1 Clare Champion Cup (1959)
1 Junior Championship
1 Minor (A) (St. John's)

The 1959 Clare Cup Winning Team was as follows:

Aidan Lynch, Paddy Kerin, Paddy Loftus, Bobby Burke, Jimmy Cronin, Hugh O'Donnell, Brendan Doyle, Colm Madigan, Johnny McCarthy, Paddy Duggan, Michael Blake, Ollie Ball, Michael Guerin, Pat Tynan, Patsy O'Loughlin.

Stephen McNamara

Éire Óg and Clare

Steeped in the tradition of Gaelic games, Stephen McNamara was raised in Coolock. His family moved to Ennis in 1979 and Stephen joined the Éire Óg Club. A unique feature about Mac is that he is the third generation of his family to win All-Ireland senior medals.

Stephen told me - *"My mother, the former Breda Power is a sister of Kerry's Ger Power and a daughter of the late Jackie Power. My grandfather was a big influence on me. I heard all the stories from him about all the great hurlers he played with and those that came later, the likes of Jimmy Langton of Kilkenny, Jack Lynch, the Mackey's, Ring, Jimmy Smyth and Matt Nugent. My interest took off from there. My interest in Gaelic football is just as big."*

Jackie Power was a member of the great Limerick team of 1933-40. Regarded as one of the most glamorous teams of all time, the side also included Mick Mackey and Timmy Ryan of Ahane. Power, Mackey and Ryan are counted amongst Limerick's greatest ever.

Naturally, Stephen was also drawn to the magic of the great Kerry football team of Ger Power, Mikey Sheehy and Eoin 'Bomber' Liston and their almost total domination. Only Dublin, Offaly and Cork could live with them during the great years of 1975-86.

The sporting tradition in Mac's lineage isn't confined to the Powers. Stephen is a grand-nephew of one of the most colourful hurlers to represent Ennis Dals, Johnny 'Joker' Coote. Joker won an All-Ireland junior medal with the Banner County in 1914 and was still playing when the Dals won the senior championship in 1928. He also played senior for Clare. Stephen's father, T. J. won two minor championships with Rovers in 1961 and 1962. T. J.'s great granduncle, Patrick Moroney, won senior football honours with the Dals in 1904.

In recent years, Éire Óg's contribution to county team selections has been modest compared to teams of the past. Yet, Stephen McNamara, Colin Lynch, Fergus Flynn and Tomas Corbett were all involved with the senior team, while Paddy Guilfoyle, Cathal Shannon and others assisted the county at U/21 level. Ronan Cooney was a member of the successful 1997 minor panel. Cooney was introduced to the fray in the games with

Stephen McNamara - a fine opportunist and tremendous goalscorer - "walking on air" following one of Clare's successes in the 1990s.

A happy group pictured at the Éire Óg 2002 social were left to right: Dessie Loftus, Henry Shefflin (Kilkenny), Liam Griffin, Stephen McNamara, Jimmy Cullinan (Newmarket), Paddy McNamara (Newmarket), Josie Nevin, Pat Daly, Seán O'Driscoll.

Antrim and Kilkenny. He was introduced as second sub in the All-Ireland Final against Galway. He broke his hand and missed the reception afterwards. Michael O'Halloran, a member of the senior winning team was thoughtful enough to visit Ronan in hospital, bringing the Liam McCarthy Cup with him. What the Clare team of the moment lack is a goal scoring forward of a 'Sparrow' O'Loughlin or a Stephen Mac. The 'Sparrow' has yet to be replaced, while McNamara set up and scored many wonderful goals for Clare at vital stages between the years of 1995 and 1999. It was his solo run in the Munster final of 1995 that led to Clare's goal. Mac went on a great solo run down the left. Clare were awarded a penalty. Davy Fitzgerald ran down the field and shot high to the roof of the net to put Clare ahead 1-3 to 0-5 late in the first half. A vital score. Should we forget the cracking goal McNamara scored in the closing stages of the Cork game in 1997, or his goal against Galway in 1999 when he finished a half chance to the net bringing Clare back into contention. His goal against Kilkenny in the 1999 semi-final was a gem. A beautiful low drop shot from Barry Murphy, flicked back by Colin Lynch to Stephen McNamara who dispatched as cheeky a goal as ever I saw to the net. I believe McNamara has yet to get the credit for these and other goals.

2003 Senior Championship

To-date Éire Óg have beaten Scariff, Kilnamona, Tubber and drawn with O'Callaghan's Mills, coming back from a four goal deficit. The goals were scored by Stephen McNamara and Niall Daly. These results keep this young, talented Éire Óg team in line for championship honours.

Honours Won (To-date)

2 All-Ireland Senior - 1995, 1997
2 Munster Senior 1995, 1997
2 Clare Senior Football 1994, 2000
1 Clare Senior Hurling 1990
1 Clare Minor Hurling 1990
2 Minor A Championships - 1989, 1991
2 Minor League - 1990, 1991
1 Junior A plus Junior League
1 Harty Cup
1 All-Ireland Senior Colleges - 1991
I U-12 hurling
1 U-12 football
1 U-14 football
1 U-16 football

John Nevin

Éire Óg and Clare

"John Nevin hurled a fine hour at centre-back and was well up to his usual high standard."
Minor Championship, Clare versus Cork.
Clare Champion (May 17th, 1963)

Like all Ennis hurlers of his era, John Nevin picked up the skills on the streets and in the many green spaces, playing miniature All-Ireland Finals. John attended the CBS primary and secondary schools lining out with their senior team, while assisting the Rovers, a tight-knit hurling club that dominated the minor and under-21 grades in the early to mid-1960s.

I got to know John quite well and we often spoke on the street about mutual interests. He often recalled the Ennis of his youth to me. *"There used to be huge carnivals across from the Friary, which included all the usual attractions, and of course the local Skiffle groups often performed entertaining the crowds. Tony Mulvey had a Skiffle group; Eddie Browne too, and Tony Butler was a member of the Satellite Skiffle group."*

Victory for an Ennis club often reverberated throughout the town. Socially, supporters may have celebrated by going to Paddy Cons or the Queen's Hotel to listen to one or more of the many Skiffle groups that proliferated during the 1950s. Ennis boasted many such groups in the form of The Alley Cats, The Aces and the Lifford Skiffle group.

Skiffle is an American folk music derived from the Blues, which was popularised in Britain and Ireland by Tony 'Lonnie' Donegan, Chas McDevitt and Nancy Whiskey.

Skiffle is a home-made music. Some of the instruments involved a washboard, a stand up bass constructed from a tea chest, a broom handle, and a length of thick string and a guitar, probably a 'Big Ben'. Lonnie Donegan, a member of the Chris Barber Jazz Band burst on the scene in 1956 with a wonderful raucous, wild and undisciplined version of an old folk song called 'The Rock Island Line'.

Many of the local Skifflers who performed at these 'cutting' sessions included 'Boston' and Declan Blake, Jesse Keane, Michael 'Tex' Keane, Michael O'Connell, Noel Carmody and Packie Vaughan. Lonnie Donegan and Skiffle paved the way for British rock in the 1960s. The Skiffle craze is something that local people will recall with great fondness.

John Nevin continues: *"The Gaiety Cinema is another great loss. I remember the matinee and the 'Early House' as we called it – we weren't allowed go to the late house. I lived in Garraunakilla and before we moved to Summerhill we played hurling on two greens, the Clearance it was called. We hurled in front of the Old Pearl factory and if the ball was hit too hard and went in to the factory premises it would be a toss up to see who would go in because there was a big Alsatian dog in there. These were great times. The town leagues were brilliant. If you didn't turn out from your own area, people wouldn't talk to you for weeks. There was also great rivalry between Rovers and St. John's. In 1961, Rovers beat Newmarket in the Minor (A) final. Newmarket, with the exception of Michael Arthur, Jim Cullinan and Pat Cronin, had the full complement that won the county senior titles in the 1960s. But we rarely beat them afterwards. We beat them with half the town. The pick of Rovers and St. John's couldn't beat them afterwards. We lost the blend when the Rovers left the scene because when we had two minor clubs we just had barely enough to field 15. Spirit made up for it, the blend was lost, the lad who*

Lifford Skiffle Group, March 1958. Left to right: *Gerry Roche, Jim Ball, Johnny Pickford, Mattsie Hogan, Frank McInerney, Noel Carmody, Andy Carmody (Jnr.), seated.*

John Nevin (4) in action for Clare in the 1967 Munster Final (Babs' Keating is the Tipperary player pictured).

could 'break the ball', the likes of Michael Flaherty at fullback. We lost all that because the best 15 hurlers don't always make up the best team."

John had the distinction of representing both Ennis CBS and St. Flannan's at Colleges level winning two Dean Ryan Cups with the latter in 1961 and 1962. In 1962, he played centre-back on the St. Flannan's team that lost to Ennis CBS (4-2 to 2-7) in an epic Harty Cup Final. The following school year, he captained Flannan's, unusual for a day boy in those years. While at St. Flannan's he graduated to the county minor scene, making his minor debut in 1961 at Nenagh with Clare defeating Galway by 7-12 to 1-5. He played three years in the under-21 grade (1964-1966) in the company of Paddy McNamara, P. J. Purcell and P. J. (Pudsy) Ryan and others. These were fine Clare sides. The 1966 team was most unlucky to lose to a star-studded Tipperary (4-6 to 3-8) in a gruelling contest with few prisoners taken.

John played in many positions both in defence and attack. Pa Howard's collection tells us that he made his senior debut for Clare on 6 October, 1963 against Cork at the Athletic Grounds, playing at wingback. John Nevin made his senior championship debut in 1964 when Clare easily defeated Limerick by 4-14 to 2-6, at Nenagh. He continued as an automatic choice until 1968. This was a fast, stylish Clare team that was most unlucky not to win a Munster Championship or National League title.

The 1968 series of games with Kilkenny were outstanding with Nevin holding the great Eddie Keher. Their magnificent performances in those championships all stand out. John Nevin was a shining light in many of those games and while inter county honours eluded him, he picked up three minor, three under-21, one senior hurling and junior football titles with Rovers, Éire Óg and Faughs. After the premature retirement of goalkeeper Paschal O'Brien, John often represented Éire Óg in goal. He later made a big contribution to the Banner Club.

Some time ago I asked Pat Brennan, a club team-mate to describe him in a nutshell. This is what he said: - *"John Nevin was a hurler to his finger tips. His positional sense rarely let him down. He played in all grades from minor to senior for Clare and matched the best corner forwards and wing forwards in the game with his silken skills. In short he was a terrific sportsman who could have been adept at any sport he chose."*

Long after he hung up his hurley, John became a very regular letter writer to the letters page of the Clare Champion regarding what he saw as the slow erosion of the values of his native town. Whether we agreed with him or not, John Nevin always had the courage of his convictions to put pen to paper.

Footnote: Lonnie Donegan had 34 'Top 20' hits in Britain during his heyday. Tony Donegan took the nickname Lonnie from Lonnie Johnson, a Blues singer from New Orleans. Johnson had a world-wide hit in 1951 with a sentimental Irish ballad called My Mother's Eyes. Some of Donegan's hits included – The Battle of New Orleans, Lost John, and Kevin Barry. While I didn't see Lonnie Donegan first time around, I did have the pleasure of seeing him live at the Cork Jazz Festival in 1989. Lonnie Donegan passed away in 2002.

Matt Nugent

Tubber, Ennis Faughs, St. Joseph's, Clare and Munster

"Matt Nugent was a class sportsman. Apart from a hurler, he was an outstanding footballer. He could have played any sport at the highest level."
Peadar O'Brien (former Kilfenora and Faughs footballer).

Matt Nugent was one of the great hurling stylists. A native of Tubber, he first came to the notice of the Clare selectors when he represented that club.

Like many Clare hurlers of his time an All-Ireland medal eluded him, though he felt the teams of 1946 and 1955 were close enough to it. Matt Nugent made his debut about 1945 and the following year he won a National League, Aras na nGael and Thomond Feis (four county championship) with Clare. An Oireachtas medal followed in 1954 when Clare defeated the great Wexford team of that era in Croke Park. However, Clare were sensationally beaten in the Munster final of 1955 by a rampant Limerick side trained by Mick Mackey. Nugent continued to assist Clare until 1959, though he made a brief comeback in 1963.

A dual player, he won four football medals with Ennis Faughs, as well as two senior hurling medals with St. Joseph's. He continued to assist St. Joseph's until 1969 when they knocked rivals Éire Óg out of the championship, though a veteran Nugent scored 2-4 for St. Joseph's.

He was an automatic choice on the Munster Railway Cup teams of 1951 to 1954 and was selected as a sub in 1955. Three of his sons played hurling at senior level. Michael represented Eire Óg and later Clarecastle. Martin wore the colours of Eire Óg with distinction from 1975 to the mid 1990s. He also wore the saffron and blue of Clare. His younger brother Tony also played with distinction for Clare from 1981 to 1985 before emigrating to the U.S.A. Tony was honoured by the Munster selectors in 1984. Another son, Sean, took a keen interest in hurling though he didn't play competitively.

When Matt Nugent lived in Marian Avenue he instructed the youngsters of that area on the finer points of the game during the long hot Summer evenings. I vividly remember Matt Nugent and Gus Whelan* bringing groups of us regularly to the Fairgreen. After a little coaching, Matt and Gus would then delicately hit the ball to us during 'backs and

Faughs Senior Champions 1952. Back row, left to right: *Matt Nugent, Michael Brooks, Michael Considine, P.J. Kyne, Paddy King, Paddy Dowling, Tony Strand, Frank Costelloe.* ***Front row:*** *Frank O'Dea, Hugh O'Donnell, Jimmy Hanrahan, Michael Garry, Gerry Moroney (captain), Tommy Moloney, Brendan Madigan, Frankie Cassidy, Murt O'Shea.*

forwards'. He continued to take an interest in all sports up to his death in 1990. He will be remembered always as a great sportsman. As the Clare Champion newspaper reported in 1969 *"Nugent's fluent stroke and quick flick split many a defence and he accepted defeat in the same way as he did victory. It would be hard to find a more perfect example of a true sportsman".*

Matt Nugent Honours Won

3 Railway Cup (Munster)
1 National League (Clare) 1946
1 Aras na nGael (Clare) 1946
2 Thomond Feis (Clare) 1946, 1956
1 Oireachtas (Clare) 1954

2 County Championships (St. Joseph's) 1954, 1958
2 Clare Cups St. Joseph's 1953, 1957
4 County Senior Football (Faughs) 1947, 1948, 1952, 1954
1 Dean Ryan (Ennis CBS) 1941
1 Intermediate Hurling Championship – 1952 – Our Lady's Hospital
1 Intermediate Football Medal – 1946 – Faughs

Matt Nugent – Fact File
Schools – Tubber National School and Ennis CBS
Clubs: Tubber (1940-1947), Our Lady's Hospital (1948), St. Joseph's Hurling Team (1949-1969). *Returned in 1969 after a long lay off.
Ennis Faughs Football Club (1946-1955)
Matt captained St. Joseph's for 17 consecutive seasons.

Player most admired – Donal O'Grady
Biggest disappointment - losing 1951 county final
Most memorable game – 1953 – Clare Cup final

Railway Cups
1951 – Munster 4-9 Leinster 3-6
1952 - Munster 5-11 Connaught 4-2
1953 - Munster 5-7 Leinster 5-5

*Gus Whelan resided for a time with his sister Maureen O'Gorman (R.I.P.) and her late husband Frank, in Marian Avenue. Gus was a noted hurler and a member of the winning Ruan team of 1960. A pen picture of the time reads – *'Gus Whelan – Left Full Back. Won minor with Ruan in 1953. One of their soundest defenders. Can be relied upon to keep his lines cleared'.*

Gus later emigrated to the United States where he died tragically. He was electrocuted on a construction site on August 30th, 1966.

St. Joseph's won their first ever senior championship in 1954 – along the way they defeated the following –

St. Joseph's 3-7 ... ... Eire Óg 0-3
St. Joseph's 7-6 ... ... Clarecastle 1-2
St. Joseph's 3-7 ... ... Ruan 3-7
St. Joseph's 6-7 ... ... Ruan 3-5
St. Joseph's 4-4 ... ... Tulla 3-4
St. Joseph's 3-6 ... ... O'Callaghan's Mills 2-2

Paschal O'Brien

Éire Óg, Clare and Munster

"Goalkeeper O'Brien was excellent his two first half saves from Michael Keating were out of the top-drawer"
Sean King-Clare Champion, June 1968

One of Clare's finest goalkeepers, Paschal O'Brien made his competitive debut for the county in November 1964. Interestingly, he played at least four times for the Clare seniors before getting his place with the Éire Óg seniors. Paschal put his selection on the county team down to John Daly (Clarecastle). A product of the CBS, he played from about the age of 5.

Paschal recalled to me, *"I had sort of stopped playing hurling but Garry Stack suggested I play in goal. Bro. (Jim) Hennessy selected me in goal for the 1963 Harty Cup team. Seanie Barry and St. Finbarr's beat us in the final. I played outfield for CBS in the 1964 campaign. Limerick CBS, the eventual winners, beat us narrowly."* The Clare team of 1964/69, though unsuccessful, was highly regarded by hurling people and media alike. My earliest memory of inter-county hurling is when Kilkenny, All-Ireland finalists of 1964 played Clare at Cusack Park. The 'Cats' as always brought the full-complement. What I remember best was a devastating display by the fair-haired Tom Walsh and the goal keeping of Paschal O'Brien and getting autographs during the interval. *"O'Brien was outstanding in goal. Were it not for some tremendous saves from O'Brien, the winners would have coasted to a more convincing victory"* (reported the Clare Champion of November 13th 1964.)

Paschal recalled: *"We should have beaten Cork in 1966. Seanie Barry once again tormented us in the replay. Again in 1969, we lost to Cork in a replay. The team of 1968 was the best I played on. Fr. Tim Tuohy had us motivated. We played great ground hurling. We beat every team in the country but won nothing."*

The National newspapers and Gaelic publications bear out the enigma that was Clare hurling. Writing in Gaelic Weekly in 1968 Dominick Davin had this to say *"Whatever way one views Clare's bid for hurling honours in 1968 it is, at least, found to be eventful. Those three national league semi-final meetings with Kilkenny set the tempo and these were followed by another nerve-tingling game against Waterford in the Munster Championship. At the crucial hurdle though, Clare repeated the role for which nature seems to have destined them and they, once again, became the great losers. For Claremen it was depressing that June afternoon in Cork. It was the time for Clare to take Tipperary and, for more than 40 minutes, it appeared if Clare would do it. Then, with that intrinsic fatality which has become their hallmark, they crumbled. Can Clare come? Will they make amends in 1969 - burying once and for all their second half inferiority complex and fear of victory? Who really knows? What we do know is that they are still the team with the potential and most definitely number two in Munster. If Tipp are to crack next year, Clare should be the team to succeed them in the province, as they are still a fast and stylish side with players of the All-Ireland calibre of Paschal O'Brien, full back Mick Considine and 'play anywhere and everywhere' Jimmy Cullinan."* In spite of this and many other good reviews this Clare team didn't make the breakthrough.

Paschal O'Brien evades the challenge of Colum Sheehan during the Cork/Clare Championship clashes of 1966.

In 1971, Paschal was selected in goal for Munster in the Railway Cup. Though he retired prematurely, he had great memories of the game and in December 1994 he recalled those memories to me. *"It was an honour to play for Clare alongside Jimmy Cullinan, Vincent Loftus and Liam Danagher. I admired Mick Roche (Tipperary), Tom Ryan (Tipp/Clare). Ryan gave a wonderful display against Roche at the Cork Athletic grounds in 1968. Vincent Loftus had great stick-work. Jimmy Smyth was a wonderful sportsman; he was coming towards the end of his career when I came on. Naoise Jordan, Johnny McCarthy, Dermot Fitzgerald, Mick O'Shea and Michael Arthur are others I hold in high regard. Mick O'Shea was a fine athlete, he could play anywhere. I retired in 1971. I'd lost the appetite. I regretted the decision, I was only 25."*

Honours Won

1 Dr. Rodgers Cup (Ennis CBS) 1961.
1 Senior Championship (Éire Óg) 1966.
2 Minor (A) Rovers.
3 Under 21 (A) - 2 with Rovers and 1 with Éire Óg 1964, 1965, 1966.

Top 10

The following ratings in hurling are based on inter-county games from St. Patrick's Day to Sunday, April 14th 1970 inclusive. We would remind readers that the ratings are based on a points system and, at the end of the year, the totals reveal the stars of the season under review.

1. Mick Roche (Tipperary)
2. Jim Treacy (Kilkenny)
3. Len Gaynor (Tipperary)
4. Pat Henchy (Clare)
5. Ted Carroll (Kilkenny)
6. Paschal O'Brien (Clare)
7. Michael Keating (Tipperary)
8. Paddy Barry (Cork)
9. Liam Devanney (Tipperary)
10. Jimmy Cullinan (Clare)

From Gaelic Sport, April 1970

Paschal O'Brien was originally picked to play in goal for Clare in the National Hurling League tie 1st November 1964 against Galway. He had previous commitments to Rovers in the Under-21 championship. Jim Ryan played in goal. Paschal replaced the Tubber man at half-time.

The Éire Óg junior team that contested the 1964 Junior A final was:

Paschal O'Brien, Aidan Tuttle, Des Neylon, Paddy Gilligan, Bernie Dilger, Micheál Casey, Brendan Doyle, Gerry Roche, Noel Pyne, Massey Dilger, Johnny Guerin, Peter Brigdale, Georgie Dilger, Paddy Duggan, Jimmy McNamara. Subs. Pat Coffey, Colum Flynn. Cratloe won by 2-8 to 3-3.

Peadar O'Brien

Kilfenora, Ennis Faughs and Clare

Peadar O'Brien.

Peadar O'Brien was born into the football heartland of north-west Clare. A native of Kilfenora, Peadar remembers stalwart Kilfenora players of the 1940s, the likes of Dermot and Tommy Hogan, P. J. Lynch and Sean Halloran, men who backboned Kilfenora football at this time. When Peadar was only 11 he went to England to school for a few years, where he was introduced to soccer and cricket. Some years later after leaving school, he worked as a railway clerk in Scotland, where he played junior soccer with Kilsyth Rangers. Later he played semi-professional with Albion Rovers in the Scottish Second Division. However, during this time he often returned to Kilfenora, where he assisted his club playing at all levels. I asked him to compare the game of soccer then with the game now. *"It's hard to judge. It was a more direct game. You tried to play in the other team's half. You got rid of the ball. It was a different type of soccer. It was more attacking. Today it's all tactics. Shortly after returning home to Clare I joined Ennis Faughs Gaelic Football team. This was about 1954. I played centre-field with Fr. Michael Considine, whom I hold in the highest regard. Other Faughs players from this era I remember include Brendan Purcell, Barney O'Connor, Mickey Butler and Dermot Leahy. I really admired Michael Garry, our goalkeeper and Murt O'Shea was a great fullback. Gerry Moroney was very tidy; his man might get the ball but he certainly wouldn't pass him. Michael Blake and Matt Nugent were outstanding sportsmen. They could have played any sport. Geoff Brennan, the Cork inter-county player also played for Faughs. The west Clare clubs probably resented us because of our pick, but we were all legal."*

After being spotted playing soccer by the Vigilante Committee, Peadar was banned from playing Gaelic for 6 months. This effectively ended his ties with Faughs. He then returned full-time to Association Football and played semi-pro with Limerick AFC* in the company of Mick Lipper and Beaver Cronin. Limerick was probably one of the first professional or semi-professional clubs to be formed in this part of the country. Later he played for Ennis United, an amalgamation of the Clare league clubs. Ennis did very well in the Limerick League and Peadar recalls wonderful players like Michael Arthur, Peter White, Audi Geres and the Hosey brothers playing for Ennis United. *"The Hoseys and Peter White were from Scotland. Audi Geres was Austrian or German and they came to Ennis to work. Naturally being brought up in soccer they were good. They had all the moves but Michael Arthur was good too. Be it at hurling, rugby or soccer, Michael Arthur just had it. He was a wonderful soccer player and was a victim of the ban on foreign games."*

Three generations of Lifford AFC - *Peadar O'Brien with his son Noel and grand-daughter Janet Dinan. Janet won two All Ireland medals with Lifford AFC in 1993 and 1994.*

Sporting prowess often breaks out in families and Peadar attributes his Gaelic football skills to his uncle, Jack O'Brien, who played for Kilfenora. Peadar's nephew is none other than James Hanrahan, who kept goal for Clare over the last decade and won a Munster Senior Football Championship medal in 1992. James is a son of Millie Hanrahan, formerly of Kilfenora. Another Kilfenora man, who kept goal for Clare is Michael Connole; like James, he too won a Munster Senior Championship medal with Clare in 1917.

Peadar's son, Noel, is another all-rounder at handball, hurling and soccer. Noel played with the great Avenue United team of the 1980s, a club Peadar regards very highly for their professional approach to the game and their fabulous attacking style of football. Peadar's grandson, George Dinan, is hugely promising at athletics, while his granddaughter, Janet Dinan, won All-Ireland Ladies Soccer honours with Lifford AFC, under the guidance of Damien Walsh. Regarding all sports, Peadar considers hurling the greatest and his favourite, though he never played the game. After leaving Gaelic football he missed the bodily contact and the camaraderie of the game, but he has great memories of his soccer days with Limerick AFC, Ennis United and Rockmount.

The Faughs team that lost the football championship replay to Doonbeg in September 1955 lined out as follows: -

Paddy Kerin (Goalie), Michael Blake, Murt O'Shea, Gerry Moroney, Peadar O'Brien, Dermot Leahy, Barney O'Connor, Tony Strand, Geoff Brennan, Bobby Burke, Jimmy Smyth, Colm Madigan, Michael 'Doc' Doherty, Brendan Purcell, Hugh O'Donnell.

George Dinan

A sporting all rounder. George has played representative hurling and Gaelic Football, while excelling at athletics.

Some of his honours to-date include:

U/16 Gold 4x200 Relay All Ireland - 2003

U/15 Bronze 4x200 Relay All Ireland - 2002

U/16 Silver Long Jump - Munster - 2003

U/16 Gold 4x200 Relay - Munster - 2003

U/15 Silver 200m Hurdles - Munster 2002

U/15 Silver 4x200 Relay - Munster - 2002

U/15 Bronze Long Jump - Munster - 2002

George Dinan.

Plus North Munster Schools - Gold/Silver/Bronze - at sprint/hurdles/long jump - relay etc. and numerous awards in Clare Athletics.

P.J. O'Dea

Kilrush Shamrocks, Faughs. Clare and Munster

I met P.J. and Mary O'Dea of Chicago in Ennis in September 1997. Naturally, P.J. was home for the All-Ireland Hurling Final. I was introduced to P.J. by his great friends Tony (R.I.P.) and Michael Butler. I was aware of P.J.s footballing prowess, I knew he played for Kilrush, Clare and Munster; but, it was hurling we spoke of. P.J. recalled his days in Ennis playing with Rovers, Dals and Faughs. The Dals, whom P.J. represented at senior level, were going badly, easily dispatched by Ruan in 1948.

P.J. O'Dea and Seán Connolly in the Munster Railway Cup colours - early 1950's.

Despite this, the Faughs juniors held Ruan to a 5-1 to 5-1 draw in the Junior (A) championship final. *"I played hurling with the Old Mill Street Rovers. They were the greatest bunch of people I ever played with. They were great characters. The old ladies inspired us. Hurling wasn't new to me. We loved hurling in West Clare. We had a good junior team in the west. We could hold our own with the best of them. Sean Mounsey was the star of the Rovers - a lovely hurler, also the Molloys, Johnny and Paschal. Tony McEnery was a very good goalkeeper. I never enjoyed anything as much as the street leagues in Ennis. They were terrific."* After the drawn Junior (A) final of 1948, the Clare Champion reported *"Faughs fielded a good back-line but lacked a good finisher like Smyth. (Paddy) Duggan outwitted his opponents but retired with a hand injury. P.J.*

O'Dea and John Keane were outstanding with Miko Ball, John Molloy and Reggie Connellan the pick of the attack."

The replay, played in a 'sea of mud' with pools of water covering many parts of the pitch, was called off mid-way through the second half with Ruan leading by 8-5 to 3-0. Despite this disappointment, Faughs captured the senior football title of 1948. P.J. recalled this season: *"My best position was centre half back and my best game ever for Faughs was in Kilfenora against a North Clare selection (Doolin), in the first round of the championship. I loved playing in the half back line. I was an attacking half back. We won in 1948. The final wasn't played until March or April 1949 because Kilkee had their holiday-makers and they would play illegally for Kilkee. I loved my time with the Faughs. We had great players in Sean Connolly, Murt O'Shea, Paddy Dowling, Tony Strand - 'a good bit of stuff'. Afterwards Matt Nugent and Jimmy Smyth played for the so-called 'League of Nations'. Gerry Keniry of Doonbeg was a big loss to the game when he emigrated. Noel Crowley, E.J. Carroll and Peter Daly were amongst the best. I think my duel with Eamon Boland (Roscommon) in the 1951 Railway Cup final is the toughest football I ever played."*

About this time Seamus O'Ceallaigh ran a series of articles on the greats of Gaelic football. Amongst those he profiled were Jackie Lyne, Padraig Carney, Bill McCorry, Frank Stockwell, James Gallagher, Gerry O'Malley and P.J. O'Dea - in-depth articles all. Jim Gallagher of Ballyshannon, Donegal and Ulster had this to say: *"I take training very seriously. I believe that brisk walking is the best means for keeping fit, apart from ball practice. I have already played against most of the star half-forwards in the country and I rate Eamon Young (Cork), P.J. O'Dea (Clare), Kevin Armstrong and Sean Gibson (Antrim) the pick of them."* Great praise indeed for the Kilrush and Faughs man, who was first selected for his county in 1946 and an automatic choice on until about 1953 when a knee injury kept him out of the game for a considerable time.

P.J. emigrated in 1954, first to England where he togged out for Warwickshire. His travels took him to the United States and he spent time in Toronto, Los Angeles and San Francisco before settling in Chicago. Every September this wonderful ambassador of sport (swimming, handball, billiards and G.A.A.) makes the long journey home on All Ireland final day. Long may it last!

Noel Pyne

St Flannan's, Rovers, Éire Óg, Clare and Munster

"The heart of the Rovers was the 'Tage'.
John 'Dugger' Kearney and P.J. Summerly were great mentors.
Many of that Rovers team went on to play for the county
and about three played for Munster".
Noel Pyne

Like many good hurlers, Noel Pyne began his hurling in the CBS street leagues. Though Noel came from Abbey Street, he lined out with the Boreen. This was the golden era of Ennis hurling. Éire Óg were county champions in 1956 and 1957. St. John's fielded a second team and John's and Rovers were amongst the top of the pile at juvenile and minor ranks. After leaving the CBS Primary School, Noel attended St. Flannan's, as was the tradition in his family. Noel played Harty Cup in 1962 and 1963. Coming through the successful Rovers nursery, he made his senior debut with Clare in the mid-1960s.

Club rivals and County team mates *Noel Pyne and Paddy McNamara (Newmarket) at the launch of 'Ballads of the Banner' October 1998.* Courtesy of Michael Keane.

Noel recalled his sporting days to me: *"I played for Rovers. Vincent Loftus approached me to play for them though my brother, Dickie played for St. John's. We lost to them in a famous juvenile final. We won Minor 'A' in 1961, 1962 and 1963 and u/21 in 1964, 1965 and 1966 and senior championship 1966 (Éire Óg), so most of us won at least 6 medals in a row. Both St. John's and Rovers were very strong. The heart of the Rovers was the 'Tage'. John 'Dugger' Kearney and P.J. Summerly were great mentors. We had great respect for the mentors. Jack Heaslip was one of the main men with Éire Óg. A very decent man, he was always available for the club. My father loved sport - golf and hurling especially. He passed it on to us."*

It's hard to believe, but Noel Pyne and Paschal O'Brien played senior hurling for Clare before getting the call up for the club. Noel and Paschal shone with the Éire Óg juniors in 1964. *"We had great fun, Aidan Tuttle was full back, Paschal was in goal, Paddy Gilligan and Des Neylon. The banter was great. Cratloe beat us in the final. Some of us progressed from there. We began building a good team about 1964. In 1966 we beat Newmarket in the senior championship. We thought we were there for a long spell. We were young and business like, but the Newmarket team was exceptional. They started to win and we just couldn't put them away, but we should have been able to take them now and again. At one time Éire Óg had about 9 players on the county team. Our best chance was the County Final of 1965. We should have won it. It was a fine County final. 1966 was a hard won county final, 3 games with Clarecastle. We beat St. Joseph's, Tubber, Newmarket, Whitegate as well".*

Noel Pyne was part of a very good Clare team from 1966-1970. Though unsuccessful, they gave us great value and great memories. When not in Cusack Park I recall Micheál O'Hehir's and Liam Campbell's commentaries from Croke Park and Thurles on the radio.

In 1969, Noel was honoured as Clare Hurler of the Year. Though this highly talented Éire Óg team failed to deliver after 1966, they served up excellent hurling against The Blues, the Magpies and Glen Rovers. In 1969, Éire Óg and Newmarket gave us a cracking Clare Cup final, with Derry Pyne hurling a great hour on Jimmy Cullinan.

After the Munster championship replay defeat to Limerick at the Gaelic Grounds in 1970, Noel Pyne retired from the game. Though Noel admits he went long before his time he has no regrets. *"Rather than retire, I probably should have taken a year off from hurling. I was only 25 when I retired. The golf was going well for me. I attempted a comeback in 1974. I trained in St. Flannan's on my own - later I played on Tony Kelly during a training session and I discovered how out of touch I was. I didn't play against Brian Borus in 1974; I felt I wasn't ready. I needed a lot more training. If I had just taken a year off I might have come back with my batteries recharged. Golf can get a grip on you. I won the Galway Scratch Cup - and the Knox Cup in 1972. I'd like to have played a few more years' hurling in the company of Sean Stack and John Callinan but I made a clean break and have no regrets".*

Honours Won

1 Railway Cup (Munster) 1969

Clare Hurler of the Year Award - 1969

1 Senior Championship, Éire Óg - 1966
3 Minor A (Rovers)
3 U/21 – 2 Rovers, 1 Éire Óg.
1 Junior (A) Football 1967

The Éire Óg team that played in the Clare Cup Final of 1969 was: -
Paschal O'Brien, Des Neylon, Vincent Loftus, Sean O'Driscoll, Joe Barry, Noel Pyne, Paul Higgins, Pat Brennan, Tom Ryan, John Dunne (captain), Paul Glynn, Derry Pyne, Eric Hanrahan, Georgie Dilger, Massey Dilger.
Sub: Martin Bradley

Noel Ryan

Éire Óg and Clare

"I played soccer with Noel Ryan at Cork Celtic. A grand fellow. I played hurling against him later. Noel played a couple of seasons with Celtic. A great man in the air".
Jimmy Barry Murphy

Noel Ryan was one of Clare's most polished hurlers during the 1970's. A versatile sportsman at all chosen sports, he represented Clare seniors at Gaelic football regularly. He played soccer with St. Michael's, Janesboro, and with Cork Celtic at league of Ireland level.

Noel Ryan.

A member of a sporting family, his brothers P.J., Tommie and Michael all represented Éire Óg at senior level, while his sister Pauline Kilmartin won an All-Ireland junior camogie medal with Clare in 1974.

A product of Ennis CBS, Noel came up through the ranks of Rice Cup, White Cup and Dean Ryan Cup. He featured on the Harty Cup teams of 1967/68 and 1968/69.

In 1970, Noel played with the very exciting Braids Utd. F.C. Later still he was selected on the Clare soccer team which captured the Oscar Traynor Youths Cup, beating Galway, Cork, Waterford and Dublin along the way. This talented side was put together by Manager Pat O'Brien and Brendan O'Loughlin. The cup final was staged at the Ennis Showgrounds with Dublin A.U.L. installed as favourites. Inspired by the Kenny brothers, Clare took the game to Dublin. The home supporters came to life when Martin Irons headed Clare into the lead after Michael Kenny had struck the crossbar. Clare were now rampant and it looked all over when Terry Walton was brought down in the box. But Michael Kenny's well-struck penalty was saved by Quinn. Clare, still on top, kept up the pressure and

Noel Ryan holds aloft the cup following Éire Ógs Intermediate Football success in 1985.

a dazzling piece of individual play by Noel Ryan, who beat four defenders before crashing the ball home to make it 2-Nil. It was a marvellous day for Clare sport and afterwards Brendan O'Loughlin described it as *"the greatest day of my life"*. The cup was presented to Steve Kenny by C.I. Liddy, Chairman of the F.A.I. junior league. Jim Younger, secretary of Dublin A.U.L. paid tribute to a fine Clare side. *"We were beaten by a very good team with a lot of talent. I was particularly impressed by Peter Webb, Steve Kenny and Noel Ryan".*

Shortly afterwards Noel Ryan was signed by League of Ireland side, Cork Celtic. He made his debut at the Showgrounds in a 2-2 draw with Finn Harps. Ryan went on to play exceptional football with Cork, scoring one or two hat tricks.

During research for my book 'Against the Wind' it was my privilege to meet and interview many celebrated hurlers. On a beautiful summer's morning in 1996 I spoke to the Cork hurling manager, Jimmy Barry Murphy. After speaking at length on the game, Barry Murphy briefly turned his attention to soccer and recalled his days with Cork Celtic, recalling Noel Ryan. *"I was out of hurling for a short time and Celtic asked me to sign. I played with Noel Ryan at Cork Celtic, a grand fellow, a great man in the air. Afterwards I hurled against him."*

In 1972, Noel returned to the saffron and blue and starred in the county's 3-9 to 3-8 win over Cork in the U/21 hurling championship. Unfortunately, Clare were pipped by Tipperary (4-10 to3-10) in the Munster final. The following year he made his senior championship debut in Clare's 3-11 to3-9 defeat to Limerick. Ryan was described in the local press as *'Clare's most polished forward.'* He played possibly his last game for Clare in the autumn of 1981 when Offaly visited Cusack Park. Before the game the Clare players formed a guard of honour for the Offaly men and team captain, Timmy Ryan made a presentation to Padraig Horan to mark the midlanders achievement in winning the All-Ireland. Clare County Board Chairman, Tadgh Murphy, officially welcomed Offaly to Ennis and the Offalymen showed their appreciation after the game when they applauded the home team as they made their way to the dressing rooms.

Noel's son, Barry has carried on the sporting tradition with League of Ireland side U.C.D. He has since moved to Shamrock Rovers.

Noel Ryan – Fact File and Honours Won.
2 County Senior Championship 1980, 1982 – Éire Óg
Minor and u/21 hurling – Éire Óg
1 Intermediate Football – 1985
1 Banner Cup
1 Junior Championship – Éire Óg - 1990
1 All Ireland youths soccer medal – Clare 1971
1 FAI junior cup medal – Janesboro – Limerick
Haughey Cup medals – St. Michael's AFC

Represented Clare at minor, Under-21 and senior hurling. A dual GAA player, Noel played senior football with Clare and played soccer for Cork Celtic in the League of Ireland in the 1971-72; 1972-1973 seasons.

Toughest opponents in hurling - Noel O'Dwyer (Tipperary), and Jackie O'Gorman, Sean Hehir and Gus Lohan

Favourite Position (centre-back). Though he generally played centre-forward or full-forward for the county.

Biggest disappointment – Losing 1975 County final

Clare Youths Soccer XI v. Dublin – June 1971

Michael Huismann, Pat O'Neill, Steve Kenny (captain), Terry Walton, Peter Webb, Gerry Gilligan, Martin Woods, Martin Irons, Noel Ryan, Michael Kenny, David Connellan.

Reserve: Matt O'Donnell at the interval. Daithi Walton (not used).

Path to the Final
Clare 1 ... ... Galway 1 - A.E.T. – Our Lady's
Clare 1 ... ... Galway 0 - Terryland Park
Clare 0 ... ... Cork 0 – Church Road, Cork (game abandoned due to dangerous waterlogged condition of pitch)
Clare 4 ... ... Cork 1 – Turner's Cross
Clare 2 ... ... Waterford 1 – Angers
Clare 2 ... ... Dublin 0 - Showgrounds

Other Ennis lads to play in various rounds and friendlies included: -

Flan Hehir, Tony Considine, Seanie Clohessy, Noel Glynn, Ciaran Earlie and the late Billy Greer. Billy played in goal in the opening round against Galway and in the semi-final win over Waterford. Tony Considine played against Galway at Our Lady's. A broken hand ruled him out of contention.

Michael 'Aoner' Sheridan

Ennis Dals, Faughs and Clare

"Sheridan, Hennessy and Kennedy combined well. Sheridan took his goal in remarkable style."
Clare v. Tipperary clash -
Opening of Newmarket-on-Fergus pitch - 1934
Clare Champion

Aoner learned his hurling at the Boys National School. A first cousin of Freddie Garrihy and Jackie Duffy, hurling was in Aoner's blood, playing minor, junior, intermediate and senior hurling for the county.

Aoner recalls *"We beat Clooney in the 1934 county final. Clooney had the pick of Ruan. Amby Power was a selector on that Clooney team. He came into T.J. Meehan's pub in O'Connell Street. T.J. was secretary of the Dalcassian club and Amby said to him on the Friday before the match 'win, lose or draw, we have the match'. T.J. got worried and decided to look up the registration and found that Peadar Dervin, a Galway man wasn't registered. I was first sub when that happened, I got my place on the starting fifteen. Paudge Hynes, Peadar Flanagan and I were about the only newcomers on the 1934 team. The bulk of the team were from the 1928/29 era".*

The importance of a nickname was brought home to Aoner when he first ran for the council elections. *"I went as Michael Sheridan and I lost by six votes. The following election I ran as Aoner and I flew in. I was on the council for 27 years and served as chairman in 1975. I really enjoyed my time in politics and was very proud of playing my part in getting a swimming pool for Ennis and the de-centralisation of government offices to the town. I was the one who put the notice of motion about the de-centralisation in progress and Ray McSharry did the rest."*

I then asked him how he received his pet name. *"When the Free State Army and DeValera were at loggerheads, I lived in Barrack Street next door to Duffy's public house. Duffy's was popular with the soldiers. I used to go in as a young lad and, if I got their backs turned, I'd take a swig of their stout. One day a soldier caught me and bought me a medium (1/2 pint). I was very young at the time and he asked me straight out 'what are you'? Now, at the time De Valera was a Sinn Feiner and the Market and Barrack Street were all Sinn Fein. I couldn't say to the soldier*

I was a Sinn Feiner so I said I was an 'Aoner'. The name stuck with me after that. You couldn't go down the market unless you were Sinn Fein."

Aoner was on and off the Clare team during the years 1936-1941. I asked Aoner who were the best hurlers he saw or admired. *"The 'Blues' without a doubt were a great club, though we beat them in 1934. They were all big men - Monty Murphy, Tony Nealon, John Joe Doyle. Club hurling was hard then. Feakle and Clooney were very good. Mick Halloran of Clooney was a great hurler. The best full-back I saw was Jimbo Higgins (Newmarket). Peadar Flanagan of the Dals was some hurler. He was a student in Flannan's when he played for us. Mickie White, Brudsy McCarthy and Paddence O'Loughlin were good. On the inter-county scene the Limerick team of Mackey's era was outstanding. Clare was the only team to hold them during a 5 year spell. I hold Martin Kennedy of Tipperary in high regard; he was a great full-forward. Lory Meagher was a great man. Jimmy Smyth had everything. After the championship success in 1941 the DALS went into a low decline. By 1945 the Faughs came into being. The name Faughs came from the Old Mill Street side, that was the Old Faughs back in my father's time at the turn of the 20th century. They had a private meeting in Moloney's house in Steele's Terrace. Ralphie (Burns) and I went over to the Faughs and we won the Intermediate championship. They should never have dropped the name Dalcassians."*

It was with the Faughs that Aoner Sheridan ended his hurling career.

Honours Won

2 County Senior medals. 1934, 1941 - Dals
1 Clare Cup 1937 -Dals
1 Intermediate - 1945 -Faughs
1 Junior (A) – Kilbeacanty

Tim Smythe

O'Callaghan's Mills and Ennis

Tim Smythe, athlete and politician, was born near Feakle in 1905. His parents died when he was young. He was reared at Clonloum, O'Callaghan's Mills, by his Aunt, Mrs. Nora Lenihan and he attended O'Callaghan's Mills primary school.

His athletic career began in May 1925 at a sports meeting in Feakle, when he finished second in the half mile event. In 1926 he won several races in the 1 – 4 mile distance. In 1927, he started training and competed with Limerick City Harriers and he was introduced to cross-country running. O'Callaghan's Mills didn't yet have a club of their own so in 1928, Tim was invited to join the Ryan Athletic Club in Thurles. During the subsequent track season he won 3-mile and 5-mile Munster championships, in addition to numerous wins in Clare, Limerick and Tipperary.

An athletic club was founded in O'Callaghan's Mills in October 1928. Tim, now with his native parish, finished in second and third place in the individual placings at the 1929 All-Ireland junior and senior championships. Taking third place in the senior competition earned him a place on the Irish team at the International cross-country championships. He later took part in the three country International series involving England, Scotland and Ireland, coming in first. In 1930, he won the first All-Ireland individual championship and once again he was chosen for the International cross-country team running at Leamington Spa. Further Munster championship successes followed and he also won the Daily Express Cup and various county sports events. In 1931, he captured the All-Ireland senior individual title.

Tim Smythe's finest hour was on 28th March 1931 at Baldoyle Racecourse near Dublin. He won the World Cross-Country Championship in a time of 48 minutes 52 seconds, 19 seconds ahead of the Englishman, Winfield. Despite the bad weather conditions, Tim had beaten some of the world's best runners including Deaken and Evenson from England. This win was the climax of his running career but he went on to win many more races. In the 1931 track season he was successful in twenty-two events, over distances from 1 mile to 10 miles and including 5,000 metres in the Ireland versus France contest. He won again in the 1932 senior cross-country championship and qualified for a place on the international team for that year's championship held in Brussels. Later that year he represented Ireland against Scotland in Edinburgh. Between 1929 – 1937 Tim won ten All-Ireland championships and was on the International cross-country team on nine consecutive occasions. He won every Munster track championship from 1-6 miles. He won hundreds of medals and prizes during his running career and continued to take part in competitive athletics until 1949.

Tim Smythe entered politics in 1948 when he was a founder member in Clare of Clann na Poblachta. He unsuccessfully contested the general election for the party. He was first elected to Clare County Council in 1950 on a Clann na Poblachta ticket. After Clann na Poblachta dissolved, he became an Independent candidate and in three subsequent elections he topped the poll. He was a member of the County Council until 1974 when he retired from politics. He was also a member of Ennis UDC from 1967 to 1974.

Tim was also involved in hurling. He was Treasurer of Clare County GAA Board from 1959 to 1963 and a member of Éire Óg hurling club. He trained the Ennis Faughs team to win the County Intermediate Championship in 1945. His innovative training methods also helped Éire Óg to win two senior titles in 1956 and 1957. Bobby Burke takes up the story *"Éire Óg was founded to arrest the decline of hurling in Ennis and after a lean year in 1952 in junior hurling, a decision was taken to enter senior ranks in 1953. Progress was painfully slow, as most of the senior panel were either in minor grade or a year or two above minor. Then Tim Smythe entered the scene. He agreed to train the team and a close association between Tim and the team started. With the passing of time this bond developed into a family relationship so that trainer and team became one. Tim never professed to be an expert on hurling and he left the finer points and tactical moves to others. Physical fitness was his responsibility and the team's performance was the proof, if proof was needed, of how well he did his job. His training methods were tough. The schedule was paced over a certain period so that there was no peaking in mid-term. If he thought a player was overdoing it, he told him to cut down."*

In addition to his athletic and political interests he was a keen huntsman and was a staunch member of the Old Mill Street Harriers, with whom he hunted every Sunday morning.

Tim Smythe married Maura Duggan of Ennis. All members of their family had sporting interests. His son, Barry represented St. Flannan's in the Harty Cup and later gave many sterling performances for Éire Óg and

Maura and Tim Smythe pictured with Seán Reid, at a social in 1973. Seán (on right) was a native of Castlefin, Co. Donegal, and a member of the Tulla Céilí Band from 1947-1965. He was also a member of the Ennis branch of Comhaltas Ceoltoirí Éireann. The branch held monthly meetings at the Queens Hotel (McKaigney's) and afterwards played sessions at my parents home in the Gort Road. Some of the musicians I remember best include P. Joe Hayes, J.C. Talty, Peter O'Loughlin, Michael Preston, Joe Cooley, Gus Tierney, Paddy O'Donoghue and of course Seán Reid. Seán who played uileann pipes and piano, passed away in the late 1970s.

Clare. He was selected on the Munster Railway cup team in 1982. Barry's older brothers, Conor and Michael, were promising hurlers at Colleges level, both representing Ennis CBS in the Harty Cup. Michael also played rugby with distinction while Maura Smythe was an outstanding athlete at Coláiste Muire.

Tim Smythe died in 1982 after a brief illness. The Tim Smythe Park, formerly the Fairgreen, is named after him.

Clare Sports Stars 1969 – selected at the Ennistymon Family Festival – June 22.

Tim Smythe (Hall of Fame)
Michael Haugh (Gaelic Football)
Tommy Flynn (Boxing)
Noel Pyne (Hurling)
Tony Lynch (Rugby)
Marie Larkin (Badminton)

Ennis' Football – A Brief History

This book is primarily about hurling and the wonderful tradition of the game in Ennis. However, Gaelic football also has a rich history in the town, and teams such as the Dals, the Faughs and more recently Éire Óg have brought sporting glory. This chapter will briefly outline some of the tremendous successes in football enjoyed by the Ennis clubs, but football deserves its own history to be written, in order to do justice to the many great sportsmen who played that game. Hopefully, we will see such a book done at some stage.

The earliest football in Ennis dates back to the turn of the 20th century and the very successful era of 1897-1911 when the Ennis Dals and Kilrush dominated the senior football championship. In 1934, Spailpín Fánach wrote the following: *"In the distant days of 1887, the name of the Ennis Dals graced the records of the GAA in Clare. Then a famous game in football was played between Ennis and Ardsollus. For a decade it continued to play in championship football, but its first rise to fame was in 1897, when it won the senior championship. This year saw the start of the memorable matches between Ennis Dals and Kilrush Shamrocks. The Dals club has an envious record, as in the eleven years between 1904 and 1914 they annexed seven senior football championships, truly a great achievement".*

Right up to the late 1920s the Ennis Dals were a formidable force and in 1929 they reached the pinnacle of their success, winning Senior Hurling honours and Clare Cup, as well as Senior Football honours and Cusack Cup. There was a wealth of sporting talent in Ennis at the time and there were eight dual players involved in both codes.

Moving on, the 1930s was a period when football went somewhat into decline. Yet the Dals still won the occasional junior title. And Ennis still produced its share of competent players. In 1941, four prominent Ennis footballers won senior football championship honours with Kilfenora. One of these players was Sean Guinnane and he recalled the choice of club was made easy due to the very friendly existing relations between the Dals and Kilfenora. The decision was a very fortunate one, as the North Clare Gaels benefited by the Ennis addition and achieved a long awaited ambition.

***Ennis Dalcassians Football team, Clare County Champions 1904. Back row, left to right:** J. Malone (President), Jim Hayes, Pako Malone, Fr. W. Armstrong, Patrick Moroney, James F. Corbett, Tom McNamara, F. McMahon. **Middle row:** Ml. Smith, Paddy Kenny, Miko Connellan, Joe W. Nono, Miko Duggan, Donat Callinan, Michael Fuody. **Front row:** Tom McNamara, – –, – –.*

By 1942, Ennis had returned to senior ranks and they were allowed to draw from the military personnel stationed at Firgrove and Rineanna, achieving moderate success. But 1943 saw changes taking place and a new hurling club to be known as '**The Faughs**' was founded. This club was confined solely to the sparsely populated Lifford area and its formation had come about due to a split in the Dalcassian Club. On 22nd July 1944, the Faughs had their first win. The Clare Champion of that week carried the following atmospheric account: "*Lifford was the scene of unusual activity on Sunday afternoon last. Many an onlooker must have watched in amazement and wondered what all the preparations were for. Horses were being harnessed to gaily painted wagonettes, shining traps and side-cars were standing in readiness for a journey, while a big crowd had assembled in the vicinity. Soon all the vehicles were filled with young men, some carrying football outfits, others equipped with musical instruments. With a cheer of good-luck from the crowd, the parade moved off. The Faughs team and their supporters had started on their victorious journey to Ballynacally. The horse-drawn vehicles, which the club had obtained for the day, accompanied by numerous cyclists, presented a sight reminiscent of the times before the advent of the internal combustion engine.*

The many footballers who made the journey from Ennis gave the team a great deal of vocal support in their victory over Caherea, whom they defeated by 0-6 to 1-1. Both the teams and their supporters were jubilant at their victory. This is understandable, as it was the Faughs' first win, this being the maiden year of the club. Previous to this, they had been beaten by Clondegad by one point after a hard game, and had forced a draw with Caherea. Great credit must go to the Faughs club on their win, as they had to overcome innumerable difficulties in fielding a team. The Faughs' perseverance and success goes to prove the old adage 'Where there's a will, there's a way'.

In 1946, new decisions were made, which were to have significant implications for Gaelic games in Ennis. At a meeting called by Jack Spellissy that year, it was decided that the Dals Club could pick for senior purposes from the entire town in hurling and the Faughs could do likewise for football. The decision paid off handsomely for the Faughs and they were about to enter a very productive period.

Prominent dual player, Sean Guinnane sums up this time when he says: *"from 1946 to 1955, a span of ten years, the Faughs held the limelight. This was a most exceptional achievement, particularly when one considers that Ennis is so far removed from what is generally termed the Football Area. For such a successful run, much credit must go to the men behind the scenes – the officials in charge in the initial stages and for most of the decade of glory were, Jack Carroll (Chairman), Tom Collins (Secretary) and Sean Moloney (Treasurer). The record of achievement speaks for itself, six senior championship final appearances, one Cusack Cup title, and one intermediate title."*

In 1947, it was expected that O'Curry's, the county champions from the previous year, would retain the senior championship. For more than 40 minutes in their semi-final clash with Faughs, this possibility looked on. The O'Curry Club drawn from Carrigaholt/Doonaha led Ennis by 3-4 to 0-5 with less than 20 minutes to go. Then in an amazing turnaround, the Faughs scored a goal and eight points to win by the narrow margin of 1-13 to 3-6. In the final, the Faughs had one point to spare over Clohanes. It was the beginning of a great era.

Faughs retained the championship in 1948, beating O'Curry's by 10 points to 4 in the final. Due to objection followed by counter objection between Kilkee and Faughs in the semi-final, over Kilkee allegedly playing illegal players, the final between Faughs and O'Curry's wasn't played until the Spring of 1949. It's possible that the delay in the staging of the final had an adverse effect on O'Curry's. The winning Faughs team produced outstanding performances from Tony Galvin, P. J. O'Dea, Murt O'Shea and Jimmy Walker.

Murt O'Shea (Faughs) leads the Clare team prior to the 1949 Munster Senior Final against Cork. The other Clare players in order include Jack Moroney, (Miltown) 2, Tommy Kelly (O'Curry's) 3, Paddy Dowling (Faughs) 4, Paddy Crohan (5). Courtesy of George Bradley (Kilkee).

The mid 1940s also marked a new beginning for the Clare County Football team and the Ennis Faughs were well represented on the county team of 1947 and 1948. In 1947, Clare reached the final of the National Football League, only to be beaten by Derry on a score of 2-9 to 2-5. Again, the Banner men made a significant impact in the 1948 National League with a run of victories. But they were halted by a strong Cork side at the quarterfinal stage. At local level, the Faughs (who had become known as the "United Nations" team) collected their second consecutive county title.

The Clare team of 1949 caused tremendous excitement when they beat Kerry in the Munster Championship at Cusack Park, Ennis by 3-7 to 1-8. The win led them to a meeting with Cork in the Munster Final, which was played in Limerick. The sense of anticipation and excitement was terrific, but on the day they were beaten by the seasoned Cork side. The defeat of the county team seems to have left its mark on the Faughs and they bowed out of the county championship, leaving the final to be contested by Miltown and Kilrush.

However, loss and disappointment were short lived for the Faughs and in 1952 they returned to the top in Clare football, defeating Kilrush in Miltown. 1953 could have been a double but they lost 1-6 to 0-7 to Miltown. John Drury, a member of the Clare minor team, was the difference. His goal from a free paved the way for victory.

Michael Garry (above) and Frankie Cassidy were amongst the prominent players on the Clare Minor Football team of 1953 that reached the All Ireland final. Michael was an outstanding goalkeeper and in the one season he played minor, junior and senior championship for Faughs and Clare. Michael Garry is pictured in 1983 following a visit home to Ennis from Australia.

1954 Controversial Final

The 1954 final between Kilrush and Faughs was never played. The County Board fixed the match for Miltown. The Kilrush delegates refused to play the match in Miltown and opted for the match to be played in Kilmihil or Kilrush. To be fair to them, they even agreed to play the county final in Ennis. However, the County Board stood firm on its decision for the venue to be Miltown. Fr. Corry said at a board meeting, *'the GAA is a democratic organisation, and matches are fixed by vote.'* But Kilrush felt that Miltown was getting everything and refused to play there. They then withdrew from the championship and Faughs were then declared county champions.

Faughs again contested the county final in 1955, barely losing to Doonbeg in a replay. Although Faughs beat Cooraclare in the final of the Cusack Cup in 1955, it was essentially their swan song and gradually the great and glorious Faughs team disappeared from the Clare Football scene.

Colm Keating.

The Faughs football team of the 1950s was an outstanding team that considerably raised the standard of Clare football. With their stylish and sophisticated approach to playing, they brought a glamour and excitement to the game which had been missing for a number of years. Amongst the other football clubs of the time, in particular the West Clare clubs, they became 'the challenge' – the club to beat. To defeat the Faughs in the 1950s was an honour for other club teams. In Clare football lore, they will be remembered as amongst the best.

The 1960s

In the 1960 Cusack Cup, the Faughs lost to Kilmihil by 1-5 to 2-0. The match finished in controversial circumstances. Following this the Faughs dropped from senior ranks for a number of years. In 1968, they won the Junior A title, defeating Michael Cusack's by 1-6 to 0-6 with players of the calibre of Paschal O'Brien, Sean Coffey and Noel Pyne. A fisted goal by John Hayes proved to be crucial, after good work by Larry Kilmartin. After the match, the Central Council representative, Jack Daly, presented the Egan Cup to the captain of the Faughs team, Sean Coffey, who came on a substitute in the second half.

This was to effectively end the 'Faughs' name, until it was revived again in 1993. But the Faughs had made an outstanding contribution to

Pictured at a Faughs victory social in 1968. Back row, left to right: *Tommy Collins, Seán Guinnane, John Hayes, Tony 'Beef' Shannon, Paul Higgins, Paschal O'Brien, Colum Flynn.* ***Front row:*** *Joe Fenwick, Seán Coffey, Donal Griffin, Paddy White.*

***Éire Og Junior Footballers c.1975. Back row, left to right:** Pat McInerney, Tommy Pilkington, Kevin Keane, Michael Ball, Kieran Earley, Ml. Nugent, John McAllister, Paddy Piggott, Dan McCarthy, Brendan Gilligan, Miko McNamara, Pat Fitzpatrick, Ml. Howard (out of shot). **Front row:** Gerard McCullough, Martin Galvin, Eric Connellan, Seanie Clohessy, David Seery, Ollie O'Loughlin, Declan Coote, Tony McMahon, Mick Barry.*

Ennis football. Following the junior success of 1968, Éire Óg fielded a senior team in the 1969 championship, losing to Miltown Malbay in a spirited match by 2-11 to 2-6. Football was essentially disorganised at this stage. But in Ennis CBS for example, Bro. Power introduced Gaelic football to the school, circa. 1966-1970. Gaelic football was new to us, but some took to it such as natural players like Paul McNamara and Alan Lewis. One didn't necessarily have to attend the CBS in order to play; it was open to players from all over the town. In 1968, Bro. Power organised under fourteen and under sixteen teams to compete in the county championship. Initiatives such as this ensured that Gaelic football was kept alive and preparation and groundwork was done for the clubs.

Then in 1972, at the Éire Óg club's AGM that year, a proposal was made by Pat Brennan and seconded by Ollie O'Regan that the club should have a football team under the auspices of the parent club Éire Óg. In that first year, the club fielded both a senior and junior team, but both teams were defeated by Kilrush. After the initial year, the club

Anne Kenneally (secretary Éire Óg) presents Pat Brennan with the 'Football Clubman of the Year Award'. The others present are Tom McInerney, Anna McInerney and Miko McNamara.

reverted to junior status. In 1975, the Junior Championship was won by Éire Óg when they defeated Lissycasey. The team to win those first honours for Éire Óg was: Frankie Tuohy, Ollie O'Regan, Joe Lynch, Paddy Brennan, Alan Lewis, Denis O'Connor, Paddy O'Sullivan, Noel Ryan, Tony Kelly, Leo Mannion, Brian Stenson, Ger O'Loughlin, Eric Connellan, Sean Heaslip, Michael Skelly.

1976 brought some success when Éire Óg won the Aberdeen Arms Cup beating Doonbeg in the final. That year, they also took the Junior B championship. The success of these years is probably due to the fact that in 1974 the football arm of the club became more structured when Micko McNamara was elected chairman and a very active committee organised the training and selection of teams. Those who came to the forefront and gave much needed expertise included Michael Howard, Denis Horgan, Christy Glynn and Martin Galvin. Indeed, special mention should be made here of Martin Galvin from Kilmurry Ibrickan who was a coach with the club in the mid-1970s. His work bore fruit as Éire Óg dominated the under 14 grade from 1975 – 1978. His charges also contested three minor finals in a row. In 1978 they lost to Kilrush, 3-6 to 3-5. In 1979, with Michael Butler and Pete Barry lording it at centre field, they defeated Kilmihil in the minor final by 2-6 to 1-7 and the following year Éire Óg lost to Kilmurry Ibrickan in a low scoring game played in Quilty. The success of these years is due in no small way to Martin Galvin, who is described by some former players as a man who had great commitment,

Two outstanding mentors, Martin Galvin (left) and Paddy Duggan, pictured at the Éire Og clubhouse.

whose aim it was to get the best out of players and whose positive attitude got lads playing Gaelic football who may not otherwise have been interested. Players at this time included Dermot O'Loughlin, Brendan Gilligan, Noel Ryan, Alan Lewis, Frankie Tuohy and Joe Lynch, a native of Castlegregory at full-back.

After winning the junior championship in 1975, the club once again went senior for two years. In 1976, a strong side drew 0-9 to 1-6 with Doonbeg in the championship. The team was criticised in the Clare Champion for not utilising the tall full-forward line of Michael Skelly, Frank Molloy and Sean Heaslip to their potential. In the replay, Éire Óg

1986 County Semi-final - *John O'Connor races through the Doonbeg defence, enroute to scoring Éire Ogs first goal. Bert McMahon, Noel Ryan and Pat Hanrahan have more than a passing interest in the outcome.*
Courtesy of Clare Champion.

lost to Doonbeg by 1-6 to 0-4. The West Clare side was best served by Senan Downes, Tommy Tubridy and Seamus Bowe.

Eire Og reverted back to intermediate in the early 1980s and with ever improving juvenile structures they have gone from strength to strength with many juvenile, junior and senior final appearances to their credit. Throughout the 1980s the club gained many new officers and mentors and those who joined in the administration during this period were Mick Barry, John McAllister, Joe Lynch. Seamus Flanagan, who had transferred from Fermanagh, was an inspirational figure on the field as well as a competent officer off it. The football club also broke new ground when appointing Anna Kenneally as club secretary in 1982 and in 1984 she became overall club secretary, which was a first for Clare.

Separate Club

At the end of 1982, football had become a strong and independent force within the club and a formidable committee was in place that believed independence from the hurlers would be to their benefit. In 1983 the footballers registered a new club to be known as the Éire Óg Football Club. Having sought and gained independence from the hurling body, they also had their share of success. The club won the intermediate championship in 1985, beating Kilfenora in a fine game at Cusack Park. With spirits high within the club, they reached the senior final in 1986

Fine action study of Pete Barry in possession, with Roibéard Lyne in support, 1986 Championship v Doonbeg.

Éire Óg pictured before the 1986 County Senior Final meeting with Cooraclare. Back row, left to right: *John O'Connor, Enda Connolly, Micheál Glynn, Roibéard Lyne, Noel Ryan, Seán Heaslip, Martin Nugent, Pete Barry.* ***Front row:*** *Shaun McCarthy, Bernie O'Brien, Tom Russell, Johnny Purtill, Patrick Walzer, Gerry Barry, Seamus Flanagan, David McCullough.*

Courtesy of County Express.

beating Doonbeg along the way. However, the team disappointed in the final, losing to Cooraclare by 2-5 to 1-5.

Even though there was a wealth of juvenile talent coming through the ranks at this period, many of these young men, possibly due to the economic downturn of the 1980s, emigrated or did not pursue the game. The club reverted back to intermediate in the early 1990s.

Many new faces emerged on the executive front of the football section of the club in the late 1980s and early 1990s, among whom were Donie Buckley, Tony Honan, Pat Fitzpatrick, Tim Caffrey and Jarlath O'Halloran at under-age. With Buckley, Caffrey and O'Halloran's coaching and tactical skills, the young charges greatly benefited on the field.

In 1993, Éire Óg sought assistance from St. Joseph's in the form of James Hanrahan, Ollie Baker, Ciaran O'Neill and James O'Connor to form a team which took the traditional name of 'The Faughs'. Hanrahan and O'Neill had made a big contribution to Clare's Munster Championship breakthrough in 1992. After reaching the quarter final, Faughs drew

***Faughs, 1994 County Senior Champions. Back row, left to right:** Francis Corey, James Hanrahan, Ciarán O'Neill, Roibéard Lyne, Brian O'Connell, Seán Lyne, Ollie Baker, Declan Tobin, Stephen McNamara. **Front row:** Tom Russell, Kenneth Hickey, Murrough McMahon, Barry Keating, Shaun McCarthy, Kieran Lynch. Courtesy of County Express.*

with Ennistymon, 2-8 to 0-14, but with Ciaran O'Neill and Dermot Cronin moved to defence for the replay, Faughs defeated Ennistymon by 1-8 to 1-4. In a semi-final clash with Doonbeg, they lost 0-11 to 1-6.

In 1994, again with St. Joseph's assistance 'The Faughs' contested and won the senior football final beating Kilrush, 1-12 to 2-6 in a replay. The same year, with the majority of the Faughs in their ranks, Éire Óg reached the Intermediate Final, but heartbreak was their lot going under to Lissycasey in the county final.

1995, however, was to be a triumphant year for the intermediate team when all before them was swept aside in a successful assault on this championship.

Football was now very much in the ascendancy in Éire Óg and much was expected from them in senior ranks. Expectations were eventually fulfilled in the year 2000 when Éire Óg for the first time gained ultimate honours in Cusack Park at the expense of the old enemy, Doonbeg. The team was managed by John Hickey with Dave Loughman, Noel Normoyle and Kieran Kelleher in the backroom team.

Éire Og Junior (A) Finalists 1996. Back row, left to right: *Paddy Guilfoyle, Rory Hickey, Leonard Keane, Shane Flanagan, David McNamara, Michael Guerin, Eoin Bradley, Matt Fennell, Liam Miniter.* ***Front row:*** *John Roche, Ger Daly, Diarmuid Kelly, Niall Keavey, Fergus Flynn, Tomás Corbett, Jack Murphy.*
*Jack Murphy was a great supporter of the Ennis teams. He had a great love of hurling. He followed Gaelic Football and soccer teams. He was also involved in The Boxing Club. He was an out and out Ennisman.
Courtesy of Mort O'Loughlin.

2000 proved to be a very successful year for football in the club when the Under-16, Minor and Under-21 titles also rested on the club shelves.

The 2001 county senior final was again reached but in a dour encounter at Quilty, Doonbeg got the better of Éire Óg, although they had looked all set at half time to retain their title.

Overall football in Éire Óg is on a sure and healthy footing. It has a great history and tradition to draw upon. There was a slight lapse in concentration in 2002. But the material is there, the commitment is there and there is hope for a very bright future.

Notes:

Successful Dals teams of the years 1897-1911 included the following: Tom Clohessy, Miko Duggan, Miko Connellan, Michael Smith, Patrick Moroney, Michael Foudy, Donat Callinan, Joe Nono, Paul Hayes, Jim Hayes, James Clohessy, Paddy Kenny, Pako Malone, Michael Madden,

Bryan MacMahon and Peter Cosgrove accept the Jack Daly Cup from County Board Chairman Fr. Michael McNamara, after the 2000 County Final.
Courtesy of County Express.

Barry Keating, a dual player with Éire Og. Barry was one of Clare's top footballers during a good spell in the 1990s.

Éire Og County Senior Champions 2000 pictured before defeating Doonbeg. Back row, left to right: *Albert Hardiman, Donie Lyne, Seán Lyne, James Hanrahan, James Ruane, Cathal Egan, Brian Fitzpatrick, Tadhg McNamara.* ***Front row:*** *Barry Keating, Bryan MacMahon, Nicky Hogan, Peter Cosgrove, Kenneth Hickey, Aidan Keane, Paul Scahill.*

Courtesy of County Express.

J. Griffey, Michael O'Leary, Patrick Considine, William Fox, Paddy Jones, Michael Corley, F. McMahon, James Casserly, James Corbett, Tom McNamara, Paddy McNamara, Tom Vaughan, Michael Carmody, Fr. Tim Monaghan, Fr. W. Armstrong, Fr. Michael Hayes, John Fahy, James Spellissy, James Frawley, Joe Moroney, Paddy Roughan, Tom McDonnell, Jack Darcy, Ned Monaghan, Luke Moroney, James McMahon, S. Keavy, Michael O'Reilly, J. Neylon, Joe Millar, Michael Slattery.
Mentors: Jim Coughlan and James Hayes.

1929 Dals Senior Football Winning Team: Joe Davis, Paul Cronin, Tull Considine (Captain), James McInerney, Larry Blake, Paddy Callinan, Michael Malone, Anthony Moroney, Jacksie Darcy, Joe Madigan, Thomas O'Halloran, Tony 'Topper' Morrissey, Jackie Duffy, Con Levin, Jack Doherty.

The 1947 Faughs team was: Tony Strand (Captain); Gerry Moroney; Tommy Hennessy; Tony Galvin; Sean Moloney; Jimmy Walker; Murt O'Shea; Christy Glynn; Reggie Connellan; Matt Nugent; Paddy Dowling; Leo Finlay; Johnny Fleming; Ralphie Burns; Sean Guinnane.
Sub: Tommy Moloney (used).

The 1968 Winning Faughs Junior Team was: John McAllister, Sean O'Driscoll, Charlie Geraghty, P. Hehir, Pat Brennan, Michael Hanrahan, Paschal O'Brien, Jim Kerins, Noel Pyne, Joe Fenwick, John Courtney, Larry Kilmartin, Tom Glynn, John Hayes, Paul Higgins.
Sub: Sean Coffey (captain).

1979 Éire Óg Minor Winning Team: David Casey, Sean Walzer, Joe Lynch, Conor Hanrahan, John Casey, Micheál Glynn, Sean Lyons, Michael Butler, Pete Barry, Tómas Mannion, Louis Galvin, Pat Lynch, John O'Connor, Michael Kenny, Jarlath O'Halloran.

1994 Faughs Team was: Brian O'Connell, Barry Keating, Tom Russell, Shaun McCarthy, Murrough McMahon, Sean Lyne (Captain), Kieran Lynch, Ciaran O'Neill, Roibeard Lyne, Ollie Baker, James Hanrahan, Declan Tobin, Francis Corey, Stephen McNamara, Kenneth Hickey.
Sub: Joe O'Muircheartaigh.

Éire Óg Winning Senior Championship Team - 2000: James Hanrahan, Sean Lyne, Donie Lyne, Tadgh McNamara, Aidan Keane, Barry Keating, Cathal Egan, James Ruane, Peter Cosgrove, Brian Fitzpatrick, Paul Scahill, Nicky Hogan, Ken Hickey, Albert Hardiman, Bryan McMahon.
Subs used: Andy Leyland and Stephen McNamara.

Short Biographical Sketches

I'd like to acknowledge the following for their contribution.

Michael Arthur, Newmarket. All round sportsman, also played rugby and soccer at a very high level. Member of the all powerful Newmarket team of late 1960's. Played for Clare from 1966/1970.

Larry Blake (Éire Óg) – One of the founders of Éire Óg, a son of Larry Snr. He represented club and county at senior level. A member of a highly respected sporting family, now living in Kilmihil.

Teresa Blake (Clooney) and Ennis, nee McNamara. A member of the great Clooney camogie team in the days of Babs (Mary Catherine) Clune, Chris Markham, Annie Conheady and the captain, Dokey McNamara. Living in Clonroad for many years, Teresa won a Munster senior camogie medal with Clare in 1944.

George Bradley (Blackweir and Kilkee) – Long serving Kilkee and Clare footballer in the days of Murt O'Shea and Paddy Dowling. Still hale and hearty, George shared his memories with me in January 2000. A brother of Richard (Birdie) Bradley.

Cyril Brennan (Ennis) – Highly popular teacher at CBS Primary from 1955 to 1994. A great teacher, Cyril had a lovely gentle way of imparting his knowledge.

Pat Brennan (Éire Óg) – played senior hurling from c. 1962 to 1973. Also represented Rovers. Pat is still involved in the game, coaching at under-age level. A brother of Michael, who served as Chairman in the past, Pat's contribution to this work is immense.

Gerry Browne (St. Joseph's) – prominent Clare hurler of the 1950s, Gerry put me right on a number of very technical points for this publication.

Kevin J. Browne (RIP) – born in Ennis in 1920. Worked as a journalist with the Independent and the Irish Press. He joined the staff of the Clare

Champion in 1970, and contributed until 1979. Kevin Browne is the author of Eamon De Valera and The Banner County. A son of Thomas and Mai Browne (nee Meehan) both of whom took an active role in the War of Independence. His article on the Town Leagues was first published in 1980. It is reproduced here with the kind permission of his daughter, Kate.

Bobby Burke (Éire Óg) – played senior for Éire Óg (1954 – 1964). Also represented Clare in senior championship and Wembley tournament, 1958. Bobby taught 3rd class for many years in the CBS, instilling a great love of learning.

John Burke (Banner). John has a long association with the Banner Club. He is their current chairman.

Denis Canty – retired Speech & Drama Teacher at St. Flannan's. Denis made a big contribution to the local radio station, West Coast Radio.

Michael Carmody (Éire Óg) – long serving club man at u/21 and senior, justifiably collecting a senior championship medal in 1980. Michael is involved with hurling at CBS primary where he teaches. A brother of Joe.

Des Carroll (Scariff) – outstanding colleges player with St. Flannan's. Des represented Newmarket at all levels before returning to his native Scariff, with whom he won 3 championships in a long career, 1945 – 1960. Represented the County team from '45 until 1955, Des captained the Banner County for at least two seasons. Now retired in Ennis.

Jarlath Colleran, RIP (Clooney), member of a well-known family who distinguished themselves with St. Flannan's. Jarlath, Noel, Raymond and Enda all played Harty Cup with Flannan's between 1976 and 1983. Another brother, Hugh, played in the 1972 Harty Cup Final. Their cousin, Philip Colleran (Clarecastle) also played senior hurling for the college. Jarlath was always obliging and helpful. He died tragically in October 2002.

Caroline Collins (Ennis). A huge debt of gratitude for her assistance with editing, re-writing, proofing, indexing, and above all for her ideas and her understanding.

David Connellan (Ennis) – Represented CBS at all colleges levels. Played Harty Cup 1970 and 1971. Won Minor Championship with the Dals in 1971.

Seán Connolly (Faughs) – A native of Galway. He represented Faughs, Clare and Munster. A contemporary of P. J. O'Dea's and Eddie Cotter's on the Munster inter-provincial team c. '51 – '53.

Elizabeth Crimmins (RIP) - Newmarket. Taught for many years in England. Born in Newmarket in 1896, a real 'Old World' lady. It was a pleasure to meet her.

Patrick J. Crimmins (Newmarket-on-Fergus) (1861 - 1937) - Patrick contributed a column called "Clare Searchlights - Notes from the Banner County" for the Limerick Leader during the years 1925 - 1936. He was father of Elizabeth Crimmins.

Michael Cullinan (Éire Óg) – better known as 'Darby'. He played at all levels for town teams. A product of Ennis CBS.

Frank Custy (Ruan) – goalkeeper during a great spell with Ruan, 1959 – 62 and beyond. Also represented Clare seniors in goal. Frank also made a massive contribution to Irish music. His family, Mary, Frances, Tola, Catherine and Nora are all involved to some extent in music.

Seán Custy (Ruan) – a brother of Frank. Won 3 senior and 1 Clare Cup during a great spell. Emigrated to New York and was part of the Clare and New York teams out there. Highly rated corner-back, Seán now lives at home.

Pat Daly (Éire Óg) - current PRO of the club. Member of a distinguished Clarecastle/Ennis sporting family, Pat is a son of the late John Daly.

Kevin Damery (Cobh) – Hurled for the 23rd Battalion, the Army team based in Dromoland. Kevin later wrote to me giving me the complete history of the 23rd Battalion.

Liam Danagher (Newmarket) – Stylish mid-field player during the years 1964 – 1971. Represented Munster on Railway Cup team. Liam was selected by genuine hurling people, at centre-field on Clare's greatest 15.

Pat Danaher (Tulla) – Represented Clare at senior level playing at wing back. County Championship medallist with Brian Borus in 1975. Pat is an authority on Clare hurling.

Bernie Dilger (RIP) (Éire Óg) – Known affectionately as Champ. An outstanding sportsman and fisherman. Everything he did, he did well. A lifelong member of the Scouts. Bernie played for Éire Óg 1953 – 1959. Captained Clare in '58. Bernie who passed away in 2002 was a brother of Michael (Gruggy) (RIP), Massey and Georgie.

Georgie Dilger (Éire Óg) – Represented CBS, St. John's and Éire Óg during a lengthy career. Extremely skilled hurler.

Massey Dilger (Éire Óg) – One of the 4 brothers from Connolly villas to hurl for Clare. Won senior honours in 1966. I spoke to him in September 1997, a joy to listen to.

Brian Dinan (Ennis) – Hurled with Rovers. A published author with Mercier Press – 'Clare and its People'. A fine writer, Brian has contributed many articles to various books and other publications including An Ennis Miscellany. 'Townies on the Ball' was written especially for this publication in December 1997.

Michael Doherty (Ennis) – Played for Turnpike and Éire Óg. Captained Michael Cusack's in London scene. His family, Paddy (RIP), Josie, Tommy, Nuala and Vera are all steeped in the tradition, being closely related to Rob Doherty of 1914 fame.

Paddy Duggan (RIP) (Éire Óg) – founder member of Club. A neighbour of mine, we talked hurling countless times. Hurled at all levels. Paddy gave a lifetime of service at under-age level.

Michael J. Fitzgerald – A native of Lower Market Street. He was born in Ennis c. 1906. He emigrated with his parents to the United States in 1920.

Michael Gallagher (RIP) (Kilkishen) – Clare FM sports reporter for many years. He had a great love of the game and gave freely of his time. He died a young man.

Esther Gilligan (Ennis) – A native of Gowran, Esther McGee came to Ennis at a young age. A great follower of Clare and Kilkenny hurling. Mother of hurlers Noel, Paddy and Brendan. Her daughter, Margaret Lacheiner was tops in her chosen sport.

Catherine Glynn (Éire Óg) – Native of Francis Street. Very prominent member of Éire Óg camogie team during the successful years 1969 – 1975. Catherine (Fitzpatrick) won All-Ireland Junior Championship with

Clare in 1974. A member of a sporting family, Margaret, Grainne, Eilish, Tom, Noel and Micheál were all involved with Éire Óg.

Christy Glynn (RIP) (Ennis Dalcassians) – Clon Road. A Dals hurler of the 1930/40s. He later served as Chairman of Éire Óg. Father of Paul, John, Michael and Edel.

Liam Griffin (Éire Óg). Long serving official with the club. Served as secretary in the past. Liam is a member of the Executive Committee.

Michael Guerin (Éire Óg) – Former hurler (1959 – 1964) and Chairman. A great club man, he gave generously of his time at under-age level. A very popular Ennisman. His son, Johnny played senior football with Éire Óg.

Peter 'Slavery' Guilfoyle (RIP) (Ennis) – A character, storyteller and quick wit. Man of jovial disposition, great follower of Ennis hurling teams.

Seán Guinnane (Ennis) – New Road. Represented the Dals at Minor. Seán later served as Vice Chairman of Éire Óg in their formative years. He is not to be confused with Seán Guinnane, the well known dual star of the 1930s.

John Hanly (Clarecastle) – A leading player in St. Flannan's golden era of 1944 – '48. Represented Clarecastle, Clare and Laois. John was a highly respected coach and former Chairman of the County Board.

Mary Hanly (Newmarket) nee O'Brien – Represented Coláiste Muire, and UCC in camogie. Mary won Ashbourne Cups with UCC in 1972 and '73. She trained the Newmarket senior hurling team in 1992.

Michael Hanrahan (Éire Óg) – Represented Clare in mid-1960s. A prominent CBS Harty Cup and Éire Óg player. A brother of Eric.

Seamus Hayes (Lissycasey) - respected journalist with the Clare Champion, at all times fair in his comments, Seamus has been with the Champion since 1973.

Seán Heaslip (Éire Óg) – Represented Clare in 1981 and 1987. A son of Jack and brother of Frannie. Seán won 3 senior championships with his club.

Kieran Hennessy (R.I.P.) (Clooney) – A long time follower of the game, Kieran was a student at St. Flannan's from 1944 – 1949. An authority on hurling, he was a great help to me during my research, especially for 'Blue is the Colour'. He died in the spring of 2003.

Jack Hogan (Newmarket) – Later played for Feakle. Jack wore the saffron and blue playing Senior Championship in 1944.

Joe Hurley (Ruan) – Club secretary from 1940 to 1945. Joe gave me the complete background on the Ruan Club.

Flan Hynes (RIP) (Ennis) – Long and illustrious club career spanning the years 1943 – 1963, with Avondhu, Faughs, and best known with St. Joseph's, during a great spell. A brother of Paddy Hynes who won senior championship with the Dals in 1934.

Kevin Keane (Kilnamona) – A formidable hurler with the amalgamation St. Flannan's during 1970s. Unlucky not to win a senior championship. Kevin represented Éire Óg at Gaelic football. He also played senior with St. Joseph's in 1969.

Michael Keane (Ennis) – A talented writer, contributed many articles to Clare Advertiser. One of the mainstays of West Coast Radio (1984 – 1988).

Colm Keating (Éire Óg) - Colm made a big contribution to Éire Óg football in the 1990s. In his own playing days he represented Faughs and Claughaun, Limerick. Colm, Gabriel and Ollie Keating were part of the Claughaun club that dominated Limerick GAA during 1967 - 1971. Colm Keating won senior medals in both hurling and football. He later contributed handsomely to the Clare soccer scene, representing both Lifford FC and Gardisette. Colm is the father of hurler/footballer, Barry Keating.

P. J. Kelly (Ennis) – well known publican in Carmody Street. Played Harty Cup with CBS. Always a great help to me with my research.

Kevin Kennedy (Éire Óg) – His career in the Gardaí took him to various parishes. A 'Journey Man' hurler he represented Brian Borus in 1975. Kevin later won senior medal with Éire Óg.

Kyran Kennedy (Éire Óg) – Chairman of Éire Óg Minor Club for some years. Secretary of development committee. Also served as secretary of club and County Board.

Donal Kenny (Rovers) – Donal was part of the outstanding Rovers minor teams of the mid-1960s. He played corner-back on the 1965 winning team. Later he turned his attention to golf representing Munster. Donal is a son of Tony Kenny, and nephew of Paddy, Stevie.

Josie Kerin (R.I.P.) Ennis. Josie played minor hurling with the Dals. After retiring from Air Traffic Control in Shannon, he contributed to the sports desk at West Coast Radio. We often travelled together to record interviews with hurling stars (e.g. Pat Fox, Colm and Conal Bonner, Pierse Piggott, Sylvie Linnane and Steve Mahon) are just some that come to mind. In 1987 Josie and I recorded many Clare greats live on air. After the demise of W.C.R. he contributed a hugely popular column to the County Express. A wonderful character, he died suddenly in January 2003.

Seán King (Ennis) – A former journalist with the Clare Champion.

Mick Leahy (Ruan) – Clare hurler of the 1950 – 1956 era. Mick played also for Tullogher in Kilkenny. He lives in Cork.

Maura Leyden (Mayo) – a huge help with typing and general suggestions.

Martin Linnane (Éire Óg) – Represented St. John's before emigrating. On returning to Ennis in 1968 became a valuable member of Éire Óg for a few seasons. Martin represented Clare at intermediate level. His father, Mick won intermediate in 1927 and senior championship in 1934.

Colin Lynch (Lissycasey) – Colin hurled for Éire Óg for close on 10 years. An outstanding member of the Clare team since 1996.

Joe Madigan (RIP) (Dalcassians & Clare Hurler) – Joe taught at CBS from 1927 – 1971. His article 'A Record Year' was first published in the Éire Óg Book 1952 – 1967.

Tony Maher (Rovers/Éire Óg) – Colleges star with CBS in 1961. 'Lory' played club hurling in Dublin. A founder member of the Banner.

Colm Mahon (Éire Óg) – Tremendous club hurler throughout the 1980s. Great leader on the pitch. Hurled for the County in 1981/1982. A son of Seán Mahon.

Jimmy Mahony (RIP) (Ennis) – 1900 – 1995 – Jimmy Mahony of old Mill Street and New York was an authority on the social, political and sporting life of Ennis during the early decades of the 20th century. In the words of Vincent Sheridan: "Jimmy made a study of everything". Jimmy died in New York in January 1995.

Frank Malone (RIP) (Ennis) – Son of Pako Malone who hurled for Clare in 1912 and grandson of Stephen Malone – a topping singer. Frank was a farrier, the third or fourth generation of farriers.. He was filmed by an RTE television crew during the making of the Telefís Scoile documentary in Ennis, about 1968. This film also featured 'Diver' McNamara. I had the pleasure of his company one afternoon in November 1995.

Gearóid Mannion (Éire Óg) – Harty Cup medallist with St. Flannan's. Won Senior Championship with Éire Óg in 1990. Brother of Leo and Tomás and son of Tom.

Joe 'Jazzer' Meaney (Ruan) – Represented his club during the great years. A regular on a very good Clare team c. 1952 – 1954. A brother of Patsy and Tony.

Tony Meaney (Ruan) – Hurled with Clare 1964 – 1966. Won all major honours with Ruan from 1959 – 1962. Tony recalled the many Ruan/Éire Óg games with great regard and affection for his opponents.

Paschal Molloy (Rovers) – Played for, and administered with Rovers during their 'heyday' with 'Dugger' Kearney.

Fr. Brendan Moloney (Scariff) – Present Dean of St. Flannan's. Student at St. Flannan's 1959 – 1964, playing colleges hurling. A member of the teaching staff since 1977. A great authority on the game.

Johnny Moloney (RIP) (Scariff) – Clare senior selector during 1940s. Johnny had a great knowledge of the game. He shared many stories with me.

Christy Murphy (Ennis) – A son of Christy Murphy of the Scout Movement and Bridie (nee Fagan). A class friend of mine at the CBS, Christy later taught at St. Flannan's and in Copenhagen.

Jimmy Barry Murphy (St. Finbarrs) – Renowned Cork hurler and footballer. Holder of 6 All-Ireland Senior Medals. Jimmy also had a spell with Cork Celtic.

Johnny McCarthy (Éire Óg) – Musician and hurler, Johnny represented club and county at all levels from 1957 – 1971. A huge help to me in the publication of this book.

Paddy McDonnell (Kilkee) – PRO of West Clare Hurling Board. A lifelong supporter and enthusiast of hurling in the Kilkee/Bealaha area.

Val McGann (Éire Óg) – Played juvenile for Kilmaley before transferring to Ennis. Val was involved with the formation of Éire Óg with whom he played senior. Played hurling in Australia with Young Irelands. A brother of Johnny McGann (St. John's), Val lives in Victoria, Australia.

Gerry McInerney (Sixmilebridge) - one of Clare's finest forwards of the 1981 - 1994 era. Wore the famous blue jersey of Munster in the Railway Cup. Gerry played a leading role in Sixmilebridge's club success of 1995/96 and though at the veteran stage, he often came from his corner to lead the attack. He is a journalist with the Clare Champion.

Joe McNamara (RIP) (Newmarket) – A brother of Patrick 'The Hound' McNamara, who played on the 1932 Clare team. Joe was a lifelong follower of hurling. He is the only man I ever met who knew the complete story surrounding the 'Cooney Case' of 1938. He had a lovely poetic way of telling a story.

Stephen McNamara (Éire Óg) – A wonderful opportunist and goal poacher. A son of T. J. who played for Rovers. Stephen holds two All-Ireland Senior medals.

Kitty McNicholas (Éire Óg) – Prime mover and organiser in Clare camogie since 1972. Has made a monumental contribution to Clare camogie since 1972.

John Nevin (RIP) (Éire Óg) – Hurled with great distinction for St. Flannan's, Éire Óg and Clare. John possessed a great love of his town. He died long before his time.

Michael Nihill (Ennis) – A founder member of St. John's. Michael spent many years in Britain before returning to Ennis. One of the founders of the Clare Supporters Club.

Michael O'Brien - A native of Granagh, Co. Limerick, Michael is current P.R.O of the juvenile town hurling board.

Paschal O'Brien (RIP) (Éire Óg) – A wonderful warm personality, Paschal played in goal for Clare (1964 – 1971). Played Railway Cup with the provincial team. He retired before his time.

Seamus O Ceallaigh (RIP) – A prolific writer on GAA matters. He wrote for the Limerick Chronicle in 1926. He moved to the Kerryman in 1934 and wrote under the name of 'Camán'. His books include 'The Mackey Story'.

Christy O'Connell (RIP) (Barefield) – Long time follower of Clare hurling teams, especially from 1928 – 1932. A brother of Alfie O'Connell who played hurling for Barefield.

John O'Connor (Éire Óg) – Gifted footballer, played senior for Clare 1985 – 1987. A great goalscorer. Also represented Avenue United at centre-forward playing alongside Michael Byrnes. Now involved with Eoin O'Neill and Clachán Music 'A Small Community'. Their ethos is to record traditional musicians of Clare.

P. J. O'Dea (Kilrush) – Highly rated Clare and Munster footballer of the 1950s. P. J. played hurling with Rovers and Dalcassians.

Simon O'Donnell (Éire Óg) – One of the founding members of the club. His brothers Hugh, Colm, and Fr. Con (RIP) were also involved with Éire Óg.

Seán O'Gorman (Ennis) – Founder member of St. John's. A winning hurling club.

Gearóid Ó hEarcáin (Éire Óg) - has coached hurling and Gaelic football from U-12 to U-21 with his club. A Clare selector with the Tony Forrestal team 1986 - 1987. He made a big contribution to Colleges hurling with St. patrick's Comprehensive College in Shannon where he teaches. Gearóid gives meticulous care to detail. He served with the minor club in the mid-1980s working closely with the late Paddy Duggan. He has a monumental in-depth knowledge of the game.

Seán O'Halloran (Bodyke) – Stylish wing back on Brian Borus winning team in 1975. Very involved with Bord na n-Óg.

Seán O Liodáin (John Leyden) (RIP) – A native of the Lifford/New Road area. Seán spent many years in England. He was a regular contributor to the Clare County Express.

Domhnall Ó Loingsigh (Kilmaley and The Banner) – current secretary of The Banner. Domhnall played Harty Cup with Ennis CBS. Member of Conradh na Gaeilge and prominent Irish language enthusiast.

Annie O'Loughlin (Clooney) – nee Conheady. Annie gave me firsthand information on the Civil War era. Wife of the late Patrick 'Duckle' O'Loughlin, who hurled for Clooney in the 1940s.

Ciarán Ó Murchadha (Ennis) – Ciarán is the author of Sable Wings Over the Land – Ennis, Co. Clare, and its wider community during the Great Famine. Editor of Co. Clare Studies, Ciarán has contributed to many publications. Ciarán holds a doctorate in history. He is a member of the teaching staff at St. Flannan's College.

Ollie O'Regan (Éire Óg) – Long serving hurler and officer with the club. Won County Championship in 1980. A brother of Michael, in Ruan.

Seamus O'Reilly (Clondegad). Dedicated G.A.A. follower and clubman. Seamus runs the County Express Newspaper and possesses an excellent photographic archive. Many of his photographs are re-produced in this publication.

Tony O'Sullivan (Na Piarsiagh) – Represented 'The Mon', Cork and Munster. A wonderful ball player and stylist. Member of the Cork team (1982 – 1994). Tony later served as a selector with Cork.

Margaret O'Toole (Ballynacally) – Played for Clondegad. Later joined Éire Óg in the mid-70s. She captained Clare to their first ever All-Ireland Camogie title in 1974.

Flan Purcell (RIP) (Feakle) – Clare centre-back – mid to late 1930s. Always positive, he had many wonderful and colourful stories.

P. J. Purcell (St. Joseph's) – Constant part of St. Joseph's teams 1961 – 1980. A purist, P. J. also played for the amalgamation St. Brendan's.

Noel Pyne (Éire Óg) – Member of well known sporting family. Highly regarded hurler and golfer. His brothers, Dickie, Derry, Liam, Louis, Brenny, Tom also played sport. Noel won Railway Cup honours with Munster in 1969.

Leo Quinlan (Sixmilebridge) – outstanding colleges hurler with St. Flannan's in 1976/'77. Played senior championship for Clare in 1981. Current coach of Coláiste Muire camogie teams.

Jim Quinlivan (Dalcassians) – a native of Tulla. Came to Ennis in 1937. Won a senior championship with the Dals in 1941.

Kurt Russell – American film star, who made his film debut as a child star in the 1963 movie It Happened at the World's Fair, starring Elvis Presley. He appeared in many TV series. In 1968 he starred in the leading role in Guns in the Heather, which was filmed mostly in Clare. In 1979 Russell played the part of Elvis Presley in the highly rated film Elvis. Kurt Russell continues to get parts in big movies.

Gretta Ryan (nee Gilligan) (Hermitage) – Gretta's brothers, John Joe and Freddie, hurled for the Rovers.

John Ryan (Cratloe) – former County Secretary. John is a GAA historian and enthusiast.

Michael 'Aoner' Sheridan (Ennis Dals) – Made debut for county in 1934. Regular on County team 1936/1941. Won 2 championship medals. A brother of the late Vincent.

Paschal Sheridan (St. Joseph's) – A member of the St. Joseph's winning teams of the 1950s. Paschal recalled the great clashes of St. Joseph's/Éire Óg, with fondness.

Jimmy Smyth (Ruan) – Represented Clare hurlers at every level from 1945-1967. Member of Munster Railway Cup team for 12 seasons. Won eight inter-Provincial medals - a record for a Clareman. Regarded by contemporaries as one of the greatest forwards of all time. Jimmy is a fine singer and the author of 'Ballads of the Banner'. He is also the editor of the 'Pa Howard Collection', a chronicle of all Clare hurling teams since 1949. His article 'Recollections of Ennis Hurling' was wirtten especially for this publication in 1997.

Jimmy Spellissy (Éire Óg) – Promising under-age hurler. Won all honours from juvenile to u/21. Played senior for a time in 1977. A founder member of the Clare Environmental Alliance. Jimmy also runs the Ennis Rock and Blues Club.

Seán Spellissy (Ennis) – Author of numerous publications including 'The Merchants of Ennis' and the 'Ennis Compendium'. Seán is a son of Jack and nephew of James 'Sham' Spellissy.

P. J. Summerly (Rovers) – Great organiser and mentor with Rovers. A brother of Anthony, Georgie and Haulie, all of whom represented the club.

Aidan Tuttle (RIP) (Ennis) – Hurler, commentator, writer, raconteur, bookmaker, and wit. Aidan was well known for his sporting videos, which he produced with Michael O'Sullivan. An all round sports follower, he died suddenly in 1987.

Brendan Vaughan (Clooney) – Lifelong involvement with gaelic games. Chairman of Munster Council from 1983 to 1986. Later PRO for County Board. In 1964 he founded Clare Primary Schools Hurling Board. Brendan was the driving force behind the re-development of Cusack Park. He also had a lengthy involvement with schools' drama – now retired from teaching.

Josie White (RIP) (Ennis) – A well known Ennis fisherman and native of the Hermitage area. Josie didn't ever hurl but took an keen interest in Rovers.

Paddy White (Ennis) – A well known barber, now retired. His shop in Market Street was a haven of hurling lore. A son of Mickie, who played for the Dals during the years 1924 – 1941.

Colm Wiley (Bodyke) – Captained Brian Borus to Championship win in 1975. Colm won many honours in the London Club scene.

Bernie Woods (Dals) – Played all grades for Ennis. Bernie represented Old Mill Street and later the Market (1948) in the Town Leagues. A brother to Andy and Jamesy, he also represented the Army Team.

Winning Senior Championship Teams

Ennis Hurling Club, essentially the Dals, but referred to in the papers as Ennis Hurling Club.

1911 – Ennis H.C. 3-1 . . . O'Callaghans Mills 1-2

(17-a-side) chosen from the following panel: Tom Clohessy, John Coleman, John Cunningham, John 'Joker' Coote, Brendan Considine, Willie (Dodger) Considine (Capt.), Michael Doherty, Freddie Garrihy, John Griffey, Grealish, Paddy Gordon, Paddy Kenny, Mack, Pako 'Brophy' Malone (Goalie), Steve Millar, Martin 'Handsome' Moloney, P. Moloney, Michael Moloney, Jim Marrinan, Dan Minogue, Michael McElligott, Neville, 'Gallery' O'Brien, O'Neill, C. O'Sullivan, M. Rochford, James 'Sham' Spellissy.

Ennis Dalcassians 3-1 . . . Newmarket 1-0
1914 Selection

Pako Malone (Goal), Jim Marrinan (Captain), Paddy Kenny, Tom Clohessy, Martin Moloney, 'Joker' Coote, Dan Minogue, Danaher, M. McNamara, M. Ensko, P. Walsh, Paddy Gordon, Brendan Considine, 'Dodger' Considine, Freddie Garrihy, Michael J. Baker, Edward 'Ted' Lucid, Jack Spellissy, James 'Sham' Spellissy.

1915 – Ennis Dalcassians 3-4 . . . Newmarket 2-4

Paddy Kenny, Martin Moloney, Tull Considine, 'Dodger' Considine, Brendan Considine, M. Hanrahan (Goalie), G. Kelly, P. Moloney, Jack Spellissy, Sham Spellissy, Paddy Connell, Ted Lucid, Freddie Garrihy, Jim Marrinan, Paddy Gordon, M. J. Baker, Dan Minogue (Captain).

1924 – Ennis Dalcassians 7-2 . . . Newmarket 3-2

Tom Blake (Goalie), Tull Considine, John Coleman, Gerry Cronin, John 'Joker' Coote, Paddy 'Boo' Doherty, Jackie Duffy, Mike Ensko, Bill 'Botch' Fahy, Eddie Fahy, Mickey Fahy, Wally Fahy, Freddie Garrihy, Paddy Guerin, Joe Hogan, John O'Leary, Joe Madigan, John Joe Murphy, Michael (Slasher) Malone, Pako Malone, James 'Sham' Spellissy, Mickey White.

1928 – Ennis Dals/Clarecastle 4-1 . . . Newmarket 0-3

Johnny 'Joker' Coote, Tull Considine (Capt.), Gerry Cronin, Peter Cronin, Paul Cronin, Tom 'Hawker' Blake, Larry Blake, Jacksie Darcy, Joe Hogan, Paddy Kenny, Jackie Duffy, Joe Madigan, William Hackett, Mickey White.

Clarecastle supplied the following: Dick Cole, Pa Corry, Christy 'Swaddy' McMahon, Patrick McInerney, Bernie Power, Vincent Murphy, Albert Murphy, John 'Poet' Russell.

1929 (Traditional Line Out)

Tom Blake, Paul Cronin, Paddy Kenny, Vinnie Considine, Jacksie Darcy, Gerry Cronin, Larry Blake, Tull Considine (Capt.), Mickey White, Joe Madigan, Michael Malone, Tony (Topper) Morrissey, Peter Cunningham, Paddy Doherty, Jackie Duffy.

1934 - Dals – County Champions Dalcassians 4-2 Clooney 3-1

Jimmy Kearney, Jacksie Darcy, Tull Considine, Paddy Hynes, Seán Harrington, Larry Blake, Gerry Cronin, Jack Quirke, Ralphie Burns, George Morgan, Peadar Flanagan, Aoner Sheridan, Mickey White, Miko Malone, Joe Madigan.

Subs: Tadhg Quirke, Tony 'Tonnie' Considine (both used).

According to Aoner Sheridan – Peadar Dervan didn't play in the County Final, though initially selected. The other panel members included: Jack 'Buster' Carroll, Christy 'Click' Houlihan, Mick Linnane, Paddy Kenny, Paddy Flynn, John Joe Quinn, Paddy Howard.

1941 – Dals County Champions, Dalcassians 5-2 . . . Clooney 2-1

Arthur Power, Ml. 'Paddence' O'Loughlin, Jim Quinlivan, John 'Brudsy' McCarthy, Ralphie Burns, Christy Glynn, Tom Neylon, Seán Guinnane (Captain), Tony 'Tonnie' Considine, Mickie White, Larry Blake, Aoner Sheridan, Johnny Fleming, Edward 'Bucky' Flynn, Bruddy Mann.

Subs: Jack Quirke, Miko Ball, Joe Madigan (all used). Seán Moloney, Tony Glynn. **Trainer:** John Hynes. **Coach:** Tull Considine.

1956 – Éire Óg 4-5 . . . Clarecastle 2-8

Pat Kirby, Gerry Moroney, Paddy Loftus, Bobby Burke, Bernie Dilger, Michael Blake, Jimmy Cronin, Mick Morrissey, Colm Madigan, Larry Blake, Gerry Cronin, Seán Madigan, Paschal Brooks, Paddy Kerin, Paddy Duggan.

Subs: Hugh Ensko, Jack Daly, Tony Keaty, Michael Dilger, Hugh O'Donnell, Aidan Raleigh also played senior championship in 1956.

Scorers: Colm Madigan (2-1), Gerry Cronin (1-1), Larry Blake (0-3), Paschal Brooks (1-0).

1957 – Éire Óg 5-9 . . . Whitegate 2-3

(Hugh) Joe Ensko, Paddy Kerin, Paddy Loftus, Bobby Burke, Bernie Dilger, Jimmy Cronin, Brendan Doyle, Pat Kirby, Gerry Cronin (Capt.), Michael Dilger, Paschal Brooks, Michael 'Doc' Doherty, Tony Keaty, Jack Daly, Johnny McCarthy.

The 1957 captain was Michael Blake. He was injured before the semi-final clash with Sixmilebridge and he played no further part in the championship. Gerry Cronin accepted the Hamilton Cup after their victory over Whitegate.

Scorers: Pat Kirby (1-4), Tony Keaty (2-1), Michael Doherty (1-1), Jack Daly (1-1), Johnny McCarthy (0-1), Michael Dilger (0-1).

1966 – Éire Og 2-8 . . . Whitegate 1-4

Paschal O'Brien, Jimo Blake, Martin Bradley, Des Neylon, John Nevin, Vincent Loftus, Pat Brennan, John Dunne (0-1) (Capt.), Massey Dilger, Noel Pyne (0-4), Dickie Pyne (0-1), Michael Hanrahan (1-0), Des Loftus, Johnny McCarthy (1-1), Tony Kinnevane.

Subs: Brendan Considine (used), Ml. 'Haulie' Casey, Gary Stack, Pat Coffey, Maurice Carey, James Ball, Seán O'Driscoll, Terry Hurson, Tom Glynn, Aidan Lynch.

1980 – played under the name of Éire Og Dals 3-10 . . . Newmarket 1-9

Seamus Durack, Paddy Kelly, Joe Barry, Tony Roche, Tony Kelly, Barry Smythe, Colm Mahon, Tony Nugent, Declan Coote (Capt.) (0-2), Michael Skelly, Seán Heaslip (0-2), Pete Barry (0-1), Martin Nugent (3-3), Noel Ryan (0-1), Seán Lynch (0-1).

Sub: Pat Lynch at half time.

Michael Carmody, John Glynn, Dermot Delaney, Michael Chandler, Louis Galvin, Francis Heaslip, Ollie O'Regan, Michael Griffin (Parnell Street), Francie Mahon, Tom Russell, Pat Hayes, John Quinn (sub Goalie), Donie Fitzpatrick, Johnny Kierse, Vinny Daly.

1982 – Éire Óg 3-8 . . . Sixmilebridge 2-9 (replay)

Seamus Durack, Joe Barry, Paddy Kelly, Micheál Glynn, Colm Mahon, Tony Nugent (0-4) (Capt.), Francis Heaslip, Declan Coote (0-2), Seán Heaslip, Pat Lynch (1-0), Kevin Kennedy, Martin Nugent (0-1), Seán Lynch (1-1), Pete Barry (1-0), Noel Ryan.

Sub: Michael Chandler (used).

Note: Michael Chandler played at centre-field in the drawn match

Éire Óg Senior Team, 2003. *This side progressed to the semi-final of the Championship, where they lost to Ballyea, 2-11 to 2-10. Ballyea met Clarecastle in a unique County Final, for the first time since 1909, two clubs from the same parish contested the Clare Senior Championship Final.* *Courtesy of County Express.*

versus Sixmilebridge. Michael Ryan and Francie Mahon were both introduced. Additional reserves – Paschal Mahon, Gerry Barry, Michael Skelly, Michael Kenny, Louis Galvin, Brian O'Connell, Jarlath O'Halloran, Eoin McMahon (sub-Goalie). Tomás English, Louis Mulqueen, Conor Lynch, Vinny Daly, Tom Russell.

1990

Eoin McMahon, Michael Meagher, Barry Smythe, Francis Corey, Tomás Corbett, Micheál Glynn (Capt.), Shaun McCarthy, Ger Cahill, Colm Mahon, Seán Heaslip, Géaróid Mannion, Gerry Barry, Martin Nugent, Pete Barry, Declan Coote.

Subs: Johnny Corbett, Declan Tobin, John Russell (all played in County Final). Stephen McNamara played in early rounds, while Colin Lynch and Tony McEnery shone in Munster Club Championship.

The panel also included Seamus Durack, Tadhg Lyne, Michael McCarthy, David McCarthy, Michael Skelly, Paul Nihill, Peter Kelly, Cathal Kilcawley, Tómas Fogarty.

Winning Senior Championship Captains

Ennis teams have contested 28 senior hurling championship finals. They were successful 14 times. The DALS have a great record. Between the years 1911 – 1941 they contested 12 deciders, winning 8. Formed in 1952, Éire Óg have to date played in 14 finals, winning 6. Thomond contested the 1903 final but they lost to Kilnamona. Faughs contested the 1899 final.

The honour of captaining the first successful Ennis team fell to Willie 'Dodger' Considine in 1911. Dodger's younger brother, Turlough (Tull) is the most decorated winning captain. Tull captained the DALS in 1924, 1928, 1929 and 1934. The DALS supplied at least 10 members of the Clare Junior panel of 1914, including Dan Minogue and Jim Marrinan. Jim Marrinan captained the DALS team of 1914, while Dan Minogue had the honour in 1915. Sean Guinnane, another dual medallist in hurling and football was captain when the Dalcassians won their last championship in 1941.

Éire Óg captured the imagination of the public when they swept all before them in 1956 and 1957. Their first piece of silverware was the Clare Champion Cup of 1955 played the following year with Paddy Duggan as captain. Michael Blake was captain in 1957 but injury ruled him out of contention in the latter stages. Gerry Cronin took over the captaincy and it was he who received the Hamilton Cup. Gerry Cronin was also captain of the team in 1956.

A new and very exciting crop of players arrived on the scene in the mid-60s. In 1966 John Dunne was captain and I vividly remember him bringing the cup to the CBS the following day and getting a half day into the bargain.

A contemporary of mine at the CBS, Declan Coote, was captain of the 1980 winning team, one of the best ever to represent the town. Tony Nugent captained the team from centreback in 1982 following in the footsteps of his father, Matt of St. Joseph's, in 1958. Micheál Glynn was skipper in 1990. A very good Éire Óg team reserved much of their best form for the Munster Club Championship, when Éire Óg went within a puck of a ball of winning the provincial championship.

Ennis Winning Captains At a Glance

Willie 'Dodger' Considine – 1911
Jim Marrinan – 1914
Dan Minogue – 1915
* Tull Considine – 1924, 1928, 1929, 1934
Sean Guinnane – 1941
Gerry Cronin – 1956
Michael Blake – 1957
John Dunne – 1966
Declan Coote – 1980
Tony Nugent – 1982
Micheál Glynn – 1990

* I'm not 100% sure if Tull captained the winning 1924 team. He certainly captained both the Dalcassian hurlers and footballers from 1925 - 1934 inclusive. "He rendered trojan work for Ennis and Clare, both on the field and in committee rooms. Others who gave sterling service to the Club during these years were Rev. Fr. Crowe (Chairman 1924 - 1931) and Paddy Mack (Vice-Chairman)". Spailpín Fanach 1934.

Snippets

- Simon Moroney the current Ennis Town Clerk has been appointed to the position of Secretary of the Munster Council of the G.A.A. Simon is the first Ennisman to be appointed to the position. A former school friend of mine throughout our days at CBS Ennis, Simon was part of the Leaving Cert Class of 1973. An extremely capable man, I'm sure all G.A.A. people will wish him the very best of luck in this new role.
- The first championship played on a provincial basis was in 1889. Clare lost to Dublin in the final. The teams lined out 21 a side.
- In 1892, teams were reduced to 17 a side. On the domestic scene, the last 17 a side county final was played between Ennis Dalcassians and O'Callaghans Mills, in 1911. The Dals won by 3-1 to 1-2. In 1912 the game was standardised to 15 a side.
- Players jerseys were numbered for the first time in the 1922 All-Ireland final. Kilkenny beat Tipperary by 4-2 to 2-6.
- Ennis Dals won the Clare Cup in 1928, 1929 and 1937. Éire Óg were successful in 1955 and 1959. Éire Óg also won The Cusack Park Féis and the Newmarket Tournament in 1959.

Paths to 1959 County Final

Éire Óg 2-7 ... ... Feakle 1-6
Ruan 12-7 ... ... Smith O'Briens 4-4
Éire Óg 4-3 ... ... Whitegate 1-3
Ruan 5-12 ... ... Newmarket 2-3
Éire Óg 2-8 ... ... Sixmilebridge 2-2
Ruan 3-6 ... ... Clarecastle 0-5
Final: Ruan 2-6 ... ... Éire Óg 0-4

Cups and Trophies

Senior Hurling Championship: Presented by Canon Michael Hamilton (1894-1969). The former Chairman of the County Board presented this cup in 1957.

Senior Hurling League: The Clare Champion Cup. Presented by Sarsfield Maguire, editor of Clare Champion in 1928. This cup succeeded the Redmond Cup for senior league. The Redmond Cup was presented by William Redmond MP c. 1905.

Under-21 (A): The Blake Memorial Cup. Presented by the Rovers HC in memory of Larry Blake Snr. and Michael Blake. First played for in 1965 for the delayed 1964 championship.

Minor (A): The O'Byrne Cup. Presented by O'Byrne Mineral Water.

Minor (A) League: The Liam Moloney Cup – presented 1974.

Junior (B): The Shannon Dairies Cup.

Under 16 Juvenile: Dr. Stuart Shield.

Under 15 Juvenile: Corn Padraig O'Caoimh.

Under 14 (Féile) Clare: Brendan Keane Memorial Cup

Under 14 ('A') All Ireland Féile: Christy Ring Trophy

Former Town Leagues: During the heyday of the Town Leagues - the cups played for were: -
The Gilroy Cup – presented by the Gardaí.
The Dr. McKay Cup or **Mackey Cup.**
McKaigney Cup – presented by Queen's Hotel.
Was a popular tournament in the early 1960s. Long discontinued.
First presented in 1957.

Inter-county Scorers

The following is a list of **some** outstanding Championship top score performances from earliest records.

* *The points are all given in modern day equivalents.*

Name	County	Score	*Pts	Opp.	Venue	Date	F. Sc
*Nick Rackard	Wexford	7-7	28	Antrim	Croke Pk	8/8/1954	12-17 to 2-
P. J. O'Riordan	Tipp.	6-8	26	K'kenny	Jones Rd	15/3/1896 *('95 Final)*	6-8 to 1-
Andy *'Dorric'* Buckley	Cork	7-4	25	K'kenny	Jones Rd	16/7/1905 *(1903 H. F)*	8-9 to 0-
Jimmy Smyth	Clare	6-4	22	Limk*	Cus. Pk	14/6/1953	10-8 to 1-
Tull Considine	Clare	7-0	21	G'way	Limk	14/8/1932	9-4 to 4-1
Mick 'Gah' Aherne	Cork	5-4	19	G'way	Croke Pk	9/9/1928	6-12 to 1-
Nicky English	Tipp.	2-12	18	Antrim	Croke Pk	3/9/1989	4-24 to 3-
Eddie Keher	K'kenny	2-11	17	Tipp.	Croke Pk	5/9/1971	5-17 to 5-1
Eddie Keher	K'kenny	2-9	15	Cork	Croke Pk	3/9/1972	3-24 to 5-1
Eddie Keher	K'kenny	0-14	14	Waterford	Croke Pk	1/9/1963	4-17 to 6-

* Recorded in 1953, Jimmy Smyth's score is a record for Munster Championship.

* It is reputed that Nick Rackard scored 5-4 v Dublin in the 1954 Championship.

* In the 1936 Clare/Cork replay Mick Hennessy scored 3 goals in 3 minutes. In the same game Paddy Loughnane (Feakle) recorded at least four goals.

* Pat Cronin is the only Clareman to date to top the National Scoring Charts. The Newmarket player achieved this in 1967 with 11-71 (104 pts) in 18 outings for the Banner County.

County Express Top Score Award

Sponsored by – Shannon Crystal – Murphy Stout – Martin Donnelly

In 1984, Seamus O'Reilly of the County Express, introduced a top score for hurling and Gaelic football championships. Gary Logue is the only Ennis hurler to top the chart to-date.

1984	Cyril Lyons (Ruan) … … … … … … … … …	1-45	(48)
1985	Val Donnellan (Feakle) … … … … … … …	2-21	(27)
1986	Val Donnellan (Feakle) … … … … … … …	4-26	(38)
1987	Val Donnellan (Feakle) … … … … … … …	3-51	(60)
1988	Val Donnellan (Feakle) … … … … … … …	3-35	(44)
1989	Val Donnellan (Feakle) … … … … … … …	5-23	(38)

1992 Éire Óg, beaten County Finalists. Back row, left to right: *Gary Logue, Pete Barry, Micheál Glynn, Mick Meagher, Declan Tobin, Colin Lynch, Martin Nugent, Gearóid Mannion.* ***Front row:*** *Shaun McCarthy, Tomás Corbett, John Russell, Seamus Durack, Barry Keating, Francis Corey, Barry Smythe.*

1990	Pat Minogue (Scariff)	5-15	(30)
1991	Mike Daffy (Ruan)	3-23	(32)
1992	Gary Logue (Éire Óg)	3-23	(32)
1993	Pat O'Rourke (Wolfe Tones)	2-19	(25)
1994	James Healy (Clarecastle)	2-22	(28)
1995	Gerry McInerney (Sixmilebridge)	3-13	(22)
1996	Mark McKenna (Scariff)	1-21	(24)
1997	Ken Ralph (Clarecastle)	4-22	(34)
1998	John McKenna (Ogonnelloe)	0-40	(40)
1999	Alan Markham (Kilmaley)	1-30	(33)
2000	Alan Markham (Kilmaley)	2-21	(27)
2001	Niall Gilligan (Sixmilebridge)	5-44	(59)
2002	Niall Gilligan (Sixmilebridge)	3-27	(36)

Gary Logue

Roll of Honour

In relation to County Senior Hurling Championship Results

A number of minor discrepancies with scorelines exist with other publications. In some parish histories the 1888 County Final is given as Ogonnelloe, 4-5 Tulla Emmets - nil. Likewise the 1896 final is often listed as Tulla Emmets, 1-6 O'Callaghans Mills, 0-3.

My own County Final results are gleaned from the pages of The Clare Journal. In some instances no score line is given e.g. 1909, when two teams from O'Callaghans Mills contested the County Final.

Sometimes the County Final wasn't played within the calendar year, making it even more difficult to obtain a result.

Club Names

It's important to list club names correctly. Faughs were known as Faugh a Ballagh Club, Ennis. In the early days of the Association, the Tulla team lined out as Tulla Emmets. In 1909 O'Callaghan's Mills fielded St. Patrick's and O'C. Mills Fireballs.

Its not clear when the Dalcassian name was first used. In 1911, the Ennis team is given as Ennis Hurling Club, yet in 1904 **Ennis Dalcassians** and Kilnamona played a 4-9 to 4-9 draw in a Cup game. We can assume then that the 1911 Ennis H.C. winning team is essentially the Ennis Dalcassians.

The 1920 final was declared null and void though Ennis Dals defeated O.C. Mills by 2-4 to 1-1. The 1923 final was unfinished, with the scores tied at Kilkishen 1-1 Feakle 1-1. The 1923 championship was awarded to Kilkishen.

1887	Smith O'Brien's - G/boy	0-3	...	Ogonnelloe	0-1
1888	Ogonnelloe	3-1	...	Tulla	0-1
1889	Tulla Emmets	2-3	...	Feakle	0-6
1890/95 – *No championship*					
1896	Tulla Emmets	3-5	...	O'Callaghan's Mills	2-6
1897	Tulla Emmets	3-8	...	O'Callaghan's Mills	1-8
1898	Carrahan – *awarded*		...	Tulla	

1899	Tulla	1-9	...	Faugh *a Ballagh Club, Ennis*	1-1
1900	Carrahan				
1901	– *No official championship*				
1902	Kilnamona	1-17	...	Barefield	2-2
1903	Kilnamona	4-14	...	Ennis Thomonds	Nil
1904	O'Callaghan's Mills	2-4	...	Tulla	0-4
1905	Tulla	2-11	...	Carrahan	0-1
1906	O'Callaghan's Mills	5-10	...	Kilnamona	0-1
1907	Scariff	4-12	...	O'Callaghan's Mills	5-5
1908	Kilnamona	0-11	...	O'Callaghan's Mills	0-10
1909	O'C Mills Fireballs		...	St. Patrick's *(O'Callaghan's Mills)*	1-2
1910	O'Callaghan's Mills	5-0	...	Tulla	3-2
1911	Ennis Hurling Club*	3-1	...	O'Callaghan's Mills	1-2
	**Later re-organised as Ennis Dalcassians*				
1912	Newmarket-on-Fergus Blues	3-3	...	O'Callaghan's Mills	3-1
1913	Tulla		...	Quin	
1914	Ennis Dalcassians	3-1	...	Newmarket-on-Fergus	1-0
1915	Ennis Dalcassians	3-4	...	Newmarket-on-Fergus	2-4
1916	Newmarket-on-Fergus	8-2	...	Ennis Dalcassians	2-2
1917	Scariff	5-2	...	Feakle	5-0
1918	O'Callaghan's Mills	7-2	...	Scariff	4-5
1919	Clonlara		...	Scariff	
1920	Ennis Dalcassians	2-4	...	O'Callaghan's Mills	1-1
	– *declared null and void*				
1921	*No County Board - no championship*				
1922	– *Championship undecided*				
1923	Kilkishen – *awarded*		...	Feakle	
1924	Ennis Dalcassians	7-2	...	Newmarket-on-Fergus	3-2
1925	Newmarket-on-Fergus		...	Tulla	
1926	Newmarket-on-Fergus	3-5	...	O'Callaghan's Mills	2-3
1927	Newmarket-on-Fergus		...	Ennis Dalcassians	
1928	Ennis/Clarecastle	4-1	...	Newmarket-on-Fergus	0-3
1929	Ennis Dals – *awarded*		...	Newmarket-on-Fergus	
1930	Newmarket-on-Fergus	6-3	...	Ennis Dalcassians	3-0
1931	Newmarket-on-Fergus	3-4	...	Ennis Dalcassians	1-3
1932	Kilkishen	6-5	...	Newmarket-on-Fergus	1-1
1933	Tulla	7-1	...	Newmarket-on-Fergus	2-1
1934	Ennis Dalcassians	4-2	...	Clooney	3-1
1935	Feakle	6-1	...	Newmarket-on-Fergus	2-3
1936	Newmarket-on-Fergus	6-2	...	Clarecastle	2-3

1937	O'Callaghan's Mills	5-2	...	Clarecastle	2-2
1938	Feakle	4-2	...	Kilkishen	1-5
1939	Feakle	4-6	...	Clarecastle	3-4
1940	Feakle	3-4	...	Clooney	2-3
1941	Ennis Dalcassians	5-2	...	Clooney	2-1
1942	Clooney	3-6	...	Scariff	3-5
1943	Clarecastle	4-3	...	Scariff	4-2
1944	Feakle	9-3	...	Clooney	0-4
1945	Clarecastle	4-7	...	Broadford	2-2
1946	Scariff	3-4	...	Feakle	2-5
1947	Bodyke	5-8	...	Clarecastle	4-7
1948					
Draw	Ruan	6-4	...	Clarecastle	5-7
Replay	Ruan	6-3	...	Clarecastle	3-5
1949	Clarecastle	4-8	...	Ruan	3-3
1950	Whitegate	5-1	...	Ruan	3-1
1951	Ruan	3-6	...	St. Joseph's	2-2
1952	Scariff	4-6	...	Sixmilebridge	2-0
1953	Scariff	5-2	...	Newmarket-on-Fergus	2-7
1954	St. Joseph's	3-6	...	O'Callaghan's Mills	2-2
1955	Newmarket-on-Fergus	3-9	...	Éire Óg, Ennis	3-3
1956	Éire Óg, Ennis	4-5	...	Clarecastle	2-8
1957	Éire Óg, Ennis	5-9	...	Whitegate	2-3
1958	St. Joseph's	3-6	...	Feakle	2-2
1959	Ruan	2-6	...	Éire Óg, Ennis	0-4
1960	Ruan	6-9	...	Scariff	3-10
1961	Whitegate	5-7	...	Newmarket-on-Fergus	3-9
1962					
Draw	Ruan	3-4	...	Sixmilebridge	1-10
Replay	Ruan	3-9	...	Sixmilebridge	2-8
1963	Newmarket-on-Fergus	6-10	...	Whitegate	3-7
1964	Newmarket-on-Fergus	8-12	...	Clarecastle	5-7
1965	Newmarket-on-Fergus	2-6	...	Éire Óg, Ennis	1-6
1966	Éire Óg, Ennis	2-8	...	Whitegate	1-4
1967	Newmarket-on-Fergus	3-10	...	Clarecastle	2-4
1968	Newmarket-on-Fergus	2-8	...	Clarecastle	1-9
1969					
Draw	Newmarket-on-Fergus	3-5	...	Clarecastle	2-8
Replay	Newmarket-on-Fergus	9-13	...	Clarecastle	3-6
1970					
Draw	Clarecastle	1-8	...	Crusheen	1-8
Replay	Clarecastle	1-7	...	Crusheen	0-5

1971					
Draw	Newmarket-on-Fergus	3-9	...	Clarecastle	2-12
Replay	Newmarket-on-Fergus	2-7	...	Clarecastle	1-7
1972	Newmarket-on-Fergus	7-8	...	St. Senan's	3-5
1973	Newmarket-on-Fergus	7-10	...	Clarecastle	4-16
1974	Newmarket-on-Fergus	1-6	...	Crusheen	2-2
1975	Brian Boru's	4-7	...	Éire Óg, Ennis	2-9
1976	Newmarket-on-Fergus	1-11	...	Sixmilebridge	1-5
1977	Sixmilebridge	1-6	...	Kilkishen	1-5
1978	Newmarket-on-Fergus	3-10	...	Clarecastle	2-8
1979	Sixmilebridge	5-11	...	St. Brendan's	0-9
1980	Éire Óg Dal gCais	3-10	...	Newmarket-on-Fergus	1-9
1981	Newmarket-on-Fergus	3-8	...	Tubber	1-10
1982					
Draw	Éire Óg	2-11	...	Sixmilebridge	2-11
Replay	Éire Og	3-8	...	Sixmilebridge	2-9
1983					
Draw	Sixmilebridge	1-10	...	Éire Og	3-4
Replay	Sixmilebridge	1-10	...	Éire Og	1-7
1984	Sixmilebridge	3-7	...	Clarecastle	1-12
1985	Kilmaley	0-10	...	Éire Og, Ennis	0-8
1986	Clarecastle	2-11	...	O'Callaghan's Mills	0-7
1987	Clarecastle	0-15	...	Feakle	0-11
1988	Feakle	1-17	...	Ruan	1-10
1989	Sixmilebridge	3-14	...	Clarecastle	1-11
1990	Éire Og, Ennis	1-5	...	O'Callaghan's Mills	1-3
1991	Clarecastle	0-14	...	Scariff	1-5
1992	Sixmilebridge	1-11	...	Éire Og	1-10
1993	Sixmilebridge	3-8	...	O'Callaghan's Mills	2-6
1994	Clarecastle	1-8	...	St. Joseph's	0-8
1995	Sixmilebridge	2-10	...	Scariff	0-15
1996	Wolfe Tones, Shannon	1-11	...	Clarecastle	0-8
1997	Clarecastle	2-11	...	St. Joseph's	0-11
1998	St. Joseph's	3-9	...	Kilmaley	2-7
1999	St. Joseph's	3-12	...	Sixmilebridge	1-12
2000	Sixmilebridge	4-9	...	Éire Og, Ennis	1-8
2001	St. Joseph's	1-15	...	Sixmilebridge	1-12
2002	Sixmilebridge	3-10	...	Clarecastle	2-8

Clare Champion Cup - Senior Hurling League

More commonly known as The Clare Cup, this was first presented to the GAA by Mr. Sarsfield Maguire of the Clare Champion in 1928 for a **senior** league competition.

1928	Ennis/Clarecastle	3-3	...	Newmarket-on-Fergus	1-4
1929	Ennis Dalcassians – *awarded* - *game unfinished*		...	Newmarket-on-Fergus	
1930	Newmarket-on-Fergus	4-7	...	Ennis Dalcassians	2-4
1931	Newmarket-on-Fergus	5-5	...	Ennis Dalcassians	3-6
1932	Newmarket-on-Fergus	8-3	...	Kilkishen	2-0
1933					
Draw	Newmarket-on-Fergus	5-1	...	Tulla	4-4
Replay	Newmarket-on-Fergus	2-7	...	Tulla	1-6
1934	Clooney	4-4	...	Clonlara	4-2
1935	Newmarket-on-Fergus	7-6	...	O'Callaghan's Mills	1-1
1936	Newmarket-on-Fergus	2-4	...	Feakle	1-6
1937	Ennis Dals - *walkover*		...	O'Callaghan's Mills	
1938	Feakle	6-2	...	Tulla	3-2
1939					
Draw	Tulla	2-3	...	Newmarket-on-Fergus	2-3
Replay	Tulla	5-5	...	Newmarket-on-Fergus	5-3
1940	Feakle	6-5	...	Clooney	0-4
1941	Clooney	5-2	...	Bodyke	2-3
1942	Scariff	4-4	...	Clooney	3-3
1943	Clarecastle	4-6	...	23rd Battalion	3-2
1944	23rd Battalion	2-5	...	Clooney	2-4
1945	Clarecastle	4-4	...	Tulla	4-1
1946	Clarecastle	4-5	...	Tulla	4-1
1947	Newmarket – *walkover*		...	Feakle	
1948	Newmarket-on-Fergus	5-3	...	Bodyke	4-1
1949	Newmarket-on-Fergus	2-8	...	Ruan	3-3
1950	Scariff	5-7	...	Newmarket-on-Fergus	3-4
1951	Broadford – *awarded*		...	Whitegate	
1952	Newmarket-on-Fergus	5-3	...	Clarecastle	2-5
1953	St. Joseph's	3-7	...	Newmarket-on-Fergus	2-3
1954	Sixmilebridge	4-6	...	Newmarket-on-Fergus	2-6
1955	Éire Og	4-6	...	Feakle	2-3
1956	Sixmilebridge	2-13	...	Ruan	2-4
1957	St. Joseph's	5-5	...	Whitegate	2-5
1958	Whitegate	3-3	...	St. Joseph's	1-5

1959					
Draw	Éire Og	3-3	...	Clarecastle	2-6
Replay	Éire Og	6-5	...	Clarecastle	4-6
1960	Whitegate	6-8	...	Scariff	2-1
1961	Ruan	5-6	...	St. Joseph's	1-2
1962	Newmarket-on-Fergus	3-4	...	Sixmilebridge	1-9
1963	Newmarket-on-Fergus	8-5	...	St. Joseph's	0-6
1964	Feakle	3-9	...	Tubber	2-10
1965	Crusheen	5-4	...	Éire Og	4-6
1966	Newmarket-on-Fergus	5-12	...	Feakle	2-4
1967	Newmarket-on-Fergus	7-14	...	Crusheen	1-3
1968	Newmarket-on-Fergus	7-13	...	Clarecastle	6-1
1969	Newmarket-on-Fergus	5-8	...	Éire Og	3-4
1970	Crusheen	2-6	...	Clarecastle	0-5
1971	Newmarket-on-Fergus	8-5	...	Éire Og	1-5
1972	Newmarket-on-Fergus	5-6	...	Crusheen	3-1
1973	Newmarket-on-Fergus	3-5	...	Éire Og	1-5
1974	Newmarket-on-Fergus	5-14	...	Brian Boru's	3-8
1975	Sixmilebridge	1-9	...	Feakle	0-11
1976	Sixmilebridge	2-9	...	Newmarket-on-Fergus	1-4
1977	Brian Boru's	2-8	...	Sixmilebridge	2-5
1978	Sixmilebridge	3-9	...	Crusheen	3-8
1979	Sixmilebridge – *decided on points system*				
1980	Sixmilebridge	2-8	...	Tubber	2-5
1981	Kilmaley	1-14	...	Tubber	3-1
1982	Sixmilebridge	3-9	...	Feakle	1-13
1983					
Draw	Clarecastle	3-6	...	Tubber	2-9
Replay	Clarecastle	3-9	...	Tubber	3-9
2nd Replay	Clarecastle	2-12	...	Tubber	2-9
1984	Clarecastle	2-14	...	Feakle	1-10
1985	Tubber	2-13	...	Éire Og	0-16
1986	Tulla	3-7	...	Sixmilebridge	4-3
1987	Feakle	2-10	...	Éire Og	2-7
1988	Feakle	2-15	...	Broadford	1-7
1989	Sixmilebridge	3-13	...	Feakle	0-10
1990	O'Callaghan's Mills	0-15	...	Clarecastle	0-11
1991	O'Callaghan's Mills	2-8	...	Scariff	1-6
1992	Clarecastle	3-5	...	O'Callaghan's Mills	0-10
1993					
Draw	O'Callaghan's Mills	1-11	...	Sixmilebridge	1-11
Replay	O'Callaghan's Mills	2-10	...	Sixmilebridge	2-6

1994	Scariff	2-12	...	Clarecastle	3-4
1995	O'Callaghan's Mills	2-11	...	Sixmilebridge	2-9
1996	Clarecastle – *walkover**		...	Wolfe Tones – *null and void*	
1997	St. Joseph's	0-13	...	Tulla	0-6
1998	St. Joseph's	1-8	...	Whitegate	0-9
1999	Ogonnelloe	0-13	...	Whitegate	1-7
2000	Sixmilebridge	1-11	...	Feakle	0-10
2001	Kilmaley	0-11	...	Clarecastle	0-7
2002	Clarecastle	2-11	...	Crusheen	0-8

* In 1996, due to Wolfe Tones involvement in the Munster Senior Club Championship Final, they declined to play in the final of the Clare Cup. The County Board awarded the cup to Clarecastle; however, the Magpies, as one would expect of a club of their stature, refused to accept the trophy in such a fashion. To the best of my knowledge the 1996 Clare Cup is null and void.

Intermediate Hurling Champions

1927	Ennis Rovers	1928	Clonlara
1929	Kilkishen	1930	Feakle
1931	Clarecastle	1932	Bodyke
1933	O'Callaghan's Mills	1934	Clooney
1935	Kilkishen	1936	Bodyke
1937	Cratloe	1938	Scariff
1939	Mountshannon	1940	Ruan
1941	Broadford	1942	Mountshannon
1943	Cratloe	1944	Ballyea
1945	Ennis Faughs	1946	Bodyke
1947	Broadford	1948	Ruan
1949	*No competition*	1950	Ruan
1951	Sixmilebridge	1952	Our Lady's Hospital
1953	*Unfinished*	1954	*No competition*
1955	*No competition*	1956	Parteen
1957	Cappagh	1958	St. John's, Ennis
1959	Whitegate	1960	Crusheen
1961/'66 – *No Intermediate Competition*			
1967	Newmarket-on-Fergus	1968	O'Callaghan's Mills
1969	Bodyke	1970	Cratloe
1971	Sixmilebridge	1972	Tubber
1973	Feakle	1974	Broadford
1975	Clonlara	1976	Tubber
1977	O'Callaghan's Mills	1978	Ruan

1979	Tulla	1980	Kilmaley
1981	Broadford	1982	Scariff
1983	Wolfe Tones	1984	Whitegate
1985	St. Joseph's	1986	Clooney
1987	Crusheen	1988	Sixmilebridge
1989	Clonlara	1990	Sixmilebridge
1991	Corofin	1992	Whitegate
1993	St. Joseph's	1994	Cratloe
1995	Ogonnelloe	1996	Bodyke
1997	Broadford	1998	Kilnamona
1999	Clonlara	2000	Crusheen
2001	Ballyea	2002	Corofin

Note: Intermediate 'B' was run on and off for a few years, the winners: -

1937	Tubber	1938	Kilmaley
1939	Sixmilebridge		
1941	Kilmaley	1942	Ballyea

Junior 'A' Champions

1926	Newmarket-on-Fergus	1927	Ennis Dalcassians
1928	Feakle	1929	Bodyke
1930	Meelick	1931	Tradaree
1932	Ruan	1933	Clooney
1934	Crusheen	1935	Cratloe
1936	Scariff	1937	Ogonnelloe
1938	Mountshannon	1939	Broadford
1940	Ballyea	1941	Crusheen
1942	Tuamgraney	1943	Tradaree
1944	Crusheen	1945	Ardnacrusha
1946	Bodyke	1947	Cappagh
1948	Ruan	1949	Cappagh
1950	Sixmilebridge	1951	Our Lady's Hospital
1952	Barefield	1953	Bauroe
1954	Parteen	1955	Broadford
1956	Cappagh	1957	Tuamgraney
1958	Kilbane	1959	Crusheen
1960	St. Joseph's	1961	Bodyke
1962	Tubber	1963	Kilmaley
1964	Cratloe	1965	Kilnamona
1966	Clooney	1967	Smith O'Brien's
1968	Parteen	1969	Corofin
1970	Killanena	1971	Broadford
1972	Newmarket-on-Fergus	1973	Clonlara

1974 Wolfe Tones
1975 Kilnamona
1976 Cratloe
1977 Killanena
1978 Smith O'Brien's
1979 Wolfe Tones
1980 Corofin
1981 Sixmilebridge
1982 Ballyea
1983 St. Joseph's
1984 Inagh
1985 Clarecastle
1986 Bodyke
1987 Meelick
1988 Ogonnelloe
1989 Kilnamona
1990 Éire Og, Ennis
1991 Ballyea
1992 Scariff
1993 Inagh
1994 Kilnamona
1995 Wolfe Tones, Shannon
1996 Kilnamona
1997 Smith O'Brien's, Killaloe
1998 Newmarket-on-Fergus
1999 Ballyea
2000 St. Joseph's
2001 Kilmaley
2002 Éire Og

Junior 'B'

1938 Clarecastle
1939 Cratloe
1940 Broadford
1941 Newmarket – *walkover*
1942 Fergus Gaels
1943 Barefield
1944 Feakle
1945 Corofin
1946 Cappagh
1947 Liscullane
1948 Barefield
1949 Ardnacrusha
1950 Smith O'Brien's, Killaloe
1951 Clonlara
1952 Tulla
1953 O'Brien's Bridge
1954 Fergus Rovers
1955 Castle Rovers
1956 St. John's, Ennis
1957 Kilnamona
1958 Crusheen
1959 Cratloe
1960 Ogonnelloe
1961 Broadford
1962 Feakle
1963 Broadford
1964 Killanena
1965 Newmarket-on-Fergus
1966 Clarecastle
1967/70 – *None*
1971 Kilnamona
1972 Crusheen
1973 Corofin
1974 Sixmilebridge
1975 Meelick
1976 Ballyea
1977 Parteen
1978 Quin
1979 O'Callaghan's Mills
1980 Ruan
1981 Crusheen
1982 Éire Og, Ennis
1983 Ennistymon
1984 Ogonnelloe
1985 Sixmilebridge
1986 St. Joseph's
1987 Wolfe Tones
1988 Clooney
1989 Scariff
1990 Tulla

1991	Feakle	1992	Kilmaley
1993	Feakle	1994	St. Joseph's
1995	Broadford	1996	Wolfe Tones
1997	Clarecastle	1998	Whitegate
1999	St. Joseph's	2000	Sixmilebridge
2001	Newmarket-on-Fergus	2002	Feakle
2003	Crusheen		

U/21 'A' Roll of Honour

The Blake Memorial Cup. Presented by Ennis Rovers Hurling Club. Inscription on the trophy reads "Corn Cuimhneacháin de Bláca – a bhronnadh ag Cumann Iomána Fánaithe na hInse."

1964	Ennis Rovers	1965	Ennis Rovers
1966	Éire Og, Ennis	1967	Newmarket-on-Fergus
1968	Newmarket-on-Fergus	1969	Crusheen
1970	Newmarket-on-Fergus	1971	Sixmilebridge
1972	Whitegate	1973	Sixmilebridge
1974	Éire Og	1975	Kilmaley
1976	Ruan	1977	Éire Og
1978	Ruan	1979	Sixmilebridge
1980	Sixmilebridge	1981	Sixmilebridge
1982	Feakle	1983	Feakle
1984	Feakle	1985	Feakle
1986	Sixmilebridge	1987	Scariff
1988	Sixmilebridge	1989	Wolfe Tones
1990	Wolfe Tones/Clarecastle – *unfinished*	1991	Wolfe Tones
1992	Cratloe	1993	St. Joseph's
1994	St. Joseph's	1995	Clarecastle
1996	Clarecastle	1997	Sixmilebridge
1998	Sixmilebridge	1999	Clarecastle
2000	Clarecastle	2001	Newmarket-on-Fergus
2002	Sixmilebridge	2003	Sixmilebridge

Minor 'A' Championship

1926	St. Flannan's College	1927	St. Flannan's College
1928	Clonlara	1929	Feakle
1930	Feakle	1931	Tulla
1932	Tulla	1933	Tulla
1934	St. Flannan's College	1935	Feakle
1936	Clarecastle	1937	Clarecastle
1938	Ruan	1939	Clarecastle

***Éire Óg Minor A Finalists 2002. Back row, left to right:** John Brennan, Niall Daly, Ronan Keane, Damien Coleman, Eoin Woulfe, Garry O'Connell, Conor McNamara, David Gallagher, Rory Hally, Tomas Craven, Eric Kelly, Adrian Flaherty, James Gallagher. **Front row:** Colm O'Callaghan, Conor Considine, John Quinn, Eoin O'Connell, Paddy Guilfoyle, Stephen Skelly, Jamie Deniffe, Fergal Brennan, Enda McNamara.*

1940	Tulla	1941	Tulla
1942	Clarecastle	1943	Ennis Dalcassians
1944	Ennis CD	1945	Ennis CD
1946	Ennis CD – *Commercial Dalcassians*	1947	Ennis CD
1948	Newmarket-on-Fergus	1949	Bodyke – *Mid-Clare Selection*
1950	Clarecastle	1951	Ennis Faughs
1952	Clarecastle	1953	Ruan
1954	Smith O'Brien's Killaloe	1955	St. John's Ennis
1956	St. John's Ennis	1957	Ennis Rovers
1958	St. Joseph's	1959	St. Joseph's
1960	Newmarket-on-Fergus	1961	Ennis Rovers
1962	Ennis Rovers	1963	Ennis Rovers
1964	Clarecastle	1965	Ennis Rovers
1966	Ennis Rovers	1967	Éire Óg
1968	Newmarket-on-Fergus	1969	Éire Óg
1970	Sixmilebridge	1971	Ennis Dalcassians
1972	Ennis Dalcassians	1973	Kilmaley
1974	Éire Óg	1975	Sixmilebridge

Henry Shefflin pictured with a group of young Éire Óg hopefuls from U/12 to U/15 after he had given a coaching session at the Éire Óg Club.

1976	Sixmilebridge	1977	Sixmilebridge
1978	Éire Og	1979	Sixmilebridge
1980	Sixmilebridge	1981	Clarecastle
1982	Feakle	1983	Sixmilebridge
1984	Sixmilebridge	1985	Sixmilebridge
1986	Clarecastle	1987	Clarecastle
1988	WolfeTones na Sionna	1989	Éire Og
1990	St. Joseph's	1991	Éire Og
1992	Wolfe Tones na Sionna	1993	Éire Og
1994	Sixmilebridge	1995	Clarecastle
1996	Sixmilebridge	1997	Sixmilebridge
1998	Newmarket-on-Fergus	1999	Clarecastle
2000	Tulla	2001	Sixmilebridge
2002	Newmarket-on-Fergus		

23 Minor 'A' titles have been won by Ennis clubs to date, be it the Dals, St. John's, Rovers, Faughs or Éire Óg.

Munster Senior Club Championship Finals

Year	Winner	Score		Runner-up	Score
1964	Glen Rovers	3-7	...	Mount Sion	1-7
1965	St. Finbarr's	3-12	...	Mount Sion	2-3
1966	Carrick Davins	2-17	...	Ballygunner	1-11
1967	Newmarket-on-Fergus	3-9	...	Carrick Davins	2-7
1968	Newmarket-on-Fergus	5-8	...	Ballygunner	4-3
1969	Roscrea	3-6	...	Glen Rovers	1-9
1970	Roscrea	4-11	...	Clarecastle	1-6
1971	Blackrock	4-10	...	Moyne-Templetuohy	3-1
1972	Glen Rovers	2-9	...	Roscrea	1-10
1973	Blackrock	1-13	...	Newmarket-on-Fergus	0-14
1974	St. Finbarr's	0-7	...	Newmarket-on-Fergus	0-3
1975	Blackrock	8-12	...	Mount Sion	3-8
1976	Glen Rovers	2-8	...	South Liberties	2-4
1977					
Draw	St. Finbarr's	3-5	...	Sixmilebridge	3-5
Replay	St. Finbarr's	2-8	...	Sixmilebridge	0-6
1978	Blackrock	3-8	...	Newmarket-on-Fergus	1-8
1979	Blackrock	0-13	...	Dunhill	1-8
1980	St. Finbarr's	2-12	...	Roscrea	1-14
1981	Mount Sion	3-9	...	South Liberties	1-4
1982	Moycarkey-Borris	1-9	...	Patrickswell	0-11
1983					
Draw	Midleton	3-6	...	Borrisoleigh	1-12
Replay	Midleton	1-14	...	Borrisoleigh	1-11
1984	Sixmilebridge	4-10	...	Patrickswell	2-6
1985	Kilruane-McDonagh	0-12	...	Blackrock	0-6
1986	Borrisoleigh	1-13	...	Clarecastle	1-9
1987	Midleton	1-12	...	Cappawhite	1-11
1988	Patrickswell	3-13	...	Mount Sion	2-13
1989	Ballybrown	2-12	...	Sixmilebridge	1-8
1990	Patrickswell	0-8	...	Éire Óg, Ennis	0-6
1991	Cashel King Cormacs	0-9	...	Midleton	0-6
1992	Kilmallock	3-11	...	Sixmilebridge	2-11
1993	Toomevara	0-15	...	Sixmilebridge	0-7
1994	Kilmallock	2-11	...	Toomevara	1-11
1995	Sixmilebridge	2-18	...	Éire Óg, Nenagh	1-7
1996	Wolfe Tones, Shannon	4-9	...	Ballygunner	4-8
1997	Clarecastle	2-11	...	Patrickswell	0-15
1998	St. Joseph's	0-12	...	Toomevara	0-8
1999	St. Joseph's	4-9	...	Ballygunner	3-8
2000	Sixmilebridge	2-17	...	Mount Sion	3-8
2001	Ballygunner	2-14	...	Blackrock	0-12
2002	Mount Sion	0-12	...	Sixmilebridge	0-10

Munster Club Hurling Championship

The winning county champions in each of the six provinces represent their respective county in this championship. However, there is an exception to every rule and in the case of Brian Borus (1975 County Champions), Éire Óg represented the county as 'Borus were an amalgamation. In 1980, Éire Óg couldn't represent Clare as they had assistance from The Banner Club. Newmarket, the beaten finalists were then nominated to represent the County.

Clare clubs have won the championship nine times, a fine record.

The following is a comprehensive list of all Munster Club games involving Clare Clubs. The competition was first introduced in 1964.

1964/1965	Mount Sion *(Waterford)*	2-9	...	Newmarket	2-5
1965/1966	Mount Sion	6-7	...	Newmarket	7-3
1966/1967	Avondhu *(Cork)*	2-8	...	Éire Óg Ennis	3-5
	Avondhu	3-14	...	Éire Óg	2-4
1967/1968	Newmarket	3-8	...	Glen Rovers *(Cork)*	4-4
	Newmarket	4-10	...	Ballygunner *(Waterford)*	3-4
	Newmarket	3-9	...	Carrick Davins *(Tipp)*	2-7
1968/1969	Newmarket	11-21	...	Liam Mellowes *(Galway)*	1-5
	Newmarket	4-9	...	St. Finbarrs (Cork)	3-2
	Newmarket	5-8	...	Ballygunner	4-3
1969/1970	Glen Rovers	5-6	...	Newmarket	3-6
1970/1971	Clarecastle	3-6	...	Patrickswell *(Limerick)*	3-6
	Clarecastle	5-2	...	Patrickswell *(Limerick)*	3-6
	Clarecastle	3-8	...	U.C.C.	2-11
	Clarecastle	3-7	...	U.C.C.	2-5
	Roscrea	4-11	...	Clarecastle	1-6
1971/1972	Newmarket	3-9	...	Portlaw *(Waterford)*	1-4
	Blackrock *(Cork)*	5-14	...	Newmarket	2-5
1972/1973	Roscrea	3-13	...	Newmarket	4-4
1973/1974	Newmarket	6-10	...	Portlaw	3-7
	Newmarket	4-7	...	Ballyduff *(Kerry)*	2-7
	Blackrock	1-13	...	Newmarket	0-14
1974/1975	Newmarket	2-10	...	Thurles Sarsfields	0-9
	St. Finbarrs	0-7	...	Newmarket	0-3
1975/1976	Moneygall *(Tipp)*	2-10	...	Éire Óg Ennis	0-6

1976/1977	Newmarket	2-12	...	Moneygall	2-10
	Glen Rovers	1-13	...	Newmarket	2-9
1977/1978	Sixmilebridge	1-7	...	Kilruane McDonagh	0-8
	St. Finbarrs	3-5	...	Sixmilebridge	3-5
	St. Finbarrs	2-8	...	Sixmilebridge	0-6
1978/1979	Newmarket	7-10	...	Dunhill *(Waterford)*	2-13
	Newmarket	3-7	...	Ballyduff *(Kerry)*	3-2
	Blackrock	3-8	...	Newmarket	1-8
1979/1980	Dunhill *(Waterford)*	3-9	...	Sixmilebridge	2-8
1980/1981	Roscrea	2-10	...	Newmarket	2-8
1981/1982	Newmarket	3-11	...	St. Finbarrs	0-10
	South Liberties *(Limerick)*	2-9	...	Newmarket	1-5
1982/1983	Ballyduff *(Waterford)*	3-8	...	Éire Óg Ennis	1-13
1983/1984	Midleton *(Cork)*	2-14	...	Sixmilebridge	0-15
1984/1985	Sixmilebridge	2-10	...	St. Finbarrs	1-7
	Sixmilebridge	4-19	...	Ballyduff *(Kerry)*	1-9
	Sixmilebridge	4-10	...	Patrickswell	2-6
1985/1986	Blackrock	1-17	...	Kilmaley	0-10
1986/1987	Clarecastle	6-12	...	Mount Sion	2-2
	Clarecastle	3-11	...	St. Brendan's	2-4
	Borrisoleigh	1-13	...	Clarecastle	1-9
1987/1988	Midleton	3-12	...	Clarecastle	2-11
1988/1989	Feakle	4-16	...	Ballyduff	1-8
	Mount Sion	1-8	...	Feakle	1-7
1989/1990	Sixmilebridge	1-18	...	Glen Rovers	4-4
	Ballybrown *(Limerick)*	2-12	...	Sixmilebridge	1-8
1990/1991	Éire Óg Ennis	2-16	...	Roanmore *(Waterford)*	1-14
	Éire Óg Ennis	2-5	...	Na Piarsaigh *(Cork)*	0-9
	Patrickswell	0-8	...	Éire Óg	0-6
1991/1992	Clarecastle	3-15	...	Ballybrown	1-5
	Cashel King Cormacs	3-11	...	Clarecastle	2-4
1992/1993	Sixmilebridge	1-15	...	Ballyheigue *(Kerry)*	1-7
	Sixmilebridge	3-12	...	Ballygunner	0-5
	Kilmallock	3-11	...	Sixmilebridge	2-11
1993/1994	Sixmilebridge	2-9	...	Lismore *(Waterford)*	1-4
	Toomevara *(Tipp)*	0-15	...	Sixmilebridge	0-7
1994/1995	Toomevara	1-12	...	Clarecastle	1-11
1995/1996	Sixmilebridge	5-11	...	Ballygunner	2-10
	Sixmilebridge	2-18	...	Éire Óg, Nenagh	1-7

1996/1997	Wolfe Tones Shannon	1-12	...	Ballyheigue	2-7
	Wolfe Tones	1-11	...	Patrickswell	0-9
	Wolfe Tones	4-9	...	Ballygunner	4-8
1997/1998	Clarecastle	1-16	...	Ballygunner	0-16
	Clarecastle	2-11	...	Patrickswell	0-15
1998/1999	St. Josephs	1-13	...	Mount Sion	0-7
	St. Josephs	0-12	...	Toomevara	0-8
1999/2000	St. Josephs	2-11	...	Toomevara	0-12
	St. Josephs	4-9	...	Ballygunner	3-8
2000/2001	Sixmilebridge	0-13	...	Patrickswell	0-12
	Sixmilebridge	2-17	...	Mount Sion	3-8
2001/2002	Ballygunner	2-19	...	St. Josephs	2-13
2002/2003	Sixmilebridge	1-15	...	Blackrock	0-16
	Mount Sion	0-12	...	Sixmilebridge	0-10

Clare Senior Football Championship - Roll of Honour

1887	Dal Gais Newmarket		...	Cratloe	
1888	Dal Gais Newmarket	0-2	...	Kilmacduane *(Cooraclare)*	0-1
1889	Kildysart William O'Brien's	0-0	...	Cunnal Gulbans *(Clooney)*	0-1
– game abandoned - replay ordered					
Replay	Kildysart William O'Brien's	0-3	...	Cunnal Gulbans *(Clooney)*	0-2
1890	Ennis Dalcassians		...	Coore – *unplayed*	
1890/1895 – *County Board Dissolved*					
1896	Killimer	0-4	...	Dal Gais Newmarket	0-3
1897	Ennis Dalcassians		...	Kilrush – *after three games*	
1898	Doora				
1899	Ennis Dalcassians	2-13	...	Clarecastle Shamrocks	0-4
1900	Labasheeda St. Patrick's	0-7	...	Kilmihil St. Michaels	0-1
1901 – *No County Championship*					
1902	Kilrush Shamrocks	0-8	...	Ennis Dalcassians	0-5
1903					
Replay	Kilrush Shamrocks	0-4	...	Ennis Dalcassians	0-3
1904	Ennis Dalcassians	0-5	...	Miltown Malbay	0-3
1905					
Replay	Miltown		...	Ennis Dalcassians	
1906					
Replay	Miltown	0-12	...	Kilrush	0-4
1907	Ennis Dalcassians				
1908	Robert Emmets Clarecastle		...	Miltown	
1909	Ennis Dalcassians		...	Cooraclare Milesians	
1910	Ennis Dalcassians				
1911	Ennis Dalcassians				

1912	Kilrush				
1913	Ennis Dalcassians	0-1	...	Cooraclare	0-1
Replay	Ennis Dalcassians	1-1	...	Cooraclare	0-2
1914	Ennis Dalcassians		...	Miltown	
1915	Cooraclare Milesians *– awarded*		...	Ennis Dalcassians	
1916	Miltown	3-2	...	Cooraclare Milesians	2-2
1917	Cooraclare Milesians				
1918	Cooraclare Milesians		...	Coolmeen	
1919	Coolmeen	0-7	...	Kilrush*	0-9
	**Though Kilrush led Coolmeen by 0-9 to 0-7 the game was awarded to Coolmeen*				
1920	County Board Dissolved				
1921	County Board Dissolved				
1922	Coolmeen	0-4	...	Kilkee	0-2
1923	Miltown	0-3	...	Kilkee	0-2
1924	Kilrush		...	Kilmurry Ibrickane	
1925	Miltown	1-2	...	Kilrush	0-3
1926	Kilkee	1-6	...	Coolmeen	0-1
1927	Miltown	2-5	...	Ennis Dalcassians	1-2
1928	Kilkee	0-5	...	Kilrush	0-4
1929	Ennis Dalcassians	1-1	...	Miltown	0-3
1930	Kilrush	1-5	...	Ennis Dalcassians	1-4
1931	Kilrush		...	Miltown	
1932	Miltown	2-4	...	Cooraclare Utd	1-6
1933	Kilmurry Ibrickane	2-4	...	Kilkee	1-2
1934	Kilrush	3-1	...	North Clare	0-2
1935	Quilty St. Mary's	2-3	...	Kilmurry Ibrickane	1-4
1936	Quilty St. Mary's	1-3	...	Kilrush	0-4
1937	Kilrush	1-7	...	Quilty	1-4
1938					
Draw	Kilrush	1-4	...	Ballyvaughan/North Clare Selection	1-4
	Kilrush received a walkover in replay				
1939	Quilty	1-5	...	Kilrush	0-2
1940	Liscannor	1-8	...	Kilrush	0-7
1941	Kilfenora	0-3	...	Kilkee Utd	0-2
1942	Kilkee	1-4	...	Ennistymon	1-3
1943	*– Final between Ennistymon/Kilkee was declared Null and Void*				
1944	Cooraclare	1-6	...	Kilfenora	1-4
1945	Cooraclare	1-5	...	Kilmurry Ibrickane	1-3
1946	O'Currys	2-0	...	Kilmurry Ibrickane	1-2
1947	Ennis Faughs	0-7	...	Clohanes	1-3

1948	Ennis Faughs	0-10	...	O'Curry's	1-4
1949	Miltown – *awarded*	0-6	...	Kilrush	1-5
1950	Kilfenora	1-4	...	Clohanes	0-3
1951	Kilrush	1-8	...	Miltown	0-4
1952	Ennis Faughs	3-3	...	Kilrush	0-3
1953	Miltown	1-6	...	Ennis Faughs	0-7
1954	Ennis Faughs – *awarded*		...	Kilrush*	
	** Kilrush refused to play at Miltown Malbay the appointed venue*				
1955					
Draw	Doonbeg	0-5	...	Ennis Faughs	0-5
Replay	Doonbeg	0-8	...	Ennis Faughs	1-2
1956	Cooraclare	1-5	...	Miltown	0-6
1957	Kilrush	4-3	...	Miltown	3-2
1958	Kilrush	0-6	...	Kilmihil	0-4
1959					
Draw	Miltown	2-8	...	Cooraclare	2-8
Replay	Miltown	1-11	...	Cooraclare	0-7
1960	Kilrush	1-8	...	Cooraclare	2-3
1961					
Draw	Doonbeg	1-5	...	Cooraclare	1-5
Replay	Doonbeg	1-6	...	Cooraclare	0-5
1962	Kilrush	1-11	...	Miltown	1-7
1963	Kilmurry Ibrickane	3-10	...	Shannon Gaels	0-11
1964	Cooraclare	2-8	...	Kilmurry Ibrickane	1-9
1965	Cooraclare	3-8	...	Miltown	2-9
1966	Kilmurry Ibrickane	1-9	...	Kilrush	1-3
1967	Doonbeg	0-6	...	Kilrush	0-3
1968	Doonbeg	0-9	...	Kilmihil	0-3
1969	Doonbeg	0-7	...	Shannon Gaels	1-1
1970	Shannon Gaels	1-3	...	Kilrush Shamrocks	1-2
1971	Shannon Gaels	1-8	...	Doonbeg	1-7
1972					
Draw	Doonbeg	0-7	...	Kilmihil	1-4
Replay	Doonbeg	0-6	...	Kilmihil	0-4
1973	Doonbeg	0-13	...	Shannon Gaels	2-6
1974					
Draw	Doonbeg	1-6	...	Kilmihil	1-6
Replay	Doonbeg	0-4	...	Kilmihil	0-3
1975	Kilrush Shamrocks	2-10	...	St. Joseph's *(Miltown Malbay)*	1-6
1976	Kilrush Shamrocks	2-7	...	Kilmihil	2-5
1977	Kilrush Shamrocks	1-7	...	North Clare	0-5

1978	Kilrush Shamrocks	3-11	...	North Clare	0-8
1979	Kilrush Shamrocks	2-9	...	Doonbeg	1-5
1980	Kilmihil	1-8	...	Doonbeg	0-5
1981	Kilrush Shamrocks	1-13	...	St. Senans Kilkee	1-10
1982					
Draw	Doonbeg	1-5	...	Kilmihil	1-5
Replay	Doonbeg	0-4	...	Kilmihil	0-3
1983	Doonbeg	0-9	...	Kilrush Shamrocks	1-4
1984	St. Senans Kilkee	0-10	...	Kilmihil	1-2
1985	St. Josephs *(Miltown Malbay)*	4-5	...	St. Breckans Lisdoonvarna	0-4
1986	Cooraclare	2-5	...	Eire Og Ennis	1-5
1987	Kilrush Shamrocks	1-5	...	Doonbeg	0-5
1988	Doonbeg	1-5	...	Kilmihil	0-6
1989					
Draw	St. Senans Kilkee	1-9	...	Doonbeg	2-6
Replay	St. Senans Kilkee	2-7	...	Doonbeg	1-8
1990	St. Josephs Miltown	1-6	...	Kilmihil	0-7
1991	Doonbeg	0-10	...	St. Josephs Miltown	0-6
1992	St. Senans Kilkee	1-9	...	Doonbeg	0-11
1993	Kilmurry Ibrickane	0-9	...	Doonbeg	0-7
1994					
Draw	Faughs	0-11	...	Kilrush Shamrocks	2-5
Replay	Faughs	1-12	...	Kilrush Shamrocks	2-6
1995	Doonbeg	0-11	...	Faughs	1-7
1996	Doonbeg	1-10	...	St. Breckans	0-7
1997	Cooraclare	1-6	...	Doonbeg	0-7
1998					
Draw	Doonbeg	2-4	...	Lissycasey	1-7
Replay	Doonbeg	1-9	...	Lissycasey	0-2
1999	Doonbeg	1-8	...	Kilmurry Ibrickane	1-6
2000	Eire Og Ennis	1-10	...	Doonbeg	0-10
2001	Doonbeg	2-6	...	Eire Og	0-7
2002	Kilmurry Ibrickane	1-5	...	Liscannor	0-6

SENIOR HURLING TITLES

Roll of Honour – Senior Hurling Titles

Club	Titles	Years
Newmarket	(22)	1912, 1916, 1925, 1926, 1927, 1930, 1931, 1936, 1955, 1963, 1964, 1965, 1967, 1968, 1969, 1971, 1972, 1973, 1974, 1976, 1978, 1981.
Sixmilebridge	(10)	1977, 1979, 1983, 1984, 1989, 1992, 1993, 1995, 2000, 2002
Clarecastle	(9)	1943, 1945, 1949, 1970, 1986, 1987, 1991, 1994, 1997.
Ennis Dalcassians	(8)	1911, 1914, 1915, 1924, 1928, 1929, 1934, 1941.
Tulla	(7)	1889, 1896, 1897, 1899, 1905, 1913, 1933.
Éire Óg, Ennis	(6)	1956, 1957, 1966, 1980, 1982, 1990. *(This gives a total of 14 titles to Ennis.)*
O'Callaghan's Mills	(6)	1904, 1906, 1909, 1910, 1918, 1937.
Feakle	(6)	1935, 1938, 1939, 1940, 1944, 1988.
Ruan	(5)	1948, 1951, 1959, 1960, 1962.
St. Joseph's	(5)	1954, 1958, 1998, 1999, 2001.
Scariff	(5)	1907, 1917, 1946, 1952, 1953.
Kilnamona	(3)	1902, 1903, 1908.
Whitegate	(2)	1950, 1961.
Kilkishen	(2)	1923, 1932.
Carrahan	(2)	1898, 1900.
Brian Borus	(1)	1975.
Kilmaley	(1)	1985.
Wolfe Tones Shannon	(1)	1996.
Smith O'Brien's Garranboy	(1)	1887.
Ogonnelloe	(1)	1888.
Clonlara	(1)	1919.
Clooney	(1)	1942. Along with Carrahan this gives the parish of Clooney 3 titles
Bodyke	(1)	1947.

SENIOR FOOTBALL WINNERS

16 Senior Football Titles have come to Ennis in the following years: -

Club	Titles	Years
Ennis Dalcassians	(10)	1897, 1899, 1904, 1907, 1909, 1910, 1911, 1913, 1914, 1929.
Ennis Faughs	(5)	1947, 1948, 1952, 1954, 1994.
Éire Óg	(1)	2000.

Martin Cronin

Martin Cronin (Ennis) a colourful character and prolific writer, contributed many pieces to The Clare Champion and County Express. The Cronin family have lived in Garraunakilla, Market Street for many generations. Martin F. Cronin whose writings are contained in this publication was born there in 1898.

Martin's grandfather James Cronin (1821-1886) married Susan McInerney. Their son James (1859-1912) married Mary Moloney (1865-1925). Martin F. was the seventh child born from this union.

Martin's brothers and sisters are as follows:

Mary Ann	15th June 1888	–	28th April 1973
James M.	4th September 1889	–	16th February 1923
John T.	22nd May 1891	–	2nd February 1948
Patrick A.	17th November 1892	–	26th March 1933
Joseph	19th August 1894	–	20th August 1978
Martin	7th November 1896	–	September 1897
Martin F.	2nd August 1898	–	24th June 1974
Bernard A.	13th June 1900	–	1st January 1956
*Frederick	3rd April 1902	–	28th July 1980
Louis	31st January 1904	–	11th March 1952
Peter	30th June 1905	–	8th August 1936
Paul	30th June 1905	–	4th April 1939
Agnes	12th November 1907	–	26th April 1909
Agnes F.	26th October 1909	–	4th February 1950
Kathleen	3rd November 1910	–	1st July 1973

*Peter Cronin of Cronin's Yard is a son of Frederick.

Club & Colleges Index

General Index

Patrons of Around the Square

I would like to sincerely thank the following for their financial help in producing this book: -

Martin Bradley, Clonroadbeg, Ennis.
Michael Brennan Insurances, Barrack Street.
Larry Brennan, Proprietor Brennan's Building Services.
Pat Brennan, Clonroadmore.
Paschal Brooks, Brooks Video, for all your video, DVD needs.
Tel. Pascal at (086) 2588565, www.brooks.video.com.
The Sports - Wedding Video Specialists.
Jackie Browne, Ardlea Road.
Declan Coote, Accountants, Kilrush Road.
Pat Coffey, Ennis and Waterford.
Clare Champion, Barrack Street, Ennis.
Clare Roof Truss, Proprietors Jessie and Liam Hogan, Gort Road.
Tomás Corbett, Limerick Road, Ennis.
J. J. Considine, Tobartaoscain, Ennis.
Collins Jewellers, O'Connell Street, Proprietor Christy Collins.
Caroline Collins, 19 St. Flannan's Terrace, Ennis.
Callinan/Walsh Construction Company Ltd., C/o Michael O'Loughlin Group, Loughville.
Peter Cronin, c/o Cronin's Yard, Upper Market Street, Ennis.
Gerard and John Curran, College View, Clonroadmore.
Cllr. Pat Daly, M.C.C., 53 Gallows Hill.
Martin 'Massey' Dilger, 5 Dalcassian Avenue, Ennis.
Geraldine and Michael Dinan, John Paul Avenue, Cloughleigh.
John Dunne, Limerick Road, Ennis.
Ennis Music Shop, Tesco Shopping Centre - Proprietor Maurice Young.
Éire Óg Hurling Club, Clonroadmore.
Martin Fitzgibbon Builders, Darragh.
Finbarr and Marion Garde, B&B, 6 Park View, Wellington Road, Cork.
Tony Garry, Westminster Road, Foxrock, Dublin.
Jarlath and Carole Gallagher, Eye Specialists, College Road.

Seanie Gleeson, Coal Merchant, Clarecastle.
Jane Guthrie, Teaskagh, Carron, RIP.
Liam Griffin, 2 Creggaun, Tobartaoscain.
Liam Harvey, Ballycarroll, Barefield.
Jack Heaslip, Wholesale and Retail Fruit Merchant, 34 O'Connell Street.
Seán Heaslip, Ballyalla, Ennis.
Noel Howard, Proprietor Howard's Shop, Newbridge Road, Lifford.
Jackie Hynes, 42, Willow Park.
David Keane, Proprietor D. K. Couriers, College Road.
Keane Company Tarmacadam, Proprietor John Keane, Knockanean, Ennis.
Peter Keane - Renoir Productions, Multimedia Specialists, Kilrush Road.
Paddy Kelly - Proprietor Kelly's Garage, Mill Street.
Leader Rural Resource Development, Shannon.
Lewmac Ltd., Proprietor Alan Lewis, Clonroad Business Park.
Loftus Brothers, Paddy, Stephen, Des, Vincent, Ennis.
Brian McMahon, Fountain.
Noel Mulhearn, Riverside, Clonroadmore.
Tom Mannion Travel. 71 O'Connell Street
Mike McDonagh, Marian Avenue.
Johnny McCarthy, 12 Kincora Park.
John McCarthy, Proprietor JMC Retail Systems, 15 Park Row, Francis Street.
Liam and Claire McNamara, Loughville.
Michael McNamara, College Green.
John O'Dea, Publican, Upper O'Connell Street.
P. J. O'Dea, Kilrush and Chicago.
Mary and Paddy O'Donoghue, Ard Mhuire, Ballyalla.
Jim O'Dowd, O'Dowd's Convenient Store, Turnpike.
Jarlath O'Halloran, Fergus Lawn, Lifford.
Paddy O'Halloran, Broadhaven, Cahercallamore.
Noel Pyne, Kildysart Road.
John and Sadie Quinn, C/o Paddy Quinn's Bar, Lower Market Street.
Patrick Quinn, Barrister, Market Street.
Declan Ryan, C/o Clare Champion, Barrack Street.
Michael Sexton, Builders, Quilty.
Michael Skelly, College Green.
Jimmy Spellissy, Tulla Road, Ennis.
Seán Spellissy, c/o The Book Gallery, Cronin's Yard, Market Street.
Shannon Development, Shannon, Co. Clare.
Alfie Sutton Lighting Centre, Clonroadmore.
Garry Stack, Drimeen, Darragh.
St. Francis Credit Union, Parnell Street.
Nora Wallace, Glenina, Gort Road, Ennis.